The City in the Islamic World

Volume 1

Handbook of Oriental Studies

Section 1, The Near and Middle East

Edited by

H. Altenmüller
B. Hrouda
B. A. Levine
R. S. O'Fahey
K. R. Veenhof
C. H. M. Versteegh

VOLUME 94

The City in the Islamic World

Volume 1

General editor
Salma K. Jayyusi

Special editors
Renata Holod, Attilio Petruccioli and André Raymond

BRILL

LEIDEN · BOSTON
2008

This book is printed on acid-free paper.

This book was subsidized by His Royal Highness Prince 'Abd al-'Azīz Ibn Fahd Ibn 'Abd al-'Azīz

On the cover: Vertical aerophoto of the two sides of the river and the médinas of Rabat and Salé. Archives of the Ministry of Housing and Urbanism.

Library of Congress Cataloging-in-Publication Data

The city in the Islamic World / edited by Salma K. . . . [et al.].
    p. cm. — (Handbook of oriental studies section 1, the Near and Middle East)
    Includes bibliographical references.
    ISBN 978-90-04-16240-2 (hardback : alk. paper) 1. Islamic cities and towns—Islamic countries—History. 2. Islamic cities and towns—Islamic countries—Social life and customs. 3. Islamic cities and towns—Islamic countries—Intellectual life. 4. Cities and towns—Islamic Empire. I. Jayyusi, Salma Khadra. II. Title. III. Series.

HT147.5.C59 2008
307.760917'67—dc 22

2008006517

ISSN 0169-9423
ISBN 978 9004 17168 8 (vol. 1)
ISBN 978 9004 17167 1 (vol. 2)
ISBN 978 90 04 16240 2 (set)

PRINTED IN THE NETHERLANDS

CONTENTS

VOLUME ONE

PART ONE

GENERAL TOPICS

PART TWO

REGIONAL ASPECTS

PART THREE

CASE STUDIES

VOLUME TWO

PART FOUR

CITY FUNCTIONS

PART FIVE

THE MODERN AND CONTEMPORARY CITY

PREFACE AND ACKNOWLEDGEMENTS

This book was initially created by the urge that has taken hold of me almost thirty years ago: to enhance the beleaguered and suppressed knowledge of Arabic culture and of Arab/Islamic civilisation outside the Arab world; to try to demonstrate the similarities but also the dissimilarities, the points of convergence and the points of divergence in major avenues of Arab and non-Arab, mainly Western, traditions, and, by this means, perhaps to help bring out the underlying unity of human cultures. This was made especially urgent by the paucity, outside the Arab world, of material representing Arabic culture, thought and literature, and Arab/Islamic civilisation.

I founded East-West Nexus/*PROTA* for this purpose, with the specific aim of providing the English-speaking world, to the best of my ability, with some of the finest manifestations of the Arab creative talent, past and present. I believe, indeed, that the creative fruits of all cultures are the rightful inheritance of all peoples, and there is confirmation of this in the interest people show in reading the novels and poems of other cultures in translation, of gazing at their monuments and works of art, of listening to their music and watching their dances and performances. It was crucial, I felt, that an attempt was made, at this juncture in time, to foster a genuine understanding of other human triumphs, and of another human civilisation, the Arab-Islamic, that has made such a contribution to the progress of world culture. A Eurocentric emphasis vis-à-vis human progress is not merely flawed. It leads further to the deepening of negative factors between peoples—something whose consequences have become only too evident in recent times. Only when the resplendent gifts, proffered by all the peoples of the world, for the furtherance of aesthetic, philosophic and spiritual goals within humanity are recognized—only then can true civilisation be finally achieved.

In my efforts to foster such understanding, I was upheld and invigorated both by a select group of colleagues in America where this work had its beginnings, and also by colleagues in Europe and the Arab world who shared this view with me.

THIS BOOK:

It was Lewis Mumford's book, *The City in History*, which first awoke in me the idea of providing, for a world audience, a volume on 'the city in the Islamic world'. In his elaborate and beautifully written book, Mumford failed to speak of a single Islamic city—as though such cities were created and inhabited outside the built world, indeed outside human history itself. He had not a word to say of centuries of a luminous civilisation, of an urbanity grounded in magnificent cities that were citadels of learning and discovery, of invention and art, boasting urban gardens and magnificent architecture—nowhere finer than in the Andalusi metropolises to which flocked so many seekers of knowledge from East and West, who having learned and translated all they could, took the fruits of their knowledge back with them to their own countries.

My own love of cities was an additional spur. As a child I was struck with awe when reading the elaborate descriptions of Jurji Zaydan (1861–1914) in his many novels, of pre-modern Islamic cities in various parts of the old Islamic empire. A Lebanese Christian, he was a genuine admirer of the heritage Arabs and other Muslims had handed down in the sphere of urban culture, and his writings were eye openers to the high level of sophistication and complexity Islamic cities had attained in their time. My young mind was imbued with images of great events, processions, palaces, libraries, of public baths and fragrant gardens, of spacious and elaborately designed mosques. Mumford's omission of all cities Islamic brought these childhood images surging back to my mind, and I resolved forthwith to bring out a specialised book on the city in the Islamic world.

However, I was faced at the outset with two major challenges: the first to obtain financial sponsorship for a work I visualised as a voluminous, comprehensive account of the Islamic city, the second to engage the interest of some of the leading specialist scholars on the Islamic city, who would undertake the specific editing of the work.

It was clear that such a major work would perforce need a subsidy. It took me eleven years to find one, when I finally sought the help of my friend, Abdallah al-Nasir, the Saudi Cultural Representative at the Saudi Cultural Mission in London. His understanding of my work in general, and of the need for disseminating Arabic culture in the world, had been always profound, manifested in a constant readiness to help whenever he could. He it was who spoke to Dr. Khalid al-ʿAngari, Minister of Higher Education in Saudi Arabia and one of the most enlightened and responsible guardians of culture in our part of the world. Dr. ʿAngari was enthused with the idea of the book and immediately assumed the responsibility for helping us accomplish the project. He spoke to his Royal Highness, Prince Abd al-Aziz ibn Fahd, who is well-known for his enthusiastic interest in Arabic civilisation and culture, and we had our subsidy.

As for identifying the proper editors, specialised in the city in the Muslim world, there was no great difficulty involved. I had read some of Professor André Raymond's excellent work, and was struck by its scope, depth and style. I had also come to know Dr. Attilio Petruccioli when he held in the 1990s the Aga Khan Chair at the MIT in Cambridge, Mass. where I live, and I had come to admire his overriding preoccupation with his vast area of specialization. He and I met several times during the mid-1990s to discuss the endeavour and to work out a provisional, preliminary table of contents for a book which was yet to be born. My friend, Professor Oleg Grabar, one of the world's most renowned Islamic city specialists, further urged me to contact Professor Renata Holod at Penn University, with a view to her becoming the third specialised editor the projected work needed. She was immediately enthusiastic about the project, lending it her wide knowledge of the subject, her characteristic precision and zest. This was a wonderful meeting of minds, fruitful, amiable and totally rewarding; and here I should like to extend my heartfelt thanks to all three of this book's specialised editors, for their insight, their precision, their creativity and their unfailing care. It was the greatest pleasure to work with them.

To the contributors for this volume we owe many thanks. Each of them gave this book the fruits of his or her own specialisation and, by their serious and meticulous effort they cooperated on giving to the world readership a rounded and comprehensive account on the Islamic city, its past and present, and the complex role it has played in the history of human civilisation. They are indeed the backbone of this work.

And we all join in thanking His Royal Highness, Prince Abd al-Aziz ibn Fahd ibn Abd al-Aziz for his most generous subsidy, which made it possible for us to collaborate in bringing this work to fruition. Our deep gratitude goes also to Dr. Khalid al-ʿAngari who proved to be a staunch supporter of civilizational projects aimed at furthering knowledge about Arab/Islamic culture, and its role as builder and enhancer of world culture. We also thank Ustadh Abdallah al-Nasser for his initiating role in facilitating this work and for his thorough understanding of the need to give Arabic culture and civilization their rightful place within contemporary world culture.

Salma Khadra Jayyusi
Editor of Islamic Civilisation Series
EAST-WEST NEXUS/*PROTA*

INTRODUCTION

Recent calamitous events have shone a light of attention and renewed curiosity on the Islamic world in a most insistent fashion. Whether it was the attack on the World Trade Center, the search for the Taliban in Afghanistan, the war in Iraq, the unsolved problem of Palestine or even the most recent assault on Beirut, all have put the Islamic world in the centre of media attention. Yet, beneath that roiled surface, there is much that warrants a deeper, more sustained look. The purpose of this book, then, is to focus on the sites of life, politics, and culture where current and past generations of the Islamic world have made their mark. These are, of course, its cities, large and small, forgotten or dynamically growing. Such an initiative is all the more important as there has been much new research on the nature of these cities in the past decades. Yet, in spite of this large body of detailed information, there are few recent volumes attempting to present a new summary or digest of it all; and none in the Arabic language.

Since this volume is a contribution of many authors, the approach must be as inclusive as possible, looking from different perspectives and with varying methods for urban studies at functions and on special or regional cases. The single leading concept, nonetheless, has been to consider the city as a living organism. The city, then, consists of parts that are deeply interconnected, with patterns of residence, circulation, public spaces, and facilities, mutually and dynamically collaborative, to yield a culture of urban life. And as any living organism, the city should be seen in continuous transformation and not in frozen images. The city has a birth and a death as well.

Unlike many previous volumes dealing with the city in the Islamic world, this one has been specially expanded not only to include snapshots of historical fabric but also to deal with the transformation of this fabric into modern and contemporary urban entities. Rather than focusing on specific historic fabrics alone, often the sites of political and nationalist image-making, attention has been drawn to the entire flow of urban processes up to and including the present, encompassing such phenomena as the introduction of wheeled transport, the impact of colonial structures and administration, and the overwhelming changes brought about by demographic migrations of recent years.

We have chosen to title this volume "City in the Islamic World" specifically to circumvent the no longer productive discourse on the "Islamic City." These issues have been debated for some decades now and are reflected in the review of the literature in the first chapter. Rather, by assembling specifically focused studies on the organic, regional, and chronological aspects of the city, we hope to bring a richer database into circulation; and from it derive a more viable view of how cities functioned and continue to function as loci of identity and culture.

While the large-scale changes in cities have been sufficiently documented by official sources and maps, the smaller-scale impact of individual decisions can now be better retrieved and made apparent. Thanks to an almost continuous stream of new publications dealing with archival data, we have a closer and closer view of the concerns and transformations of urban life. For example, the social service centres dotting the cityscapes were founded and funded by various members, male and female, of the ruling elites. These are now better known, thanks to the publication of numerous pious foundation documents (Arabic *waqf or hubus*, Persian *vaqf*). As well, continuous work on official and private family archives has illuminated aspects of urban life and change. The massive Ottoman material, including cadastral and taxation records, throws new light on regional variations. The greater availability of materials in the former soviet Central Asian republics allows for a larger comparative scope. And the increasing attention to, and availability of, family papers, whether held in chests or stored in reused olive oil dolias, allow for microanalysis down to the single domestic unit.

For the presentation of the city as a continuous and dynamic organism, study of the near past, namely the nineteenth and twentieth centuries, clearly becomes crucial. In this pursuit, all colonial archives as well as material stored in the planning offices and agencies of municipalities are invaluable. For example, the Vincennes Archives de la Guerre, Les Archives d'Outre-Mer in Aix-en-Provence, the India Office Library in London, and similar such collections can yield data that change our perceptions about the early modern city.

Materials such as cadastral surveys and insurance maps created for a different initial purpose have now begun to be utilized for the interpretation of the history of urban fabric. For example, the Pervititch map of Istanbul of 1922–1945 for fire insurance, the cadastral surveys in the French tradition at the scale of 1:500 in areas of former French control and impact (such as Syria and Algeria), and even the survey recording the church properties of Toledo, can be regarded as palimpsests of urban life. More recently, new tools applied to the analysis of urban form ranging from satellite imaging to geographic data collected through GIS and GPS have further strengthened and deepened the basic data. Further, discourse about urban form analyses has been accelerated through new centres and systems of diffusion of information. These are, for example, the Centre for the Study of the Built Environment (CSBE) in Jordan, the Equipe Monde Arabe et Méditerranée/(URBAMA/EMAM) at the University of Tours, IREMAM at the CNRS and the University of Aix-en-Provence, the School of Architecture of Bari, the Archnet website (archnet.org) sponsored by the Aga Khan Trust for Culture, and a burgeoning list of periodicals on architecture and urbanism produced anywhere from Morocco to Turkey and Iran.

While few historical studies of cities have extended their attention into contemporary time, dealing with the urban setting as it has been experienced by its users holds great promise. The urban experience has been recognized as a rich source by many writers, among them most recently Orhan Pamuk, in his *Istanbul.* More anthropologically conducted studies, such as that on Sefrou in Morocco by C. Geertz, H. Geertz, and L. Rosen also show that every urban dweller has a specific experience of a place, while sharing in even the densest environment. These experiences are very much a product of age, class, status, and gender.

The images of urban settings with their monuments as well as small-scale daily activities are windows into the social and economic life of the city. The publication and increasing accessibility of historic photographic collections such as those of the Library of Congress, the University of Bamberg Collection, and the volumes of cityscapes comparing old and new (for example, those of Morocco, gathered by Said Mouline as *Repères de la Mémoire*), anchor our ideas about individual city settings.

The method for studying urban fabric, begun by Saverio Muratori and continued by the school of Versailles, has been applied to cities in the Islamic world since the 1980's, and has brought ever-richer results. Either at the scale of buildings or at the scale of urban fabric, this method has allowed for the integration of data from maps, texts, and excavations, as is the case of the Cairo study by Philippe Panerai and Sawsan Noweir, or in several of the articles in this volume.

Contributions of archaeological investigations over the last four decades have brought to light massive detail about the construction, continuity, expansion, and usage of urban fabric. Whether in projects of rescue archaeology or in extensive horizontal exposures, chronological shifts, and changes in function are now better documented. For example, the excavations in Beth Shan have shown massive Umayyad investment in a ruinous late antique city. And Navarro Palazon's exposure of several hectares of residential fabric in Murcia has allowed a reconstruction of the medieval Islamic city. Work on the ruins of old Samarkand-Afrasiyab has brought to light palatial structures as well as the foundation of the congregational mosque (*masjid al-jami'*). Alastair Northedge has combined new mapping techniques with *sondage* and textual sources to give a newer, fuller picture of the palace city of Samarra. The investigation of Jean Passini in the basements of Toledo, coordinated with old church property registers, has mapped the first Islamic city there.

At the same time, scholars using geographical and legal texts have developed new theoretical perspectives about the use of space within the city, and about the ordering and function of urban territory. Public and private zoning, inheritance law, and concepts of urban nomenclature and administration have been investigated by a variety of scholars, among them Saleh Hathloul, Paul Wheately, and Baber Johansen. Through these efforts, Islamic civilization has been clearly re-articulated as, primarily, an urban civilization.

New urban construction at large scale has been a constant feature of the twentieth (and twenty-first) century. The fuller publication and close critique of these new entities can reveal the extent of continuities and ruptures within urban thinking and imagination. At best, these large-scale interventions can introduce environmental amelioration and psychological relief to an otherwise overburdened urban sprawl. For example, the Middle East Technical University's planting programme has been able to modify the microclimate of Ankara. The Cairo Park commissioned by the Aga Khan has inserted a massive new green presence into the brown horizon of an eighteen million—large megalopolis. New capitals for new states have created large zones of public interaction, allowing for newer methods of communication and formation of national identities. Whether Ankara within a newly constituted secular republic of Turkey of the 1930s, Islamabad and Dhaka in the new Islamic republic of Pakistan of the 1960–70s, or the new setting for the Saudi monarchy in Riyadh of the 1970s, the new city fabric holds present and future urban experience within its structure of public buildings, highways, apartments, and parks. Conservation and restoration-attempts to recuperate and reconstitute urban and territorial morphology can only be partial at this scale of change; nonetheless, they deserve attention and resources, as they are still the loci of living patterns. Whether in the territory of the hills of Hunza, or the urban fabric of Tunis, the small-scale spaces create intimate corners for life. Finally, the newest leap into myth-making futures is represented by the waterfronts in Abu Dhabi or Dubai, with scales of construction visible even at satellite level.

In introducing the material of this book and its arrangement, we have paid special attention to the fact that we see the city as an organic whole. Therefore, whatever their functions and characteristics, whether past or present, they all contribute to it. The study of the city within the Islamic world has had a long history, one that has been recounted and theorized by the late Paolo Cuneo, now updated in Part I, section 1. Included is, of course, a post-colonial critique of several key early works. André Raymond, in his consideration of the city as an Arab or Islamic city, addresses some of the problems in designating an urban entity as one or the other. Nonetheless, it is through the lens of Islamic law, when it was applied to city living, that the special characteristics of the city called "Islamic" can be discerned, as is elaborated in Part I, section 3. Based on law cases that were post-positive reactions to the situation of urban life, dealing with heights of buildings, harm to the neighbour, or more general zoning, one can ask the question whether Islamic law, the *shari'a*, modified the physical layout of the city and to what extent. This question is particularly important when considering urban organisms that have been inherited by the Islamic empires from earlier urban fabrics and traditions of city life. Part I, section 4 lays out some of the details of this inheritance. On the other hand, early in the history of Islamic expansion, there was a perceived need to found new, exclusively Muslim settlements, tied most often to army encampments and to dynastic palace cities. This dyad of city and palace continued to have special reverberation within Islamic space, and was key to the development of the idea of what is "civilized" (*tamaddun, mutamaddin*) and what is not. Thus, the new *madina*s, whether east or west, in fact, became that image of Islamic civilization. Part I, section 5 records the phenomenon of new city foundation and its role in developing an Islamic hegemony.

Dealing with the city as an organism is also dealing with a description of its functions. Thus, the city at work is a section within the volume that pays particular attention to those functions that provided it with water, communication, education, administration, public order, private retreat, and civic life. All these together assure the proper and continuous health of the organism.

The city has always functioned as the locus of religious practice for Muslims, as well as for Christian and Jewish communities within the Islamic world. Any congregational mosque had to be situated in an agglomeration of contiguous buildings designated as *madina*. Furthermore, beginning with Mecca, Medina, and Jerusalem, and including numerous, lesser but, nonetheless, important shrines, among them Karbala, or Mashhad, urban centres have been vessels for, and supporters of, piety and pilgrimage.

The kaleidoscopic composition of the *dar al-islam* obliges us to take a closer look at the regional and chronological differentiation of the city. This has become possible thanks to the variety of specialized studies. Thus, in this part of the volume, we have made an effort to represent cities ranging from the Atlantic to the Indian Ocean. Cultural geographies created regional models that encompassed ideas of space and landscape extant before Islam, and it was their relationship to new models of social life and power that have contributed to shaping the city within the Islamic world. The selection of case studies is arranged regionally and chronologically, and this arrangement is meant to bridge the "gap" between what has been called traditional and modern.

Many new cites in the early centuries of the Islamic world were founded with an intentional design. Yet, that very design has been consumed by their success as urban centres. In the end, the diagram for the city was challenged and disaggregated by the application of the Islamic legal system and usage to form a new and individualized urban fabric, in which private space was vouchsafed and public space was a feature of usage but without clear and marked boundaries. Initial diagrams for cities such as the grid, square, or circle, remain as mere memory in texts in the case of successful cities such as Baghdad or Cairo; they can only be fully recuperated from unsuccessful or abandoned sites and entities. Therefore, the archaeological recovery of the initial layout ideas and plans has been essential, as in the case of Qasr al-Hayr al-Sharqi and 'Anjar in the central lands, Qsar al-Sghir in the west, or Merv in the east. In fact, these sites can now be fertile grounds for the recuperation of surveying techniques and metrology.

While early medieval urbanism can be reconstructed only partially, the early modern city, in some cases, can be experienced as it was conceived and built. In particular, the sixteenth and seventeenth century ideas of layout and urban form are available in the Safavid and

Mughal capitals such as Isfahan, Fathepur Sikri, Agra, or Shahjah-anabad. These environments were generated out of Timurid garden and landscape thinking on an exploded scale. They also became the sites of an expansive public culture, epitomized by parades and court viewings, theatrical performances, markets, coffee shops, and banquets. The Ottomans made the Bosphorus their garden and viewing space, while the inherited city of Stambul remained a grouping of villages in an extensive cultivated landscape interspersed with monumental sultanic and elite social service complexes (*kulliye*). And similarly, in the entire Ottoman Empire, the city would remain without further planning or layout until the Tanzimat period of the nineteenth century.

The establishment of a public ferry system (Shirket-i Hayriye) in Istanbul in the 1850s marked the arrival of "modern" life. Over the horizon of the nineteenth century, city life was impacted dramatically, as the telegraph, the railroad, and public lighting also made their appearance. While these new technologies were means to a greater unification of the territory of the city, the capital in particular, and selected provincial centres as well, their adoption also ushered in closer controls. From taxes to hygiene, all aspects of "new" urban life were now within the purview of the central state government. These techniques of organization brought with them increasing European influence, if not outright control, in Istanbul as well as in Cairo. Additionally, what had been an insistently pedestrian city, with densely packed habitation zones, was now making room for the newly reintroduced wheeled transport. Systems of production previously organized through guilds disappeared in favour of imported technicians; agricultural monocultures fed an extensive export network replacing an earlier organization of territory. With the arrival and expansion of colonialist empires, many nineteenth and early twentieth century cities in the Islamic world became the recipients of a different model of urban space and social interaction. Not unexpectedly, these habits of receiving urban ideas did not stop with the colonialist era. The newly independent states have continued implanting the large-scale developments, whether commercial or state-funded, and often the least successful of European or American planning and building practices.

As a result, we are now looking at a massively changed picture of urban life. The present manner of urban planning and layout has been separated from earlier urban experiences that, in fact, had defined the Islamic world. Not only have most urban centres grown exponentially in population and territory, they have already set aside, or are at the risk of forgetting, their own past experiences with urban living. The area of historical fabric per city probably does, at best, not reach more than 10–15 percent of the built-up zone. Nevertheless, the older urban fabric still has valuable lessons to teach, among them a complexity of spatial and chronological relationships, rather than a mechanical linearity of experience. Even if only preserved as a museum of forms, it functions as a guarantor of local identity. More importantly, it serves as a repository of design principles and ideas in opposition to self-referential plans invented by "star" architects. Its potential to generate alternative models for a habitable environment has yet to be fully activated.

Renata Holod
Attilio Petruccioli
André Raymond

PART ONE

GENERAL TOPICS

SOME HISTORIOGRAPHICAL NOTES ON THE ISLAMIC CITY WITH PARTICULAR REFERENCE TO THE VISUAL REPRESENTATION OF THE BUILT CITY

Giulia Annalinda Neglia

The Orientalist Approach

At the beginning of the twentieth century European scholarship on the Islamic city was based mainly on two approaches: one who attributed the structure of Islamic cities to social and religious factors and another one who sought to describe their structure through an approach which was more dependent on an analysis of the urban structure and its physical features. The first of these approaches comes from English and particularly German Orientalist studies for which the Islamic city represented a theoretical rather than an actual horizon informed by archaeological, historical, and social interests: it was an urban system connoted by a "different" structure from the "western" one since it was based on a different social organization. The second approach comes from Orientalist studies of French derivation for which a knowledge of the Islamic city was much more immediate and tangible since it was born from the actual conquest of extensive territories around the Mediterranean. For this approach the Islamic city represented a system to be described in detail in order to be controlled politically. Actually, these two approaches were never completely separate. Instead, they constituted two different attitudes that travelled in tandem for a long time until modern historiography subjected them to a critical revision.

The origin of Orientalist studies on the Islamic city[1] springs from an interest in the cities of North Africa that was cultivated, from the

---

[1] Some of the most important works that have sketched the main lines of this debate in relation to urban studies are: M. E. Bonine, E. Ehlers, T. Krafft, and G. Stöber, eds., *The Middle Eastern City and Islamic Urbanism: An Annotated Bibliography of Western Literature* (Bonn, 1994); M. Haneda, "An Interpretation of the Concept of Islamic City," in *Islamic Urban Studies: Historical Review and Perspective*, ed. M. Haneda and T. Miura (London and New York, 1994); M. Kisaichi, "The Maghrib," in *Islamic Urban Studies: Historical Review and Perspective*, ed. M. Haneda and T. Miura (London and New York, 1994); P. Guichard, "Les villes d'al-Andalus et de l'Occident musulman aux premiers siècles

1920s onwards, by historians such as William and Georges Marçais, Roger Le Tourneau, Louis Massignon, and Robert Brunschvig. These historians described the salient features of Islamic cities from various points of view: architectonic-urbanistic and socio-economic. Though they used different approaches and methodologies in their studies, they all postulated the unity of Muslim urbanism. Using the specific knowledge derived from their research into North African cities, they formulated an urban model that was then applied to all Arab-Islamic, Turkish, Iranian, and Berber-Andalusian territories. Influenced by Max Weber's[2] and Henry Pirenne's[3] work, the descriptions of the characteristics of cities in the Islamic world had a universalizing tendency, in opposition to the descriptions of European cities.

Even though William and Georges Marçais[4] deserve credit for having shifted scholarly attention from the study of monuments to the study of the urban fabric of Islamic cities, their theories nevertheless apply the principles of urban organization verified for the Maghreb without distinction to all regions of the Islamic world. Starting from reflections on the importance of the role of religion in the codification of Islamic urban form, on the idea of conflict between urban populations and nomads, and the stagnation of Islamic society, the two Marçais hypothesized a representative model for the structure of the Islamic city based on: the presence of the congregational mosque at the heart of the city, the suq structure organized hierarchically from the mosque to the city gates and associated with the presence of specialized buildings, a divi-

---

de leur histoire. Une hypothèse récente," in *Genèse de la ville islamique en al-Andalus et au Maghreb occidental*, ed. P. Cressier and M. Garcia-Arenal (Madrid, 1998).

[2] M. Weber, *Wirtschaft und Gesellschaft* (Tübingen, 1922).

[3] H. Pirenne, *Les villes du moyen âge* (Brussels, 1927).

The two above-cited texts have considerably influenced European historians' vision of the medieval European city. Weber's theories in particular have led Orientalist historians to use a universalizing and comparative methodology to describe the structure of the Islamic city.

[4] W. Marçais, "L'Islamisme et la vie urbaine," in *Comptes rendus de L'Académie des Inscriptions et Belles Lettres* (1928), 86–100; G. Marçais, *Tunis et Kairouan* (Paris, 1937); G. Marçais, "L'urbanisme musulman," in *5e Congr. De la Fédération des Soc. Savantes d'Afrique du Nord, Tunis, 6–8.4.1939* (Algiers, 1940), 13–34; G. Marçais, "La conception des villes dans l'Islâm," *Revue d'Alger* 2 (1945): 517–533; G. Marçais, *L'Architecture Musulmane d'Occident: Tunisie, Algérie, Maroc, Espagne et Sicilie* (Paris, 1954); G. Marçais, "Considérations sur les villes musulmanes et notamment sur le rôle du mohtasib," *Recueils de la Société Jean Bodin* (Brussels) 6 (1954): 249–262; G. Marçais, "L'urbanisme musulman," in *Mélanges d'histoire et d'archeologie de l'occident musulman*, Articles et Conferences de Georges Marçais (Algiers, 1957), 219–231.

sion of the different neighbourhoods on the basis of different ethnic groups, and the absence of any type of municipal organization.

In numerous essays of a socio-economic character on North African cities, Fez in particular, Roger le Tourneau[5] confirmed the Orientalist vision of the Marçais brothers, delineating the organizational features of Islamic guilds on which his theory of the urban structure was based, and describing the characteristics of the Islamic city—the main elements of which comprised the suq, the Friday mosque, the citadel, and the city walls—as if it had sprung up spontaneously, without any plan, in opposition to the countryside, and without any change throughout what Orientalists considered as a long Middle Ages.

Louis Massignon[6] formulated a comparative theory of medieval professional guilds in Europe and medieval Islamic guilds in which he identified the basic structure of the Islamic city formalized on an urban scale in the physical structure of the suq.

Robert Brunschvig[7] adopted the Marçais' spatial model and shared the widespread tendency of Orientalist studies to define the urban form of Islamic cities as "irrational" and without any plan. In his studies he attributed this spontaneous or unplanned form to the legal and administrative organization of Islamic society which determined the modes of construction of urban forms as well as the spatial and structural relations between the different neighbourhoods.

Despite this general tendency to ignore the structural complexities and different "declinations" of each individual urban organism and to read the salient features of the Islamic city in terms of a dichotomy between a progressive European and a stagnant Muslim world, the work of these scholars represents the starting point for modern studies on the Islamic city.

---

[5] R. Le Tourneau and L. Paye, "La corporation des tanneurs et l'industrie de la tannerie à Fès," *Hespéris* 21 (1935); R. Le Tourneau, *Fès avant le Protectorat: Etude économique et sociale d'une ville de l'occident musulman* (Casablanca, 1949); R. Le Tourneau, *Fez in the Age of the Marinides* (Norman, OK, 1961); R. Le Tourneau, *La vie quotidienne à Fès en 1900* (Paris, 1965); R. Le Tourneau and H. Terrasse, "Fas," in *Encyclopaedia of Islam*, 2nd ed. (1965), 818–823; R. Le Tourneau, *Les villes musulmanes de l'Afrique du Nord* (Algiers, 1957).

[6] L. Massignon, "Les corps de métiers et la cité islamique," *Revue Internationale de Sociologie* 28 (1920); L. Massignon, "Enquête sur les corporations musulmanes d'artisans et de commerçants au Maroc (1923–1924)," *Revue du Monde Musulman* 58 (1924).

[7] R. Brunschvig, "Urbanisme médiéval et droit musulman," *Revue des Etudes Islamiques* 15 (1947): 127–155.

In the same period, while the Marçais brothers were conducting research on North African cities, the French historian Jean Sauvaget[8] was doing the same in the Middle East, using a different methodology. Indeed, modern historico-morphological research on Syrian cities changed significantly after 1934, when Jean Sauvaget published his article on Latakia. It emerged from his studies that beneath the Late Antique and Islamic urban fabric of many Syrian cities there was a Hellenistic plan with a mono-directional axis. While proposing clear and plausible schemes which were the precursors to later archaeological investigations and urban studies Sauvaget's approach to the study of the Islamic city was still considered Orientalist, since it was based on the interpretation of the structural fabric of medieval Syrian cities as the product of a progressive degradation of the classical plans beneath. Yet Sauvaget deserves credit for having had important intuitions about the morphology of the urban fabric of these cities, gleaned from his pioneering use of French cadastral surveys.

The case of the Syrian administration under the French mandate and Sauvaget's studies are emblematic due to the close temporal relation between the redaction of modern cadastral surveys and the development of urban studies based on a morphological approach.[9] A similar phenomenon is to be found throughout the colonized ter-

---

[8] J. Sauvaget, "La citadelle de Damas," *Syria* 11 (1930); J. Sauvaget, "Le plan de Laodicée-sur-Mer," *Bulletin d'Études Orientales de l'Institut de Damas* 4 (1934); J. Sauvaget, "Esquisse d'une histoire de la ville de Damas," *Revue des Etudes Islamiques* 8 (1934); J. Sauvaget, "Le plan de Laodicée-sur-Mer (Note complémentaire)," *Bulletin d'Études Orientales de l'Institut Française de Damas*, 6 (1936); J. Sauvaget, "Le 'tell' d'Alep," in *Mélanges Syriens offerts à M. R. Dussaud* (Paris, 1939); J. Sauvaget, *Alep: Essai sur le développement d'une grande ville syrienne des origines au milieu du XIXe siècle* [texte, album] (Paris, 1941); J. Sauvaget, "Le plan antique de Damas," *Syria* 26 (1949); J. Sauvaget, "L'enceinte primitive de la ville d'Alep," *Mélanges de l'Institut Français de Damas*, Tome 1, 133–159.

[9] For Syria, for example, see the cartography produced in Aleppo between 1919 and 1931 after the French survey of the urban fabric: (1919) "Alep (édition provisoire)," this is the first map of Aleppo published under the French mandate, edited by the Bureau Topographique de T. F. L. in Beirut, scale 1:5000 or reduced to 1:10000; (1926–30) cadastral plan of Aleppo compiled under the direction of C. Durrafourd (201 cadastral sheets, 133 intra muros and 68 extra muros), the sheets of the ancient city are on a scale of 1:500 and only the sheets for the central part of the suq are on a scale of 1:2000, while the citadel and the less densely populated districts are on a scale of 1:1000; (1930) "Ville d'Alep. Plan d'ensemble du territoire de la ville...," scale 1:20000; (1930) map of Aleppo, scale 1:10000; (1931) "Ville d'Alep. Plan general," four sheets on a scale of 1:5000. In Syria, the work of measuring and drawing the urban fabric was also carried out for Damascus, Tartous, Latakia, and Hama where, except for slight revisions, the 1930s French cadastral surveys are still in use, especially for cartography on an urban scale.

ritories along the borders of the southern Mediterranean, from North Africa to the Middle East. In the period in question English, but more especially French surveys become the most efficient tool for the physical description of the urban organism and a morphological approach to urban studies on Islamic city.[10] Indeed, French cadastral surveys not only constituted a means of control of landed property in the newly colonized territories, but were, more importantly, the first precise instrument for representing the urban organisms of these regions, providing a knowledge and description of the pre-modern structure and form of Middle Eastern and North African cities, and laying the foundations for later urban studies.

In general, beginning with the use of cadastral surveys in urban studies, the Orientalist approach that had characterized the Western attitude towards the study of Islamic cities which was based on an interpretation of these cities as esoteric and mysterious because little known entities was partly supplanted by a more structurally based epistemological approach, favoured by a better knowledge of the urban fabric. From this moment, interest in the physical structure of cities in these regions was no longer the exclusive domain of simplified surveys, visual representations, or literary descriptions, but became part of a more widespread interest in urban and architectonic classification carried out by colonialists, beginning in the eighteenth century with the *Description de l'Egypte* and culminating in the redaction of cadastral surveys.[11]

---

[10] For cities in Algeria and Egypt, cadastral surveys of the urban fabric were begun at the end of the nineteenth century. For Algeria, as an example, see some of the cartography for the city of Blidah: "Plan General d'Alignement de la Ville de Blida" of 1842, "Ville de Blidah" cadastral plan of 1866 or 1915, or the series of historical plans, beginning with "Blidah" in 1935. For cities in Egypt, cadastral surveys of the urban fabric began when the Egyptian Survey Authority compiled a series of maps and plans of Cairo on a scale of 1:500, 1:1000, 1:5000 at the end of the nineteenth century. The Egyptian Department of Survey has integrated the existing cartography on Cairo with the "Map of Islamic Historical Monuments in Cairo" on a scale of 1:5000 and based on a 1947 survey.

[11] In Islamic cities cadastral surveys were only introduced in the twentieth century as a direct result of European colonization. Prior to this time there were other methods for the registration of landed property and for taxation, such as the endowment property registers, called waqf in the Middle East and *habous* in North Africa. While they did not provide a cartographic reconstruction of the urban fabric, they did nevertheless give the data necessary for any attempt to reconstruct the individual property units.

These registers, which have represented the main source for important studies on the Islamic city, do not allow one, however, to describe the physical urban organism as a whole, since the waqf registers did not cover all the property in a city. Moreover,

Research publications from the same period on the physical structure of cities in those areas of the Islamic world that had not been colonized by Europeans were less numerous than those on North Africa and the Middle East, partly because of the lack of adequate descriptive tools. Though, at the beginning of the twentieth century, measured drawings of the cities of Central Asia, the Anatolian Peninsula, and Iran were made by local scholars.

The bases of urban studies on central Asian cities were laid before the Soviet Revolution by the Russian scholars W. Barthold[12] and V. A. Shishkin.[13] By studying the main Arabic and Persian written sources on central Asian urban centres in pre-Mongol medieval Russia (Turkestan), they were able to produce a cross-section of the historical topography of cities in this region.

While European scholars were studying in this period the cities of the Near East and North Africa using the Orientalist approach described above, Soviet scholars introduced the semantic fields of "feudal city" and "medieval city" and described the structure of Central Asian cities as well in terms of a dichotomy between their urban structure and that of western European and Russian cities.

As with Central Asian cities, only a few studies, when compared to the large number of studies on North African and Middle Eastern cities, were carried out in the first decades of the twentieth century on urban physical structures in Iran. Moreover, even though during the Shah's reign cadastral surveys were compiled,[14] in the first decades of the twentieth century scholarship was focused above all on the study

---

their descriptions are codified in such a way that it is not always possible to reconstruct the plan of the property in question.

For the debate on the representation of the Islamic city before the twentieth century see: D. Behrens-Abouseif, "Alternatives to Cadaster Maps for the Study of Islamic Cities," in "Urban Morphogenesis: Maps and Cadastral Plans," ed. A. Petruccioli, *Environmental Design: Journal of the Islamic Environmental Design Research Centre* 1–2 (1993): 92–95; A. Raymond, "Cartographie et histoire des villes arabes, quelques remarques générales," in "Urban Morphogenesis: Maps and Cadastral Plans," ed. A. Petruccioli, *Environmental Design: Journal of the Islamic Environmental Design Research Centre* 1–2 (1993): 22–31.

[12] W. Barthold, *Istoriko-geograficheskii obzor Irana* (St. Petersburg, 1903); W. Barthold, *Turkestan down to the Mongol Invasion* (first published in Russian in 1910; London, 1928). Later, with his excavations in Samarkand, Barthold spread throughout the future Soviet Union a methodological approach to urban studies that combined historical and archaeological enquiry.

[13] V. A. Shishkin, *Goroda Uzbekistana* (Tashkent, 1943).

[14] In Iran, too, cadastral surveys were compiled under the Shah on a scale of 1:2000.

of Iranian art and architecture or, again from an Orientalist perspective, on the archaeology of pre-Islamic strata rather than the physical structure of Islamic cities.[15]

In this period the most important urban studies were those carried out by the French urbanist Eugene E. Beaudouin and the American historian Arthur Upham Pope on Isfahan[16] which remained without sequel for many years.

Despite the fact that in Anatolia, at the beginning of the twentieth century, accurate surveys of the main cities were compiled[17] which would have allowed the further development of studies on Islamic urban structure, even here European scholarship was mainly focused either on the archaeology of Hellenistic or pre-Hellenistic sites or on the capital, Istanbul, which represented the vestiges of the ancient world and the cradle of European civilization. Thus, the strata of the Islamic phases in the construction of the city were ignored.[18] In this period, urban studies were mainly conducted by local historians for the Turkish government,[19] while research by European scholars only began

---

[15] E. Herzfeld and F. Sarre, *Archäologische Reise im Euphrat und Tigris Gebiet* (Berlin, 1911–20); G. Bell, *Palace and Mosque at Ukhaidir* (Oxford, 1914); D. T. Rice, "The City of Shapur," *Ars Islamica* 2 (1935): 174–189; A. Godard, "Isfahân," *Athâr-é-Irân. Annales du Service Archéologique de l'Iran* 1 (1937): 7–176; L. Lockhart, *Famous Cities of Iran* (Brentford, 1939); E. Herzfeld, *Geschichte der Stadt Samarra* (Berlin, 1948).

[16] E. E. Beaudouin and A. U. Pope, "City Plans," in *A Survey of Persian Art*, ed. A. U. Pope and P. Ackerman (London, 1939), 1391–1410; E. E. Beaudouin, "Ispahan sous les grands chahs (XVIIᵉ siècle)," *Urbanisme* 2, no. 10 (1933).

[17] Already in the Ottoman period accurate maps and surveys were made of Istanbul and Smyrne. Then in 1904–1906 the "Plans d'assurance d'Istanbul et de Smyrne" by C. E. Goad, scale 1:600, 1:3.600. In the first decades of the twentieth century a cadastral survey of Istanbul was compiled. In 1922–1945 the "Plans d'assurance d'Istanbul de Pervitich" was completed by J. Pervitich, on a scale of 1:250, 1:375, 1:500, 1:600, 1:1000, 1:2000, 1:2400, 1:4000. For this subject, see: P. Pinon, and S. Yerasimos, "Relevés après incendie et plans d'assurance. Les précurseurs du cadastre Stambouliote," in "Urban Morphogenesis: Maps and Cadastral Plans," ed. A. Petruccioli, *Environmental Design: Journal of the Islamic Environmental Design Research Centre* 1–2 (1993): 112–129.

[18] H. H. von der Osten, "An Unnoticed Ancient Metropolis of Asia Minor," *Geographical Review* 18 (1928); D. T. Rice, "Nicaea," *Antiquity* 3 (1929); D. T. Rice, "British Excavations at Constantinople," *Antiquity* 4 (1930); E. Mamboury and T. Wiegand, *Die Kaiserpaläste von Konstantinopel zwischen Hippodrom und Marmara-Meer* (Berlin, 1934); R. Mayer, *Byzantion-Konstantinupolis-Istanbul: Eine genetische Stadtgeographie* (Vienna and Leipzig, 1943); E. Mamboury, "Istanbul: Un nouvel élément pour la topographie de l'antique Byzance," *Archäologischer Anzeiger: Beiblatt zum Jahrbuch des Archäologischen Instituts* 49 (1934): 50–61; C. Alzonne, *Istanbul* (Paris, 1936); R. Bova Scoppa, *Stanbul* (Milano, 1933); R. Busch-Zantner, "Zur Kenntnis der osmanischen Stadt," *Geographische Zeitschrift* 38 (1932): 1–13; A. Cuda, "Stadtaufbau in der Türkei," *Die Welt des Islams* 21 (1939): 1–84.

[19] O. Ergin, *The Historical Development of Urbanism in Turkey* [in Turkish] (Istanbul, 1936).

once they were allowed access to the Ottoman archives after the fall of the Ottoman empire.

The Revision of the Orientalist approach

This initial phase of scholarship on the Islamic city, and especially of urban studies on North African cities, produced a representative model of the structure of the Islamic city that was too homogeneous. This model was subjected to an initial critical revision in the 1950s, when Edmond Pauty[20] elaborated the theories of William and George Marçais, Henri Terrasse,[21] and Henry Pirenne on North African cities and refined the models proposed by them, thereby beginning a process of classification of diverse urban structures based on geographical, social, historical, and economic factors that would predominate in the following years.

Emphasizing the role of Islam as an urban religion and proposing an urban model in terms of its divergence from the medieval European city, he suggested a distinction between spontaneous and planned cities, concluding that in most cases Islamic cities were founded by dynasties or monarchs and, thus, did not develop autonomously. Pauty's distinction not only represented the starting point for a process of revision of Orientalist studies, but also allowed scholars to focus their attention on the necessity of dealing with the actual history and form of these cities instead of their theoretical models.

In the following years, Pauty's theories were taken up by Gustav von Grunebaum, Ira M. Lapidus, Xavier de Planhol, H. A. R. Gibb, and Harold Bowen, who examined the salient features of the Islamic city mainly in terms of the socio-political organization of its inhabitants.

Gustav von Grunebaum[22] based his work on the Islamic city on the Marçais' theories (from which he partially distanced himself by

---

[20] E. Pauty, "Villes spontanées et villes créées en Islam," *Annales de l'Institut d'Études Orientales* 9 (1951).

[21] H. Terrasse, *Villes impériales du Maroc* (Grenoble, 1938); H. Terrasse, "L'architecture musulmane d'Occident," *Les Cahiers de Tunisie* 4 (1956): 137–144; R. Le Tourneau and H. Terrasse, s.v. "Fas," *Encyclopaedia of Islam*, 2nd ed. (1965): 818–823.

[22] G. E. von Grunebaum, "Die Islamische Stadt," *Saeculum* 6 (1955): 138–153; G. E. von Grunebaum, "The Structure of the Muslim Town," in "Islam: Essays in the Nature and Growth of a Cultural Tradition," *Memoirs of the American Anthropological Association* 81 (1955): 141–158; G. E. von Grunebaum, "The Muslim Town and the Hellenistic

drawing a distinction between rural villages and urban agglomerations, for which he held their theories to be valid) and, to some extent, Brunschvig's studies. Grunebaum ascribed the origins of certain elements in the urban structure—such as the narrow, winding streets—to the spontaneous, unplanned nature of Islamic cities and their internal chaos, as well as to the hectic nature of neighbourhood life. Focusing his attention on the socio-political structure of urban organization, he stressed the absence of municipal institutions and community structures, in the European sense, and even concluded that the—self-enclosed and autonomous—neighbourhoods themselves were what defined their residents as a community.

Referring to a vast geographical area, from Egypt to Central Asia, Ira M. Lapidus[23] applied a flexible analytical model to the study of the Islamic city which could be modified according to period and region, though he tended mainly to describe urban society rather than urban form. Moreover, he substituted the term "Islamic city" with either "Muslim city" or "Islamic society," while in his studies on Mamluk society in Syria he introduced the concept of a "mosaic" society: an organic network of ethnic and religious groups at the basis of urban morphology which found its essential conformation in the neighbourhood.

Gibb's and Bowen's[24] theories enriched the debate by drawing on von Grunebaum's work which made a distinction between city and rural village, and Lapidus' vision of a mosaic society.

Still from an Orientalist perspective, Xavier de Planhol[25] underlined the lack of civic government in Islamic cities and societies, and attributed this scarce civic sense to the nomadic origins of its inhabitants.

Town," *Scientia*, 1955, 364–370; G. E. von Grunebaum, "The Sacred Character of the Islamic Cities," in *Melanges Taha Husain*, ed. A. Badawi (Cairo, 1962); G. E. von Grunebaum, "The Structure of the Muslim Town," in *Islam: Essays on the Culture and Growth of a Cultural Tradition* (London, 1961).

[23] I. M. Lapidus, *Muslim Cities in the Later Middle Ages* (Cambridge, 1967); I. M. Lapidus, ed., "Muslim Cities and Islamic Society," in *Middle Eastern Cities: A Symposium on Ancient, Islamic and Contemporary Middle Eastern Urbanism* (Berkeley, 1969), 47–79; I. M. Lapidus, "Traditional Muslim Cities: Structure and Change," in *From Medina to Metropolis*, ed. C. L. Brown (Princeton, NJ, 1973), 51–69; I. M. Lapidus, "The Early Evolution of Muslim Urban Society," *Comparative Studies in Society and History*, 15 (1973): 21–50; I. M. Lapidus, "Muslim Cities as Plural Societies: The Politics of Intermediary Bodies," in *Urbanism in Islam*, ed. Y. Takeshi (Tokyo, 1989), 133–164.

[24] H. A. R. Gibb and H. Bowen, *Islamic Society and the West: A Study of the Impact of Western Civilization on Moslem Culture in the Near East*, vol. 1 (London, 1950).

[25] X. de Planhol, *The World of Islam* (Ithaca, 1959); X. de Planhol, *Les Fondements Géographiques de l'Histoire de l'Islam* (Paris, 1968).

Eliyahu Ashtor[26] and Claude Cahen[27] revised von Grunebaum's theoretical model and applied it to a different geographical region, that of Syrian and Iraqi cities in the tenth-twelfth centuries. Using the example of Damascus in the early medieval period, Ashtor sought to demonstrate the existence of an urban autonomy in Islamic cities based on the role of the *rais, muhtasib*, and *qadi*. Cahen, on the other hand, stressed that the guilds were a motive of urban dis-aggregation, due to their religious orientation which tended towards mysticism, and that civil order was maintained by organized groups of urban bandits.

In this debate on the structure of the Islamic city the theses of Shmuel Tamari[28] shifted attention from a social to a more structural perspective, reintroducing an interest in morphological data and urban structure. With his classification of Islamic cities into four types—Hellenistic-Mediterranean, Iranian-Mesopotamian, Southern-Arabian, and Residential—he demonstrated that, while the Islamic city was the result of diverse schemes and influences, it then developed autonomously, finding its own morphological individuality through time.

Equally interested in urban morphology, Sauvaget's pupil, Nikita Elisseeff,[29] carried out urban studies on Damascus, refining on the former's method and asserting the impossibility of applying Massignon's theories to Damascus, since Islamic urban form was determined by social and economic factors more than by legislative ones.

Despite these isolated attempts to extend the debate on the Islamic city to other regions of the Islamic world and to deal with it from the perspective of its physical structure, until the 1960s this debate was the almost exclusive terrain of French historians and English sociologists who continued to study North African cities in order to delineate an urban model that would be valid for all cities in the Muslim world.

---

[26] E. Ashtor, "L'administration urbaine en Syrie médiévale," *Rivista degli Studi Orientali* 31 (1956); E. Asthor, "L'urbanisme syrien à la basse-époque," *Rivista degli Studi Orientali* 31 (1958): 181–209; E. Ashtor, "Républiques urbaines dans le Proche-Orient à l'époque des Croisades," *Cahiers de la Civilisation Médiévale* 18 (1975).

[27] C. Cahen, "Mouvements populaires et autonomisme urbain dans l'Asie musulmane du moyen age," *Arabica* 5, no. 3 (1958), 6, no. 1 (1959), 6, no. 3 (1959); C. Cahen, *Mouvements populaires et autonomisme urbane* (Leiden, 1959); C. Cahen, "Y a-t-il eu des corporations professionelles dans le monde musulman classique?" in *The Islamic City: A Colloquium*, ed. A. H. Hourani and S. M. Stern (Oxford, 1970), 51–64, in which he criticizes Massignon's theories on the guild corporations.

[28] S. Tamari, "Aspetti principali dell'urbanesimo musulmano," *Palladio*, nos. 1–4 (1966): 45–82.

[29] N. Elisséeff, "Damas à la lumière des théories de Jean Sauvaget," in *The Islamic City*, ed. A. H. Hourani and S. M. Stern (Oxford, 1969), 157–177.

Many of the contributions to the debate on the structure of the Islamic city which marked the scholarship of this period were published in the proceedings of conferences, including those organized by Ira M. Lapidus in 1969[30] and Albert H. Hourani and Samuel M. Stern in 1970.[31] The latter conference in particular traced the course of these studies, in the wake of Hourani's observations on the North African origins of the model that G. Marçais extended to the whole of the Muslim world, of the impossibility of generalizing this model, and of Stern's criticisms of the theories put forward by Massignon, von Grunebaum, Ashtor, and Cahen. Stern rejected the possibility of a comparative hypothesis between medieval European and Islamic urban structure, since in the latter case autonomous organizations were still in their infancy.

After 1970, following this revision of the approach to research on the Islamic city, the debate began to diversify, due to the contribution of English and American geographers, sociologists, and architects who rejected the unified and abstract model proposed up to that time. They focused their interest, instead, on the role of religion in the codification of Islamic urban form and society, or on the structure of cities in other regions, especially the Middle East.

In this period anthropologists such as Dale Eickelman and Kenneth Brown proposed different urban models from those already delineated by sociological studies, though their research remained tied to the Maghreb. Beginning with an analysis of a neighbourhood in the city of Boujad in Morocco and comparing it with other regions, Eickelman[32] considered the theories of Massignon and Marçais inadequate to outline a definitive model of the Islamic city. Rejecting Lapidus' model of a mosaic society and his theories on the neighbourhood which were only useful for describing social rather than urban models, Eickelman identified in the neighbourhood an intellectual rather than a physical structure, based on a mutual sense of nearness and on the dynamic structure of social relations.

---

[30] I. M. Lapidus, *Middle Eastern Cities: A Symposium on Ancient, Islamic and Contemporary Middle Eastern Urbanism* (Berkeley, CA, 1969).

[31] A. H. Hourani and S. M. Stern, eds., *The Islamic City: A Colloquium* (Oxford, 1970); A. H. Hourani, "The Islamic City in the Light of Recent Research," in *The Islamic City: A Colloquium* (Oxford, 1970), 1–24; S. M. Stern, "The Constitution of the Islamic City," in *The Islamic City: A Colloquium* (Oxford, 1970), 25–50.

[32] D. Eickelman, "Is There an Islamic City? The Marking of a Quarter in a Moroccan Town," *IJMES* 5 (1974).

Brown[33] extended the work of scholars such as Lapidus, Stern, and Hourani on Middle Eastern cities to North African cities. In his essay on Salè, he moved away from Lapidus' theories and closer to Eickelman's and Gibb's ideas, demonstrating that in a city which had the typical morphological structure of a North African medina, the sense of community, autonomous organization, and solidarity was instead very strong.

In the 1980s the debate on the structure of the Islamic city became more heated and a series of conferences—especially those organized by Robert B. Sergeant (1980),[34] Ismail Serageldin and Samir el-Sadek (1982),[35] Aydin Germen (1983),[36] Kenneth L. Brown (1986),[37] Carl L. Brown,[38] Abdulaziz Y. Saqqaf (1987),[39] and Takeshi Yukawa (1989)[40]— marked the transition to this new phase of scholarship.

Since there was a growing awareness that every urban organism has its own unique identity, which is different from others in terms of geographical and historical circumstances, the perception of the impossibility of using generalizations to describe a unified model determined a change of approach and a new attitude dominated the field of urban studies on the Islamic city. The arguments which epitomize this debate are those of Eugen Wirth, Besim Selim Hakim, Jean Claude Garcin, and Janet Abu-Lughod.

Hakim[41] sought the derivation of the urban structure of cities, still generically defined as Islamic, in Islamic law. Applying a methodology similar to Brunschvig's he maintained that the general lines for the construction of the Islamic city had been determined on the basis

---

[33] K. L. Brown, "An Urban View of Moroccan History: Salé 1000–1800," *Hespéris–Tamuda* 12 (1971): 5–106; K. L. Brown, *People of Salé: Tradition and Change in a Moroccan City 1830–1930* (New York, 1976).

[34] R. B. Serjeant, ed., *The Islamic City* (Paris, 1980). Studies on Arabia and Yemen.

[35] I. Serageldin and S. el-Sadek, eds., *The Arab City: Its Character and Islamic Cultural Heritage* (Riyadh, 1982).

[36] A. Germen, ed., *Islamic Architecture and Urbanism* (Dammam, 1983).

[37] K. L. Brown, M. Jolé, P. Sluglett, and S. Zubaida, eds., *Middle Eastern Cities in Comparative Perspective* (London and Ithaca, 1986); K. L. Brown et al., eds., *Urban Crisis and Social Movements in the Middle East* (Paris, 1989).

[38] C. L. Brown, ed., *From Medina to Metropolis: Heritage and Change in the Near Eastern City* (Princeton, NJ, 1973).

[39] A. Y. Saqqaf, ed., *The Middle East City: Ancient Traditions Confront a Modern World* (New York, 1987).

[40] T. Yukawa, ed., *Urbanism in Islam: The Proceedings of the International Conference on Urbanism in Islam* (ICUIT), Oct. 22–28, 1989 (Tokyo, 1989).

[41] B. S. Hakim, *Arabic–Islamic Cities: Building and Planning Principles* (London, 1986); B. S. Hakim, "The 'Urf' and its role in diversifying the architecture of traditional Islamic cities," *Journal of Architectural and Planning Research* 11, no. 2 (1994): 108–127.

of statutory rules and regulations. Thus, Arab cities could be called Arabo-Islamic, since Islamic law functioned as a guideline both for building and for urban life.

In line with other morphological studies, Wirth's[42] theories set out to describe an urban model based on a comparison between the structures of pre-Islamic cities in North Africa, Western Asia, and the Middle East. Indeed, his theories, together with those of Sauvaget, are at the basis of morphological studies on the Islamic city. While scholarship in the Orientalist tradition used a generalized scheme, deriving from the observation of specific urban structures in specific cultural and geographic areas which then became a general point of reference for urban structures that were actually widely differentiated in terms of time and space, the work carried out by Wirth and Sauvaget brought specific morphological data, geographical differentiation, and a reading of the urban fabric to bear on this more generalized debate, thereby paving the way for modern studies on the Islamic city. Beginning with a comparative analysis of the functions and morphology of cities in North Africa and Western Asia, Wirth concluded that it was not possible to define such cities as "Islamic," since none of their characteristics could be directly related to Islam as a religion. Rather, the structure of the medieval Islamic city derived from its oriental substratum. The tree-lined routes, the cul-de-sac system, the division into separate and mutually independent neighbourhoods, the dog-leg entrances, the courtyard dwelling type were all already present in the most ancient cities of Mesopotamia. Only the suq seemed to be an element unique to the Islamic city, since it was present neither in the ancient East nor in Europe. On the basis of these considerations he suggested replacing the term "Islamic" with "Oriental," rejecting the term "Arab", since the same urban characteristics could be found in Turkish and Iranian cities.

In the same period the debate on the structure of the Islamic city was enriched by Hicham Djaït's work on al-Kufa.[43] Through a careful analysis of texts relating to the primitive city of al-Kufa, Djaït revealed

---

[42] E. Wirth, "Die Orientalische Stadt. Ein Überblick aufgrund jüngerer Forschungen zur materiellen Kultur," *Saeculum* 26 (1975): 45–94; E. Wirth, "Villes islamiques, villes arabes, villes orientales? Une problématique face au changement," in *La ville arabe dans l'Islam*, ed. A. Bouhdiba and D. Chevallier (Tunis and Paris, 1982), 193–215; E. Wirth, "Zur Konzeption der islamischen Stadt: Privatheit im islamischen Orient versus Öffentlichkeit in Antike und Okzident," *Die Welt des Islams* 25 (1985): 50–92; E. Wirth, *Die Orientalische Stadt im islamischen Vorderasien und Nordafrika* (Mainz, 2000).
[43] H. Djaït, *al-Kûfa: Naissance de la ville islamique* (Paris, 1986).

the ordered character of urban topography in the early phases of
anthropic development and demonstrated that in the case of cities
built over military encampments, the structure of the urban fabric
derived from the original military layout which was divided internally,
for political reasons, according to ethnic groups. In his theories he
criticized Wirth's approach, since it was based on purely geographical
presuppositions and had rejected the term "Islamic." He shared, in
some respects, the notion of continuity and related the structure of
the Islamic city to that of the Greco-Roman and ancient eastern city.

Janet Abu-Lughod[44] confirmed that the model of the Islamic city
so far defined was the result of an Orientalist perspective based on
the observation of a few case studies in a limited area. In her essays,
she warned of the dangers of generalizing specific morphological and
geographical data that had led the so-called Orientalists to assimilate
cities from widely differing geographical areas, and instead advanced
an idea of the formation of the Islamic city through a morphological
process based not only on legal, political, and religious systems but also
on specific cultural factors.

Robert Ilbert's[45] contribution went along the same revisionist lines.
Keeping to theoretical positions, his thesis transformed the concept of
the Islamic city into a tool for abstract analysis. Starting from an analysis
of actual morphological data, he extrapolated general concepts, identifying the Islamic city with a concept that did not correspond to actual
urban structures, but rather to the critical selection of certain features
taken out of their historical context and thereby invalidated by a series
of contrasts, due to the widely differing urban structures in question.

In order to conserve at least in part the urban model defined by
Orientalist scholars, while at the same time recognizing its tendency
to over-generalization, the French historian Jean-Claude Garcin,[46]
using the example of Cairo, based his theories on the chronological

---

[44] J. L. Abu-Lughod, "The Islamic City: Historic Myth, Islamic Essence, and Contemporary Relevance," *IJMES* 19 (1987); J. L. Abu-Lughod, "What is Islamic about
a City? Some Comparative Reflections," in *Urbanism in Islam: The Proceedings of the
International Conference of Urbanism in Islam* (Tokyo, 1989).

[45] R. Ilbert, "La ville islamique: réalité et abstraction," *Cahiers de la recherche architecturale,* nos. 10–11 (1982): 6–13.

[46] J.-C. Garcin, "Le Caire et l'évolution urbane des pays musulmans," *Annales Isla-
mologiques* 25 (1991): 289–304; D. Behrens-Abouseif, S. Denoix, and J.-C. Garcin, "Le
Caire," in *Grandes Villes Méditerranéennes du Monde Musulman Médiéval,* ed. J.-C. Garcin
(Rome, 2000).

diversification of Islamic urban development and the division of this over-simplified Orientalist model into periods. The first phase of this division corresponds to the foundation of a new urban centre or the occupation and reorganization of an existing city. The second phase corresponds to the transformation of urban centres with the advent of military aristocracies, while the third phase corresponds to the formation of the traditional city, beginning with the crisis at the end of the fourteenth century. This was a city enclosed within its defensive walls and characterized by closed-off, separate, and specialized neighbourhoods, seemingly chaotic and labyrinthine, which constituted the prototype for Orientalist generalizations.

In this context, Andrè Raymond's studies in the 1980s,[47] especially *The Great Arab Cities*, have represented a cornerstone of urban studies on the Islamic city, by rejecting the other major Orientalist prejudice, based on the notion of stagnation and a vision of Islamic cities as economically backward. In his essays on Cairo, Aleppo, and Tunis, Raymond has demonstrated that the Ottoman Empire represented a period of expansion, rather than decline, for Islamic cities. Applying a methodology that combines an historical with a morphological approach—beginning with an examination of waqf archival documents in order to obtain a social, economic, and historical cross-section of the dynamics of urban development and with the aid of morphological information on urban growth given by the position of newly founded specialized buildings within the urban fabric—he has pointed out that the general decline of Islamic cities began with European colonization after the fall of the Ottoman Empire.

Finally, in these years, a further series of conferences organized by the Aga Khan Award for Architecture resulted in the publication of proceedings and texts on the architecture of the Islamic city.[48] Even

---

[47] A. Raymond, "Signes urbains et étude de la population des grandes villes arabes à l'èpoque ottomane," *Bulletin d'Études Orientales de l'Institut Français d'Études Arabes de Damas* 27 (1974): 183–193; A. Raymond, "Le déplacement des tanneries à Alep, au Caire et à Tunis à l'époque ottomane: Un 'indicateur' de croissance urbaine," *Revue d'Histoire Maghrébine*, nos. 7–8 (1977): 192–200; A. Raymond, *The Great Arab Cities in the 16th–18th Centuries: An Introduction* (New York, 1984).

[48] J. G. Katz, ed., *Architecture as a Symbol and Self–Identity* (Cambridge, MA, 1980); L. Safran, ed., *Housing: Process and Physical Form* (Cambridge, MA, 1980); L. Safran, ed., *Places of Public Gathering in Islam* (Cambridge, MA, 1980); L. Safran, ed., *Toward an Architecture in the Spirit of Islam* (Cambridge, MA, 1980); M. B. Sevcenko, ed., *Adaptive Reuse: Integrating Traditional Areas into the Modern Urban Fabric* (Cambridge, MA, 1983); R. Powell, ed., *Regionalism in Architecture* (Cambridge, MA, 1985).

though the subject matter of these conferences was mainly contemporary architecture, they were part of the rise of a more general interest
in the study of the Islamic city as an actual physical space for research,
not an abstract, speculative model. The role of the Aga Khan Award
for Architecture has been even more important, since, together with
the above-mentioned conferences, it has made clear that a regional
approach to the study of the physical city linked to the study of the
specific morphological data, building types, and techniques of construction of the diverse regions that go to make up the Islamic world is
needed in order to overcome the Orientalist impasse in the study and
urban renewal of Islamic cities.

The regional approach

In the 1980s, when a substantial amount of knowledge on the Islamic
city and its architecture had already been acquired, it was possible to
compile a series of historical-encyclopaedic works, such as the *Encyclopaedia of Islam*[49] and the *Encyclopaedia Iranica*,[50] the precursor to which
is recognisable in the bibliography on Islamic arts and architecture
compiled by A. C. Creswell.[51]

In the same period, Paolo Cuneo's book on the Islamic city was
published.[52] This probably represents the single most systematic work on
the history of the cities and different regions of the Muslim world. Its
historical approach was associated with a regional one, while the analysis
of the most salient urban features of the different regions was conducted
on the basis of the underlying features and diverse influences that over
time had determined a diversity of urban forms. The uniqueness of
this work is confirmed by the fact that its comprehensive and organic
treatment has been equalled only recently by Paul Wheatley's work.[53]

---

[49] *Encyclopaedia of Islam*, 2nd ed. (Leiden, 1960).
[50] E. Yarshater, ed., *Encyclopaedia Iranica* (London, 1988).
[51] K. A. C. Creswell, *A Bibliography of the Architecture, Arts and Crafts of Islam, Second
Supplement Jan. 1972 to Dec. 1980 (with Omissions from Previous Years)* (Cairo, 1984), the
third volume of a bibliographic collection that began with K. A. C. Creswell, *A Bibliography of the Architecture, Arts and Crafts of Islam to 1 Jan. 1960* (Cairo, 1961); K. A. C.
Creswell, *A Bibliography of the Architecture, Arts and Crafts of Islam, Supplement Jan. 1960 to
Jan. 1972* (Cairo, 1973).
[52] P. Cuneo, *Storia dell'urbanistica: Il mondo islamico* (Rome, 1986).
[53] P. Wheatley, *The Places where Men Pray Together: Cities in Islamic Lands Seventh through
the Tenth Centuries* (Chicago, 2001).

Using a morphological and historical approach, the latter has described the urban structures of the different regions of the Muslim world both in relation to their territorial context and their urban structure.

From another perspective, Paolo Cuneo's encyclopaedic approach represents an opposite trend with respect to the more widespread one of the 1980s which consisted in an interest in specific cities in the Muslim world and was often expressed through the formation of different schools or groups of scholars with a similar methodological approach or interest in the study of the physical structure of Islamic cities.

The first identifiable school, and perhaps the one that has always been the most active in research on the physical structure of the Islamic city, is the French school, mainly oriented toward the study of cities in the regions of their ex-colonies. This school has had its main theoretical points of reference in the work of scholars such as Andrè Raymond[54] and Philippe Panerai.[55]

Using the methodology developed by André Raymond, which combines a historical with a morphological approach, the work of scholars such as Jean Paul Pascual, Robert Ilbert, and Silvy Denoix[56] has favoured an approach based on historical and archival research.

In his studies on the structure of the Islamic city Philippe Panerai has adopted the urban studies methodology developed in Italy by Aldo Rossi and Carlo Aymonino in the 1960s which they applied to Italian and other European cities. He describes the model of the Islamic city as radial, enclosed by walls, with the congregational mosque at the centre and the suqs linking it to the city gates. For Panerai the urban fabric develops in terms of autonomous neighbourhoods based on a social organization and is thus somewhat similar to the mosaic city model.

Starting from Panerai's methodology which is closely linked to an analysis of morphological data, though adopting different approaches, Pierre Pinon has mainly used historical data to trace the various phases

---

[54] A. Raymond, "Signes urbains et étude de la population des grandes villes arabes à l'èpoque ottomane," *Bulletin d'Études Orientales de l'Institut Français d'Études Arabes de Damas* 27 (1974): 183–193; A. Raymond, "Le déplacement des tanneries à Alep, au Caire et à Tunis à l'époque ottomane: Un 'indicateur' de croissance urbaine," *Revue d'Histoire Maghrébine*, nos. 7–8 (1977): 192–200; A. Raymond, *The Great Arab Cities in the 16th–18th Centuries: An Introduction* (New York, 1984).

[55] P. Panerai, "Sur la notion de ville islamique," *Peuples Méditerranéens—Mediterranean Peoples* 46 (1989): 13–30.

[56] S. Denoix, "History and Urban Forms. A Methodological Approach," in "Urban Morphogenesis: Maps and Cadastral Plans," ed. A. Petruccioli, *Environmental Design: Journal of the Islamic Environmental Design Centre* 1–2 (1993): 70–81.

of urban development, while Serge Santelli has used the measured drawing of residential buildings as a means of describing the urban structure mainly of Tunisian, but also of Middle Eastern and African cities.[57] Jean-Charles Depaule[58] has combined a descriptive-classifying approach to architecture with a sociological one, while Jean-Claude David has used a hybrid method in his study of the structure of the Islamic city. David's methodology could be considered somewhere between Raymond's and Panerai's, combining a classifying approach to the study of urban morphology, based on the measured drawing, with a historical one, based on the study of waqf documents, and a geographical one, based on statistical research. From this methodological admixture, developed in his studies on Aleppo, David has obtained a completely original synthesis that has led him to have interesting intuitions on the morphology of the Islamic city.

In France, the research centres where these studies have been carried out are: the Institut de Recherches et d'Études sur le Monde Arabe et Musulman in Aix en Provence[59] which is especially concerned with the history of the city; the Équipe Monde Arabe et Méditerranée (ex URBAMA-Urbanisation du Monde Arabe) of the French C.N.R.S. at the University of Tours, where geographers and town-planners carry out research on contemporary Arab cities,[60] and the Maison de l'Orient Méditerranéen in Lyons,[61] which is especially concerned with historico-morphological studies.

---

[57] Ph. Revault and S. Santelli, eds., *Harar, une cité musulmane d'Ethiopie/Harar, a Muslim City of Ethiopia* (Paris, 2004).

[58] J.-C. Depaule and S. Noweir, *L'habitat urbain dans l'Orient arabe, éléments d'architecture* (Paris, 1984); J.-C. Depaule, "Daily Life and Living Space in the Mashriq," in *Middle Eastern Cities in Comparative Perspective*, ed. K. Brown, M. Jolé, P. Sluglett, and S. Zubaida (London, 1986), 203–211.

[59] Groupe de Recherches et d'Études sur le Proche Orient, eds., *L'Habitat traditionnel dans les pays musulmans autour de la Méditerranée* (Cairo, 1988).

[60] Centre d'Études et de Recherches sur l'Urbanisation du Monde Arabe, ed., *Présent et avenir des Médinas*, Fasc. 10–11 (Tours, 1982); Centre d'Études et de Recherches sur l'Urbanisation du Monde Arabe, ed., *Petites villes et villes moyennes dans le Monde Arabe*, Fasc. 16–17 (Tours, 1986); Centre d'Études et de Recherches sur l'Urbanisation du Monde Arabe, ed., *Eléments sur les centres-villes dans le Monde Arabe-Material on City Centres in the Arab World*, Fasc. 19 (Tours, 1988); Centre d'Études et de Recherches sur l'Urbanisation du Monde Arabe, ed., *L'eau et la ville dans les pays du Bassin Méditerranéen et de la Mer Noire*, Actes du Colloque de Rabat, 20–22 Octobre 1988, Fasc. 22 (Tours, 1991); J.-F. Troin, ed., *Recherches urbaines sur le monde arabo-musulman—Urban Research on the Middle East* (Tours, 1993).

[61] J. Metral and G. Mutin, eds., *Politiques urbaines dans le Monde arabe*, Études sur le Monde Arabe, no. 1 (Lyons: Maison de l'Orient Méditerranéen, 1984).

In Italy interest in the study of Islamic cities began at the University of Rome, with the work of a group of scholars that included Attilio Petruccioli,[62] Florindo Fusaro,[63] and Ludovico Micara.[64] Beginning with a general interest in urban morphological data, based on the work of Saverio Muratori and Ludovico Quaroni, they initiated studies on the Islamic, especially Mediterranean, city that were characterized by a keen interest in the physical structure of urban fabric and so were close to those of Panerai's French School.

The research methodology on Islamic cities introduced by Attilio Petruccioli consists in a reading of the urban fabric using epistemological tools developed in the field of morphological and typological studies. Considering the city as a living organism, Petruccioli's research is based on the idea that the history of every city is inscribed in its urban fabric and so it is possible to decipher the various phases of its

---

[62] L. Micara and A. Petruccioli, "Metodologie di analisi degli insediamenti storici nel mondo islamico," Istituto Poligrafico e Zecca dello Stato, no. 4 (1986): 27–40; A. Petruccioli, "The Arab City neither Spontaneous nor Created," in "Environmental Design: Trails to the East, Essays in Memory of Paolo Cuneo," ed. A. Petruccioli, *Environmental Design: Journal of the Islamic Environmental Design Centre* 1–2 (1997–98–99): 22–34; A. Petruccioli, "New Methods of Reading the Urban Fabric of the Islamicized Mediterranean," in *Built Environment* (Oxford), ed. N. Nasser, 28, no. 3 (2002): 202–216; A. Petruccioli, "La permanenza della città classica nei tessuti arabi del Mediterraneo," in *L'africa romana. Lo spazio marittimo del Mediterraneo occidentale: geografia storica ed economica*, ed. M. Khanoussi, P. Ruggeri, and C. Vismara (Rome, 2002), 3:2267–2278. Since 1983 he is editor of the journal *Environmental Design: Journal of the Islamic Environmental Design Research Centre*; see especially the monographic issues "Urban Morphogenesis, Maps and Cadastral Plans" (1993) and "Urban Fabric" (1989); M. Cerasi, A. Petruccioli, A. Sarro, and S. Weber, eds., *Multicultural Urban Fabric and Types in the South and Eastern Mediterranean* (Beirut, 2007); A. Petruccioli, *After Amnesia. Learning from the Islamic Mediterranean Urban Fabric* (Bari, 2007).

He has also organized numerous conferences on the Islamic city, amongst which, annual international conferences since 1982: for example, in 1989 "History and Project: the Historic Centres of the Maghreb"; in 1991 "The Islamic Town from Cadastral Plans"; in 1999 the ISUF conference in Florence "Transformations of Urban Form: From Interpretations to Methodologies in Practice. Six International Seminars on Urban Form" with a section dedicated to "The Islamic City"; and in 2003 the conference "The Planned City" in Trani (Apulia), which included several papers on the Islamic city.

[63] F. Fusaro, *La città islamica* (Bari, 1984).

[64] L. Micara, *Architettura e Spazi dell'Islam. Le Istituzioni Collettive e la Vita Urbana* (Rome, 1985); L. Micara, "Ghadames: house and urban fabric in a Town-Oasis of Central Lybia," in *Transformations of Urban Form: From Interpretations to Methodologies in Practice. Six International Seminars on Urban Form*, ed. R. Corona and G. L. Maffei (Florence, 1999); L. Micara, "Città storica e architettura moderna in Libia. Il caso di Tripoli," in *Architettura Moderna Mediterranea*, Atti del Convegno Internazionale, Bari 10 aprile 2002, ed. G. Strappa and A. B. Menghini (Bari, 2003), 81–96; L. Micara, "Scenari dell'abitare contemporaneo: Tripoli medina mediterranea," *Piano Progetto Città*, Rivista dei Dipartimenti di Architettura e Urbanistica di Pescara, nos. 20–21 (2003): 134–141.

transformation through a structural reading of the building fabric. This approach begins with a reading of cadastral surveys and compares the data obtained from them with historical data.

Other Italian scholars, though not trained in the Roman School, have developed a similar interpretative methodology. Amongst these is Roberto Berardi. With a keen interest in the morphology of the city as a physical entity, he has managed to decipher the "alphabet" of the urban fabric of Tunis by breaking it down into its component parts.

Since the 1990s, the research centre in Italy where an interest in Islamic cities with a strong morphological orientation, continuing the tradition of Saverio Muratori's School, has been developed is the Facoltà di Architettura at the Politecnico di Bari.

In the 1980s in Germany various research groups conducted studies on Islamic, especially Middle Eastern, cities, using both an historical and a geographical approach. These were the geographers at the Institut für Geographie of the Friedrich-Alexander-Universität Erlangen-Nürnberg,[65] especially Eugen Wirth, the historians at the Orientalisches Seminar of the Eberhard Karls Universität Tübingen,[66] especially Heinz Gaube, and those at the Technische Universität Berlin, especially Dorothée Sack.

Wirth's urban studies and his theoretical definitions of the structure of the Oriental-Islamic city, already begun in the 1960s, are based on a geographical-morphological approach that defines the specificity of the Islamic city in relation to the commercial system of the suqs.[67]

Heinz Gaube's studies on the Islamic city use an analysis of historical documents and inscriptions to reconstruct the history and structure of Islamic cities in the various phases of their urban development. Based on a keen interest in the city as a physical entity, his studies have led

---

[65] A. Escher, *Studien zum traditionellen Handwerk der orientalischen Stadt. Wirtschafts—und sozialgeographische Strukturen und Prozesse anhand von Fallstudien in Marokko* (Erlangen, 1986); A. Escher and E. Wirth, eds., *Die Medina von Fes. Geographische Beiträge zu Persistenz und Dynamik, Verfall und Erneuerung einer traditionellen islamischen Stadt in handlungstheoretischer Sicht* (Erlangen, 1992).

[66] One of the main projects of scholars in this research centre is the TAVO, the *Tübinger Atlas des Vorderen Orients*, Wiesbaden 1977–1993, especially the production of a thematic cartography on the cities that have been the subject of their research.

[67] The work of German geographers that began with Wirth's research on commercial systems and bazaars, continued with M. Scharabi, *Der Bazar: das traditionelle Stadtzentrum im Nahen Osten und seine Handelseinrichtungen* (Tübingen, 1985), which is probably the most systematic text on the bazaar in the Islamic world, with a collection of images, measured drawings, and bibliographies on the commercial structure of the bazaar, divided by types.

him, in tandem with the geographer Wirth, to elaborate interesting interpretative syntheses of the urban structures of Islamic cities, especially in Syria and Iran.

Beginning with her research on the urban structure of Damascus, Sack's studies—whose methodology is based on an historical approach but with a marked orientation toward a morphological approach—are moving toward a revived interest in the archaeology of Islamic cities. Other scholars, such as the Swiss Stefano Bianca,[68] are concerned with the urban renewal of Islamic cities.

In the United States studies on the Islamic city began with Oleg Grabar's research, who was the first scholar to teach the History of Islamic Art in the USA, but were concerned more with architecture than with the city as a physical entity. An interest in Islamic architecture and urban form has become the objective of many scholars and research centres: Renata Holod[69] at the School of Art and Science, University of Pennsylvania; Nasser Rabbat[70] at the Aga Khan Program for Islamic Architecture, MIT; Gülru Necipoglu[71] at the Aga Khan Program for

---

[68] S. Bianca, *Architektur und Lebensform im islamischen Stadtwesen. Baugestalt und Lebensordnung in der islamischen Kultur, dargestellt unter besonderer Verarbeitung marokkanischer Quellen und Beispiele* (Zürich, 1979); S. Bianca, *Städtebau in islamischen Ländern* (Zürich, 1980); S. Bianca, J.-C. David, G. Rizzardi, Y. Beton, and B. Chauffert-Yvart, *The Conservation of the Old City of Aleppo*, Technical Report UNESCO (Paris, 1980); S. Bianca, "Evolution d'une politique de réhabilitation: le cas de Alep," in *La réhabilitation des cités anciennes*, Actes du Colloque International tenu à Salé les 6–9 Octobre 1988, ed. Association Bou Regreg (Casablanca, 1990); S. Bianca, *Hofhaus und Paradiesgarten: Architektur und Lebensformen in der islamischen Welt* (Munich, 1991).

[69] R. Holod, ed., *Studies on Isfahan: Proceedings of the Isfahan Colloquium, Iranian Studies* (Special Issue), no. 7 (1974), especially the article by Lisa Golembek: L. Golombek, "Urban Patterns in Pre-Safavid Isfahan" (with Comments on Urban Patterns by Renata Holod) *Iranian Studies*, no. 7 (1974): 18–48; R. Holod and Khan H. Uddin, *The Mosque and the Modern World* (London, 1997). The latter's interest in Islamic cities has led her to edit conference proceedings—for example, R. Holod, ed., *Conservation as Cultural Survival*. Proceedings of Seminar Two in the Series: Architectural Transformations in the Islamic World, held in Istanbul, Turkey, September 26–28 1978 (Cambridge, MA, 1980)—and to carry out research on archaeology and settlements in Tunisia.

[70] N. Rabbat, "Writing the History of Islamic Architecture in Cairo," *Design Book Review* 31 (1994): 48–51; N. Rabbat, *The Citadel of Cairo: A New Interpretation of Royal Mamluk Architecture* (Leiden, 1995); N. Rabbat, "The City," *Encyclopedia of the Qur'an* (Leiden, 2001); N. Rabbat, "The Social Order in the Layout of the Islamic City," *Al-Mouhandis al-Arabi* 78 (1984): 9–11.

[71] G. Necipoglu, *Architecture, Ceremonial, and Power: The Topkapı Palace in the Fifteenth and Sixteenth Centuries* (New York and Cambridge, MA, 1991); G. Necipoglu, *The Age of Sinan: Architectural Culture in the Ottoman Empire* (London and Princeton, 2005). Necipoglu is editor of the journal *Muqarnas: An Annual on the Visual Culture of the Islamic World*, founded by Oleg Grabar.

Islamic Architecture, Harvard; Irene Bierman and Donald Preziosi[72] at the UCLA Center for Near Eastern Studies, in the Art History Department, Los Angeles; and Nazar al-Sayyad[73] at the Center for Middle Eastern Studies, University of California, Berkeley, who has studied the history of architecture in relation to its urban context.

Using an approach based on the study of the history of architecture and the archaeology of the Islamic city in order to reconstruct its urban history, in 1974 Renata Holod edited the monograph on Isfahan for *Iranian Studies, The American Journal of Iranology*, thereby initiating contemporary studies on Iranian cities.

Nasser Rabbat's interest in the Islamic city, especially Cairo and Syrian cities, is based on the study of historical and archival documents which he uses as the principal means of reconstructing the history of architecture in relation to the transformation of its urban context.

Likewise, Gülru Necipoglu's studies are based on an analysis of archival documents in order to reconstruct architectural history on an urban scale. In her studies on Topkapi Palace in Istanbul, by examining the Topkapi scrolls she has been able to elucidate its spatial structure in relation to the urban context and Turkish and Islamic cultural traditions.

Beginning with Lapidus' theories on the Islamic city and a meticulous historical enquiry, Nazar al-Sayyad has examined the form of Islamic military cites and the morphology of cities in the early centuries of Islam in order to define the Arab-Islamic elements in their urban structure. His interest is now moving toward processes of transformation of the physical structure of traditional and modern cities.

In the 1980s, starting from the interest of the above-mentioned schools in specific regions of the Islamic world, the scholarship and hence the literature on the different physical forms and structures of the traditional Islamic city proliferated. This fresh approach, applied to contingent geographical, political, social, historical, and economic

---

[72] I. A. Bierman, R. A. Abou-El-Haj, and D. Preziosi, eds., *The Ottoman City and Its Parts: Urban Structure and Social Order* (New York, 1991).

[73] N. Al-Sayyad, *Streets of Islamic Cairo: A Configuration of Urban Themes and Patterns* (Cambridge, MA, 1981); N. Al-Sayyad, "Notes on the Islamic City: Aspects of Physical and Non-Physical Structure. The Costs of Not Knowing," in *Proceedings of the 1986 EDRA Conference*, ed. J. Wideman (Madison, WI, 1986); N. Al-Sayyad, "Space in an Islamic City," *Journal of Architectural and Planning Research* 2 (1987); N. Al-Sayyad, *Cities and Caliphs: On the Genesis of Arab Muslim Urbanism* (New York, 1991). Al–Sayyad is editor of the journal *Traditional Dwellings and Settlement Review: Journal of the International Association for the Study of the Traditional Environment*.

conditions, dealt with the specific—that is, not theoretical—problem of urban structure and form, and so managed to overcome the Orientalist impasse created by an over-generalized model. It has, thus, represented a methodological point of reference for modern studies on the physical structure of the Islamic city. Moreover, the interest of international research centres has acted as a springboard for a renewed interest on the part of local research centres in the morphological and physical specificity of their own urban centres.

Thanks to these combined efforts in the field, today there are many studies on the urban structures of the different regions that go to make up the variegated panorama of cities in the Islamic world, even though there is still a notable imbalance in studies on urban physical structures in favour of some regions rather than others.

Spain

In the 1980s, research on the Islamic city in Spain was mainly conducted by a Hispanic-French group of scholars. Starting from the work of the Orientalist Leopoldo Torres Balbás,[74] they used data from archaeological excavations as the main tool in their reading of urban structure. Applying a methodology that combines archaeological research with an interpretation of cadastral surveys, they produced various studies on Andalusian and Moroccan cities, thereby filling the void left by architects who had abandoned this field of research. Their work has often been part of the projects of the Casa del Velázques[75] in Madrid (the French Cultural Centre), which is concerned also (though not only)

---

[74] L. Torres Balbás, "La ciudad musulmana," *Revista Universitaria* 6, no. 25 (1938): 97–112; L. Torres Balbás, "Hallazgos arquéologicos en la alcazaba de Málaga," *Al-Andalus* 2 (1934): 344–357; L. Torres Balbás, "Excavaciones y obras en la Alcazaba de Málaga (1934–1943)," *Al-Andalus* 9 (1944): 173–190; L. Torres Balbás, "Notas sobre Sevilla en la época musulmana," *Al-Andalus* 10 (1945): 196–214; L. Torres Balbás, "Les villes musulmanes d'Espagne et leur urbanisation," *Annales de l'Institut d'Études Orientales* (Alger) 6 (1947): 5–30; Torres Balbás L., "Los contornos de las ciudades hispanomusulmanas," *Al-Andalus* 15 (1950): 437–486; L. Torres Balbás, "Estructura de las ciudades hispanomusulmanas: la medina, los arrabales y los barrios," *Al-Andalus* 18 (1953): 172–197; L. Torres Balbás, *Resumen histórico del urbanismo en España* (Madrid, 1954); L. Torres Balbás, *Ciudades Hispano-musulmanas* (Madrid, 1971).
[75] P. Cressier, "Histoire et archéologie de la ville islamique (Al-Andalus–Maroc). Les activités de la Casa de Velásquez," *Medina. Cité du Monde* 2 (1996): 104–106; P. Moret and P. Cressier, "La Casa de Velázquez y los estudios ibéricos," in *La cultura ibérica a través de la fotografía de principio de siglo. Un homenaje a la memoria*, ed. J. Blánquez Pérez and L. Roldán Gómez (Madrid, 1999), 43–47; P. Cressier, "Casa de Velázquez," in

with research on the morphology of Islamic cities in Andalusia, and the Centro de Estudios Arabes in Granada, directed by Antonio Almagro, under whose aegis numerous reconstructions of the urban structure of Andalusian cities have been carried out.

Within this general frame of reference, some of the most important work on the Islamic city in Spain has been the historico-archaeological work carried out by the following: Julio Navarro Palazón[76] on Murcia, under the aegis of the Centro de Estudios Arabes, whose task was made easier by the demolitions that have allowed him to carry out archaeological research on the urban fabric and residential buildings; Jean Passini on Toledo; and André Bazzana and Patric Cressier on Andalusia and Morocco. To these we may add Pierre Guichard's[77] historical studies on Spain, in particular Valencia, and B. Pavón Maldonaldo's[78] work on Spain in general.

Using a philological approach to the analysis of fifteenth century cadastral records, Passini's[79] studies have attempted a reconstruction

---

100 imágenes: Pasado y presente de la Arqueología española, ed. J. Blánquez Pérez (Madrid, 2000), 254–257.

[76] J. Navarro Palazón, "Siyâsa: una madîna de la cora de Tudmîr," *Annual Report on English and American Studies*, 5 (1985): 171–189; J. Navarro Palazón, "Murcia como centro productor de loza dorada," in *Congresso Internazionale delle Università degli Studi di Siena* (Florence, 1986), 129–143; J. Navarro Palazón, "Excavaciones arqueológicas en la ciudad de Murcia durante 1984," in *Excavaciones y prospecciones arqueológicas* (Murcia, 1987), 307–320; J. Navarro Palazón, *Una vivienda islámica en Murcia. Estudio de su ajuar (siglo XIII)* (Murcia 1991); J. Navarro Palazón, "Aproximación a la cultura material de Madînat Mursiya," in *Murcia musulmana*, ed. F. Arroyuelo and F. José (Murcia, 1989), 253–356.

[77] P. Guichard, *Structures sociales "orientales" et "occidentals" dans l'Espagne Musulmane* (Paris, 1977); P. Guichard, "Les Mozarabes de Valence et d'Al-Andalus entre l'histoire et le mythe," *Revue de l'Occident Musulman et de la Méditerranée* 40 (1985): 17–27; P. Guichard, *Les musulmans de Valence et la reconquête (XIᵉ–XIIIᵉ siècles)*, 2 vols. (Damascus, 1990–1991); A.-L. de Prémare and P. Guichard, "Croissance urbaine et société rurale à Valence au début de l'époque des royaumes de Taifas (XIᵉ siècle de J.-C.) Traduction et commentaire d'un texte d'Ibn Hayyan," *Revue de l'Occident Musulman et de la Méditerranée* 31 (1981): 15–30.

[78] B. Pavón Maldonado, *Ciudades hispanomusulmanas* (Madrid, 1992).

[79] J. Passini and J.-P. Molénat, "Persistance parcellaire et évolution diachronique à Tolède. L'impasse de la Bajada del Pozo Amargo et sa mosquée," in *Mélanges de la Casa de Velazquez*, 1992: 181–198; J. Passini, "Plan parcellaire et urbanistique médiévale islamique," *Le Moyen âge, Revue d'histoire et de Philologie* 1, no. 99 (1993): 27–39; J. Passini, J.-P. Molénat, and S. Sánchez-Chiquito de la Rosa, "El barrio de Santa Justa y el Mesón del Lino al final de la Edad Media," *Anales Toledanos* 31(1994): 65–122; J. Passini, "La ville de Tolède au Moyen Âge: apport du parcellaire, du texte et du bâti à l'étude du quartier de San Ginés," *Les Cahiers de Saint-Michel de Cuxá* 33 (2002): 61–66; J. Passini, *Casas y casas principales urbanas. El espacio doméstico de Toledo a finales de la Edad Media* (Toledo, 2004).

of the structure of medieval Islamic cities in Andalusia, in particular Toledo. He has paid special attention to the relation between residential building typology and urban fabric and has been able to reconstruct accurately the urban structure of these cities in the Islamic period.

Cressier's[80] and Bazzana's[81] work is based on an examination of the archaeological strata of Islamic cities in Andalusia and an analysis of cadastral records. They have attempted a reconstruction of the urban structure of cities in Andalusia and Morocco during the first phases of anthropic development. Cressier in particular has been able to investigate these urban structures without conducting excavations, by using a method similar to that of the Italian School, of reading the various phases of urban development through an analysis of the cadastral records.

Using a different methodology, Marianne Barrucand[82] has studied Spanish and Moroccan cities, in particular Meknes, concentrating her research on the history and structure of palace architecture in relation to urban context. Finally, though not concerned with the urban context

---

[80] P. Cressier, "L'Alpujarra médiévale: une approche archéologique," *Mélanges de la Casa de Velázquez* 19 (1983): 89–124; P. Cressier, "Fonction et évolution du réseau castral en Andalousie orientale: le cas de l'Alpujarra," in *Castrum 3. Guerre, fortification et habitat dans le monde méditerranéen au Moyen-Âge* (Madrid and Rome, 1988), 123–134; P. Cressier, "Le *Catastro de la Ensenada* (v. 1752): La structure des petites 'villes' islamiques d'Andalousie," in "Urban Morphogenesis: Maps and Cadastral Plans," ed. A. Petruccioli, *Environmental Design: Journal of the Islamic Environmental Design Centre* 1–2 (1993): 38–43; P. Cressier, and L. Erbati, "La naissance de la ville islamique au Maroc. Campagne 1996," *Nouvelles archéologiques et patrimoniales* 1 (1997): 13–14; P. Cressier and M. Garcia-Arenal, eds., *Genèse de la ville islamique en al-Andalous et au Maghreb occidental* (Madrid, 1998).

[81] A. Bazzana, "Eléments d'archéologie musulman dans Al-Andalus: caractères spécifiques de l'architecture militaire arabe de la ragion valencienne," *Al-Qantara* 1 (1980): 339–363; A. Bazzana, P. Cressier, L. Erbati, Y. Montmessin, and A. El Aziz Touri, "Première prospection d'archéologie médiévale et islamique dans le Nord du Maroc (Chefchaouen–Oued Laou–Bou Ahmed)," *Bulletin d'Archéologie Marocaine* 15 (1983–84): 367–450; A. Bazzana and P. Cressier, *Shaltish/Saltés (Huelva): Une ville médiévale d'al-Andalus* (Madrid, 1989); A. Bazzana, "Urbanismo e hidráulica (colectiva y doméstica) en la Saltés almohade," in *Casas y palacios de al-Andalus. Siglos XII y XIII* (Madrid and Barcelona, 1995), 139–156.

[82] M. Barrucand, *L'Architecture de la Qasba de Moulay Ismail à Meknes* (Rabat, 1976); M. Barrucand, *L'urbanisme princier en Islam: Meknès et les villes royales islamiques post-médiévales* (Paris, 1985); M. Barrucand, "Stadtgründungen als Herrschaftssymbol. Bemerkungen zur Architektur islamischer Herrscherstädte des 16. und 17. Jahrunderts," in *22. Deutscher Orientalistentag 1983 in Tübingen. Ausgewählte Vorträge* (Stuttgart, 1985), 395–403; M. Barrucand, "Die Palastarchitektur Mulay Isma'ils: Die Qasaba von Meknes," *Madrider Mitteilungen* 30 (1989): 506–523; M. Barrucand and A. Bednorz, *Maurische Architektur in Andalusien* (Cologne, 1992).

as a whole, Pedro Chalmeta's[83] studies on the Spanish market system
have provided interesting information both on the structure of Spanish
markets and suqs in general.

North Africa

From the mid 1980s there have been numerous urban studies on North
Africa cities that favour a reading of the city as a physical entity. These
studies have used the cadastral surveys compiled in the first decades
of the twentieth century as their main documentary source and have
often complemented these records with detailed measured drawings of
the urban fabric and architecture.

The cartographic representation of the urban organism deriving
from this extensive corpus of measured drawings of urban fabric and
architecture has been carried out not only by European scholars but
also by many local research centres that are concerned with the renewal
and conservation of North African medinas and has resulted in the
redaction of numerous plans of the ground floors in the medinas.[84]

In Tunisia especially, the various Associations de Sauvegarde de la
Médina which operate even for the medinas in smaller cities are pro-
moting research in collaboration with universities and international
research centres as well as the compilation of corpora of measured
drawings and the monitoring of historic centres.[85] Amongst the most
active research centres on North African cities are the AIMS (American Institute for Maghreb Studies) and EMAT (Centre for Maghrib
Studies in Tunis).

---

[83] P. Chalmeta, *El señor del zoco en España: edades media y moderna. Contributional estudio
de la istoria del mercato* (Madrid, 1973).

[84] In Tunisia, for example, ground floor plans of Tunis medina on a scale of 1:200
were executed by the Association de Sauvegarde de la Médina; ground floor plans of
Kairouan medina by Paola Jervis and Paolo Donati, redesigned by the draughtsmen of
the Association de Sauvegarde de la Médina; ground floor plans of Hammamet medina
by Mario Face; and ground floor plans of Sfax medina by Michel van der Meerschen.
In Morocco, ground floor plans of Essaouira are at present being completed by Attilio
Petruccioli and Mirco Accorsi.

[85] See, for example, the Atelier Méditerranéen Nabeul 2003 organized by the ASM of
Nabeul in order to draw up the general guidelines for the recovery of smaller medinas
in Tunisian cities, in collaboration with the Institut National du Patrimoine (Tunis), the
École Nationale d'Architecture et d'Urbanisme de Tunisi, the Institut Supérieur des
Beaux Arts di Tunisi, the École Polytechnique d'Architecture et d'Urbanisme d'Alger,
the Facoltà di Architettura del Politecnico di Bari, the Facoltà di Architettura di Palermo,
and the École d'Architecture Languedoc-Roussillon di Montpellier.

The tradition of urban studies that has seen in the measured drawing of aggregates of residential buildings the tool for describing urban form was initiated in North Africa by the work of Jacques Revault.[86] He classified residential buildings in North Africa into four types, with each type based on the same compositional principles. Despite the fact that his studies have used a lower scale of reference with respect to the subject of the present article, describing the relation between residential buildings and urban fabric and the aggregative logic of residential buildings within it, they have nevertheless constituted representative cross-sections of the entire urban fabric. The importance of such research resides in the fact that, unlike earlier studies, the Marçais' especially, which was focused exclusively on specialized buildings, Revault's work has initiated a fresh scholarly interest in residential buildings. The studies by Mona Zakariya[87] and Jean-Claude Garcin[88] on Cairo have developed from Revault's studies. Still on an architectural scale, Serge Santelli's[89] research has documented the residential buildings in this region.

Amongst the works closely linked to a reading of the physical structure of North African Islamic cities as an aggregate of residential and public buildings are Roberto Berardi's studies on Tunis.[90] They have

---

[86] J. Revault, *Palais et demeures de Tunis (XVIIIᵉ et XIXᵉ siècles)* (Paris, 1967); J. Revault and B. Maury, *Palais et maisons du Caire du XIVᵉ au XVIIIᵉ siècle*, 3 vols. (Cairo 1977–1979); J. C. Garcin, B. Maury, J. Revault, and M. Zakarya, *Palais et maisons du Caire*, vol. 1, *Époque mamelouke (XIIIᵉ–XVIᵉ siècles)* (Paris, 1982); B. Maury, A. Raymond, J. Revault, and M. Zakarya, *Palais et maisons du Caire*, vol. 2, *Époque ottomane (XVIᵉ–XVIIIᵉ siècles)* (Paris, 1983); J. Revault, *Palais, demeures et maisons de plaisance de Tunis et ses environs* (Aix-en-Provence, 1984); J. Revault, L. Golvin, and A. Amahan, *Palais et demeures de Fès* (Paris, 1985–1989); J. Revault, "Reflexions sur l'architecture domestique en Afrique du Nord et en Orient," in *L'Habitat traditionnel dans les pays musulmans autour de la Méditerranée*, vol. 1, *L'Héritage architectural: formes et functions*. Rencontre d'Aix-en-Provence, 6–8 juin 1984, ed. Groupe de Recherches et d'Études sur le Proche-Orient (Cairo, 1988), 315–321.

[87] M. Zakariya, "Typologie de l'habitat dans le Caire médiévale: contribution à l'étude de l'espace central," *Cahiers de la recherche architecturale*, nos. 10–11 (1982): 116–125.

[88] J.-C. Garcin, B. Maury, J. Revault, and M. Zakarya, *Palais et maisons du Caire* (Paris, 1982–1983); J.-C. Garcin, *Espace, pouvoirs et idéologies de l'Egypte médiévale* (London, 1987); J.-C. Garcin, "Le Caire et l'évolution urbaine dans des pays musulmans à l'époque médiévale," *Annales Islamologiques* 25 (1991).

[89] S. Mouline and S. Santelli, *Rabat. Numéro spécial du Bulletin d'Informations Architecturales* (Paris, 1986); S. Santelli, "Mahdiya," in "Urban Fabric," ed. A. Petruccioli, *Environmental Design: Journal of the Islamic Environmental Design Centre* 1–2 (1989): 54–59; S. Santelli, *Atlas des Médinas Tunisiennes* (Paris, 1992); S. Santelli, *Médinas: L'Architecture Traditionnelle en Tunisie* (Tunis, 1993); S. Santelli, *Tunis: Le Creuset Méditerranée* (Paris, 1995); S. Santelli, "L'Atelier Harar," *Archiscopie*, no. 34 (October 2003).

[90] R. Berardi, "Lecture d'une ville: la médina de Tunis," *L'Architecture d'Aujourd'hui*, no. 153 (1970–1971): 38–43; R. Berardi, "Alla ricerca di un alfabeto urbano: la medina di Tunisi," *Necropoli* 9–10 (1970): 27–48; R. Berardi, "Signification du plan ancien de la ville arabe," in *La ville arabe dans l'Islam* (Paris, 1982), 187; R. Berardi, "On the

represented an important methodological point of reference for a reading of North African cities, due to their syntactical deconstruction of the urban fabric, based on the identification of the discrete elements that shape it and the application of simple operations to them that has allowed him to determine the structure of the suqs and dwellings. Other monographic works, such as those by Paola Jervis Donati[91] on Kairouan, Marcello Balbo and Daniele Pini[92] on Salé, and Samuel Pickens[93] and Michael Bonine[94] on Morocco, are part of the growing corpus of individual research projects conducted on North African cities.

Interest in Cairo as a physical entity has developed from the studies of Laila ʿAli Ibrahim[95] and André Raymond,[96] the most eminent scholars of the architectural and urban history of this city in the Mamluk and Ottoman periods. Beginning with their studies of the waqf documents, they have developed a new methodological approach to a reading of this city's urban structure. Studying the composition of the inhabitants,

---

City," in "Urban Fabric," ed. A. Petruccioli, *Environmental Design: Journal of the Islamic Environmental Design Centre* 1–2 (1989): 8–17.

[91] P. Jervis Donati, "Kairouan," in "Urban Fabric," ed. A. Petruccioli, *Environmental Design: Journal of the Islamic Environmental Design Research Centre* 1–2 (1989): 36–53.

[92] M. Balbo, D. Pini, and M. F. Zniber, "Quelle stratégie d'approche pour la Médina de Salé?" in *La réhabilitation des cités anciennes*, Actes du Colloque International tenu à Salè les 6–7–8–9 Octobre 1988, ed. Association Bou Regreg (Casablanca, 1990); M. Balbo and D. Pini, eds., *Medina di Salè: studi e ipotesi di riqualificazione urbana* (Milan, 1993).

[93] S. Pickens, *Les villes impériales du Maroc: Fès, Marrakech, Meknès, Rabat-Salé* (Paris, 1990).

[94] M. E. Bonine, "The Sacred Direction and City Structure: A Preliminary Analysis of the Islamic Cities of Morocco," *Muqarnas* 7 (1990): 50–72. This article on the sacred orientation of the urban fabric, which rotated over time to coincide with the orientation of the mosques, is one of the more interesting essays on the urban structure of Moroccan cities, and its conclusions may be applied to other Islamic cities.

[95] L. A. Ibrahim, "Residential Architecture in Mamluk Cairo," *Muqarnas* 2 (1984): 47–59.

[96] A. Raymond, "La conquête ottomane et le dèveloppement des grandes ville arabes. Le cas du Caire, de Damas et d'Alep," *Revue de l'Occident Musulman et de la Méditerranée* 27 (1979): 115–134; A. Raymond, "Les grands *waqfs* et l'organisation de l'espace urbain à Alep et au Caire à l'èpoque ottomane (XVIᵉ–XVIIᵉ siècles)," *Bulletin d'Études Orientales de l'Institut Français d'Études Arabes de Damas* 31 (1980): 113–128; A. Raymond, "La géographie des hāra du Caire, au XVIIIᵉ siècle," in *Livre du centenaire de l'IFAO* (Cairo, 1980); A. Raymond, *The Great Arab Cities in the 16th–18th Centuries: An Introduction* (New York, 1984); A. Raymond, *Grande villes arabe à l'époque ottomane* (Paris, 1985); A. Raymond, *Le Caire* (Paris, 1993); A. Raymond, *Le Caire des Janissaires: L'apogee de la ville ottomane sous ʿAbd al-Rahman Katkhuda* (Paris, 1995); A. Raymond, "The Residential Districts of Cairo's Elite in the Mamluk and Ottoman Periods (Fourteenth to Eighteenth Centuries)," in *The Mamluks in Egyptian Politics and Society*, ed. T. Philipp and U. Haarmann (Cambridge, MA, 1998), 207–223; A. Raymond, *Cairo* (Cambridge, MA, 2000).

the spatial organization, the urban economy and facilities in Cairo in the Mamluk period, Laila ʿAli Ibrahim has demonstrated that, different from the common Orientalist notion, the residential buildings and suq grew in an ordered, not in a chaotic manner in this phase of urban expansion. André Raymond, describing the structure of Cairo in the Ottoman period, has demonstrated the urban explosion that determined its various phases of development by using waqf documents that record the foundation of new mosques and baths and by relating these new foundations to the development of the urban fabric.

Following the research carried out by Laila ʿAli Ibrahim and André Raymond, many other scholars have used waqf records as a means of reconstructing Cairo's urban history. Doris Behrens-Abouseif[97] has been especially concerned with the urban development of the northern and eastern districts of Cairo, while Leonor Fernandes[98] has used waqf documents as a means of reconstructing its architectural history. The historian Nelly Hanna[99] has reconstructed the history of the Bulaq district of Cairo, using waqf documents and the *Description de l'Egypte*. Federico Cresti[100] has carried out demographic studies on Algiers in the

---

[97] D. Behrens-Abouseif, "A Circassian Mamluk Suburb North of Cairo," *Art and Archaeology Research Papers* 14 (1978): 17–23; D. Behrens-Abouseif, "The North Eastern Extension of Cairo under the Mamluks," *Annales Islamologiques* 17 (1981); D. Behrens-Abouseif, *Azbakiyya and its Environs: From Azbak to Ismaʿil, 1476–1879* (Cairo, 1985); D. Behrens-Abouseif, "Locations of Non-Muslim Quarters in Medieval Cairo," *Annales Islamologiques* 22 (1986); D. Behrens-Abouseif, *Egypt's Adjustment to Ottoman Rule: Institutions, Waqf and Architecture in Cairo (16th and 17th Centuries)* (Leiden, 1994); D. Behrens-Abouseif, "Qaytbay's investments in the city of Cairo: *Waqf* and power," *Annales Islamologiques* 32 (1998); D. Behrens-Abouseif, ed., *The Cairo Heritage: Essays in Honor of Laila Ali Ibrahim* (Cairo, 2001).

[98] L. Fernandes, "Three Sufi Foundations in a 15th Century *Waqfiyya*," *Annales Islamologiques* 17 (1981): 141–156; L. Fernandes, "Some Aspects of the Zawiya in Egypt at the Eve of the Ottoman Conquest," *Annales Islamologiques* 19 (1983): 9–17; L. Fernandes, "The Foundation of Baybars al-Jashankir: Its *Waqf*, History and Architecture," *Muqarnas* 4 (1987): 21–42; L. Fernandes, *The Evolution of a Sufi Institution in Mamluk Egypt: The Khanqah* (Berlin, 1988).

[99] N. Hanna, *An Urban History of Bulaq in the Mamluk and Ottoman Periods* (Cairo, 1983); N. Hanna, *Construction Work in Ottoman Cairo (1517–1798)* (Cairo, 1984); N. Hanna, "La Maison *Waqf* Radwan au Caire," in *L'habitat traditionnel dans les pays Musulmans autour de la Méditerranée*, vol. 1, ed. Groupe de Recherches et d'Études sur le Proche-Orient (Aix en Provence, 1984); N. Hanna, *Habiter au Caire: La maison moyenne et ses habitants aux XVIIᵉ et XVIIIᵉ siècles* (Cairo, 1991).

[100] F. Cresti, "The Boulevard de l'Impératrice in Colonial Algiers (1860–1866)," in "Maghreb: From Colonialism to a New Identity," ed. A. Petruccioli, *Environmental Design: Journal of the Islamic Environmental Design Centre* 1 (1985): 54–59; F. Cresti, "Alger à la période turque. Observations et hypothéses sur la population et sa structure sociale," *Revue de l'Occident Musulman et de la Méditerranée* 44 (1987): 125–133; F. Cresti, "Beni

Ottoman period using travellers' accounts and the information found in the waqf registers on the number of mosques and baths.

Studies on Cairo and other Egyptian cities have also been carried out by scholars from various disciplines. Sylvie Denoix[101] has used an historical approach based on an analysis of archival and archaeological documentation. Philippe Panerai,[102] interested in the morphology of the Islamic city, has based his research on measured drawings as well as on an analysis of cadastral plans and the structural relations between the different parts of the city. Robert Ilbert[103] has studied Cairo and Alexandria from an historical perspective while also touching on morphological aspects. Jean-Charles Depaule[104] has studied the residential systems of Cairo using an approach that combines typological and sociological disciplines, while Wladyslaw B. Kubiak[105] has used historical and archaeological sources in order to describe the structure of al-Fustat.

Amongst the various research centres monitoring architecture in Cairo, the following have made important contributions: the Deutsches Archäologisches Institut in Cairo, which publishes its results in *Mitteilungen des Deutschen Archäologischen Instituts, Abteilung Kairo*, and the Institut Français d'Archéologie Orientale du Caire, which publishes its results in *Bulletin, Mémoires*, and *Annales Islamologiques*.

Abbes," in "Urban Fabric," ed. A. Petruccioli, *Environmental Design: Journal of the Islamic Environmental Design Research Centre* 1–2 (1989): 28–35.

[101] S. Denoix, *Décrire le Caire—Fustat—Misr d'après ibn Duqmaq et Maqrizi: L'histoire d'une partie de la ville du Caire d'après deux historiens égyptiens des XIV\u1d49–XV\u1d49 siècles* (Cairo, 1992); S. Denoix, ed., *Le Khan al-Khalili et ses environs. Un centre commercial et artisanal au Caire du XIII\u1d49 au XX\u1d49 siècle* (Cairo, 1999).

[102] S. Noweir and P. Panerai, "Cairo: The Old Town," in "Urban Fabric," ed. A. Petruccioli, *Environmental Design: Journal of the Islamic Environmental Design Research Centre* 1–2 (1989): 60–67.

[103] R. Ilbert, *Heliopolis: Le Caire 1905–1922—genése d'une ville* (Paris, 1981); R. Ilbert, "Note sur l'Egypte au XIX\u1d49 siècle: Typologie architecturale et morphologie urbane," *Annales Islamologiques* 17 (1981): 343–357; R. Ilbert, "Mèthodologie et idéologie: la recherche française sur les politiques urbaines en Egypte," K. Brown, M. Jolé, P. Sluglett, and S. Zubaida, eds., *Middle Eastern Cities in Comparative Perspective* (London,1986), 103–114; R. Ilbert, "Entre deux mondes: Archives et lecture d'une ville," *Revue de l'Occident Musulman et de la Méditerranée* 46 (1987): 9–12.

[104] J.-C. Depaule, *L'habitat urbain dans l'Orient arabe, éléments d'architecture* (Paris, 1984); J.-C. Depaule et al., *Actualité de l'habitat ancien au Caire: le Rab' Qizlar* (Cairo, 1986).

[105] W. B. Kubiak, *Al-Fustat: Its Foundation and Early Urban Development* (Cairo, 1987).

The Middle East

In the 1980s, following in the footsteps of a large number of French and German scholars, urban studies on Middle Eastern cities intensified and had as their general field of interest the structure of the city as a physical entity and the commercial system of the suqs.

Studies on Syrian cities developed from the research of Heinz Gaube and Eugen Wirth on Aleppo[106] in which a close examination of literary sources and inscriptions was combined with an extensive survey of specialized buildings in the ancient city from which they were able to reconstruct the urban fabric from the early centuries of the Islamic conquest onwards. The different approaches of these two German scholars, historical and geographical respectively, have been combined in the redaction of a series of thematic maps that represent the urban structure of Aleppo in the pre-modern and modern era, especially the route system and the religious, public, and commercial structures.

A further contribution to our knowledge of Aleppo has been made by Jean-Claude David.[107] Using a different methodology in his reading of the building fabric, especially the structure of the suq, pious foundations, and courtyard dwellings, he has been able to make morphological and typological deductions that can be applied more generally to other cities in the same region.

---

[106] H. Gaube and E. Wirth, *Aleppo. Historische und geographische Beiträge zur baulichen Gestaltung, zur sozialen Organisation und zur wirtschaftlichen Dynamik einer vorderasiatischen Fernhandelsmetropole*, 2 vols., Beihefte zum TAVO, B, Nr. 58 (Wiesbaden, 1984).

[107] J.-C. David, "Alep, dégradation et tentatives actuelles de réadaptation des structures urbaines traditionnelles," *Bulletin d'Études Orientales de l'Institut Français d'Études Arabes de Damas*, Tome 28, 1975 (1977); J.-C. David, "Urbanisation spontanée et planification; le faubourg ancien nord d'Alep (XVᵉ–XVIIIᵉ siècle)," *Les Cahiers de la recherche architecturale* 10–11 (1982): 14–18; J.-C. David and B. Chauffert-Yvart, *Le waqf d'Ipšīr Pāšā à Alep (1063–1653): Étude d'urbanisme historique* (Damascus, 1982); J.-C. David, "La formation du tissu de la ville arabo-islamique; apport de l'étude des plans cadastraux d'Alep," in "Urban Morphogenesis: Maps and Cadastral Plans," ed. A. Petruccioli, *Environmental Design: Journal of the Islamic Environmental Design Centre* 1–2 (1993): 138–155; J.-C. David, "L'habitat permanent des grands commerçants dans les khans d'Alep à l'époque ottomane," in *Les Villes dans l'Empire Ottoman: Activités et Sociétés*, ed. D. Panzac (Paris, 1994), 85–123; J.-C. David, *La suwayqat 'Alī à Alep* (Damascus, 1998); J.-C. David and M. al-Dbiyat, "La ville en Syrie et ses territoires: héritages et mutations," *Bulletin d'Études Orientales de l'Institut Français d'Études Arabes de Damas* 52 (2000): 17–27; J.-C. David and G. Degeorge, *Alep* (Paris, 2002).

Numerous other scholars have been concerned with the physical structure of Aleppo.[108] Anette Gangler,[109] in her monographic work based on an extensive architectural survey of residential buildings, which she then used in the compilation of descriptive maps of the urban aggregation, has analyzed the physical structure of the Bānqūsā district. Using historical data, Yasser Tabbaa[110] has produced studies and a reconstruction of the urban structure of Aleppo in the Ayyubid period.

Still speaking of Aleppo, yet again one cannot ignore André Raymond's[111] contribution to our understanding of the city's commercial and urban structure in the Ottoman period. In his reading of Aleppo he often compares it with Tunis and Cairo, and through studying waqf documents, travellers' accounts and historical topography, he has demonstrated its urban growth in the Ottoman period.

Following Raymond's studies, other architectural historians have used waqf documents to reconstruct the urban fabric of Aleppo in the same period. Antoine Abdel Nour[112] has analysed the physical structure of residential buildings between the sixteenth and eighteenth centuries, using sharia-court registers. On the basis of an analysis of archival documents and field research, Jihane Tate[113] has reconstructed the

---

[108] See also G. A. Neglia, "Persistences and Changes in the Urban Fabric of the Old City of Aleppo," *Environmental Design: Journal of the Islamic Environmental Design Centre* 1–2 (2000–2001): 32–41; G. A. Neglia, "Bab Qinnasrin à Alep," in *Bulletin of the Max van Berchem Foundation* (Geneve), n. 20 (December 2006); 3–4; G. A. Neglia, "An interpretation of the urban fabric: The structure of pre-Islamic Aleppo," in *Urban Morphology. Journal of the International Seminar on Urban Form*, vol. 11, n. 1 (2007): 43–58.

[109] A. Gangler, *Ein traditionelles Wohnviertel im Nordosten der Altstadt von Aleppo* (Tübingen, 1993).

[110] Y. Tabbaa, "Circles of Power: Palace, Citadel, and City in Ayyubid Aleppo," *Ars Orientalis* 23 (1993): 181–200; Y. Tabbaa, *Constructions of Power and Piety in Medieval Aleppo* (Philadelphia, 1997).

[111] A. Raymond, "Signes urbains et étude de la population des grandes villes arabes à l'èpoque ottomane," *Bulletin d'Études Orientales de l'Institut Français d'Études Arabes de Damas* 27 (1974): 183–193; A. Raymond, "Le déplacement des tanneries à Alep, au Caire et à Tunis à l'époque ottomane: Un 'indicateur' de croissance urbaine," *Revue d'Histoire Maghrébine* 7–8 (1977): 192–200; A. Raymond, *La Syrie d'aujourd'hui* (Aix-en-Provence, 1980); A. Raymond, *La ville arabe, Alep à l'époque ottomane, XVIᵉ–XVIIIᵉ siècles* (Damascus, 1990); A. Raymond, "Alep à l'époque ottomane, XVIᵉ–XIXᵉ siècles," in "Alep et la Syrie du Nord," *Revue du Monde Musulman et de la Méditerranée* (Aix-en-Provence), no. 62 (1990).

[112] A. Abdel Nour, "Types architecturaux et vocabulaire de habitat en Syrie au XVIᵉ et XVIIᵉ siècle," in *L'espace social de la ville arabe*, ed. D. Chevallier (Paris, 1979); A. Abdel Nour, "Habitat et structures sociales à Alep aux XVIIᵉ et XVIIIᵉ siècle d'après des sources arabes inédites," in *La ville arabe dans l'Islam*, ed. A. Bouhdiva and D. Chevallier (Tunis, 1982).

[113] J. Tate, *Une waqfiyya du XVIII siècle à Alep. La waqfiyya d'al-Ḥāǧǧ Mūsā al-Amīrī, traduction et commentaire* (Damascus, 1990).

history of a waqf and its relation to the district. Based on a reading of the waqf documents, Heghnar Watenpaugh[114] has put forward the thesis of a decentralization of the urban structure of Aleppo in the Ottoman period.

The research of a number of these scholars, especially Gaube and Wirth, has generated interest on behalf of international organizations for the conservation of the world architectural heritage, such as UNESCO.[115] This interest continues today in the constant monitoring of the ancient city by a Syro-German group GTZ/Directorate of the Old City.[116]

In the 1980s the most exhaustive research on Damascus was carried out by Dorothée Sack,[117] who used an approach to urban studies that combined historical and archival research with measured drawings of the urban fabric and the principal monuments. Her work describes the urban transformation of Damascus through the compilation of historical and thematic maps of the route systems, mosques, and suqs in different periods and identifies in the streets, neighbourhoods, water systems, and suqs the basic elements of the urban structure.

Michael Meinecke's[118] work on a district of the ancient city is more closely linked to the study of architecture, as is that of Stefan Weber[119] who has shown a typological interest in nineteenth century Damascus. Jean-Paul Pascual's[120] approach to historical inquiry, on the other

---

[114] H. Zeitlian Watenpaugh, *The Image of an Ottoman City: Imperial Architecture and Urban Experience in Aleppo in the 16th and 17th Centuries* (Leiden, 2004).

[115] S. Bianca, J.-C. David, G. Rizzardi, Y. Beton, and B. Chauffert-Yvart, *The Conservation of the Old City of Aleppo*, Technical Report UNESCO (Paris, 1980).

[116] This interest has manifested itself in a series of colloquia and conferences, amongst which: M. Fansa, ed., *Damaskus-Aleppo: 5000 Jahre Stadtentwicklung in Syrien* (Mainz, 2000). In 2005 the city of Aleppo received the Veronica Rudge Green Prize in Urban Design at GSD/Harvard for the rehabilitation of the historic centre of Aleppo.

[117] D. Sack, "Damaskus, die Stadt intra muros," *Damaszener Mitteilungen* 2 (1985): 207–290; D. Sack, *Damaskus: Entwicklung und Struktur einer orientalischen Stadt* (Mainz, 1989).

[118] M. Meinecke, "Der Survey des Damaszener Altstadtviertels as-Sālihīya," *Damaszener Mitteilungen* 1 (1983): 189–247.

[119] S. Weber, "The Creation of Ottoman Damascus. Architecture and Urban Development of Damascus in the 16th and 17th centuries," *ARAM* 9–10 (1997–1998): 431–470; S. Weber, "Der Marga-Platz in Damaskus—Die Entstehung eines modernen Stadtzentrums unter den Osmanen als Ausdruck strukturellen Wandels (1808–1918)," *Damaszener Mitteilungen* 10 (1998): 291–344, Taf. 77–88; S. Weber, "The Transformation of an Arab-Ottoman Institution: The Suq (Bazaar) of Damascus from the 16th to the 20th Century," in *Seven Centuries of Ottoman Architecture: A Supra-National Heritage*, ed. N. Akin, S. Batur, and A. Batur (Istanbul, 2000), 244–253.

[120] J.-P. Pascual, *Damas à la fin du XVI siècle d'après trois actes de waqf ottomans* (Damascus, 1983); J.-P. Pascual, ed., "Villes au Levant: Hommage a André Raymond," Numéro Spécial de la *Revue du Monde Musulman et de l2a Méditerranée* 55/56 (1990).

hand, is through an analysis of waqf documents. Applying the same methodology as Nelly Hanna in her research on Cairo, Pascual's work on Damascus has continued that of Raymond on Aleppo and Cairo, producing an accurate description of its urban form at the end of the sixteenth century.

In Syria the main research centres on the city as a physical entity are: the Institut Français de Damas[121] which has sponsored numerous urban studies and monitors many urban centres, publishing its results in the *Bulletin d'Études Orientales*;[122] the Direction Générale des Antiquités et des Musées[123] which publishes *Les Annales Archéologiques Arabes Syriennes*; and the Deutsches Archäologisches Institut which publishes the *Damaszener Mitteilungen*.

In Lebanon urban studies on Tripoli have been carried out by Hayat Salam-Liebich[124] and Nimrod Luz[125] on Mamluk commercial and religious architecture, while the Deutsches Orient-Institut in Beirut[126] studies and monitors Mamluk urban structures there.

Studies on Islamic Jerusalem have been carried out by Mahmoud K. Havari,[126bis] on Ayyubid architecture, Michael H. Burgoyne,[127] on

---

[121] Many of the more recent publications represent research of a historical or geographical kind on the main Syrian cities, amongst which: P. Canivet and J.-P. Rey-Coquais, eds., *La Syrie de Byzance à l'islam* (Damascus, 1992); S. Atassi, J.-P. Pascual, M. Kandalaft, et al., *Damas extra-muros: Mīdān Sultānī, présentation des édifices répertoriés et analyse* (Damascus, 1994); M. Dbyiyat, *Hama et Homs en Syrie centrale: Concurrence urbaine et développement régional* (Damascus, 1995); B. Marino, *Le faubourg du Mīdān à Damas à l'époque ottomane* (Damascus, 1997); Y. Roujon and L. Vilan, *Le Mīdan, actualité d'un faubourg ancien de Damas* (Damascus, 1997).

[122] See especially the monographic issue of the *Bulletin d'Études Orientales*, Tome LII–2000 (Damascus, 2001) and the article J.-C. David and M. al-Dbiyat, "La ville en Syrie et ses territoires: héritages et mutations," *Bulletin d'Études Orientales* 52 (2000): 17–27.

[123] La Direction Générale des Antiquités et des Musées, *Qā'imat al-mabānī al-athrīya al-musajjala wal-mu'adda lil-tasjīl fī madīnat Dimashq hattā bidāyat 'ām 1983* (Damascus, 1983).

[124] Hayat Salam-Liebich, *The Architecture of the Mamluk City of Tripoli* (Cambridge, MA, 1983).

[125] N. Luz, "Tripoli Reinvented: a case of Mamluk Urbanization," in *Towns and Material Culture in the Medieval Middle East*, ed. Y. Lev (Leiden, 2002), 53–71.

[126] The Deutsche Orient-Institut in Beirut (directed by Stefan Weber), together with Centre de Restauration et Conservation, at the Tripoli Town Council and the Lebanese University (Tripoli) have an interdisciplinary programme for the recovery of the ancient centre of Tripoli based on historical enquiry and measured drawings of Mamluk architecture.

[126bis] M. K. Havari, Ayyubid Jerusalem. An architectural and Archaeological Study, (Oxford 2007).

[127] M. H. Burgoyne, *Mamluk Jerusalem: An Architectural Study* (London, 1987).

Mamluk architecture, and Sylvia Auld and Robert Hillenbrand,[128] on Ottoman architecture. Their research which represents the final product of a series of historical inquiries and field surveys on Mamluk and Ottoman buildings sponsored by the Waqf Council of Jerusalem relates the architectural to the urban structure of the walled city in these crucial phases of urban development and gives indications as to the main lines of urban development for the same periods, thanks to the use of ground plans that show the distribution of specialized architecture within the urban fabric.

In this context we must also mention the monograph on the Dome of the Rock by Oleg Grabar and Sari Nuseibeh.[129] Though this work deals primarily with a single monument, in its visual and structural relation to the Holy Sepulchre, the authors also give a spatial reading of the whole of the ancient city of Jerusalem.

Today there is as yet no systematic research being carried out on residential buildings in Jerusalem. The only systematic work on residential buildings in an urban context within the same region is that on Bethlehem by Philippe Revault, Catherine Weill-Rochant, and Serge Santelli;[130] and on Palestinian urban mansions edited by Riwaq-centre for architectural conservation.[130bis]

The research centres operating in Jerusalem and monitoring its building and architectural heritage are the British School of Archaeology in Jerusalem and Islamic Waqf Department.

In Jordan the historian and archaeologist Hugh Kennedy[131] has described the passage from a Byzantine urban structure to an early Islamic one, while Donald Whitcomb[132] has studied Islamic archaeology

---

[128] S. Auld and S. Hillenbrand, *Ottoman Jerusalem: The Living City, 1517–1917* (London, 2000) and, in particular, Catalogue of Buildings by Yusuf Natsheh.

[129] O. Grabar and S. Nuseibeh, *The Dome of the Rock* (New York, 1996).

[130] P. Revault, C. Weill-Rochant, and S. Santelli, *Maisons de Bethléem* (Paris, 1997).

[130bis] D. Khasawneh, Memories Engraved in Stones. Palestinian Urban Mansions, (Ramallah 2001); Riwaq eds., Riwaq's Registry of Historic Buildings in Palestine, 3 rolls (Ramallah 2007).

[131] H. Kennedy, "From Polis to Medina: Urban Change in Late Antique and Early Islamic Syria," *Past and Present* 106 (1985): 3–27; H. Kennedy, "The Towns of Bilad al-Sham and the Arab Conquest," in *Proceedings of the Symposium on Bilad al-Sham During the Byzantine Period* (Muharram 9–13, 1404 A.H./November 15–19, 1983), ed. M. Adnan Bakhit and M. Asfour, vol. 2 (Amman, 1986), 88–99.

[132] D. Whitcomb, "Excavations in 'Aqaba: First Preliminary Report," *Annual of the Department of Antiquities of Jordan* 31 (1987): 247–266; D. Whitcomb, "A Fatimide

in the Fatimid period. The research centre operating here is the centre for the study of the Built Environment (CSBE).

In the 1980s, leaders in the debate on the physical structure of Iranian cities[133] (albeit with different approaches and methodologies and drawing different conclusions) were: Heinz Gaube and Eugen Wirth,[134] with their research on the commercial structures of the bazaars; Heinz Gaube,[135] with his research on the structure and morphology of Iranian cities; and Michael E. Bonine,[136] with his research on the relation between urban and territorial structures. In their monograph on Isfahan Gaube and Wirth have been able to draw more general conclusions concerning the historical development of the whole urban structure from their fieldwork and historical research on the structure of the bazaar. In his book on Iranian cities Gaube identifies common features in the urban structures of Isfahan, Herat and Bam and other cities in the Islamic world, which he believes are recognizable in the structure of the city walls, bazaars and mosques, as well as those features not in common, given the importance of water and the influence of ancient, non-Western, pre-Islamic circular or square urban plans. Moreover, he identifies the urban plan and structure of Isfahan in the original pre-Safavid route network and derives the square plan of the Herat city walls from the influences of Indian cosmology.

Residence at Aqaba, Jordan," *Annual of the Department of Antiquities of Jordan* 32 (1988): 207–224; D. Whitcomb, *Aqaba—'Port of Palestine on the China Sea'* (Amman, 1988).

[133] Cadastral surveys on a scale of 1:2500 that cover the whole Iranian territory. Those of the urban centres, even the minor ones, from the 1980s, are very interesting. The plans were drawn up by the National Cartographic Centre. Maps of Iranian cities are also collected in: M. Mehryar, Sh. S. Fatullayev, F. F. Tehrani, and B. Qadiri, eds., *Pictorial Documents of Iranian Cities in the Qajar Period*, Shahid Beheshti University and Iranian Cultural Heritage Organization (Tehran, 2000).

[134] H. Gaube and E. Wirth, *Der Bazar von Isfahan* (Wiesbaden, 1978).

[135] H. Gaube, *Iranian cities* (New York, 1979); H. Gaube, "Innenstadt-Aussenstadt: Kontinuität und Wandel im Grundriss von Herat (Afghanistan) zwischen dem X. und dem XV. Jahrhundert," in *Beiträge zur Geographie orientalischer Städte und Märkte*, ed. G. Schweizer (Wiesbaden, 1977).

[136] M. E. Bonine, "The Morphogenesis of Iranian Cities," *Annals of the Association of American Geographers* 69 (1979): 208–224; M. E. Bonine, *Yazd and its Hinterland: A Central Place System of Dominance in the Central Iranian Plateau* (Marburg/Lahn, 1980); M. E. Bonine, "Qanats, Field Systems, and Morphology: Rectangularity on the Iranian Plateau," in *Qanat, Kariz and Khattara: Traditional Water Systems in the Middle East and North Africa*, ed. P. Beaumont, M. E. Bonine, and K. McLachlan (Cambridgeshire, 1989), 34–57.

Herat has also been the subject of research by scholars such as Abdul Wasay Najimi,[137] Rafi Samizay,[138] and Terry Allen.[139] Using the methodology of the German School, Allen has published a history of Herat in the fifteenth century based both on fieldwork and historical research. In reference to the ancient city, and without deviating significantly from Gaube's theories, Najimi has stressed the common features Herat shares with other cities in the Islamic world: the cul-de-sacs, bazaars, and position of the mosques within the urban fabric.

The close relation between the urban structure of Iranian cities and their water systems has also been stressed by Michael Bonine, who has analyzed the relation between these cities and their surrounding environment, both natural and anthropic, and associated their regular structure with the channelling of water. Donald Whitcomb's work on Iranian anthropic structures,[140] on the other hand, like his studies on Jordan, is based on an archaeological interest in the early phases of the Islamic conquest of the region.

Finally, the work of the Iranian scholar Mahvash Alemi[141] has been directed toward a reconstruction of the physical structure of Safavid cities, beginning with an interpretation of historical documents and travellers' accounts, such as those by Pietro della Valle and E. Kaempfer. In her article on Teheran, she used a reprint of a

---

[137] A. W. Najimi, *Herat: The Islamic City* (London, 1988).

[138] R. Samizay, "Herat: Pearl of Khurasan," in "Urban Fabric," ed. A. Petruccioli, *Environmental Design: Journal of the Islamic Environmental Design Research Centre* 1–2 (1989): 86–93.

[139] T. Allen, *Timurid Herat* (Wiesbaden, 1983).

[140] D. Whitcomb, "The City of Istakar and the Marvdasht Plain," in *Akten des VII. Internationalen Kongresses für Iranische Kunst und Archäologie, München 7.–10. September 1976* (Berlin, 1979), 363–370; D. Whitcomb, "Islamic Archaelogy at Susa," *Paléorient* 11 (1985): 85–90; D. Whitcomb, *Before the Roses and the Nightingales: Excavations at Qasr-I Abu Nasr, Old Shiraz* (New York, 1985).

[141] M. Alemi, "The 1891 Map of Tehran: Two Cities, Two Cores, Two Cultures," in "Maghreb: From Colonialism to a New Identity," ed. Attilio Petruccioli, *Environmental Design: Journal of the Islamic Environmental Design Research Centre* 1 (1985): 74–84; M. Alemi, "Urban Spaces as the Scene for the Ceremonies and Pastimes of the Safavid Court," in "Mughal Architecture: Pomp and Ceremonies," ed. Attilio Petruccioli, *Environmental Design: Journal of the Islamic Environmental Design Research Centre* 1–2 (1991): 98–107; M. Alemi, "The Relation Between The Royal Complexes and Cities," in *Transformations of Urban Form. ISUF '99* (Florence, 1999); M. Alemi, "Il giardino reale in Persia e la sua relazione con il disegno urbano," in *Giardini Islamici: architettura, ecologia*. Atti del Convegno, Genova, 8–9 Nov. 2001, ed. M. Matteini and A. Petruccioli (Genoa, 2001); M. Alemi, "Giardini reali e disegno del paesaggio ad Esfahan e nel territorio iraniano alla luce dei documenti inediti di Pascal Coste," in "Opus," *Quaderno di Storia, Architettura, Restauro* (Università degli Studi Gabriele D'Annunzio a Chieti), no. 7 (2003).

nineteenth century map as her main source for a fresh interpretation of its urban morphology.

In the 1980s the debate on the structure of the Islamic city in Iraq was marked by Hicham Djaït's work on al-Kufa.[142] Using historical documents and comparing the urban structure of al-Kufa with other cities, he found the Arab characteristics of its urban morphology in the structure of residential neighbourhoods and in the relation between khitat and the central public area.

In the same years, studies on the physical structure of Baghdad from an historical and morphological perspective were carried out by C. I. Beckwith and the Iraqi Department of Archaeology in collaboration with the Iraqi-Italian Institute of Archaeology in Baghdad.

Taking into account reciprocal cultural, historical, and morphological influences, Beckwith's[143] research has traced the source of the urban model of Baghdad in the Central Asian and Iranian circular urban plan.

Starting from the 1970s, the Iraqi Department of Archaeology and the Iraqi-Italian Institute of Archaeology in Baghdad[144] have carried out an architectural survey of the monuments of the Karkh and Rusafa neighbourhoods with the aid of waqf documents and historical sources in order to delineate the historical topography of these districts.

In his studies on Baghdad and Basra from a mainly historical perspective, and especially in his work on Baghdad, Ahmad al-'Alī Sālih[145] has been able to produce evidence of the structure of its urban fabric and morphology during the Abbasid Caliphate.

Studies on the traditional urban structure of Mosul are more numerous than those on Baghdad, since the former's urban fabric has undergone only slight transformations. In this context we must mention the research carried out by Hāshim Khudayr al-Janābi and Yūsuf Dhannūb. In his work on Mosul and other Iraqi cities, Hāshim

---

[142] H. Djaït, *al-Kûfa: Naissance de la ville islamique* (Paris, 1986).

[143] Ch. I. Beckwith, "The Plan of the City of Peace: Central Asian Iranian Factors in Early 'Abbāsid Design," *Acta Orientalia Academiae Scientiarum Hungaricae* 38, nos. 1–2 (1984).

[144] V. Strika and J. Khalīl, "The Islamic Architecture of Baghdād: the Results of a Joint Italian–Iraqi Survey," *Annali* 47, no. 3, Supplement 52 (1987).

[145] A. Sālih, *Baghdād, the City of Peace: Buildings and the Residential System at the Beginning of the 'Abbasid Caliphate* [in Arabic] (Baghdad, 1985); A. Sālih, *Topography of Basra in the Early Islamic Period* [in Arabic] (Baghdad, 1986).

Khudayr al-Janābi[146] has traced from a geographical perspective the salient features of the urban structure of the old city and has produced maps of the neighbourhoods and suq. The same interest in the representation of the physical structure of Mosul has characterized the work of Yūsuf Dhannūb.[147] His studies, sponsored by the Department of Construction of Mosul, are based on a survey of public, religious, and residential buildings. Through his work of representation and classification of single buildings there emerges a cross section of the entire urban structure.

Central Asia

Until the 1980s, research on Central Asian cities was the almost exclusive domain of scholars from the ex-USSR, since non-Soviets did not have access to bibliographic sources nor could they carry out field surveys. Moreover, another problem impeded the development of studies on the historical structure of Central Asian cities on a broader scale of reference: many of the cities that had arisen next to nomadic encampments had vanished without trace. The history of the salient urban features in these regions was, therefore, often the province of archaeologists rather than scholars studying urban physical structures.

Modern studies on Islamic cities in Central Asia began with the work of A. M. Belenitskii, I. B. Bentovich, and O. G. Bolshakov[148] who from an historico-archaeological perspective sought to revise Russian and Soviet Orientalist studies on medieval Central Asian cities. *Svednevekovyi gorod Svendei Azii* included cartographic reconstructions that described the transformations of the urban structure of Merv, Samarkand, and Bukhara from the Arab conquest to the Mongol invasions.

---

[146] H. K. al-Janābi, *Der Suq (Bazar) von Baghdad: Eine wirtschafts und social-geographische Untersuchung* (Erlangen, 1976); H. K. al-Janābi, *Inner Structure of the Old City of Mosul* [in Arabic] (Mosul, 1982); H. K. al-Janābi, *Urban Geography of the City of Irbil* [in Arabic] (Irbil, 1987).

[147] Y. Dhannūb et al., *The Buildings of Mosul* [in Arabic], vols. 1–3 (Mosul, 1982).

[148] A. M. Belenitskii, I. B. Bentovich, and O. G. Bolshakov, *Svednevekovyi gorod Svendei Azii* (Leningrad, 1973); O. G. Bolshakov, *Svednevekovyi gorod Blizhnego Vostoka, VII–seredina XIIIV: Sotsial'noekonomicheskie otnosheniyai* (Moscow, 1984).

After the publication of these works, various symposia on Islamic cities in Central Asia—such as the one organized in 1989 by the Institute of History of the Uzbek Academy of Science[149]—were held in the 1980s, in which, however, the city as a physical entity was given only a marginal treatment.

In the same decade individual studies on cities in this region were carried out and made a notable contribution to their urban history: for example, A. Anarbaev's work[150] in which archaeological data were used to interpret the architectonic and urban structure of medieval Panjikant, Samarkand, and Nasaf, and the work by non-Soviet scholars, such as Ernst Giese.[151]

More recently, and partly thanks to the greater accessibility of the sources, a keen interest in the physical structure of Central Asian cities has developed and several monographs on Bukhara and Samarkand[152] have been published, especially after the International Symposium sponsored by the Samuel H. Kress Foundation and the Aga Khan Program for Islamic Architecture at Harvard and MIT.[153] The research carried out by Anette Gangler, Heinz Gaube, and Attilio Petruccioli on Bukhara,[154] for example, has been collected in a recent publication in which the various phases in the evolution of urban structure—from a large scale of reference to individual architectural monuments—are analyzed. Finally, Robert D. McChesney[155] is amongst the scholars who

---

[149] Many of the papers have been collected in R. G. Mukminova, ed., *Pozdne-feodal'nyi gorod Srednei Azii* (Tashkent, 1990).

[150] A. Anarbaev, *Blagoustroistvo svednevekovgo goroda Srednei Azii, V-nachalo XIII v.* (Tashkent, 1981).

[151] E. Giese, "Aufbau, Entwicklung und Genese der islamisch-orientalischen Stadt in Sowjet-Mittelasien," *Erkunde* 34 (1980): 46–60.

[152] G. Andriani, D. Catania, F. Gigotti, L. Guastamacchia, L. Pisano, C. Rubini, and P. Traversa, "Samarkand: the Planned City," in *The Planned City?* ISUF International Conference, ed. A. Petruccioli, M. Stella, and G. Strappa (Bari, 2003), 595–599.

[153] A. Petruccioli, ed., *Bukhara: The Myth and the Architecture* (Cambridge, MA, 1999).

[154] A. Gangler, H. Gaube, and A. Petruccioli, *Bukara: The Eastern Dome of Islam, Urban Development, Urban Space, Architecture and Population* (Stuttgart and London, 2004).

[155] R. D. McChesney, *Waqf in Central Asia: Four Hundred Years in the History of a Muslim Shrine, 1480–1889* (Princeton, 1991); R. D. McChesney, "Reconstructing Balkh: The Vakfiya of 947/1540," in *Studies on Central Asian History*, ed. D. DeWeese (Bloomington, 2001); R. D. McChesney, "Architecture and Narrative: The Khwaja Abu Nasr Shrine. Part One: Constructing the Complex and its Meaning, 1469–1696," *Muqarnas* 18 (2001); R. D. McChesney, "Architecture and Narrative: The Khwaja Abu Nasr Shrine. Part Two: Representing the Complex in Word and Image, 1696–1998," *Muqarnas* 19 (2002).

have used waqf documents to reconstruct the architectural and social history of Central Asian cities.

Anatolia

Studies on the physical structure of Islamic cities in Anatolia have developed in tandem with those on Arab and Balkanic cities in the Ottoman period, though they have been concentrated above all on Istanbul. Robert Mantran[156] was the first scholar to carry out research on the structure of Turkish cities. Starting from an analysis of archival documents, he has studied urban structure, economic life, and the different social groups in Istanbul.

Research more closely linked to the definition of the physical structure of Anatolian cities was later carried out by Dogan Kuban[157] and U. Tanyeli.[158] Kuban has ascribed the structural origin of the Turkish city to the diverse influences of Islamic, Central Asian-Iranian, Anatolian-Byzantine, and traditional Turko-Nomadic urban models. Tanyeli has developed Kuban's theses and, beginning with the classification of Anatolian cities into three types (eastern Anatolian cities enclosed by walls, eastern Anatolian cities without defensive walls, and western Anatolian cities bordering on Byzantine territory) and a reading of their urban structure, he has ascribed the origins of their most salient features to Turko-Iranian urban models and the contribution of nomadic populations. Finally, Sevgi Aktüre's[159] studies on the Anatolian city in the Ottoman period have analyzed their urban spatial structure in relation to their social and economic structures.

---

[156] R. Mantran, *Istanbul dans la seconde moitié du XVIIe siècle. Essai d'histoire institutionnelle, économique et sociale* (Paris, 1962); R. Mantran, *La vie quotidienne à Constantinople au temps de Soliman le magnifique et de ses successeurs (XVIe et XVIIe siècles)* (Paris, 1965); R. Mantran, "Foreign Merchants and the Minorities in Istanbul during the Sixteenth and Seventeenth Century," in *Christians and Jews in the Ottoman Empire*, vol. 1, *The Central Lands*, ed. B. Braude and B. Lewis (New York, 1982), 127–137.

[157] D. Kuban, "Anadolu-Türk Şehri Tarihî Gelişmesi, Sosyal ve Fizikî Özellikleri üzerinde Bazi Gelişmeler," *Vakiflar Dergisi* 7 (1968).

[158] U. Tanyeli, *Anadolu-Türk Kentinde Fiziksel Yapinin Evrim Sürecisi: 11.–15.yy* (Istanbul, 1987).

[159] S. Aktüre, *19. Yüzyil Sonunda Anadolu Kenti, Mekânsal Yapi Çözümlemesi* (Ankara, 1978); S. Aktüre, "The Islamic Anatolian City," in "Urban Fabric," ed. A. Petruccioli, *Environmental Design: Journal of the Islamic Environmental Design Research Centre* 1–2 (1989): 68–79.

Systematic urban studies on Istanbul have seen in W. Müller-Wiener's work[160] on urban and architectural structures the most comprehensive cartographic reconstructions of the city in the various phases of its anthropic development.

Maurice Munir Cerasi's work[161] on the physical structure of Istanbul, on the other hand, elucidates its morphological organization. In his research Cerasi describes the structure of the "Levantine" city, which finds in Istanbul its main point of reference, through an elucidation of the morphological and spatial relations between the different structures that comprise the urban fabric and between the urban fabric and the morphology of the site.

Halil İnalcik[162] has described Istanbul's salient urban features in relation to the structure of the Islamic city. Using the term "Islamic Ottoman" city to refer to a social model based on the *qadi* and waqf system and the idea of privacy, he has described an urban model divided spatially into residential districts with autonomous functions, and public and commercial zones, planned and controlled by a central power, with the function of connecting the residential districts.

Apart from Cerasi's and İnalcik's studies on the spatial organization of Ottoman Istanbul and the relation between architecture and urban-scape, many other studies have been carried out: for example,

---

[160] W. Müller-Wiener, *Bildlexikon zur Topographie Istanbuls: Byzantion—Konstantinupolis—Istanbul bis zum Beginn des 17. Jahrhunderts* (Tübingen, 1977); W. Müller-Wiener, "Der Bazar von Izmir: Studien zur Geschichte und Gestalt des Wirtschaftszentrum einer ägäischen handelsmetropole," *Mitteilungen der Fränkischen Geographischen Gesellschaft* 27–28 (1980–1981): 420–454; W. Müller-Wiener, "Das Kavak Sarayi: Ein verlorenes Baudenkmal Istanbuls," *Istanbuler Mitteilungen* 38 (1988): 363–376.

[161] M. M. Cerasi, "Open Space, Water and Trees in Ottoman Urban Culture in the XVIIIth–XIXth Centuries," in "Water and Architecture," ed. A. Petruccioli, *Environmental Design: Journal of the Islamic Environmental Design Research Centre* 2 (1985): 36–49; M. M. Cerasi, "Place and Perspective in Sinan's Townscape," in "Mimar Sinan: The Urban Vision," ed. A. Petruccioli, *Environmental Design: Journal of the Islamic Environmental Design Research Centre* 1–2 (1987): 52–61; M. M. Cerasi, *La Città del Levante. Civiltà urbana e architettura sotto gli Ottomani nei secoli XVIII–XIX* (Milano, 1988); M. M. Cerasi, "Città e architettura nel Settecento," in "Istanbul, Constantinople, Byzantium," *Rassegna: Problemi di architettura e dell'ambiente* 72, no. 4 (1997): 36–51; Cerasi M. M., "Type, Urban Context and Language in Conflict: Some Methodological Implications," in *Typological Process and Design Theory*, ed. A. Petruccioli (Cambridge, MA, 1998), 179–188; M. M. Cerasi, "Un Barocco di Città—trasformazioni linguistiche e tipologiche nel Settecento ad Istanbul," *Quaderni di Storia dell'Architettura* 3 (2000): 81–102; M. M. Cerasi and A.-I. Melling, "Costantinopoli tra naturalismo e prospettiva," *Rassegna di studi e notizie della civica raccolta delle stampe Achille Bertarelli* 27 (2003): 191–230.

[162] H. İnalcik, "Istanbul: An Islamic City," *Journal of Islamic Studies* 1 (1990).

by I. Aslanoglu,[163] J. Erzen,[164] J. M. Rogers,[165] A. Kuran,[166] Godfrey Goodwin,[167] Enis Kortan,[168] S. Yérasimos,[169] and Pierre Pinon,[170] who has paid special attention to the study of cadastral surveys. Amongst the scholars who have used waqf documents as their main source for a reconstruction of the urban history of Istanbul, Haim Gerber[171] has maintained, through his work on Edirne and Bursa, that the waqf

---

[163] I. Aslanoglu, "Siting of Sinans Kulliyes in Istanbul," in "Mimar Sinan: The Urban Vision," ed. A. Petruccioli, *Environmental Design: Journal of the Islamic Environmental Design Research Centre* 1–2 (1987): 154–161.

[164] J. Erzen, "Imperializing a City: Istanbul of the Sixteenth Century," in "Mimar Sinan: The Urban Vision," ed. A. Petruccioli, *Environmental Design: Journal of the Islamic Environmental Design Research Centre* 1–2 (1987): 88–97.

[165] J. M. Rogers, "Sinan as Planner: Some Documentary Evidence," in "Mimar Sinan: The Urban Vision," ed. A. Petruccioli, *Environmental Design: Journal of the Islamic Environmental Design Research Centre* 1–2 (1987): 174–191.

[166] A. Kuran, "A Spatial Study of Three Ottoman Capitals: Bursa, Edirne, and Istanbul," *Muqarnas* 13 (1996): 114–131.

[167] G. Goodwin, "Sinan and City Planning," in "Mimar Sinan: The Urban Vision," ed. A. Petruccioli, *Environmental Design: Journal of the Islamic Environmental Design Research Centre* 1–2 (1987): 10–19.

[168] E. Kortan, "The Role of Sinan's Work Within the Urban Context," in "Mimar Sinan: The Urban Vision," ed. A. Petruccioli, *Environmental Design: Journal of the Islamic Environmental Design Research Centre* 1–2 (1987): 140–145.

[169] S. Yérasimos, "Istanbul Ottomana," *Rassegna: Problemi di architettura dell'ambiente* 72, no. 4 (1997): 24–35.

[170] P. Pinon, "Les tissus urbains ottomans entre Orient et Occident," in *Proceedings of the 2nd International Meeting on Modern Ottoman Studies and the Turkish Republic* (Leiden, 1989), 15–45; A. Borie, P. Pinon, and S. Yérasimos, "Tokat: essai sur l'architecture domestique et la forme urbaine," *Anatolia Moderna* 1 (1991): 239–273; P. Pinon, "Essai de définition morphologique de la ville ottomane des XVIIIe–XIXe siècles," in *La culture urbaine des Balkans*, vol. 3, *La ville des Balkans depuis la fin du Moyen Age jusqu'au début du XXe siècle* (Paris and Belgrade, 1991), 147–155; P. Pinon, "Métamorphose d'une ville," in "Byzance-Istanbul," *Critique* 48, nos. 543–544 (1992): 712–720; P. Pinon, "La cartographie urbaine d'Istanbul et les incendies au XIXe siècle: les plans de lotissements après incendies et les cadastres d'assurances," in "La ville en Feu," Actes du Colloque du Laboratoire TMU, ed. S. Yérasimos and F. Friès, *Cahiers*, nos. 6–7 (1993): 37–44; P. Pinon, "Topographie des lotissements et transformations urbaines d'Istanbul dans la seconde moitié du XIXe siècle," in *Histoire économique et sociale de l'Empire ottoman et de la Turquie (1326–1960)*, Actes du Sixième Congrès International (Leuven–Paris 1995), 687–703; P. Pinon and S. Yérasimos, "Relevés après incendie et plans d'assurances: les précurseurs du cadastre stamboultiote," in "Environmental Design: Urban Morphogenesis, Maps and Cadastral Plans," ed. A. Petruccioli, *Environmental Design: Journal of the Islamic Environmental Design Research Centre* 1–2 (1993):112–129; P. Pinon, "Essai de typologie des tissus urbains des villes ottomanes d'Anatolie et des Balkans," in *7 Centuries of Ottoman Architecture: "A Supra-National Heritage"* (Istanbul, 2000), 174–198.

[171] H. Gerber, "The *Waqf* Institution in Early Ottoman Edirne," *African and Asian Studies* 17 (1983); H. Gerber, *Economy and Society in an Ottoman City: Bursa 1600–1700* (Jerusalem, 1988).

was an efficient instrument of urban control, while Suraiya Faroqhi[172] has been concerned mainly with the relation between the city and its urban economy.

These brief historiographical notes have attempted to trace the main lines of the debate that has characterized studies on the traditional Islamic city, starting from changes in the scholarly approach to its physical structure with the advent of regional studies in the 1980s. Despite their concise nature, and with reference to more wide-ranging critical and bibliographical works on the Islamic city in general,[173] we have sought to outline the course that has led from a revision of the Orientalist approach to contemporary urban studies. The resulting balance seems tipped in favour of a renewed interest in such urban organisms, seen in the numerous contributions of scholars and research centres, using a range of methodologies, to the study of the diverse physical forms and structures of Islamic cities.

[English translation by Lisa Adams]

---

[172] L. T. Erder and S. Faroqhi, "The Development of the Anatolian Urban Network During the Sixteenth Century," *Journal of the Economic and Social History of the Orient* 23 (1980): 265–303; S. Faroqhi, *Towns and Townsmen of Ottoman Anatolia: Trade, Crafts and Food Production in an Urban Setting, 1520–1650* (Cambridge, MA, 1984); S. Faroqhi, *Towns and Townsmen of Ottoman Anatolia, Trade, Crafts, and Food Production in an Urban Setting 1520–1650* (Cambridge, 1984); S. Faroqhi, "The Anatolian Town and its Place within the Administrative Structure of the Ottoman State (1500–1590)" in *From Mantzikert to Lepanto, The Byzantine World and the Turks 1071–1571*, ed. A. Bryer and M. Ursinus, *Byzantinische Forschungen*, XVI (1991), 209–244: S. Faroqhi, "Migration into Eighteenth-Century 'Greater Istanbul' as Reflected in the Kadi Registers of Eyüp" in *Eyüp'te Sosyal Yaşam*, ed. T. Artan (Istanbul, 1998), pp. 33–48; S. Faroqhi, "Urban Space as Disputed Grounds: Territorial Aspects to Artisan Conflict in Sixteenth to Eighteenth-Century Istanbul" in *Stories of Ottoman Men and Women: Establishing Status, Establishing Control,* (Istanbul, 2002), 219–234; S. Faroqhi, "Pious Foundations in the Ottoman Society of Anatolia and Rumelia: a Report on Current Research," in *Stiftungen in Christentum, Judentum und Islam vor der Moderne. Auf der Suche nach ihren Gemeinsamkeiten und Unterschieden in religiösen Grundlagen, praktischen Zwecken und historischen Transformationen*, ed. M. Borgolte and T. Lohse (Berlin, 2005), 223–256; S. Faroqhi, "Die historische Forschung und das frühmoderne Istanbul," in *Istanbul: vom imperialen Herrschersitz zur Megalopolis, Historiographische Betrachtungen zu Gesellschaft, Instituionen und Räumen*, ed. Yvuz Köse (Munich, 2006).

[173] See in particular M. E. Bonine, E. Ehlers, T. Krafft, and G. Stöber, eds., *The Middle Eastern City and Islamic Urbanism: An Annotated Bibliography of Western Literature* (Bonn, 1994); M. Haneda and T. Miura, eds., *Islamic Urban Studies. Historical Review and Perspective* (London and New York, 1994).

THE SPATIAL ORGANIZATION OF THE CITY

André Raymond

1. *The Hypothesis of the Muslim City*

1.1

The concept of a "Muslim" city was forged between 1920 and 1950 by the French Orientalist school of Algiers, notably by its chief protagonists William and Georges Marçais and, after them, by Roger le Tourneau.[1] It was then supplemented by Jean Sauvaget and Jacques Weulersse, of the "Damascus school."[2] This theoretical quest was accompanied by a noteworthy succession of monographs on a number of large Arab cities: by Gaston Deverdun on Marrakesh (1959); by Jacques Caillé on Rabat (1949); by Roger le Tourneau on Fez (1949); by R. Lespès on Algiers (1930); by Marcel Clerget on Cairo (1934); by Jean Sauvaget on Damascus and Aleppo (1934, 1941); and by Jacques Weulersse on Antioch (1934).[3]

All these scholars were, it will be noted, French; a fact pointed out by Stephen Humphreys who spoke of "the great French tradition of Islamic urban studies" and of "a thin but steady stream of publications

---

[1] See W. Marçais, "L'Islamisme et la vie urbaine," in *Articles et Conférences* (Paris, 1961); G. Marçais, "L'urbanisme musulman," in *Mélanges d'histoire et d'archéologie*, 2 vols. (Algiers, 1957); and R. Le Tourneau, *Les villes musulmanes de l'Afrique du Nord* (Algiers, 1957). Janet Abu-Lughod has shed a good deal of light on the development of this Orientalist tradition from the Marçais brothers to G. von Grunebaum in "The Islamic City," *IJMES* (1987). I have myself tackled this problem in "Islamic City, Arab City: Orientalist Myths and Recent Views," *British Journal of Middle Eastern Studies* 21, no. 1 (1994).

[2] J. Sauvaget, "Esquisse d'une histoire de la ville de Damas," *REI* 4 (1934); idem, *Alep: Essai sur le développement d'une grande ville syrienne* (Paris, 1941); J. Weulersse, "Antioche, Essai de géographie urbaine," *BEO* 4 (1931); and *Paysans de Syrie et du Proche-Orient* (Paris, 1946).

[3] G. Deverdun, *Marrakech des origines à 1912*, 2 vols. (Rabat, 1959–61); J. Caillé, *La ville de Rabat jusqu'au Protectorat français*, 3 vols. (Paris, 1949); R. Le Tourneau, *Fès avant le Protectorat* (Casablanca, 1949); R. Lespès, *Alger, étude de géographie et d'histoire urbaine* (Paris, 1930); and M. Clerget, *Le Caire*, 2 vols. (Cairo, 1934). For J. Sauvaget and J. Weulersse, see note 2 above.

(the majority of them by French scholars) on various aspects of the topic."[4] This is not merely a feature of scholarly sociology, of particular interest by virtue of an absence of comparable work in the parts of the world dominated by Great Britain. France was during this period a colonial power whose sway extended over the whole of the Maghreb and over the Levant; and, as such, it is not surprising that the work carried out by these noteworthy scholars should have been influenced by the spirit of the time: a spirit that led members of the dominant caste—the "ruling institution" in H. A. R. Gibb's phrase—to regard the urban realizations of subject populations (viewed as outdated and even backward) with a degree of condescension. The colonizers' profound antipathy towards the "Turkish" period which had preceded French colonization in all these parts was a further factor, inclining these scholars to discount what existed before the arrival of the French—who regarded themselves as bearers of a modern civilization with ambitions, indeed, to renew the Roman *imperium*.[5]

Such a rapprochement was hard to avoid, given that the colonized Mediterranean regions did in fact indelibly bear the mark of an ancient civilization whose lustre and prosperity were notably in evidence in a wondrous network of prestigious cities: Volubilis, Jamila, Timgad, Dougga, el-Jem, Palmyra, and Apamea were only some of the pearls among the multitude of ancient cities that developed, following the Hellenistic flowering, in the lands conquered by the Romans. Roman ways had set in place there an urbanism whose regularity, quality of municipal institutions and vigorous civic spirit were regarded as difficult to match. The existence of cities endowed with a grandiose, virtually perfect urban organization side by side with irregular Arab cities, full of an exotic charm but apparently chaotic in structure, was a spur to noteworthy works like those of Sauvaget on Damascus, Aleppo, and Latakia; but it provided food, too, for some peevish comparisons. "Nothing," wrote Le Tourneau, "is more alien to a Muslim city of the Maghreb than the rectilinear avenues of a Roman city, or of a modern city. The aerial photograph of any Muslim city gives the impression of a maze or labyrinth."[6] (fig. 1) The parallel between Roman city and

---

[4] R. S. Humphreys, *Islamic History* (Princeton: University Press, 1991), 228.
[5] An anthology of "anti-Turkism" could be made out of the work of French scholars from H. de Grammont's *Histoire d'Alger* (Paris, 1887) to J. Sauvaget.
[6] Le Tourneau, *Les villes musulmanes*, 20.

"modern" city (French, in the case of the Maghreb) is not, needless to say, fortuitous.

1.2

There is no great difficulty in defining the principles underlying the Orientalist approach vis-à-vis the Mediterranean Arab cities. Chief among these is the assumption that in a globalizing civilization like the Muslim one every phenomenon must be regarded as specifically Muslim. The Orientalists' initial training (geared chiefly towards the study of religion and its superstructures) led them naturally towards such an extreme viewpoint. R. Ilbert judiciously notes in this regard that, "it is because most Orientalists started out from a simple initial assumption...of the fundamental role of Islam in the structuring of space that they found this when they came to the subject."[7] It is not astonishing, then, to find Islam mentioned in connection with institutions, with the organization of political life, with social and economic activities, of course; but also with the physical structure of city or house, which, from this perspective, can only be designated as "Muslim."

Viewed from such a religious standpoint, *sub specie aeternitatis*, urban phenomena appear as constants within a historical continuum stretching over some thirteen centuries, and within a Muslim world covering three continents, as far as distant China. In his "Urbanisme Musulman," G. Marçais makes reference, one page after the other, to the Fustat of the Fatimids, to the Fez of the Marinids, to the Algiers of the Ottoman deys, in order to describe a city whose illustrative examples are barely more than Maghrebi and represent no more than the particular state of the *madina* (the term used by geographers to designate the ancient centres) at the beginning of the nineteenth century.

The comparison between an urbanism of Antiquity, supposedly endowed with every perfection, and a "Muslim" urbanism characterized, at first sight, by a profound irregularity and by a rejection of all intelligible rules brought Orientalists to some discouraging conclusions regarding the physical structure of cities. The observation of R. Le Tourneau, quoted above, is characteristic of this uncomprehending stance. "Besides," sighs the despondent G. Marçais (without drawing

---

[7] R. Ilbert, "La ville musulmane: réalité et abstraction," *Les Cahiers de la recherche architecturale* 10–11 (April 1982): 12.

his conclusion), "it is not that Muslims are satisfied with narrow streets that they have failed to see the advantage of the straight line as a path from one point to another."[8] This reference to the Ancient World had especially prejudicial consequences for J. Sauvaget, since it was precisely he who had studied—with precision—the structure of the great Syrian cities in the Roman period; cities whose architecture is still evident in the layout of modern Arab cities (fig. 2). Damascus and Aleppo, he says, provide only "degenerate" images (he uses the word *dégénérescence*) of the city, as reflected in what has befallen the ancient colonnaded avenue to the suq. Of this last he supplies a brilliant demonstration, supported by an eloquent diagram.[9]

Nor is the Muslim city any more endowed (J. Sauvaget once again) with the municipal institutions that marked the cities of Antiquity (and accompanied the development of the medieval western communes). This observation is one of his chief contributions to the Orientalist conception of the Muslim city.[10] Bereft of any specific administration, the city is directly subject to the authority of the prince who governs it on the principles of oriental despotism.

This concept of a dislocated city, divided into antagonistic communities, is perhaps the contribution of J. Weulersse, based on the study of a very particular city—Antioch—which was effectively divided between highly diverse communities (Sunni Muslim Turks, Alawis, and Christians) and was described by the geographer as disjointed, broken up into sectors closed in on themselves, and potentially hostile. From this finally rather local state of affairs, stemming from an exceptional confessional and ethnic diversity, J. Sauvaget derives a law that he applies to Aleppo, where, he says, in the Muslim period, we may note the "dislocation of the urban centre, its fragmentation into small cells that are individualized and particularized, sometimes even antinomic."[11] Deeply impressed by the spectacle of a Sunni Latakia plunged within a rural Alawi environment, J. Weulersse (cited above) makes a similar generalization:

> In the East, the city gives the impression of a foreign body, a cyst as it were, within the country, of a creation imposed on the countryside it dominates and exploits...As such, the economic activity of the cities

---

[8] G. Marçais, "L'urbanisme musulman," 227.
[9] Sauvaget, *Alep*, 247.
[10] Sauvaget, "Esquisse," 455–456.
[11] Sauvaget, *Alep*, 248.

gives an essentially parasitic impression. The city…consumes without producing.[12]

These different themes have been regularly sounded in connection with other cities to be found in a totally different environment.[13]

1.3

The "Muslim" city is, then, characterized above all by *what it lacks*: the regularity, regulation, and civic spirit of the city of Antiquity; the communal institutions of the medieval city. It is wedded to decline. Under the Ottomans, notes M. Clerget, Cairo "becomes slowly extinguished…allowing the fragments of its glorious past to crumble little by little…Cairo is returning…to the kind of dispersed population favoured by the first Arabs."[14] Here we are concerned only with the Ottoman period so disliked by Orientalists. J. Sauvaget, though, goes still further with the following generalization. The Muslim period, he writes, with regard to Aleppo, "is marked by no positive contribution…All that might be attributed to it is the dislocation of the urban centre." The achievement of Islam "is essentially negative." The city becomes "a loose, inorganic assemblage of quarters."[15]

Dealing as we are here with a "non-city" and a "non-urbanism," it is no surprise that, when they proceed to try and define the major characteristics of the structure of the Muslim city, the authors should find themselves a trifle short on positive criteria and should limit themselves to a listing of not very significant and sometimes not very pertinent features. They conjure up city walls, palace, or fortress (which are not truly specific characteristics), the presence of a central principal mosque (which applies equally to the central cathedral) generally linked to markets where a corporate organization is in evidence (this is found in the West), the existence of public baths (proclaimed as Muslim because necessary for the carrying out of ritual ablution, forgetting the opulence of baths in Antiquity), separate quarters, an omnipresent type of house organized around a courtyard (invariably described as "Muslim," even though its existence in Antiquity and its presence

---

[12] Weulersse, *Paysans de Syrie*, 86–88.
[13] See, for example, the reflections on the *baldi* (city-dwellers) of Algiers, described as an original population set within a different and hostile rural environment.
[14] Clerget, *Le Caire*, 1:178–180.
[15] Sauvaget, *Alep*, 247–248.

throughout the Mediterranean are commonplace realities). Gustave von Grunebaum, whose "The Structure of the Muslim Town"[16] supplied, in 1955, the standard and approved Orientalist account, considers the elements noted immediately above, but without attempting to draw from them a description of the *structure* of the Muslim town as promised in the title of his article. He gives detailed consideration to urban *institutions* (the justice of the *qadi*, the supervision of morals by the *muhtasib*), which are, as one might expect, Muslim—as is the population (or the majority at least, since religious minorities are to be found there). His conclusion, while less abrupt than J. Sauvaget's, is not unexpected: "The Islamic town did not represent a uniform type of civilized life as had the Greek or Roman town."[17] It is only fair to note, nonetheless, that G. von Grunebaum marks a clear development in certain respects vis-à-vis strict Orientalist tradition: he points out the existence of different models, in Iran and Turkestan; he notes the beginnings of decay in the organization of the world of late Antiquity; he calls attention (in the wake of the seminal article published by Robert Brunschwig in 1947)[18] to the interest of Muslim jurists regarding urban problems. The fact is that when von Grunebaum's article was written Oriental doctrine on the Muslim city was already beginning to be revised; so that, in a certain sense, the article might be regarded simultaneously as the epitome of the doctrine and its swan-song.

2. *The challenge to Orientalist viewpoints on the Muslim city*

2.1

There is nothing surprising about such a challenge. In the 1950s, the colonial era within which Orientalism had evolved was entering its final phase. France herself, the favoured site for these urban studies, closed the colonial book in the 1940s (in the Levant) and the 1950s (in Morocco and Tunisia), before the final closure in 1962 (in Algeria). The end had come for a latent Eurocentrism and for the tendency to undervalue civilizations which might, from now on, be more expediently

---

[16] G. von Grunebaum, "The Structure of the Muslim Town," in *Islam, Essays in the Nature and Growth of a Cultural Tradition* (Routledge and Kegan, 1955).

[17] Von Grunebaum, "Structure," 154.

[18] R. Brunschvig, "Urbanisme médiéval et droit musulman," *REI* 15 (1947).

viewed in terms of an understanding and analysis of differences, rather than emphasis on supposed inferiority against a Western model. It does not seem overstated to see this approximate time as marking the end of Orientalism, the latter's final major enterprise being the publication by H. A. R. Gibb and H. Bowen of their *Islamic Society and the West* (1950–57). These two introductory volumes were to be followed by a general picture of Muslim society. This venture was in fact aborted; partly because research was then insufficiently advanced to bring it to fulfilment, and partly on account of the general approach, which (as the title reflects) conformed very closely to the spirit of Orientalism who saw the East as a mirror of the West.

The reassessment—to which the historians of the Turkish school of Lufti Barkan contributed so greatly from the end of the 1930s—of the importance and interest of an Ottoman heritage assumed an equal supplementary importance, in so far as it led to a revaluation of the pejorative vision imposed by Orientalists of the Algiers and Damascus schools with respect to Arab cities prior to colonization. The development of a parallel interest in the inexhaustible archives of the Ottoman period and the progressive use to which these latter were put served to confirm that Arab cities had not, at this time, seen the generalized decline described by specialist and also that elements of administration had been in place. Specifically, this revised viewpoint cast a vivid light on the problem posed in Sauvaget's (in many ways magisterial) work on Aleppo and successfully resolved the obvious contradiction that existed between the unbelievably negative assessments he brought to bear on the Ottoman period and the glittering picture emerging from his own work—a contradiction from which he had contrived to free himself only by an unconvincing final pirouette: "The Aleppo of the Ottomans is a mere *trompe l'oeil*, a sumptuous façade behind which lie only ruins."[19]

2.2

The entry into the scholarly field of specialists from other disciplines clearly contributed to challenging the theory of the implicit primacy of Islam in studies of the city and to breaking the kind of monopoly established in these studies by specialists in religion. Historians brought

---

[19] Sauvaget, *Alep*, 239.

a more marked awareness of the need to reset the development of cities within a chronological context, stretching over twelve centuries, from the creations or refoundings of the seventh century to the end of the Ottoman period (beginning of the nineteenth). In this context, Claude Cahen's book, *Mouvements populaires et autonomisme urbain*, published in 1959, was seminal. Sociologists brought to the debate an interest in social data and pointed out that, in fact, phenomena studied from an Islamic perspective were generally urban phenomena. Geographers contributed to restating these studies in terms of space (and mapping the various aspects of this), and to reminding that the Muslim world is not merely synonymous with the Arab (or simply Maghrebi) world studied by the Orientalists. In this respect, the contribution of Eugen Wirth, recently manifested in his *Orientalische Stadt* (Mainz, 2000), has been of prime importance.

2.3

An improved knowledge of late Antiquity (to which we are especially indebted through excavations like those of J. Balthy at Apamea) confirmed the intuitions given expression by J. Sauvaget, *in extremis*, in his *Alep*.[20] The progressive disorganization of layout within Antiquity was brought to light specifically by Claude Cahen in 1958, then by Samuel Stern in 1970, and, finally and very forcibly, by Hugh Kennedy in his article "From *Polis* to *Madina*" (1970) where he notes that in the urban communities of fifth- and sixth-century Syria "there was no classical town plan to affect later growth... The 'streets' were narrow winding paths, there was no agora, no colonnades, no theatre."[21] It is, then, quite fruitless to set a flawless ancient urbanism (which no longer existed when the Arab conquest came) over against an anarchic Muslim urbanism. In addition, excavations carried out recently at Palmyra and Bet Shean have revealed significant transitional stages between the late Roman period and the Umayyad period, suggesting continuity rather than any

---

[20] See, in his *Alep*, 248 (the penultimate page of the book!), his observation on the "reduction of the framework of city life to forms more rudimentary actually set in place by the Byzantine period."

[21] Cl. Cahen, "Mouvements populaires et autonomisme urbain," *Arabica* 5 (1958): 226; S. M. Stern, "The Constitution of the Islamic City," in *The Islamic City*, ed. A. H. Hourani and S. M. Stern (Oxford, 1970); and H. Kennedy, "From *Polis* to *Madina*," *Past and Present* 106 (1985): 13–14.

brutal break.[22] The debilitating conclusion drawn from this comparison, with regard to Muslim cities, has thus lost part of its relevance.

2.4

However, it is in the discounting of any possible identification of a *Muslim* model—universal and existing, in a sense, outside time—that the revision of the Orientalist conception of the city has doubtlessly found its most radical expression. In his seminal article on Muslim urbanism Georges Marçais speaks of the cities "in Muslim lands" (defined predominantly, in climatic terms, as "countries of thirst"), and, with regard to mainly Maghrebi cities, sets forth examples ranging from the age of conquest to that of the Barbary corsairs. At the opposite end of the chain of those transmitting the doctrine, G. von Grunebaum concedes more cautiously that, "in Iran and Turkestan the original layout of the city would be somewhat different." This is not, though, allowed to hinder his dauntless traversing of the lengthy period separating the first creations of the seventh century from the Ottoman period.[23]

It is an obvious fact (so obvious there is no point in lingering over it) that the Muslim world covers an enormous territory, from the Atlantic Ocean to the Far East, that it stretches into regions whose physical nature and, above all, climate are highly various; whereas the Arab world on which the analyses of Orientalists are almost exclusively based (when, indeed, they do not restrict themselves, according to the particular case, to the Maghreb or the Mashriq) represents only a small part of this immense whole, in terms of surface area and population alike. Oleg Grabar, dealing with artistic forms (though the rationale underlying his approach is, of course, equally applicable to urban structure itself) has clearly shown the difficulty involved in using the sole concept of "Islamic" when considering phenomena and production with respect to regions as various in their historical and cultural traditions, and in their natural characteristics, as those of the "Muslim world" in its widest sense, from Morocco to China, and from Central Asia to tropical Africa.[24] How, after all, are we in the cases of the Maghreb or

---

[22] Khaled Asʿad, "Ikhtishaf . . . suq fi Tadmur," *Annales Archéologiques Syriennes* 37–38 (1991); Yoram Tsafrir and Gideon Foerster, "Urbanism at Scythopolis-Bet Shean," *Dumbarton Oaks Papers* 51 (1997).

[23] G. Marçais, "L'Urbanisme musulman"; von Grunebaum, "Structure."

[24] O. Grabar, "Reflexions on the Study of Islamic Art," *Muqarnas* 1 (1983): 8.

Indonesia to tackle the problems of providing a city or dwelling with water from a solely Islamic perspective?

Equally thorny is the problem of a-temporality that appears to be entailed in describing a city as a kind of unvarying entity, from the time Islam was preached to the dawn of the nineteenth century. This calls irresistibly to mind J.-Cl. Garcin's questions about the Muslim house which cannot be provided with "an interpretation *ne varietur*," and his enlargement on the subject: "Analogous observations might be made on the 'interpretation' still too often accorded to 'the Muslim city' and the way it is laid out."[25] It is because they have placed themselves beyond time that Orientalists—and indeed most contemporary interpreters—have behaved as though the ancient city whose remains they had before their eyes provided a directly usable image of the "classical" (medieval) city, when in fact it is merely the "modern" (i.e., largely Ottoman) version of the city, shaped by three or four centuries. The "classical" city can only be *reconstructed*, by means of an analysis basing itself on ancient sources. The history of these cities has been too lengthy and has entailed too much contrast for it to be provided with a trans-historical, truly homogeneous interpretation.

2.5

These considerations lead one to think that there is no "Muslim" city of the kind Orientalists have wished to identify. Moreover, the attempt, frequently made, to search out elements in the Quran or in Tradition, which might form the basis for the description of such a city, have produced little more than a meagre harvest of general prescriptions about the protection of private life or the constraints of neighbourhood. The only truly significant text that can be produced is the oft-invoked *hadith* of Muslim: "If you are in disagreement about the width of a street, make this of seven cubits."[26] In contrast, judicial or jurisdictional decisions made by judge or *faqih* have, over the centuries, enriched reflection on the city. This is clearly shown in the work of Robert Brunschvig and,

---

[25] J.-Cl. Garcin, "Habitat médiéval et histoire urbaine," in *Palais et Maisons du Caire, I, Epoque mamelouke*, J.-Cl. Garcin et al. (Paris: CNRS, 1982), 216.

[26] See, for example, the interesting study by B. S. Hakim, *Arabic-Islamic Cities* (London, 1986). See the observation by J. Berque, *L'Islam au temps du monde* (Paris: Sindbad, 1984), 206: "To derive more on the matter from the Quran or the Sunna would surely be to go beyond any reasonable extrapolation."

more recently, of Baber Johansen.[27] Although J. Sauvaget has written of the lack of interest and the ignorance of the *'ulama* in this sphere, they did contribute to forging an urban doctrine; but this is, of course, a matter of history, not of theology.

Both this explicit negativity, and the minute critique of false characteristics propounded to define the "Muslim" city have opened the way for a certain nihilism. Having eliminated the irregular road system and the cul-de-sac (found in the ancient East), the house with central courtyard (which is also found in Antiquity) and the division of the city into quarters, Eugen Wirth concluded that the suq, the central business district, is probably "the only and fundamental distinctive criterion for the Near Eastern City which can be considered as Islamic cultural heritage." His proposition is, accordingly, to "renounce the term 'Islamic city' and to prefer the more general 'Oriental city'... Islam seems to be more the inhabitant or occupant of Middle Eastern urban systems than the architect."[28]

It seems to me that this is going too far and I would suggest, bearing in mind the variables of time and place indicated above, that an attempt be made to describe an Arab city that is largely Mediterranean (but naturally also including Iraq, Arabia, and Yemen), taken during the final period of its development, from the beginning of the sixteenth century and before the great mutations produced from the nineteenth century onwards. The profound linguistic and cultural unity of the region under consideration, its community of historical destiny over this period, the existence of still widespread remains of the cities of this time (supplementing the exceptional wealth of Ottoman documentation)—all these things give rise for hope that these "traditional Arab" cities will present sufficient common features and original characteristics for a genuine "urban system" to be demonstrated with regard to them; one that can, of course, be usefully set against other systems—Balko-Anatolian, Irano-Afghan, Moghul, and so on. The work of which this article is part aims, in fact, to make a contribution to such comparisons.

---

[27] Brunschvig, "Urbanisme médiéval"; B. Johansen, "The Claims of Men and the Claims of God," in *Pluriformiteit en verdeling* (Nijmegen, 1980), and "The All-Embracing Town and its Mosques," *Revue de l'Occident Musulman et de la Méditerranée* 32 (1981).

[28] E. Wirth, "The Middle Eastern City: Islamic City? Oriental City? Arabian City?" (Lecture given at Harvard University, 1982), typescript, page 9.

The twofold limitation, spatial and temporal, that we take upon ourselves will not, of course, solve every problem, especially the one Orientalists have thought to be able to tackle from a religious perspective. The notion that there is a common urban domain, at any rate from Morocco to Afghanistan, does not rest solely on the impression of a vague set of common features or of a sense of "déjà vu." Certainly there is, far beyond the Arab domain, a common urban one: certain urban structural characteristics to which we shall return (a concentration of markets in the heart of the city, the existence of enclosed quarters, the statistical predominance of dwellings with central courtyard) will be found from Marrakesh to Herat. But there is nothing specifically Muslim about such features. Sometimes they predate Islam. They are bound up with the fact that these diverse regions where the natural constraints are fairly similar are occupied by populations whose commonly shared characteristics (notably concern for the protection of family life) are broadly determined by their religious affiliation; occupied by populations whose social and professional life is deeply affected by the existence of institutions which themselves bear a Muslim character (justice, *hisba*). In short, these cities are (as Wirth noted) Muslim because they are inhabited by Muslim populations. Yet this statement takes us no further along the road to the definition of any particular urban structure that might exist. It is in the bringing together of features, some of which are not specific to the Muslim sphere and others of which exist in other Muslim countries, that we may hope to conjure up the picture of an original urban system for which "traditional Arab city" seems the most appropriate designation. As Jacques Berque observes: "The meaning of a whole lies not in its elements, but in the way it effectively combines these."[29]

3. *The structure of the traditional Arab city*

If we limit our inquiry to a corpus of large Arab cities situated from Morocco to Iraq, and from Syria to Yemen, in the period from the sixteenth century to the beginning of the nineteenth (which, for virtually all of them, represents the period of Ottoman domination), the major

---

[29] Berque, *L'Islam au temps du monde*, 219.

features of urban structure appear fairly constant and exhibit a rationale such that we are justified in speaking of a coherent *urban system*.[30]

3.1

The basic features are the very marked separation existing between zones of economic activity and zones of residence, and the very strong centrality of urban organization (fig. 3). This structure determines the existence of two strongly contrasted zones: a "public" zone occupying the city centre and a "private" zone chiefly devoted to residence. The researches of Baber Johansen have shown how Hanafi jurists were perfectly aware of this division of the city, in connection with the reparation due for crimes where the perpetrator remained unknown (*qasama*). In the "public" zones, those marked out by the presence of a broad avenue, a large market or an important mosque, responsibility fell on the political authorities. In the "private" zone, a residential district with cul-de-sacs, the people living in the neighbouring houses were to answer for the consequences of any crime committed there.[31]

The urban centre was organized around the pairing constituted by the main suqs, generally set out around the "covered market" (*qaysari-yya* or *bedesten*, according to region), and the principal mosque. This was well demonstrated by Louis Massignon in his studies on Iraqi and Moroccan cities, where he stressed the role of the goldsmiths' market (*sagha*), commonly the place where currencies were exchanged. The layout is a standard one: the "mother-cell" of Fez, in the city of the Qayrawanis, is made up "of two mosques, the sanctuary of Moulay Idris and the Mosque of the Qayrawanis, and a central market, the Kisariya."[32] At Aleppo, the market district is set out around the Great Mosque and the suqs that constitute the *qaysariyya*. It is in this district that major and international trade takes place—whence the necessity of the moneychangers' market. In Cairo, a street bearing the significant name "street of clipped coinage" (*al-Maqasis*), situated behind the *sagha*, recalls these functions. Especially precious, costly articles were sold in

---

[30] I have tackled these problems in *Grandes villes arabes à l'époque ottomane* (Paris: Sindbad, 1985), and in "La structure spatiale de la ville," in *Sciences Sociales et Phénomènes Urbains dans le Monde Arabe*, ed. M. Naciri and A. Raymond (Casablanca, 1997).

[31] B. Johansen, "Eigentum, Familie," *Die Welt des Islams* 19 (1979): 19–24; idem, "Claims of Men," 64–66.

[32] Le Tourneau, *Fès*, 122, plan on page 375.

the "covered market," which was sometimes an enclosed construction, or a grouping of markets (Aleppo) and caravanserais (Khan al-Khalili in Cairo). Here were find numerous caravanserais (*funduq, khan, wakala, samsara*, according to the city), where international and wholesale trade were transacted. Also in this centre were markets (suqs) specializing in large-scale trade. Crafts of special importance might also be found there, despite the nuisance this must have presented for neighbours; an example of this is the presence of the *nahhasin* (makers of copper utensils and traders in these) in Cairo. These trades were organized on the principle of strict specialization, which found expression in a division into professional bodies and a fairly rigid geographical distribution.[33] The presence of the Great Mosque, which was also a university, some-times of international standing (as, for example, with the Qarawiyyin in Fez, the Zaytuna in Tunis, and al-Azhar in Cairo), made this quarter a district marked out by religion and culture alike. Al-Azhar, the chief centre for higher education in the Arab world, brought together a hundred or so teachers and three thousand students.

By contrast, the presence in this "hyper-centre" of the political power and the administration was not uniform in character. The most important courts were to be found there situated, usually, in the main mosques, as were a number of "administrative" services; in Cairo, the *dikkat al-hisba* was close by the trading zone that the *muhtasib* was sup-posed to supervise. Quite often, though, the higher authorities (sovereign or governor) were settled on the edge of the city (Cairo, Damascus), or even right outside (the Bardo in Tunisia); this was for reasons of security (so as to be safely away from possible popular uprisings) or of convenience (so as to have available the necessary space to lodge their troops). Thus, in Aleppo, the Ottoman pashas had abandoned the Cita-del to take up residence outside the walls, in the monastery of shaykh Abu Bakr. Algiers is exceptional in having a remarkable concentration of the organs of power in the centre of the city: the palace of the dey (*Janina*); the *dar al-sikka* (mint); the *bayt al-mal* (financial administration); the premises of the *shaykh al-balad* (city administration); the prison of the *mizwar* (police); and so on.[34] Only at a very late date (in 1817) was the Janina transferred to the Qasba, in the upper city, for reasons at once

---

[33] I shall return to these economic functions in more detail in a second contribution to this work, "The Economy of the Traditional City."

[34] T. Shuval, *La ville d'Alger vers la fin du XVIIIème siècle* (Paris: CNRS, 1998), 164–172.

of internal security (fear of unrest among the janissaries) and external security (the risk of naval bombardment), thus placing Algiers in the most common situation.

The central district was commonly crossed by relatively broad and regular streets grouped around a central thoroughfare ("Straight Street" in Damascus, of Roman origin, the Qasaba in Cairo (fig. 4), laid out by the Fatimids, the main street crossing Algiers from Bab ʿAzzun to Bab al-Wad); around a number of parallel streets (in Aleppo on the line of the ancient street, from Bab Antakiya to the Citadel); or around a network of virtually orthogonal streets (in Tunis). Relatively straight, rectilinear streets linked the central zone to the city's gates, allowing quite easy access—essential for economic activity—to the commercial centre. In Tunis the plans clearly show how these essential dual thoroughfares unfold towards the gates of Bab al-Banat and Bab Suwayqa in the north, Bab al-Bahr in the east, and Bab Jadid and Bab al-Jazira in the south.

The dense nature of the commercial centres (large markets and especially caravanserais) permits a fairly precise demarcation of these centres whose dimensions naturally varied according to the importance of the cities and to their economic activity: a little over 2 hectares in Algiers, 6 in Tunis, 9 in Damascus, 10 in Mosul, 11 in Aleppo, 12 in Baghdad, but around 60 in Cairo, the second city of the Ottoman Empire in terms of population and activity. The importance of these centres, along with their very marked individuality vis-à-vis the organization of the city, sometimes led them to be accorded a particular name: as, for instance, with the Mdineh in Aleppo, with Qahira in Cairo (in the centre of the Fatimid foundation which, in fact, stretched out fairly extensively beyond the economic central zone proper) (fig. 5), with the Rabʿ in Tunis (a name applied to virtually the whole of the covered suqs surrounding the Zaytuna).[35] The number of economic establishments and the link with the Great Mosque account for the common stability of these centres which, for the most part, have not changed their location from the most ancient times up to the modern age; the Qasaba, the central thoroughfare of the Fatimid city, was still the heart of the city of Cairo in the sixteenth century. Only a single

---

[35] On the Tunis *rabʿ*, see the analysis by A. Henia, *Propriété et stratégies sociales à Tunis* (Tunis, 1999), 240–246. Shuval is quite right (*Ville d'Alger*, 182) to make an upward correction of my assessment (above one hectare) for the area of the economic centre in Algiers.

case is known of the centre being moved. This was in Mosul, where the suqs, set normally around the Great Mosque, were moved and set up close to the Citadel and to the spot where the great trade route crossed the Tigris. The circumstances of this, and the reasons for it, are unclear.[36]

Such a highly centralized structure gave the city considerable suppleness; for, in any period of expansion, the central zone of the markets and the Great Mosque could grow by biting into the residential districts stretching around them. A case in point occurred during the Ottoman period which saw a considerable expansion of the great Arab cities of the Empire. In Aleppo this urban development took the form of a virtual doubling of the Mdineh, from 6 to 11 hectares. In Cairo, similarly, the zone of major economic activity grew from around 40 hectares to around 60.

3.2

Beyond this central region stretched the city's "private" zone, chiefly devoted to private dwellings. It was this zone that saw the development of the "quarters" (*hawma, hara, mahalla*, according to the particular city) that are one of the distinctive features of the Arab city. They were relatively enclosed in most cases, communication with the outside being by a single street, this main thoroughfare (*darb*) then branching into the interior in usually irregular streets and ending, finally, in cul-de-sacs (fig. 6). The separation of one quarter from a neighbouring one was effected not by a wall but by a back-to-back structure joining the final houses of the quarter to the final houses of the quarters abutting. The gate (*bab*) allowed the quarter to be closed at night, this providing a sense of security; but it was not a thorough-going defence against an attack from outside. The quarters were modestly equipped for inhabitants' daily lives: with an oven, sometimes with a bath and an oratory (*masjid*). But the essential feature was the *suwayqa* (minor market) of which J. Sauvaget has provided classic descriptions for Damascus and Aleppo. This unspecialized market catered for the daily needs (food, articles for common use) of the population which bought in any further provisions from the city suqs.

---

[36] Dina Khoury, *State and Provincial Society in the Ottoman Empire: Mosul* (Cambridge: University Press, 1997), 202–203.

The irregularity of the streets and the abundance of cul-de-sacs which has so intrigued Orientalists was thus a local phenomenon within the city, one answering to the various needs of the population living in the city's quarters, and not a general characteristic. We have noted how in the centre and towards the gates traffic was catered for by direct, regular thoroughfares. Within their quarters, the inhabitants could be content with irregular streets and cul-de-sacs which, in point of fact, were conducive to their security. The only communications they needed were with the city centre where their active life was passed and where they fulfilled their chief religious obligations (Friday prayer); they had no need of direct contact with the outside. Each quarter consisted of a kind of population pocket, open only towards the centre. In actual fact, the cul-de-sacs represented statistically a little less than half of the road network, their development being restricted to within the quarters: 52 per cent of the road system in Fez and 41 per cent in Aleppo. In Algiers there was a very marked contrast between the lower city, corresponding to the centre (24.5 per cent cul-de-sacs) (fig. 7), and the upper city, where the indigenous population lived (59.9 per cent) (fig. 8). The cul-de-sac was thus a functional feature, localized within a specific sector of the city.

The quarters provided dwelling for a population that could hardly have exceeded around a thousand inhabitants (around 200 families), so that they lived there in a familial environment, akin to a village where everyone knows everyone else; under the supervision of shaykhs, but above all, no doubt, thanks to a self-surveillance that made a major contribution to security. Potential troublemakers, people of bad morals, could, where necessary, be made subject to measures of expulsion that might be submitted to the authorities (some cases went as far as Istanbul). These quarters were the scenes of an active collective life, with familial celebrations (circumcision), collective festivities (a ceremony based around a local saint), rejoicings and processions (like the Damascus 'arada); these were enlivened by groups of "youth" (futuwwa) who might possibly transform themselves into self-defence groups or might activate traditional rivalries with groups from other quarters, leading to outright pitched battles, sometimes conducted outside the city.[37]

---

[37] For various aspects of the life of the quarters, see especially J. Lecerf and R. Tresse, "Les 'Arâda de Damas," *BEO* 7–8 (1937–38); and Nawâl al-Messiri, "The Concept of the Hâra," *Annales Islamologiques* 15 (1979).

This division into quarters should not be regarded as a totally negative factor, inclining the city towards fragmentation and anarchy, as
suggested by J. Sauvaget and J. Weulersse. On the contrary, such a division was an element that assured the city's stability, made for effective
government of the population; it was conducive to its administration in
the zone where the greatest part of the population lived and certainly
helped facilitate the urbanization of newcomers recently arrived from
the rural zones.

3.3

A further characteristic of the city's spatial structure was the fairly
rigorous graduation of activities and residence from the central district
out towards the extremities of the city. It was noted above how the city
centre brought together the most lucrative economic activities, especially
those linked to international trade (trade in cloths, and in particular
products like coffee, which had begun to play a considerable part in the
economy of the region). From this centre, activities tended to spread
outwards through the city on a principle of decreasing importance:
the less important the trade, the closer to the periphery. Here on the
edge would be found activities requiring a good deal of space (rope-
makers, mat-makers, traders in grain or other foodstuffs) or giving rise
to nuisances not easily tolerable in the centre (ovens, slaughterhouses,
tanneries).[38] Any modification of a trade's geographical position within
this system may be interpreted as a sign of its progress (if coming
closer to the centre) or its decline (if moving further out). A recently
introduced activity, like the major trade in coffee, found its immediate
spot in the centre of Cairo by virtue of its economic importance; the
62 *wakala* devoted to this business which appeared in the first half of
the seventeenth century are all to be found close by the Qasaba, near
the Khan al-Khalili, the Gamaliyya quarter, and al-Azhar.

An organization of this kind was so logical and corresponded so
clearly to a "natural" spread of the activities in question that it might
be viewed as broadly spontaneous in character. Such a finding must be
qualified, nonetheless, in the light of what we know about the regular
activities of the *muhtasib* and of the judges specifically concerned with
the inhabitants' welfare; in the light, too, of surviving records of inter-

---

[38] See further in "The Economy of the Traditional City," in this present work.

vention by the authorities in the most serious cases. The removal of the tanneries in Aleppo, Cairo, and Tunis to more outer districts—made necessary by a phase of urban development—sprang from a decision made at the highest level of the political authority.

Such graduation seems, likewise, to characterize the way in which the city was divided with regard to the residence of the different social strata. This has been shown in various recent studies, which, on this point, portray a situation totally at odds with the Orientalist thesis of a social mix stemming from an egalitarianism supposedly characteristic of Muslim society. Jacques Revault's research on high-grade dwellings in Tunis clearly shows how the residences of the élite described by him are localized in a district immediately around the central zone (fig. 9). In her work *Habiter au Caire*, Nelly Hanna identifies three zones, moving from the city centre outwards, that have witnessed the development, respectively, of a prosperous dwelling, an average dwelling and a modest dwelling. Studying the various kinds of ancient construction in the city of Aleppo, J.-C. David localizes them as follows: in the centre, close to the Mdineh and the Citadel, a zone of high-grade dwellings; in a district further out a zone of more modest dwellings; and in the peripheral zones a popular dwelling.[39] Such an arrangement is thoroughly logical. The bourgeoisie of merchants and shaykhs stuck to the zones near the centre, site of the markets and the great mosque-university where they carried out their activities. In those zones characterized by a great density of construction, land was scarcer and more expensive, while the peripheral zone, generally given over to poor and polluting economic activities, was devoted to popular dwelling. Nelly Hanna has calculated the annual rent for a piece of land of a hundred cubits as 171 paras in the centre of Cairo, 76 in the intermediate zone, and 17 on the periphery. The average prices for the houses she studied (which merely, of course, represent a sample, with the most substantial ones over-represented) amounted, respectively, to 20,684, 8,931 and 4,825 paras in these same zones.[40]

In the districts close to the centre, then, was to be found a rich, bourgeois dwelling of the type that has been well studied in Fez, Tunis, and Cairo: characterized by its development around a central

---

[39] J. Revault, *Palais et maisons de Tunis*, 4 vols. (Paris: CNRS, 1967–78); N. Hanna, *Habiter au Caire* (Cairo: IFAO, 1991); J.-Cl. David, "Alep, dégradation et tentatives actuelles de réadaptation," *BEO* 28 (1975).

[40] Hanna, *Habiter au Caire*, 185–207.

courtyard, by vast dimensions permitting a specialization of rooms, and by an elaborate decoration. The presence of a collective dwelling of the *rab'* type (blocks rented out in apartments) facilitated access for the Cairo middle class to the zones close to the centre.[41] Likewise, constructions of the caravanserai type (*funduq, khan, wakala*) frequently played this role for the middle class in Cairo and other great cities. In the "intermediate" districts, houses potentially retained the general character of the house with courtyard, but on a reduced scale. More elementary houses without a courtyard, of the kind studied by N. Hanna in Cairo, were also found.[42] On the periphery a poor type of dwelling developed, comprising elementary houses (one or two rooms),[43] or else a communal dwelling of the *hawsh* kind: a courtyard surrounded by very rudimentary shacks.[44] Still more precarious dwellings of the "shanty town" type very probably existed—though of these, for obvious reasons (fragility of materials and improvised nature of the construction), no trace has remained. The existence, in Fez and Tunis, of toponyms like al-Nuwayl, designating "mud huts covered with a thatched roof" in the districts on the fringes of the cities, is significant.[45] We may note in passing how much this variety of dwellings is at odds with the Orientalist conception of a uniform Muslim house with courtyard—of which most of the examples studied, especially in Fez, Algiers, Tunis, Cairo, and Aleppo, are actually mansions, large or small, relevant only to the middle and wealthy classes of these cities; and that is not to mention the kind of tall dwelling lacking in a courtyard of which we have so many examples around the Red Sea.

---

[41] J. Revault et al., *Palais et demeures de Fès*, 3 vols. (Paris: CNRS, 1985–92); Revault, *Palais et maisons de Tunis*, 4 vols. (Paris: CNRS, 1967–78); B. Maury et al., *Palais et maisons du Caire, II, Epoque ottomane* (Paris: CNRS, 1983); A. Raymond, "Le rab'," *Mélanges de l'Université Saint-Joseph* 50 (1984).

[42] N. Hanna, "Bayt al-Istanbuli," *Annales Islamologiques* 16 (1981).

[43] This poor dwelling is little known for the obvious reason that it has left no trace. One might, paradoxically, refer to the medieval one revealed by the excavations of W. Kubiak and G. Scanlon at Fustat. (*Final Report on Fustat C*, 1989.)

[44] The *hawsh* is precisely described in the *Description de l'Egypte (Etat Moderne II–2)* (Paris, 1822): E. F. Jomard, "Description de la ville du Kaire," 662, 696; M. de Chabrol, "Essai sur les moeurs," 516–517. For a Hijazi variety, see S. al-Hathlul, *Al-Madina al-'arabiyya al-islamiyya* (Riyadh, 1994), 86.

[45] Raymond, *Grandes villes*, 323.

3.4

The arguments developed above have already called attention to the importance of segregational factors which—with respect to the spatial organization of the traditional Arab city—are simply an expression of the profound inequality of the social structure. Recent researches have shown, in this regard, just how erroneous the Orientalist conception of an egalitarian society was: one that, in some degree, realized the religious equality existing within the community of believers. What is so striking when studying the realities of the social life of Muslim societies in the modern age is, on the contrary, the depth of social inequality. Perusal of the inheritances preserved for us by the court registers (*mahkama*) shows the marked difference existing between rich and poor. Moreover, these registers mainly inform us about the patrimonies of the most comfortably off; those of the poorest classes naturally eluded any kind of record following these people's deaths. In Cairo, during the two decades immediately preceding 1700, the proportion of the most insignificant inheritance to the most substantial is that of 1 to 10,000. In Damascus, around 1700, the proportion is 1 to 4,000. Whatever the imperfections of this kind of calculation (which involves patrimonies rather than incomes), the margin is obviously a wide one. When we apply to this comparison an index designed to measure social inequality, that of Gini (whereby 0.00 represents an equal distribution and 1 an absolute inequality), the resulting figures indicate a very strong inequality: the index is 0.74 for Cairo and Damascus round about 1700—a significantly similar figure which appears to confirm the reliability of such calculations. For Algiers at the end of the eighteenth century, the index of social inequality, at 0.80, is higher still.[46]

---

[46] A. Raymond, *Artisans et commerçants au Caire au XVIIIème siècle* (Damascus: IFD, 1974), 2:375; C. Establet and J.-P. Pascual, *Familles et fortunes à Damas* (Damascus: IFD, 1994); C. Establet, J.-P. Pascual, and A. Raymond, "La mesure de l'inégalité sociale dans la société ottomane," *JESHO* 37 (1994); Shuval, *Ville d'Alger*, 141–142. By way of comparison, in Algiers at the end of the eighteenth century, the 10 per cent most substantial inheritances shared 74 per cent of the total amount. In France, in 1996, 10 per cent of households accounted for 50 per cent of patrimonies. (*Le Monde*, 2 March 1996.) We might also mention Cairo, where, in 1996, according to M. Kharoufi ("Mobilité du centre ville au Caire," in Naciri and Raymond, *Sciences Sociales*, 167), 20 per cent of the population appears to have had use of 40 to 50 per cent of the *national income*.

When compared to those for other societies and other periods, these figures point to an inequality so huge that it is hardly surprising it should find expression in the spatial structure of the city. Many writers, reluctant to abandon Orientalist theses, have hesitated to accept a reality that appears beyond argument when we view the city overall, from a broadly statistical viewpoint, as has been done for Tunis, Cairo and Aleppo. The graduation outwards, from zones of prosperous dwellings in the city centre to zones of poor dwellings on the periphery, appears a perfect illustration of those differences whose importance has been underlined above, even though many individual examples may, of course, be supplied of rich and poor persons living side by side.

These tendencies towards a segregational organization likewise appear in the customary grouping of religious and ethnic minorities; something which should not be regarded as a specifically Ottoman feature, even if the phenomenon was effectively accentuated by the Ottoman practice of the autonomous running of communities. The formation of enclosed quarters for Christians and Jews is a fairly general feature in which the concern to live a separate, homogeneous communal existence with one's own kind—a concern broadly shared by the dominant element (Muslim) and the dominated element (*dhimmi*s, or "protected people")—played an important role alongside the wish of the dominant group to keep different communities apart (so as to supervise them as necessary) (fig. 10). This situation is general in the large Arab cities. What does vary greatly is the geographical siting of the communities within the city itself. When, though, they possess a certain importance and are markedly distinctive, "minority" Muslim communities are grouped together in the same way: the Kurdish quarter of Salhiyya, in Damascus, provides a very ancient example of this. In some cities, grouping by community goes to extreme lengths; this is the case in Jerusalem, with its Muslim, Christian, Armenian, and Jewish sectors, and Antioch, where the city is divided into Turkish, Christian, and Alawi sectors, their siting reflecting their respective political and social importance—the Turks, as the dominant element, occupying the centre, and the Alawis, a poor and ill-treated minority, being thrust out to the edges of the city.

By reason of the dominant caste's natural propensity to remain somewhat exclusive (reinforcing its concern to keep itself apart from the "masses"), the quarters of the élite were often voluntarily segregated: the Mamluk élite in Cairo isolated itself in this way, in the district of the Birkat al-Fil pool, to the south of Qahira; then, in the eighteenth century, in the district of another pool, the Azbakiyya, situated broadly to the west of the urban centre.

3.5

We cannot conclude this description of the structure of the Arab city without tackling the problem of its administration, especially as this is an area where Orientalists, led by Jean Sauvaget, have been very negative—maintaining that the Muslim city received little administration, or even none at all. Rather more thorough studies have shown that this supposed under-administration on the part of the political authorities was a mere myth. The re-siting of the tanneries in Cairo or Tunis, a crucial event in the sphere of urban structure, was ordered at the highest level (the Sultan for Cairo, the Bey for Tunis). The development of the Mdineh in sixteenth-century Aleppo stemmed from successive, even coordinated, action by the pashas of the province. If the activity of the *muhtasib*s has been clearly recognized, especially in al-Andalus, R. Brunschvig and B. Johansen have pointed out the role of the *qadi*s in the running of the city[47] on a more elementary level. Increased interest vis-à-vis the institution of the waqf/*hubus*, in its more specifically urban aspects, has demonstrated the crucial role this played in the organization of the city.[48]

Above all, we are beginning to appreciate the importance of the part played by the communities (*tawa'if*) administered by their shaykhs in the running of the city and the administration of the inhabitants. The extreme diversity of these (professional bodies, geographical communities within their quarters, religious and ethnic communities), together with the variety of geographical zones through which they were spread (central districts for the professional bodies, residential districts for the communities in their quarters) means that they comprised tight networks able to ensure a multiple control over the lives of inhabitants and over urban life. Cairo contained more than 250 professional bodies and 100 communities within quarters, plus various religious and ethnic *tawa'if*s. It is here, perhaps, that we should seek the equivalent of institutions of "civil society" whose apparent absence so worries specialists in the political sciences.

---

[47] See their articles quoted above, notes 18 and 27.
[48] A. Raymond, "Les grands waqfs et l'organisation de l'espace urbain," *BEO* 31 (1979). On general aspects, see *Le waqf dans l'espace islamique*, ed. R. Deguilhem (Damascus: IFD, 1995). On these problems see my contribution, in the present volume, on the administration of the city.

4. *Conclusions*

It, therefore, seems that, with respect to the vast Mediterranean Arab domain, we may indeed speak of an *urban system*; one whose coherence sits ill with the speculations of Orientalists about the supposed disorder of the Muslim city. The dislocation diagnosed by J. Sauvaget and J. Weulersse springs from a negative interpretation of the city's division into separate units. If we take, however, into account the city's unarguable success (and its development even, in the period under consideration here), we might also say that these cells, far from threatening the city's overall unity, were actually, each in its own sphere, conducive to the organization and running of the whole. Even in the apparently extreme cases of Jerusalem and Antioch, so utterly split into their multiple religious and ethnic communities, a federating element was at work to ensure the overall functioning; the part played by the market quarter in providing the link between apparently disparate components is evident enough.

In any case, it is not at all clear in principle how cities utterly formless and anarchic, like those described by J. Sauvaget in his most extreme theses, could have stood the test of centuries. We rather need to acknowledge the existence of a strong internal structure underlying the development of these cities into modern times—notably in the case of Aleppo with whose destiny the historian has concerned himself while making no attempt to resolve the glaring contradiction between a disaster he proclaims and a greatness that shows through almost despite himself. It is the very internal logic of their organization and their capacity to evolve—no doubt, with a certain robustness in the face of time's vicissitudes—that have rendered so lasting and so successful the most noteworthy examples of this urban system, from Marrakesh to Baghdad.

LAW AND THE CITY

Besim S. Hakim

This contribution on the law and the city is about the interaction of societal values—which in Islamic culture are directly rooted in religion—with decision-making, the production process, and the resulting built form. The context of the discussion is holistic, beyond the building scale, to produce a clear understanding of the relationship of the part to the whole, the building to its immediate surroundings and to the urban scale. An understanding of the reciprocal effects of the overall built environment and the various levels of the environment, down to single buildings and their design, is crucial to a comprehension of architecture and the city in the context of Islamic culture.

The levels of the environment to be stressed are: the city, neighbourhood, clusters of buildings, and the single building. That order is not always critical to the following discussions, but the relationship between levels should be kept in mind, particularly when trying to interrelate the impact of values underlying decision-making and the nature of the production and construction processes.

Pre-Islamic precedents

The Near East has witnessed in its history developments in law since the most ancient civilizations. Well-known and relatively late examples from Mesopotamia are the laws of Hammurabi, King of Babylon, who reigned from 1792 to 1750 B.C.[1] There has also been a long and ancient tradition of respecting local customs. Pre-Islamic settlement patterns, building typologies, construction techniques, and related decision-making processes influenced the emergent pattern of built form in Islamic cultures. Some Muslim scholars interpret one of the verses in the Quran, the holy book of Islam, as an instruction to accept local

---

[1] For a detailed study of Babylonian laws see G. R. Driver and J. C. Miles, eds., *Babylonian Laws*, vol. 1, *Legal Commentary* (London, 1952).

traditions and conventions, provided they do not contravene Islamic values, ethics, or law. The Quran is considered by Muslims to be the word of God as revealed to the Prophet Mohammed. The applicable verse (from Surah, or chapter, 7 titled Al-A'raf, verse number 199) uses the Arabic term *urf* to refer to an established local tradition for how something is to be done.

Contemplation of the complex plan pattern raises the question of how the common wall problems were addressed and resolved (figure 1). Islamic law addressed this and other problems related to this pattern and type of construction. Pre-Islamic legal precedents existed, as evidenced by the work of some scholars.[2]

Formation of urban models

The Prophet Mohammed proclaimed Islam soon after 610 A.D. in Mecca, 450 km. (280 miles) south of Medina, where the Prophet finally settled in 622 A.D. That date represents year 1 of the Islamic calendar. The next decade in Medina which came under the guidance and leadership of the Prophet is considered very important as a source of example and precedent for all aspects of Islamic community living, including building. A number of cases are recorded of the Prophet's attitude to specific problems related to building activity. This is also true of the caliphs who succeeded him, including Umar bin Al-Khattab, the second caliph, who ruled during the period of 634 to 644 A.D. This guidance concerning building proved to be particularly crucial for the Maliki School of Law which evolved under Malik bin Anas (712–795 A.D.) who lived all his life in Medina. Followers of his School of Law live to this day in the *maghrib* countries of Libya, Tunisia, Algeria, Morocco, Andalusia on the Iberian peninsula until the early 1500s, and in Sub-Sahara Africa.

During the first three centuries of Islam a number of schools of thought and approaches to law were formulated. Under the Sunni

---

[2] Ibid. Also see my detailed study "Julian of Ascalon's Treatise of Construction and Design Rules from Sixth–Century Palestine," *Journal of the Society of Architectural Historians* 60, no. 1 (March 2001): 4–25. The contents of this treatise draw from Near Eastern customary laws and Roman law. For a comparison of a case that deals with a party-wall that has fallen down and how similar legal solutions addressed this problem from the Neo-Assyrian and Islamic periods, see p. 72 of my "Arab-Islamic Urban Structure," *The Arabian Journal of Science and Engineering* 7, no. 2 (April 1982): 69–79.

branch of Islam the survivors are grouped into four schools: Hanafi, Maliki, Shafiʻi, and Hanbali. Followers of Sunni Islam constitute the majority in the Muslim world, although in Iran, parts of Iraq, and some communities in Syria and Lebanon, the people are followers of Shiʻism and have their own school of law. It is important to note that the legal differences about building are minor and result from different interpretations by the various schools of law. Thus, the discussion based on the Maliki School in North Africa would largely hold true for other regions of the Muslim world.

Eighty-three years after the Prophet's death in June 8, 632 A.D. Islam already encompassed a vast territory stretching from the shores of the Atlantic Ocean and the Pyrenees to the borders of China—an area greater than Rome's at its zenith. This was achieved under the leadership of Abd al-Malik (685–705 A.D.) from his seat in Damascus and his four sons who succeeded him. Across this vast geographic area, three factors influenced the nature of building and planning as it evolved within the framework of Islamic civilization. First, the urban models of pre-Islamic cultures and civilizations in territories converted to Islam influenced the evolution of the structure and form of subsequent Islamic cities. This was particularly true in the region known as the Fertile Crescent and in Iran. Second, the camel was the primary means of transportation, predominating in the Middle East between the fourth and sixth centuries A.D.[3] This important and often forgotten factor had a major impact on the street system and urban form of the Islamic city. Third, the location of most territories of the Islamic world between latitudes 10 and 40 and the resulting similarity in macroclimatic conditions contributed toward certain unifying influences in building practice.[4]

Some historians agree that three discernible urban models evolved within the framework of Islamic civilization. These are the renewed or remodelled pre-Islamic city, the planned and designed city, and the spontaneously created and incrementally grown city.[5]

---

[3] See Richard W. Bulliet, *The Camel and the Wheel* (Cambridge, MA, 1975).

[4] For the climatic advantages of the courtyard house type, which was the most widespread in the Islamic world, see D. Dunham, "The courtyard house as a temperature regulator," *The New Scientist*, September 1960: 663–666. For innovation of cooling systems in arid regions see M. N. Bahadori, "Passive cooling systems in Iranian architecture," *Scientific American*, February 1978, 144–154.

[5] See Edmond Pauty, "Villes spontanées et villes créées en Islam," *Annales de l'Institut d'Études Orientales* 9 (1951): 52–75; and Jean Sauvaget, "Esquise d'une Histoire de la

The renewed city is found most often in previously held Roman territories and is exemplified by Damascus and Aleppo. Earlier structures
and configurations were altered to suit the social requirements of the
Muslim community. The pre-Islamic Southwest Arabian model of isolated multi-storey structures, such as Sana'a, and particularly prevalent
in Yemen, is also classified under this model. Research is required to
determine why this type did not spread beyond the few localities in
which it arose.

The second type of city was pre-planned and designed by Muslim
rulers to be the capital of a dynasty or, more typically, as the seat
of a palace complex and its related facilities. A prime example of a
preconceived city palace complex constructed as a complete entity
was the original round city of Baghdad, while Al-Abbasiyah, south of
present Kairouan, was a palace complex; neither survives today. The
model influencing the plan and design of this second type of city can
generally be identified by the geographic location. In the case of the
mashriq (eastern regions), pre-Islamic models had a distinct influence,
whereas in the *maghrib* (western regions), the influences on the ruler and
his experiences determined the model and approach followed. After the
collapse of a dynasty, the tradition was to abandon this type of city or
palace complex, with the result that today they remain as ruins or are
completely obliterated and require restoration by archaeologists.

The third model of the Islamic city proved to be the most enduring and pervasive, and today most of the older areas of capitals and
major towns in the Muslim world evolved out of this model. The best
examples of the old quarters or *medina* survive in the *maghrib* countries;
in some instances, they are severely threatened today by the automobile.
Although the organizational principles of this model predate Islam by
at least 2500 years and were particularly common in southern Mesopotamia, the strength, characteristics, and longevity of this city type
reflect the manner in which building activity was pursued in Islamic
society (figure 2).

ville de Damas," *Revue des Etudes Islamiques* 8, no. 4 (1934): 421–480; and his two-
volume study on *Alep: Essai sur le developpement d'une grande ville Syrienne des origins au milieu
du XIX siecle* (Paris, 1941).

Understanding urbanism as process and product

Viewing the city as a process and a product is an effective analytical evaluation and planning tool and is indispensable for the study of the Islamic city. The process encompasses decision-making in building activity as guided by Islamic values. It can best be appreciated by viewing the dynamics of building decision-making as affecting two levels of the city: citywide and neighbourhood. Decisions about the citywide level were usually made by the ruler or government; they concerned the birth, growth, and revitalization of a city, and would include the location of the primary mosque, the distribution of the land in the projected boundaries of the city to various ethnic, familial, or tribal affiliations, and the location and configuration of the city's gates and walls. All of these were the result of decisions taken in the first few years of a city's founding.

Other typical primary decisions occurring during a city's growth involved the building of major public buildings such as mosques and public baths, or the location of new cemeteries. Revitalization activity often took place under the leadership of ambitious rulers and governments during eras marked by security and prosperity. Site conditions and the location of determining factors, such as water and natural features useful for defensive purposes, had an impact on macro decision-making and, hence, the resulting urban form.

The dynamics of decisions made at the level of the neighbourhood tended to be of a different nature and the results were of immediate significance. The effect of numerous micro decisions by citizens of a neighbourhood on urban form was indirect and usually obvious only on an aggregate basis, whereas the results of the larger decisions by rulers—such as the location of major mosques, of the *suq* (market) and its configurations, and of important industries tended to be individually discernible. Building decisions at the neighbourhood level had an impact on both the initiator and on immediate neighbours. Building activity and decisions involved the relationships and interdependence of people, and more specifically neighbours; such activity was therefore the concern of Islamic law.

Examining the city as a product clarifies how a complex, heterogeneous, and sophisticated built form is achievable with a simple set of physical organizational components and a related mechanism of verbal communication used in building decisions. The essential urban elements found in most cities of the Islamic world are the courtyard building, the street system, and the elements above the street.

The Courtyard Building. This is the basic module used for housing and public buildings. The ratio of building area to plot is 1:1. In housing, the courtyard takes up approximately 24% of the ground coverage, and the building is one, two, or occasionally three stories in height. Public buildings differ in their ratio of courtyard size to ground coverage, and the height is one story, as in mosques, but frequently is two stories, as in a *funduk* or *khan* (hostels for merchants). It should be noted that the Prophet affirmed the use of this plan type by building his mosque/residence soon after his arrival in Medina in the form of a square courtyard structure.

The Street System. Street systems are primarily of two types: the through, open-ended street which was considered a public right of way and had to be at least wide enough for two packed camels to pass; and the cul-de-sac which, according to Islamic law, is considered to be the private property of the people having access from it to their front doors (figure 3).

Elements Above the Street. The elements usually found above the street were a *sabat,* a room bridging the street, and the buttressing arches spanning between walls on either side of the street to provide structural strength and support for both opposite walls (figure 4).

In addition to this basically simple set of organizational elements, the Islamic city evolved a sophisticated communication system in the form of a language or vocabulary of building design that operated at all levels of the built environment. At the level of the city, it identified urban elements such as building types, public squares, and other uses. At the building level, it identified spatial configurations and related uses, as well as details of construction, decoration, and symbolic motifs. An important attribute of this language was that it integrated a physical component's form and function into its name. This vocabulary was known and popular amongst most segments of society involved in building activity, and it was an effective communication device between users and builders. Regional variations in the design vocabulary existed, but the language was unified by the similarity of the built form and its constituents.[6]

---

[6] For a detailed presentation of a design language at the urban level, see Chapter 2 "A design language: urban and architectural elements" of my book *Arabic-Islamic Cities: Building and Planning Principles*, 2nd ed. ([1979] 1986; London and New York, 1988), 55–101. [Available from Books on Demand, UMI, Ann Arbor, MI].

The fiqh *and formation of the rule system*

The development of rules for neighbourhood building activity became the concern of the science of *fiqh* from its very early development.

Fiqh is the Arabic term for jurisprudence or the science of religious law in Islam. It concerns itself with two spheres of activity: *ʿibadat*, dealing with matters concerning ritual observances; and *muʿamalat*, the legal questions that arise in social life (e.g., family law, law of inheritance, of property, of contracts, criminal law, etc.), and problems arising from building activity and related procedures. The latter were viewed by the *fiqh* in the same light as other problems resulting from human activities and interaction. In essence, therefore, *fiqh* is the science of laws based on religion and is concerned with all aspects of public and private life and business.

The bulk of the knowledge developed by the *fiqh* for most aspects of human relationships, including those of building activity, appeared in the first 300 years of Islam, although subsequent generations developed and refined it. The source for most rules stemmed from Quranic values and from the Hadith, which are the sayings and tradition of the Prophet, particularly during the decade of his leadership and rule in Medina.[7] Note that the recorded nature of most rules in the *fiqh* literature is implicit in the numerous cases also recorded that include the judgments of local *qadis* (judges) and the opinions of *muftis*.[8]

A set of rules documented in the literature of the Maliki School of law is identified and discussed elsewhere.[9] Some of those can be briefly itemized:

• Avoid harm to others and oneself.
• Accept the concept of interdependence.
• Respect the privacy of the private domain of others, particularly avoiding the creation of direct visual corridors.
• Respect the rights of original or earlier usage.
• Respect the rights of building higher within one's air space.

---

[7] The term Sunnah is more commonly used to mean the total traditions of the Prophet, including his deeds and life-style, as well as his sayings.

[8] A *mufti* is a specialist on the law who can give authoritative opinions on points of doctrine. His considered legal opinion is called *fatwa*.

[9] See Chapter 1 "Islamic law and neighbourhood building guidelines," in my book *Arabic-Islamic Cities* (full citation in note 6 above), 15–54.

- Respect property of others.
- Neighbours have the right of pre-emption of an adjacent property.
- Seven cubits as the minimum width of public through-streets (to allow two fully loaded camels to pass).
- Avoid placing the sources of unpleasant smells and noisy activities adjacent to or near mosques.

In addition, other rules on the behaviour of the individual and community operate as a self-regulating mechanism. A prime example is the concept of *beauty without arrogance*, which strongly influenced the manner in which exterior facades and elevations of buildings were regarded and treated. This concept is attributed directly to the Prophet Mohammed in the form of the saying, "No person with an atom of arrogance in his heart will enter paradise." According to Muslim, a renowned Hadith scholar, a man said: "A person likes to wear good clothes and shoes." The Prophet answered: "God is beautiful and He loves beauty." By tradition, and allowing for beauty without arrogance, an owner usually decorated only the front door of a building, to express his attitudes and identity. In contrast, the interiors of buildings were decorated, particularly the facades of the courtyard. The sophistication or level of such decoration depended on the financial ability and taste of the owner.

Quranic verses and sayings of the Prophet, which were used as the source for building guidelines, can be found elsewhere.[10] In most cases these verses and sayings were specifically pointed out by the author of a *fiqh* manuscript to back up or elaborate on the reasons and rationale behind a *qadi's* decision or an opinion of a *mufti*.

The role of local customs ('Urf)

Up to the early years of the twentieth century, we find that within the Islamic world two types of rule systems operated simultaneously. The centrally imposed system, and the localized, community-based customary rules. Both types of "rule system" have had their impact on the traditional built environment of Islamic societies. Ideas and stipulations

---

[10] See Appendix 1 "Selected Quranic verses and sayings of the Prophet" of my *Arabic-Islamic Cities* (full citation in note 6 above), 142–157.

from the former tended to create a unity of concepts and attitudes to the built environment in the various regions of the Islamic world. The latter tended to influence the details and architectonics of the local built form. These two types of rules operating simultaneously contributed to the phenomenon of the diversity of settlements of sub-regions of the Islamic world, yet unified by the general concepts and attitudes which all regions shared. Essentially, resulting in uniqueness at the micro-level and certain commonalities at the macro-level.

The majority of pre-Islamic Arab societies in Arabia regulated their lives in response to deeply rooted meta-customs known to different tribes in the region and to localized customs followed by a specific tribe. The former usually emanated from religious beliefs and helped to regulate inter-tribal conflicts, such as the concept of *haram* and *hawtah*: essentially the demarcation of space into sacred and profane areas where in the sacred area certain types of activities and behaviour are prohibited.[11] An example of localized customs is the manner in which the *fitra* (an instinctive impulse or innate understanding) generated building solutions which had local specificity and character. A large number of those customs, both at the meta and local levels, continued during the Islamic era because they did not contravene Islamic values and ethics as stipulated in the texts.

Islamic law underwent gradual development and reached maturity during the latter half of the third Islamic century, that is, by around 900 A.D. The sources of law which all Sunni schools of law agree on are the Qur'an, Sunnah (the Prophet's sayings and deeds), *ijma'* (opinion based on consensus of majority of learned Muslims), and *qiyas* (judgment based on reasoning by analogy). In the case of the Hanafi, Maliki, and Hanbali schools, they added *istihsan* (deviation from a common ruling regarding a problem to a ruling based on special circumstances). The Hanbali, and especially the Maliki schools added the concept of *al-istislah* or *al-masaleh al-mursala* (addressing those problems which the primary sources have not addressed before and which require solutions tailored to the special circumstances of time and place). *'Urf* (customs), as a source of legislation, was especially recognized by the Hanafi and Maliki schools and was for practical reasons accepted by all schools in

---

[11] See R. B. Serjeant, "Haram and Hawtah, the Sacred Enclave in Arabia," in *Melanges Taha Husain*, ed. Abdurrahman Badawi (Cairo, 1962). Reprinted in R. B. Serjeant, *Studies in Arabian History and Civilization* (London, 1981).

one aspect or another. For the '*urf* to be followed, it has to be "correct" (that is, it must not contravene clearly specified Islamic laws and prohibitions). Traditional building activities and methods of construction were primarily shaped by local customs, affecting the specificity of design resulting from the art and construction practices of a locality.[12]

Fiqh principles (Qawaʻid Fiqhiyya) *encourage proscriptive rules*

There are over one hundred principles upon which Islamic jurisprudence is based.[13] The following are seven, chosen because they have had a direct effect on the traditional built environment. They are here woven together to portray their cumulative rationale:

1. The basis for action is the freedom to act,
2. stimulated and judged by the intentions for those actions,
3. which are constrained by the prevention of damages to others.
4. However, it is sometimes necessary to tolerate lesser damages so as to avoid greater ones.
5. Older established facts must be taken into account by adjusting to their presence and conditions.
6. People's customs must be respected and followed,
7. however, time might change those customs and new solutions will be needed.

When applied to the context of the built environment these principles provided the freedom to act and build restrained by certain limits. They are thus proscriptive in nature, allowing the liberty to generate solutions to specific local problems in response to the site and the conditions around it. An equilibrium is established on the site where the "best" solution is achieved for a specific micro-condition at a specific period

---

[12] For a thorough analysis of how the ʻurf contributed to the diversity of architecture and urban form of traditional cities in the Islamic world, see my study "The Urf and its role in diversifying the architecture of traditional Islamic cities," *Journal of Architectural and Planning Research* 11, no. 2 (Summer 1994): 108–127.

[13] Mustafa Ahmed Al-Zarka, *Sharh al-Qawaʼid al-Fiqhiyya*, 2nd ed. (Damascus, 1989). The author is the son of Ahmed bin Muhammad al-Zarka (d. 1938) who wrote the first edition of this book. For a literature review and an extensive bibliography see the article by Wolfhart Heinrichs, "*Qawaʼid* as a genre of legal literature," in *Studies in Islamic Legal Theory*, ed. Bernard G. Weiss (Leiden, 2002), 365–384.

in time. Diversity is, thus, achieved in the built environment so that every locality and street becomes unique in character and contributes substantially to its identity. This in turn contributes to the richness of the total built environment. People's customs are fully incorporated in the manner they build and can express their world-view in built form. The system also recognizes and adapts to changes in those customs across time.

There are numerous aspects of the built environment which can clarify the working of this system. Two concepts are introduced and briefly defined. One is the spatial concept of the *fina'* which is the space enveloping a building, usually in the range of 1 metre (3 feet) in width, and which surrounds all the exterior configurations of a structure. Within it the owner has certain rights and responsibilities. The other is a physical entity called the *sabat*, which is a structure bridging a public right-of-way and is constructed for additional space. There are specific rules which must be adhered to for construction, especially the manner in which the supports are resolved. The working of these and many more examples as governed by the above principles is available elsewhere.[14]

A simulation of the building process

To appreciate the interaction between the mechanisms of the building process, consider the following simulation which includes one example for each component of a five-part framework devised by this author to represent the physical factors that shaped the traditional Islamic city, particularly at its neighbourhood level. This framework encompasses all building activity issues touched on in the *fiqh* literature of the Maliki School of Law. The components are: (1) streets, including through streets and cul-de-sacs, and related elements; (2) locational restrictions of uses causing harm, such as smoke, offensive odour, and noise; (3) overlooking issues, including visual corridors generated by doors, window openings, and heights; (4) walls between neighbours and their rights of ownership and usage; and (5) drainage of rain and waste water.

---

[14] See pages 27–30 of my *Arabic-Islamic Cities* (full citation in note 6 above). For how we can learn from traditional concepts, processes and techniques see my article "Learning from traditional Mediterranean codes," in *Council Report III/IV*, published by The Town Paper (Gaithersburg, MD, 2003), 42, 43, 63.

Imagine that a man wants to build on a vacant lot or to reuse a site on which a dilapidated house stands. If the intention is to rebuild a structure for the same use, then he can proceed with no objections; if the plan is to build a public bath or bakery, however, then he will more than likely be faced with objections from the neighbours. The reasons given are that such new public uses will create harm in three ways; (1) by generating additional traffic on the street(s) providing access to the facility, thus, causing the people living nearby to have to adjust to this new condition; (2) by the nuisance of the smoke generated; and (3) by diminishing the value of the adjacent houses because of the impending adjacent public uses and the nuisances that will result. Two frequently cited sources supporting these complaints are used by the *fuqaha'* (plural *of faqih*, a jurisprudence scholar), for preventing the change in use. The Quran says: "And diminish not the goods of the people, and do not mischief in the earth working corruption" (26:183). From the sayings of the Prophet comes: "Do not harm others or yourself, and others should not harm you or themselves" (cited by Ahmad and Ibn Majah).

After exploring other uses for the site, the owner decides to build a house. He asks a local builder to construct it; the two will communicate with each other about the design requirements by using the local design language. This is done by identifying each part according to its name in the design language. To illustrate, examples from the local language in the Tunis region are used: the owner requires one *skifa* (entrance lobby with entry doors placed so that no one can see directly into the courtyard from the outside), with two *dukkana* facing each other (built-in benches provided in the *skifa*, traditionally used by the male owner or occupant to receive casual visitors or salesmen). He specifies that the *wust al-dar* (open courtyard in the centre of the house) should have under it a *majin* (cistern for the collection of rainwater from the roofs), and one *burtal* (a colonnaded gallery off the courtyard giving importance and sometimes sun protection to the room behind) off the main room. Around the courtyard he asks the builder for three *bit trida* (simple rooms) and one *bit bel-kbu u mkasar* (a primary room common in middle- and upper-middle-class houses), which is usually located opposite the entrance to the court. This primary room is divided into (1) a central alcove called a *kbu*, usually containing built-in seating and elaborate wall and ceiling decorations, and used to receive close relatives and friends; (2) two small rooms symmetrically located on each side of the *kbu* called *maqsura* and used as bedrooms; and (3) two alcoves, constructed opposite each other, with built-in beds and/or storage. The built-in beds could be placed on one or both sides of the alcove and are usually framed with a decorative wooden structure called *hanut hajïam*. This listing could continue on to the smallest details of decoration and finishes (figure 5).

If the house is relatively complex, then the builder will more than likely sketch out the plan and any other details, but for his own use and not to communicate with the owner. When the design language is not adequate for both owner and builder to clarify a point, then either one, but more commonly the owner, takes the builder to see a house to indicate what he has in mind.

The builder is expected to know about the customs and traditions of building practice and the principles to be followed and respected. Surprisingly, the detailed implications of building rules were not common knowledge among the lower ranks of builders. Often, references are made in ancient manuscripts to implemented building decisions that were violations and were later ordered by the local judge *qadi* to be demolished or corrected in response to a neighbour's complaints. It seems, however, that the more established and older builders with many years of experience who were often hired by affluent clients had detailed insights of the rules.

Having determined the usage of the site and using the design language for planning purposes, the builder and owner examine the likely effects on their requirements and decisions of existing surrounding buildings. If a window exists on one of the neighbour's walls, for example, then its location had to be taken into consideration in the building of the new house because of the respect for the principle of the earlier rights of usage. The new owner of the house had the responsibility to avoid creating a direct visual corridor from the existing window into his private domain; in effect he had to pre-empt problems that could arise from having visual access to his house.

Rather than building another adjacent wall, a neighbour's wall could be used to insert beams for support. This practice was specifically encouraged by the Prophet: "A neighbour should not forbid his neighbour to insert wooden beams in his wall" (cited by Abu Hurairah). Nonetheless, there were elaborate guidelines to be respected for using a neighbour's wall and for the associated problems of subsequent maintenance rights. For example, the ratio of the wall to be used depended on its ownership. In the case of rebuilding a dilapidated house, correct identification of the ownership of adjacent walls was therefore crucial. Careful examination of the wall was guided by criteria that determined whether ownership was single or joint. The most common of these criteria was to discover the nature of the *akd* or wall bond at the corners

or junction of two walls, by examining the materials and mortar to
resolve whether the two walls were built together. This practice which
was sanctioned by the Prophet is traceable to the decade of 622–632
A.D. in Medina and is still followed today in the older parts of Islamic
cities under the local customary law, or *'urf*.

The problem of drainage of rain and wastewater also had to follow
certain rules and guidelines. Drainage of rainwater was a particularly
delicate problem because excess water was not to be barred from others.
This principle is directly attributed to two sayings of the Prophet: "If you
deny excess water, you will deny the benefits of pasture" (cited by Abu
Hurairah), and "Muslims are partners in three things: water, pasture,
and fire" (cited by Abu Dawood and Ibn Majah via Ibn Abbas).

As to the relationship of houses to streets, assume that one side of
a house adjoins a through street and the owner wants more space.
One option is to build a *sabat* (room bridging the street). To support
the structure on the opposite side, the owner could acquire permission
from the owner of the facing building, but the granting of such permission was not totally irrevocable and, thus, this alternative depended
on the owner's perception of his future relationship with his opposite
neighbour. More than likely, the owner would choose to use columns
for support, keeping himself and his heirs totally independent of his
neighbour. Another option would be to use columns for supporting
both sides, opening up the future possibility of being able to sell the
sabat to the owner of the opposite building, and generally upgrading
the marketability of the house.

The preceding illustrations provide only an overview of the issues
involved in the typical building process of a house. Many other cases,
some of them extremely involved, may be found elsewhere.[15] This
discussion is adequate, however, to illuminate the fact that the built
form was a direct outcome of the dynamics of decision-making, using
specific mechanisms and governed by *fiqh* rules derived from Islamic
values embodied in the Qur'an and the Hadith.

Conclusion

I shall conclude this contribution with two discussions. The first assumes
that the traditional system offers a great deal to learn from for our

---

[15] See Chapter 1 of my *Arabic-Islamic Cities* (full citation in note 6 above).

contemporary period and for the future. The second suggests numerous areas for further research that are necessary to develop our knowledge and understanding of the workings of the traditional system and, by extension, enable us to develop a comprehensive theory of the traditional Islamic city.

Learning from the past. The traditional system of building and of urban activities in most cities of the Islamic world was an incremental and constantly rebalanced process of development involving the synthesis of religious and socio-cultural conventions. The system was self-regulating, so that any significant departure or contravention of the rules and conventions created a situation where corrective action had to be undertaken; in the absence of such action, the intervention of the *qadi* (local judge) provided the prescription for normalizing the conflict within the system, in line with the established norms and rules operational in the community.

Specifically, three experiences are valuable to the contemporary context. The first is the importance of the legal framework as the prime shaper of the urban environment, particularly environments at the level of the neighbourhood. Certainly this is also true today with zoning ordinances, subdivision regulations, and building codes. However, the nature of the legal framework is where the Islamic city can provide fresh insight. The *fiqh* building rules were derived from societal values based on religious beliefs and were supported by adequate elaboration of the intent of each rule. Specific numerical prescriptions were not indicated and only rarely cited as an example of how a specific problem ought to be resolved. In essence, the rules functioned as performance criteria, as opposed to contemporary building and planning laws which are based on standards. The former is qualitative, intent- oriented, and responsive to changes in requirements or site conditions, whereas the latter is quantitative, numerically oriented, and not responsive to changes in requirements or location. Not only is the performance criteria approach more sophisticated in terms of addressing each building problem within its own context, but the aggregate results it helps to create as built environment are diverse and complex. Laws based on standards address all problems uniformly, with results of repetitiveness and monotony in the built environment. The best examples are the thousands of suburbs that were developed in the West, particularly in the United States during the twentieth century, and especially since World War II.

The second lesson is the use of a building "design language" as a communication and design-decision-making aid. The components of the language integrate the three-dimensional form and function of the design element being communicated. This mechanism helps the user and builder to communicate with each other. It also preserves and perpetuates design-configurations and forms which have proved their durability through experience without hindering diversity in the individual design solution.

The third primary lesson is in the nature of the physical organization. As mentioned earlier, the system of courtyard buildings serviced by cul-de-sacs and through streets pre-dates Islam; however, Islamic civilization developed and refined this system and spread it across a vast geographic area, aided by the simultaneous development and acquisition of *fiqh* knowledge as it pertained to interventions in the built environment. Some highlights of the attributes of this organizational system follow. The courtyard plan form is able to accommodate diverse uses. The densities created in housing are efficient without sacrificing the privacy of the individual unit. Streets as an access network are maximally utilized, as in the example of the central portion of Tunis Medina. All streets take up 12.5% of the gross built up area and only 13.3% of those are cul-de-sacs serving 28.5% of all buildings, i.e. a relatively low proportion of cul-de-sacs serving a high proportion of buildings. *Sabat*s (rooms over streets) are used to create extra space for private users, simultaneously providing cover to the public in the streets. In the central portion of Tunis Medina, 8% of all streets are covered by *sabat*s, in addition to 7.5% covered by vaulting, providing coverage to a total of 15.5% of the city's streets.

There are numerous attributes in addition to those mentioned above, such as the use and details of decoration and ornament in the realm of art. Another important attribute which has received some attention before is the energy saving attributes of the built form within the context of an arid region, aided by energy saving practices and devices such as the wind tower, air vent, cisterns for storing water and keeping it cool, and the ice maker.[16] Other practices were the collection and storage of rainwater in cisterns under the courtyard of buildings, the

---

[16] Refer to the references in note 4 above, and see the numerous examples from Iran in E. Beazley and M. Harverson, *Living with the Desert: Working Buildings of the Iranian Plateau* (Warminster, Wilts, England, 1982).

effective use of basements as living quarters during the hot season, and the recycling of building materials.

Although this discussion addresses Islamic environments, there are universal benefits; it is hoped that the value of this information will be of interest and use to peoples of other cultures today and in the future. Amos Rapoport clearly points out the relevance and importance of this information, when he says:

> The broader our sample in space and time, the more likely we are to see regularities in apparent chaos, as well as to understand better those differences that are significant. Thus, the more likely we are to see patterns and relationships, and these are the most significant things for which to look. Being able to establish the presence of such patterns may help us deal with the problem of constancy and change.... It is very important to understand constancies as well as change, since our culture stresses change to an inordinate degree. Also, if apparent change and variability are an expression of invariant processes, this is extremely important because the reasons for doing apparently different things remain the same.[17]

Areas for further research. The following suggestions for study and research are not exhaustive, but should be considered as an essential preliminary list of topics which are necessary to be undertaken for generating the knowledge and the building blocks, so that a serious attempt can take place in constructing a theory of urban form in Islamic cultures. The list suggests topics dealing with the settlement level followed by those of relevance at the cluster/neighbourhood level, and then those of value at the single building level. Some of the suggestions are of significance to all three levels combined, and some to two levels. The list of topics follows:

1. Pre-Islamic conceptions of the urban settlement and the city in the Near East and especially in the western region of the Arabian Peninsula. How did the Arabs who were converted to Islam apply the concepts in establishing new settlements and in adapting existing towns and cities, such as the case of Damascus and Aleppo? To my knowledge, no substantive studies are available which address patterns in land tenure, ownership rights, and control of space, and how those patterns affected the configurations of buildings, streets, and the alignment of shops in commercial areas and markets.

---

[17] A. Rapoport, "Cultural Origins of Architecture," in *Introduction to Architecture*, ed. J. C. Snyder and A. J. Catanese (New York, 1979), 18.

2. The process of land demarcation and sub-division in the early formation of Islamic cities. This is the initial process undertaken for allocating land to public and private uses. Did the allocation of private land precede considerations for the layout of public right-of-ways? What was the technique in undertaking this task? Or was the process in the reverse direction?[18]

3. A detailed study of the principles and workings of land allotment, *iqta'*, and revivification, *ihya'*, of land within and on the fringes of settlements. The Prophet applied the principle of *iqta'* in Medina soon after he settled there. There are abundant descriptions of that example in the Arabic literature and it should be possible to reconstruct what occurred at that time using a process of simulation based on the available information.[19]

4. The process of territorialization of land, *ikhtitat*, in the initial and early formation of the quarter, *mahalla*, or neighbourhood level. After land was allotted to a group of people, they were responsible for its territorialization into clusters of plots and allocating adequate land for access which eventually became the streets and cul-de-sacs. Since this phenomenon occurred during the early formation of most Islamic cities, it is difficult to find adequate and reliable information describing this process. Yet it is very important to develop a number of alternative scenarios for purposes of constructing theory.

5. How did the institution of *waqf* function in terms of its impact on buildings and by extension on urban form? What was the impact on the processes of growth and change? There are a large number of studies on the institution of *waqf* which originates with the teaching of the Prophet. An important saying by him is "If you wish,

---

[18] J. Akbar attempted to explain this in his "Khatta and the territorial structure of early Muslim towns," *Muqarnas* 6 (1989): 22–32. The effort addresses important issues and should be viewed as a good start. More extensive research is needed. Here the techniques and skills of archaeologists would be most valuable. A good example of an earlier study is by archaeologist J. Schmidt, "Strassen in Altorientalischen Wohnge-bieten: eine Studie zur Geschichte des Städtebaus in Mesopotamien und Syrien," *Deutsches Archäologisches Institut Abteilung Baghdad: Baghdader Mitteilungen* (Berlin) vol. 3 (1964): 125–147.

[19] See the book *Wafa al-Wafa*, by Nuraldin al-Samhudi (d. 1505), 4 parts in two volumes (Beirut, 1955). As for the principle and implementation of *Ihya'*, information based on the legal literature of the predominant Islamic schools of law *Madhahib* aided by on site archaeological investigations of cities which were influenced by a specific school of law would clarify the workings of this principle.

retain its origin (*habbasta aslaha*) and provide it as charity" cited by al-Bukhari. The Hanafi School of Law defines the *waqf* as: "the detention of the corpus from the ownership of any person and the gift of its income or usufruct, either presently or in the future, to some charitable purpose."[20] Most of the studies available deal with specific buildings designated as *waqf* but, to my knowledge, there are no studies which attempt to explain the impact of a large number of buildings and real estate on the city as a whole, its processes of growth and change, and the consequence on urban form across time.

6. What were the various types of tenure and ownership of land and buildings? What was the effect of taxation on the various types of tenure? There is a great deal of information available regarding these questions in the classical Arabic sources and more recently in late nineteenth century Ottoman sources. A sketchy attempt to address these issues was published, but to my knowledge no extensive studies are available which tackle these questions.[21]

7. The institution of *hisba*: what was its jurisdiction and responsibilities, and its impact on urban management? What were the overlap and/or interaction with the judge's (*qadi*'s) realm of jurisdiction? There are a number of well-known *hisba* manuals from the eastern *mashriq* and western *maghrib* regions of the Islamic world which should be carefully examined for answering these questions. Further clarifications will emerge from a process of detailed study and analysis of these manuals.

8. Local customs (*'urf*) in design and building construction were a primary engine affecting decision-making and the choice of design solutions in a specific locality. The School of Law (*madhab*), having the jurisdiction in a locality, sanctioned those customs, provided the custom did not contravene principles of Islamic law (*Shari'a*). Research is required for a comparative analysis of "solutions" which

---

[20] H. Cattan, "The law of Waqf," in *Law in the Middle East*, ed. M. Khadduri and H. J. Liebesny (Washington, D.C., 1955).

[21] See M. Serageldin with W. Doebele and K. ElAraby, "Land tenure systems and development controls in the Arab countries of the Middle East," in *Housing Process and Physical Form*, Proceedings of Seminar Three held in Jakarta, Indonesia, March 1979, sponsored by the Aga Khan Award for Architecture (1980), 75–88.

were generated within the umbrella of the various schools of law and the manifestation of those solutions in physical terms, particularly noting the differences in solutions to similar problems. This research would rely on cases of rulings by customary law as recorded by local judges (*qadis*) and in the compilations of specialists on law (*muftis*), aided where feasible by onsite investigations.

9. Field research of numerous cities within major regions of the Islamic world which are designed to document the design language (linguistic *'urf*), indicating the sources for the terms, their meaning, and the actual physical configuration and arrangements which the vocabulary of the local design language referred to, including their implication for the design of buildings and the shaping of urban form. Comparative study of the results of these surveys would greatly enhance our understanding of the built form qualities of those cities.[22]

10. Symbolic manifestations occurs at different levels of the built environment, the design and details of decorations in various locations of a building, such as part of the main entrance, around windows, and on the walls surrounding the interior courtyards. In a locality embedded in religious associations, the location of a mosque, water wells for public use, and other elements in the settlement is influenced by historical and religious associations. Comparative research of such examples in various regions of the Islamic world is necessary.[23]

11. Mathematics, geometry, surveying, and engineering techniques, which were used in building design and construction. Little serious research on these interrelated aspects has been undertaken. Recent scholarship is very encouraging, however this area of investigation is open to a great deal of research possibilities.[24]

---

[22] For a detailed discussion of what is the "design language" see chapter 2 of my book *Arabic-Islamic Cities* (full citation in note 6 above). For what is the "linguistic *'urf*" see my article "The 'Urf' and its role..." (full citation in note 12 above).

[23] See chapter 4: Symbolism and Form, of my edited study *Sidi Bou Sa'id, Tunisia: A Study in Structure and Form*, (Halifax, N.S., 1978) [Available from Books on Demand, UMI, Ann Arbor, MI]. That chapter analyzes symbolism in that village at three levels: (i) the village, (ii) entrances, windows, and steps, and (iii) surface embellishments such as plaster carvings, stonework, and tiles.

[24] See the articles by W. Chorbachi, "In the Tower of Babel: Beyond symmetry in Islamic design," *Computers and Mathematics with Applications* 17, no. 4–6 (1989): 751–789; and Alpay Özdural, "Omar Khayyam, Mathematicians, and Conversazioni with Artisans," *Journal of Society of Architectural Historians* 54, no. 1 (March 1995): 54–71; and the

12. Building materials and construction techniques. What were their attributes and limitations? How and in what context were materials used separately or in combination with others? For what purposes and how was recycled material used? What were the structural limitations of materials, and how did builders innovate within those constraints?

13. Traditional energy-saving practices and techniques, for example, the utilization of water, cooling devices such as wind towers, and methods for disposing of human and animal excrement. Although research on these topics is mostly available for Iran, very little has been done for other regions. Comprehensive studies are needed to understand design solutions used for dealing with conditions in different climate zones and topographical features.

14. A study which focuses on the use of the courtyard in the design and planning of houses, with particular attention to its use as a customary inherited element, i.e. when used unconsciously as a customary practice without concern to its design potentials vs. its intentional use as a device embodied with design possibilities and opportunities for climate control.

15. An atlas of Islamic cities in various regions of the Islamic world which would document: (i) city maps drawn in the same format, using the same system of colours, and supplemented by the necessary aerial photographs; (ii) morphological patterns at the levels of the city, neighbourhood, and building clusters that would include, for example, the patterns of public through streets and private cul-de-sacs, and the analysis of the typology's strengths and weaknesses. Certain peculiarities would also be studied, such as the preference for the location of a small mosque (*masjid*) at the strategic junction of a fork in the street system;[25] and (iii) study of building types drawn to the same scale and presented in plans, elevations, and sections.

---

published manuscript of Ca'fer Efendi, *Risale-i Mimariyye: An early 17th century Ottoman treatise on architecture*, trans. Howard Crane (Leiden, 1987).

[25] The utilization of this type of junction, which results from the convergence of two streets into one, within this morphological type can also be traced as far back as 2000 B.C. in Ur, southern Mesopotamia. See Exhibit 2 of my article "Arab-Islamic Urban Structure," *Arabian Journal for Science and Engineering* 7, no. 2 (April 1982): 69–79; Also the street analysis in Chapter 3: Spatial Structure and Built Form, in my *Sidi Bou Sa'id, Tunisia*, 19–56 (full citation in note 23 above).

I hope that the above list of topics will be valuable for those concerned with the lack of a theory of urban form in traditional Islamic cities. Topics addressing other detailed aspects can be developed and added. It is important to stress that we are at a point in the development of this field which necessitates co-operative efforts to address the above issues. Cooperation can be achieved in many ways, through: (i) effective and accessible communication tools, such as the World Wide Web pages of the Internet. Web sites can be created by individual scholars and institutions where the latest research is summarized and/or made available for downloading to personal computers; (ii) focused symposia and conferences; and (iii) testing in contemporary projects by recycling the principles underlying traditional ideas and procedures.[26] If all these are carried out, then an achievement of this magnitude will not only be of immense value to the Islamic world and its numerous sub-cultures, but it will also be a significant contribution to our understanding of urbanism and the urban phenomenon as a cultural expression within a global context.

---

[26] I have constructed a framework for action which was published in the article "Urban design in traditional Islamic culture: Recycling its successes," *Cities* 8, no. 4 (November 1991): 274–277. On June 7, 1997 I delivered a keynote address at a Vision symposium in Riyadh, Saudi Arabia, which was organized by Arriyadh Development Authority (ADA), on the occasion of the completion of phase 1 of a three-phase planning process known as Metropolitan Development Strategy for Arriyadh (MEDSTAR). One of the proposals I made in that address was based on the principle of bottom-up decision-making at the neighbourhood level. This principle was operational in all traditional cities and settlements in the Islamic world and was replaced, in the case of Saudi Arabia, by a top-down decision-making structure during the mid years of the twentieth century as a result of Western influences and for reasons related to local political preferences. My proposal was to create neighbourhood organizations whose task would be to coordinate decisions affecting the well being of a neighbourhood including matters related to design and planning. This would create a situation where neighbourhoods would be encouraged to compete with each other for the best ideas and designs which would alleviate or solve pervasive and common problems, such as safety in neighbourhood streets, greening of streets by planting and maintaining trees and shrubs, and creating pleasant pedestrian paths which would ensure the safety and protection of women and children. My other proposal was to rewrite the city's planning codes in a manner, which will utilize the wisdom inherent in the traditional codes, in lieu of trying to fix codes which were formulated in the early 1980s and which have proved to be inferior, as it is evident in various parts of the city. I have also addressed similar issues for the context of historic towns in the Maghrib countries of North Africa in a lecture titled: "Reviving the Rule System: An approach for revitalizing traditional towns in Maghrib," at the conference titled "The Living Medina: The Walled Arab City in Architecture, Literature, and History" held in Tangier, Morocco, June 1996, sponsored by the American Institute of Maghribi Studies (AIMS). It was subsequently published by the same title in *Cities* 18, no. 2 (April 2001): 87–92.

INHERITED CITIES

Hugh Kennedy

Many, if not most of the cities which existed in the early Muslim world had existed in one form or another before the coming of Islam. There were important exceptions: Kufa and Basra in Iraq, Fustat in Egypt, Qayrawan in Tunisia, and, of course, Baghdad and Samarra were all founded through government action to provide bases for Muslim settlers and suitable new centres for government. Other new towns seem to have emerged more gradually in response to new patterns of power and settlement: Murcia in eastern Andalus, Fez in Morocco, Mosul in northern Iraq, Shiraz in Fars, and Kirman in southern Iran are all examples of this latter pattern. Political authority was also wielded from ancient centres: Córdoba, Damascus, Rayy, and Merv are all cities whose origins were lost in the mists of antiquity.

The inherited cities of the early Islamic period are an especially interesting field of study because they give us an opportunity to examine how the coming of a new élite language and religion and the emergence of new political and military systems affected the structures of everyday life.

Archaeological evidence necessarily provides the foundations for this enquiry but in the way of things it is very patchy and does not always answer the questions we are asking. Many of the cities the Muslim state inherited are still thriving today and their past is difficult to recover beneath the modern streets and buildings. Damascus, Jerusalem, Aleppo, Córdoba, and Bukhara are all sites where the centre of the ancient city remains the centre of urban life today. But there are a significant number of other sites which survived from antiquity into the Islamic period but which have subsequently been deserted. Among these Jerash in Jordan (probably de-urbanized in the ninth and tenth centuries), Nishapur in northeastern Iran, and Merv in Turkmenistan (both effectively deserted after the Mongol conquests of 1218–20) are sites where the ancient and early Islamic cities are wide open to archaeological investigation. Balkh would be the same, if political conditions in Afghanistan were more encouraging for archaeology. In some other cities, the urban centre has moved, thus allowing the site of the ancient and early Islamic city to be investigated. Such is the case at Samarqand where the walls and citadel of the old city, destroyed at the time of the Mongol invasions, lie just outside the modern city developed by the Timurids and their successors. Fustat presents a complex picture where the Roman fortified citadel, dating from the reign of Trajan (98–117), was expanded by the foundation of the Muslim city to the north in the seventh and eighth century while this in turn was largely deserted during the twelfth century as the centre of urban life moved further north to Cairo, eventually allowing both Roman and early Islamic centres to be investigated by archaeologists.

The archaeological evidence varies widely and different sorts of material enable us to ask different questions. Broadly speaking, we can make a division between the stone built cities of the ancient Byzantine lands and the mud-brick and rubble cities of the Sasanian east. The largely brick built cities of early Islamic Egypt are only just beginning to be investigated. Spain and North Africa had some late antique urban centres in stone, though in general these have been subject to less thorough investigation than the material from Syria.

The importance of these distinctions between regions and construction techniques is that they fundamentally shape the sort of questions we can ask about the aspect of inherited cities and the way they changed, stone architecture enduring more than mud. In all provinces of the caliphate, we can make general observations about the distribution of cities and which ones thrived and which declined, but the nature of the evidence is quite varied. At a more specific level, the picture varies considerably from area to area. In Syria, and to a lesser extent in the Muslim west, we can look at the urban topography of some cities, that is to say that we can observe how street plans and the design of individual buildings evolved. In sites like Jerash[1] and Baysan[2] we can observe the evolution of the street scene and even in a city like Aleppo, continuously overbuilt to the present day, we can make meaningful judgments about the way in which the street plan did, or did not change, with the coming of Islam. Such precision is rarely possible from the Muslim east. Even from sites like Samarqand, Merv, and Qasr-i Abu Nasr where there has been some scientific excavation of the urban built environment,

---

[1] On the street plan of Jerash, Carl H. Kraeling, *Gerasa: City of the Decapolis* (New Haven, 1938).
[2] Yoram Tsafrir and Gideon Foerster, "Urbanism at Scythopolis-Bet Shean in the Fourth to Seventh Centuries," *DOP* 51 (1997): 85–146.

the information yielded has been limited. The excavations in the old city of Merv present late Sasanian housing but give little indication of later evolution, if any; Samarqand gives some information about the evolution of an élite centre, Qasr-i Abu Nasr the layout and evolution of a small urban nucleus within the walls of the citadel. Despite these limitations, the eastern Islamic material can give us a sense of the macro-geography of the city, the extent to which pre-Islamic cities expanded in the early Islamic era or changed their sites.

In this chapter, I would like to examine three main areas of the early Muslim world, greater Syria (Bilad al-Sham), Iran and the Muslim East, and the Muslim West, looking first at the distribution of inherited cities and then at the morphology of individual sites.

The cities of Bilad al-Sham[3]

It is the area of Bilad al-Sham, the Levantine provinces, which had been ruled by the Byzantines that we find the clearest evidence about the cities the Muslims inherited. Of the larger cities in the area, Damascus and Jerusalem survived and remained important cities in the early Islamic period. Damascus certainly expanded in the period because of its political role as capital of the Umayyad caliphate from 661 to 750 and, although we know little about the urban, as opposed to the monumental, history of early Islamic Jerusalem, its position as a cult centre would suggest that urban life continued.

The other provincial capitals fared less well. Antioch had been the capital of the whole of the late Roman East, one of the great cities of the Empire and seat of one of the four ancient patriarchates of the Christian church. Evidence, both written and archaeological, suggests that the city had been in decline, economically and physically since the mid-sixth century, but it retained its political primacy until the end of Byzantine rule. The city survived into Islamic times as a middle-sized

---

[3] The literature on Roman and Islamic Syria is vast. For an introduction to Syria in antiquity see Warwick Ball, *Rome in the East* (London, 2000) and Kevin Butcher, *Roman Syria and the Near East* (London, 2003). For changes in late antiquity, Clive Foss, "The Near Eastern Countryside in Late Antiquity: a review article," *JRA*, Supplementary series, 14 (1995): 213–234; Idem, "Syria in Transition, A.D. 550–750," *DOP* 51 (1997): 189–270. For the changes in the early Islamic period, Hugh Kennedy, "From Polis to Medina: urban change in late antique and early Islamic Syria," *Past and Present* 106 (1985): 3–27.

provincial town[4] but in the long term it must have suffered from the
rise of nearby Aleppo, itself an ancient city but one which grew rapidly
in the centuries after the Muslim conquest. Chalcis survived as early
Islamic Qinnasrin and there was new early Muslim settlement outside
the walls of the classical city. For a while, it remained important politically as capital of the *jund* which bore its name but even before the end
of the Umayyad period it, too, was being supplanted by Aleppo as the
most important city in the area.

Apamea had continued to be an important political centre until the
end of the sixth century but it suffered grievously from its sack by the
Persians in 573. The city put up little resistance to the incoming Muslim
armies and the ancient metropolis of Syria II was reduced to the size
and status of a small country town. Further south, the urban centre of
Scythoplis/Baysan, capital of Palestine II, continued to be developed
with new streets and porticoes until the end of the Umayyad period,
though, as with other cities, this may represent continuing vitality in
only a small part of the area of the ancient city.[5]

The cities of the coast suffered most from the new political circumstances as the Mediterranean became a war zone rather than a means
of communication, though it must be remembered that the Persian invasions of the first decade of the seventh century had already disrupted
much of the ancient commerce. In addition to suffering the damage
wrought by the reduction of sea commerce, Beirut had been ruined
by an earthquake in the mid-sixth century. It may have recovered from
that but any such recovery has left no trace in either the literature or
the archaeological record.[6] The geographer al-Yaʿqūbī says that Beirut,
along with other coastal towns like Tripoli, Jubayl, and Sidon were
inhabited by Persians (*Furs*) transported there by the first Umayyad
caliph Muʿawiya b. Abi Sufyan.[7] This suggests that, although the sites
were still inhabited, there was little or no continuity of population.
Tyre and Caesarea both seem to have remained important urban
centres until the early seventh century and Caesarea was the only city
where there was prolonged resistance to the Muslim invaders. After

---

[4] See Hugh Kennedy, "Antioch: from Byzantium to Islam and back again," in *The City in Late Antiquity*, ed. John Rich (London, 1992), 181–198.
[5] See Hugh Kennedy, "Gerasa and Scythopolis: Power and Patronage in the Byz-antine Cities of Bilad al-Sham," *Bulletin d'Études Orientales* 52 (1997): 199–204.
[6] Linda J. Hall, *Roman Berytus: Beirut in Late Antiquity* (New York, 2004).
[7] Al-Yaʿqūbī, *Kitāb al-buldān*, ed. Michaël Jan de Goeje (Leiden, 1892), 327.

the Muslim conquest, both sank into comparative obscurity and, like Antioch, any importance they did have was due to their military or political role rather than their commercial vitality. It was not until the early eleventh century that the coastal ports of the Levant began to expand once more with the appearance of western merchants in the eastern Mediterranean.

Bostra, capital of the province of Arabia, never became important in Muslim times. Its continued commercial importance in the late sixth century is suggested by the Bahira legend which describes the youthful Prophet Muhammad coming to the city as part of the trading caravan from Mecca and being impressed by the teaching of the saintly monk. But we know from other sources that it had been sacked by dissident Ghassanids in the late sixth century and in Umayyad times it lost any political importance it may still have had to nearby Damascus.[8] The most southerly of the ancient capitals, Petra, is never mentioned in the accounts of the Muslim conquest, nor is there any archaeological evidence for new construction after the mid-sixth century. The recently excavated great church was destroyed by fire in the mid sixth century and never subsequently rebuilt.[9] This negative evidence suggests that the city had entirely lost its urban character a hundred years before the coming of the Muslims.

If few of the major political centres of the late Roman Empire survived as major cities in the Islamic period, there seems to have been more continuity among the smaller towns, especially those away from the coast. As is often the case for this period, the archaeological evidence is more revealing than the scanty literary sources for the first two centuries of Islamic rule. From this we can see that a city like Jerash continued to be inhabited throughout the Umayyad period. New housing was constructed and a large new mosque built to house what was presumably an expanding Muslim population.[10] The citadel at nearby Philadelphia/Amman was extensively rebuilt and by the mid-eighth century boasted an imposing new palace, a mosque, baths and élite houses while another congregational mosque was constructed in the lower town. All this gives an impression of urban vitality which

---

[8] Maurice Sartre, *Bostra: des origines à l'Islam* (Paris, 1985).
[9] Zbigniew Fiema, et al., *The Petra Church* (Amman, 2001).
[10] For a preliminary report on this important discovery, Alan Walmsley, "The Newly-Discovered Congregational Mosque of Jarash in Jordan," *Al-'Usur al-Wusta: The Bulletin of Middle East Medievalists* 15 (2003): 17–24.

finds no little echo in the written sources. Similarly, the continuing, or revived, commercial importance of Palmyra/Tadmur is suggested by the development of a new suq along the old colonnaded street that had formed the spine of the Roman city.

It is only in Bilad al-Sham that the archaeological record enables us to make some assessment of the impact of the Muslim conquests on the built environment and architecture of the towns, and here we enter into the debate about the nature of late antique cities. The question of the shape and appearance of the late antique city has been the subject of lively controversy. There used to be a tacit assumption that the classical city with its regular plan, broad colonnaded streets, and monumental buildings survived almost unaltered until the coming of Islam introduced a new sort of "Islamic city" with narrow winding streets, blank-walled houses, and no public buildings apart from the mosque. Recently this picture of abrupt change has been challenged and modified. It is clear that the regularity and monumentality of the classical city, if it had ever existed in any sort of pristine state, had changed and developed in late antiquity. Many of the monumental buildings of the classical era, the theatres and huge baths, had fallen into disuse, not maintained in the changed circumstances. Even more significant was the closure and ruination of the great temples, a process begun in the mid-fourth century and largely complete by the beginning of the sixth. These temples had formed the central point of many town plans; the sacred ways which led to them were also the broadest and most prestigious streets and the arches and propylaea which added dignity to these processional routes were central features of the townscape. The abandonment of the pagan temples in a city like Jerash in the fifth and sixth centuries meant disruption of the entire urban fabric. And, of course, the rise of Christianity meant new religious buildings inserted into the ancient city, creating new routes and spaces.

It was not just the monumental buildings that changed in late antiquity. The broad streets and regular open spaces on the ancient city began to be eroded and encroached upon by housing and retail spaces. In towns throughout the Levant, the streets of late antiquity came to look increasingly like the narrower lanes of the archetypal, though later, Islamic city. The evolution was far from complete. In provincial capitals like Scythopolis, the governors laid out new streets and squares in the sixth century and when the Emperor Justinian gave orders for the restoration of Antioch after the disastrous earthquake of 540, he made it clear that it was to be a classical city of the old sort, with stoas, agoras, theatres, and baths. When the same Emperor extended the *cardo* of Jerusalem towards the Nea Church he was building, he laid out a broad, straight colonnaded street of which Augustus or Hadrian might have been proud.

Of course, the coming of Muslim rule naturally affected towns. The most obvious difference was the appearance of a new sort of religious building, the mosque. The impact of the mosque on the cityscape varied greatly from city to city. In Damascus the Umayyad mosque occupied the great temenos which had previously enclosed a pagan temple and a Christian cathedral. In Jerusalem, the vast precinct of Herod's temple which may have been derelict since the destruction of the building after the Roman conquest of A.D. 70 became the centre of the Muslim cult with the construction of the Dome of the Rock and the Aqsa mosque. In both these cases the new religious monuments occupied traditional sacred areas.

Both these cases were unusual. In other cities the mosque was built in an area that had hitherto been residential or commercial. Once again the clearest evidence comes from Jerash where we can see the emplacement of the Christian cathedral of the fourth century and the mosque of the seventh or eighth in the existing urban structure. The mosque, only discovered and partially excavated in the last two years, was a large, rectangular, hypostyle building, erected by a crossroads in the classical street plan that seems to have been the centre of the early Islamic settlement. In Aleppo the mosque, in the heart of the suqs, may have occupied the site and adopted the footprint of an ancient forum, just across the street from the cathedral. In some cities there are literary records suggesting the sharing of sacred space between Christians and Muslims, the mosque occupying part of the church. This picture receives striking archaeological support from the small Negev town of Subeita, where the tiny mosque occupied part of narthex of the south church without, apparently, interrupting the functioning of the Christian building. Both church and mosque fell into ruin together when the town was abandoned, probably in the eighth or ninth century.

The effect of the Muslim conquest on the ancient street plan has been much debated and is a central issue in the emergence of the "Islamic city." In his pioneering study of Aleppo,[11] Jean Sauvaget argued that

---

[11] Jean Sauvaget, *Alep* (Paris, 1941).

the classical street plan remained virtually intact until the tenth century when a period of anarchy and lack of firm government allowed merchants to build their stalls in the centre of the street and so create the suq as it has existed to the present day. Recent archaeological work has shown that this picture needs to be modified. The *sūq* in the colonnaded street at Palmyra, which in many ways confirms the changes suggested by Sauvaget, dates from the late seventh or eighth century, some two hundred years before the time he proposed. A startlingly new perspective is suggested by recent evidence from Scythopolis. In the city centre there was a broad, straight street flanked by arcaded porticoes. On stylistic grounds this was dated to the Byzantine period and seen as evidence of the continuing commitment of the authorities to the norms of classical urban planning. However, excavations have uncovered a mosaic inscription showing beyond doubt that the street was constructed by the local governor on the orders of the Caliph Hisham in the 730s.[12] Not only were the Muslim authorities constructing an urban feature of clearly classical aspect, the governor was acting as his pre-Islamic predecessors would have done, to beautify and enhance the built environment of the city and creating an inscription to commemorate his actions and the patronage of the ruler who had ordered it.

The evidence from Bilad al-Sham suggests that the coming of the new Islamic dispensation did affect the appearance and function of cities but that these changes were in many ways the continuation, variation, or acceleration of change which were already in progress before the new religion was born. Unfortunately, the nature of the evidence makes it very difficult to see if this pattern was repeated in other areas of the Caliphate.

The cities of Iraq

Like Bilad al-Sham, ancient Iraq was a land well endowed with cities. Some of these were major political centres, notably the great capital at Ctesiphon, which the Arabs called al-Mada'in (the cities) because it seemed to have so many different parts to it. Many others were smaller provincial towns which have left little trace in the archaeological record, in no little part due to the fact that they were built of mud

---

[12] Tsafrir and Foerster, "Urbanism at Scythopolis," 139.

brick. Scientific investigation of these sites has been almost entirely confined to field surveys. This can be very useful in suggesting the overall areas of settlement in certain periods, but cannot give us any idea of the use made of inherited street plans or building types. The early Arab geographers give almost lyrical descriptions of the prosperity of small towns like Dayr al-'Aqūl and Fam al-Silh with their mosques and palm trees clustered on the banks of canals. Many of these towns were not, by Mesopotamian standards, ancient settlements at all but had developed during the great expansion of agriculture in the area that had occurred during the Sasanian period. The characteristic urban settlement of the Sasanian period was the small market town rather than the great metropolis.

A typical town of the area was Nahrawan,[13] where the road to the Iranian plateau crossed the canal of that name. Ibn Rustah, at the beginning of the tenth century, describes arriving at Nahrawan, "through which a canal flows," after travelling for four leagues from Baghdad through continuous palm groves and cultivated fields. "On the west bank (of the canal) are suqs, a congregational mosque and water wheels (*nawafir*) which irrigate its fields. There is also a congregational mosque on the east side and around the mosque are caravansarais (*khanat*) for pilgrims passing through the town."[14] The town is also said to have housed a large Jewish community. Field survey suggests that the west bank settlement was already in decline by the tenth century, and by the time Muqaddasi was writing in the late tenth century the east bank mosque was the only one still in use. By the eleventh century, the site was effectively deserted.

In Sasanian times, Uskaf Bani Junayd[15] was the largest town in the Diyala river basin after the capital, al-Mada'in itself, covering about four square kilometres. It continued to be inhabited in the early Islamic period and, unusually for the small towns of the area, boasted an Umayyad-period palace, presumably built for the Banu Junayd lords who gave their name to the Arab town. At the same time a mosque was built over abandoned Sasanian constructions. This early Islamic prosperity did not last: surface survey suggests that by the tenth century the settlement only covered about twenty hectares, a twentieth of its

---

[13] Robert Adams, *The Land Behind Baghdad: a History of Settlement on the Diyala Plains* (Chicago, 1965), 91–92.

[14] Ibn Rustah, *al-A'laq al-nafisa*, ed. Michaël Jan de Goeje (Leiden, 1892), 163.

[15] Adams, *The Land Behind Baghdad*, 95–96.

greatest extent in the Sasanian period. And this settlement, at the heart
of the old city, must have been surrounded by mounds of rubble. At the
end of the eleventh century a little minaret was added to the mosque
and the rooms of the palace were divided by rough partitions to house
occupants of much lower status. After that the ancient settlement was
entirely abandoned.

Ctesiphon (Ar. al-Mada'in) was indeed a number of cities.[16] Ardashir
I had founded a roughly circular city officially called Weh-Ardashir.
This seems to have remained the centre of government and the winter
residence of the Sasanian Shahs until the middle of the fifth century
when the Tigris shifted its course and divided the city in two. It was
probably after this that a new Ctesiphon was developed to the south
and east of the round city and it was here that the Sasanians, probably
in the sixth century, created the great arched reception hall, still known
today as the Ivan-i Kisra (Iwan or portico of Chosroes). The Sasanian
palace astonished early Muslim builders and has survived, at least in
part, to the present day. Parts of the city continued to be inhabited
after the Muslim conquest. However, it lost its political role with the
foundation of the Muslim new towns of Kufa and Basra: this transition
is given symbolic form as the gates of Ctesiphon are said to have been
removed to Kufa. The establishment of Baghdad must have been a
further blow. At the end of the ninth century it was still a prosperous
market town with two congregational mosques and a *sūq*[17] but it was
probably abandoned during the eleventh. Excavation on the site has
been patchy and it is difficult to assess the extent to which Sasanian
structures were reused and adapted in the Muslim period.

The inherited towns of Iraq suffered from the establishment of new
Muslim cities. Kufa and Basra attracted settlers away from the old
towns and the development of the megalopolis of Baghdad sucked
commerce and ambitious inhabitants away from the old centres. But
it was above all the decline in the irrigation systems from the ninth
century onwards which destroyed the prosperity and vitality of the
towns.[18] By end of the eleventh century, virtually none of the towns

---

[16] For an overview of the history of the city with full bibliography, J. Kroger, s.v.
"Ctesiphon," in *Encyclopaedia Iranica*. Also s.v. "Ayvan-e Kesra," which gives a sketch
plan of the site.

[17] Ibn Rustah, *al-Aʿlaq*, 186.

[18] David Waines, "The Third-century Internal Crisis of the ʿAbbasids," *Journal of
the Economic and Social History of the Orient* 20 (1978): 282–303; Hugh Kennedy, "The
Decline and Fall of the First Muslim Empire," *Der Islam* 81 (2004): 3–30.

the Muslim conquerors had inherited from the Sasanians still existed as urban settlements.

Cities of Iran

As in the cases of Syria and Iraq, our understanding of the way in which the Muslims used and developed the cities they inherited is constrained by the nature of the archaeological evidence. Despite recent work in Merv[19] and Samarqand,[20] and some earlier soundings and surveys in Fars in Istakhr and Gur/Firuzabad, there is not a city in greater Iran, which has been explored sufficiently to give us an overview of change through this period. We have not, for example, been able to recover the detailed plan of a major urban mosque from the pre-Seljuk period[21] or to see how new religious buildings fitted into the existing urban fabric.

In some areas, the pre-Islamic cities were replaced by newly founded centres. The clearest example of this comes from Fars in Southwest Iran where the Islamic new town of Shiraz supplanted the ancient urban centres. The site of Shiraz itself seems to have shifted from the hill-top fortress now known as Qasr-i Abu Nasr to the nearby site of modern Shiraz in the plains.[22] This process of what might be termed *decastellamento*, the move from the small, fortified site to the larger, open position may be typical of other Iranian cities. Other Farsi towns survived as small centres and Gur/Firuzabad became an important political capital again in the tenth century. In the province of Kirman to the east, the Sasanian and early Islamic capital at Sirjan had been replaced by Kirman city by the eleventh century.

In some of the provincial capitals of Fars (Istakhr, Arrajan, Bishapur, Gur/Firuzabad, and Darabjird) there is archaeological evidence for the

---

[19] Georgina Hermann, *Monuments of Merv* (London, 1999).

[20] Frantz Grenet, "De la Samarkand antique a la Samarkand islamique: continuités et ruptures," *Colloque International de Archéolgie Islamique, 1993* (Cairo, 1998), 387–402.

[21] The only partial exceptions are the Tarik-khana at Damghan of the eighth or ninth century and the mosque at Na'in, probably of the tenth. Neither of these, however, was a major city nor is it clear how the mosques fitted in to the contemporary urban context. On the early mosques of Iran see Barbara Finster, *Frühe Iranische Moscheen* (Berlin, 1994).

[22] On Sasanian and early Islamic Shiraz, Donald Whitcomb, *Before the Roses and Nightingales: Excavations at Qasr-i Abu Nasr, Old Shiraz* (New York, 1985).

establishment of early Islamic settlements alongside the existing Sasanian cities, contingent extensions.[23] At Istakhr the early Islamic city was a walled enclosure some 400m square, with a mosque and a bazaar in the centre. At Bishapur, part of the early Islamic settlement lay in the gardens to the west of the Sasanian monumental city but evidence also suggests that some of the formal architecture of this Sasanian royal site was adapted to be used as mosques. In the round city of Gur, the early Islamic settlement seems to have occupied a segment of the original enclosure. In the case of the five provincial capitals of Fars, the written and archaeological evidence demonstrate continued occupation, and perhaps expansion, in Sasanian and early Islamic times, followed by decay and desertion from the eleventh century on.

In Khurasan the cities which had been important in the pre-Islamic period continued to be centres of population and political power down to the Mongol invasions. Rayy, Nishapur, Merv, Balkh, Bukhara, and Samarqand all throve on their Sasanian sites, though, as we shall see, they changed in other ways. In Khwarazm, Kath remained the provincial capital and on the steppe frontier to the southeast of the Caspian, Jurjan remained a city of importance.

Continuity of site did not mean continuity of urban topography. Throughout the region we see Sasanian cities expanding far beyond their ancient fortified nuclei and developing new suburbs, suburbs which sometimes came to replace the old city as centres of power and high status dwelling.

Probably the clearest example of this is the city of Nishapur.[24] The city that the Arab conquerors found consisted of an ovoid citadel or *quhandiz* on one side of a rectanctular *shahristan* or inner city. These were both surrounded by mud-brick ramparts which can be clearly distinguished in aerial photography. There is no evidence of an extensive *rabad* or outer city beyond these limits. Bulliet calculates the area of the city to have been approximately 17.6 hectares and, using a density of

---

[23] See Donald Whitcomb, "Trade and Tradition in Medieval Southern Iran" (Unpublished Ph.D. thesis, University of Chicago, 1979). I am very grateful to Professor Whitcomb for having provided me with a copy of this. On urbanism at Bishapur, see R. Ghirshman, *Fouilles de Châpour: Bîchâpour I* (Paris, 1971), 21–36; on Arrajan, Heinz Gaube, *Die Südpersische Provinz Arragan: Küh-Gilüyeh von der Arabischen Eroberung bis zur Safawidenzeit* (Vienna, 1973); on Darabjird, Peter Morgan, "Some Remarks on a Preliminary Survey in Eastern Fars," *Iran* 41 (2003): 323–338.

[24] See Richard Bulliet, "Medieval Nishapur: a topographic and demographic reconstruction," *Studia Iranica* 5 (1976): 67–89.

between one and two hundred people per hectare, suggests a population of between 1,760 and 3,520: this was, as he remarks, "scarcely more than a garrison for protecting the trade route through Khurasan."[25]

During the nine-month siege of the city by the troops of Abd Allah ibn ʿAmir at the time of the first Muslim conquests a mosque was built outside the walls of the city and after it was taken, another mosque was built on the site of the chief fire temple, a symbolic appropriation of the chief religious site. In the three centuries between the Arab conquest and the descriptions given by the geographers, al-Istakhri and Ibn Hawqal, the city expanded enormously. A large new mosque, known as Jamiʿ al-ʿatiq or the Old Mosque, of which traces can still be identified, was constructed to the south of the city. A new commercial quarter was developed immediately to the west of the old city. This is described in the Arabic sources as a *murabbaʿa* and it would seem to have taken the form of a crossroads with markets along each of the four streets which led from it; this seems to have been an early example of the *charsū* (*chahar sūq*, or four markets) which was to be characteristic of later Iranian towns. By Ibn Hawqal's time the markets seem to have stretched for about two kilometres from east to west.

On the other sides of the market from the old city, the Muslim authorities constructed a *Dar al-imara* or government house at an unknown date in the first two Islamic centuries. It is noteworthy that the new centre of government was not in the old *quhandiz* fortress but in an apparently unwalled site some two kilometres away. In the early ninth century, under the rule of the Tahirids, Nishapur became the capital of the entire province of Khurasan and an entirely new official quarter, the Shadyakh was constructed some further to the west.

By the late tenth century, when the city reached its maximum extent, it was probably about six kilometres across. Bulliet estimates a built up area of roughly 1,680 hectares. This would give a population of up to 336,000 but allowing for open spaces and low densities in some areas, he is inclined to suggest a population of between 110,000 and 220,000.[26]

Many of the same trends can be seen in the history of Merv. Merv was a major city, the principal Sasanian outpost on the northeast frontier of the Empire and the seat of the *marzban* who was responsible

---

[25] Bulliet, "Medieval Nishapur," 87.
[26] Bulliet, "Medieval Nishapur," 88.

for the defence of the area. As at Nishapur, the ancient city comprised a roughly oval citadel (known here as the Erk Kale or Citadel Castle), which was situated on one edge of a sub-rectangular *shahristan* nowadays called Gyaur Kale (Castle of the Unbelievers). Despite the similarities of form, everything at Merv was on a vastly greater scale than Nishapur. The citadel alone is about 20 hectares, larger than both *quhandiz* and *shahristan* of Nishapur combined. The rectangular city is about two kilometres square. This would give an area of around 400 hectares and, using Bulliet's multipliers, between 40,000 and 80,000 inhabitants, though it is not clear that the whole area within the walls was ever built up, still less clear that it was built up at the time of the Muslim conquest in 650.

As at Nishapur, the first centuries of Muslim rule of Merv saw the expansion of the city beyond the walls of the Sasanian site. A whole new quarter with mosques and markets grew up to the west of the old walled enclosure along the banks of the Majan canal. It was here that Abu Muslim built his great new *dar al-imara* after he took control of the city in the name of the Abbasids in 747. As at Nishapur again, this extension remained unwalled throughout the early Islamic period and was only fortified during the reign of the Seljuk Malik Shah (1072–92). Meanwhile, the ancient citadel was neglected and gradually fell into complete disuse and much of the rectangular Gyaur Kale was used for industrial purposes (steel making) or was simply abandoned.

In Samarqand the process was different. Here the old *quhandiz* was abandoned but the mound on which it stood became the site of the new mosque and when Abu Muslim built a new *dar al-imara* in Samarqand, he chose to construct it high on the flanks of the ancient citadel. New commercial quarters grew up outside the ramparts of the old city.

Merv is one of the rare sites where we can find something of Sasanian domestic architecture and this is important because in the old Gyaur Kale, the Sasanian city, an area of housing has been uncovered which shows what might be thought of as a traditional Islamic street, narrow and winding and bordered by small courtyard houses, the same general plan, in fact, that could be found in Iranian cities right down to the twentieth century. The Sasanian houses seem to have been the last built on the site and we cannot see how, if at all, the coming of the Muslims affected the built environment they had inherited.

The pattern of urban development from the comparatively small Sasanian core to the much more extensive early Islamic city is a common feature of Iranian urban history. Archaeology plays its part in uncovering these trends but literary evidence often points in the same direction.[27] On the basis of his analysis of textual evidence, Richard Bulliet has argued that, "the ninth century witnessed the most rapid growth of cities in Iranian history."[28] Without exception, these were inherited cities, expanded far beyond their ancient cores: there were virtually no Islamic new towns in the Iranian lands of the caliphate.

Explanations for this phenomenon vary. Watson has suggested that improved agricultural techniques and new crops allowed the development of a market- orientated agriculture which in turn permitted the development of very large cities.[29] This view has been criticized by Bulliet who argues that the importance of these changes was marginal at best.[30] He argues that the key factor is conversion to Islam which encouraged, even forced, converts to leave their rural communities, where the old beliefs and social ties still ruled, and move into the Muslim environment of the city. This is an attractive hypothesis but it may underestimate the importance of state structures. The early Islamic state made regular cash payments to a large number of people, mostly in the military: it created, in fact, a very numerous salariat. This was a market no enterprising tradesman or would-be cook and bottle-washer could afford to neglect. Merv, for example, was where the military campaigns against the rich cities of Transoxania were organized in the eighth century, it was here that the soldiers were paid and it was here that they sold their shares of the booty in the markets: no wonder immigrants from all over Khurasan flocked to the newly expanding market areas to cash in. On a larger or smaller scale, this pattern must have been repeated all over the Islamic East.

It can also be argued that the political and military elites moved into cities after the Muslim conquest. The admittedly scanty evidence suggests that great Iranian families of the Sasanian period lived in rural castles and palaces and that the major fire temples were in rural locations, often remote from urban centres: the Sasanian kings were

---

[27] Richard Bulliet, *Islam: the View from the Edge* (New York, 1994), 73–75.
[28] Bulliet, *Islam*, 77.
[29] Michael Watson, *Agricultural innovation in the early Islamic world* (Cambridge, 1983), 132–136.
[30] Bulliet, *Islam*, 67–70.

crowned in Ctesiphon, but the religious part of their inauguration took place in Shiz (Masjid-i Sulayman) in the Zagros mountains, far to the north-east. Apart from Ctesiphon and Bishapur, there is little evidence for elite residences within the walls of Sasanian towns.

Al-Andalus and the Muslim West[31]

In Roman times, the Iberian peninsula boasted a significant number of cities, some of them among the most important in the entire empire. Many of these sites came under Muslim rule in the years following the initial conquest of 711. Of the major provincial capitals, Braga (Gallaecia) was never really settled by the Muslims and Tarragona (Tarrconensis) was in a frontier zone and seems to have been mostly deserted in the early Islamic period. Toledo (Carthaginensis), Mérida (Lusitania) and Seville (Baetica) all became significant Muslim centres. In addition, Zaragoza, a Roman city, which had not been as important in classical times, became the centre of Muslim power in the Ebro valley and Córdoba, again a second rank city in the Roman hierarchy became the capital of the whole of al-Andalus.

The extent to which the Roman cities of the peninsula had retained their urban aspect through the troubles of the fifth century and more than two hundred years of Visigothic rule is not clear. There is almost no evidence for Visigothic building within cities, either ecclesiastical or secular, and in many sites it is difficult to find any traces of occupation during this period. While many Muslim cities occupied the sites of their ancient predecessors and sheltered within the remains of the late Roman walls, it is only in Zaragoza and the small Andalusian city of Ecija that we can find traces of the survival of the regular street plans of the classical period, although at Zaragoza, this apparent continuity masked major changes in the physical structure of the city in late antiquity.[32] While the Umayyad capital at Damascus preserved the

---

[31] For late antique cities in the Iberian peninsula see Michael Kulikowski, *Late Roman Spain and Its Cities* (Baltimore and London, 2004). On early Islamic cities in the peninsula and Morocco, Vincente Salvatierra Cuenca, "The Origins of al-Andalus," in *The Archaeology of Iberia*, ed. Margarita Diaz-Andreu and Simon Keay (London, 1997), 263–278; Patrice Cressier and Mercedes Garcia-Arenal, eds., *Genèse de la ville islamique en al-Andalus et au Maghreb occidental* (Madrid, 1998). For a more general introduction to urbanism in al-Andalus, Basilio Pavón, *Ciudades Hispanomusulmanas* (Madrid, 1992).

[32] See Kulikowski, *Late Roman Cities*, 244–249.

outlines of classical planning, these seem to have been entirely lost in
the Umayyad capital of Córdoba. This disappearance of urban plan
and fabric may be evidence for a real hiatus in urban life in the fifth
and sixth centuries.

The story of Córdoba is especially revealing in this respect.[33] The
ancient city had bordered the northern bank of the Guadalquivir river
at the end of the Roman bridge. At the end of the third century, a
large palatial complex, known to the twentieth-century excavators as
the Cercadilla, was constructed.[34] This probably served as the palace
of the provincial governor and the local administrative centre. Some
of the decorative materials were spolia from the now disused theatre
and it is possible that some of the old city intra-muros fell into ruin at
this time and the remaining population clustered in the southern area
close to the banks of the river. Here a large church of San Vicente was
constructed at the bridgehead as well as a later palace for the governor.
It was this complex which became the centre of Muslim power when
the governor al-Hurr b. ʿAbd al-Rahman al-Thaqafi established the city
as his capital in the city in 716 and constructed a new palace to the
west of the existing urban centre. Al-Samh b. Malik al-Khawlani, governor between 719 and 721 undertook a major programme of repairs,
restoring the Roman bridge, which seems to have been in ruins, and
sections of the Roman walls. He also established cemeteries and two
musallas (prayer places) in the suburbs. It was probably during the rule
of Yūsuf al-Fihri (748–56) that the Christians were deprived of the
main church of San Vicente which was converted into a mosque. The
earliest sections of the present building of the Great Mosque date from
786 when the first Umayyad Amir, ʿAbd al-Rahman I, demolished the
existing structure and used the materials to construct a purpose built
mosque.[35] From this time on the Christians and Jews were relegated to
churches and synagogues in the suburbs and the old city was completely
Islamized. In the tenth century, the population seems to have increased

---

[33] For Córdoba see Manuel Acién Almansa and Antonio Vallejo Triano, "Urbanismo
y Estado islámico: de *Corduba* a *Qurtuba-Madinat al-Zahara*," in Cressier and Garcia-
Arenal, eds., *Genèse* 107–136.

[34] For the Cercadilla and its effect on the city, Kulikowski, *Late Roman Spain*,
114–120.

[35] For a recent account of the mosque with further bibliographic references, Marianne Barrucand and Achim Bednorz, *Moorish Architecture in Andalusia* (Cologne, 1992),
39–46; on the use of classical and Visigothic spolia, Patrice Cressier, "Les chapiteaux
de la Grande Mosquée de Cordoue," *Madrider Mitteilungen* 25 (1994): 257–313.

very considerably and new suburbs were constructed on a large scale,
especially to the west of the city. As in many eastern examples, these
new suburbs remained unfortified. The drift to the west culminated
in the foundation of the new palace city of Madinat al-Zahra in the
mid-tenth century, some five kilometres away.

The antique legacy of the city of Toledo within the medieval fortifications has been obliterated beyond recall. In Seville we can only
find a few traces; it has been suggested that there was a forum on the
site of the Plaza San Salvador and that site of the church itself was a
Christian basilica, then the first mosque of the city, traces of which can
still be seen, until it became a Christian church once more. Mérida was
one of the great Roman cities of Spain and its magnificent ruins still
testify to its antique grandeur. By the time of the Muslim conquest its
main claim to fame was probably the shrine of Santa Eulalia, whose
cult brought pilgrims thronging to the city.[36] It was perhaps because of
this communal identity that the city is said to have put up a prolonged
resistance to the invaders. After the conquest it seems as if the local
elites soon converted to Islam and that city life continued within the
old Roman walls. Traffic across the Roman bridge, which still survives,
brought trade to the city. Some time around middle of the ninth century,
the shrine of Santa Eulalia was abandoned and the relics removed and
this seems to mark the end of Christianity as the dominant religion in
the city. The Amir ʿAbd al-Rahman II was determined to impose central
control over the *muwallad* (native Muslim) aristocracy of the city and in
855 he ordered the construction of a citadel by the river on the site of
a *xenodochium* built in Visigothic times to house pilgrims.[37] In this castle
he based a garrison of troops sent from Córdoba. It also contained a
cistern, which became the main water supply of the town when the
Roman aqueducts fell into disuse. When the Méridans continued to
be restive, Muhammad I ordered the demolition of the old city wall
and the city, thus exposed, began to decline and never became one of
the great cities of al-Andalus. When the caliphate of Córdoba split up
in the early eleventh century, it was not Mérida but the Islamic new
town of Badajoz which became the capital of the Taifa kingdom and
which controlled the area.

---

[36] On late antique Mérida, see Kulikowski, *Late Roman Cities*, 91–92, 290–293.
[37] Barrucand and Bednorz, *Moorish Architecture*, 27.

Morocco was much less urbanized than al-Andalus at the time of the arrival of the Muslims. With the exception of the northern coastal cities of Tangier and Ceuta, the country had been abandoned by the Roman administration in 285. Despite this, urban life continued in Volubilis, the best-preserved ancient city in the area.[38] In the late sixth century, the perimeter wall was shortened and much of the old monumental centre was left outside but some of the domestic quarters of the city were still lived in. The Muslims seem to have adopted the city as a base in the area and there is some numismatic evidence that there was an Abbasid garrison in second half of the eighth century. The first of the Idrisid rulers took it as his capital and the city seems to have expanded beyond the late antique walls and a new quarter with a bathhouse emerged. No trace of any mosque has yet been found and tradition says that Idris (d. 789) chose to be buried outside the city. The role of Volublis/Walila as capital of the first Muslim state in Morocco was brought to an end with the foundation of Fez and the inherited city was soon deserted for a new one.

The governance of the inherited city

The question of how far the Muslim conquests affected the social structure of the cities they inherited is a difficult one to answer. Clearly there was in many cases a new elite, a ruling class drawn from the dominant Arab/Muslim community. People who had previously been distinguished and respected citizens would have found their properties confiscated while they themselves were forced to pay the shameful poll-tax or even became slaves. The story of the Hamdani family of Isfahan may be typical. The first member of the family we know of was a landowner (*dehqan*) called Ajlan who had property in the rural area around the city, which consisted of two small urban nuclei, one called Yahūdiya and another called Jayy. When the Arab armies came to the area, he was taken prisoner and transported to the Muslim metropolis of Kufa in Iraq. Here he converted to Islam. He had two sons born in Kufa but when they grew up they returned to Isfahan and reclaimed

---

[38] See Aomar Akerraz, "Recherches sur les niveaux islamiques de Volubilis," in *Genèse*, ed. Cressier and Garcia-Arenal, 295–304 and Ahmed Siraj, "Vie et mort d' une cité islamique," in the same volume, 285–294.

their father's lands. They did not become country squires as he had
done, but moved into the developing city where one of them became
an authority on Islamic law and tradition, which is how we come to
know about them.[39]

It is impossible to know how far the experience of Ajlan and his family was typical and, in more general times, how much continuity there
was between urban elites in the period before and after the Muslim
conquests. We can see the example of the family of Sarjun/Sergius
in Damascus who served the early Umayyads as financial officials and
whose history we know a little about because the last recorded member
of the family was the great theologian, St John of Damascus.

At an institutional level, the cities the Muslims inherited had little to
pass on. Neither the Byzantine nor the Sasanian world had a tradition
of civic autonomy at the time of the Islamic conquests. In the first
two and a half centuries of the Common Era the cities of the Roman
Near East had enjoyed a high degree of local self-government, choosing
their own councils, collecting their own taxes, and minting their own
copper coinage. From the crisis of the third century, these structures
disappeared: real power in the late antique city was exercised by the
governor appointed by the imperial authorities, taxes were collected
by the imperial bureaucracy, and the copper coinage disappeared. The
abolition of the temple cults on which so much civic patriotism had
been focused simply accelerated the process and though the Christian
bishop was a leading citizen and the cults of the local saints could
provide a focus for local patriotism, they did not enjoy the institutional
status of the vanished town councils.[40] In the Iranian world, any lingering traditions of civic government brought in by the Macedonian
colonists of Alexander's army were long since extinct. There might be
rich and influential local citizens, but there were no institutional structures through which they could articulate their power. In this sphere
the coming of Islamic rule simply continued late antique practice. It
is not until the tenth and eleventh centuries that we find civic leaders
ruling towns and then only in certain areas, northern Syria, and al-
Andalus for example, where the other political structures were weak.
In these areas the *qadi* sometimes emerged as a real representative of

---

[39] Bulliet, *Islam*, 78–79.
[40] For the effects of different power structures in two late antique cities, Hugh Kennedy, "Gerasa and Scythopolis: Power and Patronage in the Byzantine Cities of Bilad
al-Sham," *Bulletin d'Études Orientales* 52 (2000): 199–204.

local interests but, in contrast to the Italian cities of the same period, there never developed any political theory or institutional structures to sustain this fragile autonomy.

Conclusions

The idea that the Arab armies burst in on and destroyed the static and unchanging world of antiquity is very misleading. The Muslim conquerors of the seventh and eighth century came to rule over rapidly changing societies. This picture of change is as true of the cities of these areas as it is true of any other aspect of life. In the ex-Roman areas, the classical cities whose ruins we visit and admire and whose image still represents a certain sort of perfect urbanism, had changed almost out of recognition: it was the narrow winding streets and churches, large and small, that the Muslims inherited, not the fora, colonnaded streets, and monumental buildings. The fate of these inherited towns varied enormously, from expansion and renewed vigour in the cases of Aleppo, Merv, or Córdoba, to virtual extinction in Caesarea, Istakhr, or Volubilis. Some cities were destroyed by the development of Islamic new towns nearby which sucked their vitality and drew away their inhabitants: Ctesiphon/al-Mada'in could not survive the building of Baghdad, nor could Istakhr thrive in the shadow of Shiraz. In many cases the fate of cities was decided by political decisions: those cities that became centres of government and Arab settlement developed and prospered. This was not just because they became official cities where the bureaucrats and military lived but because in the early Islamic state, the government and its functionaries were the most important generators of economic activity. Courts of caliphs and governors alike spent money on buildings and fine textiles, ceramics and metal work. The soldiers and bureaucrats went into the suqs to buy the necessities of everyday life and such luxuries as they could afford. Merchants and craftsmen flocked to provide goods and services and the government town expanded into a business and commercial centre. The inherited cities formed an essential foundation to the urbanism of the early Muslim world but the ways the Muslims used this inheritance varied enormously from place to place.

FOUNDED CITIES OF THE ARAB WORLD FROM THE SEVENTH TO THE ELEVENTH CENTURIES

Sylvie Denoix

The subject of founded cities has application to the fairly extended period within which cities of major significance were created. As such, the present contribution deals not with any specific age but with social phenomena arising at moments of history that may be far distant from one another and may exhibit a variety of facets. Depending on the precise time they were created, these settlements are reflections of one or another dynamic (the Muslim conquest, for example, or the accession of a new dynasty) and are peopled by one or another type of society. Herein lie, already, initial elements of differentiation.

Since the topic of founded cities concerns the initial moment only, not the development of these cities down the centuries, we shall in each case limit consideration to a study of the original age or of successive foundations on the same site (the latter case permitting a study of these phenomena over a particular period of time)—even though these cities do, like other cities, develop from the point of view of population, functions, spatial organization, and so on. The first questions, therefore, are to establish what the founders' urban project was and what appearance the city bore at that time. A further point is that the accession of a dynasty was often the occasion for the foundation of cities designed to act as capitals. The subsequent progress of the dynasty in question will obviously be crucial for the expansion of these particular cities.

Moreover, even if part of the monuments and the street network date from the original period of the cities under study, there is no question of searching for traces of hypothetical origins in these; it is not our purpose, therefore, to study the medinas and ancient quarters as they have come down to us.

There were, throughout history, so many cities founded by the Arabs that it would be an illusory exercise to try to make an exhaustive list, still more to attempt to consider them all. The aim here will simply be to bring out the different types of foundation, and, also, to provide a few short accounts concerning certain of these foundations—those that have, perhaps, most caught the imagination of later writers.

Thus, cities that turned out to have no future—like the city-camp of Jabiyya, the Umayyad city of ʿAnjar, or the city-fortress of Qalʿat Bani Hammad—left less impression on people's minds than Kufa, Basra, or Baghdad.

We know the expansion of Islam took effect within highly urbanized lands, and that a certain number of cities there (Antioch, Aleppo, Damascus, Alexandria, and so on) were inherited from previous civilizations. In the earliest times, the conquerors—coming to these places with their mounts and their camels, and being organized into tribes unaccustomed to urban life—preferred other types of settlement, city-camps, which were more suited to their present social organization than the former cities in which they settled. Nevertheless as a sign that their first choice was not a mark of mistrust, they even chose one of these, Damascus, as the capital for their first dynasty. At the time of the Conquest, under the caliphate of ʿUmar b. al-Khattab, Muslims had as supreme guide a man who remained in Arabia, and who issued orders regarding both small practical details and crucial decisions (the site of a provincial capital, for instance) through letters conveyed by mounts to troop commanders; nor had the Arabs yet assimilated the cultural characteristics of the civilizations they conquered. In the first decades they established themselves, therefore, in new settlements more adapted to most of the combatants' way of life and more in accord with the expectations of the Medinan caliph. As for the first caliphs outside Arabia, the Umayyads, they opted for local continuity by choosing Damascus as their capital. Even so, they built small mansions for themselves in the Syrian Desert; domains where they lived with their attendants in their own way, hunting and enjoying worldly pleasures at a certain distance from the populations they governed. These foundations are not cities and will not, accordingly, be considered here.

Subsequently, Muslims both populated cities in existence before their arrival and founded urban centres of greater or lesser importance. It was often the accession of a new dynasty that provided the opportunity for these new foundations.

As with any subject of study, our knowledge of these cities is dependent on available documentation. For most of the cities in question, there are no contemporary texts for the initial era. Neither the foundations of the period of Muslim conquest nor those subsequent to it had any direct witnesses supplying accounts of facts and descriptions of places. We are, therefore, virtually always obliged to work through the mediation of later sources. Thus, the first account of the foundation of Baghdad dates from 278/891—more than one century, that is, after the events described. We also have available early writings for which the manuscripts are lost, but which we can read as handed down by subsequent authors. For instance, taking Baghdad once more, we have Ibn Sarabiyun, Hilal al-Sabi, and Ahmad b. Abi Tahir Tayfur, who were quoted by Khatib al-Baghdadi (see F. Micheau, infra). For Basra we have ʿUmar b. Shabba al-Madaʾini, Saji, and Ibn ʿArabi. And we have knowledge of Fatimid Qahira thanks to Ibn Tuwayr, who was quoted by the fourteenth–fifteenth century writers Ibn al-Furat and al-Maqrizi,[1] Qalqashandi, and Ibn Taghri Birdi. Ibn Tuwayr, it should be noted, is similarly not a witness to the foundation of Qahira, since he is writing at the end of the period of the Fatimid caliphs and the beginning of the Ayyubid dynasty. In view of this, archaeology is an especially precious tool for our understanding of the phenomenon of founded cities where excavations have taken place involving these high periods.

Not only are sources not always available from direct witnesses. Over and above this, founded cities—mythical because original, and, by virtue of this, exerting a special force on the imagination—have been liable to give rise to particular representations. Such cities are often said to have originated with a saint or, sometimes, with a conqueror. In all cases, the myth is there to glorify the initial period. Something of the *baraka* from this period then falls in turn on the later inhabitants and the sources, even those written centuries later, contain the echo of these representations.

1. *Cities founded in the period of Conquest and the urban creations attendant on these*

The cities founded in the period of the Muslim Conquest were city-camps (*misr*, plural *amsar*) set up by a commander and his troops on strategic sites at the crossing of routes, thus, allowing control of a whole region. The first of these (al-Jabiyya in Syria, Basra and Kufa in Iraq,

---

[1] The parts of Ibn Tuwayr's text quoted by Maqrizi have been published by Ayman Fuʾad Sayyid.

and Fustat in Egypt) were erected under the first two caliphs, that
is, at the very outset of Islam, a period when it was felt necessary to
keep a link with Arabia. "No river [*bahr*] between you and me!" wrote
'Umar b. al-Khattab, with general application.[2] The sites chosen were,
therefore, at points of contact between the old world of the Arabs and
the new conquered lands.

A common process is evident in these establishments. The conquerors set out an encampment on a carefully selected site. However,
with the outcome of the war still uncertain, there was no guarantee
the camp would become a city. As such, it was impossible to initi-
ate any ceremonial for foundation; those who were there contented
themselves with a camp serving as a base for the mounts and for the
combined tribes while the Conquest went on. Then, with the battles
won and the region made secure, they established themselves more
permanently on the site where they had first settled provisionally. This
process explains the lack of any ritual for cities born in the Conquest
period. It is rather a question of an encampment for tribes at war; one
which then became permanent once victory was felt to be assured and
a lengthier settlement became possible: allotting plots of land (generic
term *khitta*, plural *khitat*) on a final basis (this model of equipment is the
takhtit, or *ikhtitat*), building in sustainable material, and equipping the
site with an institutional infrastructure that provided the territory with
some buildings of a political and cultural nature, i.e., the governorate
headquarters (*dar al-imara*) and the mosque. Areas not allotted (*fada* at
Fustat, *sahara* at Kufa) were reserved.

These urban establishments give rise to the following question:
do the particular means of social organization entail the land being
occupied in particular ways? One section of the Arabs (and even of
the converts of non-Arab origin, the *mawla*s) making up the population of these camp-cities—notably those of highest status, like certain
Yemenis, or like the Qurayshis, some of them formerly Companions
of the Prophet—were former city-dwellers. A case in point is the
élite of Fustat, people like 'Amr b. al-'As, 'Uqba b. Nafi', Kharija b.
Hudhafa (all Qurayshis), or Maslama b. Mukhallad (a Yemeni previously settled in Medina). Another case is the élite of Kufa, those such
as Talha, Zubayr, Usama, the Prophet's son-in-law, 'Amr b. Harith

---

[2] For the case of Kufa, see Baladhuri, *Kitab futuh al-buldan* (Beirut: Maktabat al-
Hilal, 1973), 270.

Khuza'i, Sa'd, Abu Musa Ash'ari, and so on. These city-dwellers, thus, developed urban establishments. In contrast, members of tribes not urbanized before the Conquest (the greater part of the combatants) were not city-dwellers but Yemenis or northern Arabs coming, in tribes, from the *badiyya*, whether they had been sedentary there or not. This population established itself in encampments on grants of land allotted to them tribe by tribe, whereas the aristocracy among the conquerors received individual grants for urban occupation. This dual system of allotment wherein grants were, in some *misr*s, called, respectively, *khitta*s and *dar*s (for Fustat) or *qati'a* (for Kufa) had previously been instituted by the Prophet himself in Medina.[3] As for the social group of *mawla*s, indigenous non-Arabs, it found protection alongside the Arabs in a relationship of patronage; such people were, for the most part, rural dwellers who became urbanized by settling in *misr*s on lands granted to their "masters," and espousing the tribal rivalries of these. In the long run, members of tribes adopted the urban model of the camp-cities élite, and became urbanized accordingly.

Basra

The building of a new city raises the issue of an earlier permanent population, and of the urban influence of older centres. Basra was erected on the remains of a Persian site in Lower Mesopotamia, a site the Arabs named al-Khurayba ("the small ruin"). Even so, it may be regarded as a new creation, in so far as little remained of the previous establishment when the Arabs settled on the site. As for influences, might Qaryat al-Faw,[4] an Arabian village situated around 680 kilometres to the south of present-day Riyadh, have been one of the models for Basra?

Events unfolded according to a classic pattern. In 14/635 the conquerors set up an encampment. In 17/638, three years after this initial settlement, under the caliphate of 'Umar b. al-Khattab, the military commander 'Utba b. Ghazwan chose this location as a permanent site, to serve as the base for a further advance of the Conquest towards Fars,

---

[3] "The Prophet himself in Medina . . . granted the *khitta*s for the different tribes and the *dar*s for individuals." Hathloul, *Al-Madina 'l-islamiyya* (Riyadh, n.d.), 54.
[4] Abdul-Rahman Attayib al-Ansariy, "Qaryat dhat kahl: al-Fau," in *Sciences Sociales et Phénomènes Urbains dans le Monde Arabe*, ed. M. Naciri and A. Raymond (Casablanca: Fondation du roi Abdul-Aziz Al Saoud et les sciences humaines, 1994), 13–22.

Khurasan, and Sijistan. In due course the spoils from these territories
reached Basra, and the new city-dwellers had the means to set in place
the elements of a high-grade urban infrastructure.

Various types of building material correspond to different stages of
the settlement: simple twined reeds, of the kind found on the banks of
the Euphrates, for a provisional dwelling; constructions of unfired brick,
as a sign of a slightly more permanent settlement; finally, in 50/670,
under the governorate of Ziyad b. Abi Sufyan, fired bricks. It was at
this point that the urban centre was set in place, with the provision
of such things as the governorate headquarters, the mosque with the
Muslim Treasury, the *bayt al-mal*, and a river port on the Euphrates.
The centre included services like canalizations of water. As with other
camp-cities, we are dealing here with a settlement of conquerors on
the offensive, having no need of defensive walls.[5] The classic institutions
are there, too: a governorate (the governor fulfilling the function of
imam), a police force, and so on. For the tribes the city was divided into
"fifths" (*khums*, plural *akhmas*), each of the five branches (Ahl al-ʿAliya,
Tamim, Bakr b. Waʾil, ʿAbd al-Qays, and Azd) having its territory, on
which settled the allies, the converts, the *mawali*, etc. This kind of land
occupation endured for quite some time. Thus, the first rampart of
Basra, dating from the Abbasid period, embraced the extensive area
of the city occupied by the tribes and their mounts. The second—that
of 517/1123—would take account of a genuinely urban fabric, and
would be built "two kilometres *within* the old one destroyed around the
end of the 5th/11th century."[6]

It was close to Basra that there took place one of the seminal events
of Muslim history: the celebrated Battle of the Camel (Jumada II
36/November–December 656), where ʿAʾisha, Talha, and Zubayr
opposed ʿAli following the assassination of the third caliph, ʿUthman.
This event was important for Basra, for those supporting the two sides
(the governor, ʿUthman b. Hunayf, and the chief of police, Hukaym
b. Jabala, favouring ʿAli on one side, and Hurqus b. Zubayr al-Saʿdi, a
Companion, favouring ʿAʾisha, Talha, and Zubayr, on the other) took
stands regarding the symbolic positions (direction for prayer), and this
gave rise to conflict. As such, the Arab imagination returns to the

---

[5] Basra was indeed to remain without a surrounding defensive wall for around a
century and a half. A wall, with a ditch alongside, was built in 155/771–2, during the
difficult period of the stabilization of Abbasid power.

[6] Charles Pellat, s.v. "Basra," in *Encyclopédie de l'Islam*, 2nd ed. (Leiden: Brill; Paris:
Maisonneuve, 1975), 1:1118.

Basra of the initial century as one of the first scenes where original history unfolded.

Kufa

Kufa, contemporary with Basra, was founded on an arm of the Euphrates in 17/638, apparently on a virgin site by the conqueror Sa'd b. Abi Waqqas. Is it practicable, in the absence of contemporary sources, to attempt a reconstitution of the first settlement? Tabari—following the same procedure as for establishing a hadith, i.e., by providing a chain of transmission stretching back to the age in question—provides a suggested description of the original Kufa; and a number of scholars, including Massignon and, more recently, Hichem Djaït, have ventured an interpretation.

How are we to view these later texts? Apparently an exchange of letters led the Caliph to propose a stable settlement for the army and to provide it with an urban standard. Sources note a letter from 'Umar to Sa'd, saying: "Establish a place of settlement [dar al-hijra] for the Bedouins that are with you."[7] Further, "he commanded that the manahij[8] should be of forty cubits; that passing them broadwise of thirty cubits; that between the two of twenty cubits. The streets [al-aziqqa] should be of seven cubits. Without this there is nothing. The parcels of land [al-qata'i'] of sixty cubits."[9] The impression is thus given of a hierarchical, planned road network, conceived by the Caliph, then brought into being before lands were allotted.

Tabari also tells us that the first thing to be sited and built at Kufa was the mosque (wa awwal shay' khutta [khutita] wa buniya hina 'azamu 'ala 'l-bina' al-masjid). This, however, somewhat contradicts what he had said previously, whereby, quite clearly, the streets and the parcels of land were worked out before any building began. Such a paradoxical presentation indicates a pre-conceived text, and this is confirmed by the version of Baladhuri, who says, plainly: "They assigned the plots [in Kufa]; the people divided the places among themselves; the tribes settled in their establishments and its [Kufa's] mosque was built, this in

---

[7] Tabari, 1:2360, quoted by Fred Donner, *The Early Islamic Conquests* (Princeton: University Press, 1981), 227.

[8] Louis Massignon supposes this to mean "alignment of tents." See his "Explication du plan de Kûfa," in *Mélanges Maspéro* (Cairo: IFAO, 1935–40), 3:345.

[9] Abi Ja'far Muhammad b. Jarir Tabari, *Tarikh al-rusul wa 'l-muluk*, ed. Ibrahim Muhammad Abi 'l-Fadl (Dar al-Ma'arif), 4:44.

the year 17." (*fa-ikhtattaha wa aqta'a al-nas al-manazil, wa anzala al-qaba'il manazilihim wa bana masjidaha wa dhalika fi sana sab'at 'ashar.*)[10]

More precisely, Ya'qubi[11] relates how the settlement of the conquerors took two forms: collective land grants (*khitta*, plural *khitat*) for the tribes, and other, individual grants (*dar*, plural *adur*, or *qati'a*, plural *-at*) for chiefs like Usama b. Zayd or Jubayd b. Mut'im, sited around the mosque. Fred Donner[12] supplies a list of these. The tribes had cemeteries (*jabbana*) on their allotted lands, areas without buildings, which also served for assemblies. Massignon[13] enumerates these.

Baladhuri's account has a meandering structure, and one can understand the difficulty encountered by his readers. Having described the splitting up into grants of land and the building of the mosque in 17, he returns to 'Umar's celebrated instruction as to the choice of site ("no river between us"); then comes the order in which grants are allotted: *wa wala al-ikhtitat li 'l-nas* ("then followed the allotting of grants of land to the people"—not to the tribes). Any mention of building is subsequent to this, under Ziyad, i.e., in 50/670. To reconcile the traditions—the account of Sayf transmitted by Tabari—we may say that there was at Kufa planning and allotment of plots, followed by buildings; all of this taking place over the course of the year 17.

The final outcome of these operations was a central area (*midan*) with the following: the governorate headquarters; the mosque (*jami'*); the palace (*qasr*) excavated by Muhammad Ali Mustafa;[14] some suqs; the individual land grants (*dars*) of the "aristocracy"—those, for example, of 'Amr b. Hurayth, Walid b. 'Uqba, Mukhtar, Khalid b. Urfuta, and Abu Musa (mapped, for the Umayyad period, by Hichem Djaït);[15] some suqs. *Manahij* fanned out from this central area and served the areas designated for the grants of land allotted to the tribes (the Thaqif, the Hamdan, the Asad, the Nakha, the Kinda, the Azd, the Muzayna, and so on),[16] with their mosques (*masjids*) and their cemeteries (*jabbanas*). At

---

[10] Baladhuri, *Kitab futuh al-buldan*, 270.

[11] Abu 'l-Abbas Ahmad Ya'qubi, *Kitab al-buldan* (Leiden, 1892), 310.

[12] Donner, *Early Islamic Conquests*, 228.

[13] Massignon, "Explication," 347–348.

[14] Muhammad Ali Mustafa, "Preliminary Report on the Excavations in Kufa during the Third Season," *Sumer* 19 (1963).

[15] Hichem Djaït, *Al-Kūfa. Naissance de la ville islamique* (Paris: Maisonneuve et Larose, 1986), 302.

[16] Donner, *Early Islamic Conquests*, 229.

the outlet of the road going north was the Dar al-Rizq, where the booty was stored. Hichem Djaït has suggested a cartographic representation of this, more ordered than Massignon's.[17] How far was this urban model an original one, and how far was it subject to the influence of pre-existing cities in the region, like Hira, the capital of the Lakhmids?

In the Arab imagination, Kufa is not simply one of the urban creations of the period, haloed with the prestige of the Conquest. It is also the place where the Alid dispute sprung up—and, also, the place linked to the dispute involving the discontented *mawali*, those non-Arabs converted to Islam and expecting, thereafter, a position on a par with that of their former masters. Thus, along with Abu Muslim, they proclaimed Abu 'l-Abbas caliph in 749. Quite apart from the famous school of grammar, which was of some significance given the Arabs' passion for their language (the first Arab book to be published was the *Kitab* of Sibawayh, a book of Arabic grammar), Kufa was in evidence in various intellectual fields: calligraphy (Kufic, the script of the first Qurans, was born there), prose, with the collections of the *khutba*s of 'Ali, poetry, and so on.[18]

Fustat

As with the other *amsar*, Fustat witnessed no actual foundation; rather an initial, unformalized settlement, then, later, a decision that here should be the capital of the province of Muslim Egypt.

The facts are well known. In 640, the Arab army, on its way to conquer the western part of the world under the command of its leader 'Amr b. al-'As, set up an initial encampment at the foot of a Byzantine bastion, Egyptian Babylon, whose Coptic name the Arabs understood as the "Stronghold of Wax," Qasr al-Sham'. The site, around twenty kilometres to the south of the apex of the Nile Delta, is a strategic one; the key point dividing Upper and Lower Egypt. The army, organized by tribes, settled in a vast encampment covering 750 hectares. Once this bastion had been taken, a section of the troops left to conquer Alexandria, the capital of Byzantine Egypt, while the rest occupied the land already under conquest.

---

[17] Djaït, *Al-Kūfa*, 302; Massignon, "Explication," 360.
[18] Massignon, "Explication," 343–344.

We can understand the process thanks to a legend. The conquerors
set up their encampment at the foot of a small Byzantine fortress called
Babylon, conquered it, then left to wage war at Alexandria. As they
were about to leave, the commander, 'Amr, discovered that a female
pigeon had settled on the top part of his tent (called *fustat* in Arabic—the
legend is thus specifically concerned to establish an Arabic etymology
for the toponym, which actually comes from the Greek *fossaton*, meaning ditch). He refrained from decamping, so as not to disturb it, and,
when he returned victorious and Fustat became the first Muslim capital
of Egypt, he forthwith took as his plot the site where his tent was still
in place. Through this small story we see how the allocation, the division of grants of land between the combatants, was only carried out,
in the *amsar*, subsequent to the conquest of the province in question.
The initial settlement was merely provisional so long as the outcome
of the fighting was unknown. Once the Arabs were masters of the
region, they could organize themselves and allot properties on a final
basis.

Following the victory, the decision was made by Caliph 'Umar not
to set the capital of the Egyptian province too far off; and, Alexandria
being situated beyond the western arm of the Nile, he chose Fustat.
This was now a matter of final settlement, and of the "foundation" of
the new capital, albeit with no real ritual, since people were already
there. It was precisely at the time each tribe received a plot (*khitta*,
plural *khitat*), whether at the place where they were encamped at the
time of the siege or after the tribe and its mounts had moved out (see
the tribal displacements mapped by W. Kubiak).[19]

'Amr and his companions settled in the centre of the site, on lands
allotted specifically to individuals: the *dar*, plural *adur*.[20] These former
inhabitants of cities built very swiftly, their dwellings also being designated *dar* (but with the plural form *dur*)—an indication, long overlooked, that this homonymy of the term *dar* embracing two entities,
one regarding land, the other regarding buildings. These dwellings
were sometimes of more than one storey, on the model of local, and

---

[19] Wladyslaw Kubiak, *Al-Fustat. Its Foundation and Early Urban Development* (Cairo:
American University of Cairo Press, 1987), 176.
[20] On this sense of the term *dar*, see Sylvie Denoix, "Note sur un des sens du terme
dâr," *Annales Islamologiques* 25 (Cairo: IFAO, 1991): 285–288. For Fustat specifically, see
Sylvie Denoix, *Décrire le Caire. Fustât-Misr d'après Ibn Duqmâq et Maqrîzî*, Etudes Urbaines,
3 (Cairo: IFAO, 1992), 73–80.

also perhaps Yemeni, habitations, but inquiry was nonetheless made of the Caliph whether such elevation was permissible. The first necessary infrastructure was also set in place: a mosque (the Jamiʿ ʿAmr); a small bath, the Hammam al-Far; some streets (the best known, running alongside the mosque, was the Street of the Lanterns—Zuqaq al-Qanadil). Here, then, was an initial urban centre in the camp-cities of Fustat. It was very quickly realized that some city-dwellers had been overlooked—such as Wardan, the Persian freedman of ʿAmr b. al-ʿAs—who had a right in principle to their urban grants, and a second urban core was established around a suq (Suq Wardan), a little further to the north. In Fustat, therefore, as in the other *amsar*, there was a dual system of land occupation corresponding to two juxtaposed types of social organization. On the one hand, there was an urban occupation comprising "public" buildings,[21] a street network and individual grants of land, allotted to the élite: former city-dwellers in Arabia, *mawla*s of various origins and converted Copts, all of whom built their houses on their apportioned lots. On the other hand, there was an extensive occupation comprising collective grants of land allotted to the tribes. This enormous area remained a vast encampment for a while. Then a section of these troops left Fustat to continue the conquest further west, and those who remained became urbanized by joining the centres (around Zuqaq al-Qanadil and Suq Wardan), which were becoming larger and more dense.

The political events of the empire had their repercussion for the urban organization of Fustat. The Abbasids, when they acceded in 750, did not wish Fustat to remain the capital of the province of Egypt; while not destroying it, they created an urban centre to the north of the first organized site, where, in accordance with the proven system of land grants, they allotted plots to the members of their army. The new settlement, designated as al-ʿAskar ("the army"), was endowed with the customary facilities: governorate headquarters and mosque. Then, in 868, the governor Ahmad b. Tulun seceded, founded his own dynasty (which lasted to the extent of one descendant) and created his urban centre, on the same principle of a central area for the aristocracy with

---

[21] Two fifteenth-century writers, Maqrizi and Qalqashandi, relate that the first appearance of the *dar al-imara* in Fustat dates from the Abbasid period. This is noted by Kubiak, *Al-Fustat*, 129. "There was no special residence for the seat of government until the ʿAbbasid period, when, for the first time, *dar al-imara* was built at al-ʿAskar. Before this...each governor resided in his private house."

the prince's residence (a sumptuous palace with a garden that included pavilions and a menagerie) and the mosque, then an outer area comprising grants allotted to the army contingents and hydraulic facilities (an aqueduct). The grants were called, in this case, *al-qata'i'* (singular *qati'a*), and gave their name to the site. The vast scale of the mosque, still to be observed in the urban fabric of present-day Cairo, and its minaret with external spiral stairway, were inspired by the mosque of Samarra'. The secession, however, was displeasing to the central power, and al-Qata'i' was razed, except for the mosque and aqueduct, in 905.

2. *Cities founded in later centuries*

Following the period of Conquest, with the caliphate no longer centred at Medina, there was a change in the strategies whereby Muslim armies were implanted. They could be sited further from the capital (at Qayrawan, leading the conquest further west, or, in Iraq, at Wasit, to assert the imperial presence in the face of Alid unrest; or, by way of contrast, in Syria, for a local urbanization or for semi-urban domains under the Marwanids: al-Ramla (around 714), 'Anjar and Jabal Says (711–15), Rusafat al-Sham (723), Qasr al-Hayr al-Sharqi (728), 'Amman (724–43), and Mshatta (743).[22] On the morphological level, we find sometimes elements of infrastructure (citadel, ramparts), sometimes a type of urban organization (a segregation of the princely city vis-à-vis the city of common mortals), which distinguishes these places from the foundations of the first age. Later, new foundations—Abbasid Baghdad and Samarra', Fatimid Qahira, Idrisid Fez, and so on—were often undertaken in accordance with a dynastic project.

Qayrawan

In 50/670, so legend has it, the Muslim commander 'Uqba b. Nafi' took the bold step of settling his caravan (*al-qayrawan*) in central Ifriqiya (the ancient Byzacium). The year 50 was already late in the chronology of the Conquest. Initially, two other caravans settled in the region, but

---

[22] I take this list from Donald Whitcomb, "Amsar in Syria? Syrian Cities after the Conquest," *Aram* 6, no. 1–2 (1994): 13–33.

it was 'Uqba's encampment which, in 62/682, became Dar al-Hijra (the place of settlement of the *muhajirin*, those who had left Arabia).[23] Al-Qayrawan was chosen as capital of the Ifriqiya province of the Umayyad empire, rivalling Carthage; rivalry presented by the legend of how 'Uqba tamed the snakes that had invaded the site, just as the Bishop of Carthage, St Cyprian, had asserted his power over the savage beasts.

Governors (*wali*, plural *wulat*) came there from Damascus to establish themselves and, notwithstanding the disturbances caused by the Khariji Berbers, Qayrawan came to assume the role of provincial capital and economic and religious centre. When first founded, Qayrawan was a *misr*, a city-camp, with an urbanized centre comprising a few brick buildings, such as the great mosque, founded in 50/670, the governorate headquarters, and the dwellings of a few inhabitants. In the beginning, at least, part of the site was occupied by a more or less provisional encampment where the conquerors settled with their mounts. At its foundation, "Qayrawan was conceived as a great city destined to bring together all the Arabs of Ifriqiya."[24] This coming together did not in all cases mean a permanent abode, and the Arabs in question were the conquerors, a section of whom continued their westward march.

Qayrawan was numbered among the cities having sufficient prestige to attract princes or caliphs, though these preferred to set themselves somewhat apart. The closeness of these princely centres did, nonetheless, play its part in developing commercial and craft activity in Qayrawan.

Al-'Abbasiyya was founded in 184/800, about five kilometres to the southeast of Qayrawan, by the emir of Ifriqiya, Ibrahim b. al-Aghlab. There was a palace (in which Charlemagne's ambassadors came to bring their gifts for Harun al-Rashid), a hippodrome, a mint (*dar al-darb*) where gold dinars and silver dirhams were struck, official workshops for weaving (*tiraz*), a mosque in the Mesopotamian style,[25] places for commercial transaction, baths, and hydraulic installations. The city was, thus, endowed with the necessary infrastructure for fulfilling all

---

[23] Mondher Sakly, "Kairouan," in *Grandes villes méditerranéennes du monde musulman médiéval*, ed. J.-C. Garcin, in conjunction with J. L. Aranaud and S. Denoix (Rome: Ecole française de Rome, 2000), 58.
[24] Ibid., 61.
[25] Ibid., 81.

the functions of a capital. When it lost this role, however, with the
foundation of Raqqada by Ibrahim II, al-ʿAbbasiyya fell to the level of
an insignificant small town. Raqqada, similarly, found its fate following that of the Aghlabid dynasty. The Fatimists' propagandist ʿUbayd
Allah, who had paved the way for the accession of their first caliph,
abandoned Raqqada when he had al-Mahdiyya built.

Sabra 'l-Mansuriyya, eponymous with the Fatimid caliph al-Mansur
(reigned 334/945–336/948), was sited less than two kilometres to the
south of Qayrawan; it comprised palatine complexes set amid gardens.
This Fatimid city was enclosed within walls pierced by gates, but the
commerce and craftwork were at Qayrawan, and, as Sakly notes,[26] it
initially lacked a mosque. Here, as elsewhere, political events had their
effect on urban development and the city would undoubtedly have
witnessed a more significant development, if the Fatimids had not left
to settle in Egypt (361/972) and to take as their capital the city of
al-Qahira that they had founded in 358/969. As far as capitals were
concerned, the future of the dynasty in question was obviously a crucial
factor. After the Fatimid princes had left for Egypt, Sabra 'l-Mansuriyya
did not immediately fall into decline; with a view to saving it, Badis the
Zirid ordered that the commerce and craft sited at Qayrawan should
be transferred there. In fact, the Fatimids' departure did not simply
reduce Sabra to insignificance; it also spelled decline for Qayrawan,
well before the Hilali invasions. If, indeed, Qayrawan had remained a
capital—a status it lost under the Almohads in favour of Tunis—it is
conceivable there would have been an expansion, and that the urban
fabric would have stretched unbroken from Sabra to Qayrawan, with
the latter losing its status of princely city and melting into the general
agglomeration, as was the case with Fustat-Qahira—instead of which,
historians speak of the contraction (*ikhtisar*) of Qayrawan. Thus, after
the Hilali invasion, ramparts were built there enclosing a smaller area.
Without in any way underestimating the effects of these Bedouins
surging into the Maghreb, it might be hypothesized that the Fatimids'
departure for Egypt profoundly affected Qayrawan, which had already
found itself lessened before the Hilalis arrived. After their invasion, it
was felt necessary to be sheltered by walls; and, since new ones had
to be built, then the city could as well be enclosed in accordance with

---

[26] Ibid., 81.

its true dimensions which, after the departure of the Fatimids and the transfer of craftwork to Sabra, were far more limited.

If some foundations—such as Qayrawan, which had the status of capital or a neighbour of capitals from its beginnings up to its decline at the end of the fourth/tenth century—became great cities, others did not fare so well, either failing to rise above the level of mere small towns, or becoming extinguished once their founder had left them, as was the case with the princely cities of al-'Abbasiyya or Raqqada (264/877), even though the surface area of these new cities might have been considerable (around a hundred hectares for Sabra 'l-Mansuriyya, and still greater, apparently, for Raqqada).[27]

Wasit

Wasit, a foundation sited in Lower Iraq half-way between Kufa and Basra (whence, according to one tradition, its name "The Mid-Point") on the west bank of the main arm of the Tigris was the work of the Umayyad governor of Iraq, al-Hajjaj (75/694–95/713). There was already a city (Kaskar) on the East bank, and soon the two joined to form a single entity, simply called Wasit thereafter.

This city, founded after the Conquest, in 83/702 or 84/703, was not a *misr*. There was no huge encampment at Wasit, only a garrison; at the beginning, it was a question simply of lodging the Syrian troops occupying Iraq. Its construction took around three years and was exceedingly costly. The buildings constructed there—governorate headquarters and mosque—were designed to portray the Umayyads as political and religious rulers in Iraq. It suited their purpose of making a show of their power in an Iraq largely conquered from the Alids. The governor resided there until 97/715, and coinage was struck there up to the end of the Umayyad period.

Even if it was not the seat of a dynasty, the foundation was in effect a political project. Its impact was sufficient for the palace of al-Hajjaj, square in design and topped by a green dome, to be copied by al-Mansur when he built his own palace in Baghdad. The mosque joined to the governor's palace served, likewise, as the model for the caliphal foundation of the eighth century.

---

[27] Ibid., 61.

Baghdad

It was the second Abbasid caliph al-Mansur (reigned 136/754–158/
775)—the Abbasids had previously been installed at Kufa—who had
Baghdad built on the west bank of the Tigris, on a site where buildings already existed, in particular, numerous Christian monasteries.
The construction of the Abbasid capital began in 145/762—twelve
years, that is, after the beginnings of the dynasty—and was effectively
an imperial political project.

More than for any other city, sources describing Baghdad need to be
read with caution. What are we to make of the description of the round
city? And of the dimensions provided (a circumference of between
4,000 and 20,000 "black cubits")? Numerous writers (Duri, Le Stange,
Donne, Massignon, Herzfeld, Susa, Lassner, and so on) have attempted
reconstitutions. Beyond the shape and the precise dimensions of the
new princely city, what we know is that the city's spatial organization
had been conceived in advance. We are dealing with an agglomeration
gigantic right from the start, its heart a city girdled with a wall circular in form and pierced by four monumental gates: Bab Basra to the
southwest, Bab Kufa to the southeast, Bab al-Khurasan to the northeast,
and Bab al-Sham to the northwest. From these, four avenues fanned
out, arched thoroughfares leading to an open central square with the
palace and mosque. Al-Mansur's palace was constructed on the model
of the Umayyad palace at Wasit, with a green ceramic dome, and it
was enclosed by a gate named the "golden gate." Northwest of the
square were the guards and the dwelling of their commander, and the
chief of police. Around the square were the residences of the Caliph's
children, the treasury, the administrations for post, land tax (*kharaj*), seal
and war, the kitchens, and so on. Other "utilities" were sited in the
city, such as the prison between Bab Kufa and Bab Basra. The wall
was a piece of sophisticated defensive work. There was a preliminary
wall with towers; there was an outer ditch, and the four monumental
gates were each equipped with several iron doors. To achieve this surrounding structure, special bricks were manufactured, of one cubit in
length. Channels were dug, as wells serving the round city and the
suburbs from the water of the Tigris or Euphrates, and this allowed
sumptuous gardens to be cultivated. Ya'qubi[28] gives the names of the

---

[28] Ya'qubi, *Kitab al-buldan*, 240 *et seq.*

streets: "Street of the Police," "Street of the Women," "Street of the Water Carriers," "Street of the Muezzins," and so on.

The whole programme is there: a perfect form, the power at the centre, the effective manifestation of Islam in the mosque adjacent to the palace of the prince-imams, great axes leading to gates opening out on to the four corners of the empire. The scale of the works was likewise imperial. The sources enumerate the experts from among the different professions (Ya'qubi gives the mythical figure of 10,000 workmen), including astronomers.

From the beginning Baghdad stretched beyond the round city: four suburbs, with their markets and baths, were created at the start, with an urbanist to work out their development. As in the *amsar* of the first times, the occupation rested on a principle of allocating land grants (*qati'a*), individual for Arabs or *mawla*s, collective for the army, within or outside the walls. Ya'qubi provides a list of these.[29] It does not exclude individual properties, for traders for instance.

From the outset the population was multi-confessional: Zoroastrians (*majusi*, whence our word "mage"), Jews, and Nestorian Christians had numerous establishments in the city to which they came from all parts of the Muslim world. It is known that they played a crucial part in the extensive translation of Greek learning into Arabic, via Syriac. As for Muslims, these, coming as they did from throughout the empire, were ethnically diverse. The Abbasid political project was, nonetheless, to unify the culture of their subjects by means of the Arabic language, whether they were speakers of Persian, of a Turkic language (like the Turkomans), or of any other language.

The round city was simply an initial foundation. Thereafter palatine agglomerations acted as focal points and as the centre for new urban quarters. In 157/773, again on the west bank of the Tigris, al-Mansur constructed a palace outside the round city; this gave rise to the quarter of al-Karkh. Then, for his son and heir al-Mahdi, he built another still larger palatine complex on the East bank, and this gave rise to the Rusafa quarter. From this time on, the city saw extensive development on the East bank, with the Shammasiyya and Mukharrim quarters.

---

[29] Ibid., 243–254.

From 221/836 to 279/889, the Abbasid caliphs, completely over-shadowed by their viziers, sought to escape these by founding a palatine city 60 kilometres north of Baghdad: Samarra'. When they returned, they settled for good on the East bank, where, on the same principle as before, palaces acted as foci around which quarters subsequently formed. It was no longer, though, a question of caliphal foundations. The Barmakid viziers had in fact been taking more and more power. One of them, Ga'far, built the Qasr al-Ga'fari to the south of al-Mukharrim, and, from 279/891, Caliph al-Mu'tadid took residence there. To the north of this palace, al-Mu'tadid built the Qasr Firdaws, and, to the south, the Qasr al-Taj, which became the residence of the caliphs thereafter.

Baghdad was, thus, at once a city where resided the Abbasid princes, the court and the army—the last made up largely of Turks from central Asia—and a great popular city possessing an infrastructure for trade, institutions, worship, and the transmission of knowledge. It was a popular capital where economic prosperity and a high intellectual level went hand in hand, and where the presence of an army (formed by strangers, moreover) was liable to lead to conflict with a rich, educated population. This problem, among others, induced the caliphs to search for another capital from 220/834–5 on.

Samarra'

It was a custom of the Abbasid caliphs to go hunting on the East bank of the Tigris, 125 kilometres north of Baghdad. A first attempt at urban foundation, on the model of the round city, had been undertaken there under Harun al-Rashid in 180/796, but had led to nothing.[30] In 221/836, Caliph Mu'tasim (d. 227/842) founded his new caliphal city over a pre-Islamic settlement; specifically, over a monastery.

Excavations of the city, of which 35 hectares remained in 1924,[31] and a reading of later sources (chiefly Ya'qubi's *Buldan*) have revealed, or made us aware of, a number of palaces, hippodromes, mosques and markets, a long avenue of 3.5 kilometres, and a river port with wharves

---

[30] Alastair Northedge, "Samarra'," in *Encyclopédie de l'Islam*, 2nd ed. (Leiden: Brill, 1995), 1074.

[31] E. Herzfeld, *Ausgrabungen von Samarra. I. Der Wandschmuck der Bauten von Samarra und seine Ornamentik* (Berlin, 1923). See also Northedge, "Samarra'."

along the Tigris. According to these sources, the army had obtained grants allocated according to ethnicity: to the East of the avenue for the Turks, and to the west, on the bank of the Tigris, for those "coming from the West"—the Maghariba, probably from Egypt. It was under al-Muʿtasim's successor, al-Wathiq, that Samarra' ceased to be a provisional camp and became a true city, with numerous avenues, an economic infrastructure (various markets, especially for slaves), an administrative infrastructure (headquarters for land tax [*diwan al-kharaj al-aʿzam*], police headquarters [*majlis al-shurta*], prison), and numerous palaces with lands set aside for hunting, stables for the caliph's stud-farm, and hippodromes of a considerable size (more than ten kilometres long). The residence of Caliph al-Mutawakkil, the Qasr al-Haruni, at one point lodged Turkish units.[32] Between 235/849 and 237/851, a new mosque was built, with its famous minaret with spiral staircase around the central frame, from which Ibn Tulun drew inspiration for his building in Cairo.

This urban dynamism came at a price, and the caliphs' unheard of expenditure, especially that of al-Mutawakkil, was a burden on the treasury. On the other hand, the caliphs' isolation among the army corps actually made them more vulnerable to military revolts, which might extend to sacks of the palatine city. It is why 279/892 the caliphs returned to Baghdad.

Qahira

Qahira, like Baghdad, was a caliphal dynastic foundation. In 969, the Shiʿite Fatimid caliphs, until then established in Ifriqiya, sent their army, commanded by Jawhar the Sicilian, to conquer Egypt. The purpose of this (never realized) was to maintain their thrust eastwards as far as the Baghdad of the Sunni caliphs. Once the conquest had been achieved, Jawhar's mission was to found a city on the pattern of the Fatimid capital of that time, Sabra 'l-Mansuriyya. He chose a site around four kilometres north of Fustat, at a reasonable distance from the unhealthy edges of the Nile, on the east bank of a channel dug out by the Roman emperor Trajan that connected the Nile to the Red Sea.

---

[32] Northedge, "Samarra'," 1075.

As at Fustat, writers have handed down a legend giving a crucial role to a bird. In the absence of the Caliph, still back in Ifriqiya, the city's ritual founding was entrusted to astronomers practising a kind of divination—not, it should be said, a typically Muslim ritual—to establish the ideal moment for the foundation to take place. They observed the stars from a special spot. Small bells were attached to ropes, which were held by posts surrounding the city. These bells, so those directing the operation envisaged, were to be rung the instant the stars declared themselves favourable. Unfortunately, a bird of ill omen, a crow, perched on the ropes and set the process off: the bells tinkled, and the work was set in motion. It so happened that the warlike planet Mars, or al-Qahir (whence the name given to the foundation), was then at its zenith. The astronomers predicted that Qahira, the Martial one, would end in war, conquered by a dynasty coming from the world of the Turks.

What is the myth telling us here? On the one hand that a ritual foundation took place and that, in the absence of the Caliph, the heavenly powers were invoked and matters were taken from the hands of those empowered to make the decision. Was the prince's absence perceived as being so prejudicial? On the other hand, that the first step was to demarcate the city: the works in question were not, initially, the erection of any building like a mosque or palace, or the laying out of streets, as the Romans had done in their own foundations, or the division into parcels of land as the Arabs had done in theirs. The very first act was, with a degree of ceremony, to separate the caliphal city from the rest of the country. What we see, then, is that the chief characteristic of Fatimid princely cities was realized more fully at Qahira than anywhere else. That characteristic is their splendid isolation (brought about by distancing the caliphal city from the popular city, and by means of a fortified surrounding wall protecting the city from all intrusion); for, wherever they had been, the Fatimids had never been original inhabitants, and they saw their power from an élitist viewpoint. In their Ifriqiyan foundations, al-Mahdiyya and Sabra 'l-Mansuriyya, as now at al-Qahira, the city was reserved for princes and for the princely court and army. There, too, was found what was necessary for courtly life.

The first element was the wall, which set apart these sacred princes from their subjects. Protocol made them unreachable, excepting only processions organized with great pomp outside the caliphal city so that the common herd could wonder at this élite and venerate it. On these rare occasions (for example, at the festival marking the breaking of the

Channel dike), the caliph, his vizier and the court would leave Qahira according to a perfectly forethought ceremony.[33] The other crucial element of these foundations was the palace. At Qahira there were two large complexes, sited on either side of a pre-Islamic roadway now named Bayn al-Qasrayn ("Between the two palaces"). The palatine complex to the east was reserved for the caliph and his close relatives, while the one to the west, giving on to a great garden, Bustan Kafur, was allocated to the caliph's successor who would be designated in advance. Another building was a mosque that was slightly less central than the palaces: the al-Azhar mosque. As in the other capitals of this dynasty, there was a distribution of land plots (*hara*, plural *-at*) to the ethnic groups that made up the army: Berbers, Daylamis (from south of the Caspian Sea), Turks, Sudanese, and so on.

Later, the wall was rebuilt and other mosques were erected: within the walls, al-Aqmar and al-Hakim (which was beyond the walls when originally built, but was brought inside by the new wall development); outside the walls, al-Salih Tala'i', to the south of the south wall, and al-Guyushi on the mountain, the Muqattam, to the southeast. If the Fatimid palaces have vanished, destroyed by the Sunni Ayyubid princes who succeeded them, the mosques, by contrast, are still there today, as is the wall and the layout of a number of streets that still give form to the quarter.

Fez

Fez is one of the cities shaped by the political events of a country and of the succession of dynasties. In 789, Idris b. 'Abd Allah, eponymous founder of the Idrisids, created an initial urban centre where Berber tribes settled. In 809, Idris II welcomed five hundred Qayrawani horsemen for whom he established a new city, al-Alya, on the other bank of the river. In 818, some Andalusis, driven from the suburbs of Cordoba by the Umayyad caliph al-Hakam, settled in the first city. The best known mosques of Fez are those of the Qayrawanis (al-Qarawiyyin) and the Cordobans, but they were not the first. They were preceded by those of the descendants of the Prophet, the *shurafa'*, and of the shaykhs, *al-ashyakh*. That said, the al-Qarawiyyin madrasa was one of

---

[33] See Sanders, *Ritual, Politics and the City in Fatimid Cairo* (Cairo: State University of New York Press, 1994).

the oldest and most prestigious of all centres for the teaching of the
religious sciences of Islam.

Each entity had its wall (the Qayrawanis and Cordobans were often
in conflict) and its mosques, and each struck its coinage.[34] The two cities were not to be joined into one, until the Almoravids built in 1070
a single surrounding wall with numerous gates. This wall was to be
destroyed by the Almohad caliph in 1146, then rebuilt in 1212. They
built, in 1204, also the city's first citadel (*qasaba*). Finally, in 1276, the
Marinids founded a "new Fez" (Fas al-Jdid), or "white city" (madinat
al-Bayda'). The city remained capital up to 1549, at which date the
Sa'dis took Marrakesh as their capital.

We have here a special kind of urban model: one whereby the city
became organized very early on around a number of centres, and
where we find a specific element of urban infrastructure, the citadel.
This would occur again in a good number of cities in this intermediate
period, during which a military aristocracy, whose members were often
strangers, held power. This is the urban model Jean-Claude Garcin[35]
has called "the horsemen's city," where, in the East, the citadel meets
not only "the political necessity of isolating the Turkish horsemen from
the indigenous masses" but would also seem to reflect the influence
of Iranian cities, "through which the Turkish régimes passed before
winning the Muslim countries of the Mediterranean." In most cases
this did not mean the foundation of a new city containing this urban
infrastructural element, but rather the construction of a citadel within
an already existing city; such was the case in Damascus in 1076, in
Aleppo in the middle of the following century, and in Cairo, under
Saladin, in 1176. The equivalent configuration occurred at Fez: from
the rise of the Berber dynasties on, the citadels became part of the
urban landscape.

Given the way successive dynasties have left their mark there, it
is easy to understand how, in the Maghrebi imagination, "Fez is an
emblematic city whose history merges with that of the country and
of the Idrisid dynasty...Fez embodies a strong Sharifi ideology...As

---

[34] On the particularity of the double foundation, and some reflections on the
cities of the old Maghreb, see Halima Ferhat, "Remarques sur l'histoire des villes et
la fragilité du tissu urbain avant le xvᵉ siècle," in Naciri and Raymond, *Sciences sociales
et phénomènes urbains*, 97–103.

[35] Jean-Claude Garcin, "Le Caire et l'évolution urbaine des pays musulmans," *Annales
islamologiques* 25 (1991): 289–304.

the focus of Idrisid Sharifism, and of its diaspora that gave legitimacy to regional Sharifisms, Fez has effectively contributed to a spiritual unification of Morocco."[36]

Conclusion

The founded cities of the Arab-Muslim world correspond to various types, whether in terms of urban pattern or population, according to the periods in which they were created. Those of the period of Conquest, the *amsar*, allowed tribes of diverse origin, and potentially in conflict with one another, to live together; and they accorded shelter both to city-dweller and non-city-dweller, the latter being obliged to adapt to a new way of life. This form of population conditioned the ways in which the land was occupied and the physiognomy of these camp-cities at the initial period; excepting an urban core, or a number of urban cores, with "public utilities": governorate headquarters and mosque, even a bath, the first suqs of the Muslim world, and the dwellings of "notables." While the foundation ritual accorded to most new cities might be lacking (for reasons stated above), these centres were developed with what Hichem Djaït terms an "urbanizing intention,"[37] stemming, in the first instance, from the central power in Medina.

The urbanizing intention was clearly present in all those founded cities where the central power remained in evidence. These cities were an effective reflection of particular projects: at the outset, with the camp-cities, to house the conquering army and to give expression to the existence of a centralized administration bound to Islam; in the Umayyad period, to articulate the power and splendour of the princes, something already discernible in Wasit. The will of the central powers is still more in evidence in the great caliphal or dynastic foundations of later periods. If astronomers presided at the beginnings of foundations, when they were ritualized, urbanists became a necessity for these cities—notably for Baghdad, which had been conceptualized beforehand.

---

[36] Halima Ferhat, "Fès," in Garcin, Arnaud, and Denoix, *Grandes villes méditerranéennes*, 232.

[37] Djaït, *Al-Kūfa*, 89.

Clearly, then, the founded cities considered here reflect a political project. Muslims conquered the world and settled it; or else dynasties wished to manifest their pre-eminence through material signs, and urban foundations were a means of demonstrating their lustre. These cities also made their impact on the minds of contemporaries or those who came after: on those who lived in them, or visited them, even on those whose sole acquaintance with them was from a description read in books. They impressed people, too, because part of the civilizational capital of Arab-Muslim culture had been put to use there.

The camp-cities of the Conquest period clearly made a considerable impression on the Classical Arab imagination. As such, references in sources from the Abbasid or Mamluk periods sometimes reflect major difficulty in viewing these cities retrospectively. Ibn Duqmaq, for instance, an Egyptian writing at the beginning of the fifteenth century, describes the city of Fustat without making proper distinction between what is applicable to his own age and what belongs to the age of Conquest; there is complete fusion with this matrix period.[38] In keeping with such scholarly irrationality, these sources transmit some wondrous legends. We have already seen those relating to the first beginnings of Fustat, Qahira, and Qayrawan. Quite apart from the pleasure of reading such delightful texts, and the chance of gaining some insight into the way their authors' minds work, these writings do sometimes afford hints that more rational texts fail to bring to light. And, if founded cities have, as a class, furnished a framework for fabulous stories, it is the city of Baghdad that has most gripped the Arab imagination. It has been the subject of books describing its wonders (such as the *Kitab fada'il Baghdad al-'Iraq*, by the Persian Yazjard b. Mihmandar), and its most sumptuous period, that of Caliph Harun al-Rashid, is the setting for a large part of the stories in the *Thousand and One Nights*. The protagonists of the *Nights* move in the streets and markets of the city and in the sumptuous palaces created on the banks of the Tigris.

The affective, even emotional relationship the inhabitants had with their city, or that the Arabs had with the founded cities, can also be grasped in terms of *lieux de mémoire*. One of the great collective passions of the Arabs concerns the Arabic language and knowledge of it; and it is the cities that have witnessed the development of the great literary disciplines. At Basra it is told how (Bedouin language being deemed

---

[38] Denoix, *Décrire le Caire*.

the purest) Arab grammarians went on to the *mirbad*, at the time of the fair where Arab Bedouins were trading, in order to record the way they expressed themselves. Thus, from 750 to 847, "the nerve centre of literary life is Iraq, especially the cities of Basra, Kufa and Baghdad."[39] Moreover, the existence of a capital with princes who esteemed literature, poetry, and learning and played the part of patrons, as at Baghdad, where the Caliph opened a "House of Wisdom," could not but reinforce these *lieux de mémoire* that the founded cities represented.

Additional bibliography

The modest scale of this article precludes the provision of any complete bibliography for each of the cities considered. The reader is therefore referred to the bibliographies set out in the following works:

For Qayrawan, Baghdad, Fustat, Cairo, and Fez, the reader may consult the bibliographies assembled respectively by Mondher Sakly, Françoise Micheau, Ayman Fu'ad Sayyid, and Roland-Pierre Gayraud, Jean-Claude Garcin, and Halima Ferhat in *Grandes villes méditerranéennes du monde musulman médiéval*, ed. J.-C. Garcin, in conjunction with J. L. Arnaud and S. Denoix (Rome: École française de Rome, 2000).

In addition:

For Baghdad, see K. 'Awwad and A. 'Abd al-Hamid, *A Bibliography of Baghdad* (Baghdad, 1962).

For Basra, see Charles Pellat, "Basra," in *L'Encyclopédie de l'Islam*, 2nd ed. (Leiden: Brill; Paris: Maisonneuve, 1975), 1:1117–19.

For Kufa, see Hichem Djaït, *Al-Kûfa. Naissance de la ville islamique* (Paris: Maisonneuve et Larose, 1986).

For Samarra', see Alastair Northedge, s.v. "Samarra'," in *Encyclopédie de l'Islam*, 2nd edition (Leiden: Brill, 1995).

---

[39] Katia Zakharia, *Histoire de la littérature arabe* (2003), 27.

PART TWO

REGIONAL ASPECTS

THE OTTOMAN CITIES OF THE BALKANS

Pierre Pinon

The city of which we are speaking here is a formation consisting of morphological structures and urban fabrics. It is the city, on the one hand, of the general organization of quarters, major road layouts and urban facilities; and, on the other, that of residential fabrics, of secondary layouts and parcel divisions, and of facilities within quarters. We shall, in the first place, describe these structures and fabrics, but we shall, of course, also try to understand them in relation to ethnic, economic, social, and judicial phenomena. Our objective is, however, less to explain than to reveal. It is in not at all evident that a society produces its urban spaces from a clear consciousness of its own structures as applied to space. It does so in a confused manner and has, above all, to adapt its own needs and conceptions to the city it has inherited. A more modest procedure would be to observe in what fashion spatial structures, in this case urban morphologies, are able to bring to light phenomena that then become more or less easily explicable. In this way the study of urban forms in the Ottoman world may, with the help of other procedures, contribute towards a definition of what the Ottoman city is, and towards distinguishing certain areas within the Ottoman Empire; distinguishing, for instance, between "central provinces" and Balkan and Arab ones, as is currently done.

A problem of definition always arises, moreover, in attributing the name "city" to a historical or geographical entity. Can there be one kind of city only, in a period extending over several centuries? Is that the case for the Ottoman city from the end of the fifteenth century to the beginning of the twentieth? Could it be true for an area covering several natural regions which has lived through different pasts? Is that the case with the Balkan city?[1] In any case, the very notion of city—with the exception of new cities founded and evolving in a unique historical

---

[1] See the illuminating reflections on the matter by G. Veinstein, "La ville ottomane: les facteurs d'unité," in *La ciudad islámica. Ponencias y communicaciones* (Zaragoza, 1991), 65–92, and "La ville ottomane," in *Sciences sociales et phénomènes urbains dans le monde arabe,* ed. M. Naciri and A. Raymond (Casablanca, 1997), 105–114.

context over a certain period—stands in opposition to a definition that
would enclose it within a narrow chronological period. If we wish to
speak of a "purely" Ottoman city, we shall need to restrict ourselves to
cities founded *ex nihilo*, from the end of the fifteenth century onwards,
and this will immediately exclude Bursa, Edirne, and Istanbul: three
capitals constructed within Graeco-Roman cities. The long period is
visibly evident in the urban form; each physical state is merely the heir
of a preceding one and has been adapted to new requirements. Rather
than speaking of Ottoman cities, we should speak of "Ottomanized"
cities, since the Ottoman Empire contained cities with pasts as diverse
as Graeco-Roman, Byzantine, Arab, and Seljuq.

Ottoman Cities

Traditionally, a division is made between Anatolian and Balkan cities,
and between Arab cities of the Mashriq and the Maghreb—that is, if
they are not all thrown together into an "eastern" whole.[2] Appearances
do indeed plead for such a fusion (some would say confusion): "anarchic
layout," an inextricable network of narrow, twisting streets (often cul-de-
sacs), the existence of central bazaars, and the dominance of mosque
minarets in the landscape. Such a picture may border on caricature
(in the past a slightly contemptuous one), but is it totally false? Only a
thorough analysis of structures and fabrics would be able to affirm it;
and such an analysis is often difficult to undertake because old city plans
(preceding the transformations of the twentieth century) and precise
ones are lacking; or at least they are rarely accessible. A true study of
urban fabrics is only possible through the use of cadastral plans; they
alone reveal the parcel divisions which provide a truly intimate picture,
which allow us to read the traces of earlier structures, to decrypt the
land divisions, and to discover the ways houses were implanted. These
cadastral plans have, however, appeared only in recent times (at the
end of the nineteenth century or in the twentieth) and it is difficult to
gain access to them, unless one visits the land registries of all the cities
and is given authorization to take a copy.

---

[2] On the notion of the "eastern city," see E. Wirth, "Die orientalische Stadt. Ein
Überblick auf grund jüngerer Forschungen zur materiellen Kultur," *Saeculum* (1975):
45–94; idem *Die orientalische Stadt im islamischen Vorderasien und Nordafrika* (Mainz, 2000).
Anatolian and Balkan cities are not specifically dealt with in these studies.

As a working hypothesis, we shall suppose that the terrain of Ottoman cities—the definitions and distinctions involved—may be deciphered through one of these cities' elements, namely the urban house; given that the latter is far better known than the city itself. Easy to recognize (even if many have disappeared some decades since), to study and to classify by type, the Ottoman house of the eighteenth and nineteenth centuries has for some fifty years been the subject of a multitude of monographs and syntheses,[3] from Bosnia to Turkey, by way of Serbia,[4] Bulgaria,[5] or Macedonia.[6] A look at the plans and photographs (leaving aside comments sometimes inspired by nationalism) is sufficient to reveal the astonishing unity in the aspect and distribution of Ottoman houses, outside the Arab provinces and Southeast Turkey. The distribution of Ottoman houses with *hayat* or *sofa*[7] reveals that the division is not the one we might in principle expect: namely, that between Turko-Balkan and Arab worlds. During the eighteenth and nineteenth centuries (our knowledge of houses before this is poor), the Balkans did not as a whole have the Ottoman house with all its characteristics—part of Albania partially escaped the influence[8] which was still fainter in Wallachia.[9] Moreover, not all houses in Turkey are Ottoman, in the sense of being organized around a *hayat* or *sofa*, (despite statements aimed at giving them a "Turkish" character).[10] For instance, old houses in Cappadocia and the oldest houses in Kayseri (fifteenth–seventeenth centuries) are distributed according to an inner courtyard and an *iwan*

---

[3] See especially A. Arel, *Osmanli konut geleneginde tarihsel sorunlar* (Izmir, 1982), and D. Kuban, *The Turkish Hayat House* (Istanbul, 1995).

[4] See, for instance, J. Krunic, *Kuca i varosi u oblasti Stare Raske* (Belgrade, 1994).

[5] See, for instance, B. Georgieva, I. Ivanchev, and L. Peneva, *The Old Bulgarian House. Interior, Architecture, Design and Furnishings* (Sofia, 1980) [in Bulgarian], and B. Lory, *Le sort de l'héritage ottoman en Bulgarie: l'exemple des villes bulgares* (Paris, 1985).

[6] D. Gabrijan, *Makedonska Kuca* (Ljubljana, 1957), and, more recently, the monographs published in Athens by Melissa Editions for Northern Greece.

[7] For a more precise definition of *hayat* and *sofa*, see A. Borie and P. Pinon, *La maison turque*, supplement to no. 94 of the *Bulletin d'Informations Architecturales*, 1985.

[8] If the houses of Skodër are visibly Ottoman with their *çardak* (a variant of the *hayat*), those of Tirana are arranged around a closed *divana*, while those of Kruja, Berat, and especially those of Gjirokastër have a *çardak* apartment set on a tower according to an original plan.

[9] The *çardak* is frequently present, and there is even a house with *sofa* in Bucharest (Melik house built in 1760).

[10] It should be noted nevertheless that, in these marginal areas of the Balkans or Turkey, the exterior aspect (overhanging roofs, corbelling), the interior decor (cupboards called *dolap*), and the arrangement of rooms (*oda*), are strongly influenced by Ottoman domestic architecture.

(eyvan), and those of Konya by a *mabeyn* (enclosed *iwan*). The houses of
Upper Mesopotamia (Diyarbakir, Mardin, Urfa) have inner courtyards,
iwan and *qaʿa*. The houses of Antioch have a courtyard and a *qaʿa* and
are in fact very similar to those of Northern Syria, i.e. following the
Mamluk tradition. As for the houses of the Black Sea or the Anatolian East, these may be of the Caucasian type (Erzurum). Hence, the
eastern front of the classic Ottoman house (with the exception of some
*konak*s of Ottoman notables) halts at a wavy line going from Antalya to
Tokat, by way of Mugla, Afyon, Ankara, and Amasya;[11] though Ottoman influence is not, it should be said, absent from Northern Syria[12]
or Lebanon,[13] particularly at the end of the nineteenth century or the
beginning of the twentieth.

Is this border (obviously not watertight, since there are overlapping
areas where several types co-exist), which demarcates an area of distribution of the Ottoman house covering the Balkans (Bosnia, Bulgaria,
Macedonia, Thessaly, with the beautiful Ottoman houses of Sarajevo,
Plovdiv, Ohrid, Kastoria, or Ambelakia) and Northeast Anatolia (Bursa,
Safranbolu, Amasya, Tokat, Kütahya, Afyon, or Kula), equally valid in
the urban field? If this is the case,[14] then the Balkans, with regard to
the forms of cities, will be a mere sub-group of a group also includ-
ing Northwest Anatolia. Providing a name for this group is not easy.
It excludes not only the Arab provinces, but also Cappadocia, the
Caucasian regions, and Upper Mesopotamia. We may call it "Turko-
Balkan," with the qualification that Christians are predominant in the
Balkans, while Turks are, obviously, numerous in Southeast Turkey.
We have, then, to be satisfied with this dividing line between, on the
one hand, a world that is "Turko-Balkan" (for want of a better term),
and, on the other, an "Arabo-Ottoman" world.[15] Hence, in respect of

---

[11] See Borie and Pinon, *La maison turque*.

[12] See J.-Cl. David, "Nouvelles architectures domestiques à Alep au XIXᵉ siècle:
expressions locales d'un phénomène régional?" in *La maison beyrouthine aux trois arches.
Une architecture bourgeoise du Levant*, ed. M. F. Davie (Beirut, 2003), 217–243.

[13] See Kfouri, "La maison à hall central au Liban: origines, influences, identités,"
in Davie, *La maison beyrouthine*, 33–55.

[14] This has long been our hypothesis. See P. Pinon, "Essai de définition morphologique de la ville ottomane des XVIIIᵉ–XIXᵉ siècles," in *La culture urbaine des Balkans,
3, La ville des Balkans depuis la fin du Moyen Age jusqu'au début du XXᵉ siècle*, Académie Serbe
des Sciences et des Arts, Institut des Études Balkaniques (Paris–Belgrade) (Belgrade,
1989; 1991), 147–155.

[15] On "Arab-Ottoman" cities, see A. Raymond, *Grandes villes arabes à l'époque ottomane*
(Paris, 1985).

architectural typologies and urban morphologies, the Ottoman Empire needs to be divided into two major parts and not three. It is perhaps not immaterial to note that the "Arabo-Ottoman" part (again, for want of a better term) of Turkey is the one where Seljuq architecture is present (from Divrigi to Mardin, by way of Konya and Kayseri), and especially where the Byzantine substratum was early covered over by the Arab and Seljuq conquests. By contrast, the "Turko-Balkan" part (from the ancient Bithynia to Serbia) is the one where Byzantine dominance persisted the longest. The existence of "Arabo-Seljuq" and Byzantine bases would appear to lie at the origin of this clean division with regard to architecture and the Ottoman city.

The "Ottomanization" of Balkan cities

When the Ottomans took power in Northwest Anatolia, and when they conquered the Balkans and Constantinople, cities were numerous; they barely needed to found new ones. As such, we should speak of Ottomanized rather than of Ottoman cities in the strict sense—at least with regard to urban forms, which are partly inherited and rarely reconstructed.

The Ottoman city of the Balkans is more often than not simply an adaptation of the Byzantine city; and this led, over the centuries, to transformations or extensions of some importance. Thus, to speak of Ottoman Balkan cities means, on the one hand, attempting to identify the potentially diverse origins of Balkan cities prior to the Turkish conquest, and, on the other, describing and interpreting developments from the conquest up to the beginning of the twentieth century.

We shall regard the Ottoman Balkans as a very extended region stretching from Bosnia to Thrace, and from Peloponnesia to Wallachia; and we shall then examine this region's urban development from the fifteenth century up to the beginning of the twentieth.

What precisely is "Ottomanization"? We shall make a distinction between the large cities (which are subject to transformation) and the small ones (which are subject to extension). With the exception of Constantinople and Salonica, there were no very large cities in the Balkans prior to the conquest. In the case of Salonica, which had preserved its ancient road layout structure, Ottomanization consisted in converting numerous churches into mosques (even the mausoleum of Galerius), the installation of neighbourhood facilities (such as *hamams*)

and, especially, the development of a Turkish upper quarter which, up
to the nineteenth century, was to be distinct from the remainder of the
city not only by virtue of its "eastern" plan, but by the vivid colouring
(reserved for Muslims, throughout the Empire) that characterized its
houses, as opposed to the grey of "minorities" (Greeks and, here, especially Jews). In Constantinople,[16] a city already very much depopulated
and in ruin, urbanization was progressively achieved through populations deported from all over the Empire, without the land walls ever
being completely reached. Here practically all the churches (beginning
with Hagia Sophia) were successively appropriated and transformed
into mosques (after having served, temporarily, as residence for the
relatives of Sultan Mehmed II). There was, however, no architectural
modification except for the *mihrab* and the minaret. The nucleus of the
future Great Bazaar was rapidly set in place near the Seraglio (Eski
Saray). The conqueror's mosque was constructed on the site of the
Holy Apostles. At the end of the fifteenth century, a new geography
was defined by the setting in place of mosques (*vakif* concession) with
their *medrese* and their dervish monastery (*zaviye*), and also of the new
quarters they brought in their wake (the establishments of merchants
and craftsmen around the Bazaar, and of soldiers close by the walls or
the sea). These quarters would appear to have taken the form of villages more or less detached from each other. The first cadastral plans
(established in the second half of the nineteenth century on account of
the great fires)[17] show, prior to reconstruction involving the European
form of land division, a structure made up of one or two main streets
(matrices) bordered by a narrow, deep parcel division whose origin,
model, and date of establishment all remain unknown.[18] At the end

---

[16] See S. Yerasimos, "Istanbul ottomana," in "Istanbul, Costantinopoli, Bisanzio,"
Rassegna 72 (1997): 25–36.

[17] See P. Pinon and S. Yerasimos, "Relevés après incendie et plans d'assurances: les
précurseurs du cadastre stambouliote," in "Urban Morphogenesis. Maps and Cadastral
Plans," *Environmental Design* 1–2 (1996): 112–229; P. Pinon, "Topographie des lotissements et transformations urbaines d'Istanbul dans la seconde moitié du XIXe siècle,"
in *Histoire économique et sociale de l'Empire ottoman et de la Turquie (1326–1960)*, Collection
Turcica, vol. 8 (Louvain and Paris, 1995), 687–703; idem, "Trasformazioni urbane tra
il XVIIIe il XIX secolo," *Rassegna* 72: 52–58.

[18] This is the type of urban fabric we called G in our "Essai de typologie des tissus urbains des villes ottomanes d'Anatolie et des Balkans," in *7 Centuries of Ottoman
Architecture, "A Supra-National Heritage"* (Istanbul: Turkish Chamber of Architects, YAYIN,
2000), 185–186. However, we do not know whether these are urban fabrics established
by the Ottomans after the conquest, or if they correspond to fabrics more specifically

of the sixteenth century, all the great imperial *külliye* (monumental complexes, including mosque, *medrese, hamam,* and perhaps *imaret* and hospital)—Süleymaniye, Beyazit, Fiehzade, Selimiye—were in place on the crest of the Istanbul Peninsula.

From the fifteenth–sixteenth centuries onwards (or in the seventeenth and eighteenth centuries, depending on the regions involved), cities were considerably developed and extended beyond their walls; new quarters (*varosh*) appeared around their mosques[19] (or around their monasteries, as in Wallachia). At the same time, markets were created close by the Byzantine walls, as the specification of a quarter for trade was fundamental to the Ottoman city and to the Muslim city generally.[20] This configuration, consisting of a Byzantine fortress, a bazaar (or *çarsi*) and residential quarters, was developed in Bursa and was then reproduced in Edirne, Athens, Jannina, and Shkodër (Albania).[21] The market, surrounded by caravanserais (*han*), is omnipresent in Ottoman Balkan cities, from Sarajevo to Plodiv, from Skopje to Jannina, and exists under various names derived from "*çarsi*" (*carsija* in Bosnia or Macedonia) and from "bazaar" (*pazar* in Albania). Albania and Kosovo, for instance, still have numerous bazaars,[22] in Gjirokastër, Elbasan, Pec, and Gjakove, perhaps including a *bedesten* (or *bezistan*, meaning an enclosed market), as in Shkodër, Berat, Skup, Prizren, or Pristina. This *çarsi* is generally composed of a regular and dense network of alleys lined with wooden shops. More rarely, as in Kruja, it is linear, constituting the backbone of the city.

After the manner of Anatolia, the Balkans became mostly covered with religious monuments (mosques in every quarter) or civil monuments (such as the *imaret* of Kavala). In the new quarters or in the old ones, due to the phenomenon of architectural renewal, the Ottoman house took its place along the streets, especially in the eighteenth and nineteenth centuries, creating an urban landscape that would later be designated

---

used by minorities in their quarters, since, in the current state of research, they are found only in Greek, Armenian, or Jewish quarters.

[19] On Albania, for instance, see E. Riza, "Aperçu sur l'urbanistique de la ville albanaise (XIIᵉ–XXᵉ siècle)," *Monumentet* 17 (1977): 47–73.

[20] On the structures of the Ottoman city, see M. Cerasi, *La città del Levante. Civiltà urbana e architettura sotto gli Ottomani nei secoli XVIII–XIX* (Milan, 1986).

[21] It is likewise found in Anatolia, at Afyon, Kütahya, and Tokat.

[22] See E. Riza, "Les ensembles des marchés et leur restauration," *Monumentet* 15–16 (1978): 117–38; S. Shkodra, *La ville albanaise au cours de la Renaissance nationale, 1813–1912* (Tirana, 1988).

as typically "Turkish" (the "old Turkish quarters" of the tourist guides).
From Ohrid to Plovdiv, from Verria (in Greece) to Tetovo, and as far
as Bucharest, roads lined with houses with corbelling (*çikma* in Turkish)
and overhanging roofs are closely similar, with only slight differences of
detail, even though the structures of the urban fabrics may differ; and
they are also similar to those in Bursa, Tokat, or Kütahya.

Ottoman urban fabrics of Balkan cities

Ottoman cities, as they appear in the most ancient plans known to
us, dating, with the exception of Cairo (thanks to the plan drawn up
by surveyors in Bonaparte's expedition), back to the mid-nineteenth
century, appear at first sight to be a mere sub-group of a hugely extensive group that comprises Arab, Persian, or even North Indian cities.
Without surrendering to commonplace or caricature, we may say that
the Ottoman city is organized around a great mosque which is close
to the market and the caravanserais, and that it is made up of a residential urban fabric almost without hierarchy, with a small number of
"matrix" streets in irregular layout and alignment, and with numerous
cul-de-sacs.[23] Without entering the debate on the role of cul-de-sacs in
designating "eastern" urban fabrics (there are, as we know, numerous
cul-de-sacs in medieval Mediterranean cities which were never Muslim,
as in Sardinia, at Sassari),[24] we believe that cul-de-sacs in "eastern" cities
are structural, whereas in medieval western cities (where they are also
found), they are circumstantial, that is, simply answering to particular
situations. Moreover, in the latter they do not exist when they can be
avoided, whereas in "eastern" cities they are a major constituent of
the very genesis of ordinary urban fabrics. In the case of Istanbul, in
fact, sixteenth-century texts distinguish between main streets, streets
leading to quarters, and functional streets within the quarters.[25] Some
of these latter ones may, of course, be cul-de-sacs.

---

[23] We shall return in more detail to this problem, which we have already tackled
in our "Essai de typologie."

[24] Cul-de-sacs may even be numerous in medieval western cities, as in Alsace, for
example. See Fr. Himly, *Atlas des villes médiévales d'Alsace* (Strasbourg, 1970).

[25] Yerasimos, "Istanbul ottomana," 28.

To resolve the problem fully we should use cadastral plans, or at least ancient plans representing land parcelling.[26] However, the lack of this type of plan for the Balkans (with rare exceptions like Sarajevo) makes such a procedure impossible in the current state of research. In any case, studies of urban fabrics are (outside Greece) extremely rare. Those published on urban morphology limit themselves to exploiting plans where only streets and buildings are shown. Hence, it is impossible in most cases to know either the form of parcels (geometry, proportions), or the general network of parcel organization (known as "generating lines" and their "figures").[27] In the majority of Ottoman or, more generally, "eastern" cities, and even in the most apparently complex plans, these generating lines frequently form regular figures which stand in characteristic opposition to the irregular network of public roads.

The most easily identifiable category of urban fabrics is that of cities founded in ancient times and having an orthogonal plan. Salonica is the best-known example; here, as in several cities of Northern Syria (Damascus, Aleppo, Latakia, Antioch),[28] the Hellenistic network is, despite some variations in the detail, particularly well preserved in lower quarters (Greek and Jewish). In Salonica, where (as in most colonial Hellenistic cities), the block module is 150m by 100m,[29] the size of parcels (around 50 m in depth) was sufficient to take Ottoman houses aligned along the streets with their gardens at the back (as was the case with subsequent buildings in the twentieth century, after the 1917 fire).[30] The other, less evident, example is that of Edirne (Adrianople, *Adrianopolis*) where the ancient network of orthogonal roads remained in place in the Greek quarter of the citadel (*Kaleiçi*) until the 1905 fire; we can reconstitute this through analysis of the plan drawn up by Colonel

---

[26] In the case of Turkey, an exceptional document exists: namely, the plan of Suphi Bey (1862).

[27] See Pinon, "Essai de définition morphologique"; idem, "La transición desde la ciudad antigua a la ciudad medieval. Permanencia y transformación de los tejidos urbanos en el Mediterráneo oriental," in *La ciudad medieval: de la casa al tejido urbano*, ed. J. Passini (Cuenca, 2001), 179–213.

[28] Traces of the ancient orthogonal network are still clearly visible, if less well preserved, in other Ottoman cities, especially in Turkey at Urfa, Izmir, and Bursa. See P. Pinon, "Survivances et transformations dans la topographie d'Antioche après l'Antiquité," forthcoming among proceedings of a colloquium entitled *Antioche de Syrie. Histoire, images et traces de la ville antique* (Lyon, 2001).

[29] See M. Vickers, "Hellenistic Thessaloniki," *Journal of Hellenic Studies* 92 (1972).

[30] See A. Yerolympos, *The Replanning of Thessaloniki after the Fire of 1917* (Thessaloniki, 1995).

Osmont in 1854.[31] Thus, in the cases of Salonica and Edirne, it is the
ancient plan that reveals the general network of the urban fabric. The
development of this fabric was effected through adaptations (variations
in the road system through private space encroaching on public space),
through the laying out of new roads, and by re-dividing the parcels.
The case of Constantinople remains hypothetical; here the ancient and
Byzantine plans were probably preserved in a certain number of road
systems as they still appear in the 1882 plan (published by E. K. Ayverdi).
The present topography was extensively modified by land division after
fires in the second half of the nineteenth century. The phenomenon
is discernible in the quarters of Süleymaniye, Koca Mustafa Pasa and
the valley of the old Lixus,[32] where perfectly straight, perpendicular
or parallel streets reveal the layout of large late Roman avenues (the
city of Constantine and Theodosius) and sometimes even fragments
of ancient orthogonal road networks.

The first morphological characteristic of Ottoman cities following
the creation of the Empire is the absence of a wall. The *pax ottomana*
liberated cities from this constraint. The consequences of this opening
were numerous. City plans were no longer conditioned by an imposed
frontier that limited extension and implied that the layout of main streets
had to pass through the gates. In the open city the plan was developed
with more freedom. This does, however, not mean that constraints
ceased to exist: the orography remained, which meant there were slopes
to skirt around; the hydrography remained, which meant there were
rivers to go alongside or to cross by bridges (another obligatory kind of
passage). Even so, this limitation of the physical constraints allowed the
road network to assume more easily a functional distribution spreading
outwards from a desired centrality: that of the great mosque (or the main
church) and of the merchants' and craftsmen's quarter. Paradoxically,
the form of the Ottoman city which was often presented as anarchic
(a feature it shared with all "eastern" cities) accords well with its own
functionality, setting an extremely dense commercial centre against a
distended residential periphery.

Once liberated from its limits, it was also liberated from contiguity
that was neither obligatory nor desired. If the Turks brought an original

---

[31] Architectural Archives, Vincennes. See A. Yerolympos, *Urban Transformations in
the Balkans (1820–1920): Aspects of Balkans Town Planning and the Remaking of Thessaloniki*
(Thessaloniki, 1996), 78–82.
[32] See Pinon, "Transición."

dimension to the city, it was that of a link with nature.[33] There was no house without a garden. The ideal—for house, *kösk*, or palace—was that of the detached building. Even mosques and monastery churches were isolated within enclosures. Houses might often be aligned with the street on one of their sides,[34] which was not in fact the front through which one entered (direct entrances giving on to the street appeared only at the end of the nineteenth century); but there was always a front courtyard-garden and a garden to the side or back. Terracing was generally confined to central quarters, to a few main streets. The Ottoman urban habitat (in the Balkans and Northwest Anatolia) was generally dispersed, which is something rare in the history of cities before the appearance of modern suburbs. The open city allowed the Ottomans to develop garden cities, from Sarajevo to Batak or Koprivstica (in Bulgaria), from Verria or Trikala (in Greece) to Bucharest, in large and small cities alike.

The road network of Ottoman cities, like that of all "eastern" cities, was only weakly hierarchical. It was limited to main streets (or "matrix" streets) and to roads (alleys or cul-de-sacs) for local use; there was hardly anything between the two. This gave the first European travellers an impression of chaos—one which, in reality, merely entailed misperception of an order different from their own (an apparent disorder concealing order). In any case, the "matrix" streets, while they might provide a number of major arteries, were not in any deep sense crucial to the urban fabric. Once past the first sets of houses, there was a different system of distribution. It was the configuration of parcelling that dictated an assemblage threaded through by alleys. If the road layout in the residential quarters might be considered irregular, the parcelling was generally regular.[35]

Moreover, these "matrix" roads are rare: they amount to four or five in the large cities, one or two in the small ones. In some cases there may be just the one, as in Kruja or Verria, where a trading street threads its way within a dispersed habitat.

---

[33] See Cerasi, *La città del Levante*, 223–241.

[34] With the apparent exception of Bucharest, where houses are often isolated in their parcels (the 1846 Borroczin plan).

[35] See Pinon, "Transición," 182–186.

The most frequent "matrix" system is that of a "fan," whereby a space is distributed from a central, or obligatory, point towards the urban margins, these matrices then being continued by roads.

Generally the bazaar was adjacent to the citadel (*hisar*); this pairing frequently constitutes the centre of the fan, as in Edirne, Skodër,[36] and Skopje[37] (where the centre is reinforced by the presence of a bridge over the Duna or the Vardar), in Novi Pazar or in Pec.[38] This bridge alone could result in the formation of a junction, as on the left bank of the Marica in Plovdiv;[39] this is indeed a universal physical feature in the history of urban forms (specifically, in other places besides the Ottoman world, beginning from urban gates). The junction allows the directing of branch roads to the ends of a single street (as in Verria, where an old wall still remained), or the distribution of an isthmus site as in Kastoria (here too there was an old gate). The feature may become more complex, with two fans, one starting from the fortress-bazaar pairing, and another providing a transverse link, as in Jannina. When the bazaar or the citadel do not back on to a hill or a river, the fan may spread through 180 degrees to form the fully radiating system that we find around the episcopate and bazaar in Kozani (in Greece), around the central fortress in Plovdiv (right bank), or in Sofia. Because the road network is highly centralized, direct links between quarters which have a degree of autonomy are rare.

These quarters are internally served by local roads; the rationale of their layouts is impossible to grasp without knowledge of the parcelling. In fact, the formation of large irregular blocks is perhaps related to the previous existence of enclosures or "quarters" of parcels now beyond analysis. The system of cul-de-sacs is easier to explain, since it is certainly not specific to the Balkans. Cul-de-sacs are of three types, which are found throughout the Ottoman Empire, including the Arab provinces:

— direct short cul-de-sacs serving houses set at a secondary depth behind the houses lining a street; mostly from "matrix" streets, as in Skodër (Perash quarter), Sarajevo, or Skopje;

---

[36] 1923 plan according to E. Riza.
[37] 1914 plan according to Mikailovitch (1929).
[38] See Krunic, *Kuca i varosi u oblasti*.
[39] 1891 plan by J. Schnitter.

– longer cul-de-sacs with recesses to provide access to the heart of large
  blocks, as, again, in Skodër and Skopje, and in Plovdiv, Kozani,[40]
  Trikala[41] or Sofia;[42]
– cul-de-sacs serving peripheral dead-end quarters, as in Skodër (Tepe
  quarter), Sarajevo, Jannina,[43] Kozani (at the feet of the hills) or
  Trikala. Cul-de-sacs are found in all the quarters of Skopje, in the
  Turkish, Greek, or Slav quarters. However they can be rare, as in
  Verria.[44]

The series of "matrix" streets, streets for local use and cul-de-sacs often
forms a highly ramified system, branching out like a tree: concentrated
at the centre and distended at the periphery (Kozani, Plovdiv, Sofia)
thanks to the absence of a wall, which allows a progressive extension
on to the rural framework (roads, parcels).

The outline of the blocks is by no means easily explained. The block
has no internal structure specific to it. Its form results from the layout
of streets for local use, streets whose rationale generally eludes us. In
some cases it may be presumed that local streets and alleys follow the
layout of rural roads. This is especially noticeable in peripheral quarters where we can compare urban and rural fabrics and observe that
they are similar in structure.[45] These blocks are frequently quadrangular. However, most Ottoman blocks, large or small, have an irregular
polygon form. We may imagine that these blocks were created from
properties that were progressively divided—built first at their centre,
then progressively divided into lots, the central parcels being accessed
by fairly long cul-de-sacs served by peripheral streets (on the edge of
the initial properties), these latter then joining the "matrix" streets as
they could. As such, the outlines of blocks will be those of the original
large properties. Increasing density will have been the factor leading to
the division into parcels and to the new road layouts.

These observations may be synthesized by reference to the example
of Sarajevo.

---

[40] Nineteenth-century plan reconstituted by S. Avgerinou-Kolonia.
[41] According to F. Tsapala-Bardouli.
[42] The 1878 plan.
[43] According to N. Rogoti-Kyrioupoulou.
[44] According to N. Kaloghirou.
[45] Demonstration of this may be made in the case of some Ottoman cities, such as
Ayvalik on the Aegean coast of Turkey. See Pinon, "Transición," 177–179.

Sarajevo

Bosna-Saray is the only city of the Balkans to have been founded by
the Ottomans, and it is also one of the rare cities for which we possess a detailed plan[46] representing the parcelling. Thus, we have here a
privileged example from which we can attempt to develop a synthesis
of the morphology of Balkan cities. The Turks took possession of the
place in 1428–1429 and settled there in 1435–1436.

    With the exception of the citadel quarter (*Vratnik* quarter), which was
the initial site of the *saray* of Ishak Beg, the city, mainly developed in the
sixteenth–seventeenth centuries on the two banks of the Miljacka, was
an open one. It was a green city: "The city is full of gardens," wrote
the traveller M. Quiclet, who passed through in 1658.[47] "Few houses do
not have their own garden, and they are all filled with fruit trees."

    The road network converged towards the *çarsi*, fanning out towards
the North and the East (palace quarter) and on the left bank (starting
from the *Carevi* bridge), and using a more orthogonal system towards
the Northwest (a "matrix" street parallel with the river, and perpendicular streets).

    The *carsija* was set alongside the first caravanserai (the present *Kolobara
han*), successively linked to other caravanserais, baths, and the mosque
of Hüsrev Beg (1530).[48] It was arranged around the crossing point of
two main streets (*Saraci* and *Bascarsija*) and was the site of two *bezistan*s
(the *Brusa Bezistan* founded by Rustem Pasha (1551) and that of Hüsrev
Beg (in the form of an *arasta*).

    The 1882 plan allows a close analysis of the urban fabric. Cul-de-sacs
are few in the northern quarters, which were perhaps not developed
before the eighteenth century. They are essentially of the first and
third types defined earlier. We especially find short cul-de-sacs on the
northern bank of the *Cemalusa ulica* in order to provide access to the
large blocks that line it. In the Kovaci quarter, several long cul-de-sacs
give on to the large "matrix" street that crosses the northern quarters
(in a continuation of the *Bascarsija*). This allowed the division of large

---

    [46] *Austrian cadastral plan* by L. Tautcher, A. Krezevic, and J. Matasic (Vienna,
1882).
    [47] *Voyage à Constantinople par terre* (Paris, 1664).
    [48] For the history of Sarajevo and its monuments, see R. Pelletier, *Sarajevo et sa région*
(Paris, 1934).

parcels into small strips (courtyard, house garden) having the regularity of divided lots.

The Palace quarter provides an example of the regularity of parcel division to be noted in numerous "eastern" cities, even though it is cut diagonally by the street leading from the *carsija* to the Visegrad tower. The Elava quarter, for its part, shows how the urban fabric became set within the rural structure (still a universal phenomenon); the alleys, on an almost orthogonal network, follow the layout of the limits of the original parcelled blocs.

Hence, by the end of the fifteenth and sixteenth centuries, the urban structure and the fabric have been set in place to form one of the finest preserved images of the Ottoman urban landscape in the Balkans.

Understanding the unity of Ottoman cities

Despite some variants, the picture of the "eastern" city drawn by E. Wirth is applicable in part to the Ottoman city of the Balkans, Anatolia, and the Mashriq. Certainly the Turko-Balkan city is a good deal less dense[49] (especially on its periphery); and the urban landscape, dominated by overhanging roofs and corbelling, and by numerous openings to the streets, has a very different aspect. But the structures and urban fabrics seem essentially similar. How are we to explain this unity?

Certainly, research should be directed and reflection developed on the basis of the relation of the house to the parcel and to the street. In the Ottoman city—and in the Balkans less than elsewhere—houses are not always aligned with the streets; or else they are aligned by a side other than the main façade (at least before the end of the nineteenth century, the penultimate phase in the westernization of the Ottoman house).[50] They are terraced only in a few main streets (in which case the façade necessarily gives on to the street directly accessed from the entrance); or, at a later date, in the wake of the same phenomenon

---

[49] Denser central quarters are, of course, found in the Balkans (Plovdic), but above all in Turkey (Istanbul—the Fener or Kumkapi quarters before the fires of the second half of the nineteenth century—Bursa, Afyon, or Kütahya).

[50] The final phase being the adoption of the apartment block, as seen in the Galata quarter from the end of the nineteenth century. The central *sofa* nonetheless remained for a while longer.

of westernization. In the "eastern" city, and hence in the Balkan city, alignment and terracing are secondary, whereas they constitute the very basis of the form of "western" cities.

If terracing is absent or fails to play a fundamental role, this is because it is secondary with respect to the conception of the house. Terracing does not define the nucleus of the house with a courtyard or the house surrounded by a garden. In "Arab-Ottoman" houses with a central courtyard, the connection with terracing is the way in which the ends of the rooms surround the courtyard, which is itself always geometrically regular. In the "Turko-Balkan" world, this role is assumed by the garden, or else by the independence of the ground floor, which is adapted to the form of the parcel, vis-à-vis the first floor, which is always geometrically regular, too. In both cases, the system of cul-de-sacs, structural and not circumstantial (as in the West), also diminishes the role of alignment.

The parallelism between houses with courtyards and houses "with a garden" is not in fact fortuitous. In the beginning (fifteenth-sixteenth centuries), Ottoman houses were probably houses with courtyards (at least in Istanbul); then, progressively, the courtyard was transformed into a garden, isolating the dwelling, but without the conception of the house as enclosed unit coming into question in its relation to alignment and terracing. No doubt it is this pre-eminence, in "eastern" cities,[51] of house against roadway that explains the particular conception and configuration of the urban fabrics in question.

In the specific case of "Turko-Balkan" cities, the infrastructures (road system and parcels) appear to have remained eastern up to the end of the nineteenth century, despite a westernization that began, in the eighteenth century at least, with the multiplication of windows giving on to the street, then with main façades giving directly on to the street. This would have facilitated the passage to the western city with its terraced alignment.

These reflections confirm that the Ottoman city (or at least the "Turko-Balkan" one) is situated, geographically of course, but also historically, between East and West.[52]

---

[51] Nothing indicates in fact that this system is specifically Islamic or even Eastern, since we find one of a similar kind in the Theatre quarter in Delos, and this is Hellenistic.

[52] See P. Pinon, "Les tissus urbains ottomans entre Orient et Occident," in *Proceedings of the 2nd International Meeting on Modern Ottoman Studies and the Turkish Republic* (Leiden, 1989), 15–45.

IRANIAN CITIES

Heinz Gaube

1. *Introduction*

1.1. *The Setting*

In 1960, L. Lockart republished his book *Persian Cities* (first published
in 1939: *Famous Cities of Iran*), a meagre description of twenty-three
Iranian cities, which did not contribute at all to an understanding of
Iranian urbanism. Even so we still are far away from understanding
all the rules that underlay the development of Iranian cities. In 1979,
I tried to approach the problem on the base of fieldwork and broad
investigations into literary sources (Gaube 1979). Due to the political
changes in Iran, I was not able to widen my horizon. Thus, in this
chapter I shall trace the development and shape of the traditional
Iranian city, i.e., the city as it was before the 1920/30s when drastic
changes reshaped the appearance of Iranian cities as well as all the
cities in the Near East. After an introduction which deals with the
geographic and hydrologic preconditions as well as with the development of urbanism in Iran two characteristic cities will be presented and
analysed, exposing, due to location and history, different methodological
approaches. I shall start in the west with Isfahan where different stages
of development can be isolated, and an original planning concept, that
of the round Iranian city, can be detected. The main emphasis will be
put on the pre-Safavid period, since Safavid Isfahan will be dealt with
in another chapter of this book. Then I shall go to the east, to Herat
in present day Afghanistan. This city represents the Eastern Iranian
type of city. My approach is not descriptive, but methodological. In
presenting these two cities I want to show, how fieldwork and bookwork
can come together.

Iran is a country of deserts and barren, high mountains. In only a
few places one finds contiguous settlements covering wide areas. The
country is part of the Eurasian mountain belt which runs from the
Iberian Peninsula, through the Alps, the Balkans, the Carpathians,
the Taurus and Pontus, and the Iranian highland rims of the Elburz

and Zagros. Iran is also part of the arid belt of the Old World which stretches from the Sahara in the west across the Arabian Peninsula and the Iranian plateau to the deserts of Central Asia in the east. These two belts which traverse the Old World intersect in Iran. Thus, mountains and deserts are the two elements that determine the appearance of Iran. Mosaic-like, they intermingle, forming continuously varied combinations.

The bulk of the Iranian population lives in numerous oases of different sizes and in settlements scattered along the foothills of the high mountain chains. By far the greatest part of the settlements with more then 100.000 inhabitants is located either near the foothills of the Iranian highland rims of the Elburz and Zagros or in intermountain basins. Almost all large cities are located in regions not favoured with sufficient annual precipitation. Thus these cities could only come into being and grow where the water supply was assured from sources other than rainfall. Some of them take their water from rivers. The most significant example of this group of cities is Isfahan, which owes its enormous growth potential to the water reserves of the Zāyandah-Rūd. Most Iranian cities, such as those cities south of the Elburz and east of the Zagros, depend, however, on ground water, which is brought from the foothills of the mountains by way of *qanāt*s.

The *qanāt* is a subterranean aqueduct. It collects groundwater in the alluvial fans at the foot of high mountains and carries it, following the descent of the terrain, to settlements and fields. This art of creating artificial springs by water tunnels originated most probably around 1000 B.C. or some time later in the Iranian and Armenian highlands. It led to a radical change in the settlements pattern by opening to man new areas hitherto unpopulated and can be considered the base of Iranian urbanism. The introduction of the *qanāt* created one of the bases on which the first world empire in history, the Achaemenid state, could be built. The establishment of a network of overland roads, with posts for the army for communication, administration, control, and trade, was only possible after the introduction of the *qanāt*.

1.2. *Origins*

As its most apparent feature, the city has been walled in almost all civilizations and periods of history. This was considered necessary in order to protect the houses and businesses within the city, as well as its riches. The city not only provides protection, it is the seat of government, the centre of intellectual and religious life, the locus of economic activities, and the dwelling place of a population engaged in these urban functions. As a consequence, in addition to the wall, a "real" city had a temple, originally the seat of religious and political leadership. Later a differentiation took place, and as a new feature, the citadel, seat of the political leadership, was introduced. Crafts and trade were concentrated in special areas (Mumford 1966; Weber 1958).

On the Iranian plateau and the neighbouring areas to the east and northeast urbanization started much later than in Mesopotamia. Whereas in Mesopotamia since the late fourth millennium B.C., cities characterized by walls, temples, and other monumental buildings as well as special areas for trade and crafts developed, in Iran and neighbouring areas to the east and the northeast "proto-urban" settlements developed in the Bronze Age, i.e. before ca. 2000 B.C. These "proto-urban" settlements had monumental buildings and some special areas for certain crafts but missed other characteristics of the city. Settlements of this type were excavated between Fars, Kirmania, Sistan, and southern Turkestan (Tosi 1977). This statement, of course, is based on the archaeological evidence, which is far from complete or representative. In the future, archaeological fieldwork may reveal characteristics of settlements in Iran and the neighbouring areas we cannot think of today.

At the end of the second/beginning of the first millennium B.C., Medes and Persians emigrated from the north into present-day Iran. From this period on we can speak of Iranian cities in the proper meaning of the word. The earliest representations of these cities are only shown schematically on Assyrian reliefs. However, by drawing upon Herodotus' (I, 96–99) description of Agbatana, the Hamadan of today, which was the capital of the Median state, the first Iranian state, we can get an idea of the essential elements of the Median city. Herodotus writes: "...*the Medes...dwelled in scattered villages....*" King Deioces (ca. 727–675 B.C.) "*required them to build a single great city now called Agbatana, the walls of which are of great size and strength, rising in circles one within the other. The plan of the place is that each wall should out-top one beyond it by the battlement. The nature of the ground, which is a gentle hill, favours this arrangement in some degree, but it was mainly affected by art. The number of the circles is seven, the royal palace and the treasuries standing within the last.*"

Herodotus describes Agbatana as a round city. An Assyrian relief from the eighth century B.C. where the Median city of Kishesim is depicted conforms to the urban principles described by Herodotus. Here we see a sequence of walls rising one above the other and we may assume the highest wall to be the wall of the palace. This location of the palace and/or the temple at the highest point of the settlement seems to have been one of the characteristics of early Iranian cities.

Alexander the Great's victory over the Achaemenides diffused Greek ideas as far as India. The numerous cities he and his successors founded in Iran and neighbouring areas followed the western Hippodamean grid pattern. A variation of this plan is the plan of some cities in the eastern and northeastern Iranian hemisphere, e.g. Herat and Bukhara, where, dominating a grid, a central cross of two intersecting main streets determines the plan. The origin of this schema is not clear yet. It might be a variation of the Hippodamaen schema. It might be of Indian origin or influenced by Chinese principles of planning. Alexander's successors, the Seleucides, were followed by the Iranian Parthians, who preferred to build round cities. A good example of this change is the city of Marv in Turkestan. It was founded by Alexander, destroyed 293 B.C., and rebuilt as a Hippodamean city by Antiochos I (280–261 B.C.). In the Parthian period this settlement was surrounded by a wall roughly round in shape (Gangler–Gaube 2003, 36). The most impressive example of a round Parthian city, however, is Hatra in northwestern Iraq (Andrae 1908).

The first Sasanian city founded by Sasanian Ardashir I (226–240 A.D.), Ardashir-Khurra (Firūzābād, near Shiraz), has a perfectly round shape (figure 1). The site is unexcavated. In its centre are remains of a temple-like structure. Similar Dārāb, not far away from Ardashir-Khurra, unexcavated like the latter. Here, the perfectly circular wall encircles two large rock formations. On one of these are the ruins of a castle. Most likely there was a temple on the other.

Ardashir's son, Shāpūr I (240–271 A.D.), built his capital Bishāpūr northwest of Ardashir-Khurra. After his spectacular victories over the Romans, many Roman prisoners of war were brought to Iran. They were employed in the building of Bishāpūr. They left their imprint, as the Hippodamean plan of the city indicates (figure 2). They also exerted a strong influence on the decorative arts in Shāpūr's time. In his capital, mosaics were recovered which resemble those of the same period from Antioch, and the style of rock relief changed in Shāpūr's time from the flat, graphic Parthian style, which still can be seen at the reliefs of Ardashir, to a more plastic and narrative style in the period of Shāpūr.

In summary, in pre-Islamic Iran different plans were used to lay out cities: the round plan, the grid or Hippodamaen plan, and, as a variation of the latter, the Eastern Iranian plan. In addition to these principles, which we can detect in the present plan of some of the cities of Iran, a large number of cities was destroyed and rebuilt many times that we only can determine planning activities of later periods.

2. Isfahan

2.1. The development up to the eighth century: Yahūdiyya, Jayy, and Khūshinān

Isfahan situated at an elevation of ca. 1.500 metres, is a city surrounded by deserts and semi-deserts. The essential precondition for agriculture and urban growth in such a situation is a sufficient water supply. This is provided for the city and its hinterland by the Zāyandah-Rūd which has the most abundant water flow of all the rivers of the land-locked Iranian interior.

Although Isfahan is actually favoured by nature, it did not become, by itself alone, a centre towering over other Iranian cities. Its location almost midway between the two great emporia of Damascus and Aleppo in the west and Samarqand and Bukhara in the east, made it a centre for the exchange of goods and ideas from the east and west of the Islamic world, and its central position in Iran predestined it to become the capital of the empire under two mighty Dynasties, the Seljuqs (1037–1157) and the Safavids (1502–1736). These two functions, the one as emporium, the other as capital, manifested themselves in the bazaar and in the courtly buildings which gave Isfahan the reputation of an oriental Versailles.

Since no archaeological work of a larger extent has been done in Isfahan, we can only speculate about the location and shape of Gabae/Aspadana, the Achaemenide predecessor of the later Isfahan. In the post-Achaemenid centuries, this place is mentioned in literary sources under the name of Aspahān (Marquart 1921, 27–30). Also, the abbreviation ASP for Aspahān appears on Sasanian coins from the fourth century onward (Göbl 1968, Tab. XVI).

The first to provide us with information, which enables us to form an idea of how Isfahan developed up to the tenth century A.D., are Arab geographers and historians who wrote at the time and later. According to these sources, the Muslim Arabs conquered the region around Isfahan in the middle of the seventh century A.D. They encountered two cities, Yahūdiyya ("the Jewish city") and Jayy. Yahūdiyya is the ancestor of present-day Isfahan, while only a few ruins, a debris mound, and a medieval bridge over the Zāyandah-Rūd, about eight kilometres south-east from the centre of present-day Isfahan, bear witness of ancient Jayy. The most reliable source, the local historian Abū Nuʿaim (early eleventh century) attributes the founding of Jayy to the Sasanian kings Pērōz (459–486 A.D.) and Khosrō I (532–579 A.D.). We learn from the same author that Sasanian Jayy was not continuously inhabited but served as a fortified refuge for the inhabitants of the neighbouring unfortified settlements (Abū Nuʿaim, 15). Inside the city walls Khosrō I had constructed some buildings. Ibn Rustah (161), an Arab geographer who wrote around 903, mentions an old citadel in Jayy. According to another Arab author, Ibn an-Nadim (240), who wrote around 987, some old Pahlavi manuscripts were found in Jayy. This would suggest that we should think of Sasanian Jayy not only as a fortified refuge but also as an administrative centre of its hinterland.

After the Muslim conquest of Iran, the Arabs built their first Friday Mosque in the region of Isfahan at Jayy (Māfarrūkhi, 42). The decision to build the mosque in Jayy rather than in Yahūdiyya was governed by rational and strategic reasons. Due to its fortification and the open spaces enclosed within the wall, Jayy was most fitted to serve the Arabs as a military camp.

Shortly after 767 the seat of the governor was transferred from forti-fied Jayy to Khūshinān, a village situated between Jayy and Yahūdiyya. Here the governor Ayyūb b. Ziyād erected a palace and opposite to it a Friday Mosque on the bank of the Nahr Fursān, a canal which can no longer be precisely located (Abū Nuʿaim, 16). In addition to these two structures, Ayyūb ordered the construction of a large bazaar on the outskirts of Kushinān facing in the direction of Yahūdiyya. Along with this government-sponsored programme, extensive private buildings were constructed. Soon the houses of Kushinān became contiguous with those of Yahūdiyya (Abū Nuʿaim, 16). Having grown together with Yahūdiyya, Khūshinān was forced to compete with this city. Some cities founded by the Muslims under similar conditions succeeded in becoming the new centre of a larger agglomeration; Khūshinān did not. Yahūdiyya was at this period already so filled with pulsating life that eventually it absorbed Khūshinān. As early as 773 this process was so advanced that a new Friday Mosque, the third in the region of Isfahan, was built in Yahūdiyya on the location of the present day Friday Mosque of Isfahan (Abū Nuʿaim, 17).

The transfer of the centre of activity in the area of Isfahan from Jayy/Khūshinān to Yahūdiyya is confirmed by numismatic evidence. There are coins struck between 695 and 746 with the mintmark of Jayy, whereas all later coins bear the mintmark of Isfahan (Walker 1956, LXf.). The Arab geographers of the tenth century describe Jayy simply as a small village in the region of Isfahan and do not mention Khūshinān at all. They describe Yahūdiyya, however, as the most important place of the region of Isfahan. They describe its *madina* (the circumvallated inner city), with the Friday Mosque in the centre of the bustling bazaar, which was visited daily by large crowds of people with wares from kingdoms far and near (Le Strange 1966, 202–207).

2.2. *The development up to the sixteenth century*

2.2.1. *The Friday Mosque and the old maidān*

Our discussion of the development of Isfahan up to the eighth century had to be of a general nature. However, from the time that the urban centre was transferred to Yahūdiyya, that is, to the centre of the present-day old city of Isfahan, information becomes richer. In addition to the literary sources, we now have as further important evidence the basic shape of the city's plan, and, to a lesser degree, some buildings.

A geographical analysis of the main features of the city's plan reveals that in Isfahan three ground plans have been used, characterized by different orientations of their main axes (figure 3). They reflect each of the three important periods of the growth of the city. Within the oldest of these ground patterns, which is characterized by streets running from southwest to northeast and from southeast to northwest, are to be found both the Friday Mosque and the old *maidān* (the large square southeast of the Friday Mosque). These streets originate in a centre, the Great Mosque and the old *maidān*, and run radial to gates. Adjacent is the area of the earliest Islamic building period which stretches out to the southwest, south, and northwest of the Friday Mosque.

As already mentioned, the construction of the Friday Mosque was begun in 773. Of this building, and of the structure rebuilt in the tenth century, nothing remains above ground. Almost all of the halls surrounding the courtyard of the mosque now were built in the first half of the twelfth century. At that time, following extensive fire damage, an almost entirely new mosque had to be built. In the course of this construction work the hall-mosque of the Arab style was transformed into a four-*Iwān* structure, which since then has been the typical style of the Iranian mosque.

The old *maidān* (figure 4) is the other important element in the layout of medieval Isfahan. Today, this square is built over with simple workshops and warehouses, but its original shape can be reconstructed. It was surrounded by mosques, madrasas, palaces, an elaborate bazaar, and a royal music pavilion. Most of these buildings could still be seen in the seventeenth century, albeit in ruinous condition (Chardin 1711, 146). A *maidān* was originally a horse-race course and polo field. The word *maidān* is of Iranian origin and has a Persian synonym in *asprēs* (Herzfeld 1968, 22f.). In the compound form, *maidān asfris (=asprēs)* the old *maidān* of Isfahan is mentioned in medieval Arabic sources (Yāqut IV, 713). *Maidān*s were located on the outskirts of many Iranian and Iraqi cities. That *maidān*s were the ideal sites for markets too is obvious, since horse races or polo games did not take place every day.

Up to the eighth century, the old *maidān* of Isfahan was located at the edge of the settlement. Thus, there is no reason not to date its origin back into pre-Islamic times. As a consequence of the construction activities in Khūshinān, the *maidān* was no longer at the outskirts of Yahūdiyya but in the centre of the new urban unit formed by Yahūdiyya and Khūshinān (figure 5). Then, in the course of extensive building activities that took place in the eleventh century in all these areas, which are characterized by the second street scheme (figure 3), the old *maidān* became definitely and for a long time to follow the undisputed centre of the city. Engelbert Kaempfer, a German traveller who visited Isfahan in 1684, stresses the central position of the old *maidān* in describing it as: *forum antiquum in media urbe veteri.*

In the eleventh century at the latest, when Isfahan was the capital of the mighty Seljūq empire, the old *maidān*'s original functions as a sports and commercial site were supplemented by a third function brought about by its central location: it became the religious and administrative centre of the city. The old *maidān* remained as the centre of the city until the sixteenth century. Then, the new *maidān* was built which was modelled after the old *maidān*. The new *maidān* became the administrative centre of the city and attracted much of the trade, especially in highly valued goods. The old *maidān* continued to exist, however, as the second centre of Isfahan. Today it is still evident that the main axes of intra-urban communication of the pre-motorized age converge from the periphery of the city on the magnet of the old *maidān*.

2.2.2. *The main axes of intra-urban communication*

These main axes of intra-urban communication were those of the Middle Ages. In the tenth century wall the most important of the city gates were situated along these axes. A putative location of some of these gates can be dared (figure 6). More details cannot be produced. This must not surprise us at all since already in the seventeenth century the medieval city gates no longer had any function. The city had grown beyond the medieval walls, and the Safavids did not defend their empire at the gates of their capital but at its extreme borders, be they Central Asia, western Iraq, or Eastern Anatolia. Anyhow, there is no question that pre-Islamic and early Islamic Isfahan had a polygonal to round shape. The four main axes of old Isfahan were still, at the beginning of this century, lined for long stretches with shops and workshops, forming the bazaar of the city. That they are of high antiquity is shown by the fact that, on account of the sediment collected over the centuries, they run two and more metres above the level of the courtyards on both sides of them. Along these great roads linear bazaars had already been built by the tenth century (Nāsir-i Khusrau, 122). Those in the north and northwest are still partly preserved. The street running from the west gate in a northeastern direction became, after 1600, part of the main bazaar axis. Another bazaar was located toward the east of the old *maidān*. At the northeastern corner of the old *maidān* are the vestiges of another bazaar, which can be clearly distinguished on a 1924 map and on old aerial photographs (lithographed map of Isfahan compiled for Riżā-Khān in 1302/1924; Schmidt 1940, pl. 27). We may consider it to be the old *qaisariyyah* "le vieux marché imperial" of which Chardin (146) speaks in the seventeenth century. There is no recognizable street leading from the old *maidān* toward the southeast. Literary sources allow us to conclude that here, in the Islamic new city, stood a number of religious buildings (especially madrasas) and large mansions with gardens (Māfarrukhi, 83; Yāqut, I, 677). Such extensive usage of the southeastern parts of the city did not necessitate a main axis between the citadel and the old *maidān* in the Middle Ages. Through the determination of the main lines of intra urban communication and their intersection point, the old *maidān*, all those parts of the medieval city, which formed its skeleton, are isolated.

The change of the political conditions in Iran after the decline of the Saljuq empire in the middle of the twelfth century deprived Isfahan of its function as capital city. In 1244 the city was captured by the Mongols, and the year 1387 marks the definitive end of an

almost 800-year-long period of prosperity for Isfahan in Islamic times.
In this year, Timur conquered the city and ordered his soldiers to sack
it. Many of the inhabitants were killed on that occasion. In 1414 a
second sacking took place, and in 1474 Isfahan was reported to have
only about 50.000 inhabitants.

2.3. *The development up to 1700*

2.3.1. *Shāh ʿAbbās I: Maidān-i Shāh*
During the rise of the Safavid state in the beginning of the sixteenth
century, first attempts to rebuilt Isfahan were undertaken by the first two
shāhs of this dynasty, Ismāʿil (1502–1524) and Tahmāsp (1524–1576).
These two rulers integrated their buildings into the medieval plan of
Isfahan. Their main concern was the reconstruction and the embellishment of the area around the old *maidān*. Here they had erected no
fewer than five buildings. In addition to these they built two mosques,
one madrasa, and one *hammām* along the street going from the old
maidān in a southwestern direction (Gaube 1979, 82f.).

In the winter of 1597 Shāh ʿAbbās I, shāh of Iran since 1587,
decided to transfer his capital from Qazvin in northwestern Iran to
Isfahan. This decision brought Isfahan in the course of only a few
years to the highest point of its development and made it a capital of
intercontinental importance, where envoys and merchants from Europe
met those from the Far East.

In a very short period of time ʿAbbās and his advisors had laid out
the basic concept of how to rebuild and enlarge the city. Their plans
directed the development of Isfahan along new paths and are comparable in their extent only with the foundation of the early Islamic city
of Isfahan in the eighth century. Unlike the sultans who had earlier
ruled from Isfahan, and who had sometimes lived in the old city, ʿAbbās
decided not to live in the old city at all. He built his court on the
southwestern edge of the city of those days. In this he followed trends
known already in the Saljuq period, that is, to built royal compounds
near the river (Māfarrukhi, 53–56). ʿAbbās went further, however,
and created a new religious and economic centre at the fringe of the
sixteenth-century city. He thus forced further development of Isfahan
into new directions.

The nucleus of ʿAbbās' planning was once again a *maidān*, since
this was the ideal layout to unify the most important functions of a

city as the administrative, religious, intellectual, and economic centre. However, what had been developed at the old *maidān* in the course of centuries was now recreated in a planned way. Behind the arcades running around the *maidān* there were, in the east, west, and south, bazaar lanes with shops and workshops. The northern edge of the square was lined with coffee houses whose upper floors were used as hostels and brothels (Chardin 1711, 43–50; de Bruin 1714, 147f.; Olearius 1656, 554–558; Tavernier 1679, I, 442–447).

In four places, in the middle of the south and north sides and on the east and west sides, slightly off the centre towards the south, showy portals break the continuity of the facades. The portal on the south side leads into the Shāh Mosque, the "new" Friday Mosque, as it was called in the time of the Safavids. At the east side of the *maidān* is the portal of another mosque, the Lutfallāh Mosque.

2.3.2. *The palace complex*

Facing the Lutfallāh Mosque, at the west side of the *maidān*, stands the ʿAli Qāpu, the "High Gate," the reception palace of ʿAbbās I and his successors. In the seventeenth century the ʿAli Qāpu was the entrance to the wide palace area which was adjacent to the *maidān* on the west. It extended westward as far as the Chahār-Bāgh boulevard. In this palace area there were harem buildings, the private living quarter of the royal family, and pavilions in large parks as well as kitchens, storage sheds, chicken houses, and workshops which ʿAbbās and his successors had built.

West and south of the royal palace area on both sides of the Chahār-Bāgh and at the river as well there were mansions of the courtiers, whom ʿAbbās I had ordered to build in that location. The Chahār-Bāgh, which crosses the governmental district, leads to one of the most beautiful bridges in the world, the ʿAli-Vardi-Khān Bridge. Its builder, ʿAli Vardi Khān, was one of the closest associates of Shāh ʿAbbās I. Beyond this bridge, the Chahār-Bāgh led to an enormous royal country residence, the Hazār Jarib. Around 1700 Shāh Sultān Husain, the last ruling Safavid, built to the west of Hazār Jarib another large palace garden complex, Farah-Ābād. Both of these complexes have since disappeared (Beaudouin 1933, 1–47).

ʿAbbās I ordered the building of the settlement of New Julfah, also to the south of the Zāyandah Rud. Here he settled Armenians from Julfah, and other parts of Armenia. ʿAbbās transferred these people for both strategic and economic reasons. He wanted to create a belt

of burned earth in the northwest of his empire in order to protect
it against the Ottomans. However, ʿAbbās was also conscious of the
industriousness and mercantile skills of the Armenians and he wanted
them to contribute to the economic vitality of the city.

2.3.3. *The bazaar north of the new maidān*

The bazaar north of the new *maidān* is located to the south of the area
where the pre-Safavid and the Safavid city impinge on each other (for
details cf: Gaube-Wirth 1978). The monumental portal of this bazaar
looks very much like the portal of the Shāh Mosque opposite it at the
south end of the *maidān*. Through the portal one enters a two-storied
bazaar lane, the *qaisariyya*. This was the royal monopoly market in
which, in the seventeenth century, fine fabrics were sold. In the middle
of this lane there is a high dome. Underneath the dome to the right is
the royal mint, while to the left one enters the shāh's caravanserai. This
largest caravanserai of the city had a total of 140 rooms. At the end of
the seventeenth century cloth merchants from Tabriz, Qazvin, Ardabil,
and India used the ground floor rooms. On the upper floor jewellers,
goldsmiths, and engravers had their shops and workshops. North of
the shāh's caravanserai there was a similar caravanserai now in even
worse condition than the first. The area east of these caravanserais is
divided into squares by a system of bazaar lanes, which intersect under
high domes, the *chahār-sus*. Although a great deal of rebuilding and
restoration had taken place since Safavid times, we can still detect the
master plan of the time of ʿAbbās I. The original plan for the bazaar
included two parallel lanes running north and south which intersected
with three running east and west. North of this bazaar which, as a
whole, was called *qaisariyya* in the seventeenth century, there was a hospital, and next to it a caravanserai, which ʿAbbās I had founded with
the purpose of providing funds for the hospital. Both structures have
since disappeared. Further to the north, an emir of ʿAbbās I, Jārchi-
Bāshi, built a mosque and a caravanserai. They are built following the
orientation of the second street scheme, which goes back to the early
Middle Ages. The plan originating from the new *maidān* and the older
pattern interfere with each other in this area and create a bi-polarity
old-new *maidān*.

The layout of the streets and lanes in and around the new *maidān*
characterizes the third of the older street patterns, the Safavid. We find
it in the southeastern sector of the city, in the area that we know was
destroyed in pre-Safavid times, as well as west of the old *maidān*, an

area with the same fate. At the intersection, north of the buildings of
Jārchi-Bāshi, is the contact point between the fields of gravity of the
old and the new *maidān*. The new *maidān* was not able to achieve such
prominence that it became the sole urban centre of Isfahan. This was
due, above all, to the fact that the highly venerated old Friday Mosque
continued to be, in spite of the new Friday Mosque on the new *maidān*,
the most important mosque of the city, attracting crowds of people to
the area of the old *maidān*. It is fortunate that this decisive transfer of
gravity did not occur, because this bi-polarity between the old and the
new *maidān* led to an organically stable amalgamation of the Safavid
new city with the pre-Safavid old city.

3. *Herat an Eastern Iranian City*

3.1. *Nineteenth century Herat*

Herat (figure 7) is the westernmost large city of Afghanistan. It is situated
in a fertile river oasis and surrounded by a multitude of villages. Due
to its geographical position, the city was a gateway to India. Alexander the Great had passed through it, as had the trade between India,
Central Asia, and the Near East up to very recent times. Although
Herat's history is a succession of ups and downs, the city never had
to share the fate of many other Iranian cities, that is, to suffer, on the
one hand, a partial depopulation or, on the other, to be razed to the
ground never to be inhabited again.

As there are good and reliable descriptions of Herat in the nineteenth
century and the beginning of the twentieth, we can easily form an idea
of what the city looked like about a hundred years ago. There are even
some old maps, the most informative of which is the one by a German
officer, Oskar von Niedermayer (1924), who led a small military expedition to Afghanistan in 1916/17. From Niedermayer's map we can see
that the city was nearly square in plan, measuring 1.500 metres from
east to west and 1.600 metres from north to south and was oriented to
the cardinal points of the compass. It was surrounded by a wall in front
of which a wide and deep moat ran around the city. There were five
gates in the wall, one in the middle of the west-, south-, and east-side
and two in the north-side. Four streets led from the west-, the south-,
the east-, and from the western gate in the north-side and met in the
centre of the city under a domed structure, the *chahār-su*. They were

12 to 15 feet wide and formed the bazaar of the city. Caravanserais were situated near the chahār-su and south of it. To provide drinking water for the bazaar and the adjacent sections of the city there were, in several places of the city, huge reservoirs covered by high domes.

The *qal'ah*, or citadel, was located in the western part of the northern section of the city adjacent to the city wall. Here was a modest palace. In times of peace the governor of Herat resided not in the *qal'ah* but in a palace in the city itself next to the Great Mosque. Near the palace were large stables, a state workshop, a granary, and barracks. In the northeastern quarter of the old city, the Great Mosque was and is located. In the second half of the fifteenth century the mosque was completely rebuilt and at this time acquired the basic features of its present shape.

The residential quarters cover most of the area of the old city. The access to these residential quarters is provided by the four main streets, the bazaar; off these main streets branch secondary streets, which cross the quarters roughly in the north–south and east–west directions. To say that the plan of these streets was originally based upon a grid pattern does not appear to me an unfounded interpretation. Inside the residential quarters there are many religious buildings, mosques, *ziyārāt*s (shrines). Without exception the greater mosques are almost all situated on the fringe of the quarters. The *ziyārāt*s are real or presumed tombs of saints where one prays in the hope of having one's wishes come true. They are found in great quantity inside and outside the old city. In the *Risālah-yi Mazārat-i Harāt*, a book published in 1892, almost 300 *ziyārāt*s are listed and described. I know of no other city that could boast of such a high number of shrines.

3.2. *Early medieval Herat*

On examining the literary sources on the topography of Herat, we find that the features described above are not only valid for the nineteenth century, but are essential characteristics of the early medieval city as well. The most comprehensive description of the city in the tenth century is found in the books of two Arab geographers, those of Istakhri (around 951, 149–151) and Ibn Hawqal (around 977, 366). The following picture of Herat in the tenth century may be drawn from these sources.

A wall, constructed like all the other buildings from mud brick, enclosed the city. Its circumference was about four kilometres. In front of the wall was a moat. Through four gates in the middle of each wall four high roads left the city. The gates faced the cardinal points of the compass. Beginning at each gate a bazaar led into the centre of the city. The citadel was placed inside the city walls and had four gates, which were oriented in the same manner as the city gates and bore the same name. The location of the Great Mosque certainly did not change. At the turn of the century the administrative complex, the governor's palace, stables, granary, and state workshops lay at the *qibla* of the Great Mosque. The medieval authors tell us that there was a prison adjacent to the Great Mosque. Prisons, as a rule, were not erected at random but were generally located where the ruler and his soldiers resided.

3.3. *The Plan according to fifteenth century sources*

The fifteenth century sources, especially Izfizāri, who in 1492 wrote a history of Herat, indicate that the form of the inner city of Herat has much remained the same since the tenth century.

Isfizāri begins his history of Herat with a geographical introduction, on the basis of which the following picture of Herat may be sketched (Izfizāri, 77–79). The circumference of the city walls was 7.300 Herati feet. The distance between the opposite gates was 1.900 feet, which proves that the city had a square plan. A moat surrounded the wall. In the middle of the north-, west-, south-, and the east-sides of the wall as well as the northeast there were gates. From the four gates in the middle of each side, bazaars ran to the *chahār-su* in the centre of the city. The bazaar in the north was built of baked bricks. Thus we may presume that the other bazaars were built of mud bricks.

In each of the bazaars were caravanserais. The Great Mosque was located between the east and the northeast gates. Isfizāri reports that in pre-Timurid times the Kart King Muʿizz al-Din (1330–1370) surrounded the city with an additional outer wall measuring about six kilometres square. Timur, who had destroyed this wall, did not rebuild it because he considered it impossible to defend.

The evidence presented so far is quite sufficient to draw the following conclusions: both the plan of the inner city of Herat and the locations of the most important buildings—the bazaar, the Great Mosque, the administrative buildings, and the citadel—have undergone only minor changes at most since the tenth century. This permanence distinguishes Herat from other cities of the Irano-Iraqi architectural region, where the location of the central sections of the cities' extension were considerably changed through the centuries. The square plan according to which Herat was built has not been found in the plan of cities of the same size west of the two inner Iranian deserts, but we find it in other cities of the Eastern Iranian cultural sphere inside present day Iran and as far as Bukhara.

3.4. *Examples of Eastern Iranian cities*

3.4.1. *Bam*

The two most famous cities of pre-Islamic Sasanian Iran, Firuzābād (Ardashir-Khurra), the capital founded by Ardashir I (224–241) and Bishāpur, the capital founded by Ardashir's son Shāpur I (241–272), have very different and very distinct plans. Firuzābād (Ghirshman 1962, 123) is a round city, and Bishāpur (Ghirshman 1962, 138) is a rectangular city with a grid pattern of regular intra urban streets. The Sasanian round city has its immediate predecessor in the "Parthian" round city of Hatra (Andrae 1908) in present day Iraq, which in turn has its predecessor in round cities of the Ancient Near East. The planning concept of Bishāpur originates in the fact that this city was built by Roman prisoners of war. It is a foreign concept, which in post-Sasanian times was not repeated in western Iran. But the concept of the round city survived into post-Sasanian times. The most famous example is the round city of Baghdad, built by the caliph al-Mansur (754–775; Creswell 1958, 161–182). The original plans of Isfahan and its twin city Jayy were also round or roundish (Gaube 1979, 67–72).

But if we turn to eastern Iran, we encounter different principles in city planning. The Iranian province east of Fārs is Kirmān, and in the very east of this province, on the road, which circles south around the Lut desert to Sistān, the small city of Bam (figure 8) is located. In the Middle Ages Bam was famous for its textile industry. It was a rich and flourishing city. The inner city, the *madina*, dominated a famous citadel. A wall with four gates protected the *madina*. The four gates were orientated towards the points of the compass. A *rabad* lay outside the *madina*, and palm groves lined the whole settlement (Gaube 1979, 112).

In the thirties of the twentieth century the old city of Bam was given up. The inhabitants moved to the new city south of the old city, and the old city became a kind of museum city. In the plan of the present circumvallated old city a rather regular network of streets, orientated

north-south and east-west, becomes apparent, and different stages
of growth can be isolated. The original *madina* had a square shape,
the citadel lying in the north within the city wall. Later the city was
extended to the east, and very late a second extension was added in
the northwest. Thus, medieval Bam had a square shape, a citadel at
the edge of the *madina* and four gates, which most probably were in the
middle of each side and were connected by a regular system of streets.
Bam seems to be the most western example of what we call "Eastern
Iranian Cities."

3.4.2. *Zaranj*

As the example of Bam showed, east of the inner Iranian deserts we
find cities that follow a planning concept similar to the plan of Bishāpur.
Originally Bam had a square form and a regular system of intra-urban
streets, which ran parallel to the city walls. This is surprising, and, since
western influences can be excluded, it needs an explanation. One of
the most famous cities of Eastern Iran is Zaranj, the old capital of
Sistān, located east of Bam near the modern border between Iran
and Afghanistan on Afghani territory. The name Sistān is derived from
Sijistān or Sakastān, the land of Sakas, a Central Asian people, who
immigrated into this region from Central Asia in the first century B.C.
Under the Sasanians Zaranj was an important city, and in the ninth
and tenth centuries it was the capital of the Ñaffārids (861–1003) who
in their heydays controlled almost all of Iran. In 1383 Zaranj was
destroyed by Timur and never revived.

An aerial photo (Fischer 1974, 2, figure 72) of Zaranj shows the outline of a city which consists of two parts, a square with the remains of
a citadel in one of its corners and a slightly irregular rectangle added
to the one side of this square. The square part must be the *madina*.
This *madina* had according to Ibn Hauqal and al-Istakhri, who give the
best description of Zaranj in the tenth century (Gaube 1991, 208–210),
five iron gates. On the side facing the direction of Fars (west) were
two gates, the "new" gate and the "old" gate. The remaining three
gates were facing the other three points of the compass. This allows
only one interpretation: the *madina* of Zaranj had originally four gates
facing the four points of the compass. This *madina* was extended to
the south by a *rabad*, and, before the tenth century, the entire city was
circumvallated.

3.4.4. *The Origin of the plan of Eastern Iranian cities*

How did this particular plan of the inner cities of Herat, Bam, and Zaranj develop and where should we search for its roots? One thinks immediately of Greco-Roman cities. Influenced by this prototype, cities and city-like settlements were founded in the areas west of Iran in the early Islamic period, e.g. Anjar in Lebanon and Aqaba in Jordan. Each of these two settlements had a rectangular shape and main arteries originating from gates in the middle of each of the four walls which intersected in the middle of the settlement forming a cross (a survey in: Wirth 2000, 39–44).

In Iran Islamic foundations of this type are unknown. There, however, we encounter small rural settlements with square or rectangular shape, the so-called *qal'a* settlements. Their similarity with the inner city of Herat, however, is limited to some formal aspects. Because of their much smaller size and different organizational set-up, they can only be compared with settlements of the same type in Central Asia. *Qal'a*-villages of high antiquity are known in this region (e.g. Nerasik 1966). Whereas in Iran there is almost no similarity between the *qal'a* villages and the cities, in Central Asia we encounter city plans with formal similarities with *qal'a* villages and structural similarities with Herat. This, for example, is valid for the plan of the Seleucid inner city of Parthian Marw (Pugachenkowa 1958, 42). On the one hand it is related to the Parthian *qal'a* settlement of Tobrak-Kala (Pugachenkova 1965, 43) by insulae, a clearly defined axis, and a citadel at the edge of the city. On the other hand, Marw is related to Herat by the square city wall orientated according to the cardinal points of the compass, four overland roads, leaving the city through four gates in the middle of each side, and a citadel, located at the northern edge of the city inside the city walls. West of the old inner city of Marw, a similar, but less regular city arose in the Middle Ages (Pugachenkova 1958, 191). It also had two clearly defined axes and a citadel in the northeastern corner inside the city wall.

Pre-Islamic and medieval Marw must be seen as a city representing the same type of city as Herat. Thus there seems to be ample reason to speak of an eastern Iranian-Central Asian city type which stretches from the southern fringes of the Iranian Lut desert, east of the Lut and the Kawir to the cities of Central Asia, of which Marw and Bukhara are excellent examples. The question we have to ask now is, does the plan of inner cities like those of Bam, Zaranj, and Herat originate from Central Asia or from somewhere else? Herat represents this type of city in its purest form, and Herat is geographically located between two areas of possible origin of this type of city: India to the southeast and Central Asia and/or China to the northeast.

A possible Indian influence cannot be excluded, since close cultural contacts between India and Iran existed since very old times and reached a pinnacle in the Sasanian period. And, in fact, a search through ancient Indian literature, which is rich in treaties on architecture and urbanism, is rewarding. In the *Manasara* (Acharya 1934), an architectural manual which most scholars date back to the first century B.C., we find the following principles on city planning:

> *The ideal Indian city is orientated in the direction of the cardinal points of the compass. Each city is surrounded by a wall, inside of which a citadel is located. Outside the wall there is a moat. Generally there are four city gates, one in the middle of each of the four sides. Inside the walls and adjacent to them, wide streets circle the city. In addition there are two broad streets, which connect the opposite gates of the city. They cross each other in the centre of the city, where there is a temple or a hall for the inhabitants to congregate. Thus the city is divided into four quarters each of which is again further divided by lanes. Along the two main streets which cross in the centre there are houses, on the ground floors of which are shops. The rest of the city consists of living quarters.* (Shukla 1938, 1: 247–248).

The plan of Herat follows the principles of city planning laid down in this book in seven of its eight characteristic features. Thus, there is a probability that Herat was laid out according to a plan that originated in India, crossed Afghanistan, and reached Central Asia. But this is only *one* probability. The direction of influence could have been opposite, too: from Central Asia and/or China to Eastern Iran.

A very voluminous, recently published study conveys a comprehensive survey of the origins and formal development of the Chinese city and the philosophical as well as religious roots of Chinese city planning. In the introduction to his book the author emphasizes: "It is certainly no surprise to find the 'archaic' world concept of the well-organized cosmic order as the archetypical model of settlement and the whole oikoumene, the world inhabited by sedentary societies. In China this was expressed and formulated in the pattern of the 'Magic Square,' which is also well known as the mandala of Buddhism. This is the ninefold square, called in Chinese jingtianzhi = the well-field system of the holy field of nine squares. This 'Magic Square' was used by the legendary culture hero, Yü the Great, the founder of the first (the Xia) dynasty, as an ideal frame for dividing China into nine provinces. It is also used by the Duke of Zhou as the pattern for the layout of the sacred capital of the Zhou dynasty at the end of the second millennium B.C. Up until the twentieth century it was used as the layout for the so-called 'holy field' where the emperor, as the 'first farmer' of his people, ploughed the first furrows at the beginning of spring each year..." (Schinz 1996, 9).

All over the more than four hundred pages of his book the author tries to superimpose the concept of the "Magic Square" on Chinese cities of different periods and different parts of China. I must admit I lack the ability to follow many of his verbal and graphical arguments. But one fact becomes evident, the concept of the Eastern Iranian city, as it was exposed above, and the concept of the Chinese city, have only two things in common: the geometrical division of the city space and the geometrical outline of the city walls. The main feature of the inner organization of the Eastern Iranian city, the division into four equivalent quadrants, formed by crossing main streets in the centre, is not existent in the Chinese city. The same is true for the citadel which is the characteristic feature of the Eastern Iranian city but which is missing in the Chinese city.

To conclude: there are three possibilities to explain the typical form and inner organization of the Eastern Iranian city: 1. Independent, autochthon development in the region; 2. Indian influence; 3. Chinese influence. Chinese influence can be excluded to a very high degree. With a certain degree of probability Indian influence is to be considered. But is it not also possible that this type of city developed in Khurasan, Bactria, Transoxania? Despite the fact that an autochthonous development in the region cannot be proven with a very high degree of probability, it cannot be excluded either. To organize a newly founded city according to geometrical principles is self-evident. This is proven for cities of the Ancient Near East as well as for cities of Ancient Egypt. And the Greeks did the same in their newly founded cities. Thus, geometrical regularity cannot be used as a mean to construct developmental dependence. We have to look at organizational elements beyond a geometrical regularity. In our case these elements are the two shop-lined main streets, which cross in the centre of the city, the gates in the middle of each side of a (as a rule) square city and the citadel. At the moment the question whether we have to look at the Eastern Iranian city as the product of an autochthonous development or as a city type which developed under Indian influences cannot be answered in a satisfactory way. There are at least two problems to be solved before an answer can be given. The first is a precise dating of the quoted text from the *Manasara*. If this text is old, and that means older than the first century B.C., then an influence from Eastern Iran/Central Asia on Indian city planning, which must be considered too, becomes less probable and the opposite influence becomes more probable. The second would be precise archaeological soundings in a city like Herat. If these soundings could prove that the plan of Herat, as we can analyze and reconstruct it at the present time for the early Middle Ages, is more or less the plan of the Herat of the time before Alexander the Great, that means the plan of the Achaemenid city of Aria (old Persian: *Haraiva*), which is present day Herat, then we would have a sound proof for an autochthonous development.

Bibliography

Abu Nuʿaim, Ahmad b. ʿAbdallāh. *Kitāb akhbār Isbahān*. Edited by S. Dedering. Leiden, 1934.

Andrea, W. *Hatra*. Berlin, 1908–1912.

Beaudouin, E. E. "Isfahan sous les grands chahs (XVIIᵉ siècle)." *Urbanisme* 2, no. 10 (1933): 1–47.

Chardin. *Voyages en Perse et autres lieux de l'Orient*. Amsterdam, 1711.

Creswell, K. A. C. *A Short Account of Early Muslim Architecture*. Harmondsworth, 1958.

de Bruin, C. *Reizen over Moskovien door Persien en Indien*. Amsterdam, 1714.

Fischer, K., ed. *Nimruz*. Bonn, 1974–1976.

Gangler, A., H. Gaube, and A. Petruccioli. *Bukhara: The Eastern Dome of Islam*. Stuttgart and London, 2003.

Gaube, H. *Iranian Cities*. New York, 1979.

———. "Die Quellen zur Karte B VII 6: 'Die Kernländer des ʿAbbāsidenreiches' und ihre Auswertung." In *Von der Quelle zur Karte*, ed. W. Röllig, 199–216. Weinheim, 1991.

Gaube, H., and E. Wirth. *Der Bazar von Isfahan*. Wiesbaden, 1978.

Ghirshmann, R. *Bîshâbour*. Paris, 1956/1971.

Ghirshman, R. *Iran. Parther und Sasaniden*. Munich, 1962.

Göbl, R. *Sasanidische Numismatik*. Braunschweig, 1968.

Herzfeld, E., and G. Walser, eds. *The Persian Empire*. Wiesbaden, 1968.

Ibn Hawqal, Abu 'l-Qāsim b. Hasan. *Kitāb Surat al-ard*. Beirut, n.d.

Ibn an-Nadim, Muhammad b. Abi Yaʿqub. *Kitāb al-fihrist*. Edited by G. L. Flügel. Leipzig, 1871–1872.

Ibn Rustah, Ahmad b. ʿUmar. *al-Aʿlāq an-nafisa*. Edited by M. de Goeje. Leiden, Izfizāri, Muʿin al-Din Muhammad. *Rawdāt al-jannāt fi ansāf Harāt*. Edited by M. K. Imām. Tehran, 1338/1960.

al-Istakhri, Ibrāhim b. Muhammad. *Kitāb masālik al-mamālik*. Edited by M. M. al-Hini.

Kaempfer, E. *Amoenitatum exoticarum politico-physico-medicarum*. Lemgo, 1712.

Le Strange, G. *The Lands of the Eastern Caliphate*. London, 1905.

Lockart, L. *Persian Cities*. London, 1960.

Māfarrukhi, Mufaddal b. Saʿd. *Kitāb mahasin Isfahān*. Edited by J. al-Husaini. Tehran, 1312/1933.

Acharya, P. K. *Architecture of Mānasāra*. London, 1934.

Marquart, J. *Erānšahr nach der Geographie des Ps. Moses Xorenacʿi*. Berlin, 1901.

Mumford, L. *The City in History*. Baltimore, 1966.

Muqaddasi, Muhammad b. Ahmad. *Kitāb ahsan at-taqāsim*. Edited by M. de Goeje. Leiden, 1906.

Nāsir-I Khusrau, Abu Muʿin. *Safarnamah*. Edited by M. Dabirsiyāqi. Tehran, 1344/1966.

Nerasik, E. E. *Selʾskije poseleniya afrigidskogo Choresma*. Moscow, 1966.

Niedermayer, O. V. *Afghanistan*. Leipzig, 1924.

Olearius, A. *Vermehrte Moscowitische und Persische Reisbeschreibung*. Schleswig, 1656.

Pugachenkowa, G. A. *Puti raswitija architektury juschnogo Turkmenistana pory rabowladenija i feodalisma*. Moscow, 1958.

Pugachenkowa, G. A., and L. I. Rempel. *Istoriya iskusstv Uzbekistana*. Moscow, 1965.

Schmidt, E. F. *Flights over Ancient Cities of Iran*. Chicago, 1940.

Schinz, A. *The Magic Square—Cities in Ancient China*. Stuttgart, 1996.

Shukla, V. A. *Vástù Sástra*. Chandighar, n.d.

Tavernier, J. B. *Les six voyages de Jean Baptist Tavernier, en Perse et aux Indes*. Paris, 1679.

Tosi, M. "The Archaeological Evidence for Protostate Structures in Eastern Iran and Central Asia at the End of the 3rd Millenium B.C." In *Colloque Internationaux du C.N.R.S. No. 567: Le Plateau Iranien et L'Asie centrale des origins à la conquêt Islamique*, 45–66. Paris, 1977.

Walker, J. *A Catalogue of the Arab-Byzantine and Post-Reform Umaiyad Coins*. London, 1956.

Weber, M. *The City*. Glencoe, 1958.

Wirth, E. *Die orientalisch-islamische Stadt*. Mainz, 2000.

Yāqut, Yaʿqub b. ʿAbdallāh. *Muʿjam al buldān*. Edited by G. Wüstenfeld. Leipzig, 1866–1873.

INDIAN CITIES

Marc Gaborieau

This paper is devoted to a general presentation of the Islamic cities of India. This term "India" is here taken in the historical sense of the whole of the Indian subcontinent or South Asia, which has been divided after 1947 into seven political units (Schimmel 1980; Gaborieau 1986, 7–8). Only three of them, situated in the margins of the subcontinent, are now ruled by Muslims, namely Pakistan, Bangladesh, and the Maldives; the heartland, with India and Nepal, is ruled by an overwhelming Hindu majority, while Buddhists govern Sri Lanka and Bhutan. The ever-increasing proportion of Muslims to the total population of the subcontinent is now around 29%. The total Muslim population in 2001 reached about 400 hundred million people; each of the three biggest countries sheltering about one third of it: the Muslims, thus, make up 97% of the population in Pakistan, 90% in Bangladesh, and 13% in India. In the small countries one finds 7.5% in Sri Lanka, 3% in Nepal and Bhutan, but 100% in Maldives. Muslims are now politically marginal in the subcontinent; but this was not the case during the six centuries—to which this paper is mainly devoted—which preceded the advent of the British.

I will proceed in the following way. After a presentation of the historical context and a few general considerations, I will survey the various types of towns found in Muslim India and finally analyze the main research themes which have dealt with the subject.

1. *Historical context: six centuries of Muslim hegemony*

This marginalization of Islam was brought about by the British conquest at the end of the eighteenth century, and even more by the Partition of the subcontinent in 1947. But one must keep in mind that Muslim dynasties had been hegemonic for six centuries before that time. After the first inroads of Muslim merchants and conquerors on the Western coast between the seventh and the tenth century, the Turkish dynasty of the Ghaznavids, based in what is now Afghanistan, established in the eleventh and twelfth centuries a firm stronghold on the Indian soil, in the Indus basin—roughly speaking in the territory now covered by Pakistan—with its southern capital Lahore. The next decisive step was the conquest of Delhi, in the Ganges basin, at the end of the twelfth century: it opened the way for the rapid takeover of the whole of the subcontinent in a little more than a century and the establishment of a Muslim hegemony exercised by Turkish and Afghan dynasties which was to last up to the advent of the British. During this period India was an integral part of the *dâr al-islâm*; far from being marginal in the Muslim world, it had an important demographic, economic, and cultural weight, which increased after the destruction of Baghdad by the Mongols.

This paper is devoted mainly to these six centuries of Muslim hegemony in India, since very little is known of the urban history of Muslim India before the foundation of the Delhi Sultanate in the beginning of the thirteenth century. This long tormented period can be divided into four stages: the dream of a unified Indian Muslim empire never became a reality except perhaps briefly under the Mughal emperor Aurangzeb in the second half of the seventeenth century; the two attempts at political unification—with the Delhi Sultanate and the Mughal empire respectively—were each followed by a period of disintegration.

The first unsuccessful attempt at unifying India was made by the Delhi Sultanate from the beginning of the thirteenth to the second half of the fourteenth century (Gaborieau 1995a; Jackson 1999); it resulted at best in "a collection of sub-kingdoms" both Hindu and Muslim (Jackson 1999, 87) whose allegiance to the centre was shaky; they often rebelled.

A series of such rebellions from 1338 on brought the end of this political construction about and started a second period of independent regional sultanates which was to last up to the middle of the sixteenth century (Gaborieau 1995a, 2002a). The initiative came from the Eastern province of Bengal, in the Ganges Delta, which became independent in 1338. Then the governor of the Deccan, the Southern plateau, founded the Bahmanid Sultanate which was later to be divided into five different kingdoms: Bidar, Berar, Ahmadnagar, Bijapur, and Golconda; to the South of the latter two sultanates flourished the powerful Hindu kingdom of Vijayanagar (1336–1565). On the Western coast the provinces of Khandesh, Gujarat, and Sind became also independent. The inner land of Northern India was divided between Malwa on the west of

Delhi, Jaunpur on the east, and finally Delhi itself which was by then only one of the twelve regional sultanates into which Muslim India was divided; after the pale Sayyid dynasty it was ruled by the powerful Afghan dynasty of the Lodis who shifted the capital to Agra in 1505. The sack of Delhi by Timur in 1398 may conveniently be considered as marking the end of the disintegration of the Delhi Sultanate. This age of provincial sultanates should not be considered as a period of decadence, but as an era of growth and competition, both economic and cultural, which resulted in the development of new urban centres with an increased artistic production.

The second and more successful attempt at political unification was brought about by the Mughals in the sixteenth century (Richards 1993; Gaborieau 2002b). They had to assert themselves successively against two powerful Afghan dynasties in the north (the Lodis and the Surs) and to reckon with the Portuguese presence on the sea. The first two representatives of this new central Asian dynasty—Babur who conquered Delhi first in 1526 and his son Humayun who was long exiled in Persia by the Sur dynasty—had a limited impact on India. It is only with Akbar (1556–1605) that a new imperial construction was started with an effort to build a centralized state and to bring the whole of the subcontinent under its authority. This work, continued by his son Jahangir (1605–1627) and his grandson Shah Jahan (1628–1658), the builder of the Taj Mahal, culminated in the long campaigns of Aurangzeb (1658–1707) in the Deccan, which brought under the Mughal sway the last autonomous sultanates of Bijapur and Golconda, but failed to annex the territory south of it and to check the rising power of the Hindu Marathas who were instrumental in the fall of the empire. The degree of centralization of the Mughal empire is a debated question: the classical view—brought forth and popularized by the Aligarh school—of a centralized fiscal despotism (Ali 1966; Habib 1999) has been recently questioned (Alam and Suhrbrahmanyam 1994 and 1998, 12–16): it remains that the economic prosperity and the building activities of the dynasty contributed considerably to the shaping of an Indian urban landscape which is still visible.

At the death of Aurangzeb in 1707, the disintegration of the empire had already started and in less than three decades the centralized administration had collapsed to give way to autonomous provincial units (Alam 1986). They could be governed either by the families of former Muslim province governors who styled themselves as nawabs— i.e. *nawwâb*, an intensive form of *nâ'ib*, meaning representative (of the emperor). Such was the case in Central and Eastern India with the principalities of Awadh, Bengal, Carnatic, and Hyderabad, to which may be added a variety of kingdoms created by Afghan adventurers (Gommans 1995) scattered over Northern and Western India like Rampur, Farrukhabad, Tonk, and Bhopal. These new principalities could be also be ruled by non Muslims, as was mostly the case in Western India with the Marathas in the South, the Jats west of Delhi and the Sikhs in what is now Pakistan. During these decades—which may be called the Nawwabi period—these principalities, although politically autonomous, maintained a formal allegiance to the puppet Mughal emperor who was confined in his Red Fort palace of Delhi. The British East India Company which had taken its first hold in India by supplanting the Nawab of Begal was theoretically at first a vassal of the emperor and maintained this fiction up to the Mutiny of 1857 when Queen Victoria replaced the Mughals as Empress of India. This last phase of Muslim domination—comparable to the earlier period of provincial sultanates—should not be mistaken for an era of decadence (Alam and Suhbrahmanyam 1998, 55–68): it witnessed considerable economic development; the competition between the new political formations, endowed with substantial financial means, stimulated building activities and artistic creativity which continued for a long time after the British established their domination on the subcontinent between 1765 and 1818.

This British period was in a way a prolongation of the Mughal and Nawwabi periods: many towns continued to prosper. Such was the case of Lahore and Karachi, now the two great towns of Pakistan, and of Dacca (Ahmed 1991), now the capital of Bangladesh. In India one could cite the example of Mughal provincial capitals like Patna and Allahabad, or of a Nawwabi town like Lucknow. But the most interesting case is Delhi, a Muslim capital since the end of the twelfth century, which was again chosen by the British to become the site of a new gigantic imperial capital, New Delhi, inaugurated in 1931: striding over the ruins of several of the former seven juxtaposed Muslim capitals, it was contiguous to the Mughal capital of Shahjahanabad, from then on styled as Old Delhi. The British also originated at least four types of new towns. The first one consisted of the capitals of their three "presidencies" (main administrative subdivisions): Bombay, Madras, and Calcutta, the latter being also the imperial capital from 1765 and 1931: they were at the same time administrative towns, ports and commercial cum industrial cities, and quickly evolved into megalopolises. They became the biggest agglomerations of the subcontinent with Karachi (which was the capital of Pakistan from 1947 to 1959) and Dhaka (present capital of Bangladesh). The second category was that of "junctions," new commercial and industrial towns which sprang up at the crossing of important railway lines, like Kanpur in Northern India in the middle Ganges valley. Thirdly, there were "cantonments," i.e. garrisons towns which evolved into full fledged cities, like Rawalpindi which still shelters the headquarters of the Pakistan army and was the capital of Pakistan between 1959 and 1969, before the creation of the new town of Islamabad nearby. Finally the famous "Hills stations," situated in lower mountain areas, where the higher British officials spent the hot summer months; we may cite as examples Darjeeling, Nainital, and the most famous of them, Simla (Spate 1957, 192–193) in the Himalayas.

Independence and Partition in 1947 did not fundamentally alter the urban pattern, except for the spectacular development of the main towns of the newly created Pakistan: Karachi in the Western wing (now Pakistan proper) and Dacca (Ahmed 1991) in the Eastern wing (independent Bangladesh since 1971). A curiosity of these two new countries was the creation of purely artificial capital towns built on an orthogonal geometrical pattern: Islamabad and the administrative new section of Dhaka. In the whole of the subcontinent, although many towns like Delhi (Dupont *et al.* 2000) and the other megalopolises reached a spectacular size, the population remained mainly rural; in the most urbanized country of the subcontinent, India, the proportion of the urban population to the total population grew only from 18% to about 30% since independence.

2. *General considerations*

During the period of Muslim hegemony which ended in the second half of the eighteenth century India was already densely populated: the current estimation is between 100 and 150 million people for the Mughal period (Moosvi 1987, 393–406). Muslims however remained always in a minority and were conscious of being in a minority, but they left no figures: at the time of the first enumeration, the British census of 1872–1874, they made up a little less than 20% of the total population. It may be surmised that during the Mughal period their proportion was around 15% (against 29% nowadays).

They made, however, a great impact on urban life. As a whole, a greater proportion of Muslims than Hindus is urbanized: 27% against 18%, according to the Indian census of 1961; this statement should not hide the fact that the majority of Indian Muslims are—and presumably have long been—rural. The foundation of the Delhi Sultanate stimulated urban growth and the development of a large urban population. Although no statistics are available, reports of foreign travellers puts the population of the great Mughal towns at several hundred thousands for each of them; on the basis of such reports and of fiscal documents, the school of historians of Aligarh Muslim University has estimated that the proportion of the urban population (Hindus and Muslims confounded) was around 15% (Moosvi 1987, 305). These guesses are the only reasoned ones available; their credibility will be examined in the fourth part of this paper.

In popular conceptions, reflected in modern vernacular languages like Hindi, the urban phenomenon is linked with Islam. Words designating villages (*gâûn*) and lower administrative subdivisions (*pargana*) are local Indian ones, while those for subordinate administrative headquarters (*qasba*), commercial areas (*bâzâr*), and bigger towns (*shahar*) are all borrowed from Persian and Arabic; it is only in the twentieth century that the Hindus, in an effort to de-Islamize the language, have replaced current words like *shahar* by learned Sanskrit ones like *nagar* to mean "town." However, this does not mean that the Indian civilization ignored urbanization before the advent of Islam. On the contrary, when Muslims reached India, there had already existed a several thousand years old tradition of town building—probably linked with the Mesopotamian civilization: the present town of Patna in Bihar is on the site of Pataliputra, the capital of the Buddhist emperor Ashoka of the third century B.C., described by Greek travellers: there existed a learned theory of town planning in the Sanskrit tradition, the principle of which can still be seen underlying medieval towns in Nepal and in South India. One question to be raised in this paper will be that of how much pre-existing Hindu models influenced the development of urban life in the Muslim period.

Most of what has been written about Islamic towns in Muslim India relied on accounts of foreign travellers or on descriptions and studies of the colonial period. The primary Indo-Persian sources are far from having been properly tapped (see however Naqvi 1968 and 1972), except in special cases like Delhi, which has been studied both extensively over time (Frykenberg 1986; Spear 1994) and more specifically for the Mughal period (Blake 1991) and the Deccan city of Firozabad (Eaton and Michell 1990).

The state of the research on Indian Muslim cities is not very advanced (Gaborieau 1989). While there are older (Marshall 1922; Brown 1956) and more recent (Asher 1991; Koch 1991) synthetic works on architecture, only inadequate preliminary surveys exist for urban studies, and they are not exclusively devoted to the period of Muslim hegemony (e.g. Ballhatchet and Harrrison 1980; Banga 1992). Scholars have been more interested in the trees than in the forest, i.e. more in the individual monuments than in the town (Asher 2000, 121). Discipline-wise, the studies of towns were done mainly by art historians and general historians; urban geography took long to start (see the remarks of Spate 1957, 191–196); urban anthropology made its way only recently (Kumar 1988). And very few cities have been thoroughly studied all over the Muslim period: the multiplication in recent years of studies on Delhi through ages (Frykenberg 1986; Blake 1991; Gupta 1981; Spear 1994; Dupont *et al.* 2000) is an exception. Therefore, we do not have at hand a corpus of scholarly works substantial enough to provide a ground for generalizations: I can only provide a survey of the present state of research, tentative statements on the main features of the Indian Muslim towns, and an inventory of the current themes of research as well as of the unsolved and of the neglected questions. In the absence of synthetic works, the bibliography is very dispersed and cannot be exhaustively quoted in this short essay: I will only mention the main reference works and the publications dealing with the examples I quote.

3. *Types of towns*

A well grounded typology being impossible for the time being, I will only list the four main descriptive categories used by scholars in order to give a glimpse of the various types of towns encountered: capitals, lower level administrative towns, commercial towns, pilgrimage towns. It should be clear that these are not discrete categories, each town having several functions: I have classified them according to the most important function which presided on the development of a given city.

3.1. *Capital towns*

The best-known and best-studied cities of Muslim India are those who have been used by sultans, emperors, and nawabs to govern their dominions.

Many of them go back to the period of the sultanates which was a great era of town building. The most famous of them is Delhi which was successively the siege of a united Sultanate and, after Timur's invasion, of the local Sayyid and Lodi dynasties, before being finally reconstructed as a Mughal capital in the middle of the seventeenth century, as we shall see presently. Each of the dynasties built a new city by the side of the preceding one, so that Delhi presents, on the remains of an obscure Hindu town, no less then seven juxtaposed Islamic cities, all in deserted ruins except for the Mughal capital of Shajahanabad (Sharma 1964; Frykenberg 1986; Spear 1994). This chain-abandonment of cities raises the question—discussed in the next part of this paper—of how far Islamic cities of India were permanent settlements or only temporary camps. Similarly, the first great Sultanate of the Deccan, that of the Bahmanis, built three successive capitals (Michell 1993) in different locations: Gulbarga, Firozabad (Eaton and Michell 1990), and Bidar (Yazdani 1947).

The twelve provincial sultanates which emerged from the Delhi Sultanate and from the Bahmanis (see historical sketch above) had each its inherited or newly founded capital. The best known of them are the following ones: the first Portuguese travellers have left a vivid description of Gaur, the capital of Bengal in the east (Bouchon and Thomaz 1988; see also Eaton 1993); in the west Ahmedabad, founded as the capital of Gujarat Sultanate, and also an important commercial centre, remained prosperous to this day through the Mughal empire and the colonial period (Gillion 1968; Markovits 1995); in the Deccan, Golconda, now in ruins but once famous for her diamonds, has been amply described by the European travellers, while Bijapur is known for her Sufis (Eaton 1978); Agra, founded in the middle of the fifteenth century by the Lodi dynasty of Delhi, became famous when Akbar turned it a century later into one of the capitals of the Mughal empire (Gupta 1986).

The Mughals who often lived in camps (Gaborieau 1995b) built also several capitals in a variety of locations to suit political, strategic, or religious motivations. In the second half of the sixteenth century, Akbar left Delhi and elected as his first capital Agra, which he extended and embellished. For ideological reasons, i.e., for the legitimation of his dynasty through the Chishtiyya Sufi order, he built around the tomb of the saint Salîm Chishtî the short-lived Fatehpur Sikri (Koch 1991, 56–60; Petruccioli 1988). At the end of his reign, to suit his campaigns in Kashmir and Afghanistan, he moved north and built a last—still well preserved—capital in Lahore on the site of the previous Ghaznavid town (Khan 1993). It was left to Shâhjahân (1628–1658) to build from 1638 the greatest and entirely planned Mughal capital of Shahjahanabad, which was then styled New Delhi, but became Old Delhi when the British built their own New Delhi (Blake 1991; Ehlers and Krafft 1993; Koch in this volume).

The emergence of new regional states in the eighteenth century was also the occasion to develop or to create new royal and administrative towns which may be labelled as nawwabi capitals. Two have remained famous outside India: the city of Hyderabad in the Deccan, once a suburb of Golconda, which was developed by the Nizams, a Sunni dynasty which managed to survive as princely state throughout the British period (Mackenzie Shah in this volume); Lucknow, new capital of a Shia principality in the middle Ganges valley, where Iranian influence was preponderant (Cole 1989; Graff 1997). Murshidabad in Bengal, once the prosperous seat of another Shia dynasty, has now sunken into oblivion. Arcot, headquarter of a Sunni principality in Tamilnad, on the Southeastern coast of India is still remembered. But more famous still now are the capitals of the new Afghan states of Western India like Farrukhabad (Gommans 1995, 128–131), Rampur, and Bhopal.

3.2. *Lower administrative towns*

Between the capital and the village there was a chain of administrative centres which in the Mughal period—which formalized older classifications—comprised three levels (Trivedi 1998, chap. I). First, headquarters of the provinces (*sûba*), which sheltered a miniature replica of the central government with the governor (*sûba-dâr*) or viceroy (*nawwâb*) as representative of the emperor. At the middle level were *sarkar*s, intermediary subdivisions, which we may call districts. They were systematized by Akbar on the basis of former attempts. At the lowest level stood, since the beginning of the Delhi Sultanate, the *pargana*s, a kind of county, consisting of a collections of villages under the smallest administrative town called *qasba*.

To my knowledge there is no specific study of the towns of the first level. Dacca (Dhaka in the new spelling), now the capital of Bangladesh, which was created as a province headquarter by the Mughals in the beginning of the seventeenth century, may be chosen as an example: in this new city, in addition to the governing nobility, the Mughals attracted merchants and scholars and developed their own architectural style quite different from the previous regional architecture of Bengal (Karim 1964; Eaton 1993, 149–167). Most provincial capitals, like Patna, were, however, older towns.

The middle and lowest levels are treated here together; for no specificity seems to be assigned to *sarkâr* headquarters which, like *pargana* headquarters, are small towns. Curiously enough scholarly attention has been drawn mainly to this last level of the *qasba*, which remained well into the Mughal and British periods the focus of administrative, commercial, and cultural life in the countryside; the Muslims were usually in a majority in these small towns, while they were in a minority in the surrounding rural areas (Richards 1993, 194–196). Historians have been interested first in the administrative setup; for instance Batala in the Panjab, which was founded in 1465, had a population estimated between 15,000 and 18,000 in the beginning of the eighteenth century; each religious community had its own demarcated area with distinct quarters for each caste and occupational group; there were the offices of the revenue officials and of the judge (*qâdî*) appointed by the provincial authorities; artisan production and commerce enriched the town, which was also the favourite residence of Muslim scholars and Sufis (Grewal 1975). Studies of other towns have underlined the economic importance of these small towns (Bayly 1980 and 1983) as well as their cultural and religious importance which increased from the second half of the seventeenth century when grants to judges and scholars became hereditary (Alam 1986, 110–117).

The history of the *qasba*s of Northern India has been pursued through the nineteenth century (Pandey 1984), and even up to the end of the twentieth century. A Franco-Indian team headed by Gérard Fussman of the Collège de France has produced what may be considered the most thorough study of an Indian Muslim city, which includes detailed computerized mapping (Sharma 1999; Fussman *et al.* 2003). This *qasba* is Chanderi, founded during the Delhi Sultanate and once the secondary capital of the provincial sultanate of Malwa. During the Mughal period, it was the headquarter of a *sarkâr*; its importance diminished during the British period and in 1901 its population had sunk to 4,000 souls. But it grew again after the independence, reaching about 20,000 at the end of the twentieth century. Its prosperity was mainly based on the hand weaving of silk muslin saris that were considered as the finest in India, even above those of Benares. This not yet fully published collective study covers the history, the economy, and the social anthropology of this town. One third of the population is Muslim, comprising a majority of 2/3 low status artisans, mainly weavers, and a minority of 1/3 elite. Around 12% of the population consists of merchants belonging to the Jain religion (an ascetic sect derived from Hinduism) who nearly monopolize the trade of the town, including a large part of the financing and commercialization of the silk saris. The rest of the population is Hindu belonging to 38 different castes, the two most numerous being the Brahmins (11%) who work as priests, teachers, white-collar employees, or traders, and the untouchable Kolis who are weavers. Of special interest in this study is the detailed computerized mapping of the social groups, showing clearly, as we shall see later, the location of each religious community, and of each caste or group of castes of comparable status within each community—for Muslims have also castes (Gaborieau 1993).

3.3. *Commercial towns and ports*

There is no single type of commercial town in India. Many inland cities which had also a political role were mainly known for their commercial importance: Multan in Pakistan which tapped into Afghan trade; Patna in Northern India was at the start of Himalayan networks; Burhanpur mediated the trade between Northern India and the Deccan. Let us remember that pilgrimage towns like Benares had also a large commercial importance (Couté and Léger 1989).

The types of coastal towns varied from area to area. Well known from the time of early Muslim travellers are the ports of the western province of Gujarat; first Cambay (Kânbaya) where a colony of Muslim merchants was patronized by Hindu governors before the town was conquered and administered by the Muslims at the end of the thirteenth century; because of silting, it was gradually replaced by Surat which became in the sixteenth and seventeenth centuries the main Muslim port of the Western coast from which pilgrims would embark for Mecca. Ports of the southwestern coast of Kerala where Muslims have always been the subjects of Hindu rulers present another type where the community of Muslim merchants, settled in a separate part of the town, had acquired a sort of monopoly of the maritime trade, as was the case, for instance, in Calicut (Bouchon 1988) and Cannanore. Muslims also developed their own commercial towns in Tamilnad, along the Coromandel Coast of Southeastern India (Bayly 1989, 77–86), the most famous of them being Kayalpattinam; they are almost exclusively Muslim and are richly endowed by the rich Maraikâyyar merchants, each quarter having its own mosque and its network of women's lanes running behind the houses. Because of the difficulty in finding deep waters in the ever moving Ganges-Brahmaputra delta, a new port developed in Eastern Bengal across the Bay of Bengal along the coast of the Burmese province of Arakan when, in 1666, the Mughal definitively wrested Chittagong from the Arakanese kings (Eaton 1993, 234–238) and turned it into the most important strategic and commercial port of the area. It remained this way throughout the British period and in independent Bangladesh.

3.4. *Religious and scholarly towns*

This is a residual category, for there is no great Indian Muslim town known mainly as a pilgrimage centre. However, a few cities of modest size are mainly known through the tombs of famous saints who attract crowds of pilgrims. Two of them are particularly famous. The oldest one, mentioned since the end of the thirteenth century, is Bahraich where Ghâzî Miyân was buried who, according to his legend, was killed while fighting a holy war against the Hindus; he is venerated by hundreds of thousands of pilgrims who address him to obtain rain for agriculture and to cure diseases like leprosy and sterility (Gaborieau 1996). From the reign of the Mughal emperor Akbar in the second half of the sixteenth century, Ajmer, which shelters the tomb of Mu'în ad-Dîn Chishtî, became the most frequented place of pilgrimage for the whole of Muslim India and a town grew around the tomb. It should not be forgotten that the ephemeral Mughal capital of Fatehpur Sikri was build by Akbar around a place of pilgrimage, namely, the tomb of Salîm Chishtî by whose intercession the emperor got a son to perpetuate his dynasty. Other places which are renowned for their political and economical importance are also important pilgrimage towns: such is the case in India with Delhi which houses, in particular, the greatest Chishtî saint, Nizâm al-Dîn Awliyâ (d. 1325), with Gulbarga in the Deccan which houses the shrine of the famous Chishtî Gesu Darâz (m. 1422), with Multan in Pakistan as the seat of the Suhrawardiyya order, and with Gaur and Pandua in Bengal (Eaton 1993, 176–177). Important Hindu holy towns are also important for Muslims: for instance, Benares where a quarter of the population consists of Muslims (mainly weavers of silk saris). This town has been the subject of the only monograph of urban anthropology devoted to a Muslim population (Kumar 1988; Couté and Léger 1989).

Another type of religious towns is that built by religious sects for the shelter of their own members in isolation from the rest of the Muslim community. The "utopian *madînas*" built by the millenarist sect of the Mahdawîs in the fifteenth and sixteenth century were the first known examples; but they have been destroyed by persecution (Maclean 2000, 241). Similar modern ventures were, however, started by the sect of the Ahmadiyya in the twentieth century: the first one in Qadian (Qâdiyân), now in India, as the first headquarter of the sect which had to be abandoned at the time of partition (Spate 1957, 189–192); a new headquarter was built in Rabwah in Pakistan, near Lahore. Similarly, the politico-religious party of Maududi has constructed its own community town, first in Pathankot (now in India) and, after partition, near Lahore.

Starting in the second half of the nineteenth century, another development of the colonial period was the growth of scholarly towns which sprang up around Muslim universities: the most striking examples are Deoband for the traditionalists and Aligarh for the modernists; in the latter, the attraction of the University has led to the growth of the Muslim population which is now about half of the 400,000 total population, quite an unusual proportion in India. Similarly, the foundation of a Muslim nationalist university in the Delhi suburb of Okhla has led to the growth of a town that is mainly Muslim.

4. *Research themes*

After this survey, let us analyze the main themes of research which have appeared in the publications concerning Islamic cities of India and point out unsolved questions and gaps in them in order to indicate further avenues of research.

4.1. *Towns or camps?*

Let us dispose first of a controversy considering the ephemeral character of the Islamic cities in India. On the basis of remarks made by some Europeans travellers, which compared the Mughal capitals to military camps, undue generalizations were made regarding the ephemeral

character of the towns constructed by the Muslims. It is true that the
Mughal capitals had in their layout something of the military camp
(Gaborieau 1995b); and it cannot be denied either that, in the case
where the emperor had left, part of the nobility and its retainers who
followed him deserted, thereby, the capital diminishing its population
drastically. But variation in the size of the population does not necessarily mean abandonment. Actually, few cities have been completely
deserted: in the Deccan, only Firozabad and Bidar were completely
emptied of their population, but this is due to the dismemberment of
the Bahmani Sultanate and the rise of the capitals of the new smaller
states, like Golconda and Bijapur, who grew out of it; Golconda—a
formidable hill fortress but ill provided with water—was definitely
abandoned in favour of Hyderabad only after the Mughal conquest
of 1687 when it had lost its strategic utility; in the north, it is only in
Bengal that Gaur and Pandua were deserted in favour of the Mughal
Dacca and of the post-Mughal Murshidabad. Of the four Mughal
capitals, only Fatehpur Sikri was abandoned and for the reason that the
town was in many ways atypical: it was situated out of the way, with
no sufficient water, while other Mughal capitals were on the bank of
rivers. It was also a folly of Akbar built on a pilgrimage place at the
time of a mystical crisis, but could never fulfill any real administrative
and commercial function; once the emperor deserted it, it became an
empty shell. By contrast Agra, Delhi, and Lahore, built on the site of
former Sultanate towns, prospered to this day. Delhi contains seven
juxtaposed cities, six out which are now deserted: but the site was never
really abandoned, each dynasty constructing a newly planned town by
the side of the former ones; even when it ceased to be a capital and
was superseded by Agra and Lahore in most of the sixteenth and the
early seventeenth century, it never ceased to be an important centre for
the economic, religious, and cultural life. Finally, most of the Islamic
cities of India were permanent: such was the case of inherited cities
like Multan, Lahore, or Patna, but also of newly founded towns like
Ahmedabad, Ajmer, or Dhaka.

4.2. *Rate of urbanization*

The main question discussed by the historians of the Aligarh school—
projecting into the past the question of the colonial censuses—was
that of the rate of urbanization: on the basis of the reports of the
Western travellers and of fiscal documents, the school of historians of

Aligarh Muslim University has estimated that the proportion of the urban population (Hindus and Muslims confounded) was around 15% (Moosvi 1987, 305; Habib 1999, 83–85). These guesses, the only reasoned ones available, may, however, have been inflated for ideological reasons (Islam 1991). For the Aligarh school it is axiomatic that Muslim conquest accelerated the rate of urbanization, that the towns had an economic role comparable to (or even greater than) contemporary European cities, and that the British period was a time of massive de-urbanization. In fact, there is no ground to substantiate such ups and downs. Considering that the census registered a growth of the urban population from 9.3 in 1881 to 16.1 in 1951, it would be more reasonable to estimate that the population of the towns in the Mughal period did not exceed 10%.

4.3. *Administration*

Another common theme of political and administrative history is the question of urban government. Indian historians have emphasized the fact that Muslim India compares very badly with Europe where towns became enfranchised early on. On the contrary, Indian towns had no political autonomy: they were directly under the authority of the king who was locally represented by a kind of police officer called by the Indian name of *kotwâl*: he had a police force at his disposal; he enforced law and order and public morality, controlling prostitution and the sale of intoxicants; he carried out the commands of the king and spied on his behalf; carrying out the orders of the *qâdî*, he supervised prisons, had death sentences executed, and pilloried miscreants (Sarkar 1920, 93–97; Qureshi 1966, 203–206; Singh 1985; Bosworth 1986; Gaborieau 1995b, 31–32; Trivedi 1998, 187–188). He combined in a way the duties of the police officer and of the classical *muhtasib*. It is only in 1659 that Aurangzeb revived this orthodox office, but, according to the reports of travellers, the real power in the towns continued to vest in the *kotwâls*.

The town was traditionally divided into largely self-contained quarters or *muhallas*, each inhabited by specific religious, ethnic, or caste groups. To reach the individual families of these groups, the *kotwâl* had to go through the appointed head of each of these quarters which was recognized as their representatives (Qureshi 1966, 205–206). How this mediation worked is not known.

4.4. *Lay out and planning*

Except for a few entirely planned cities like Firozabad in the Deccan or Fatehpur Sikri and Shajahanabad in the north, towns usually grew slowly, as in the case of Agra or Lahore. It is, therefore, often difficult to find a coherent pattern. This difficulty is compounded by the presence of mental images which do not correspond to reality: for instance, a representation of Lahore on a route map as a symmetrical town with the fort in the middle may correspond to the ideal model of the army camp, but is very far from the actual Mughal town where the fort is in the northern corner near the wall and the former bed of the river (Naqvi 1968, plate facing cover page; Gaborieau 1995b, 26, 29). Such an eccentricity of the fortress is found not only in Shajahanabad and Agra, but also in Sultanate towns like Ahmedabad (Markovits 1995). For the Deccan, Firozabad betrays a similar eccentricity towards the river (Michell 1993). But it is too early to offer generalizations on Islamic town planning in India. However, Attilio Petruccioli, in a bold essay entitled "Ad quadratum...," has attempted to put forward some common features of Deccani Muslim towns, notably the orthogonal intersection of the main thoroughfares, pointing to an ideal division of the town into the quarters, like in the ideal image of paradise (Petruccioli 1993). The research of Susan Gole on Indian maps and plans is of a great help in the understanding of the layout of the towns (Gole 1989).

4.5. *Urban texture, social hierarchy, and spatial segregation*

Related to town planning is the question of the distribution of the social groups in the towns. Since most of the buildings have disappeared, and since the descriptions of the original sources are not precise on this point, it is difficult to reconstruct the urban texture, especially as far as the lower classes are concerned: it is impossible to know, for instance, how the artisans lived and worked—even in the not so remote Mughal period. Historical anthropology can be made only tentatively by extrapolation from contemporary observations and from colonial descriptions.

Three features should be noticed. First, the basic urban texture was made less of homogeneous lines of houses than of juxtaposition of estates of the rich nobles, replicas in miniatures of the emperor's palace, each with an army of retainers, servants, and artisans (Blake 1991); the common people lived, as they could, in mud houses between the mansions of the noble (Gaborieau 1995b, 25–26), so that, according to the French seventeenth century traveller François Bernier, Shahjahanabad looked like "several villages joined together (...) and like an army camp rather better and more comfortably placed than in the countryside" (Bernier 1981, 184–185). In addition, there were bazaars, and most probably reserved areas for unclean artisans, since in the Mughal period at least one normative text enjoins the *kotwâl* to allocate "separate quarters in the town for noisome and despised trades like those of butchers, corpse-washers and sweepers" (Bosworth 1986, 280; see also Qureshi 1966, 206).

Second, there was clearly a hierarchy with a higher town near the royal palace where the house of the high class people, of the nobility, was located, and of a lower town to which the lower classes were relegated in the opposite part of the city: this is noted episodically in the sources; an attempt has been made to elaborate on this question from a map of Shajahanabad dating from the first half of the nineteenth century (Malik 1993).

Finally, people were spatially segregated according to religious communities, ethnical origins, and castes. Such segregation is mentioned repeatedly in the sources, but we lack sufficiently detailed data to reconstruct social maps. A glimpse at traditional towns like Chanderi may, however, help to imagine the past (Sharma 1999, detailed colour map on p. 123): the three religious communities (Muslims, Hindus, and Jains) live in distinct areas; for the Hindus and the Muslims, who are socially differentiated, higher caste people live in areas distinct from the lower castes. Weavers are regrouped in special areas where again Hindus and Muslims artisans have clearly distinct quarters. The same remarks can also be made about Benares, and especially the quarters reserved for the Hindu and Muslim artisans (Kumar 1988, 63–82; Couté and Léger, 11–38).

4.6. *Interior and exterior: the limits of the town*

A town cannot be defined only by itself, but must be seen in relation to its exterior. The historiography of the Aligarh school has mainly considered the socio-economic relations to the rural countryside (which of course are very important), but has bypassed the more critical questions of the contribution the immediate surroundings of suburbs, markets, and shrines made to the definition of the town from strategic, ritual, and cultural points of view.

Physically the limits of the town were marked by defensive walls usually reinforced by moats, as in the case of Bijapur. The most impressive remaining ones are perhaps those of Bidar which have been preserved with all their gates as they stood in the middle of the sixteenth century, after the latest improvements were introduced to resist gun fire (Yazdani 1947). It is known that part of the socio-economic life of the town was prolonged beyond the walls with densely populated suburbs which contained warehouses and markets (Naqvi 1986, 148).

The religious and cultural life also extended beyond the walls in whose proximity often the tombs of saints and kings were found: visiting these tombs was part of the socio-cultural life. To take again the example of Shajahanabad, the eighteenth and nineteenth century literature insists on the importance of these visits in which women and men equally partook, particularly on Thursday nights and Fridays and on the festivals for the saints. For there were many places to visit outside new Delhi, in particular two sites which had been much beautified by the later Mughals: first, the complex of Qutb al-Dîn Bakhtiyâr Kâkî (d. *c.* 1235), the patron saint of Delhi, in Mehrauli, near the oldest Muslim town, and the famous Qutb Minâr in the Southwest; then, in the Southeast, the area around the tomb of Nizam al-Dîn Awliyâ (d. 1325) which, to this day, remains the most lively centre for the religious and cultural life of Delhi Muslims and contains also important Mughal tombs; the most important funeral complex, which contains also the oldest Mughal monuments in Delhi, is the monumental complex built over the remains of emperor Humayun (d. 1556); situated in the middle of a Mughal garden, it could also be used as a country residence by the imperial family (Asher 1991, 43–47). These "sorties" outside the walls were the routine of the Muslim life in Indian cities. An anthropologist has even made the case that for Benares regular outings in the morning or on festive days are still an integral part of life for both Hindus and Muslims (Kumar 1988, 83–110).

But there is another religious and juridical aspect which has been seldom mentioned (Gaborieau 1995b, 30–31). The walls are not only a physical defensive limit; they have also a religious significance in canonical Islam for community prayers. The regular Friday prayer is conducted in the cathedral mosque which is located inside the wall, usually, in the higher part of the town near the ruler's palace; exceptional prayers, like the prayers at the end of the month of fasting and of the sacrifice, as well as the prayer for rain in time of drought, have to be performed outside the walls, in a place called in Arabic *musallâ*, but known in India by its Persian equivalent *'id-gâh*. Such an external prayer-ground is a regular feature of Indian Islamic towns from the time of the Delhi Sultanate down to the present day; it usually consists of an open ground large enough to accommodate thousands of men; the direction of the *qibla* is marked only by a wall in the west with a *mihrâb* but can also be a more elaborate structure (Asher 1991, index under 'Idgâh). Shajahanabad had such an *'id-gâh* (Asher 1991, 202, 235). There the emperor would go, riding on an elephant and accompanied by the highest nobles and even, in the first half of the nineteenth century, by the British residents, to attend the festival prayers (Gaborieau 1995b, 30–31). These festivals had, of course, also a political significance, since they marked the days at which the allegiance to the emperor would be renewed.

Finally, we may ask whether this canonical limit, marked by the distinction of two kinds of prayers, is not also a religious limit separating pure and impure activities. I raise this question in comparison with the Hindu towns where a religious and magical external limit must be kept outside of which the houses of the untouchable castes lie. Based on the existing evidence, it is difficult to come to a definite conclusion (Gaborieau 1995b, 31–32); but is seems that, according to the only scholar who raised the question in connection with Shahjahanabad (Naqvi 1986, 147–148), impure professions were indeed pushed towards the periphery of the cities, but not located outside the walls, still inside, where one could find wine-shops and slaughter houses; there does not seem to have been a well defined magico-religious line dividing the interior and the exterior, as was the case for the Hindus. More research is, therefore, still needed to arrive at a satisfactory definition of the limits of the town.

4.7. *Imported and local models: Hindus and Muslims*

Finally, we have to deal with the speculations about the models Muslims used to build their cities in India. Most of what has been written is based on the assumption that there are two distinct cultural Muslim and Hindu traditions clearly identifiable through classical texts written in Persian and Sanskrit respectively.

Based on this assumption, we have on one side the scholars who argue that Indian Muslims employed Persian architects and town planners and that some of their towns were built according to Iranian models which owe nothing to the Indian context. Such is the case for instance, according to George Michell, of the Deccan city of Firuzabad, the square plan of which resembles that of Herat: it "can be understood only within the Persian context" (Michell 1993, 190).

For some other cities, however, Hindu models have been invoked. According to Stephen Blake, Shajahanabad—the plan of which resembles an ark where the real centre is the emperor's palace in the northeastern corner—consciously reproduces a Hindu model which owes nothing to Iranian inspiration (Blake 1991; see comments in Gaborieau 1995b, 32–34).

But for most of the other cities, like Bidar with its circular plan, it is difficult to make such a clear-cut pronouncement. And it is usually agreed (Michell 1993; Petruccioli 1993) that there was much synthesizing of the two traditions. I would add that tracing the origins of the various elements in each case would be difficult, for, contrary to recent ideological constructions of the fundamentalists, be they Hindu or Muslims, the two traditions are not as opposed as is usually conceived: the analogies they establish, for instance, in the domain of the social and spatial hierarchy, often render it difficult to trace the exact origin of a given feature. Take, for instance, the assumption that the traditional Hindu town as well as the Muslim one is based on the centrality of the king's palace flanked by the most important religious buildings; these central structures marked also the higher part of the town inhabited by the higher classes, while lower classes are relegated to the other part of the town, or even outside of it.

Conclusion

This brief survey has underlined both the immensity of the domain which Islamic cities of India represent and the paucity of studies. Almost everything remains to be done. We may notice that the researches have been concentrated on a few towns which were mainly capitals, Delhi having the pride of place. Perhaps the greatest amount of scholarship has been devoted to Fatehpur Sikri, an abandoned and atypical city, which has fascinated the historians because of its connection with Akbar's politico-religious ideology. But it is not sure that this peculiar case enlightens us much concerning Indian Muslim urban history. Detailed studies—still awaited—of other Mughal capitals like Agra and Lahore would probably be more rewarding. Small towns have also selectively attracted research. Middle level towns have been much neglected and more research should be done on them. Curiously enough, small towns or *qasba*s have often been better studied than bigger cities.

Concerning themes of research, more studies would be needed on the administration of the town, on the town texture, and the distribution of communities and castes; and more generally, studies on the religious considerations which contributed to define the interior structure of the town as well as its external limits. To accomplish this, an urban anthropology of Muslim India would have to be developed.

Finally, against the present trend of religious antagonism, it is necessary to insist on the analogies between Hindu and Muslim traditions; it is only through these analogies that one can understand how the adherents of the two religions could live in the same towns which were often jointly constructed and developed. Let us cite, at the end of this paper, the example of Lahore: built by Akbar and Jahangir, it has kept the typical layout of the Mughal capital; for more than half a century, until 1849, it was the capital of a Sikh kingdom; at the end of the British period, the majority of the population consisted of Hindus who had to leave at the time of Partition. It is only after 1947 that Lahore became almost entirely Muslim, with the only exception of a small group of former Hindu untouchables, mainly sweepers who had converted to Christianity and were still treated as untouchable by the Muslims.

References

Ahmed, Sharifuddin, ed. 1991. *Dhaka: past, present, future*. Dhaka: Asiatic Society of Bangladesh.

Alam, Muzaffar. 1986. *The crisis of the Mughal empire in Mughal India: Awadh and the Punjab, 1707–1748*. New Delhi: Oxford University Press.

Alam, Muzaffar, and Sanjay Subrahmanyam. 1994. L'État moghol et sa fiscalité. *Annales HSS* 1: 189–217.

———. 1998. *The Mughal state, 1526–1750*. New Delhi: Oxford University Press.

Ali, Athar. 1966. *The Mughal nobility under Aurangzeb*. Bombay: Asia Publishing House. (Rev. ed., New Delhi: Oxford University Press, 1997.)

Asher, Catherine B. 1991. *Architecture of Mughal India*. The New Cambridge History of India 1: 4. Cambridge: Cambridge University Press.

———. 2000. Mapping Hindu-Muslim identities through the architecture of Shajahanabad and Jaipur. In *Beyond Turk and Hindu: Rethinking religious identities in Islamicate South Asia*, ed. D. Gilmartin and B. Lawrence, 121–148. Gainesville: University Press of Florida.

Ballhatchet, Kenneth, and John Harrison, eds. 1980. *The city of South Asia: Pre-modern and modern*. London: Curzon Press.

Banga, Indu. 1992. *The city in Indian history.* Delhi: Manohar.

Bayly, Christopher A. 1980. The small town and Islamic gentry in North India: The case of Kara. In *The city of South Asia: Pre-modern and modern*, ed. K. Ballhatchet and J. Harrison, 20–48. London: Curzon Press.

———. 1983. *Rulers, townsmen and bazars: North India in the age of British expansion, 1780–1870.* Cambridge: Cambridge University Press.

Bayly, Susan. 1989. *Saints, goddesses and kings: Muslims and Christians in South Indian society, 1700–1900.* Cambridge: Cambridge University Press.

Bernier, François. 1981. *Voyage dans les États du Grand Mogol.* Edited and introduced by France Bhattacharya. Paris: Fayard.

Blake, Stephen P. 1991. *Shajahanabad: The sovereign city in Mughal India.* Cambridge: Cambridge University Press.

Bosworth, C. E. 1986. Kotwâl. In *Encyclopaedia of Islam.* 2nd ed., vol. 5: 279–280. Leiden: E. J. Brill.

Bouchon, Geneviève. 1988. Un microcosme: Calicut au 16ᵉ siècle. In *Marchands et hommes d'affaires asiatiques dans l'Océan Indien et la Mer de Chine, 13ᵉ–20ᵉ siècles*, ed. Denis Lombard and Jean Aubin, 49–57. Paris: EHESS.

Bouchon, Geneviève and Filipe Thomaz. 1988. *Voyage dans les deltas du Gange et de l'Irraouady, 1521.* Paris: EHESS/Fondation Gulbenkian.

Brown, Percy. 1956. *Indian architecture: Islamic period.* 5th rev. ed. Bombay: Taraporevala.

Cole, Juan R. I. 1989. *Roots of North Indian shi'ism in Iran and Iraq: Religion and state, 1722–1859.* Berkeley: University of California Press.

Couté, Pierre-Daniel, and Jean-Michel Léger, eds. 1989. *Bénarès: Un voyage d'architecture.* Paris: Editions Créaphis.

Dupont, Véronique, Emma Tarlo, and Denis Vidal, eds. 2000. *Delhi: Urban space and human destinies.* Delhi: Manohar.

Eaton, Richard M. 1978. *Sufis of Bijapur, 1300–1700: Social roles of sufis in medieval India.* Princeton: Princeton University Press. (Repr. New Delhi: Munshiram Manoharlal, 1996.)

———. 1993. *The Rise of Islam and the Bengal Frontier, 1204–1760.* Berkeley: University of California Press.

Eaton, Richard M., and George Michell. 1990. *Firuzabad: palace city of the Deccan.* Oxford: Oxford University Press.

Ehlers, Eckart, and Thomas Krafft, eds. 1993. *Shâhjahânâbâd/old Delhi: Tradition and colonial change.* Stuttgart: Franz Steiner Verlag.

Frykenberg, Robert E., ed. 1986. *Delhi through the ages: Essays in urban history, culture and society.* New Delhi: Oxford University Press.

Fussman, Gérard, Denis Matringe, Eric Ollivier, and Françoise Pirot. 2003. *Naissance et déclin d'une qasba: Chanderi du Xᵉ au XVIIIᵉ siècle.* 3 vols. Paris: De Boccard.

Gaborieau, Marc, ed. 1986. *Islam et société en Asie du Sud.* Collection Purushârtha 9. Paris: EHESS.

———. 1989. Les recherches sur les aires culturelles non-européennes en habitat et urbanisme: Importance pratique et théorique. *Architecture et comportement* 5 (3): 193–206.

———. 1993. *Ni Brahmanes ni ancêtres: Colporteurs musulmans du Népal.* Nanterre: Société d'ethnologie.

———. 1995a. L'islamisation de l'Inde et de l'Asie orientale. In *Etats, sociétés et cultures du monde musulman médiéval, Xᵉ–XVᵉ siècle*, Tome I, *L'évolution politique et sociale*, ed. Jean-Claude Garcin et al., 431–459. Paris: Presses Universitaires de France.

———. 1995b. Villes de toile et villes de pierre: Les capitales mogholes étaient-elles des camps? In *Cités d'Asie*, ed. Pierre Clemént, Sophie Charpentier, and Charles Goldblum, 15–34. Marseille: Editions Parenthèses. (*Cahiers de la recherche architecturale*, nos. 35–36 [1994].)

——. 1996. Les saints, les eaux et les récoltes en Inde. In *Lieux d'islam: Cultes et cultures de l'Afrique à Java*, ed. Muhammad Ali Amir-Moezzi, 239–254. Paris: Éditions Autrement.

——. 2002. a) chap. 2, The Indian states: The sultanates; b) chaps. 5–10, The Mogul Empire (1556–1739). In *A history of modern India, 1480–1950*, ed. Claude Markovits, 23–40; 79–183. London: Anthem Press. (Translation of Claude Markovits, ed. *Histoire de l'Inde moderne, 1480–1950*. Paris: Fayard, 1994.)

Gillion, K. L. 1968. *Ahmedabad: A study in Indian urban history.* Berkeley: University of California Press.

Gole, Susan. 1989. *Indian maps and plans from the earliest times to the advent of European surveys.* New Delhi: Manohar.

Gommans, Jos J. L. 1995. *The rise of the Indo-Afghan empire, c. 1710–1780.* Leiden: E. J. Brill.

Graff, Violette, ed. 1997. *Lucknow. Memories of a city.* Delhi: Oxford University Press.

Grewal, J. S. 1975. *In the by-lanes of history: Some Persian documents from a Persian town.* Simla: Indian Institute of Advanced Studies.

Gupta, I. P. 1986. *Agra: The Imperial capital: Urban glimpses of Mughal India.* Delhi: Discovery.

Gupta, Narayani. 1981. *Delhi between two Empires, 1803–1931: Society, government and urban growth.* Delhi: Oxford University Press.

Hambly, R. G. G. 1968. *Cities of Mughal India.* New York and Delhi.

——. 1982. Towns and cities: Mughal India. In *The Cambridge economic history of India. Volume 1: c. 1200–c. 1750*, edited by Tapan Raychaudhuri and Irfan Habib, 434–451. Cambridge: Cambridge University Press.

Habib, Irfan. 1999. *The agrarian system of Northern India, 1526–1707.* 2nd rev. ed. New Delhi: Oxford University Press. (1st ed., Bombay: Asia Publishing House 1963.)

Islam, M. Mufakharul. 1991. Urbanisation and urban centres in Mughal India: some general comments. In *Dhaka: Past, present, future*, ed. Sharif uddin Ahmed, 584–594. Dhaka: Asiatic Society of Bangladesh.

Jackson, Peter. 1999. *The Delhi sultanate: A political and military history.* Cambridge: University Press.

Karim, Abdul. 1964. *Dacca, the Mughal capital.* Dacca: Asiatic Society of Pakistan.

Khan, M. A. 1993. *The walled city of Lahore.* Lahore.

Koch, Ebba. 1991. *Mughal architecture: An outline of its history and development (1526–1858).* Munich: Prestel.

Kumar, Nita. 1988. *The artisans of Banaras: Popular culture and identity,* Princeton: Princeton University Press.

Maclean, Derryl. 2000. La sociologie de l'engagement politique: Le Mahdawîya indien et l'État. In *Mahdisme et millénarisme en Islam*, ed. Mercedes Garcia-Arenal, 239–256. Aix-en-Provence: Édisud. (*Revue des Mondes Musulmans et de la Méditerranée*, nos. 91–94 [2000].)

Malik, Jamal. 1993. Islamic Institutions and Infrastructures in Shâjahânâbâd. In *Shâjahânâbâd/old Delhi: Tradition and colonial change*, ed. Eckart Ehlers and Thomas Krafft, 43–64. Stuttgart: Franz Steiner Verlag.

Markovits, Claude. 1995. L'adaptation d'un espace urbain traditionnel à des fonctions nouvelles: Le cas d'Ahmedabad (Inde). In *Cités d'Asie*, ed. Pierre Clément, Sophie Charpentier, and Charles Goldblum, 47–56. Marseille: Editions Parenthèses. (*Cahiers de la recherche architecturale*, nos. 35–36 [1994].)

——, ed. 2002. *A history of modern India, 1480–1950.* London: Anthem Press. (Translation of Claude Markovits, ed., *Histoire de l'Inde moderne, 1480–1950*, Paris: Fayard, 1994.)

Marshall, John. 1922. The Monuments of Muslim India. In *The Cambridge history of India*, vol. 3. Cambridge: Cambridge University Press.

Michell, George. 1993. Firuzabad: Palace city of the Bahmanis. In *Islam and Indian Regions*, 2 vols., ed. Anna Libera Dallapiccola and Stephanie Zingel-Avé Lallemant, 1:185–191. Stuttgart: Franz Steiner Verlag.

Moosvi, Shireen. 1987. *The economy of the Mughal empire c. 1595: A statistical study.* New Delhi: Oxford University Press.

Naqvi, Hamida Khatoon. 1968. *Urban centres and industries in upper India, 1556–1803.* London: Asia Publishing House.

———. 1972. *Urbanization and urban centres under the great Moghals.* Simla: Indian Institute of Advanced Studies.

———. 1986. Shahjahanabad, the Mughal Delhi: An introduction. In *Delhi through the ages: Essays in urban history, culture and society*, ed. R. E. Frykenberg, 142–151. New Delhi: Oxford University Press.

Pandey, Gyanendra. 1984. 'Encounters and calamities': The history of a north Indian Qasba in the nineteenth century. In *Subaltern Studies III*, ed. Ranajit Guha. Delhi: Oxford University Press.

Petruccioli, Attilio. 1988. *Fathpur Sikri: La città del sole e delle acque.* Rome: Carucci Editore.

———. 1993. 'Ad Quadratum': Notes on Deccani town planning. In *Islam and Indian Regions*, 2 vols., ed. Anna Libera Dallapiccola and Stephanie Zingel-Avé Lallemant, 1: 193–202. Stuttgart: Franz Steiner Verlag.

Qureshi, Ishtiaq Husain. 1966. *The administration of the Mughul Empire.* Karachi: University of Karachi.

Raychaudhuri, Tapan, and Irfan Habib, eds. 1982. *The Cambridge economic history of India. Volume 1: c. 1200–c. 1750.* Cambridge: Cambridge University Press.

Richards, John F. 1993. *The Mughal empire.* The New Cambridge History of India, vol. 1: 5. Cambridge: Cambridge University Press.

Sarkar, Jadunath. 1920. *Mughal administration.* Calcutta: M. C. Sarkar.

Schimmel, Annemarie. 1980. *Islam in the Indian subcontinent.* Leiden: E. J. Brill.

Sharma, K. L. 1999. *Chanderi, 1990–1995.* Paris: De Boccard.

Sharma, Y. D. 1964. *Delhi and its Neighbourhood.* New Delhi: Archaeological Survey of India. (2nd rev. ed. 1974.)

Singh, M. P. 1985. *Town, market, mint and port in the Mughal empire.* Delhi: Adam Publishers.

Spate, O. H. K. 1957. *India and Pakistan: A general and regional geography.* 2nd ed. London: Methuen; New York: E. P. Dutton.

Spear, Percival. 1994. *Delhi: Its monuments and history.* 3rd ed. New Delhi: Oxford University Press. Updated and annotated by Narayani Gupta and Laura Sykes. (1st ed. 1943.)

Trivedi, K. K. 1998. *Agra: Economic and political profile of a Mughal Suba, 1580–1707.* Pune: Ravish Publishers.

Yazdani, G. 1947. *Bidar: Its history and monuments.* (Repr. New Delhi: Oxford University Press, 1974.)

THE OTTOMAN TOWN
(FIFTEENTH–EIGHTEENTH CENTURIES)

Gilles Veinstein

In the present state of our knowledge, dealing with the Ottoman town consists primarily in pondering the very notion of "Ottoman town," not only in terms of contents, but also of application: is there a unique type of town characteristic of the Ottoman Empire as a whole that could naturally be stamped as "Ottoman town", or are there sufficiently marked differences between towns that would justify a distinction between different types throughout the empire?[1] Which type would it then be most suitable to select as the Ottoman town and what would be the most appropriate geographical location for it?

There is apparently one generally accepted answer to this question to which most researchers tend to rally, at least implicitly: there exists a spontaneously established distinction between, on the one hand, Mashreq and Maghreb towns, whose kinship goes without saying and which are not Ottoman towns but "Arabic towns in the Ottoman era"—to use André Raymond's words—and, on the other hand, the towns of "central" (relative to the capital) or better yet "nuclear," provinces of the empire, which are the real Ottoman towns. In other words, the dividing line places Arabic provinces on one side, Anatolia and Rumelia (Asia Minor and the Balkans) on the other. This means that the discrimination is based on ethno-cultural grounds and that it opposes the cities of the Arabs to those of the Turks. This can only suit nationalists on both sides who, to this day, have picked up and developed the theme without moderation. One must add that scholars more or less external to these ideological preoccupations naturally tend to embrace and reinforce this distinction insofar as it corresponds to a similar division in academics that opposes Arabic and Turkish specialists and, more precisely, specialists of the Ottoman Empire: the empire

---

[1] Cf. G. Veinstein, "La ville ottomane: les facteurs d'unité," in *La Ciudad Islamica*, Institucion Fernando el catolico (Saragossa, 1991).

purportedly had two kinds of towns, those pertaining to Arabic Studies
and those pertaining to Turcology...

It is precisely this "evidence" that we must question first through an
a priori reasoning consisting in reviewing the various factors that may
have influenced urban processes in the Ottoman Empire.

Beforehand, one must note a fact that raises a number of reflections:
all these towns belong to one and the same empire. True, this empire,
built "on three continents," according to the accepted way of saying,
stretches far enough latitudinally and longitudinally to offer great variety
in natural conditions, and marked differences in climate and available
construction material cannot but affect housing. There is a clear distinction between zones of stone architecture—Syria, southeastern Anatolia,
and the Kayseri region—and zones of wooden architecture. Wood was
the main material when in good supply, as in the traditional houses of
Istanbul and the *yalı* of the Bosporus, and when in short supply was
used only for building the framework, which was then filled in with
miscellaneous material.

At the same time, the sultans of Istanbul were not first in bringing
political unity to these disparate regions: these had all been part of the
Roman and Byzantine empires whose heritage at the time of the Ottomans' arrival was more or less recent and vivacious in some regions or,
on the contrary, buried under subsequent strata. In any case, the effect
of this common filiation on the urban landscape of the Ottoman era is
very concrete, not only because of the, sometimes spectacular, presence
of antique and Byzantine monuments in most of these towns, but also
because of subsisting traces in the topography of Roman road patterns
(which have survived to this day). What is a well-known phenomenon
in many Western towns, notably in northern Italy, attested as well in
several cities of the Mashreq, thanks to Sauvaget's work, is also found in
Salonica, Nicaea, or Rhodes or, as P. Pinon demonstrated, in Izmir,
in the ancient Turkish quarter around the agora or, to a lesser extent,
in Bursa, in the citadel quarter.[2]

As for the Ottoman period itself, the towns of the empire share, as
a whole, the fact that they belong to the same period, thereby gener-

---

[2] Cf., among others, J. Sauvaget, "Le plan antique de Damas," *Syria* 26 no. 3–4
(1949): 314–358; G. Mansuelli, *Urbanistica e architettura della Cisalpina romana* (Brussels,
1971); P. Pinon, "Les tissus urbains ottomans entre Orient et Occident," in *Proceedings
of the 2nd International Meeting on Modern Ottoman Studies and the Turkish Republic, Leiden,
April 21–26, 1987*, ed. E. Van Donzel (Leiden, 1989), 17.

ally partaking in technical and socio-economical developments whose impact extends far beyond the boundaries of the Ottoman world. In our opinion, Wirth's work on the development of urban economic centres in the Muslim area gives a good example of those general phenomena linked to a specific period. The perfecting of these centres, marked by the adjunction of caravansaries with internal courts that had so far been placed near city gates, started in the late fourteenth and early fifteenth centuries and culminated in the highest achievements and most elaborate monumental buildings of the period between the sixteenth and nineteenth centuries. This was not, however, restricted to the Ottoman area; it also spread to the Safavid area and other states, albeit in rudimentary or altered forms.[3]

Ottoman towns also experienced specific conditions connected to their integration into the empire. Contrary to long-standing and tenacious prejudices about the Ottoman regime, these conditions were far from unfavourable to urban growth as a whole, though one must concede that they benefited specific towns unevenly, depending on these towns' position in the political-administrative, strategic, and economic system of the empire. In any case, integration into this immense and powerful structure was *a priori* propitious to prosperity: first, it brought relative order and security both inside the empire and in its relationships with its neighbours, a situation which generally favoured communications and economic activity. Of course, the *pax ottomanica* was sometimes disrupted: banditry was never entirely curbed and frontiers (which fluctuated over time) were always more exposed to troubles. Second, starting with the late sixteenth century, central authorities loosened their grip, even if they sometimes were efficaciously taken over, on a reduced scale, by local governments.

The empire simultaneously gave birth to a very large domestic production and consumption market relatively unified in legislative, fiscal, administrative, monetary, and linguistic terms and, in addition, stimulated by developing relations with the West as well as by the regular

---

[3] Cf. E. Wirth, "Zum Problem des Bazars (*suq, çarşı*). Versuch einer Begriffbestimmung und Theorie der traditionellen Wirtschaftszentrums der orientalisch-islamischen Stadt," *Der Islam* 1974: 203–260, 1975: 6–46; id., "Die orientalische Stadt. Ein Überblick aufgrund jüngerer Forschungen zur materiellen Kultur," *Saeculum*, 1975: 45–94. Cf. also X. de Planhol, "Sur la genèse du Bazar," in *Régions, villes et aménagement. Mélanges jubilaires offerts à Jacqueline Beaujeu-Garnier* (Paris, 1987), 445–474.

exchanges with the rest of the Eastern world—this aspect of Ottoman trade is still the least known and has long been underestimated.

A factor of urban growth, this commercial dynamism particularly fostered the extension of urban trade centres, and in most of them, the reinforcement of typical infrastructures, bazaars, *bedesten*s, markets, *han*s.[4]

As recent works following those of Inalcik demonstrate, the Ottoman authorities evinced more interest and complacence than has been said toward the interplay of economic forces they were facing (as indicated by commercial treaties concluded at all epochs, facilities granted to big merchants with regard to the constraints inherent to the guild system, and the involvement of numerous dignitaries with business). However, the Istanbul sultans' interest was larger in scope: they were openly interested in the city and developed a proactive urban policy that was implemented in various ways and at different levels: granted deportation (*sürgün*) was undertaken in response to political considerations (aiming to prevent the formation of centres of resistance, particularly in newly conquered territories), it was also a clear response to the authorities' concern for the settlement or resettlement of certain towns and for revitalizing their economic activity by providing them with necessary manpower and technical skills.[5] Mehmed II's initiatives in revitalizing Istanbul in the morrow of the conquest are well known: Muslim, Christian, or Jewish elements from various parts of Anatolia and Rumelia, the Greek islands, and the Crimea were forcibly resettled with a new status in the neighbourhoods and houses of ancient Byzantium.[6] The conqueror's successors also endowed their capital with all sorts of craftsmen and artists brought back from their military campaigns. This was particularly true of Selim I who took much from Mamluk and Persian cities. It is true that, in the cases where these measures

---

[4] Cf. S. Faroqhi, *Towns and Townsmen of Ottoman Anatolia: Trade, Crafts and Food Production in an Urban Setting, 1520–1650* (Cambridge, 1984), 23–48. M. Cezar, *Typical Commercial Buildings of the Ottoman Classical Period and the Ottoman Construction System* (Istanbul, 1983).

[5] Cf. particularly Ö.-L. Barkan, "Osmanlı imparatorluğunda bir Iskan ve Kolonizasyon metodu olarak sürgünler," [Deportation used as a settlement method in the Ottoman Empire] *Istanbul Üniversitesi Iktisat Fakültesi Mecmuası* 6, nos. 1–4 (1949–1950): 524–569. N. Beldiceanu, *Recherche sur la ville ottomane au XVᵉ siècle. Étude et Actes* (Paris, 1973), 36–44.

[6] Cf. H. Inalcik, "The Policy of Mehmed II toward the Greek Population of Istanbul and the Byzantine Buildings in the City," *Dumbarton Oaks Papers* 23/24 (Washington, 1969), 231–249.

applied to townsmen and not to country people, they did not lead to an overall increase, but to a redistribution of the urban population toward privileged areas. In any case, they contributed to a certain standardization of production throughout the empire, particularly in art. Though of a different nature, the Sultans' reception of the Jews expulsed from Spain, Portugal or Italy and later, of *conversos*, their successors—whether it be the expression of a certain tolerance or of consummate pragmatism—lead this time to similar results in numerous towns scattered in various parts of the empire, starting with Salonica, Istanbul, and Safed. For that matter, the empire always remained open to all types of refugees, who—and this is particularly true of those that people in the West called renegades—played a role in its technical and scientific evolution, whose fruits benefited the towns.

The authorities' direct interest in architectural, and, more generally, urban matters was clearly manifest in the institution, in the early sixteenth century at least, of a corps of palace architects (*mi'mâr-i hâssa*),[7] which, toward 1535, comprised twelve architects, one carpenter and one tile roofer (*kiremetchi*).[8] It was headed by a chief architect (*mi'mâr bashı*). This position was held by the great architect Sinan from 1539 to 1588 with the magnificence that we know. This powerful figure who enjoyed a position close to the sovereign did not limit his competence to the palace or even the capital since he controlled all great civil, military and religious construction work financed by the sovereign and his entourage. For long-distance orders, he merely drew a sketch that a member of the corps executed at the place in question. This explains the incredibly high number and ubiquity of the works attributed to Sinan.[9] Starting with the early seventeenth century, architects were placed by the central government as local representatives of the *mi'mâr bashı* in a great number of Ottoman towns. They had at their levels the same competence in city planning as their senior in the capital, that is, they controlled all the guilds related to the building trade. It appears

---

[7] Cf. S. Turan, "Osmanlı Teşkilatında Hassa mimarları," [Official Architects in the Ottoman Organization] *A.U.D.T.C.F. Tarih Araştırmaları Dergisi* 1, no. 1 (1963): 157–202.

[8] Cf. Ö. L. Barkan, "H. 933–934 (M. 1527–1528) Mali yılına ait bir bütçe örneği," [Budget sample for fiscal year 1527–1528] *Istanbul Üniversitesi Iktisat Fakültesi Mecmuası* 15, no. 1–4 (1953–1954): 329.

[9] Cf. A. Kuran, "Suleyman The Magnificent's Architectural Patronage," in *Soliman le Magnifique et son temps*, ed. G. Veinstein, Rencontres de l'École du Louvre (Paris, 1992), 217–223.

that in a good number of places, the local architect had to give prior agreement to all construction projects, and he sometimes happened to distribute available construction material among skilled craftsmen. While the initial role of the *muhtasib* was gradually reduced and he was turned into a subordinate tax collector who sometimes farmed his office, the local architect became invested with his urbanistic competence.

It was clearly the case for the chief architect in the capital. He was responsible for implementing the sultan's urban regulations and, in most cases, probably inspired them.

This abundant corpus, elaborated between the mid-sixteenth century and the Tanzimat era, is known to us—at least concerning Istanbul and to some extent Mecca—thanks to the numerous documents published by Ahmed Refik and Osman Nuri, and more recently synthesized by S. Yerasimos.[10] The latter emphasizes the documents' definitely "customary" character, inspired by the State's concern for public utility as opposed to the principles of the *shari'a* that were geared toward protecting private interests. Here we can observe the Ottoman administration's same determination to regulate all aspects of urban matters minutely as in so many other domains: height zoning, front features (canopy roofs and corbels were theoretically banned), prescribed and proscribed materials, prohibited areas, etc.

A good number of these principles admittedly correspond to openly expressed security concerns: wood and housing developments were proscribed for fear of fire hazards; neighbourhoods were protected from aggressions by gates; illegal and marginal constructions and *han*s sheltering singles were banned for fear of clandestine immigration; building against the external side of ramparts was forbidden (in cities liable to be besieged, this ban aimed to avoid facilitating the besieger's task, as in Algiers or sixteenth-century towns on the Croatian border), but other motivations were put forward concerning eighteenth century Istanbul, namely that the city walls must be used as a firebreak; traffic around gates and ladders must not be blocked; lastly, it was recom-

---

[10] Osman Nuri, *Mecelle-i Umur-i Belediye* [City Code] (Istanbul, 1922); A. Refik, On altıncı asırda *Istanbul hayatı, 1553–1591* [Life in Istanbul in the sixteenth century] (Istanbul, 1935); id., *Hicri onbirinci asırda Istanbul hayatı, 1000–1010* (Istanbul, 1931); id., *Hicri onbirinci asırda Istanbul hayatı, 1100–1200* (Istanbul, 1930); id., *Hicri onucuncu asırda Istanbul hayatı, 1200–1255* (Istanbul, 1932); S. Yerasimos, "La réglementation urbaine ottomane (XVIe–XIXe siècles)," in *The 2nd International Meeting...*, op. cit.: 1–14.

mended not to give a bad impression to foreign ambassadors arriving to Istanbul.[11]

In another study, Yerasimos states that the repetition of the same bans across the centuries is evidence of their total inefficacy. He ascribes this situation to the protection of private interests by the *qadis*, who gave priority to the *shari'a* over the sultan's regulations. If this is so, reality must have resembled more what was proscribed than what the sultan and his architects advocated.[12]

This is true at least of "informal," private, architecture and more generally, of what is sometimes called "micro-urbanism" or "infill."

On the other hand, only through official architecture could the sovereign successfully leave his mark and the *mi'mâr bashı* put his principles into practice. Instituting pious endowments helped finance the projects, but also determined what types of construction must be undertaken: religious and charitable buildings, utilities, which were built not as separate elements but jointed to each other to form "complexes" (*külliye*), and which exerted a structuring effect on entire sections of the urban fabric. The Ottoman sultans and their families were great founders of urban waqf, whose number increased in the sixteenth century when the State's wealth was at its highest, and the tradition was maintained afterwards when the women of the dynasty, mothers and wives of the sovereigns, were particularly active in this area in the seventeenth and eighteenth centuries.[13] High dignitaries and provincial governors followed the lead. In these conditions, the waqf played a decisive role not only in ornamentation but also in the improvement of services and the development of Ottoman towns. Entire areas could be remodelled according to a general plan following the construction of a large-scale foundation. This can be illustrated by examples both from the Mashreq and the Balkans, namely, the foundations by two Damascene governors, Sinan and Murad Pasha, in the late sixteenth-century, and those of Gazi Husrev Bey, governor of Sarajevo in the early sixteenth century.[14]

---

[11] Decree of May 2–June 7, 1722, published by O. Nuri, op. cit.: 1089, quoted in Yerasimos, art. cit.: 7. On the ban on building around city walls, both inside and outside, see Başbakanlık Arşivi, Istanbul, *Muhimme Defteri* 3, no. 82.

[12] S. Yerasimos, "À propos des réformes urbaines des Tanzimat," in *Villes ottomanes à la fin de l'Empire*, ed. P. Dumont and F. Georgeon (Paris, 1992), 17–32.

[13] Cf. L. P. Pierce, *The Imperial Harem, Women and Sovereignty in the Ottoman Empire* (Oxford, 1993), 198–218.

[14] Cf. B. Djurdjev, s.v. "Bosna," *Encyclopédie de l'islam*, 2nd ed., 1:1301–1305. A. Handzić, "O formiranju nekih gradskih naselja u Bosni v XVI stoljecu," *Prilozi za orijentalnu*

Whether they were due to objective conditions or to a more or less determined and efficient action on the part of central authorities, the factors favouring urban growth that we have just reviewed had an overall impact, but there is no doubt that they unevenly benefited specific regions and towns. In this respect, Istanbul was certainly privileged, being both the main centre of attraction for all the empire's commercial exchanges and the primary object of imperial solicitude in terms of settlement, supplies, facilities, development, and beautification. This explains why historic Middle-Eastern metropolises (Cairo, Aleppo, Damascus) rank far behind Istanbul in the classification of the empire's main cities. Stunted by their proximity to the capital, Anatolia and Rumelia only had medium-sized towns at best—Bursa, Salonica, and Edirne.[15] We have also seen that the urban regulations that we know of concern the capital almost exclusively and we do not have a very clear vision of how they were implemented in other places. As for the influence exerted by the *mi'mâr bashı's* architectural models in the Arabic provinces of the empire, A. Raymond's survey shows how limited it was quantitatively and chronologically: he only noted down some fifteen monuments in the Ottoman style, among which nine date back to the sixteenth century, three to the seventeenth, and three to the eighteenth. Besides, the two sole monuments of the Maghreb, the New Mosque in Algiers and the Sidi Mehrez Mosque in Tunis, are more recent (dating from 1660 and 1686 respectively) and they express the will of their local sponsors to affirm their ties with the Porte symbolically, and not the control of Istanbul's official architects.[16] These remarks suggest that aside from all other considerations, the greater or lesser distance from the capital was per se a factor of differentiation among Ottoman towns, but it is not possible at this point to evaluate its significance exactly.

---

filologiju 25 ([1975] Sarajevo, 1977): 133–169; in German: "Ein Aspekt der Entstehungs Geschichte Osmanischer Städte im Bosnien des 16 Jahrhunderts," *Südost-Forschungen* 37 (1978): 41–49; J.-P. Pascual, *Damas à la fin du XVIᵉ siècle d'après trois actes de waqf ottomans*, vol. 1 (Damascus, 1983).

[15] Cf. Ö. L. Barkan, "Essai sur les données statistiques des registres de recensement dans l'Empire ottoman," *Journal of Economic and Social History of the Orient* 1 (1958): 9–36.

[16] A. Raymond, "L'architecture dans les pays arabes à l'époque ottomane," in *Histoire de l'Empire Ottoman*, ed. R. Mantran (Paris, 1989), 684–688.

Moreover, we have last to consider a factor of unity between the towns of the empire that many would agree is decisive, to wit, Muslim towns, or at least towns under Muslim domination (many of them, and this does not solely apply to the Balkans, had large minorities, or perhaps even non-Muslim majorities). Scholars who adhere to G. E. Von Grunebaum's and G. and W. Marçais' view that, as a doctrine, juridical system, and more generally as a culture, Islam determines a specific city model which they call "Muslim town," will tend to liken the Ottoman town to the Muslim town ("Eastern" or "Levantine" town, in the words of historians of the Balkans) and will not *a fortiori* distinguish among Ottoman towns. And yet, we do note divergences between the Hanafite, Malakite, and Shafeite schools of jurisprudence that shared the empire's regions and cut off the Mashreq both from central provinces and the Maghreb, but it is nevertheless true that these differences had little effect on the towns aside from well-known divergences in the styles of mosques and minarets. Of more significance are perhaps the variations in antiquity and the conditions of Islamization in the regions: we are definitely dealing here with a contrast between Arabic and central provinces. On the one hand, there are regions where Islamization took place several centuries before Ottoman domination and is interconnected with the Arabic language and culture. In the central provinces one must distinguish between central and eastern Anatolia, where Islamization, though much more recent than in the Arabic provinces, took place before the Ottomans' arrival and developed in a culture strongly influenced by Persia; lastly, northern and western Anatolia and the Balkans, where Islam was brought by the Ottomans themselves, in a form descending from Anatolian Islam and therefore, marked by Persian culture.

These different situations engender obvious divergences, at least in architectural styles and terminology, though not necessarily in the reality the latter denotes: the terms *bazar*, used for the commercial centre and *bedesten* (corrupted form of *bazzistan*), used to designate the covered market where precious goods were traded and well looked after, are commonly used in the empire's towns. But differences in naming definitely separate Arabic from central provinces: in central provinces, the *han*'s or *kervansaray*'s, which were simultaneously warehouses, inns for travellers and merchants, and centres for specialized wholesale trade, are not designated with the synonyms used currently in Arabic provinces (*qaysariyya, funduq, wakala*, or *ukala*). Central provinces only use the term *dükkan* to designate shops, to the exclusion of *hanut*; streets and parts of specialized streets lined with shops are called there *charshı* and not suq. The matter is purely linguistic, for all these terms designate the same commercial entities.

If we attempt now to recapitulate the common features shared by all Ottoman towns, as well as the slight differences that we occasionally pointed out, we are inclined to postulate that these towns are certainly closely related (to wit the above urban economic centre) but, as we saw, some disparity is also possible, in terminology and architectural style, for instance. But if we want better to evaluate the impact of partly identical and partly different conditions on the basic particulars of the respective urban fabrics, we must leave the speculative level and move on to concrete comparisons of the data: drawing of the general plan, plot plan, built-up surface, circulation area; but also the spatial distribution of functions and of the population according to wealth or ethno-religious identity (most towns showed diversity in that respect, which brought the Mashreq closer to central provinces than to the Maghreb).

This type of exercise naturally entails that specialists of the different areas engage in a dialogue above the academic division between Arabic and Ottoman specialists mentioned above, but also, that the research on both sides be done at the same pace and in similar directions. To our view, this has been insufficiently done, at least until recently. Whether or not cities of the Arabic and central provinces are fundamentally different, it is clear that they have been studied rather differently by different people. This disparity must and can be corrected: if only by the very fact that all the cities in question belong to the same period and the same political-administrative structure, the conditions for their study, both fieldwork and archival research, are by and large analogous. In this respect, the Maghreb is at a relative disadvantage compared to the rest of the empire, since the Istanbul bureaucracy never undertook census registers in the area, which is also the case for other Arab countries (Egypt, Hedjaz, part of Iraq). Furthermore, there are apparently fewer surviving *qadi* registers there.

Fieldwork is more advanced in Arabic provinces, thanks notably to the "French school" (a fact not unrelated to the colonial situation, of course), but recourse to Ottoman archives is infrequent, either because they were lacking (as the Ottomans did not take the census in Cairo, Algiers, Tunis, Baghdad, Mecca, and Medina) or because they were not accessible, at least at the start: hence the care with which these scholars assessed the population level of a given town and its evolution on the basis of concrete "urban signs" (built-up surface, types of habitat, number of *hammams*, variation in the surface of *khutba* mosques, movement of tanneries) when they adapted the methods elaborated by Torrès Balbas, the historian of Medieval Spain's Muslim towns. This inevitably paved the way to most concrete investigations.[17]

On the contrary, monographs on traditional towns (before nineteenth-century reforms)[18] are legion in the Turkish field, but tend to be more "bookish," to be overwhelmed by the overabundance of Turkish archival material, to conform to what has been called "document fetishism" (Halil Berktay), and ignore the treatment of questions, particularly those related to urbanism. In the best of cases, when they do not fall within the province of local scholarship (with both its merits and limitations), they are contributions to institutional and social history rather than studies on urbanism proper (Beldiceanu, Inalcik, Mantran, Todorov, Ergenç, Gerber, Faroqhi). It seems even that historians of Arabic towns, notably A. Raymond, A. Rafeq, and A. Abdel-Nour, took the lead again in the exploitation of qadi registers: which is not to say that these sources have not been the subject of pioneering works in Turcology in a long time (Inalcik, Barkan, Jennings, Todorov, Ergenç, Özdemir, Faroqhi, Gerber), but, to our view, their authors and others later on did not clearly care to study these materials in the framework of the town's spatial structures and the distribution of its population.

For all that, there is no need to exaggerate and the gap between the two approaches tends to be reduced: during the last decades, there have been sufficiently numerous and serious studies on the concrete aspects of the town in central provinces to allow us to begin to draw comparisons

---

[17] Cf. L. Torrès Balbas, "Extension y demografia de las ciudades hispano-musulmanas," *Studia Islamica* 3 (1955). A. Lezine, *Deux villes d'Ifriqiya* (Paris, 1971). A. Raymond, "Signes urbains et étude de la population des grandes villes arabes à l'époque ottomane," *Bulletin d'Études Orientales* 27 (1974).

[18] Reforms of urban institutions in the Tanzimat era and the general context of the second half of the nineteenth century changed the conditions in Ottoman city planning: we are not considering this period in which the unity of the Ottoman city acquired new characteristics, nor the literature on the subject, especially recent: cf. the handlist provided in the work referenced above, edited by P. Dumont and F. Georgeon.

with Arabic towns on these points (urban habitat,[19] physical structures,[20] facilities,[21] urban fabric).[22]

In a synthesis of the first results of research on the urban fabric, P. Pinon[23] concludes that the real division does not obtain between cities of the Arabic and central provinces, but that the dividing line crosses Anatolia, approximately linking Izmir with Erzurum, or more precisely, Antalya with Erzurum. Thus, it contrasts the Balkans and northwestern Anatolia on the one hand with southeastern Anatolia on the other, the latter being joined to the "Arabic," i.e., Near Eastern and Maghrebine, side, this rapprochement having no ethnic or nationalistic connotation. This split is verified by the habitat. The Balkans and northwestern Anatolia are the seat of the so-called "Turkish" house (also called by certain authors "Ottoman," "Bulgarian," or even "Byzantine"): it is a house with a *hayat* or *sofa*, i.e., a central hall lined with rooms; the house is two-storied, with a solid podium, made of

---

[19] Cf. Balcı, *Eski Istanbul evleri ve Bogaziçi yalıları* [Old Houses of Istanbul and Residences of the Bosporus] (Istanbul, 1975); R. Osnan, *Edirne evleri ve konakları* [Houses and Palaces in Edirne], ed. A. S. Ünver (Istanbul, 1976); N. Araz, "Eski Bursa evleri," [Bursa's Old Houses] *Sanat Dunyamız* 4, no. 10 (1977): 6–21; B. Çetinor, "Eski Ankara evleri," [Ankara's Old Houses] *İlgi* 8, no. 27 (1979): 7–13; A. Arel, *Osmanlı konut geleneğinde tarihsel sorunlar* [*Historical Questions on the Traditional Ottoman Habitat*] (Izmir, 1982); S. H. Eldem, *Turk evi Plan Tipleri* [Layout Types of the Turkish House] (Istanbul, 1954); id., *Türk evi. Osmanlı Dönemi* [The Turkish House: Ottoman Period], vol. 1 (Istanbul, 1984). S. Faroqhi, *Men of Modest Substance: House Owners and House Properties in Seventeenth-Century Ankara and Kayseri* (Cambridge, 1987); A. Borie and P. Pinon, "La maison turque," *Bulletin d'Information Architecturale*, suppl. to no. 94 (1958); id., "La maison ottomane: une centralité inachevée?" *Les Cahiers de la recherche architecturale*, no. 20–21 (1988); id., "Maisons ottomanes à Bursa," in *L'Habitat tradtionnel dans les pays musulmans*. Actes du colloque tenu à Aix-en-Provence en 1984, III (Paris, 1991); P. Pinon, "Le voyage d'Orient de l'architecte Jean-Nicolas Huyot (1817–1820) et la découverte de la maison ottomane," *Turcica* 26 (1994): 211–240.

[20] Cf. notably G. Tankut, "The Spatial Distribution of Urban Activities in the Ottoman City," *TA* 3, 211: 245–265; id., *Nauplia-Anabolu-Napoli di Romania: A Structural Analysis* (Ankara, 1978).

[21] Cf. notably C. Orhonlu, *Osmanlı İmparatorluğunda Şehircilik ve Ulaşım üzerine Araştırmalar* [Studies on City Planning and Communications in the Ottoman Empire], ed. S. Ozbaran (Izmir, 1984); K. Ceçen, *Istanbul'da Osmanlı Devrinde Su Tesisleri* [Water supply Installations in the Ottoman Period] (Istanbul, 1979).

[22] S. Aktüre, "17, Yüzyıl başından 19, Yuzyıl ortasına kadarki dönemde Anadolu Osmanlı şehrinde şehirsel yapının değişme süreci," [The Transformation Process of the Urban Structure of the Ottoman Town between the early seventeenth and the mid-nineteenth Centuries] *Mimar Fakültesi Dergisi* 1, no. 1 (1975): 101–128; id., *19, Yuzyıl sonunda anadolu kenti mekansal yapı çözümlesi* [The Dissolution of the Spatial Structure of the Anatolian Town at the End of the Nineteenth Century] (Ankara, 1978); M. Cerasi, "Il tessuto residenziale della città ottomana (secc. XVII–XIX)," *Storia della città* 31–32 (1985): 105–122.

[23] "Les tissus urbains ottomans...," art. cit.

wood or of a wooden supporting frame filled in with mixed materials, covered with a sloping overhanging roof, with projecting corbels, and painted in bright or soft colours. Lastly, it is extrovert, with numerous windows and sometimes the door opening onto the street. Specimens of this type have survived in Afyon, Bursa, Kula, Birgi, Tokat, Ankara, as well as in Istanbul, Edirne, Plovdiv, Melnik, Kastoria, Ambelakia, and Sarajevo. However, one must keep in mind that these houses do not antedate the eighteenth and nineteenth centuries and have already undergone Western influence. The more ancient Ottoman house is not well known. It was apparently more introvert, and in this, was closer to the "Arabic" house, which has a central court (qa'a) and is dominant in Aleppo as well as in Anatolian towns, south of the dividing line defined above: Diyarbekir, Urfa, Mardin, or Kayseri.

P. Pinon also observes that the works attributed to the *mi'mâr bashı* Sinan are rare, not only in Arabic provinces, as already noted, but also south of the same line (only a few monuments can be found in Konya, Kayseri, Payas, and Diyarbekir).

Lastly, the cleavage applies to the layout and *morphology* of the town (in the sense used by P. H. Panerai) in a way not unrelated to the differentiation in the habitat, which, as we have said, increased over time. Unlike Western, even medieval, towns, all Ottoman towns undoubtedly share common features, such as less continuous circulation zones geometrically and topologically and more irregular plots which emerged over time as private housing and concerns, undoubtedly encouraged by Islamic law, encroached upon public land. However, while the morphology of the towns of southeastern Anatolia is very similar to that of the cities in the Mashreq and Maghreb, as far as it is possible to generalize (the layout of Kayseri, Konya, Urfa, and Diyarbekir closely resembles that of Aleppo and Mosul, for instance), there are perceptible differences in the Balkans and northwestern Anatolia: easy-to-locate continuous great axes serving the centre and prolonged by main roads (these axes are more numerous than in "Arabic" towns); straighter and longer dead-end streets; less densely settled habitat (the houses are inside gardens and share only one wall with their outer limits), but, and this is yet another difference, this scattered type of housing was partially connected to the street by façades.

P. Pinon then concludes that there did exist an original urban type, halfway, so to speak, between the "Arabic" and "Western" towns. If this analysis is confirmed by future studies and comparisons, then the term "Ottoman town" will be legitimately used to refer to this type of town.

PART THREE

CASE STUDIES

BAGHDAD IN THE ABBASID ERA:
A COSMOPOLITAN AND MULTI-CONFESSIONAL CAPITAL

Françoise Micheau

The history of Baghdad divides itself into three phases: first, the prestigious capital of the Abbasid caliphs from the time of its foundation in 145/762 by al-Mansur up to its conquest by Mongol armies in 656/1258; then, for centuries, a simple provincial metropolis; and finally, since 1921, the capital of the kingdom of Iraq, whose dramatic reality assails us with daily images of devastation. Here we are interested only in the first of these periods.[1]

Nothing, however, remains of the capital of the Abbasid caliphs, since monuments and urban fabric have, with a few exceptions, disappeared. Fires, floods, destruction, wars, invasions and, more simply, the wear of centuries have erased all trace of caliphal edifices, which were often in unfired brick. Thus, Baghdad has become a capital with no "site of memory." Numerous specific studies touching on the city's monuments have accompanied campaigns of architectural survey and restoration.[2] From these we see that the oldest monumental remains date back to the sixth/twelfth–seventh/thirteenth centuries, and are extremely scarce. The most important is the Mustansiriyya madrasa founded in 630/1232. It was abandoned in the seventeenth century and very crudely restored in 1945 and 1960. Today it houses a museum. We may add four isolated minarets, the Qasr ʿAbbasi, built perhaps by the caliph al-Nasir (575/1180–622/1225), two doors of the Mustazhir wall (Bab al-Wastani and Bab al-Talism), and lastly a few tombs. We hardly

---

[1] On the history of Baghdad in the Abbasid era, see especially G. Le Strange, *Baghdad during the Abbasid Caliphate* (Oxford, 1900; new edition London and Dublin, 1972); *The Encyclopaedia of Islam*, new edition, vol. 1, s.v. "Baghdad"; special issue of the journal *Arabica* 9 (1962); special issue of *Al-Mawrid* 8, no. 4 (1979) [in Arabic]; F. Micheau, "Bagdad," in *Grandes villes méditerranéennes du monde musulman médiéval*, ed. J.-Cl. Garcin (Rome, 2000), 87–112.

[2] V. Strija and J. Khalil, "The Islamic Architecture of Baghdad. The Results of a Joint Italian-Iraqi Survey," *Annali Instituto Universitario Orientale*, 1987, suppl. no. 52; M.-O. Rousset, *L'archéologie islamique en Iraq. Bilan et perspectives* (Damascus, 1992).

ever think of the number and magnificence of the palaces, mosques, and princely houses of the medieval city.

Even the toponymy and layouts of streets have not preserved the memory of ancient times. The layout of the wall built in 488/1095 by al-Mustazhir alone remained just as it was from the end of the fifth/eleventh century to 1870, when it was destroyed apart from the two gates mentioned earlier.

Moreover, the plans of Abbasid Baghdad are mere reconstructions based on the data provided by ancient Arab geographers. They are highly hypothetical, all the more so in that the waterway of the Tigris and the urban space have undergone major transformation over the centuries. The relevant pioneer work, which remains a reference point to this day, is that of Le Strange. However, Le Strange did not himself regard his plans, established by period and by quarter, as definitive: "My plans of mediaeval Baghdad are, to a certain extent, tentative."[3] Since the 1950s, Iraqi scholars have conducted important work on the city's history and topography. They have enriched the Orientalist's[4] data, supplied further detail, and sometimes corrected it.

Though some repairs were made during recent excavation work, there was no attempt at an archaeological dig. Moreover, the investigations still possible at the beginning of this century, when the greater part of the site was covered with agricultural or wasteland, are no longer possible on account of the progress of urbanization.

Hence, our knowledge of Abbasid Baghdad is based solely on written sources. These are, fortunately, numerous, and have been extensively used by modern historians. The three most important descriptions of the Baghdad of the Abbasid period are by al-Yaʿqubi, Ibn Sarabiyun, and al-Khatib al-Baghdadi. The first of these authors opens his *Kitab al-buldan*, written in 278/891, with his famous account of the foundation of the "Round City" and the precisely established list of all concessions and their beneficiaries.[5] Ibn Sarabiyun (or Ibn Serapion) provides, for the beginning of the fourth/tenth century, an accurate description

---

[3] Le Strange, *Baghdad*, p. xi. See pp. 352–356 for an explanation of the method followed.

[4] Especially A. Susa and M. Jawad, *Dalil mufassal li kharitat Baghdad* (Baghdad, 1958); S. al-ʿAli, *Baghdad Madinat al-Salam: Al-janib al-gharbi*, 2 vols. (Baghdad, 1985); and a number of contributions in *Al-Mawrid* journal.

[5] Al-Yaʿqubi, *Kitab al-buldan*, Bibliotheca Geographorum Arabicorum 7, ed. M. J. Goeje (Leiden, 1892), 237–254; trans. G. Wiet, *Les pays*, Publications de l'Institut Français d'Archéologie Orientale. Textes et traductions d'auteurs orientaux, 1 (Cairo, 1937), 9–43.

of the channels in Baghdad; this has been the starting point for all attempts at reconstituting the urban topography.[6] As for al-Khatib al-Baghdadi (d. 463/1071), he introduces his biographical dictionary, entitled *Ta'rikh Baghdad*, with a valuable description of the city, which takes the form of a collection of traditions derived from previous authors rather than being a testimony to the city of the fifth/eleventh century.[7] Texts by other important geographers of the Abbasid period, such as Ibn Hawqal and al-Muqadassi, are notably less rich.[8] By contrast, the description of Baghdad by Ibn 'Aqil (d. 513/1119) provides precious information about the city after the Seljuq conquest.[9] The testimonies of subsequent geographers and travellers such as Ibn Jubayr, who passed by the city in 581/1185, Yaqut, who, in 623/1226, wrote his "geographical dictionary," or Ibn Battuta, who stayed in the city in the eighth/fourteenth century, above all attest to the city's decline from its times of splendour; but they do also provide complementary indications that are sometimes useful.

The historical works are, obviously, very numerous. They supply a large number of topographical references, and they provide especially the possibility of writing an institutional and social history of the city. Without making any pretence at being exhaustive, we may list here some of the most important: the *Annals* (*Ta'rikh al-rusul wa 'l-muluk*) of Tabari (d. 310/923); the *Meadows of Gold* (*Muruj al-dhahab*) by Mas'udi (d. 345/956); the *Experiences of Nations* (*Kitab tajarib al-umam*) by Miskawayh (d. 421/1030); and the *Muntazam* of Ibn al-Jawzi (d. 597/1200). The *Memoirs* of the courtier al-Suli (d. 335/946) also provide rich indications. As for biographical dictionaries, or *tabaqat*—including the *Ta'rikh Baghdad* by al-Khatib al-Baghdadi, already mentioned with regard to

---

[6] G. Le Strange, ed. and trans., "Description of Mesopotamia and Baghdad, written about the year 900 A.D. by Ibn Serapion," *Journal of the Royal Asiatic Society*, 1895: 1–76, 255–315.

[7] The purely topographical part was edited and translated by G. Salmon, *L'introduction topographique à l'histoire de Bagdâdh* (Paris, 1904), and by J. Lassner, *The Topography of Baghdad in the early Middle Ages* (Detroit, 1970), 43–118.

[8] Ibn Hawqal, *Kitab al-Masalik wa 'l-mamalik*, Bibliotheca Geographorum Arabicorum 2, ed. J. H. Kramers (Leiden, 1938), 164–65; trans. G. Wiet, *Configuration de la terre* (Paris and Beirut, 1964), 233–234; al-Muqaddasi, *Kitab Ahsan al-Taqsim*, Bibliotheca Geographorum Arabicorum 3, ed. M. J. de Groeje (Leiden, 1877), 119–121; eng. trans. B. A. Collins and M. H. al-Tai, *The Best Divisions for Knowledge of the Regions* (Reading, England, 1994), 108–110.

[9] Description preserved in the *Manaqib Baghdad*, a work attributed to Ibn al-Jawzi, trans. G. Makdisi, "The Topography of eleventh-century Bagdad: Materials and Notes," *Arabica* 6 (1959): 185–195.

its introduction—these supply material for major social investigation
that has yet to be realized.[10]

The history of Baghdad overlaps broadly with that of the caliphal
dynasty; according to Le Strange, "the history of the city is that of
the Abbasid Caliphate." This statement was echoed by Lassner: "(The)
pattern of growth was determined by the character of the city as
the administrative center of the realm."[11] In fact, the times of urban
splendour coincide with those of caliphal flourishing.

The Abbasids, a new dynasty claiming to be from the family of al-
'Abbas, uncle of the Prophet Muhammad, signalled their decisive break
with the preceding dynasty, that of the Umayyads who had derived
their strength from Syria and taken Damascus as their capital, by looking towards Mesopotamia and beyond this, towards Iran. By founding
a new capital in Baghdad, following some very temporary choices of
other sites in Lower Iraq, Caliph al-Mansur not only established the
base of what was to become one of the world's most prestigious cities
but also gave the history of the countries of Islam a new orientation:
from this point on, the centre of the caliphal empire was far from the
Mediterranean regions; fixed rather in the East, close to Persia, with
its wealth and goods, both material and cultural, in men, soldiers and
scholars.

The descriptive sources, especially that of Ya'qubi, cannot too highly
praise the "Round City" founded in 145/762 by Caliph al-Mansur: in
the centre of a huge esplanade, with no other buildings, rose a palace
topped by an immense green dome. Alongside it was the great mosque.
Houses reserved for the élite of government employees and officers were
pushed out to the perimeter. Four streets crossed this ring of building
and were closed off by four gates: those of Basra, Kufa, Khurasan, and
Syria. This monumental complex, with its moat, walls, and fortified
gates, must, when seen from the outside, have aroused fear and respect.
The circular form, probably derived from earlier Mesopotamian models,
is noteworthy for its symbolic significance: the seat of the new dynasty
was set in the centre of a circle opening via four gates on to the area

---

[10] Vanessa Van Renterghem, in December 2004, defended her thesis prepared
under my direction and devoted to the Baghdadi élite during the first Seljuq century
(forthcoming, Paris, les Indes Sarantes, 2009). Thorough research into biographical
dictionaries has allowed her to establish an extensive database of more than 2,000
personages.
[11] Le Strange, *Baghdad*, 301; Lassner, *Topography of Baghdad*, 177.

of domination: to the south, the shores of the Arab-Persian Gulf and the Indian Ocean; to the east, the Iranian plateaux and the steppes of central Asia; to the north and the west, Upper Mesopotamia, Anatolia, and Syria. The geographer Ya'qubi quotes a seemingly prophetic speech by al-Mansur about the central role of Baghdad:

> Here will arrive and drop anchor ships coming over the Tigris from Wasit, Basra, Ubulla, Ahwaz, Fars, Oman, Yamama, Bahrain, and neighbouring regions. Here will arrive merchandise that will be transported along the Tigris, coming from Mosul, Diyar Rabi'a, Azerbaijan, and Armenia. Here, too, will arrive goods transported by ships on the Euphrates, coming from Diyar Mudar, Raqqa, Syria, the [Syrian] marches, Egypt, and from the Maghreb. This city will also be on the populated routes from Djibal, Isfahan, and the provinces of Khurasan. Praise be to God who reserved this capital for me and left it unknown to all my predecessors![12]

This city was the heart of the world, but it was also the heir of past civilizations. According to a tradition specifically recorded by al-Tabari and by al-Khatib, al-Mansur is said to have ordered the demolition of the palace of Khusraw in Ctesiphon in order to use its material for the construction of the "Round City." This account, though improbable, reflects the will of the new caliphs to gather the heritage of the Sassanids and call the inhabitants of this lost empire to allegiance.

The "Round City" of al-Mansur has aroused the keen interest of historians, no doubt on account of its original architecture. However, in the absence of any remains, historians have failed to agree either on its dimensions (estimated at 2 to 3 kilometres in diameter), or on its exact siting, or on its precise arrangement. They tend to see the original city only in terms of this monumental complex, which was, in reality, no more than a kind of "palace city," a palatial complex, "the Caliph's personal domain, comprising the area, his residence, and the governmental machinery."[13] However, al-Mansur conceived a real city, giving land concessions (qati'at) to the members of his military and civil entourage. The description of Ya'qubi shows a willed urbanism, with vast public spaces set aside in each quarter:

> For each head of sector [rub', that is, one of the four sectors around the "Round City"] was fixed the area of land to give to each man and his

---

[12] Al-Ya'qubi, Kitab al-buldan, 237–238; Wiet, Les pays, 10. This text provides an authentic description of the major channels of communication converging on Baghdad at the time al-Ya'qubi was writing.

[13] Lassner, Topography of Baghdad, 144.

followers, and the space that should be set aside for shops and markets in each suburb (rabad). They were ordered [to allot] spacious locations for shops, so that each suburb would have a general market with trades of every kind; to provide for avenues (sikak), streets (durub), passages (nafidha), and other ways in each suburb [a space] equivalent to that of the houses; to name each street after the officer or famous person living in it, or else after the city [of origin] of the inhabitants; to give avenues (shawari') a width of 50 black cubits [around 50 metres] and streets (durub) a width of 16 cubits [around 8 metres]; to build in every suburb markets, streets and mosques sufficient for all the people in the neighbourhood (nahiya) and the quarter (mahalla).[14]

These concessions lay at the origin of vast quarters on the west bank, of which al-Karkh, to the south of the "Round City," was by far the most important and the most populated.

Following the foundation of the "Round City" and its neighbouring quarters on the west bank of the Tigris, the city developed and was structured on the basis of successive palatine constructions. In fact, the civil war between al-Amin and al-Ma'mun, the sons of Harun al-Rashid, marked by several months of fighting in the Abbasid capital in 198/814, resulted in serious devastation. The "Round City," already abandoned by the caliphs as a place of residence, fell into final ruin, and this space found itself incorporated into the urban fabric.

Following the reign of al-Mansur, two other foundations contributed to the expansion of the urban space. First of all, the palace of al-Khuld, built in 157/773 to the north of the "Round City," along the Tigris. Then a large complex designed for his heir al-Mahdi, comprising a palace and a mosque and situated on the east bank of the Tigris. This palace was at the origin of the Rusafa quarter, and even of the development of the city on the east bank, with the quarters of al-Shammasiyya to the north and Mukharrim to the south.

During the second civil war in 251/856, Caliph al-Musta'in encircled the city with an enclosure comprising, on its east bank, three quarters (al-Rusafa, al-Shammasiyya and Mukharrim, from Bab al-Shammasiyya to Suq al-Thalatha'); it continued on the west bank from Qati'at Umm Ja'far to the Humayd palace. This wall is often presented on plans as a durable element of the urban topography, but all indications are that it swiftly disappeared, since it was mentioned neither in the descriptions of Arab geographers nor by chroniclers of work undertaken by al-Mu'tadid.

---

[14] Al-Ya'qubi, Kitab al-buldan, 242; Wiet, Les pays, 18–19.

Following their return from Sammara', in the last years of the third/ninth century, the Abbasid caliphs settled once more on the east bank, but more to the south, where, thanks to enlargements, adjunctions and reconstructions, they formed an important compound comprising three main palaces:

– The Ja'fari, or Ma'muni, or Hasani palace. These various denominations are justified by the history of the place: the palace was built originally by the Barmakid vizier Ja'far to the south of the Mukharrim quarter. Then it was inherited by al-Ma'mun, who embellished it and gave it to his vizier Hasan. Al-Mu'tadid resided in it from 279/891, having first considerably enlarged it.
– The Firdaws palace, built by al-Mu'tadid, upstream from the Hasani palace.
– The Taj palace, founded by al-Mu'tadid, downstream from the Hasani palace. It was completed by his son al-Muqtafi (289/901–295/907) and enlarged by al-Muqtadir. It became the main caliphal residence, and it was linked, by an underground passage, to the Thurayya palace, or palace of Pleiades.

These prestigious constructions were not the only ones. Inside the caliphal enclosure were numerous palaces, pavilions rather, such as the Shajara palace (the palace of the Tree) which owed its name to the silver tree in its centre, or the Jawsaq palace, with its famous basin with tin facing. They were surrounded by luxurious gardens, polo grounds, and racecourses even an area for hunting and a zoological park. Among all the suggestive descriptions offered by Arab sources, we shall retain the following:

> Al-Qahir possessed, in one of the palace courtyards, a small garden planted with orange trees, which he imported from India via Basra and Oman. The branches of his trees were intertwined and heavy with red and yellow fruits, shining like stars, on a ground of exotic plants, balsamine and flowers. There were gathered, in this place, turtledoves, doves, blackbirds, parrots, and other birds from every country. In this magnificent garden, al-Qahir liked to drink and gather his courtiers. Al-Radi, on succeeding him to power, shared the same predilection for this garden and, like al-Qahir, made it his usual place for his feasts and gatherings.[15]

---

[15] Al-Mas'udi, *Muruj al-dhahab*, ed. and trans. C. Barbier de Meynard and J. Pavet de Courteille, *Les prairies d'or* (Paris, 1816–77), 8:336–337.

The configuration of palaces, and their interior organization and ornamentation, remain unknown. However, the famous account of the Greek embassy received in 305/917 by the vizier Ibn al-Furat and by Caliph al-Muqtadir, in the Taj palace, describes a succession of open-air courtyards with dark passageways giving on to vast audience halls where took place sumptuous and complex ceremonials.[16]

Palaces, belvederes, and gardens made up the Dar al-Khilafa, where the sovereign lived surrounded by his court and guards, far from people and bustle. This reserved space, often designated in sources by the word *harim*, was enclosed within a wall whose exact date of construction is unknown to us. A "Grand Avenue," named al-Shari' al-A'zam, led from Bab al-Shammasiyya, in the north of the city, to the suq al-Thalatha' in the south; from there it went on to Bab al-'Amma (the "Gate of the People"), which was the main entrance to the Dar al-Khilafa. This road was used by ambassadors, prestigious prisoners, by caliphs for their solemn entrances and exits, and by official processions of emirs and high officials.

In the second half of the third/ninth century, the Buyids brought their own distinctive mark to palatine urbanism. In 350/962, Mu'izz al-Dawla built a huge complex near Bab al-Shammasiyya, partially rebuilt by 'Adud al-Dawla; and Baha' al-Dawla, having confiscated the palace of the chamberlain Mu'nis, situated in the suq al-Thalatha', transformed it into a sumptuous residence that was adopted by the Seljuq sultans and took the name of Dar al-Mamlaka (or Dar al-Saltana). Caliph al-Nasir, however, had this symbol of sultanic tutelage destroyed in 587/1191. The precise, detailed history of the emiral and sultanic palaces remains shrouded in obscurity.

With the protection of the princes, the élite built sumptuous residences. Let us cite some examples: the palace of the emir Humayd (governor of Iraq during the reign of al-Ma'mun), built on the banks of the Tigris river and immortalized by the poet 'Ali ibn Jabala; the palace of al-Tahir (the famous general of al-Ma'mun), which was, during the third/ninth century, the residence of the chief of police, and subsequently a mausoleum for more than one caliph; the palace of Faraj (a slave of Hamduna, concubine of Harun al-Rashid), described as one of the most beautiful of the Shammasiyya quarter; the palace of Ibn

---

[16] Al-Khatib al-Baghdadi, trans. J. Lassner, *Topography of Baghdad*, 86–99. See J. Sourdel-Thomine, "L'art de Bagdad," *Arabica* 9 (1962): 449–465.

Muqla (vizier to Caliph al-Muqtadir), whose construction cost 200,000 dinars and which was endowed with a huge garden of 3 hectares.

Palaces moved according to vicissitudes of the power of caliphs, viziers, emirs, and sultans, doubling and multiplying like the sovereignty itself, making way for other constructions when their masters left them. On the ruins of the palace of al-Khuld, for instance, 'Adud al-Dawla had built the famous hospital that bore his name. To take another example, the site of the "Round City," destroyed during the civil war between al-Amin and al Ma'mun, was covered, from the fourth/tenth century, by the urban fabric. In contrast to other cities, Baghdad did not, despite the importance of the Dar al-Khilafa quarter, have a fixed seat of power occupied by successive sovereigns. It was a city with multiple nuclei which projected itself from its original centre, the "Round City," by the creation and enlargement of palaces within an urban landscape in constant transformation.

Ibn Khaldun, with his usual perspicacity, perceived this complex morphology—a characteristic, in his eyes, of imperial capitals:

> Then, when the town has been built and is all finished, as the builder saw fit and as the climatic and geographical conditions required, the life of the dynasty is the life of the town. If the dynasty is of short duration, life in the town will stop at the end of the dynasty. Its civilization will recede, and the town will fall into ruins. On the other hand, if the dynasty is of long duration and lasts a long time, new constructions will always go up in the town, the number of large mansions will increase, and the walls of the town will extend farther and farther. Eventually, the layout of the town will cover a wide area, and the town will extend so far and so wide as to be (almost) beyond measurement. This happened in Baghdad and similar (cities).
>
> The Khatib mentioned in his *History* that in the time of al-Ma'mun, the number of public baths in Baghdad reached 65,000. (Baghdad) included over forty of the adjacent neighbouring towns and cities. It was not just one town surrounded by one wall. Its population was much too large for that. The same was the case with al-Qayrawân, Córdoba and al-Mahdîyah in Islamic times. It is the case with Egypt and Cairo at this time, so we are told.[17]

The mention by Ibn Khaldun of forty towns and cities (*mudun wa amsar*) poses a much-discussed problem: was this immense capital divided into quarters? At its foundation the city was divided into *rabad*, a term

---

[17] Ibn Khaldun, *The Muqaddimah: An Introduction to History*, trans. Fr. Rosenthal (London, 1958), 2:235–236.

usually translated by suburb, given that the built spaces were situated outside the "Round City." It is not even debatable that, later on, the city was constituted of units—streets and quarters—often assembling a population of the same geographical origin, same confession, and same professional activity. The distinction in the landscape between rich and poor sectors was well marked, as underlined by Ibn ʿAqil: "Some roads were the exclusive residence places of persons of dignity: Darb al-Zaʿfaran in the Karkh used to be inhabited, not by craftsmen, but rather by the merchants of dry-goods and perfumes; Darb Sulayman, in the Rusafa used to be exclusively for *qadis*, *shuhud*-notaries and elegant merchants."[18]

On a larger scale, the opposition between the two banks is highly marked: the east bank gathered, around the palaces, the sumptuous residences of great courtiers, high government employees and emirs, while the west bank seems to have been more popular and animated, with a large Shiʿite population. Generally, chroniclers use the expression "inhabitants of the two banks" to signify that the whole population is concerned. The passage from one bank to another was ensured by two or three pontoon bridges (depending on the period in question); built constructions were impossible on account of the river's frequent flooding. These bridges were important public spaces. Exposed along these much-frequented passages were the bodies of famous people who had been executed.

It is hard, in contrast, to know if the city of Baghdad in the third/ninth-fourth/tenth centuries was divided into quarters properly speaking. In fact, it is important to distinguish between, on the one hand, the quarter as a physical unit, possibly a social one (without any fixed boundaries or precise sub-divisions), and, on the other, the quarter as an autonomous administrative entity. A number of factors—the mention of shaykhs of quarters, the clear differentiation in certain texts between the city of Baghdad as such (the city of al-Mansur and its immediate surroundings) and the other built zones (particularly al-Karkh), the existence of several great mosques—argue in favour of a division of the agglomeration into a number of clearly distinct entities.

At the end of the fourth/tenth century, in fact, six great mosques, or *jamiʿ*, which should be distinguished from simple mosques or oratories (*masjid*), numbering 30,000 on the west bank and 15,000 on the

---

[18] Makdisi, "Topography," 195.

east bank according to al-Yaʿqubi—gathered the Muslim community
for Friday prayer. There were four on the west bank and two on the
east bank:

- Al-Mansur mosque, in the old "Round City," rebuilt by Harun
  al-Rashid in 192–193/808–809 and enlarged by al-Muʿtadid in
  280/893.
- The mosque of the Umm Jaʿfar quarter; this small mosque was
  enlarged in 379/989 to become a *jamiʿ*.
- The Harbiyya mosque, situated in the north of al-Karkh, was, in
  383/993, accorded the status of *jamiʿ* by Caliph al-Qadir.
- The Baratha mosque in the southwest of al-Karkh; this high place
  of Shiʿism was destroyed on the order of al-Muqtadir, then rebuilt
  and enlarged in 328/939 by the grand emir Bajkam; Caliph al-Mut-
  taq solemnly inaugurated it to mark the return of the Sunna to this
  holy place.
- The mosque of the Rusafa quarter, built by al-Mahdi in 159/775.
- The mosque of Dar al-Khilafa, often called jamiʿ al-Qasr, was built
  by al-Muktafi in 289/901.

The existence of a number of great mosques is, no doubt, the religious
expression of urban gigantism: the cultural needs of several hundreds
of thousands of adult male Muslims made necessary this derogation
to the usual rule respected, i.e., that there should be one great mosque
per city. In Baghdad, however, as in other places, the multiplication of
great mosques may also be explained by urban compartmentalization
within autonomous quarters.

From the fifth/eleventh century on, the source testimonies become
explicit. Ibn ʿAqil states clearly: "I will not describe to you what you
might find hard to believe. I will simply give you a description of my own
quarter, which is but one of ten, each the size of a Syrian town, namely
Bab al-Taq."[19] The nine other quarters are: Suq al-Silah, Mukharrim,
Suq al-Dabba, Nahr Muʿalla, Dar al-Khilafa, Bab al-Maratib, Bab al-
Azaj, and al-Maʾmuniyya on the east bank; and, on the west bank, one
quarter only, that of al-Karkh.[20] According to the Andalusi traveller
Ibn Jubayr, who stayed in Baghdad for a time in 581/1185, the city

---

[19] Makdisi, "Topography," 185.
[20] According to Makdisi, "Topography," 196.

then comprised "seventeen quarters (*mahalla*) each forming an isolated city." The question is whether this is (as Lassner states) a phenomenon of differentiated urban growth characteristic of the caliphal capital, or whether it is rather (as Cahen suggests) a new development. In this case, the united city would have been divided from the Seljuq period on, being progressively replaced by a group of semi-autonomous quarters separated by ravaged land, waste land and gardens. Hence, the social differentiation would have been accentuated.[21]

In any case, the city gradually declined as the caliphs' power was reduced by the emirs, and as political troubles and popular revolts multiplied. Even though new constructions were still enriching the urban landscape in the Seljuq period, even though economic activity carried on, especially in the very active Karkh quarter, Ibn Jubayr describes a largely devastated city. The invasions of Hulagu in 656/1258, and of Tamerlain in 803/1401 were a fatal blow to the city. In 841/1437, al-Maqrizi writes: "Baghdad is in ruin; there are no more mosques, believers, call to prayer or market. Most of the palm trees have dried up; most of the channels are blocked. It can no longer be called a city."[22] Even if the pride of this Egyptian intellectual in his own city of Cairo, then in full expansion, spurred him on to exaggerate somewhat, his testimony shows clearly enough the irremediable decline of the caliphal capital, which had become a mere provincial metropolis. In fact, the city was successively under the domination of the Ilkhanids (up to 740/1339), the Jala'irids (up to 813/1410), the Turkomans (up to 914/1507), and the Ottomans in 941/1534, following several decades of conflict with the Persians for possession of the city. The traveller Tavernier who visited Baghdad in 1652 gave the extremely low number of 15,000 inhabitants.

Let us return to the Abbasid period in order to underline, like all medieval authors, the gigantic dimensions of the capital in the third/ninth-fourth/tenth centuries. In reality, the numbers they provide spring more from a perception of the city's exceptional character than from exact measurements. The tone is given by an amusing passage by al-Tanukhi in the compendium of literary anecdotes written by this *qadi* in the fourth/tenth century:

---

[21] See Lassner, "Municipal Entities and Mosques," in *Topography of Baghdad*, 178–183 (see also pp. 176–177); and Cl. Cahen, "Bagdad au temps de ses derniers califes," *Arabica* 9 (1962): 295.

[22] Quoted by J. Aubin, "Tamerlan à Bagdad," *Arabica* 9 (1962): 308.

In the year 360/970–1 in the house of the Qadi Abu 'l-Hasan Muhammed b. Salih b. ʿAli al-Hashimi b. Umm Shaiban we were discussing the vastness of Baghdad and the number of its inhabitants in the days of Muqtadir [a caliph who reigned from 295/908 to 320/932], as well as its buildings, streets, lanes, the size of the place, and the multitudinous classes of the inhabitants.

[After the author has mentioned a work by Bayazajard, estimating the numbers of *hammams* in Baghdad at ten thousand and the number of sacks of wheat, barley and other foodstuffs necessary for the daily provisioning of the city at between thirty and forty thousand, and another participant has mentioned the work of Ahmad ibn al-Tayyib on the same subject, the *qadi* Abu 'l-Hasan takes up the tale:]

That is indeed an enormous amount, of whose truth I have no knowledge; still I have witnessed facts therein in connection wherewith the statements of Yazdajird and Ahmad b. Tayyib are not improbable, though we have not counted so as to be able to attest their accuracy. Only, a short time ago, in the year 345/956–7 when Muhammed b. Ahmad known as Turrah, farmed Baduraya, he took great pains with its cultivation. Once we made a calculation of the number of *jaribs* of lettuce sown there this year, and computed roughly how much lettuce was brought into Baghdad from Kalwadha, Qutrabull and other places in the neighbourhood. It came to two thousand *jaribs*. Now we found that on every *jarib* six sorts were sown, and that of each sort so many roots were plucked—this I do not remember. On each *jarib* then there were so many roots. The average price of lettuce at the time was twenty stalks for a dirhem. The average amount earned by a *jarib*, produce and price being both considered, was 350 dirhems, valued at twenty-five dinars. Two thousand *jaribs* then gave fifty thousand dinars. All of this was consumed in Baghdad. What then must be the size of a city wherein in one season of the year one sort of vegetable was consumed to the value of fifty thousand dinars![23]

With the aim of showing the extraordinary extension of the Abbasid capital, al-Khatib al-Baghdadi recorded several traditions in a chapter entitled "The Length and Width of the Two Sides of Baghdad, the Total Area, and the Number of Mosques and Bathhouses."[24] One piece of this data is often cited by modern historians: an area of 43,750 *jaribs* in the third/ninth century, 16,750 of which were in the eastern part and 27,000 in the western part. Equivalence problems, irritating and insoluble at once, render uncertain the interpretation of the number of

---

[23] Trans. D. S. Margoliouth, *The Table-Talk of a Mesopotamian Judge*, Royal Asiatic Society, Oriental Translation Fund, new series, vol. 28 (London, 1922), 69–70.
[24] Lassner, *Topography of Baghdad*, 107–110.

43,750 *jarib*s (between 5,000 and 7,000 hectares).[25] It has nevertheless been used to calculate the number of inhabitants. However, trying to estimate the size of the population from the area of the city is a method filled with pitfalls, since it supposes knowledge of the area but also of the density of the population. Despite this, several modern historians have made the venture. Hence, Lassner proposes 40 inhabitants per hectare by dividing by 5 the known density of Constantinople (200 inhabitants per hectare in the fifth century)—Baghdad being far less densely populated because of the surface occupied by gardens and palaces. Having estimated the area of the city at 7,000 hectares, he arrives at the result of 280,000 inhabitants.[26]

In this chapter on city dimensions, al-Khatib al-Baghdadi, as is his habit, adds several traditions indicating the number of mosques, the number of bathhouses, but also the quantity of soap and oil necessary for the population during festivals. According to one of these traditions, going back to Muhammad ibn Yahya al-Suli (d. 335/946), the city had 60,000 public bathhouses, each served by five servants (a bath attendant, a steward, a swapper, a stoker, and a water carrier); i.e., a staff of 300,000 people. For each *hammam* there were five mosques, each corresponding to at least five people. Thus, the number of mosques was 300,000 and that of the population one million and a half. These exorbitant numbers have, it seems to me, no specific meaning, resulting from a form of arithmetical emphasis designed to show the abnormally populated character of the "megapole." The medieval authors appear to have a worrying facility to multiply a number by ten so as better to mark the size: hence the number of 3,000 mosques, already approximate, but likely enough if compared to the 785 mosques of Fez[27] and 684 mosques of Aleppo,[28] was subjected to this phenomenon of arithmetical emphasis by jumping from 30,000 to 300,000.

The Iraqi historian Duri starts from a far less elevated number, that of 1,500 *hammam*s given by Hilal al-Sabi for the end of the fourth/tenth

---

[25] 5,000 hectares according to Le Strange, *Baghdad*, 324–326; 5,900 according to A. A. Duri, "Baghdad," *Encyclopaedia of Islam*, 1; 7,000 according to Lassner, *Topography of Baghdad*, 157–158.

[26] Lassner, *Topography of Baghdad*, 159–160.

[27] Survey undertaken during the reign of the Almohad caliph al-Nasir (595/1199–610/1213) and quoted in al-Jazna'i, *Zahrat al-As*, trans. into French by A. Bel, *La fleur de myrthe* (Algiers, 1923), 81–82.

[28] According to the geographer Ibn Shaddad, quoted in A.-M. Eddé, *La principauté ayyoubide d'Alep (579/1183–658/1260)* (Stuttgart, 1999), 559, n. 675.

century, and from the indication given by the same author according to which each bathhouse services 200 houses; he estimated that each house had an average of five people, thereby reaching the number of one and a half million inhabitants in Baghdad at the time of its greatest extension.[29]

It is impossible to set a figure between these two extremes, ranging between 300,000 and a million and a half inhabitants. However, Baghdad at the time of the Abbasids was certainly a heavily populated city; Constantinople alone, during the same period, was able to compete with it.

Baghdad was a new creation (even if some Aramaean establishments did exist before the foundation of the caliphate), and, as such, the population was originally exogenous. The list of concessions and their beneficiaries shows the different sectors to have been inhabited, simultaneously, by civilians and soldiers, mostly Arabs and Persians. Apart from the elite—Abbasid family, descendants from companions of the Prophet, courtiers, government employees, military leaders—the city of al-Mansur was mostly populated by craftsmen and workers (to the number of a hundred thousand according to al-Ya'qubi), by merchants and, above all, soldiers. These were gathered according to their city or region of origin: Kufa, Yamama, Fars, Kirman, Khurasan, Khwarizm, Bukhara, Marw, Balkh, Kabul, Sughd, Isbijab, Khuttal, Jurjan, Farghana. Note the preponderant place occupied by Iran in this enumeration.[30] It seems, then, that the make-up of the Baghdadi population stems from the voluntary occupation of non-indigenous elements and hardly at all from the population of neighbouring villages and rural zones.

Thereafter the population increased due to natural growth and immigration. Biographical dictionaries, especially the *Ta'rikh Baghdad*, provide material for a study of the origin of scholars and men of religion who settled in Baghdad, attracted by the material and cultural possibilities the caliphal capital offered. Such a study, though, remains to be realized. Even so, some work on matters of detail permits us to underline the characteristics of this emigration. In the second/eighth–third/ninth centuries, Baghdad was the great pole towards which a

---

[29] Duri, "Baghdad."

[30] S. al-'Ali has sketched out the ethnic and social groups present in early Baghdad: "The Foundation of Baghdad," in *The Islamic City*, ed. A. H. Hourani and S. M. Stern (Oxford, 1970), 87–103. See also *Baghdad Madinat al-Salam*, cited above.

number of scholars and men of letters were drawn.[31] The majority
came from the cities of Lower Mesopotamia, notably Basra and Kufa,
and from Upper Mesopotamia, Syria and Egypt, but above all from
various regions of Iran. In the following centuries, the movement continues, with the same characteristics, even though, with the division of
the Abbasid Empire, regional dynasties were formed whose capitals
sought to compete with Baghdad.[32]

The force of attraction of the Abbasid capital seems to have been
extremely great, even though limited to the Arab and Persian Near
East. However, the voluntary migrations that characterize an élite
free to move, and attracted by the conditions offered by the capital,
were minor in comparison to imposed migrations: those of craftsmen
recruited by the caliphal power to enhance the prestige of the capital;
those of slaves of various origins—black, Slav, Turkish, Berber—who
contributed greatly to cross-breeding within the population, through the
manumission of slaves and employment of concubines; and finally, and
above all, those of soldiers, bought or captured in large numbers on
the borders of central Asia to form the essential numbers of the army
following the reform of Caliph al-Muʿtasim (218/833–227/842).

Consequently, Baghdad became a cosmopolitan city, if by this term
is meant the co-existence, within one urban agglomeration, of multiple
populations with various ethnic origins and cultural traditions. Three
groups dominated: Arabs, Persians, and Turks. However, cosmopolitan-
ism in Baghdad was not accompanied by multi-lingualisim, even though
other languages were in private or liturgical use. Arabic imposed itself
as a spoken language and as a language of culture—an indication that
the Abbasid caliphs' project to integrate multiple populations within
one political and cultural whole had been successful. Nevertheless, the
importance of Persians, especially in the administration, is reflected
in Baghdadi life by the dissemination of traditions of Iranian origin:
literary traditions, which were opposed by pure Arabs in the move-

---

[31] See the maps showing the division of men of learning established by F. Micheau
in "L'intermédiaire arabe?" in Eléments d'histoire des sciences, ed. M. Serres (Paris, 1989),
158–159; in the second/eighth–third/ninth centuries, 25 men of learning, out of the
26 in these two centuries, lived in Baghdad.

[32] Hence, according to the same study, Baghdad in the fifth/tenth–sixth/eleventh
centuries had 16 scholars, whereas there were 18 in the Muslim West, 10 in various
cities of the Arab Near East, and 12 in the Iranian metropolises. In the seventh/
twelfth–eighth/thirteenth centuries, these numbers were, respectively, 3 (for Baghdad),
14, 18, and 12.

ment known as *shu'ubiyya*, and popular traditions, such as the Iranian New Year holiday (the Nauruz), which was one of the big festivals in Baghdad, celebrated in June around bonfires.

For their part, the Turks, having become preponderant in the army, brought a new distinctive mark to Baghdad society. The appearance of these hardened, rough soldiers in the reign of al-Mu'tasim led to troubles that spurred the caliphs to leave Baghdad for a time and to settle in a new capital, Samarra', built further to the north, on the banks of the Tigris. After the caliphs' return to Baghdad, in the final years of the third/ninth century, the Turkish contingents and their leaders, the emirs (*amir*, plural *umara'*), played an ever more important role in political life, progressively eclipsing the viziers. The history of Baghdad in the fourth/tenth century is dominated by fights between the military factions.

Baghdad in the Abbasid period was a cosmopolitan city but also a multi-confessional one, where Muslims, Christians, Jews and Zoroastrians lived together.

The Nestorian Christian community was particularly numerous, active and well organized.[33] It was partially of local origin, having been enlarged by the arrival of Christians attracted by the riches and advantages of the capital. The Catholicos Timothy, who had campaigned with the inhabitants of Baghdad during his election in 780, left his residence in Ctesiphon for the caliphal city. The Nestorian patriarch was an eminent personage with access to court and formed part of the city's notables. Thus, the courtier al-Suli noted in his journal the death of the Catholicos Ibrahim as one of the events marking the year 325/936–7. Jacobites and Melchites were likewise present, but did not have the same importance.

Christians owned some twenty churches and monasteries, among which were Dayr Durta and Dayr al-Kibab on the west bank, Dayr Darmalis, Dayr Samalu, and, above all, the celebrated Dayr al-Rum, built during the reign of al-Mahdi, which became the Catholicos' burial place in the Shammasiyya quarter on the east bank. These monasteries were places of sociability and leisure, and were visited by Muslims

---

[33] See the studies by J.-M. Fiey, especially *Chrétiens syriaques sous les Abbassides surtout à Bagdad (749–1258)* (Louvain, 1980) [C.S.C.O., 420 Subsidia, 49]; M. Allard, "Les chrétiens à Bagdad," *Arabica* 9 (1962): 375–388; Al-Abb Butrus Haddad, *Kana'is Bagdad wa diyaratuha* (Baghdad, 1994).

as well as Christians, as is confirmed by the descriptions of the *Kitab al-Diyarat*, composed by al-Shabushti at the end of the fourth/tenth century:

> This monastery is located on the most elevated point in Baghdad, to the east, near the house built by Ahmad ibn Buwayh the Daylami, near the Gate of al-Shammasiyya. Its situation is excellent. It is a most agreeable monastery, with numerous trees and gardens. Near the place, there is a marsh and reeds. This monastery is large and is inhabited by monks, priests and ascetics. It is one of those places we visit for leisure, and where we go to drink and to take walks.
>
> The festivals of Christians in Baghdad are divided between the various well known monasteries. Among these festivals are those of the [four] Sundays of Lent…the fourth is that of the Darmalis monastery, and the festival of this monastery is the most beautiful. The Christians of Baghdad gather there, and they are followed by all those who enjoy entertainment and leisure. People spend days there and go there at night, except during the festivals.[34]

Like the Christians, Jews, numerous in Mesopotamia before the Arab conquest, came into Baghdad. The Exilarchs settled at the caliphal court, and the major scholars of the two great Talmudic schools of Sura and Pumbedita resided permanently in these, probably from the third/ninth century on. Baghdad attracted, at that time, students and scholars from Egypt, the Maghreb, Spain, Italy, and the Byzantine empire. If the power of Jewish financiers in economic life was overestimated at the time, it is certain that the two great families, the Banu Natira and Banu Harun, sometimes allies and at other times rivals, dominated the community, and a number of their members were bankers to caliphs and viziers.[35]

Zoroastrians, that is, adepts of the dualistic religion of Ancient Persia, are less known but were undoubtedly present. There was a street named *darb al-Majus*, meaning street of the Zoroastrians. In the sixth/twelfth century, the *nisba* al-Majusi was borne by Muslim traditionalists simply because they lived in that place. It is believed that originally Persians

---

[34] Trans. G. Troupeau, "Les couvents chrétiens dans la littérature arabe," *La Nouvelle revue du Caire* 1 (1975): 265–279, quoted in A.-M. Eddé, F. Micheau, and Chr. Picard, *Communautés chrétiennes en pays d'Islam du début du VIIe siècle au milieu du XIe siècle* (Paris, 1997), 204.

[35] G. Vajda, "Le milieu juif à Bagdad," *Arabica* 9 (1962): 389–393; and, especially, D. S. Sassoon, *A History of the Jews in Baghdad* (Letchworth, 1949).

gathered there and maintained their cult.[36] Al-Suli reports how, in 332/943, rich Jewish and Zoroastrian merchants left the capital because of the insecurity that reigned there.[37]

Finally, Muslims, though assuredly forming the majority, were nevertheless not a united community. On the contrary, at a time when Islam was seeing its reference texts, dogma and rites, law and practices, being developed, the Abbasid capital crystallized the currents then being affirmed. Without going into the various aspects of the history of Muslim thought, which would be beyond our purpose here, mention should be made of two of these groups that particularly marked social life in the Abbasid capital.

The Shi'ites were numerous on the west bank. They seem to have gathered a number of supporters from among the popular circles in these quarters, and—considering the role they played in riots—to have provided an ideological framework for their social demands. The domination, from 334/945, of the great Buyid emirs, who were Twelver Shi'ites, naturally favoured Shi'ite practices, particularly the celebration of Ashura'. This official commemoration of the death of Husayn in Kerbela, a day of great mourning for Shi'ites, was turned into a festival by the Sunnis, who dressed up in new clothes and organized banquets.[38]

Another well organized group, and very visible in the urban history, was that of the Hanbalis. We know that Ibn Hanbal had, in the years 820–850 (he died in 241/855), imposed a rigorous conception of Islam based on resort solely to the Quran and the Tradition of the Prophet as opposed to movements giving a larger place for rational reflection and openness to other cultures. The Hanbalis, thus, played a crucial role in the fight against Mu'tazilism, imposed on the *qadis* as official doctrine by Caliph al-Ma'mun in 212/827, and they made a major contribution to its condemnation by Caliph al-Mutawakkil at the beginning of the latter's reign in 234/848. They then enjoyed the support of the caliphs who saw in them valuable defenders of caliphal doctrine. In everyday life, they frequently intervened as preachers, often esteemed by the

---

[36] On the meaning of *majus*, see the article entitled "Madjus," in the *Encyclopaedia of Islam*. I have taken the attestation and explanation of the *nisba* al-Majusi provided in the dictionary of Sam'ani (d. 562/1166), *Al-Ansab* (Hyderabad, 1981), 12:99.

[37] Al-Suli, *Kitab al-Awraq*, trans. M. Canard (Algiers, 1946), 2:88.

[38] According to A. Mez, *The Renaissance of Islam* (London, 1937), 69.

humble people, but also as defenders of values and ideas, opposed to any form of innovation.

> In this year 323/934–5, the activity of the Hanbalis became great and their influence was reinforced. They forcibly entered the dwellings of military leaders and humble people, and, if they found wine, they scattered it; if they found a singer, they beat her and broke the instruments. They intervened in the operations of sale and purchase; they also intervened when men walked in the company of women and young people. The moment they saw them, they asked them who the person was that was accompanying them, and, if the information was withheld, they beat them and took them to the Chief of Police, testifying to their immorality.[39]

We have an exceptional testimony about the Hanbali group during the Seljuq period: Ibn al-Banna', a Baghdad notable, lived on the east bank of the Tigris, and kept a journal about his daily activities and observations, not, no doubt, designed for publication. This teacher, a traditionist and Hanbali jurist, had two teaching circles, one at the great mosque of the palace, the other at the great mosque of al-Mansur. He was also private tutor to the family of the rich merchant Ibn Jarada. The family ceremonies, marriages and indeed funerals, the arrival of merchant convoys, even the return of the pilgrimage caravan, were privileged moments when bonds were created and expressed between eminent Hanbalis, merchants, and the learned.[40]

Baghdad, with its extensive buildings, substantial population, and the co-existence of highly diverse ethnic, social, and religious groups, also appears as a fragile city, regularly devastated by disasters and riots.

Urban risks such as accidents, floods, and fires were particularly important, and chroniclers do not fail to mention these dramatic events. Here are some examples:

> The pontoon bridges ensuring the obviously vital passage between the two banks of the Tigris were fragile. In 282/895, the structures supporting the roadway gave way under the weight of those crossing. More than a thousand perished in the Tigris. A similar accident took place in 330/942, when masses gathered to attend the Caliph's departure.[41]

---

[39] Ibn al-Athir, *al-Kamil fi 'l-ta'rikh*, 8:307.

[40] Ed and trans. from a fragment preserved (with respect to the year 460/1068–9) by G. Makdisi, "Autograph Diary of an eleventh-century Historian of Baghdad," *Bulletin of the School of Oriental and African Studies* 18 (1956): 9–31, 239–260, and 19 (1957): 13–48, 281–303, 426–443.

[41] Al-Mas'udi, *Muruj*, 8:170; and al-Suli, *Kitab al-Awraq*, 2:50.

Even more serious was the flooding of the Tigris, which regularly devastated the more exposed quarters. At periods of high water, the Tigris rises up to 34.60 metres, so that the presumed site of the "Round City," at 35 metres, was in constant danger of being submerged. The Karkh quarter, situated on an elongated hillock between 36 and 44 metres, was not always spared, and high waters could be devastating, as in 270/883, when 7,000 houses were destroyed by the torrents.[42] The east bank, for its part, was relatively protected by earth levees amounting to or exceeding 36 metres. This no doubt underlay the extension of the city on the left bank. The risks of floods were nonetheless real and made necessary the regular maintenance of the dikes.[43]

Equally devastating were fires, which could result from an incident or from riots. To take one example from a long series, in 362/972 trouble broke out, and al-Karkh was set on fire; 17,000 people died, and 300 shops, numerous houses, and 33 mosques were destroyed by the fire.[44]

Urban fragility was also economic. Feeding such a large population implied vast supply networks. Baghdad drained the agricultural surplus and the fiscal revenues of the whole of Sawad. Indeed, development of the city, as that of all the ancient cities of Mesopotamia, would not have been possible without the presence of this rich hinterland. However, ensuring a regular supply seems to have become more and more difficult. The necessary but fragile equilibrium between the city and the territory that feeds it must have been broken in the fourth/tenth century. Shortages and epidemics, rare before 320/932, became frequent after that date. Chroniclers mention grain crises in 323/934, 324/935, 329/940, 330/941, 331/942, 332/943, 334/945, 336/947, 337/948, etc., and these often led to crowd movements and scenes of looting.

Insecurity seems to have been endemic because of the presence of numerous marginalized groups. The *'ayyarun*, poor people carrying on small trades, or vagabonds without fixed employment, were first mentioned during the civil war between al-Amin and al-Ma'mun. Subsequently they become a major topic in the Baghdad chronicles of the third/ninth-fourth/tenth centuries. These trouble-makers, also called *fityan* or *shuttar*, emerge from the shadows in periods of relaxation by

---

[42] Al-Tabari, 3:2, 105.

[43] E. de Vaumas, "Introduction géographique à l'étude de Bagdad," *Arabica* 9 (1962): 243–244.

[44] Ibn al-Athir, *al-Kamil*, 8:462.

the authority and of public riots; then they commit multiple acts of vandalism and looting. The ethnic dimension (bond with the *futuwwa*) and the social significance (crime or revolt of the destitute) of the unrest they caused have been the object of contradictory assessment. At times they had such power that they took the place of the urban authority and exerted pressure on the rich population; hence in 421/1030–425/1033, al-Burjumi, a particularly powerful leader of the *'ayyarun*, succeeded in defying the authorities and imposing his own rule. At other times, these marginalized people were taken up by the state, which incorporated them into the police or used them as a combat force.[45]

From a reading of the chronicles, the history of Baghdad seems full of popular revolts whose demands were, at once, religious, political and social: riots led by the Hanbalis, conflicts between Shi'ite and Sunni, revolts against the rich, anxiety in the face of the Byzantine re-conquest, displeasure at the exactions of government employees, hostility towards the military, protest from soldiers because of delays in their pay.[46] Baghdad suffered greatly from this constant insecurity and from the popular outbursts. Insecurity seems to have been particularly serious in the first half of the fourth/tenth century, to the extent that, on several occasions, a number of rich inhabitants left the city to seek refuge elsewhere, while others closed the gates to their streets and merchants organized night watches. In the years 323/934–328/940 alone, we may note the following from the *Memoirs* of the courtier al-Suli:

- popular protest against a rise in the price of bread;
- mutiny of the Turkish regiments demanding their pay;
- a huge fire in the Karkh quarter;
- a fresh riot because of the high prices of supplies, resulting in a confrontation between people and army;

---

[45] On the *'ayyarun*, see Cl. Cahen, "Mouvements populaires et autonomismes urbains dans l'Asie musulmane au Moyen Age," *Arabica* 6 (1958), especially 34–44 and 47–52; S. Sabari, *Mouvements populaires à Bagdad à l'époque abasside. IXe–Xe siècles* (Paris, 1981), 77–100; A. Cheikh Moussa, "L'historien et la littérature arabe médiévale," in "L'œuvre de Claude Cahen. Lectures critiques," *Arabica* 43 (1996): 152–188.

[46] Sabari, *Mouvements populaires*. See also the lists established by M. Canard for the fourth/tenth century in "Baghdad au IVe siècle de l'Hégire (Xe siècle de l'ère chrétienne)," *Arabica* 9 (1962): 283–285; by H. Laoust, "Les agitations religieuses à Baghdad aux IVe et Ve siècles de l'Hégire," in *Islamic Civilisation, 950–1150*, ed. D. S. Richards (Oxford, 1973), 169–185; and by E. G. Heilman, *Popular Protest in Medieval Baghdad. 295–334/908–946* (Princeton, 1978).

- protests led by the Hanbalis against the celebration of the Iranian festival of Mahya;
- scandal aroused by the arrest of a Jewish banker;
- a number of armed attacks by thieves subsequently condemned to death;
- violent flooding of the Tigris;
- unrest stirred up by the protests of Daylami soldiers.

Maintenance of order required that the authorities should supply the city, prevent a rise in the price of bread, and resort constantly to force, but also watch over people's welfare. There were few riots in the reign of the Buyid emir Mu'izz al-Dawla, because, on becoming master of the city in 334/945, he brought prosperity, managing to have bread sold at one dirham per 20 pounds. He also introduced new shows, wrestling championships in public squares, swimming competitions in the Tigris, or races.

> One of the amazing things which occurred in the time of Mu'izz al-Dawla was the inauguration of racing and wrestling. This came about because Mu'izz al-Dawla was in need of runners whom he could appoint as couriers to traverse the distance between him and his brother Rukn al-Dawla at Rayy. They traveled that long distance in a short time.
>
> Mu'izz al-Dawla would offer prizes to those who excelled in the races, consequently, the *ahdath* of Baghdad and the poor were attracted to this and became preoccupied with it giving their sons over to racing. As a result, there developed two main runners for Mu'izz al-Dawla. One was known as Mar'ush, the other as Fadl; each could run over thirty parsangs in a day, from sunrise to sunset, retracing the distance between 'Ukbara and Baghdad. Along every mile of the road there were people urging on these two. They became the Imams in running, and the sport took its name from them. The people developed two factions around them.[47] [These two factions took the form of solidarities between quarters and confessional solidarities (Shi'ite and Sunni).]

Beyond these tumultuous realities, Baghdad incarnated for the inhabitants of the *dar al-islam* the dream of a single caliph gathering all Muslims within a single *umma*. Even though the Abbasids never truly realized the unity of the Muslim world, this did not prevent their capital from becoming, in the collective imagination, the centre of the world:

---

[47] Ibn al-Jawzi, *Muntazam*, trans. in, *The Buwayhid Dynasty in Iraq. 334 H./945 to 403 H./1012: Shaping Institutions for the Future*, ed. J. J. Donohue (Leiden and Boston, 2003), 343–344.

If I start with Iraq [writes al-Ya'qubi at the beginning of his *Book of Countries*], it is simply because it is the centre of this world, the core of this earth. I mention, in the first place, Baghdad, because it is the heart of Iraq, the most important city, which has no equal in the East or West of the earth, either in its vastness, or in its importance, prosperity, abundance in water, or in its healthful climate. It is inhabited by the most diverse people, whether from the city or the country; it is the destination of those emigrating from all countries, far and near; from all parts, numerous are those who have preferred it to their own nation. All the peoples of the world have a quarter in it, a centre of dealing and trade. This is why there is, united in it, that which does not exist in any city of the world.[48]

Al-Khatib, who introduces his *Ta'rikh Baghdad* with a long description of the city, takes up the same themes when writing in the fifth/eleventh century, at a time when Baghdad could no longer claim, politically, economically, or culturally, to play the same role as it had done two centuries before:

In the entire world, there has not been a city which could compare with Baghdad in size and splendour, or in the number of scholars and great personalities. The distinction of the notables and general populace serves to distinguish Baghdad from the other cities, as does the vastness of its districts, the extent of its borders, and the great number of residences and palaces. Consider, the numerous roads, thoroughfares, and localities, the markets and streets, the lanes, mosques and bathhouses, and the high roads and shops—all of these distinguish the city from all others, as does the pure air, the sweet water, and the cool shade. There is no place which is as temperate in summer and winter, and as salubrious in spring and autumn. The very great population also distinguishes it from all other cities.[49]

These representations set Baghdad as a unique city, placed at the centre of the universe, as a city-world that recapitulates all the qualities and riches of other cities. They are less the result of analysed realities than symbolic in nature, especially after the weakening of caliphal power.[50] They are powerful nonetheless, and have remained, up to our present

---

[48] Al-Ya'qubi, *Kitab al-buldan*, 233–234; Wiet, *Les pays*, 4.

[49] Al-Khatib al-Baghdadi, 108–109.

[50] On the symbolic representation of "mégapole," such as city-worlds in the Arab sources, see F. Micheau in collaboration with P. Guichard, "Les sources pour les mégapoles orientales," in *Mégapoles méditerranéennes*, under the direction of Cl. Nicolet, R. Ilbert, and J.-Ch. Depaule (Paris and Rome, 2000), 685–704.

day, strongly present in the imagination of Arabs, expressing as they do nostalgia for a prestigious past and symbolizing as they do the dream of a unified Muslim *umma*. If Baghdad is, in the stone, a city "without memory," it remains, for Arabs, "a place of memory."

MARINID FEZ: ZENITH AND SIGNS OF DECLINE

Halima Ferhat

Situated in the plain of the Sais, at the intersection of the major axes linking the different regions of the country, Fez was for centuries the capital of Morocco. The city was, it is true, lacking in a navigable waterway, but the Almohads had created a dockyard on the river at the place known as al-Habbalat, three kilometres to the east, and for a time small boats ensured a link with the Atlantic. The project of the Marinid Abu ʿInan was more ambitious but failed to last; nevertheless, two large vessels were built in this spot. It was the Maghrawa princes (end of the ninth to the middle of the twelfth centuries), so maligned by the chroniclers, who contrived to endow the town founded by their Idrisid enemies with its resolute city character. Fez kept its privileged status under the Almoravids and the Almohads whose official capital was Marrakesh. But the Marinid period was indisputably the most brilliant and the most fertile; and many monuments still bear the mark of this dynasty.

We have a relative abundance of information about this period which saw, at one and the same time, the city's zenith and the appearance of signs of stagnation, even decline. Historians, travellers, theologians, poets, and other scholars have left descriptions of the Marinid capital that have the advantage of supplementing one another. Leo Africanus, chronologically the last of these, devotes sixty-two pages to his adopted home, and it is hard to call Fez to mind without falling into a paraphrase of this trenchant, precise description; his book was published in Venice in 1550. Fez was, however, already undermined from within and threatened by the Saʿadis.[1]

---

[1] (J.) Leo Africanus, *Description de l'Afrique*, trans. E. Epaulard (Paris, 1956), 1:179–241. The information in the *Buyutat Fas* (Rabat, 1972), a short treatise attributed to Ismaʿil ibn al-Ahmar, leaves the reader puzzled. Are we dealing with notes designed to serve as the outline of a work perhaps never completed? The loose style and the anachronisms give the impression that the author (or authors) has dipped undiscerningly into some scattered and sometimes contradictory sources. See *Buyutat Fas* (attributed to I. Ibn al-Ahmar).

The present city has preserved its medieval configuration, even though the ramparts and the gates have undergone several transformations. The number of gates has increased or decreased throughout the city's history. Some have been walled up, others—like Bab al-Kanisa, mentioned by al-Bakri, which became Bab al-Khukha—have changed their names.[2]

All the relevant writers, vying in their superlatives, have paid homage to this city known to be endowed with such exceptional advantages. "There is no city," declares the fascinated author of *Zahrat al-as*, "no country, that does not have representatives in Fez. They engage in trade, live there, and are active there. Traders, along with craftsmen, have come there from every region, and every kind of commercial dealing is gathered there."[3] The mystic Ibn ʿAbbad, a man not easy to please, notes the capital's intellectual role: "Fez is the mother of the various parts of the Maghreb...it is from her that order and corruption alike spread to the other cities."[4] Ibn al-Khatib, well known for his Andalusi chauvinism, sings the praises of this splendid city without stint. Finally, Leo Africanus who had visited so many countries concluded: "Nowhere, either in all of Africa, or in Asia, or in Italy, have I seen a market where so many kinds of goods are to be found. It is impossible to set a value on it all."

Fez was closely bound up with the Mediterranean and its chief ports, such as Sabta and Badis, over the Sahara, and Bilad al-Soudan, via Sijilmassa. The relentless hostility of the Marinids towards Tlemcen is partly to be explained by the wish to lay hands on those gold routes over which so much ink has been spilled.

In the Middle Ages, Fez was an indisputably opulent city, known for its dynamism and for the sophistication of its inhabitants. The buildings were well constructed, beautiful, and elegant. It produced, manufactured and sold a large variety of goods and took in others which it then redistributed; its trade was particularly prosperous. Its province supplied it with grains, fruit and men. The village of Bhalil provisioned it with firewood and coal; the Banu Yazgha supplied it with cedarwood

---

[2] H. Berrada, *Fès de Bab en Bab* (Casablanca, 2002). This small guide gives a clear impression of the complex framework of gates and ramparts in Fez.

[3] ʿAli al-Gaznai, *Zahrat al-as* (Rabat, 1967), 34; Abu-al-Hasan ʿAli El-Djaznai, *La fleur de myrte*, Arabic text, with annotated translation by Alfred Bel (Algiers, 1923). The work centres on the Qarawiyyin mosque, but does not speak of the Marinid New City. See also al-Gaznai, *Zahrat*, 72–73.

[4] N. Nwyia, *Ibn ʿAbbad de Ronda (1332–1390)* (Beirut, 1961), 150.

that was extensively used for building; the villages of Madchar Shatibi
and Dimnat al-Baqul sent the salt used by the tanneries abundantly.
Numbers of small centres functioned as simple dependencies and taxes
were levied from these to finance the embellishment of the capital.
Even Meknes was unable to escape this ascendancy, and the revenues
from its olive oil works allowed certain monuments to be erected in
the White City.[5]

Water: chief endowment of Fez, and its ornament

The role of rivers and springs was crucial, and there had been major
works of canalization in the city since remote times; basins, tanks, water
jets, and fountains (bila, fwara, saqqaya)[6] were regularly noted, and writers
reiterated longingly how Fez, with 360 springs, was richer in water than
Damascus. Thanks to this water, the streets were regularly washed.[7]

Chroniclers attributed exceptional virtues to the city's water. Luke-
warm in winter, it was cool in summer; it facilitated the removal of
internal stones and cured certain skin diseases. Wad al-Jawahir (the
river of pearls) owed its name to its precious shells and provided large
quantities of fish.

Princes and patrons endowed the quarters, the streets, and the monuments with fountains that were not simply designed to provide water,
but were also true masterpieces decorated with zallij, those celebrated
earthenware squares glazed in iridescent colours. Impressive numbers of
structures equipped with running water are attributed to Abu 'l-Hasan:
fountains, naturally, but also drinking-troughs, rooms for ablution, basins,
tanks in the mosques, etc.[8] The houses of notables had long been supplied with water, and the finest of them had "richly decorated" fountains
and tanks used as pools for swimming in the hottest season.[9]

This water was the glory of the new royal city. An innovation of
the Marinid kings was the installation of the enormous water-wheels

---

[5] A. Ibn Ghazi, *Rawd al-hatun fi akhbar Maknasat al-zaytun* (Rabat, 1964). Fez produced
olives to the value of 50,000 dinars, almost double the production of Meknes, which
reached 35,000. Ibn Ghazi settled permanently in Fez in 856 A.H. (1452 A.D.).

[6] See Dozy, *Supplément aux dictionnaires arabes*, 1:137, 2:289.

[7] Al-Gaznai, *Zahrat*, 34. In the time of Leo Africanus the streets in Fez were still
being washed (*Description*, 1:228).

[8] S. A. Ibn Marzuq, *Al-Musnad*, ed. M. J. Viguera (Algiers, 1981), 417–441.

[9] Leo Africanus, *Description*, 1:182–183.

that enabled them to irrigate the palace and the multiple gardens they maintained at such great expense.

Muhammad ibn al-Hajj, inventor of the hugely famous and much described[10] *dawlab*s (water-wheels) was brought from Granada. The son of a mudejar from Seville, he was expert in the mechanical arts. He installed the great wheel with its numerous buckets and a secret mechanism, along with other norias, such as the one in the Mosarra.

Despite its abundance, the distribution of water among houses was strictly regulated, being controlled, like the upkeep of canalizations, by the *muhtasib* and by experts. The rich vocabulary in this field has not yet been the subject of study. However, the aspect of the city did change considerably over two centuries: the springs and watercourses were no longer open to the sky; they had now been covered by buildings. The ownership of water was the subject of numerous lawsuits between the city-dwellers and the peasants of the surrounding districts.[11]

Thanks to irrigation, Fez produced an abundance of fruits and vegetables, along with the flowers for which the inhabitants had a fondness. Ibn 'Abbad, a stranger in the city, complained of his woeful lodging, "where there were neither trees, nor lights, nor flowers." The Fassis were, it seems, particularly attracted by places where they could walk and go on picnics and rustic outings.

Dynamic minorities

Overpopulated as it was, the city was short of places to live. Moreover, shared dwelling was frequent, and wretched suburbs co-existed with the splendid palaces described by both al-'Umari and Leo Africanus.

The Jewish minority was as powerful as it was old-established, and some of its members exercised important functions at court. They were especially prominent in trade and in the working of precious metals, to the point of stirring up envy. Jewellers, goldsmiths, moneychangers,

---

[10] Ibn al-Khatib, *Al-Ihata fi akhbar Gharnata* (Cairo, 1973–79), 2:139–141; Ibn al-Hajj Numayri, *Fayd al-'ubab* (Rabat, n.d.), 20, 25; Leo Africanus, *Description*, 1:234–235, attributes the works to a Genoese merchant (?); G. S. Colin, "L'origine de norias de Fès," *Hesperis* 13 (1933): 156.

[11] M. Mezzine, *Fas wa badiatuha. 1549–1637* (Rabat, 1986).

they were suspected of fraud at times of monetary crisis, and conflicts of interest were sometimes the cause of tragedies.[12]

Funduq al-Yahud was one of the oldest places in the city, along with Dar al-Kaytoun, which gave its name to a branch of the Idrisid Sharifs. From al-Bakri on, chroniclers repeated constantly that Fez was the city of the Maghreb where Jews were the most numerous. Ibn al-Khatib noted how "the descendants of Shem and Ham" had settled themselves in Fez and lived there as good neighbours.[13] The influx of Jews expelled from Spain increased this minority's importance. The substantial amount of taxes they paid was a sign at once of their numbers and their wealth.

Relatively little is still known about Christians present in the city. Knights in the service of successive dynasties, captives, diplomats, and renegades do, though, seem to have been numerous. The chroniclers who note the foundation of a Christian quarter in the White City, Rabad Nasara, state that, before this time, they lived within the old city. The word 'alj (plural 'uluj) already seems, in Fez, to have denoted "renegades" or converted Christians.

"Municipal" institutions

We do not have any *hisba* document available that is specifically devoted to the city of Fez at this time. The function was undoubtedly a prestigious one, since the official poet al-Malzouzi was appointed to the post. Leo Africanus is distressed at its degradation and regrets the changes that have set in: "In the past it was entrusted only to men who were competent and of good repute. Nowadays, sovereigns accord it to common, ignorant people."[14]

The *muhtasib* supervised order, cleanliness, and hygiene. He kept a watch on fraud among the traders and supervised the interests and health of the inhabitants; he prevented the occupation of public spaces threatened by the proliferation of *sabat*s (covered streets), and so on.

---

[12] M. Kably, *Société, pouvoir et religion au Maroc à la fin du Moyen Age* (Paris: Maisonneuve et Larose, 1986), 274.

[13] Ibn al-Khatib, *Mi'ya al-ikhtyar* (Rabat, 1977), 79; Leo Africanus, *Description*, 1:234.

[14] Leo Africanus, *Description*, 1:207.

One of the most important aspects was the checking of weights and measures. During the rule of the Marinids, standard indications of length were set on the walls of the *muhtasib*'s office, for the supervision of precious fabrics and cloths.[15] The building materials used (wood but also easily inflammable rushes and palms) accounted for the frequency of fires and their disastrous effects. Once fire had broken out, indeed, it was virtually impossible to keep it under control, and *hisba* documents are silent on the measures to be taken in such a case.[16]

There was a health service concerning itself with the presence of lepers. Compelled to reside in lazar-houses, the sick people were a source of constant anxiety to the city-dwellers who on two occasions demanded the removal of these ghettos. Set up close to Bab al-Khukha, then removed to Bab al-Shari'a, they were compelled to move once again, when the inhabitants complained of miasmas and of refuse that might contaminate the water sources.

In the interests of hygiene, it was forbidden to slaughter animals outside the abattoirs (*gurna*), and the transportation of meat was, in principle, strictly controlled by the *muhtasib*. The blood, considered as being taboo, was not to soil passers-by, and in these narrow, perpetually crowded streets, the task cannot have been an easy one.

The White City: Marinid capital

With Fez conquered and its Almohad governors driven out, the Marinid princes began by installing themselves in their enemies' fortress, the Qasba of Flowers. In March 1276, however, they inaugurated the construction sites for the White City whose foundation marked, according to Ibn Khaldun, the distinctive beginning of the new dynasty. This city came to be added to the urban agglomeration made up by the Old Fez which had already comprised two quite distinct cores, one on the side of the Qayrawanis, the other on the side of the Andalusis.[17]

Celebrated by all the chroniclers, this foundation was a true capital, designed to symbolize the glory and power of the new dynasty. We are

---

[15] A. Bel, *Inscriptions arabes de Fès* (Paris, 1917).

[16] *Dhakhira al-saniyya*, attributed to Ibn Abi Zar' (Rabat, 1972), 73.

[17] R. Le Tourneau, *Fès avant le Protectorat*, new edition (Rabat, 1987), 2:837–842; H. Ferhat, "Fès," in *Les Grandes Villes méditerranéennes du monde musulman médiéval* (Ecole Française de Rome, 2000), 215–232.

dealing here not with a simple royal residence or a purely administrative complex.

This royal city was named al-Madina al-Bayda, the White City, but the population of Fez swiftly gave it another name, Fez-Jdid, which it has preserved.[18] A girdle of ramparts, built first of all to shut it off from the Old Fez which kept its aspect of a twofold city. It contained the palace, along with its multiple, vast dependencies, the principal mosque, barracks, stables, and, finally, a city in the proper sense, with its mosques, its trading centres and other suqs, its residential quarters, and its *hammams*. The most important state services were transferred there.[19]

A new mint, *Dar-Sikka*, competed with, or supplanted, the old workshops. Workmen and employees worked and lodged there, as did the goldsmiths, jewellers, lawyers, secretaries, etc. Also to be found there was the Christians' suburb (*Rabad al-Nasara*) and the Jewish quarter. Christians in the service of the dynasty had, up to that time, been lodged in the old city, along with the Jews. These latter had been transferred following a series of attacks.[20]

The great mosque had every care lavished on it, and seemed designed to rival older places of worship. It was endowed with a valuable *minbar*, an impressive chandelier with 187 holders, a *maqsura*, etc.

Ambitious, determined builders that they were, the Marinid kings multiplied their foundations and spent without stint on the adornment of monuments—spurred on, it would seem, by the desire to eclipse the achievements of the Almohads. This competition is well illustrated by the Qarawiyyin mosque. The Marinid *qadis*, notably Muhammad ibn Abi Sabr Ayyub, carried out work in this place of worship out of which the Almohads had made the principal religious edifice of Fez.[21] The décor of buildings became ever more sumptuous and Marinid architecture found its own distinctive stamp.

The Marinid *hammams* were very beautiful structures that have never been equalled (though sometimes imitated), even though their scale

---

[18] Leo Africanus, *Description*, 1:232–233.

[19] Ibn Fadl Allah al-ʿUmari, *Masalik al-absar*, trans. and annotated Gaudrefoy-Demombynes (Paris, 1927), provides a lengthy description of the White City.

[20] *Dhakhira*, 96–161.

[21] Al-Gaznai, *Zahrat* (Rabat, 1967), 45–67; al-Qirtas (Rabat, 1973), 60–66. These writers supply a detailed description of Marinid architectural innovations (new domes, ʿAnza, a small building in the courtyard to indicate the direction of prayer, etc.). See D. Maslow, *Les mosquées de Fès et du Nord du Maroc* (Paris, 1937).

remained modest. The most beautiful appears to have been the *hammam* of the royal city. Al-'Umari, quoting Ibn Sa'id, assures us that only the sweating-rooms of Fez were supplied by springs.[22] Those dignitaries who found mixing with others distasteful had *hammam*s in their houses. In contrast to the East, the baths in Fez had no private booths allowing notables to avoid mixing in the common rooms—those frequented by the lower orders so decried by censorious chroniclers (*'amma*).[23]

The new edifices were equipped with accessories that demonstrated how technical innovations remained important. Putting aside the architectural details involved, we may point out the celebrated clepsydra (*al-magana*) installed in one of the madrasas of Abu 'Inan; a number of other clocks functioned in other religious establishments. To protect believers from the sun, a linen cloth velarium was unfolded, using an ingenious system of ropes, in the courtyard of the Qarawiyyin mosque. In the same courtyard was built a shelter for the vast bell, weighing ten quintals that had been seized at Gibraltar in 1333.

Improved astrolabes, clocks adjusted to the solar year, ingenious hydraulic devices, a model of the city of Gibraltar—there was no inclination that wasn't satisfied with reproductions of what had always existed. Automata often featured among the gifts presented by foreign ambassadors, especially the Genoese. There were frequent exchanges with the Muslim world, headed by Egypt, as also with Genoa, Castille, and Aragon; no delegation would be likely to introduce itself empty-handed.

Situated outside the palatial complex, al-Mosarra was a vast space sited to the northwest of the city; here military parades and other march-pasts took place, along with sports involving horsemanship. There were several pavilions there, including the Golden Tower (al-Dhahab); Abu 'l-Hasan would go there twice a week to attend military manoeuvres and jousts where the best, most skilful knights would face one another.

Zawyia al-Mutwakkilya, created by Abu 'Inan, was designed to take in travellers who arrived after the city gates had been closed. According to testimonies, including that of al-Numayri, this edifice was an architectural masterpiece with its gardens and fountains. Unfortunately, not the smallest trace of the monument now survives. The Marinids created or restored numerous gardens, parks, and *riyad*s. The palaces

---

[22] Al-'Umari, *Masalik*.
[23] Leo Africanus, *Description*, 1:189–190.

called Rawd al-Ghizlan and Bustan Amina have kept their fame, but a good number of others mentioned in the texts have not yet been identified.

The Qaysariyya and the hegemony of trade

It was trade, with its various branches, that marked out the history of the city and the mentality of its inhabitants. Specialized markets were already noted in the Idrisid period. The Qaysariyya, an architectural agglomeration extending over a vast area, apparently underwent several transformations before becoming the impressive Marinid market. It was "a small town surrounded by walls," with a complex system of supervision, and it was also a focus of competition and tensions between Muslim and Jewish traders.

The Qaysariyya was given over to luxury articles: silks, jewels, spices, and perfumes, sashes, harnesses for horses, threads for embroidery, European cloths, etc. The description of Leo Africanus, given at a time when the country was in crisis, gives an idea of the wealth of these markets.[24] A good many other places were devoted to less exalted trade, and less care went into their building; the *tarbi'as* were modest squares sometimes surrounded by galleries and reserved for specific kinds of trade, particularly in textiles.

The *funduqs* of the city fell into two categories: those serving to lodge merchants and those serving above all for the storage of goods, generally sited close to the city gates. While some *funduqs* belonged to particular people, the most substantial ones made up part of foundational assets, including the famous wax *funduq*.

The commercial talents of the Fassis aroused prejudices whose echo is to be found from the twelfth century; the poet al-Bakki became renowned for his satires on their avarice, and Ibn al-Khatib viewed them as pragmatic, self-interested, and bereft of a sense of hospitality.[25] Ibn 'Abbad complains of the cruelty of being in exile in this opulent city whose wealthy inhabitants remained indifferent to the loneliness of strangers.[26] The Fassis were recognized as possessing a sharp intelligence,

---

[24] Leo Africanus, *Description*, 1:198–199.
[25] Anon, *Kitab al-istibsar* (Alexandria, 1958), 182; al-Maqqari, *Nafh al-tib*, ed. I. 'Abbas (Beirut, 1968), 3:324.
[26] Nwyia, *Ibn 'Abbad*, 49.

a redoubtable skill in trade, a frantic love of gain, but also knowledge and a piety bordering on the pharisaical.

Wealth advertised itself, and the properties of the city-dwellers extended over a vast district around the city. The division of properties among the great city families was reflected in the topography of Fez, whose streets, *riyad*s, *funduq*s, *hammam*s and suqs would bear the name in question. The history of the Banu 'l-Hajj, the Slalgi and the Banu Maljum merged with the history of the city.[27]

Private houses were built high, with two, three, or sometimes four storeys. Those of traders and notables were richly decorated with multi-coloured *zellij*s and contained gardens. The city was, however, overpopulated, and writers were inclined to take little notice of modest dwellings.

Public demonstrations and royal ostentation

The Marinid apparatus and Marinid pomp were expressed through extravagant expenditure. Royal audiences were carefully choreographed, for the sovereign needed to make public advertisement of his power and authority.

The royal cortège displayed a solemnity designed to impress. The finest horses were harnessed with gold and precious stones, and the saddles were embroidered with gold thread. The cortège would advance to the sound of drums and other musical instruments. A profusion of multi-coloured standards would be unfurled, dominated by the white that was the dynasty's distinguishing mark. There are plenty of descriptions of these processions, of which the reception accorded to King Muhammad V of Granada was an example.[28]

The different professional bodies were invited to celebrate these solemn events. Freed from its toil for the occasion, the population would flock to gaze at the sovereign's public appearances—departures and arrivals, receptions of ambassadors—but also to rejoice in the circus games and the displays of equestrian prowess.

The Marinids officialized the celebration of the Mawlid and gave it an unprecedented lustre; nothing was spared to make this anniversary

---

[27] *Al-Istibsar*, 203, 204, 205; *Buyutat*, 44, 49.
[28] Ibn al-Khatib, *Nufadat al-jarab* (Cairo, n.d.), 184–185.

a sumptuous event. There are many descriptions. Ibn Marzuq, author of the *Musnad*, attended several years in a row, and his testimony is supplemented by that of Leo Africanus. There was food abundant in quality and quantity, fruit, delicacies, cakes made from honey and sugar, sumptuous rooms, and illuminations. The night was enlivened by recitation of al-Busayri's poem *Al-Burda*, by contests in singing, and by reading or psalmody of the *mawlidiyyat*.

The glory of the Prophet was reflected back on to the reigning prince, who distributed his liberalities to the *ahl al-Bayt* (descendants of the Prophet) and other dignitaries. For the city's poor, the festival was a chance to feast abundantly. They were able to take advantage of the leftovers from these gigantic banquets, and they received alms and the unused candles and wax. Soon the Marinids added to the celebration of the Prophet's birth the commemoration of the seventh day, the day of "baptism," if the expression is permissible.

Fez may indeed have been founded by the Idrisids, descendants of the Prophet, but it was the Marinids who arranged and encouraged the installation of the Sharifs and accorded them privileges. The popular veneration for the family of Idris was already noted by the author of *Al-Istibsar* in the Almohad period, but it was the policy of Marinid funding that allowed the formation of a veritable caste.[29]

The organization of the Sharifs into a formal body, jealous of its acquired interests, was swift. The palace sent emissaries to invite authentic Sharifs to come and settle in the city; and the influx of eastern Sharifs attracted by Marinid generosity was a noteworthy feature.[30] Pensions and a variety of privileges were granted them, and these exempted them from the need to earn their livelihoods in any difficult or base professions. A *naqib* (or *mazwar*), from among their number, was charged with watching jealously over their genealogy and with preventing intruders from enjoying the same advantages. Muhammad ibn 'Imran al-Juti, an Idrisid from Fez, was the first holder of the title. Thereafter, the Sharifs were no longer subject to the civil jurisdiction but began to have their own jurisdictions.

---

[29] Al-Gaznai, *Zahrat*, 29; Kably, *Société, pouvoir et religion*, 219, 99; H. Ferhat, "Chérifisme et enjeux du pouvoir au Maroc," *Oriente Moderno* 18 (1999): 473–483.

[30] H. L. Beck, *L'image de Idris II, ses descendants de Fas et la politique chérifienne des sultans Mérinides* (Leiden, 1989); F. R. Mediano, *Familias de Fez (SS. XV–XVII)* (Madrid, 1995).

The departure of the caravan for Mecca, the *rakb*, was another moment that allowed the integration of religion with power and with trade. The formation and departure of the *rakb* was an impressive spectacle. Pilgrims from the different regions were not the only people involved. Ambassadors, princes, and a large number of traders made up part of the caravan, along with envoys of the kings bearing gifts destined for the princes of the East. Subjects could, thus, marvel at the splendour of their sovereigns and the extent of their relations with the legendary eastern lands, especially Egypt and the holy places.

Circus spectacles (a distant echo of Rome) were regularly organized. There were fights between lions and bulls. In spite of precise descriptions, we still cannot locate the Marinid arenas, and their similarity with the present-day corrida remains a matter of speculation. In reality, the lions in these "games" faced the bulls under the direction of tamers protected by kinds of wooden "barrels." The advantage was not always with the king of the forest. Wounded lions were apparently dispatched with arrows.

An unprecedented intellectual activity

Following the downfall of Cordoba and Seville and the decline of Marrakesh, Fez became the principal focus of attraction for élites from every corner.[31] The city was a crossroads where every important Maghrebi personage made a more or less extended stay. Banu Ziyan princes from Tlemcen, Nasrids from Granada, Hafsid princes, but also ambassadors, travellers, mystics, students or straightforward parasites, along with most of the famous personages of the age, made a stay there or else settled permanently. The autobiography of the author of the *Muqaddima* is a valuable testimony regarding the city's intellectual circles. There is abundant information about these learned circles that gravitated around the princes, especially around Abu 'l-Hasan and Abu 'Inan. The Marinid court was a highly open one, and the kings neither were nor could allow themselves to be miserly. The gift was part of the system of government, and the women of the court also took part in this. Before his departure for Granada, Ibn Battuta

---

[31] M. Benchekroun, *La vie intellectuelle marocaine sous les Mérinides et les Wattasides* (Rabat, 1974).

admitted that the king's mother "sent me some gold pieces that were very useful to me."[32]

Isma'il ibn al-Ahmar, banished by his cousin, the king of Granada, lived in a gilded exile and consorted with men of letters in court and city alike. A prolix writer, he was one of the dynasty's poets and historiographers. His work provides a valuable testimony of the groups where men of letters were to be found. He acknowledged that the king of Fez took upon himself all the expenses for his marriage with his cousin.[33]

Ibn 'Abbad, a talented disciple of Ibn 'Ashir of Salé, attracted the attention of the court in spite of his extreme modesty. His commentaries on al-Hikam brought him great success and made a major contribution to the diffusion of Shadhilism. Imam and preacher at the Qarawiyyin, he took part in the official Mawlid ceremonies. His sermons and commentaries were a great literary event. His talents, his love of solitude and his aversion to trifling fashionable questions set him apart from others.

This élite of birth and knowledge animated cultural life. This dynamic group of writers and thinkers knew one another, consorted with one another, esteemed, envied, hated one another. They had unhesitating recourse to the denunciation and petty spite of which Ibn al-Khatib was a victim. Ibn al-Khatib's friend to whom he addressed a letter on the birth of a child was none other than Ibn Khaldun.[34] The brother of Ibn Khaldun, Yahya, was the historiographer of the Banu 'Abd al-Wad of Tlemcen, the Marinids' brothers and enemies, and he made a stay in Fez. The accounts of Ibn Battuta which we esteem so highly aroused more suspicion and mocking comment than enthusiasm.

In Fez, too, resided a throng of fine minds come from every corner: from neighbouring tribes like the Fishtala and Makkuda, from other Maghrebi cities like the grammarian Ibn Ajarrum, the Banu 'l-'Azafi princes, from Sabta, but above all from al-Andalus and from Tlemcen.

Besieged on a number of occasions by the Marinid sovereigns, the latter city functioned as a counterpart to Fez, and hostile or friendly

---

[32] Ibn Battuta, *Voyages*, ed. and trans. C. Defremery and B. Sanguinetti (Paris, 1968), 2:383.

[33] I. Ibn al-Ahmar, *Natir al-juman*, ed. M. R. Daya (Beirut, 1976); A. L. de Premare, *Maghreb et Andalousie au XIVe siècle* (Lyon, 1981).

[34] Ibn al-Khatib, *Nufadat*, 131.

exchanges remained as important as they were regular. The élites of Tlemcen moved constantly between the two cities, fleeing prosecution by the prince of one city to seek the protection of his rival.

When, in 1282, the Marinids occupied Tlemcen, the city of his birth, Abu 'Abd Allah al-Abili chose exile and travelled to the East. When he returned to his homeland, he hastened to leave once more, so as to avoid re-entering the service of Sultan Abu Hammou. He took refuge in Fez, with the Jew Khalluf al-Maghribi, who taught him esoteric sciences ('ilm ta'alim). We find him next in Marrakesh, with Ibn al-Banna, then among the Haskoura of the High Atlas with Ibn Taroumit, before finally becoming the pivotal figure in the scholarly circle of Abu 'l-Hasan whom he accompanied on the Tarifa and Tunis expeditions before dying in Fez in 1356.

From Tlemcen, too, came the Banu 'l-Imam brothers, protégés of Abu 'l-Hasan. Brought up in Tunis, they had a violent confrontation with Ibn Taymiyya while staying in the East.[35] Their Banu Marzuq fellow-citizens played a part of prime importance, and it is thanks to one of them that we are so well informed about the exploits of al-Hasan to whom he was very close. From Tlemcen, likewise, was the family of one of the city's most important qadis, al-Maqqari.

Emigrants from al-Andalus played a prime part in every sphere, the importance of this minority being explained by the inexorable Christian advance and the internal crises of the Kingdom of Granada.

The madrasas are the monuments that still maintain the glorious memory of the Marinids. There was indeed a madrasa founded by a rich scholar in Sabta, but the institution, with its rich buildings and its teachers paid by the ruling power, was very much a Marinid innovation. Most of the madrasas in Fez were the work of this dynasty whose princes vied with one another in foundations and gifts.[36] Thus, in 1337, at great expense, a lump of marble weighing 143 quintals was imported from Almeria for the basin of the Sahrij Madrasa. The transportation of this block required the most heroic exertions.[37]

Fez prided itself on the considerable number of books to be found there, even if most of the Almohad workshops which produced paper had disappeared. The importing of European products which had

---

[35] Ibn Khaldun, *Le Voyage d'Orient et d'Occident*, ed. A. Cheddadi (Paris, 1980), 54; Ibn Mariam, *Al-Bustan* (Algiers, n.d.), 123–26, 214–19.
[36] M. Manouni, *Waraqat* (Rabat: Publ. Fac. Des Lettres, 1983).
[37] Al-Gaznai, *Zahrat*, 37.

now become a necessity gave rise to a series of *fatwas*.[38] While private libraries were not uncommon, those of the mosques and the madrasas derived from royal or private legacies, and plenty of writers presented copies of their works by means of waqf. Ibn Khaldun bequeathed the Qarawiyyin a manuscript of his monumental historical work.

At court and in the city alike, people needed no encouragement to write verses. Most of these poems, though, were the work of paid rhymesters: poetry competitions brought poets together when the opportunity arose. In 1363 (Rabiʿ II, 764), a large number vied to celebrate the sword of Idris I which was to be placed in the minaret of the Qarawiyyin and serve as a talisman for the city. If poetry was very often inspired by circumstances, many writings stemmed from hope of a reward in ringing, tested currency. After the manner of the kings, powerful ministers maintained their own courts of extollers,. The generosity, even mad prodigality, of the Banu ʿUthman, a dynasty of dignitaries, was appreciated by the courtiers and poets who constantly celebrated their open-handedness. Valuable for the study of the city's history, these works are liable to grate on the nerves of the present-day reader with their overdone homage and panegyric of the powerful.

Ibn Battuta and his editor sought to outdo everyone in their celebration of the glory and merits of king Abu ʿInan. Ibn Juzay constantly intersperses his account with praises that border on the toadying. After the reign of Abu ʾl-Hasan, that of Abu ʿInan is set forth as the reign of justice, equity and order; the prince's talents are praised as beyond the normal: of outstanding valour on the battlefield, he lays the lion low, surpasses every king in the world in every sphere. It is affirmed, too, that "in all these sciences our master holds the first place," and that "his handwriting surpasses in beauty all the decorations of the holy tomb."[39]

The classes of the most famous masters attracted the élites and were often an opportunity to make useful acquaintances and penetrate the circles of power. Princes, sons of dignitaries, but also gifted students, rubbed shoulders there. Social rise was still achieved through knowledge! And yet renowned scholars like ʿAbd al-ʿAziz al-Qarawi ventured to make vehement criticism of the fiscal policy of Abu ʾl-Hasan.

---

[38] H. Ferhat, "Le livre instrument de savoir et object de commerce," *Hespéris-Tamuda* 32 (1994): 53–62.

[39] Ibn Battuta, *Voyages*, 2:369, 372.

Taking over from the Andalusi cities whose heritage it claimed, Fez
was a glittering centre where wit and culture were especially esteemed.
Everything was discussed there: methods of teaching already threatened
with stagnation, Sufi approaches, the morality of the common people
(*'amma*), and also taxation and Sharifism.

The Mawlid, at once an official and a popular festival, was at the
centre of a major debate revolving around the value of this "innovation." Was it a good or a bad *bid'a*?[40]

The supervision of knowledge through the institution of the madrasas did not escape criticism. Abu 'Abd Allah al-Maqqari, a disciple of
al-Abili and chief judge of Fez, disputed the merits of these official
colleges that threatened the dynamism and freedom of masters and
students alike and were harmful to learning.[41] Ibn 'Abbad, who attacked
the avarice and intellectual sloth of his contemporaries, seems to have
been alluding to these paid teachers.

The Sufi current which had formerly flourished in the Almohad
capital moved to Fez, undergoing changes that attracted to it scholars
and even courtiers; despite their creed, the saints did not shun closeness
to power. It was at Fez that Ibn Khaldun wrote his treatise on Sufism,
the famous *Shifa al-sa'il*.[42] Ibn al-Khatib devoted his *Rawdat al-Ta'rif* to
the same subject.[43]

Thanks to two exceptional testimonies, we are relatively well informed
about these circles.[44] The Sufis watched over order, denounced the
iniquity of taxes, the maladministration of foundational assets (waqf),
and sometimes attacked the prince directly. Some took a specific interest in the world of craftsmen whom they ventured to censure. We may
discern in this current a proselytizing spirit. A holy personage fashioned
a special prayer (*wird*) for craftsmen. Ibn al-Hajj devoted the fourth and
final volume of his *Madkhal* to the world of work.[45]

---

[40] H. Ferhat, "Le culte du prophète au Maroc au XIIIᵉ siècle: organisation du
pèlerinage et célébration du Mawlid," in *La religion civique à l'époque médiévale et moderne*
(Ecole Française de Rome, 1995), 89–97, idem, *Sabta des origines au XIVᵉ siècle* (Rabat,
1993), 454–457.

[41] Kably, *Société, pouvoir et religion*, 283.

[42] R. Péres, *La Voie et la Loi ou le Maître et le Juriste* [trans. from *Shifa al-sa'il*] (Paris,
1991).

[43] H. Ferhat, *Le soufisme et les zaouyas au Maghreb. Mérite individuel et patrimoine sacré*
(Casablanca, 2003).

[44] A. Ibn Qanfud, *Uns al-faqir* (Rabat, 1967); al-Hadrami, *Al-Salsal al-adhb* (Salé,
1988).

[45] Ibn Qanfud, *Uns*, 74, 77; Ibn al-Hajj, *Al-Madkhal* (Beirut, 1972).

Certain Sufis were prepared to act as intermediaries between the rulers and their subjects, at the risk of arousing indignation or provoking the jealousy of their peers. Consorting with princes was, indeed, viewed as especially bad.[46] Abu 'l-Hasan Lijai, a scholar and mystic, devoted his life and his income to works of benevolence, letting nothing stand in the way of his efforts to help the poor and allay conflicts.

Despite his official responsibilities, Ibn 'Abbad constantly denounced bad governance, the iniquity of taxes, and the avarice of scholars whose cupidity and opportunism he did not hold back from denouncing: "It is not, it must be said, to struggle against the public misguidance of our poor contemporaries that they have taken on this function [of *faqih*]. Rather, they have seen in it an excellent means of acquiring the goods of this world."[47] Indeed, such criticisms are not new, but they do reflect a politico-social reality whereby dubious fortunes could be accumulated.

Abu 'Abd Allah al-Maqqari, from a rich Tlemcen family that combined knowledge and wealth, and ancestor of the author of *Nafh al-tib*, was an all-powerful *qadi* and a prestigious teacher, who did not hold back from criticizing his sovereign.[48]

Al-Abili, a philosopher attracted by the esoteric sciences, denounced the official institution of the madrasas. His interest in Shi'ism made him suspect, but we lack sufficient information to understand his flights, his clandestine behaviour, and the persecutions he endured.

For all the intellectual brio, such essential disciplines as medicine and philosophy began to stagnate; the hospital (or hospitals; *maristan*) was functioning, but our information remains insufficient. The author of *Al-Musnad* who entitles a chapter of his work "foundation of *maristans*" contents himself with noting Abu 'l-Hasan's restoration of a *maristan* founded by his father.[49] In so far as we can glean the names of physicians attached to the court, it would seem that they were primarily interested in dietary matters and the art of preserving health; the works of Ibn al-Khatib (who was, let us remember, a physician) are testament

---

[46] H. Ferhat, "Saints et Pouvoir au Moyen âge au Maghreb: entre le refus et la tentation," in the collection *L'autorité des saints en Méditerranée occidentale* (Tunis, 1998).

[47] Nwyia, *Ibn 'Abbad*, 150. Ibn 'Abbad became the patron of the shoemakers, and his commentaries on the *Hikam* still enjoy the same success.

[48] Al-Maqqari, *Nafh*, 3:203–209.

[49] Ibn Abi Zar', *Al-Anis al-mutrib bi rawd al-qartas* (Rabat, 1972).

to this. The Black Death did indeed give rise to a few treatises, but it revealed, above all, the powerlessness of practitioners.

The absence of philosophy is virtually total. Hunted down by the *fuqaha'*, the discipline had become a dangerous one—the misfortunes of al-Abili are witness to this. Under suspicion of heresy, he was forced more than once to conceal his beliefs.

There was an ambiguous current of learning, involving mathematicians like Ibn al-Banna, astrologer-astronomers like Ibn Qanfud, Sufis, and Jewish scholars like Ibn Makhluf.

Abu Zayd al-Lijai, known for his asceticism and his charitable works, devised a hydraulic astrolabe which Ibn Qanfud, himself an astronomer attracted by Sufism, regarded as an exceptional invention.[50]

A society in decline?

The power and popularity of the Sharifs became a threat to the ruling authority; the revolt of al-Juti illustrates the political emergence of this caste well.[51] From the fifteenth century on, the "discovery" of the tomb of Fez's founder led the city to focus around two places of worship: the Qarawiyyin mosque and the sanctuary of Moulay Idris.

In the fourteenth century, *hubus* assets were considerable, and royal donations were added to private bequests. They comprised mills, *hammams*, fountains, public ovens, and *funduqs*; their income was designed to ensure the upkeeping of mosques, hospitals, and madrasas. Expenditure, however, was no less substantial: the foundation and upkeeping of the madrasas and hospitals and mosques, salaries, illuminations, alms, pensions for the Sharifs, and also misappropriations—all these threatened the patrimony. Forty employees, among them a number of muezzins, supervised the upkeeping and proper working of the Qarawiyyin mosque alone. The squandering of this income, including abuse over lighting, led to the *qadi* 'Abd Allah al-Fishtali refusing to set foot in the great mosque until an end was put to the wasting of public assets in the purchase of wax and oil.[52] Public property fell

---

[50] Ibn Qanfud, *Uns*, 68.
[51] M. García-Arenal, "The Revolution of Fas in 869/1465 and the death of Sultan 'Abd al-Haqq al-Marini," *BSOAS* 41 (1978): 43–66.
[52] Ibn al-Khatib, *Al-Ihata*, 2, 1:33.

into disrepair for want of upkeep, and Gaznai was already noting, in a flourishing city, several gates condemned, mechanisms broken down, and places of worship neglected.[53]

The death of Abu 'l-Hasan coincided with the rise of powerful families. His son Abu 'Inan, for all his panache and ambitions, was effectively strangled by his vizier al-Fududi. A number of his successors were deposed or assassinated by these high dignitaries. These grand viziers from the great Marinid tribes, al-Fududi, al-Sadrati, al-Yabani, were followed by the Banu Wattas, who finally supplanted their cousins and seized power for themselves.[54]

The present toponyms of Fez reflect a long history and send an echo of tragic events (rebels hanged or burned), or of the residence of eminent persons; and the cemeteries crystallize this long history.[55] They also preserve the memory of activities or functions that have vanished or are in the process of vanishing. The houses where illustrious personages stayed are still shown: the house of the Banu 'l-Hajj, for instance, where the qadi 'Iyad of Sabta once lived, the mosque of Abu Madyan, the present patron saint of Tlemcen, and the house of Ibn 'Abbad.

Vanished or vanishing professions, like the tyalun (makers of sieves) and sbitriyyun (shoemakers) have left their names to quarters, funduqs, or mosques.

Disquieting signs were already to be discerned.[56] Abu 'l-Hasan suffered a fearful defeat at the hands of Arab tribes in Ifriqiya and Christians in al-Andalus. His scholars and his army were decimated by the Black Death. He finally died in exile in the High Atlas, having been driven out by his own son, the no less famous Abu 'Inan. Disreputably acquired fortunes provoked scandal, and moralists constantly denounced these parvenus who had accumulated wealth by blameworthy means. A class of holy men, in the minority till then, began to assume prominence. These odd devotees concerned themselves less and less

---

[53] Al-Gaznai, *Zahrat*, 80.

[54] Al-'Umari, *Masalik*, 153 and note 3; Kably, *Société, pouvoir et religion*, provides a detailed analysis of the rise of powerful personages within the Marinid political system.

[55] One might cite Ibn 'Ayshoun Sharrat's *Rawd al-'atr al-Anfas*, and al-Kattani's *Salwat al-Anfas*, which focus on the history of the city by reference to its cemeteries.

[56] M. J. Viguera, "Le Maghreb mérinide: un processus de transfèrement," in *La signification du bas Moyen Age dans l'histoire et la culture du monde musulman* (Edisud, 1976), 309–322.

with religious practices. Neither the indignation of the orthodox nor
the censure of scholars could prevent their success, which was to assert
itself over the centuries.

Fez remained, nevertheless, the acme of refinement. The reception
accorded to the Sa'adis by the Fassis speaks eloquently. They regarded
these Bedouins who dressed in drapes and furnishing fabrics purloined
from fine houses as scandalously boorish. They accused them of strut-
ting around in absurd, gaudy outfits.[57] It was a couple in the service
of the Marinids who apparently initiated them in the proper way to
behave. This man and this woman taught them, it seems, how to dress,
comb their hair, sit, bear arms, prepare food, present it, eat, etc. The
opposition of the population of Fez was scathing: confronted with the
Sa'adis, they remained nostalgic for the Banu Marin and their Banu
Wattas cousins. According to one adage, there was nothing worthwhile
outside these two dynasties.[58] Chroniclers ceaselessly exalted the virtues
of these builders, who were attentive to the opinion of theologians,
benefactors of the city—even if the historical reality was far from corresponding to this idealized vision.

The testimony of Leo Africanus, writing at the end of the rule of the
Wattasid branch of the Marinids, is a homage to this city that continued
to resist despite the crises shaking the country, despite the recurrent
anarchy, and the Iberian peril.[59] The territory contracted, and, despite
considerable effort, the gold routes escaped from the control of Fez.
A lack of gold was, indeed, already making itself felt, and monetary
crises multiplied.

Before concluding, we might mention one curious feature that continued to exist in Fez, this highly devout city, home to the theological
sciences. A number of writers note the existence of talismans designed
to protect the monuments and the inhabitants. The phobia about
figural representation seems not to have bothered the orthodox: there
is a figurine representing a bird holding a scorpion's tail in its beak,
there are apples to protect against reptiles.[60] Another statuette guards

[57] Anon, *Tarikh al-dawla*, ed. A. Benhadda (Rabat, 1994), 28–30.

[58] E. Destaing, "Les Beni Merin et les Beni Wattas (légende marocaine)," in *Memorial
H. Basset* (Paris, 1928), 1202.

[59] Velentim Fernandez, *Description de la côte d'Afrique de Ceuta au Sénégal*, trans. P. de
Cenival and Th. Monod (Paris, 1938); Damiao de Gois, *Les Portugais au Maroc de 1495
à 1521* (Rabat: Editions R. Ricard, 1937).

[60] Al-Gaznai, *Zahrat*, 93; Ibn Abi Zar', *Al-Anis*, 5.

against swallows nesting in the mosques. Copper lions have water flowing from their mouths. There is a clock in the reception room where
female figurines leave their cases to mark the hour.[61] Such indications
compel us to reconsider certain preconceived ideas.

---

[61] Manouni, *Waraqat*, 269–270.

THE SPATIAL ORGANIZATION OF TUNIS MEDINA AND OTHER ARAB-MUSLIM CITIES IN NORTH AFRICA AND THE NEAR EAST

Roberto Berardi

Many years ago the study of Tunis Medina (see Appendix) became the occasion for me to explore an urban reality for the first time with original instruments conceived entirely with that aim in mind. It was not so much a matter of understanding the space of the medina through the differences, which this collective artefact showed with regard to my historical and practical knowledge of western cities. It was more a matter of trying to understand how a space defined as urban is organized within the historically specific culture that constructed it. I was lead to this condition of *tabula rasa* by the realization that the spatial experience of Tunis Medina awoke in me echoes, impressions of differences, the desire to forge analogies, and a sense of disorientation. These sensations revealed to me, above all, that my formal education had never gone deeply enough to arrive at any real knowledge of the cities I had visited or studied. It was, thus, in a fresh relation with this reality that I would have to construct the appropriate tools needed to explore it.

The history of urban societies never materializes automatically in the physical organization of their cities. Nor have cities belonging to relatively homogeneous cultural areas appeared and developed in the course of time following uniform and easily recognizable patterns. Until the twelfth and thirteenth century the European Middle Ages were a virtually unknown terrain, except in scattered fragments, and it included both the later degradation, or simply evolution, of older urban bodies as well as settlement processes that were engulfed by successive phases of urbanization. So I am not looking for a model or a prototype, but rather the *order* that a given *space*—the space of the defence, of the commercial and production activities, and the religious and social convictions of a given urban culture—has imprinted on all preceding ones, either by absorbing or cancelling them. In the case in question, this culture was just one of the many Arab-Muslim cultures on the shores of the Mediterranean; but it was important for me to be able to give a cogent analysis of *this particular* city.[1]

More recently I have examined the topography of Aleppo and Damascus in the extremely accurate French cadastres,[2] and compared the planimetrical organization of the Syrian capital in 1932 with the topographical survey carried out by Wulzinger and Watzinger in 1912. I have also utilized measured drawings of the Fez suqs and Aleppo by Stefano Bianca, one of Sfax by M. Van Der Meerschen, and one of Kairouan by Paola Jervis and Paolo Donati. This work has led me to develop the hypotheses that I had formulated during my earlier research, and it has enriched the image I had formed of a conscious organization of space along the Mediterranean coast in various Arab countries. Nevertheless, I do not intend to affirm that a *type*, or that just *one* type of Arab-Muslim city exists, nor that all Arab-Muslim cities are alike. The Arab-Muslim world is vast enough, in time and space, to have been both distinct from and confluent with other, earlier urban experiences. The relations of the Arab peoples with ancient Syria and Mesopotamia began before the dawn of written history. The Arabian territories saw the cohabitation of pastoral and nomadic cultures with urban, mercantile, and peasant cultures, with which the nomadic life came to be integrated through trade, travel, and military expeditions.

In *Città, Materia del Tempo* I attempted to trace the extraordinary affinities between these ancient, founding realities—built with much of what we find in the urban and architectonic organization of Tunis Medina, but also of Fez, Kairouan, Sfax, Aleppo, and Damascus—yet without being able to detect a common identity in the material configuration of these different cities.[3] Perhaps it would be more interesting, to fol-

---

[1] In this essay I have consulted and referred to my earlier publications: "Lecture d'une ville: La Médina de Tunis," *L'Architecture D'Aujourd'hui*, 1970–1971; "Espace et Ville en Pays d'Islam," in *L'Espace Social de la Ville Arabe*, ed. Dominique Chevallier et al. (Paris, 1979); *Signification du Plan ancien de la Ville Arabe* in *La Ville dans l'Islam*, ed. Abdelwahab Bouhdiba and Dominique Chevallier (Tunis and Paris, 1982); *Città, Materia del Tempo* (Florence, 1995); *Della Città dei Fiorentini* (Florence, 1992); *Capri, Portolano della città* (Florence, 1994); "L'Architettura delle Città nelle Epoche di Formazione dell'Occidente Cristiano e dell'Islam," in *Architetture e Città del Mediterraneo tra Oriente e Occidente*, ed. Alireza Naser Eslami (Genoa, 2002).

[2] See Jean Claude David's work on Aleppo and its cadastral records, especially his essay "La Formation du Tissu de la Ville Arabo-Islamique; apport de l'Etude des Plans cadastraux de la Ville d'Alep," in "Urban Morphogenesis," *Environmental Design* 1–2 (1993).

[3] Yet we can not ignore the fact that many elements of the ancient Sumerian, Akkadian, Babylonian, and Assyrian cities were systematically taken up and applied

low the trade routes, wars, and cultural transformations that led to the diffusion throughout the ancient world—from Mesopotamia to Crete to Archaic Greece—of certain forms of urban spatial organization, its architectural components, and route patterns. Until the innovations of Hippodamus brought about a revolutionary notion of space with regard to the legacy of the past: it is as if, from that moment, the art of building the city knew a divergence between a Greco-Roman notion of space in the West and the persistence of a Mesopotamian and Persian notion of space in the Near East.

We seem to be able to verify this hypothesis through a chronological study of the *type* of dwelling with an internal patio, and all its vicissitudes and variations, from the fourth–third millennium in Uruk, Ur, and Nippur to Assur, Ancient Persia, Susa, and Parthia, on the one hand; and from Archaic Greece (for instance Phylakopi)—where the megaron, already present in prehistoric Anatolia, is combined with an internal courtyard, blind alleys, and the absence of open public spaces—to the houses in Delos, Olinth, Miletus, and Priene, on the other. Here, despite an apparent similarity due to the presence of an internal courtyard, another chapter in the history of urban domestic space begins (a variant now independent of *type*) to be followed by the Italic, and later, Roman *domus*.

I have mentioned both my own work and my sources in order to make explicit my research methodology, which is based on the conviction that, in their physical configuration, cities are *logoi*, that is, they give material form to a *general order* of urban spatial composition.[4] In the case of Tunis Medina the principles and strategies used in its realization, in terms of architectonic and urban space, seem as clear as a set of rules to me. Yet we can neither say whether these rules refer to social ideologies and historical traditions, nor whether they represent the final evolution in terms of a "forever possible" Arab-Muslim and

---

to the Arab-Muslim cities in question: apart from the dwelling *type*, in a series of often complex variants with multiple courtyards, devices such as the dog-leg entrance, the blind alley as a form of aggregation around one or more important buildings, and the commercial streets near the gates of the great Assyrian cities are just some examples. In Susa in the Achaemenid period we note, next to the rigid layout of Darius' palace (composed of a summation of courtyard dwellings of varying sizes, store-rooms, and hypostyle halls, like all imperial palaces in the ancient Near East), a less rigid urban spatial organization and a freer experimentation with multiple-courtyard dwellings, both large and small.

[4] This material form conforms to the general order through the variation of its parts, yet with a fundamental respect for the principles governing it.

later Arab-Ottoman space. We can only say that the models of spatial composition for housing, trade, and production seem, in terms of reciprocal inclusion or exclusion, to date back to well before the advent of Islam—or Rome and Ancient Greece even—in the lands of the first Arab Conquest: Egypt, Syria, Iraq, and North Africa.

As already mentioned, in the archaeological survey of Mohenjo-Daro there seem to be patterns of interdependence between mono- or bi-cellular dwellings and larger, more complex building organisms that we could call palaces.[5] These seem to form groups, or units, which are repeatedly proposed. If the architectural models do not correspond to those of the urban experience analysed here, nevertheless, the clusters of larger houses and bi-cellular dwellings and the conception itself of a route network internal to the large built-up areas situated within the major route system cannot be considered foreign to the later spatial organization of Arab-Muslim cities in the Mediterranean.

Just as language—or writing, which is the material imprint of classifying, narrating, evaluating, and computational thought—conserves within itself the ancient roots that link diverse peoples and cultures descending from more or less remote civilizations, so cities—which are the imprint left by urban civilizations on the land—contain within themselves, in built form, the initially unrecognizable memory of all their pasts.

The methodological tool on which I have relied is the measured drawing of the city, in which the cadastral boundaries cease to delimit property and become filled instead with an architectonic organization of space. This in turn is open to interpretations, in which time and custom act as basic variables through the changes they have wrought on

---

[5] For Mohenjo-Daro see especially A. Sarcina, "House Patterns at Mohenjo-Daro," *Mesopotamia* 13–14 (1979). If the Cretan palaces at Knossos, Phaestus, and Mallia seem to be palace-cities due to their functional complexity and the arrangement of the buildings that go to make up the palace complex, then the Sumerian and Akkadian palaces of the third millennium BC reveal a similar conception of architecture: that is, the palace complex as a *closed* city, and the actual extended city around it as having a different organization, both in terms of scale and layout. In this context, Zimrilin's palace in Mari is a good example. The urban space seems implicit in the general organization of the palace, made up of internal courtyard units linked by labyrinthine corridors, fortified entrances, groups of store-rooms, a series of artisans' workshops, archives, deposits, and sanctuaries. The whole is organized on a grid-like pattern, starting with a series of atrium-s, vestibules, entrance courtyards, and courts of honour that lead to the throne room and sanctuary. Despite their differences, the Caliph's palaces of the Abbasid period and later take up, with variations, this model.

the urban organism. All this happens by means of the organization of *space*, so that an urban society and the history of its city are glimpsed through a limpid transparency, so to speak, or through a hypothesis and inquiry. The measured drawing is not just a complement to the cadastral survey of a city; it is also a *visit* in which the mental acumen of the draughtsman, the experience acquired through the exploration of a given space and the relationship established with those who live there play a crucial role.

For this reason, not even the measured drawing is an absolute mirror-image of reality, but is rather a text to be deciphered through the discovery of those elements which, when combined on the basis of recognizable laws, produce a set of variables that can be traced back to a *general law*. The interpretation of a measured drawing only works, if it gives rise to an epistemological system in which all the elements are connected through a relation of coherence and correspondence, linking the smallest detail to the most complex organization, the simplest spatial component to a global sense of urban space. This seemingly theoretical, *a priori* affirmation is really the result of a *practical* knowledge on the basis of which we may then come to formulate a theory. The city in the measured drawing thus becomes a *corpus* of knowledge that can be tapped by many forms of analysis and interpretation.

The purpose of my own measured drawings was to examine the ways in which an urban space is realized; to examine the architecture of the city and the city as the general organization of a space constructed by a society projected through time and change. I do not claim to identify the continuity or discontinuity of a *history* in these measured drawings, though I may touch upon it or indeed provide its material elements. I have managed to glimpse this history through the spaces I have explored, and the conjunctions and disjunctions I have been able to discern in *them*.

Tunis Medina: its spatial configuration

In my initial endeavour to understand the nature and modes of composition of the built environment of Tunis Medina I attempted to describe accurately the practical and conceptual foundations that form the compositional basis of all the architecture of this city and perhaps even of most Arab cities in the Mediterranean and Near East (see Appendix).

In the beginning was the *basic element*: the *unit*, three walls, a floor, and a covering. At the same time the primary system of architectonic organization came into being: an *open space* surrounded by walls, which we might consider the negative of the first and which seems to be the basis of all later architectonic genesis of urban space. In the case of the *dwelling type*—an essential and universal component of all cities—the first two acts are followed by a *reticulated organization* of different kinds of units around an open space. The differentiation of the units establishes the *type*, the *dar* (*house* but also *lineage* and *family*), which is invariable, as opposed to the variables of ownership or inhabitants. This type is able to organize most of the urban space, either by following a double linear sequence or by "gemmation" around a narrow access lane.

The units around a central space can be doubled or combined, or they can form series and clusters. The *skifa* and *driba* take shape; these architectonic elements provide a link between the house and the spaces that can be freely traversed. Moreover, they are ways of controlling who comes into the house from the outside. The courtyard[6] is called the heart of the house (*wust ad-dar*)—since it is the space where all the members of the extended family gather, where guests are received and where internal passageways converge—though it is, nevertheless, external with regard to the *bait-s*[7] (rooms built around this central core) where the life of the various members of the extended family is conducted in private, according to age, status, domestic duties, children's education, and so on. The house (*dar*) is like the embryo of a small village (*douar*), which like the former is the living space shared by family clans.

If the courtyard is lengthened and the units are aligned on the two longer sides, the result is a segment of a suq, terminating in a gate at either end. The end units are always doubled and are laid out at an angle with respect to one another in order to allow for a similar series at different angles. In many cases the suq units are doubled vertically and have a cellar. Their grid-like composition forms a *fondouk* of two or more storeys, with the upper one used as the living quarters. This type of *fondouk* is not very common in Tunisia, though it was once in Sfax, for instance (as described by Mourad Rammah in *Ifriqia*), in Cairo, Damascus, Baghdad, and even Venice and Istanbul.

---

[6] The courtyard may have a stone facade in an expressive architectural language, using the motif of the arcade, and sometimes with inlaid work.

[7] In the ancient Semitic languages *bait* meant a temple or a place sacred to a divinity.

The suq segment can generate linear sequences by a summation of the units, and these, too, form a network; the segments intersect, though they remain, nevertheless, closed off by a gate at either end. The different segments correspond to different crafts, or different kinds of merchandise on sale, which were never traditionally in competition. Thus, even a linear series of units is organized on the principle of creating internal, empty spaces that are invisible from the outside and are difficult of access. This reticular system—that is, the creation of a triangular or quadrangular intersection of a series of units, at the centre of which is a courtyard, or the summation of a succession of units in both orthogonal directions—is always generated by the basic act of placing one or more empty spaces *at the centre*, around which the succession of units is organized. Both house and suq are the result of such an articulation.

When applied to a succession of units this reticular system can create either the entire space of the suqs or a new building: the *fondouk*, the workshop of a group of artisans (for the manufacture of textiles, leather and copper goods, wickerwork, and so on); or the *oukala*, a temporary residence for those who have not yet found a house in the city or suburbs. The most articulate expression of this system and of a parallel sequence of simple units is the *kaisariyye*. In the case of Tunis, from the Ottoman period onwards, it was entirely dedicated to the production of *chéchia*s, the profits from which were collected and administered directly by the sultan or bey.

The *kaisariyye*[8] is a covered enclosure with gates, in which a portion of the *suq* network is contained. The sequences of units here either face or back onto one another in parallel fashion. The empty space is limited to the passage of men and merchandise. While the *fondouk*s, madrasas, *hammam*s, *midha*s, *mesjed*s, *oukala*s (and occasionally small groups of houses) are situated in the empty space created by the network of suqs, the *kaisariyye* is a large, completely self-enclosed building covered by a single vaulted roof, similar to a bazaar and distinct from the rest of the suqs, despite being composed of the same elements. We can

---

[8] See, for example, Louis Massignon, *Les Corps de Métier et la Cité Islamique* (Paris, 1920): "The kaisariyye is a closed environment, with sturdy gates and a kind of great hall where imported merchandise and the precious materials of the various guild corporations are kept." See also the accurate description by Gustav von Grunebaum in "Die Islamische Stadt," *Saeculum* 6, no. 2 (1955).

compare this with the measured drawing of Fez around the great Qarawiyyin mosque.[9]

The Qarawiyyin Mosque is surrounded to the north by dwellings served by interminable blind alleys, which seem to group together the more secluded clusters of larger houses or houses arranged in succession along both sides of an alley, in an inner zone far from the public thoroughfare. This kind of spatial organization of the streets and grouping together of extended families is standard and is also found in Aleppo, Damascus, and throughout the Maghreb, particularly in Tunisia. These very long blind alleys are rare in the Central Medina in Tunis, while they are more frequent in the Bab el Souika suburb. The routes that link the more important streets are often divisible in discrete segments and can be barricaded or closed off in case of rioting unleashed by a *foutouwa*, for instance.[10] In such cases the main routes (from the gateways to the mosque, or from gate to gate) are broken up for defence purposes into sections akin to a series of parallel dwellings served by isolated segments of street networks. *Whole areas of the city, thus, become fragmented, closed off and inaccessible.*[11] In peaceful times, however, the main routes regain their value as a circulation system within the long rows of houses flanking them.

In Fez, too, the *kaisariyye* of precious materials and jewels, between the mosque and the Moulay Idriss mausoleum, forms a compact building made up of a succession of parallel units dovetailing with the other suqs. In the measured drawing of Fez we see how the segments of a suq can generate a number of pseudo-*foundouks*, as in the *djellaba* and carpet suqs, which form closed organisms around an internal courtyard. In Sfax these formations around a blind alley or a small "square" are common in both suqs that link Bab el Djebli and Bab el Diwan, even though there are proper *foundouks*, too, as in the case of the blacksmiths' suq and others.

A further morphological similarity with the spatial organization of Tunis is the parallel arrangement of two rows of units (see the blacksmiths' and dyers' suqs in Tunis). These units invariably produce a kind of courtyard onto which may face a prayer hall (see the carpenters' and other suqs in Fez). In Tunis, Fez, and Sfax the *fondouks* are

---

[9] See Stefano Bianca, *Urban Form in the Arab World* (New York, 2000).
[10] A *foutouwa* is juvenile violence coming from a *zaouia*.
[11] See Stefano Bianca, op. cit.; also Jean Claude David op. cit.

situated both within the network of suqs and around their perimeter, as well as near the city gates and outside them. The same goes for Kairouan, where the morphology of the Bab el Tunus environs is an exemplary case. There is also a similar spatial organization in Aleppo and Damascus.[12]

In the measured drawing of Kairouan 30 years ago—a fragment of a city with a long history of devastation, contraction, and transformation—the staples[13] for caravans and their merchandise are concentrated between Bab el Tunus and the citadel, generating outside the city gate a kind of immense "ante-gate," an open space guarded by the troops based in the *kasbah*, or citadel. The gate itself is a market, like Bab el Menara and Bab el Djedid in Tunis, and near the open space of the grain market rises the suburb that encircles the city centre to the west and northwest and faces onto the open space with the *oukala*s for foreigners who cannot spend the night in the city.

According to Paola Jervis[14] the wide route that today crosses Kairouan from Bab el Tunus to Bab el Djelladin (with the cattle market at the far south–southeast end), like a breach in the otherwise compact city, was linked to the specific commercial function of Kairouan: once a place of rest and exchange for nomad and semi-nomad caravans with their cargoes of slaves and textiles, today transformed into a tourist itinerary where rural products (leather, wool, and pulses) are bought and sold. The author also mentions a tanners' suq near Bab el Djelladin and a blacksmiths' suq to the north of the central suqs; outside the walls to the west are brick and pottery kilns, while to the east are the wool-weavers in two staples near the Mosque of the Confraternity. The same segregation of noisy, dirty and dangerous work occurs in all the Islamic cities I have ever explored.

Kairouan and Sfax (more than Tunis, Aleppo, or Damascus) both present this scheme of a *centre* with a linear morphology, going basically in one direction (northwest, southeast for both). In Sfax this centre is situated between two parallel rows of suqs linked by other, smaller ones, to which may be added a parallel network that includes the mosque and extends to the Bab el Diwan gate, itself like a great *fondouk* from which

---

[12] See especially the measured drawing of part of the main street between Bab Qisnareen and the Bimaristan Arghun, published by Stefano Bianca (op. cit.), which I have integrated with the cadastral records from Aleppo.

[13] Staples are authorized places of trade for foreign merchants.

[14] See Paola Jervis, "Kairouan," *Environmental Design* 1–2 (1989).

one enters and leaves the city. In Damascus and Aleppo many of the
suqs, arranged in parallel rows, include a hybrid *fondouk-suq* (between
parallel suqs facing one another) with its own gate and completely invisible from the outside. Since the markets concentrated near the Great
Mosque in these two cities are covered by a kind of continuous roofing,
a space is created in which no one direction prevails and in which the
unity of the myriad parts is affirmed by a sense of disorientation, as in
a hypostyle hall: for instance, the prayer hall of an important mosque
or even the *maghzen* of an important staple.

The morphology of the Tunis suqs is closer to that of Damascus and
Aleppo than Kairouan or Sfax, though the extensive network of suqs
in Tunis Medina thins out near the Bab el Bahr and Bab el Intjemmi
gates[15] (between the *kasbah* and the Central Medina) in the stretch
called Rue de la Kasbah. The stretch called Rue Djamâa el Zitouna,
on the other hand, bends back like an elbow with the name of Rue
des Selliers and ends at Bab el Menara, which is formed by a market
and organized like a great entrance *skifa* to the city.

After this comparative description—and more especially in the case
of Tunis Medina—we need to examine the route connections, other
than the more or less accessible and segmented street network of the
suqs. In other words, we must enter the *city of family clans*, the space
of women and children, where men only spend the night. This is the
vital heart of the city, where its population is renewed and formed
together with its religious precepts and the solidarity of its citizens.
This city is made up of a dense mosaic of dwellings which are conceived as an *enclosure* erected around a courtyard providing light, air,
and rainwater. In Tunis—but also in Aleppo and Damascus as far as
I have been able to observe in the cadastral records—there are three
different types of dwelling:

1) *Those aligned along a route*, which are open to everyone and connected
   to other similar ones, or to which access is not prohibited. They open
   onto the street by means of a dog-leg atrium (*skifa*) that prevents a
   direct view of the courtyard, where all the activities of family life are
   carried out: preparing semolina, drying vegetables to be conserved,

---

[15] I have used the name given by Robert Brunschvig—in *La Berbérie Orientale sous
les Hafsides* (Paris, 1947)—to the gate that opened onto the medina from the kasbah. I
have also based my reconstruction of the original boundaries of Bab el Djedid suburb
on the same text.

doing laundry, educating the children, and so on. The courtyard is the largest area in the house and is shared by all the women and children of the household. It is surrounded by three or four rooms (*baits*), which in their most complete form constitute an upside-down T. The shaft of the T is a kind of living room, while the ends of the crossbar are occupied by beds on trestles. The central part is called a *qbou* and terminates opposite the entrance in a rectangular niche furnished with chairs and shelves. Next to this niche are the doors to two smaller rooms (*maqsouras*), which may have a staircase leading to an upper room situated above one side of the crossbar and from which the head of the household can observe the activities in the courtyard, or simply shut himself off to read.

In Tunis this arrangement is frequent, especially in the larger houses of wealthy families. In others the *qbou* niche is reduced to a small recess in the wall. In Sfax this *type* is rarer, while in Kairouan it is common, both in the small suburban houses and the larger, more affluent ones. Each house is composed of three or four *baits* organized in a grid-like pattern around the courtyard.[16] The houses do not have façades looking onto the street, but onto the court-yard, sometimes in smooth stone or coloured marble, often with colonnaded arcades, especially in the fifteenth–seventeenth century dwellings. That which in the West is meant for the admiration of passers-by—the façade—is here reserved for the inhabitants and their guests. The beauty of the house is reserved for the family; only the wooden front door, decorated with rivets, framed by lintels and a carved sandstone arch, suggests the family's status. As far as the layout is concerned, the house follows the same reticular organiza-tion as the *fondouks*, *oukalas*, the urban fabric and mosque even, in a network of smaller units (*baits*) around the courtyard. Precisely

---

[16] Almost all the residences of the Omayyid and Abbassid Caliphs visibly contain *in nuce*, in their court apartments, the layout of the family dwelling, with the *baits* organized on a reticular pattern around a great central hall (or courtyard): Qasr al-Qarrâna, al-Qastal, Qasr al-Mushatta, and the Omayyid palace in the citadel of Amman, where blind alleys (corridors and galleries) and *iwans* appear in the rigid geometry of the architecture; Qasr al-Khayr al-Chargi, almost a village, with its peristyle dwellings; Ukhaydir, the most complex, where all the elements developed in the early centuries of this civilization are present and where one can imagine the genesis of the T-shaped *baits* from the amalgamation of an *iwan* with a part of its own side-wings. The *iwan* and an incipient form of T-shaped *bait* were also found in the dwellings excavated by Gabriel Marcel at Fustat.

because it is a family dwelling it can be doubled or tripled, while
enclosing its privacy in the protection of an *impasse*.

2) *Those which have an entrance on a public route but are set back behind a driba*,
and look inward to the cluster of houses. The *driba* opens onto a *skifa*
and this in turn opens onto the courtyard of the dwelling. Apparently
these houses are not as old as the ones surrounding them, having
perhaps been built on wasteland. They can be as rich and complex
as those described below. They may have a service courtyard and
are sometimes adjacent to a blind alley.

3) *Those which are adjacent to or at the end of a blind alley*; they are usually
large and are sometimes connected to others by means of passageways from one courtyard to another. They have a service courtyard
for lavatories and are sometimes connected directly to a *fondouk*
belonging to the owner. These dwellings turn their back on the public
or semi-public routes. They are built in the innermost zones of the
street networks and the blind alley only reaches them *across a distance*
or by means of a *change of direction* (a *driba* or *skifa*); that is, in terms
of an ever-increasing separation from the public thoroughfare. One
might be tempted to think that a blind alley has always represented
the original settlement area of an extended family, or a clan with
a common ancestry. Robert Bruschvig has demonstrated, however,
that from the fourteenth century onwards there were quite strict
laws prohibiting anyone owning property next to a blind alley from
opening a door onto it.

Thus not even the morphology of the blind alley represents an immu-
table social and spatial reality, but follows changes in ownership and
human relations, introducing variations, however slight, in the conformation of the alley and its use. Nevertheless, the larger, wealthier, and
more complex houses are grouped at the end of the blind alley and
the law traditionally prohibits the construction of doors near the end
of the alley or facing existing ones, unless the oldest property owners
agree otherwise. In Cordova, the consent of all the neighbours was
traditionally required for the opening of a new door onto the alley, or
the closure of the entrance to the alley with a gate.[17]

If we examine the measured drawing of any Arab-Muslim city in
North Africa or the Near East, we can see that next to the simple and

---

[17] See Robert Brunschvig, "Urbanisme Médieval et Droit Musulman," *Revue Des
Études Islamiques*, 1947.

straight *impasses* there are others which are fragmented and branch off at various points. These are the offshoots of increasingly narrow lanes whose genesis is sometimes the result of a building that has collapsed. Then, in the course of time, another building rises over the ruins, due to neglect or the material impossibility of removing the rubble. I do not wish to sustain that the genesis of the *impasses* is this and only this, but simply that I have observed such situations in Tunis. And the reverse, too, in the agglomeration of houses around Fondouk el Henna, bounded by Suq el Blat, Rue du Mufti, and Rue Sidi Ali Azouz: halfway along the present Rue Djamâa Ghourbal a great eighteenth century house must have risen over the ruins of a small mosque, without using the prayer hall, however, which is now open to the sky. This hall was still in ruins when I made the measured drawing. The exit of the lane onto Rue du Mufti, spanned by an arch (*sabat*), seems to have had a gate at one time, while the exit onto Rue Sidi Ali Azouz at the opposite end no longer shows any such traces. The other lane that traverses this cluster of houses, Rue el Nayer, ends at Suq el Blat with another arch which may have had a gate. Thus, the decision of one or more groups of families or neighbours could turn a relatively permeable space into a completely closed-off zone, protected from whatever might happen in the public thoroughfares, Rue Sidi Ali Azouz and Suq el Blat. A further example is to be found in the neighbourhood block bounded by Rue el Khomsa, Rue de la Medersa Slimania, Suq el Blat, and Rue du Tresor, where a narrow lane that once linked Rue de la Medersa Slimania and Rue du Tresor has been incorporated in the adjacent buildings and, in sections, completely privatized for the use of seventeenth-eighteenth century houses. The presence of large *maghzens* suggests that there was once a *fondouk* here.

Such ambiguity—and impermanence—of the rights of entry, passage, and use is visibly possible in all the side streets linking what I have called the *main routes* that seem to cut through the physicality of the urban space, connecting every gate both with a network of suqs and with another gate. This Y or V configuration, which indicates the two-way character of every route, is accompanied by a more or less compact alignment of *mesjeds*, *zaouias*, *madrasas*, *hammams*, ovens, and small suqs selling foodstuffs.

These main routes are neither defined by their size nor by the conspicuous nature of the buildings lining them. Discretion is the first rule of an urban aesthetics in which what is important is hidden from sight: the Djamâa el Zitouna behind the walls and vaults of the suqs (though the type of merchandise on sale—perfumes, clothes, carpets, and books—signals its presence without revealing it); the *mesjed*s and *zaouia*s indicated merely by a door frame in the white limestone wall; the red and green door of the *hammam*s and the parti-coloured laundry drying on the roof. The continuous and direct route from one gate to another, or from a gate to a suq, exists, but it is never straight, and is expressed through the smallest *signs*, which are nevertheless easy recognizable for those who live there. It is the frequency of these signs, together with the help of passers-by and shopkeepers that allows one to get one's bearing and arrive at one's destination.

When we visit a western city what gives us our bearings is not so much the regular network of streets (in which we may easily get lost) as the great architectural monuments that soar above the lower buildings—cathedral spires, medieval towers, elaborately decorated pediments, domes silhouetted against the sky—or the sudden burst of light that heralds a square at the end of a street.

In Tunis, on the other hand, the web of main routes establishes a network of intersections that the more internal, secondary routes develop further. The steep street, ascending or descending, the string of mosques, ablution halls, and inns are the clues this space provides for those who traverse it, together with the query addressed to the passer-by (the best way to get one's bearings in my opinion). The distinct impression of anyone who walks along these lanes is that they are all alike and that they all hide an invisible world behind their walls. Thus the fundamental web-like organization is experienced by everyone who crosses the city. And it is precisely this forgotten, unexpected *order* that disoriented so many nineteenth century European travellers who considered it irrational and meaningless.

The network is formed, not by streets, but by the intersections of architectural organisms: for instance, the walls of two buildings that are separated by a passage. Within the network itself there may be madrasas or even *fondouk*s, sometimes connected directly to a wealthy residence, as we saw around the Great Mosque in Tunis.

Other signs connote the city gates,[18] for instance: a market outside the city proper, yet within the architecture of the gate, such as Bab el

---

[18] See Louis Massignon, "Les Corps de Métiers et la Cité Islamique" (a lecture given at the Collège de France on 4/2/1920) in *Revue Des Études Islamiques*, 1950: "The city functions merely as an extension of the markets. It is the crystallization of the market, which is transformed into a centre where the various materials bought and sold are crafted by artisans. Indeed, the weavers' workshops, the mills, the dye-works, and the

Menara and the destroyed Bab el Djedid in Tunis; a mosque; the cell of a holy man; a *fondouk* in the immediate vicinity; an *oukala*; a citadel. Thus the gate extends its *baraka* (defensive might, protective energy, but also hospitality) both within and without. The gate is still a gate, but it is also part of the urban apparatus of welcome and selection. It is forbidden to enter armed or in a vehicle; merchants may lodge in the suqs where there are the appropriate *oukala*s, or in a *zaouia* linked in some way to their birthplace or religion. The space is thus full of rules and regulations that make it the expression of a particular society in a historically determined moment.[19]

Yet again, the main routes, as indicated in the city plan, can be read, even experienced, in different ways. As we have seen, the open, accessible route can be replaced by a fragmented one, when one or more *sabat*s are barred in order to isolate areas where civil disorder has erupted due to a *foutouwa*, or where there is a popular uprising against certain political events. The same thing can happen on a smaller scale to the lanes that link one main route to another, thus affecting whole residential areas and the entrances to the *impasses*. Since this is possible anywhere and everywhere, by closing gates or barricading *sabat*s, the city knows this kind of space too, in which no one route can guarantee a free passage in any direction, in which any section of a street can become a dead-end and the space infinitely fragmented. This is just what happens at night when the gates to each section of the suqs are closed.

What is outside, what is removed, is extraneous to the ever-more restricted community, from the urban community to the tribe, to co-nationals, blood relations, family clan. Yet this "outside" implies an "inside": the system of suqs, a place of exchange between citizens, and between merchants and foreigners, under the watchful eye of the law. The degree of separation varies, and the very same devices that bring it about are also those that lessen or indeed cancel it. Thus the *skifa* is certainly not made to

---

sawmills are naturally situated outside the city gates, as in Fez, for example. I refer you to a Muslim encyclopaedia that gives a detailed account of the craft guilds, since it was compiled by an Ishmaelite sect in the eleventh century. It is entitled *'Ikhwân al-safa'* and it gives a kind of philosophical classification of the different vocations in the Muslim world, according to materials, work-place, working hours, and tools."

[19] Cf. Ibn Jobeir, *Voyages* (Paris, 1949): "The kadi must place an honest and virtuous man, someone who knows the law, outside every city gate. This man must arbitrate between persons who are in disagreement...He must keep an eye on the fresh hides and meats that are sold outside the city gates."

welcome the outsider, and if it opens onto a *driba* and the *driba* onto a
blind alley, then the degree of separation is at its most extreme. Nevertheless, the *skifa* is often next to a room that does not communicate
either with the courtyard or the *baits* where the family lives, and so it
can be used to receive and welcome the outsider; like the *scrittoio* in
European palaces, half-inside, half-outside, situated between the street
and the house, and used for staff and clients. The whole urban space
thus seems saturated with two possible meanings, which are opposed
but not always irreconcilable.

So we are in the presence of a fluid space, yet one which is penetrable only under certain conditions and in certain zones, through
degrees or levels of access and vigilance; a negotiable space, yet one
without architectural signs, apart from the minaret of the congregational
mosque, visible only from the outside, from the hills or roads leading to
the city. Within the city everything is internalized; everything is known,
though not offered to the gaze, for it is only from the inside that the
city reveals itself in recognizable forms to the foreign eye. Yet even this
"inside" is broken up and reassembled by temporary prohibitions and
familiarity with them, in other words, by the practices and customs of
urban social life. The elected form of community life that allows for
social selection is indeed "urban": the space for non-citizens is in the
suburbs, where they can shake off their established habits and acquire
those of a citizen; the space for citizens is in the centre of the city with
their crafts and wares. Nomads must remain outside the gates, organizing caravans and contracting the price to pay for their protection on
a journey across the deserts.

Exchange is the relational agent that eliminates foreignness. It takes
place within the network of units which, as they intersect, can form
either a single, penetrable body, or else an impenetrable labyrinth of
closed gates. The system of suqs[20] is a permeable space open to the
"other," it is a *topos* within which vital communication takes place.
Otherwise the city would be an opaque receptacle and have no relation
with other human societies.

The system of suqs and *fondouks*, the Great Mosque and madrasas
(theological-juridical schools) constitutes a kind of body within the body

---

[20] The suqs form a kind of internal boundary within the city, in-between the
residential areas, represented by the "void" of the streets where trading activities take
place.

of the city, often extending between two gates, and represents the space of men, and their vocation as merchants or *savants*. We could call this system the place of accepted practices and of the production of religious knowledge that has immediate social relevance.[21] It is the place of activities that give shape to exchange, of the exercise of crafts and the production of wares. It is the place of social cohesion that manifests itself in the mosque, but also beats out the rhythms of the day with its codes and rules. In every city, in every workshop and staple, or thereabouts, is a guild mosque. In Damascus and Aleppo it was once quite common to find a shrine in the centre of a *fondouk* courtyard.

This intricate web, spun of interlacing segments—suqs, shrines, and madrasas, the Great Mosque hidden behind the workshops, the most important staples concealed behind a door—animated by voices and footsteps, presents itself to a foreigner's perception as an indecipherable labyrinth, an infinite sameness, a space of disorientation, in which the underlying scheme does not surface or manifest itself. This space is all context, uniformity, in which the eloquence of an architectural monument is stifled, our apprehension of it problematic.

The whole city appears as an inexhaustible repetition of itself; a compact, uniform, indivisible spatial whole. This perception of the Arab-Muslim city as a whole or unity that cannot be broken down into its various parts—and in which the juxtaposition of identical parts does not generate serial monotony, but rather the sense of belonging to a single, yet articulate space expressive of a *norm* materialized in its construction—easily takes us back to the Omayyid or Abbassid palaces. Here the *apparent geometry* of clear and distinct elements, and of their distribution, generates the same ambiguous sense of a reality that continually eludes us visually, while never relinquishing the clarity of its *nomos*.

The written account of the foundation of the first cities of Basra and Kûfah is more suggestive of the layout of a palace around its mosque than it is of a topological survey of a thirteenth–sixteenth century medina. Besides, we are unaware of all that has taken shape on the sites we study, and how many transformations the concept itself of built space has undergone from the eighth century to the present. We can

---

[21] Cf. Louis Massignon (op. cit.): "It is an absolute certainty that an exchange of knowledge and learning around the mosque—that is, belonging to a specific community of intellectual "providers" and clients, a community that organizes forms of welcome for visiting scholars—has made the university the guild corporation *par excellence*."

only know the immediate, and a few fragments of the remote, past.
And we are obliged to compare our categories of judgement with the
products of a civilization that flourished in a period in which western
civilization was undergoing its most profound crisis of identity. Arab-
Muslim civilization has certainly influenced us, is part of us, yet it is
still too little known. For this reason I decided many years ago to try
and decipher it, knowing full well that I could only do so from within
my own culture.

When, out of an insatiable curiosity about the origins, or one of
the origins, of this space, I reread the *Tradizione della fondazione della
città di al-Kufâh*:[22]

> When it was decided to found the city of al-Kufâh, Saʿd bʾabi Waqqas
> sent for abdul-Hayyag and informed him of the wishes of the Caliph
> concerning the dimensions of the streets. The main streets (al-mahaniʾ)
> were to be 40 dziraʿ long; their branches 30; the secondary routes 20;
> finally, the lanes (al-aziqqah) were never to be narrower than 7 dziraʿ. The
> blocks were to be 60 dziraʿ except for the Banu Dabbah block...
>
> First the boundaries of the mosque were fixed...the measurements
> were fixed by a man...who from the centre of the square shot an arrow
> in one direction and another in the opposite direction; the space in-
> between the two points where the arrows fell was reserved for the mosque;
> beyond these points anyone could build their dwelling. With the distances
> thus established, a square was laid out based on the shooting of an
> arrow...Around the mosque the city of al-Kufâh was laid out. Behind
> the mosque (fil wadʾah min al-sahn) 5 main streets (mahanigʾ) were laid
> out; at the front, in the direction of the qibla, facing the midday sun, 4
> mahanigʾ were laid out; 3 mahanigʾ were laid out on the east side and
> the same on the west side, placing boundaries everywhere to differenti-
> ate them from the land that could be built on. Around the mosque, in
> separate neighbourhoods, the Muslim peoples settled, divided according
> to the tribe to which they belonged. To the north: the Sulaym and Thaqif
> settled in two streets; nearest the mosque, the Hamdan in one street and
> the Bagitah in another; the Taym al-Lat and the Taqlib in the last of
> the five streets.

...and I try to determine to what extent an eighth century foundation
might be the prelude to the urban spaces I have studied, and what traces
of it might remain in the urban fabric, past and present, I seem to see
elements that 1300 years have not completely erased. The classification
of the streets as main streets, branches, minor branches, and lanes is

---

[22] Tabari, I., *Ibn Abbas*, quoted in L. Caetani, Annali dell'Islam, IV, Rome, 1949.

not casual, but represents a fundamental order planned within a freer serviceability ("beyond these points anyone could build their dwelling"), applying criteria of social and ethnic uniformity, and therefore of relative segregation, within the urban space. The "Muslim peoples" settle on either side of the same street; so we can imagine two parallel rows of houses along the *free zone* of the street. Tabari's text mentions *blocks* (or groups of houses?), *secondary routes* and *lanes* (it would be interesting to know the original meaning of the terms). The secondary routes seem to develop an intricate network of junctions recognizable in all the cities in question. Do we not glimpse in this description features or aspects of the urban space that has come down to us?[23]

In the "Plan de la ville de Tunis dressé par Colin en 1860" Tunis Medina appears in its tripartite form: the Central Medina is enclosed within its own walls, while it is encircled to the south, west, and east by a second circuit of walls, which encompasses the suburbs and is linked to the defensive walls of the *kasbah* to the west–southwest and west–northwest. The latter opens onto the Central Medina, but not onto the suburbs, through an eastern gate. On the eastern side of the Medina are pools and canals, the outline of Avenue de France and Avenue Bourguiba, perhaps the remains of the shipyard, and the railway station of the Goulette-la Marsa-Gammarth line. In this area there are no city walls; in their place are marshlands and the Lake of Tunis.

Two of the suburbs (*rbats*), Bab el Djedid and Bab el Souika, do not communicate, except via the marshlands to the east; that is, by leaving the city and entering it again through another gate. They are linked, however, by what I have called the main routes, within the Central Medina, which may be reached via the gates in common to the Central Medina and the suburbs. The latter have their own outer gates, often overlooking the cemeteries, and flanked by *fondouks* and *mesjeds* or *zaouias*. Each suburb has its own mosque, equivalent to the main mosque, Djama el Zitouna: the Sidi Béchir Mosque, the Sidi Mahrez Mosque, and the Saheb Ettabaa Mosque.[24]

---

[23] This space is naturally quite different today from the original, since both took a long time to reach completion.

[24] I mention the Sidi Mahrez Mosque as an important peripheral mosque since the development of at least a part of the northern area of the Central Medina (around the Suq el Grana and the Mosque of the Holy Founder, protector and promoter of the integration of the Jewish community) seems to date to the thirteenth century.

None of these three urban agglomerations have squares. Place Hal-faouine, in the French survey of 1898, still did not exist in 1860. In its place there was a group of buildings which was later demolished. Place Bab el Souika did not exist either. In the suburb to the south, the empty, level areas served as grain and horse markets. At Bab el Bahr there was a sort of "ante-gate," while the foreign staples were situated beyond this gate, outside the city walls.

In this period Tunis Medina, together with its suburbs, counted 110,000 people and 22,000 families. If its temporal duration, until the advent of the French Protectorate, is that of the Ottoman Empire and traditional time, then the Medina is heir to the metropolis of the ancient world and the pre-industrial era. Or so it seems to me. Vegetable gardens and cemeteries (Muslim, but also Jewish and Christian) are scattered around its walls. Beyond these are orchards and woodlands, especially towards Djebel Houst to the north, and eastwards, along the road to Ariana and Biserta, and the road to Marsa.

In looking at these early plans of Tunis, executed by European topographers,[25] our impression is one of a built *mass* incised by deep fissures branching out into other, narrower ones. It is as if the original space of the city and suburbs were a *solid* that the routes had cut through in its weaker parts, while the buildings had been forcibly wedged into this solid rather than into the empty spaces.

In actual fact, Tunis Medina is composed of architectonic modules based on the most standard geometrical pattern: quadrangles open to the sky at the centre, which may be houses, staples, inns, or religious institutions respectively. Even the more important mosques have the same layout, internal articulation, and traditional geometry. And yet their composition in units seems like an *intarsio* in which topological procedures replace the Euclidean geometry so dear to the West and virtually inherent in its urban identity.

It is still difficult for me to say just what this solid is, within which the elementary geometry of the buildings must adapt itself to unexpected obstacles, bend, recede, advance. The only valid hypothesis seems to be that this solid is *time*; in other words, the material conditions that different historical periods have imposed upon discrete building initiatives,

---

[25] That is, before a detailed plan on a scale of 1:250 of all the building groups enclosed within a network of routes, or at least those in the Central Medina, was drawn up under the French Protectorate, and a cadastral plan (in several sheets) on a scale of 1:1500 of the medina and its suburbs.

whether these be new buildings or re-buildings. Of course, sometimes communication networks would have been blocked by rubble that was never removed, while in other cases it would have seemed logical to link branches of blind alleys to which an obsolete division into family nuclei and clans no longer corresponded. Apart from neglect, phenomena such as earthquakes and fires would have created new and unexpected situations. In order to affirm this, however, a diachronic knowledge of the different intersecting and overlapping temporal phases—that is, reliable dating—would be needed.

The excavations at Nippur carried out by Donald E. McCown and Donald P. Hause[26] (relating to the period from the fourth to the second millennium) are a pertinent example of the development and intersection of segments of a city across two millennia, the spatial organization of which has marked affinities with those described above. In the excavations of the residential districts in Ur (third millennium), the route system—with communication routes inside the city and hierarchies of blind alleys—creates an urban space of impressive congruence, just as in Nippur earlier. The dog-leg entrance (*skifa*) is the norm, both in houses and places of worship. Here, too, we find the important houses set back from the street by means of covered passages, and the most important houses, those with two or three courtyards, located deep within the built fabric. A thousand years later the situation is virtually the same.

Whatever the transformations and substitutions of meaning wrought by time, it seems that the tools for remodelling and reorganizing urban space have not changed and have acted as a constant in the *intarsio* design of ancient cities as well as their more recent configurations. Only the acquisition of new models—nineteenth century European to be exact—and the allure of their diversity and novelty have been able to supplant the ancient ones, when traditional customs paled in the face of the imposition of European settlements right next to millenary cities.

In his now classic article[27] Robert Brunswig identified a juridical principle—*finâ* or the free space surrounding or facing a building, which the owner of the building has a special right to use—recurrent

---

[26] Donald E. McCown and Donald P. Hause, *Excavations at Nippur*, University of Chicago Oriental Institute Publications, vol. 57 (Chicago, 1967).
[27] See *Urbanisme Médiéval et Droit Musulman*, in op. cit.

in the judgements of the *sâfi'iti kadi* and, in watered down form, in the
fiqh mâlikiti treatises. That is, the demolition of a building occupying
part of the street[28] is not obligatory if many years have passed since its
construction, if no one has objected to it, or if no one knows why it
was built, even though such a building is considered unlawful according to a Hadith of the Prophet. Thus, physical space and juridical
space are not defined by the same restrictions. Unwritten law sees, in
the empty space, the clash or establishment of rights that make it a
space full of *potential*. The rubble from a house that has collapsed can
only be removed with difficulty. There are no municipal services for
that purpose, and it is very difficult to establish who should pay the
removal costs.

The many abandoned ruins in Muslim cities were the natural place
to dump all kinds of rubbish. And the legal profession has had to take
on the unpleasant consequences. They do not condemn the practice
in itself and they do not formally prohibit it. If, in a specific case, an
unauthorized use of someone else's property can be identified, by what
right can its use be prohibited altogether in agglomerations where there
is no public cleaning service?

Many of the blind alleys in Arab-Muslim cities would, thus, seem
to be the result of these and similar violations which later became
legitimate due to the amount of time that had elapsed between the
occupation of a piece of land and its indictment, or indeed the absence
of any such indictment. Likewise, the transformation of streets with
two exits into blind alleys represents a *de facto* transformation in the
use and control of space, given that the blind alley is considered the
common property of those who have a door opening onto it, either
with or without their neighbours' consent.

Ownership, property, and neighbourhood are juridical and spatial
categories, though it is easy to see how such categories came to be
used to refer to social customs, the habits of close-knit groups and
the consolidation of agreements or prohibitions that are all expressed
spatially.

Certainly, everything that has been said so far is not just about
the spatial organization and system of laws and civic obligations that

---

[28] Such a construction is made possible by the belief in a *finâ'*—a kind of "aura"
of availability, impalpable but real, that extends from the space of the house to the
immediate vicinity.

characterize Tunis Medina and other Arab-Muslim cities. Something comparable is to be found in every society in which the slow evolution of property laws leaves the problem of everyday practices temporarily unresolved. In Italy, for instance, in the passage from the early Middle Ages to the fifteenth century, and then from the fifteenth to the eighteenth century, the appropriation of land of uncertain ownership, which was apparently, perhaps even legally, neither public nor private, reduced the number of side streets linking the more important streets, and saw the narrow *chiassi* (lanes) that separated the houses and isolated the more important properties from the minor, serial buildings swallowed up by the larger *palazzi*. In Florence, for instance, these are all recognizable, both inside and outside later constructions.

Even the legal and civic status of medieval European courtyards, connected to the public street via covered passageways, is similar to that of the blind alleys on the opposite shores of the Mediterranean. A similarity, not a mere imitation of Arab-Muslim urban culture, which was known to Italian merchants through their travels and which had reached its most mature expression when the renascence of the European city was still in its infancy. In the medieval European city, too, there was a physical separation between the world of the family clan and the public world of the merchants; but it was a vertical separation, perhaps deriving from the turreted city, which had not yet completely disappeared. So from the thirteenth century onwards in Europe there was a ground-floor city, which was completely open, and an upper-floor city, which was completely closed.

Another customary practice confirms the particular vision of the organization of built space that we find in Tunis Medina and, likewise, in other Arab-Muslim cities: no door can open directly opposite that of another house, just as no inner door can open directly onto a courtyard. (The *fondouks*, on the other hand, have an entrance that gives directly onto the street, or blind alley, without a *skifa*.) Every house projects its own *harim*—that is, the defence of its own uniqueness and intimacy—onto what is considered a public space. So it is possible to tie pack animals and leave bundles next to one's door, or let groups of clients wait on a *doukana*.

Instead of an appropriation of public space, this practice suggests a concept of built space that is not defined by property boundaries, but entails the potential extension of every building towards *the rest*: a form of *possible* intervention in a space which, rather than belonging to a

collective body, is considered communal, or *shared* by many. The blind
alley, with its extensions branching off in different directions—starting
with the "stem" that links it to a public thoroughfare, main route or
junction—seems to express this type of classification of spatial components. The dead-end of each blind alley denotes both the extreme
privatization of the houses situated there and all kinds of relations of
kinship and solidarity that can at any moment form a barricade, making access impossible.

The blind alley is the space used freely by the women and children of
the houses that open onto it; like another *wust ad-dar*, only on a larger
scale in terms of kinship and solidarity. Taken together, the branches of
the original blind alley seem to indicate a network of close relationships,
which were originally perhaps much wider (tribal even) and were later
broken up and replaced by others, grouped together in a different form
of inclusion or exclusion. Even the outlying houses that make up the
complex and interesting structure of main routes and intersections can
become part of the morphology of the blind alley on certain occasions.
For instance, when a revolt calls for a fragmentation of the space, by
locking communal gates or barricading passageways.

Sometimes, when the rubble from a building that has collapsed is not
removed, this can affect the layout of the routes. A similar effect may be
produced by certain social phenomena, such as a common origin from
a given geographical area, devotion to the preaching of a holy man, or
political rivalry between different neighbourhoods—especially in these
cities where the courts were non-existent, or else more concerned with
civil order than with safeguarding urban integrity and hygiene.[29]

Thus at the heart of the image of urban space there seems to be a
category of ambiguity, or ambivalence, that makes of it both a unified
whole and a *realm of distinction*; a distinction based on ancestry, origins
(whether from a nomad or sedentary culture, for instance), and the
socio-religious interpretation of the realities of citizenship and foreign-

---

[29] Cf. Gustav von Grunebaum, *Medieval Islam* (Chicago and London, 1946, 1953,
1971): "One shouldn't be surprised, therefore, if the inhabitants of an Islamic city
haven't developed any real administrative machinery... Under state administration a
rudimentary neighbourhood organization continued to exist; this was merely a continuation of tribal customs, the desire to be guided by the head of one's tribe. The
population continued the late antique tradition of the guilds, organizing themselves
into a large number of groups in which everyone could find a place... In 1923 there
were still 164 guilds in Fez, 115 in Marrakesh, and 106 in Meknes."

ness.[30] So every citizen is sometimes an outsider (with respect to the house or *impasse* of other groups, or the staples for foreigners), at other times a welcome guest, or the serene member of the group or groups to which he belongs.

Perhaps precisely because of this ambiguity, or ambivalence, urban space acts as an *agent of transformation*. What seems even more relevant is that in the course of time different social organizations have conceived and realized a spatial order which has never been abandoned and which has left an indelible mark on every segment of space in the Arab-Muslim city, whatever its origins.

Dignitaries and clients, merchants and artisans, rich and poor, religious foundations, but also citizens and not-yet-citizens, religious and legal authorities, city centre, and suburbs for rural immigrants and their preparation for citizenship (just as in European, especially Italian, cities in the twelfth and thirteenth centuries) go to make up this multifarious, often divided, yet strongly cohesive universe that assumes concrete form in the construction of urban space. This *distinction*, this attribution of meaning forged in the urban melting pot, invests entire geographical areas, from the fortified and protected centres to the *kasbah*s and trading and military zones: weekly fairs (Suq el Khemis, Suq el Arba, Houmt Suq, etc.), streets under surveillance, *rbat*s, shipyards, ports, waterways, and pirate routes, traditional routes across deserts and seas, caravanserai, routes made safe through an alliance with nomadic tribes. This is the potentially boundless net cast by this civilization, materially and culturally, over the changing geography of its own affirmation.

(English translation by Lisa Adams)

---

[30] Even in crafts and trade; von Grunebaum translates a part of the *Ihwân al-safâ*: "...the crafts are differentiated in terms of prestige when one considers them under the following five categories: (1) the materials used: here the goldsmith and perfumer are at the top of the scale; (2) the finished product: here builders of complex instruments like astrolabes are at the top; (3) the demand that makes their work necessary: here weavers, agricultural workers, and masons are preferred; (4) general usefulness: here those who run the baths and the rubbish collectors are vital for city hygiene; and (5) those who are to be taken as they are, in terms of their particular skill, without considering their usefulness, etc: magicians, painters, and musicians are justified by their talent."

THE MAMLUK CITY[1]

Doris Behrens-Abouseif

From Fustat to al-Qahira

Cairo under Mamluk rule (1250–1517) was a major Muslim city and one of the largest in the world. Its evolution from the Ayyubid double capital Fustat-Qahira to the Mamluk metropolis was a tremendous transformation shaped by the intensive patronage of the ruling establishment. After having legitimized their rule by victories against the Crusaders and Mongols, the Mamluks set out to pursue a pious patronage of unparalleled dimensions. The magnitude of their endowment of mosques, colleges, khanqâhs, and other charitable foundations was coupled by urban expansion and a florescence of architecture in the cities of their empire. The Mamluk capital Cairo, seat of a shadow Abbasid caliphate installed by al-Zahir Baybars, succeeded Baghdad as the foremost capital of the Muslim world.

Mamluk Cairo covered a gigantic area that stretched from the mausoleum of Imam Shafi'i in the south, to the Dome of Yashbak, in what is today 'Abbasiyya in the north, and from the Nile to the desert in the east. This area was not a homogenous agglomeration however. When the Mamluks came to power in 1250, Cairo was an unfocused double agglomeration, which consisted of the old capital Fustat, the Arab foundation and its subsequent satellites, and al-Qahira, the Fatimid city founded in the tenth century which was gradually losing its exclusive palatial character. Salah al-Din planned to unify Fustat with al-Qahira by encompassing them in a set of walls connected with his citadel and future princely residence on the Muqattam hill, between al-Qahira to the north and Fustat to the south. Instead of the fusion envisaged by Salah al-Din, al-Qahira thrived as the Mamluk capital and metropolis, expanding on all sides without fully merging with Fustat.

---

[1] This article is inevitably very similar to chapter 8 in my book *Cairo of the Mamluks.*

The first monuments of the Mamluks indicate that the preference given to al-Qahira over Fustat took some time to materialize; however, from the outset the sultans expanded the buildings of the royal residence at the Citadel. The earliest buildings of the Mamluk period were the mausoleum dedicated to the last Ayyubid sultan al-Salih Najm al-Din Ayyub and a funerary madrasa, both founded in the same year, 1250, by Shajar al-Durr, al-Salih's widow, and herself the first sultan of the Mamluks for three months. The madrasa was built in the cemetery of Sayyida Nafisa to the southeast of the Citadel, in the vicinity of Fatimid shrines, notably the mausoleums of Sayyida Nafisa and Sayyida Ruqayya.[2] Near her madrasa and mausoleum, Shajar al-Durr built a *hammam* and a palace with gardens. No other ruler had been buried in this cemetery before; Shajar al-Durr's choice of the site could have been motivated by its vicinity to the royal residence in the Citadel and also to tombs of female saints. Her husband's mausoleum was erected beside his madrasa at Bayn al-Qasrayn Street in al-Qahira. The allegiance of the first Mamluks to the last Ayyubid sultan al-Salih, epitomized in this memorial building, enhanced the significance of Bayn al-Qasrayn with its inherited regal and religious traditions. As in the past, this site continued to be the heart of the Egyptian capital also under the Mamluks. The toponym Bayn al-Qasrayn, Between-the-Two-Palaces, referred to the Fatimid palatial centre and to Mamluk palaces built later in this area.

Shajar al-Durr's successor and her second husband, al-Mu'izz Aybak (r. 1250–57), preferred to build his madrasa (1256–7) in the area of southern Fustat, near the Nile shore, facing the Nilometer on the island of Rawda.[3] Its endowed estates, a double *hammam*, an apartment complex (*rab'*), a large commercial building, and a piece of land, were located nearby. This was the first and last Mamluk royal foundation in the capital to be built that far south. Sultan al-Mu'izz Qutuz (r. 1259–60) chose a different site by erecting his madrasa in the vicinity of the Citadel, in the quarter of Hadarat al-Baqar, where Sultan Hasan later erected his mosque.[4]

During the reign of al-Zahir Baybars (r. 1260–77), Fustat continued to enjoy religious and monumental patronage; the sultan's interest in

---

[2] Maqrîzî, *Khitat*, 1:343; Behrens-Abouseif, "Lost Minaret."
[3] Maqrîzî, *Sulûk*, 4:302; Ibn Duqmâq, 4:92; Ibn Taghrîbirdî, *Nujûm*, 7:14.
[4] Ibn Iyâs, I/1:308.

developing the island of Rawda by restoring al-Salih's fortress and palace and adding a new Friday mosque, and his foundation of a large Friday mosque in 1273 between Fustat and al-Qahira, at Mansh'at a-Maharani, were propitious to the development of the old capital.[5] However, Baybars' madrasa at Bayn al-Qasrayn (1262–3), close to that of his master al-Salih Najm al-Din, and his mosque at Husayniyya in al-Qahira's northern suburb signaled the shift of royal patronage to the north.[6] Although Baybars does not seem to have had schemes of urban development, his decision to multiply the *khutba* or Friday sermon in the capital, waiving the Shafi'i doctrine of his Ayyubid predecessors that restricted the number of Friday mosques to one for each agglomeration, had a significant decentralizing effect on the city.

While the sultan established two major religious foundations in al-Qahira, some of his prominent civil servants, the Banu Hanna family of powerful and wealthy viziers and bureaucrats originating from Fustat, demonstrated their attachment to the old capital by endowing it with a number of religious and commercial buildings.[7] Also, the emir Mu'izz al-Din Aybak al-Afram (d. 1296), who started his career under al-Salih Najm al-Din launched a great urban development project in the southern outskirts of Fustat. Making use of the land added by the shift of the Nile bed, which created a new road along the river, he transformed part of the pond called al-Birka al-Shu'aybiyya into a walled garden equipped with a dam to protect it against the Nile flood, and he sublet the remaining land for the construction of residences. He also built a *ribat* and a mosque.[8]

The foundation of Sultan al-Mansur Qalawun (r. 1279–80) confirmed the supremacy of al-Qahira. His complex, which included a madrasa, mausoleum, and a large hospital, was built in 1284–5 at Bayn al-Qasrayn facing the madrasas of al-Salih Najm al-Din Ayyub and al-Zahir Baybars. With these three royal monuments, built in close proximity and surrounded by the commercial structures of their endowments, the heart of the Fatimid city became the cultural and commercial centre of the Mamluk metropolis. The hospital of Qalawun continued to be the major medical centre of pre-modern Egypt until the early nineteenth century. To acquire building material for this complex, Qalawun

---

[5] Ibn Duqmâq, 4:119; Maqrîzî, *Khitat*, 2:298.
[6] Maqrîzî, *Khitat*, 2:299, 378; Ibn Taghrîbirdî, *Nujûm*, 5:161f.
[7] Ibn Duqmâq, 4:101; Maqrîzî, *Khitat*, 2:298f., 370, 427, 429.
[8] Ibn Duqmâq, 4:55, 78, 101; Maqrîzî, *Khitat*, 2:158f., 165, 298.

dismantled al-Salih's citadel and palace on the island of Rawda, after Baybars had restored them, thus depriving the island and the opposite Fustat shore of their aristocratic residential character.[9]

The shift of the Nile bed to the west that had just come to a halt by the fourteenth century added land to the metropolitan area, and created new urbanization potentials in al-Qahira's northern and western outskirts. Unlike Fustat, built along the Nile shore, al-Qahira was built further east along the Canal or Khalij, which connected the Nile with the northeastern outskirts; its mouth was located opposite the northern tip of the island of Rawda. Al-Qahira expanded far beyond its Fatimid walls, which gradually disappeared behind buildings. From greater Fustat only the quarter around the mosque of Ibn Tulun, at the very northern periphery of the old capital, was integrated into al-Qahira with the Saliba artery connecting the Citadel to the Khalij. South of Saliba street an urban gap separated al-Qahira from Fustat.

Navigation on the Nile had always been important to Egypt's economy; Fustat continued to harbour ships carrying agricultural goods from Upper Egypt and merchandise from the Red Sea trade, which in the thirteenth and fourteenth centuries passed via Qus to the capital and further to Alexandria and Damietta on the Mediterranean shore. Mamluk Fustat was an industrial area with pottery kilns, oil and sugar presses, and a shipyard. Other luxury crafts seem also to have existed there, such as textiles and a carpet industry mentioned in the fourteenth century.[10] From the nine madrasas built in Fustat during the Mamluk period only that of Aybak was a royal foundation.[11] The others were founded by emirs, bureaucrats, and merchants. The mosque of 'Amr, however, which enjoyed the status of the first Muslim sanctuary on Egyptian soil, was repeatedly restored. The scarcity of royal foundations and the absence of Fustat in the itinerary of royal ceremonial processions, confirm the marginality into which it gradually fell.

The southern cemeteries, which had developed in connection with Fustat, were maintained because of their religious significance due to the presence since the early Islamic period of saints' tombs. With al-Qahira's expansion new cemeteries with princely religious foundations

---

[9] Maqrîzî, *Khitat*, 2:183f.
[10] Maqrîzî, *Khitat*, 2:72.
[11] This excludes the madrasas of Sanjar al-Jawli and Sarghitmish along the Saliba street. Denoix, *Décrire le Caire*, p. 95f.

emerged in the desert on the northeastern side of the city and to the southeast of the Citadel.

Baybars and Qalawun's foundations were soon followed by other royal buildings in al-Qahira: al-Nasir Muhammad's madrasa (1295–1304), Baybars al-Jashankir's *khanqâh* (1306–10), and the multifunctional complexes of al-Zahir Barquq (1384–86), al-Ashraf Barsbay (1425), al-Mu'ayyad Shaykh (1415–20), and Qansuh al-Ghawri's (1504–5).

The Urban Patronage of Sultan al-Nasir Muhammad

Maqrizi described with nostalgia the reign of al-Nasir Muhammad as the golden age of Cairo's history.[12] Cairo's development during this period was favoured by the sultan's exceptionally long reign (1293–4, 1299–1309, 1310–41), which was a period of political stability and peace, propitious for economic expansion. Most importantly, al-Nasir Muhammad was spurred by an urban vision, through which he conceived and designed the capital in terms of a cityscape rather than individual monuments. Ambitious projects of civil engineering were a substantial factor in his building programme. With a number of additional bridges built during the reign of al-Nasir, the Canal or Khalij was no longer al-Qahira's western boundary, the western bank being opened to merge with the main city. The Canal and the ponds it supplied in the western, northern and southern suburbs, were flooded by the Nile during the summer and filled with greenery during the rest of the year, once the flood receded. This landscape attracted residential quarters at the same time as it provided venues for leisure and pastimes. The canal also provided Cairo with drinking water.

Al-Nasir pushed forward the urbanization of the western Khalij bank by digging in 1325 a new canal parallel to the main one, which it joined north of Baybars' mosque. The new canal nurtured the old one and connected Cairo with the village of Siryaqus, about twenty kilometres north of Cairo, where al-Nasir Muhammad built a great *khanqâh* with his mausoleum and a hippodrome along with residential structures.[13] Between the two canals al-Nasir dug the Nasiriyya pond, which became a magnet for new aristocratic mansions. The creation

---

[12] Raymond, *Cairo*, Chapter 3; Harithy, "Patronage."
[13] Williams, "Siryaqus."

of the Siryaqus complex was not directly connected to Cairo's urban growth; the pleasance complex was related to the sultan's hunting ground, and the *khanqâh* fulfilled a pious vow after al-Nasir recovered from an ailment while he was once in this neighbourhood. However, being on the caravan road coming from Syria, the Hijaz, or beyond, Siryaqus must have provided an architectural foretaste to the visitor entering Cairo.

The sultan orchestrated his metropolitan schemes with his emirs whom he urged to build, encouraging them with legal privileges on the land and with material support. He thus transformed the Birkat al-Fil or Pond of the Elephant into an aristocratic residential area which included the mosques of the emirs Ulmas (1329–30), Qawsun (1329–30), Bashtak (1336).[14] The area around the mosque of Ibn Tulun, the old Qata'i', which became a satellite of the greater Fustat, had already been revived by Sultan Lajin after a long period of neglect by his renovation of this mosque in 1296 and his construction of a hippodrome in its vicinity. The emir Salar had built a palace at Qal'at al-Kabsh and a funerary madrasa (1303–4) nearby along Saliba Street.

Al-Nasir's urban vision is further demonstrated by his scheme for the transformation of the quarter of Hadarat al-Baqar beneath the Citadel, northwest of the Rumayla Square, where Sultan Hasan later erected his madrasa. He designed a palace complex with the idea of creating a spectacular architectural vista for himself to admire from his palace at the Citadel. It consisted of an ensemble of two palaces for his favourite emirs and in-laws, Yalbugha al-Yahawi and Maridani and four great "stables" for the emirs Qawsun, Tashtumur, and Aydighmish.[15] Such stables must have been important palaces like the one called Istabl Qawsun, the monumental ruins of which still attest to its grandeur,[16] and the palace of Baktimur, called Istabl Baktimur, which occupied the site of Sultan Lajin's hippodrome.

The great building boom of al-Nasir's reign included the cemeteries. Given Cairo's location between the Nile and the desert, it was natural that the cemeteries were located on the eastern desert side rather than along the green Nile shores. The religious foundations attached to the mausoleums of the Mamluk aristocracy bestowed an urban character

---

[14] Salmon, chapter 5.
[15] Maqrîzî, *Khitat*, 2:71–73.
[16] Garcin et al., pp. 51–59.

on the cemeteries. Referring to the cemetery southeast of the Citadel, Maqrizi wrote:

> The amirs followed by the military and all other people built tombs, monasteries, markets, mills and baths so that southern and eastern cemeteries were urbanized. Roads multiplied and streets were pierced. Many wished to dwell there because of the magnificent palaces that were erected there and which were called tombs, and because of the charities bestowed upon the inhabitants of the cemeteries.[17]

The Citadel founded by Salah al-Din, and completed by his successors, to be the center of administrative and political power, evolved into a palace-city under the Mamluk sultans. The Mamluk additions to the Ayyubid fortress extended the southern section with a palace complex that commanded a panorama encompassing the two cities al-Qahira and Fustat with their cemeteries and far beyond. The Citadel, perhaps the largest of its kind in the medieval world, has often been described as a city in itself, with its palaces and offices, barracks, dwellings and shops. Al-Nasir Muhammad replaced the old palaces and the mosque of the Citadel with new buildings. His mosque (1318–35) facing the monumental palaces, the Great Iwan (1310–11) and Striped Palace, al-Qasr al-Ablaq (1313), remained for centuries the major landmarks of the royal residence.[18] For the construction of the Hawsh, which comprised private apartments overlooking a pasture ground for cattle and sheep, al-Nasir initiated the gigantic undertaking of carving it out of the Muqattam hill, the plot on which the complex was erected. In addition to the aqueducts, his project to conduct water from the Nile up to the Citadel, through a canal and hydraulic installations, faced insurmountable difficulties, and was abandoned.

The Citadel had a dynamic impact on the development of the southern quarters of al-Qahira, attracting to its neighbourhood the markets of the horses and weapons to supply the demands of the military aristocracy and the army. Princely religious foundations spread along the streets that connected the Citadel to al-Qahira's southern gate, Bab Zuwayla.

During al-Nasir's reign eight mosques were built at Husayniyya, six in the northwestern outskirts including Bulaq, six in the southwestern

---

[17] Maqrîzî, *Khitat*, 2:444.
[18] On the Citadel in the Mamluk period, s. Casanova, Behrens-Abouseif, "Citadel," and Rabbat, *Citadel*.

zone, ten within al-Qahira, 16 between Bab Zuwayla and Ibn Tulun, four in the southern cemetery and three in the Fustat-Rawda area.[19]

The Friday mosques in the suburbs were planned to form nuclei for new quarters, or to consolidate areas still in the process of urbanization. The emirs usually built mosques near their residences, creating small urban entities that included commercial structures. When Emir Husayn built his mosque on the western Khalij shore, he built a bridge near it and even took the controversial decision to pierce a gate in the city's west wall, in order to attract worshippers.[20] Whereas the immediate northern and southern expansions proved to be durable and consistent with the city's natural needs, the western expansion, except for Bulaq and the street leading to it, did not survive the crises of the late fourteenth century.[21] The area around al-Nasir's greatest mosque, built in 1312 along the Nile shore facing the island of Rawda, was abandoned prior to Maqrizi's time.[22]

The mosque of Sultan Hasan built in 1356–62, while introducing a new dimension to Mamluk religious architecture, interacted through its monumental scale with the Citadel and the Rumayla square it faced. Built on the site of the palace his father al-Nasir Muhammad had erected to create an architectural vista for himself to admire from the Citadel, its design and proportions satisfied such expectations. Its function as a combination of mausoleum, Friday mosque, and madrasa, was an innovation that became henceforth the rule for all subsequent royal foundations.

The mosque of Sultan Hasan was the culmination of a period of building activity, which went on beyond al-Nasir's death in 1341 despite the great calamity or Black Death in 1348. Cairo is estimated to have lost during the Black Death between one-third and two-fifths of its population.[23] The building zeal of the Mamluk aristocracy could go on because such catastrophes helped replenish the State Treasury, which was the ultimate heir, thus releasing funds for new foundations. According to data from the 1950s,[24] Cairo inherited from the three decades following al-Nasir's death an important number of religious

---

[19] Raymond, *Cairo*, p. 136.
[20] Maqrîzî, *Khitat*, 2:307.
[21] Ayalon, "The Muslim City" and "The Expansion and Decline."
[22] Maqrîzî, *Khitat*, 2:304.
[23] Dols, p. 169ff.
[24] This list is based on Creswell's *Brief Chronology* and the "Index of Mohammedan Monuments" of the Egyptian Antiquities Organization.

monuments attributed to the following patrons: Aslam al-Baha'i
1344–45, Aydumur al-Bahlawan 1346, Aqsunqur 1346–47, Qutlbugha
al-Dhahabi 1347, Arghun al-Isma'ili 1347, Tughay 1348, Manjaq al-
Yusufi 1349, al-Kharrubi 1349, Shaykhu (mosque) 1349 and (khanqâh)
1349, Sarghitmish 1356, Nizam al-Din, 1356, Sultan Hasan 1356–63,
Badr al-Din al-'Ajami 1357, al-Jamali Yusuf 1357, Tatar al-Hijaziyya
1360, Bashir Agha al-Jamdar 1360, Mithqal 1361–62, Taibugha 1366,
Sultan Sha'ban's mother 1368–69, Asanbugha 1370, anonymous 1370,
Uljay al-Yusufi 1373, Ibn al-Ghannam 1373, and al-Baqari 1374. This
list does not include monuments that disappeared much earlier, such
as the madrasa built by Sultan Sha'ban in 1375 near the Citadel and
destroyed by his successor Sultan Barquq in 1411.

The Circassian Period

Maqrizi's nostalgic praise of al-Nasir's reign and his gloomy perception
of his own time, the first two decades of the fifteenth century, led historians to equate the entire Circassian Mamluk period with decline. Maqrizi
was looking at a city that was still suffering from Timur's invasion of
Syria in 1400, which heavily affected the Mamluk economy, and from
a series of natural catastrophes alongside political instability. Many of
Cairo's quarters and markets were abandoned or devastated. However,
neither the building zeal of the ruling establishment nor the quality of
the constructions dropped in times of economic crises. The reign of
Sultan Barquq (r. 1382–90) and his fifteenth century successors al-Nasir
Faraj (r. 1405–12), al-Mu'ayyad Shaykh (r. 1412–21), al-Ashraf Barsbay
(r. 1422–38), al-Zahir Jaqmaq (r. 1438–53), al-Ashraf Inal (r. 1453–61),
al-Zahir Khushqadam (r. 1461–7), al-Ashraf Qaytbay (r. 1468–
96), al-'Adil Tumanbay (1501), Qansuh al-Ghawri (r. 1501–16) might
not have all been prosperous, however they added religious monuments
to the Mamluk capital, most of which survived, and attest to the continuing vigour and innovation of the building craft.

During the fifteenth century, Bulaq's status as a port, coinciding
with the growing importance of the Mediterranean trade, increased; it
became a commercial and industrial centre with a number of mosques
and palaces.[25] Ibn Taghribirdi reported intensive urbanization activities

---

[25] On Bûlâq see Hanna.

that filled the desert area northeast of Cairo and Bulaq already prior to Qaytbay's reign.[26] No less than eighty mosques were built in the capital between 1412 and 1516.[27] Extant buildings point to an intensive period of construction also in the vicinity of the Citadel.

The northern cemetery, which had included so far only emirs' mausoleums, began to also attract royal foundations: Faraj ibn Barquq (r. 1400–11), Barsbay (1432), Inal (r. 1451–56), Khushqadam (r. 1461–67), Qaytbay (r. 1472–74), al-Zahir Qansuh Abu Sa'id (1498), and al-'Adil Tumanbay (1501) built their funerary structures there. Except that built by al-Zahir Khushqadam,[28] these have all survived to the present day. With time, the layout and architecture of the cemetery acquired increasingly urban features, emphasizing the facades and following the street perspective, as the buildings of Barsbay, Qaytbay, and Qurqumas (r. 1506–7) demonstrate.

Urban embellishment was also on the programme of Circassian sultans and emirs. Al-Mu'ayyad Shaykh built a new pleasance complex at Kaum al-Rish, a northern suburb along the canal, which included a new palace, called al-Khamas Wujuh or Pentagon, built on the ruins of a Fatimid palace of the same name.[29] He encouraged his courtiers to build residences nearby to be close to his court when he was there.[30] One of his high-ranking bureaucrats, 'Abd al-Ghani al-Fakhri, demolished in 1417 all buildings along the Nile shore between the quarter of Maqs in the north and Qantarat al-Muski in the south—an area which Maqrizi described as equivalent to a Syrian town—in order to set up a garden near his residence.[31] Sultan Barsbay cleared the area around the Rumayla square, and Inal was praised for having enlarged the main artery at Bayn al-Qasrayn Street when he built his rab' with a double hammam in 1457 behind the line of the previous buildings. He moreover gave instructions to prevent obstructions, and to demolish all buildings that obstructed the roads along the Nile shore.[32]

---

[26] Ibn Taghrîbirdî, *Nujûm*, 11:186f.
[27] Raymond, *Cairo*, p. 179.
[28] This monument did not survive; its exact foundation date is not known nor the circumstances of its vanishing.
[29] Ibn Taghrîbirdî, *Nujûm*, 14:94, 105f.; Ibn Taghrîbirdî, *Hawâdith*, 2:217; Maqrîzî, *Sulûk*, 4:526, 528, 538, 541.
[30] Ibn Taghrîbirdî, *Nujûm*, 14:105.
[31] Maqrîzî, *Sulûk*, 4:386.
[32] Ibn Taghrîbirdî, *Nujûm*, 15:118; idem, *Hawâdith*, 2:307.

During the reign of Sultan Khushqadam, the great secretary Janibak, launched an ambitious project of landscape transformation; it consisted of a walled garden covering an area of 120 *faddâns* i.e., ca. 130 acres facing the island of Rawda with a quay. The garden was set on the site of a pond that was filled in by pulling down a mound nearby. On its northern end, at Qanatir al-Siba', the emir built his palace and on its southern end he established a sufi complex overlooking the Nile.[33]

Qaytbay's building programme was characterized by extensive restoration works of religious and secular monuments in the capital. In addition to his funerary mosque in the southern part of the northern cemetery and another mosque at Qal'at al-Kabsh, he restored the mosque of 'Amr at Fustat, the mausoleum of Imam Shafi'i, the shrine of Sayyida Nafisa, the Azhar mosque, and a number of Mamluk mosques.[34] Moreover, he upgraded the urban waqf estates of previous foundations by restoring and reconstructing their commercial structures and dwellings,[35] thus revitalizing the commercial infrastructure of the city. In the Citadel he restored the monuments of al-Nasir Muhammad: the aqueduct, the Great Iwan and the mosque whose dome he rebuilt. He transformed the Hawsh area, which used to be the harem of the Bahri Mamluks, adding new structures to it and making it the venue for his audiences. Whereas the sultan himself was concentrating his efforts on the rehabilitation of monumental heritage rather than designing new urban schemes, his most powerful emirs, Azbak min Tutukh and Yashbak min Mahdi, pursued ambitious urban transformations.

An aspect of Mamluk princely urbanism in Cairo throughout the entire period was the expansion of the suburbs that filled urban gaps and extended the metropolitan area. The emir Azbak, commander-in-chief of Qaytbay's army, launched a project that was to transform and rehabilitate the western bank of the Khalij. He dug a large pond to the south of a predominantly Coptic quarter, filling an area that had been so far poorly urbanized and which was at that time run down. Along the southern shore of the pond Azbak founded a quarter with a palace, a mosque, apartment buildings and commercial structures including shops, a *qaysariyya*, and a double *hammam* built on both sides

---

[33] Ibn Taghrîbirdî, *Hawâdith*, Part 3, pp. 566–69, 766–68; *Nujûm*, 16:323; Ibn Iyâs 2:406.

[34] Al-Sakhâwî, 6:201ff.: Ibn Iyâs, 3:329.

[35] Behrens-Abouseif, "*Waqf* and power."

of a new street. The project began in 1476 (it was completed in 1484) and was named Azbakiyya after the founder.[36]

Another major urban project was launched by Yashbak min Mahdi, the Great Secretary. He built on the northern outskirts of Husayniyya/ Raydaniyya a complex of residential and commercial structures along-side a domed mosque (1480) reached through a long elevated passage. The quarter overlooked a depression that turned into a pond during the Nile flood. On the desert side, he built his mausoleum. Only the domed mosque, known today as Qubbat al-Fadawiyya, has survived.[37]

Yashbak's name is also associated with an urban reform that divided minds at that time. In 1477–8 he launched an embellishment campaign for the capital to celebrate Qaytbay's return from a visit to Syria by issuing orders for people to paint their facades and remove all encroachments along the streets. Although the historians praised the initiative, it did provoke uproar among those who had to remove their illegal constructions, which had become a traditional feature of the city. Sultan al-ʿAdil Tumanbay (1501), although he ruled for only a hundred days, contributed to the expansion of the Raydaniyya area near the Matʿam al-Tayr with what seems to have been a substantial religious-funerary complex, comparable to that of Qurqumas erected in the northern cemetery in 1506–7, with residential structures and warehouses.[38] Only the domed mausoleum has survived.

At the very end of the Mamluk period and notwithstanding the Ottoman advance, Sultan al-Ghawri dedicated great attention as well as funds to prestigious building projects. At the intersection of the main avenue with the street leading to the al-Azhar mosque he built a funerary complex straddling the main street, displaying ingeniously urban-integrated architecture. The mosque with its minaret on one side of the street faces the mausoleum with its adjoining *khanqâh* and the *sabil-maktab* on the other. Between them a small piazza covered with a wooden roof was designed to include a market with booths and shops.

The proliferation of Mamluk religious and scholarly institutions did not diminish the status of al-Azhar as the first sanctuary of al-Qahira. Baybars re-established its *khutba* after it was abolished by Salah al-Din.

---

[36] Behrens-Abouseif, *Azbakiyya*, pp. 3–25.
[37] Behrens-Abouseif, "A Circassian Mamluk suburb."
[38] Evliya Çelebi, pp. 397, 484, 1043. A description is included in the archive of al-Bâb al-ʿÂlî, 265/230:171f.

Its curriculum was enlarged to include additional disciplines, and philanthropic services, due to endowments and donations from the Mamluk establishment and ordinary individuals. The institution continued to attract students from abroad and from the provinces. The building was regularly consolidated and embellished; in the Bahri period Taybars (r. 1309–10) and Aqbugha (1340) and in the Circassian period Jawhar al-Qanqaba'i (1440) built madrasas adjacent to it. Qaytbay consolidated the building and added to it two gates and a minaret, and al-Ghawri added a minaret. Other major sanctuaries, such as the mosque of 'Amr at Fustat, the mausoleums of Imam Shafi'i and Sayyida Nafisa were likewise restored and maintained on a regular basis.

Waqf, Building, and Maintenance

The mosques of the Mamluks were largely financed by urban estates. Although the foundation of Friday mosques contributed to stretch the urban boundaries and upgrade neighbourhoods, not all great waqfs were conceived to include all endowed commercial structures and dwellings around the mosque. Rather, the most common pattern in a royal foundation was that of diversified investments. Al-Zahir Baybars endowed his madrasa at Bayn al-Qasrayn with a large apartment complex near Bab Zuwayla, as well as a qaysariyya and a house in other quarters. Part of al-Ashraf Khalil's endowed estates to the benefit of his madrasa and his father's mausoleum consisted of rented land in the western suburbs alongside a variety of commercial structures in the capital and land in Syria. Al-Nasir's estates for his madrasa in the city or his khanqâh in Siryaqus were also mixed, including agricultural land, commercial structures and factories in Alexandria and Syria. The waqf of Sultan Hasan's madrasa consisted mainly of agricultural land and villages in Egypt and Syria. Qaytbay's and al-Ghawri's waqfs also consisted of a mixture of dispersed commercial structures and agricultural land. The diversified investments allowed the patrons to rehabilitate dilapidated estates and upgrade marginal areas all over the city. Through their creation of new quarters or upgrading of old ones, or simply by adding commercial structures and dwellings wherever needed, the ruling establishment renewed the urban fabric.

The sultan and the great emirs, by being ex officio the overseers of the great administration of the waqfs of their predecessors, could play an active role in the preservation of architectural heritage. They often appeared personally to oversee public works of vital significance, in particular civil works concerning the Nile; on such occasions, the emirs contributed with their resources and with the participation of their mamluks and members of their households. The sultans often went on inspection tours, looking after the construction of their mosques as well as other urban matters. Jaqmaq's and Qaytbay's inspection tours were a characteristic feature of their rule.[39]

The intensive building activities of the Mamluk establishment in the capital must have been coordinated by some form of urban planning due to the centralization of the building craft in the hands of the sultan and his surroundings. The great builders among the sultans are likely to have established a consensus with their subordinates regarding individual building projects. Moreover, the emphasis on the foundation of complexes or quarters rather individual buildings implied *per se* a certain amount of planning.

Although the qadis, the police prefect (*wâlî*) and the market inspector (*muhtasib*) were involved in the administration of the capital, the continuous and direct interference of the sultans assisted by their emirs, making ad-hoc choices and decisions, shaped the city's functions and morphology to a great extent. Inal's initiative to widen the main avenue at Bayn al-Qasrayn and Yashbak's measure to eliminate encroachments along its streets, demonstrate the direct involvement of the ruling establishment in matters of urban order and aesthetics. At the same time, they indicate that only the authority of a sultan or a powerful emir could be effective enough to implement order or introduce reforms.[40] However, the chroniclers regularly report that the sultans took the liberty to obstruct the road with their own buildings or to appropriate by dubious methods waqf estates from their predecessors. The positioning of Qaytbay's funerary mosque in the cemetery shows that he must have diverted the road to enhance the approach to his complex, as did Qansuh Abu Saʿid years later.[41]

With the exception of al-Nasir Muhammad's royal village at Siryaqus, none of the other sultans or emirs built residences or summerhouses in the provinces or in other Egyptian cities. On their hunting and other excursions and travels they dwelt in elaborate encampments. The

---

[39] Jawhari, *Inbaʾ*, 202, 244, 405.
[40] Raymond and Wiet, p. 54f.
[41] Ibn Iyâs, 3:437, 425.

Mamluk aristocracy lived continuously in Cairo, either in their urban mansions or in villas in the outskirts along the shores of the ponds, the Khalij, or the Nile. Quite often the emirs' palaces were not their private property but owned by the State, which they could enjoy as part of their remuneration and which was to return to the sultan upon their death or dismissal. Some belonged to waqf estates, their rent being part of the revenue of pious foundations. The palaces continued to be occupied for centuries, albeit not on a hereditary basis, being regularly remodelled and transformed.

The palaces of the Mamluk emirs were located in various areas within the premises of the Fatimid city and in the suburbs, notably in the southern quarters along the Saliba artery and the pond called Birkat al-Fil. Although the sources refer to places favored by the emirs and other notables such as the shores of the ponds, there was no exclusively aristocratic quarter in the Mamluk capital. Waqf descriptions of Azbakiyya and other quarters indicate that they were planned with palaces near ordinary dwellings of various sizes alongside shops and commercial buildings. The mamluks and other members of an emir's household would dwell in the same quarter.

The growth in the number of mosques with the status of *jâmiʿ* or Friday mosques in the fourteenth century was a response to al-Nasir's ambitious schemes to expand the urban area. After sultan Hasan integrated the madrasa with the Friday mosque the multifunctional complex caught on in a big way. In the fifteenth century, not only sultans and emirs but also civilians of various backgrounds could found Friday mosques; at the same time earlier *zâwiyas* and madrasas were endowed with the *khutba* and new ones included it automatically. The proliferation of congregational mosques and multifunctional complexes led to saturation in the late fifteenth century, so that even Sultan Qaytbay could only build neighbourhood mosques, reduced in size and function. This development was accompanied by the adoption of residential features in religious architecture, with the mosque adopting the shape of a reception hall, and the living units in the form of a *rabʿ*.

Unlike many other Islamic cities, Cairo's domestic architecture was not introverted. The *rabʿ*, a typical form of dwelling for the middle class, consisted of apartments built above a row of shops or a commercial structure with a courtyard.[42] These apartments, mostly duplexes with

---

[42] Ali Ibrahim, "Middle-class Living Units."

an individual roof, preferably overlooked the street whenever access was available. Likewise, in mansions and palaces, the windows of the main hall or *qâ'a* opened onto the street. The *qâ'a*, which occupied the entire height of the house and was surrounded by smaller rooms on multiple stories, was the heart of the residence, whereas the courtyard—rather than being the centre of domestic life like the patio of the Syrian or Maghrebi house—included various service facilities, including a stable. In larger residences a second courtyard might fulfill the function of a garden.

Cairo received its drinking water from the Nile through the Khalij. Water was conducted to the Citadel through aqueducts and waterwheels. Pious foundations had their own *sabîls*, or water houses, which provided water to the public on a philanthropic basis. Since the late fourteenth century the *sabîl* was integrated architecturally in all religious buildings, usually at a corner and surmounted by the *maktab* or boys' primary school. Others, along with troughs for the animals, were independent structures. Houses and commercial buildings had cisterns, wells, and waterwheels. The cisterns were filled yearly during the flood season with water carried by camels or donkeys. Ambulant water-carriers sold water on the streets.

Open Spaces and Hippodromes

Maqrizi enumerates open spaces called *rahba*s often used as markets. Hippodromes multiplied in the Mamluk period, they often functioned as outposts of the Citadel, hosting, beside polo and military tournaments, princely weddings, congregational prayers, or even the sultan's audiences. The hippodromes were walled, often combined with gardens, and they included pavilions and residences.[43] The Rumayla square at the foot of the Citadel, which stretched between the Hadarat al-Baqar with its aqueduct, near Sultan Hasan's mosque, and Bâb al-Qarâfa, the gate of the cemetery, included a major hippodrome, and was the venue where public events, such as parades and the celebration of the departure of the pilgrimage caravan, took place. It was an Ayyubid foundation rebuilt by al-Nasir Muhammad, who used it as a falconry ground, to review the royal horses, celebrate the two great religious feasts, and for congregational prayers. At the very end of the Mamluk

---

[43] Maqrîzî, *Khitat*, 2:197–200, 228.

period, Sultan al-Ghawri refurbished the hippodrome to make it an outpost of the Citadel; he connected it with hydraulic installations to provide water for a pool and a garden planted with imported trees, and he built there pavilions and residential structures for his audiences and festivities.

The northern cemetery was originally a hippodrome, the Maydan al-Qabaq, built by al-Zahir Baybars. In 1267 he built there a kind of dais (mastaba) connected to a falconry (Mat'am al-Tayr). Al-Nasir transferred the falconry to southern Fustat at Birkat al-Habash, and allowed instead the cemetery to spread. However, a mastaba-hippodrome in the northern part of the cemetery continued to be mentioned in the chronicles to the end of the Mamluk period, as a venue of tournaments, parades, and various regal ceremonies.[44]

Al-Nasir Muhammad demolished two other hippodromes, set by his predecessors al-Zahir Baybars and al-'Adil Kitbugha, and replaced them with the Maydan al-Mahara located at Qanatir al-Siba' between the two canals and another one at Bustan al-Khashshab between Fustat and al-Qahira along the Nile shore. With the exception of Siryaqus, which was abandoned in the Circassian period, the hippodromes established by al-Nasir continued to serve the Mamluk court; they were regularly restored by subsequent sultans.[45]

Streets and markets

Apart from the Citadel, the Mamluks did not fortify Cairo, the Egyptian capital being defended far beyond its own territory. They rather maintained the fortifications of Syrian and Egyptian coastal cities; Syria was the buffer zone between Egypt and any possible invaders. The Mongol and Timur's raids, which inflicted much damage on Syria, were halted there before they could reach Egypt. The main battle with the Ottoman conquerors was also fought there at Marj Dabiq near Aleppo.

The built area of Mamluk Cairo covered a huge area with varying demographic density. According to Garcin's estimation, the population of the Egyptian capital Fustat-Qahira in 1517 amounted to c. 270,000.[46]

---

[44] Behrens-Abouseif, "Northeastern Extension."
[45] Maqrîzî, *Sulûk*, 4:529; *Nujûm*, 14: 95, 96, 99.
[46] Garcin, "Note sur la population du Caire."

Mamluk Cairo displayed the traditional Islamic street pattern with a few major arteries connected to winding streets and lanes ending in cul-de-sacs. Maqrizi's hierarchy of streets includes the *hâra*, *khutt*, *zuqâq*, and *darb*, the latter being a lane closed by a gate. The *hâra* was a large district with many quarters, whereas the *khutt* was a quarter. The map shows the main artery from Husayniyya down to Bab Zuwayla, where it bifurcates eastwards into al-Darb al-Ahmar street leading to the Citadel, and southwards to the pond Birkat al-Fil, and, after it crosses Saliba, continues further to the cemetery of Sayyida Nafisa, where it bifurcates westwards to Fustat and eastwards to the southern cemetery. On the west side, the bridges of the Khalij connected the city with Bulaq and the Nile shore.

The major markets stretched along the thoroughfares from Husayni-yya in the north to the Citadel and further to Saliba in the south. They consisted of shops and booths built beneath *rab*'s or mosques or along their facades. The most prestigious markets were in the area of Bayn al-Qasrayn around the major royal mosques. They included the major commercial buildings of the *khân*, *qaysariyya*, and *wakâla* type, which functioned as specialized markets or factories as well as banks and stock markets.[47] Besides the trade of local and imported luxury goods, slaves, and agricultural products, a characteristic feature of Cairo's market streets, reported by many travellers, were the food stalls, and the cooks and peddlers, who sold cooked meals.

Virtually all commercial structures in al-Qahira's central market streets alongside their dwellings were the property of the great waqfs of the sultans and emirs, which financed their religious foundations at the same time as they provided revenue for themselves and their descendants. The Mamluk aristocracy and their officials controlled much of the urban trade.[48] A sultan or emir could force the transfer of a market or a group of craftsmen to his own premises, and merchants could be forced to purchase and sell certain goods at prices dictated by the sultan. The great markets provided the court with luxury and ceremonial articles. The famous Mamluk inlaid metalwork was pro-duced in the bazaar before it disappeared in the fifteenth century, and the enamelled and gilded glass lamps and vessels could also have been made in the glass markets (*zajjâjûn*) mentioned by Maqrizi. The

---

[47] Raymond and Wiet, *Marchés*.
[48] Labib, p. 184ff.

historian refers to markets of designers (rassâmîn),[49] who served various arts and crafts. Also ceremonial gowns and weapons were produced in the city. The merchants and craftsmen of the central markets were tenants and not the owners of their shops and workshops, as were most inhabitants of all types of domestic and residential structures, including mansions and palaces.

The non-Muslim minorities were able to maintain their pre-Islamic sanctuaries in Fustat and in the outskirts of Cairo. Greek churches and a synagogue built in al-Qahira during the Fatimid period could maintain themselves. The Mamluks did not allow the dhimmîs to found new religious buildings, but only to restore the old ones. For the Copts, who worked in the commercial centre and dwelt in some of al-Qahira's quarters along the Khalij and in the western suburbs, the churches of Fustat no longer corresponded to their demographic concentration. The situation was different for the Jews, who had a synagogue at Harat Zuwayla, which was the main Jewish quarter behind the complex of Qalawun. Whereas some quarters were predominantly inhabited by non-Muslims, there were many mixed areas so that no strict segregation seems to have existed between the communities.

The Metropolitan Style

The involvement of the ruling aristocracy in the city's commerce, and the potentials of the waqf system, that led the Mamluks to invest in urban estates, dedicating their revenue to their private and pious foundations, had a significant impact on the city's image. With their mosques, dwellings, hammams, shops, and caravanserais integrated in princely patronage, Cairo's main streets must have had a homogenous princely character, with no room left for common building projects.

The Mamluks inherited a capital with a long history of unchallenged status as the capital of Muslim Egypt whose urban and architectural traditions did not fail to inspire them. The supremacy of the street aesthetic was a characteristic feature of Cairene architecture since the Fatimid period further cultivated by the Mamluks. They used the device, already applied in the Aqmar mosque (1125), to split the axis of the mosque's façade from that of the Mecca-oriented interior in order

---

[49] Maqrîzî, Khitat, 2:101, 105.

to adjust the building to the street and not disturb its alignment. This approach to the street perspective was elaborated in their religious-funerary monuments, which were designed to emphasize the domed mausoleum and its positioning with optimal visibility from the street,[50] as well as its harmonious relationship to the minaret. As a result, the Mamluk religious complexes display a large variety of layouts individually conceived to fit in their urban environment. These features, which combined inherited traditions with princely commemorative obsessions, shaped the inimitable metropolitan style that remained exclusive to the capital. Ayalon's observation that "few military aristocracies in Islamic history were as bound to the capital and as closely identified with it, in almost total disregard of the other towns, as were the Mamluks in relation to Cairo,"[51] is confirmed by the sultans' regular appearance in the streets and their direct involvement in the capital's urban development and maintenance. The exclusive and intimate relationship between the Mamluk ruling aristocracy and their capital contributed to shaping Mamluk Cairo as a singular phenomenon or, as Ibn Khaldun said, "a city beyond imagination."

Bibliography

Abu-Lughod, Janet. *Cairo: 1001 Years of the City Victorious*. Princeton, 1971.
Ali Ibrahim, Laila Ali. "Middle-class living units in Mamluk Cairo." *Art and Archaeology Research Papers (AARP)* 14 (1978): 24–30.
Amîn, Muhammad Muh. *Al-Awqâf wa'l-hayât al-ijtimâ'iyya fî misr (648–923/1250–1517)*. Cairo, 1980.
Ayalon, David. "The Muslim City and the Mamluk Military Aristocracy." In *Proceedings of the Israel Academy of Sciences and Humanities* 2 (1968), 311–29.
———. "The Expansion and Decline of Cairo under the Mamluks and its Background." In *Itinéraires d'orient: hommages à Claude Cahen*, edited by R. Curiel and R. Gyselen, 14–16. Paris, 1994.
Behrens-Abouseif, Doris. "A Circassian Mamluk suburb in the Northeast of Cairo." *Art and Archaeology Research Papers (AARP)* 14 (1978): 17–23.
———. "The Northeastern Extension of Cairo under the Mamluks. *Annales Islamologiques* 17 (1981): 157–189.
———. "The Lost Minaret of Shajarat ad-Durr at Her Complex in the Cemetery of Sayyida Nafisa." *Mitteilungen des Deutschen Archäologischen Instituts, Abteilung Kairo* 39 (1983): 1–16.
———. *Azbakiyya and its Environs, from Azbak to Ismâ'îl: 1476–1979*. Cairo, 1985.

---

[50] Kessler, "Funerary Architecture."
[51] Ayalon, "The Muslim City," p. 319; idem, "Studies," p. 205.

——. "Locations of non-Muslim Quarters in Medieval Cairo."*Annales Islamologiques* 22 (1986): 117–132.

——. "The Citadel of Cairo: Stage for Mamluk Ceremonial." *Annales Islamologiques* 24 (1988): 25–79.

——. "Gardens in Islamic Egypt." *Der Islam* 69, no. 2 (1992): 302–312.

——. "Le Acque del Cairo: Scenario e Stile di Vita di una Città Islamica." In *Il Teatro delle Acque*, edited by Dalu Jones, 31–41. Rome, 1992.

——. "Al-Nâsir Muhammad and al-Ašraf Qâytbây, Patrons of Urbanism." In *Egypt and Syria in the Fatimid, Ayyubid and Mamluk Eras*, edited by U. Vermeulen and D. De Smet, 257–274. Leuven, 1995.

——. "Qâytbây's Investments in the City of Cairo: Waqf and Power." *Annales Islamologiques* 32 (1998): 29–40.

——. Cairo of the Mamluks. A History of the Architecture and its Culture, London, 2007.

Behrens-Abouseif, Doris, Sylvie Denoix, and Jean-Claude Garcin. "Le Caire." In Garcin, *Grandes Villes Méditerranéenes du Monde Musulman Medieval*, 177–213.

Casanova, Paul. "Histoire et description de la citadelle du Caire." *Mémoires publiés par les membres de la Mission Archéologique Française au Caire* 6 (1891–1892).

Clerget, Marcel. *Le Caire: Etude de géographie urbaine et d'histoire économique*. 2 vols. Cairo, 1934.

Creswell, K. A. C. *A Brief Chronology of the Muhammadan Monuments of Egypt to A.D. 1517*. Cairo, 1919.

Denoix, Sylvie. *Décrire le Caire d'après Ibn Duqmâq et Maqrîzî*. Cairo, 1992.

——. "Topographie de l'intervention du personnel politique à l'époque Mamlouke." In Denoix et al., *Le Khan al-Khalili*, pp. 33–49.

Denoix, S., Charles Depaule, and Michel Tuchscherer. *Le Khan al-Khalili. Un centre commercial et artisanal au Caire du XIIIᵉ au XXᵉ siècle*. 2 vols. Cairo, 1999.

Dols, Michael. *The Black Death*. Princeton, 1977.

Evliya Çelebi. *Seyahatnamesi. Misir, Sudan, Habeş (1672–1680)*. Istanbul, 1938; Arabic translation by Muhammad 'Ali 'Awnî. Cairo, 2003.

Garcin, Jean-Claude. "Habitat médiéval et histoire urbaine à Fustat et au Caire." In *Palais et maisons du Caire, I: époque mamelouke (XIIIᵉ–XVIᵉ siècles)*, edited by J.-C. Garcin, B. Maury, J. Revault, and M. Zakariya. Paris, 1982.

——. "Le Caire et l'évolution des pays musulmans à l'époque médiévale." *Annales Islamologiques* 25 (1991): 289–304.

——. "Note sur la population du Caire en 1517." In Garcin, *Grandes Villes Méditerranéennes du Monde Musulman Medieval*, pp. 205–213.

——, ed. *Grandes Villes Méditérranéennes du Monde Musulman Medieval*. Rome and Paris, 2000.

Hamza, Hani. *The Northern Cemetery of Cairo*. Cairo, 2001.

Hanna, Nelly. *An Urban History of Bûlâq in the Mamluk and Ottoman Periods*. Cairo, 1983.

al-Harithy, Howyda. "The Patronage of al-Nasir Muhammad ibn Qalâwûn." *Mamluk Studies Review* 4 (2000): 219–44.

Humphreys, Stephen. "The Expressive Intent of the Mamluk Architecture of Cairo: a Preliminary Essay." *Studia Islamica* 35 (1972): 69–119.

Ibn Duqmâq. *Kitâb al-intisâr li wâsitat 'iqd al-amsâr*. Bulaq, 1314/1897–98.

Ibn Taghrîbirdî. *Hawâdith al-duhûr fî madâ 'l ayyâm wa'l-shuhûr*. Edited by W. Popper. Berkeley, 1931.

——. *al-Nujûm al-zâhira fi mulûk misr wa'l-qâhira*. Cairo, 1963–71.

Ibn Iyâs. *Badâ'i' al-zuhûr fî waqâ'i' al-duhûr*. Edited by M. Mustafâ. Wiesbaden and Cairo, 1961–75.

Jomard, J. "Description de la ville et de la citadelle du Kaire." In *Description de l'Egypte par les savants de l'Expédition Française: Etat Moderne*. Paris, 1812.

Kessler, Christel. "Funerary Architecture within the City." In *Colloque International sur l'Histoire du Caire (1969)*, 257–67. Cairo, 1972.

Lapidus, Ira. *Muslim Cities in the Later Middle Ages*. Cambridge, MA, 1967.

Al-Maqdîsî, Abû Hâmid. *Al-Fawâ'id al-nafîsa al-bâhira fî bayân shawâri' al-qâhira fî madhâhib al-a'imma al-arba'a 'l-zâhira*. Edited by Amâl al-'Imarî. Cairo, 1988.

Al-Maqrîzî. *Kitâb al-mawâ'iz wa'l-i'tibâr bi dhikr al-khitat wa'l-âthâr*. Bulâq, 1306H.

Massignon, Louis. "La Cité des Morts au Caire: Qarâfa-Darb al-Ahmar." *Bulletin de l'Institut Français d'Archéologie Orientale (BIFAO)* 57 (1958): 25–79.

Meinecke-Berg, Victoria. "Quellen zur Topographie und Baugeschichte in Kairo unter Sultan al-Nasir Muhammad b. Qalâwûn." *Zeitschrift der Deutschen Morgenländischen Gesellschaft*, Supplement 3, 1977: 539–550.

——. "Historische Topographie des Viertels." In *Die Restaurierung der Madrasa des Amîrs Sâbiq ad-Dîn Mitqâl al-Ânûkî und die Sanierung des Darb Qirmiz in Kairo*, edited by Michael Meinecke et al., 18–28. Mainz, 1980.

——. "Cairo, the Changing Face of a Capital City." In *Islam, Art and Architecture*, edited by M. Hattstein and P. Delius. Königswinter, 2004.

Mubârak, 'Alî. *Al-Khitat al-jadîda al-tawfîqiyya*. Bûlâq, 1306/1888–89.

Pauty, Edmond. *Les Hammams du Caire*. Cairo, 1933.

Rabbat, Nasser. *The Citadel of Cairo*. Leiden, 1995.

Raymond, André. *Cairo*. Translated by William Wood. Cambridge, MA, 2000.

——. "Cairo's area and population in the early fifteenth century." *Muqarnas* 2 (1984): 21–32.

——, and Gaston Wiet. *Les Marchés du Caire (Traduction annotée du texte de Maqrizi)*. Cairo, 1979.

Ravaisse, Paul. "Essai sur l'Histoire et sur la Topographie du Caire d'après Maqrîzî." *Mémoires de la Mission Archéologique Française au Caire* 1, no. 3; 3, no. 4 (1886–1889): 409–489; 33–114.

Rogers, J. M. "Kâhira." *Encyclopaedia of Islam*. 2nd ed. Leiden, 1978.

Salmon, Georges. "Etudes sur la topographie du Caire: Kal'at al-Kabch et Birkat al-Fil." *Mémoires de l'Institut Français d'Archéologie Orientale* 7 (1902).

al-Shishtâwî, Muhammad. *Muntazahât al-qâhira fî 'l-'asrayn al-mamlûkî wa'l-'uthmânî*. Cairo, 1999.

Warner, Nicholas. *The Monuments of Historic Cairo*. Cairo and New York, 2005.

——. *The True Description of Cairo: A Sixteenth Century Venetian View*. 3 vols. Oxford, 2006.

Wiet, Gaston. *Cairo: City of Art and Commerce*. Oklahoma, 1964.

Williams, John Alden. "Urbanization and Monument Construction in Mamluk Cairo." *Muqarnas* 2 (1984): 33–45.

ISLAMIC JERUSALEM OR JERUSALEM UNDER MUSLIM RULE

Oleg Grabar

In drawings by eighteenth and nineteenth century travellers or in photographs from the second half of the nineteenth century until the fifties of the twentieth century, Jerusalem was always presented in the same fashion. It was shown from the southwest, from the southern spur of the Mount of Olives, where natural height and bareness of occupation allowed the visitor to see the city in its totality, on the other side of a deep valley filled with tombs. Beyond the realm of the dead, there was a squarish area outlined by massive and well-preserved walls with few visible gates; the one most easily seen from that angle, the Golden Gate handsomely outlined on the walls of the city, had been blocked since the seventh century and may never in fact been used as an entrance. That city seemed to be artificially perched on top of a craggy and stony uneven terrain. Inside, partly covered with trees, the large and open Muslim holy place known as the Haram al-Sharif, "the Noble Sanctuary," occupies the southeastern corner of the walled enclosure. It harbours the startling and imposing Dome of the Rock and, to the south of it, a large congregational mosque known as the Aqsa Mosque, also with a high dome. Crowded streets and buildings occupied the rest of the city, but the fairly modern domes of the ancient Holy Sepulchre, purposefully framed by the minarets of two small mosques, or the much more recent domes of Ashkenazi and Sephardic synagogues were clearly visible. Later in the nineteenth century, the tall Lutheran and Catholic towers served to identify yet another religious presence in the holy city as well as to evoke western Christian preeminence. No external sign or symbol identified the sectarian allegiance of these buildings, but local inhabitants knew what they were, because they were part of the fabric of the city, the indispensable means to its meaning and to its life. Most of those who came to Jerusalem were also aware of their existence, but the knowledge of the pilgrims was probably restricted to the monuments of their own faith or even of a specific segment of their faith.

This walled city acquired its present shape in the sixteenth century and, while much has been done over the past five hundred years to alter or to repair its individual parts, on the whole the character of its basic structure remains the same; even the electric lights of evening and night spectacles which have changed the looks of so many historic cities are absent from the walled city of Jerusalem. They have only reappeared on the western side of the city to satisfy the needs of a new tourism, just as the seventh century lights were left on the slope of the Mount of Olives that would lead the pilgrims into the Holy City. Changes in the urban structure of Jerusalem occurred mainly outside the walls, as mostly foreign institutions—schools, hospitals, monasteries, institutes of all sorts, later hotels and administrative buildings—were constructed in the more open and relatively free spaces to the north and west of the city. Small clusters of houses or single estates, usually fairly large ones, appeared there as well and formed the core of what later became villages and eventually were incorporated, not always willingly, into a megalopolis in the making.

What creates the originality, in fact the uniqueness, of Jerusalem is not its late nineteenth and twentieth century growth which it shares with hundreds of other urban centres, but two unique features characterizing the Old City. One is that its present shape was created under the leadership or rule of Muslims over a Roman imperial transformation of an ancient Jewish city. And the other is that its contents were Muslim, Jewish, and Christian in proportions and importance that varied according to the ebb and flow of history and with an increasing presence of secular functions and structures from the middle of the nineteenth century onward. No other holy city in the world is holy, in one way or the other, to three different, if historically and theologically related, systems of faith and practices of belief.

How did it happen? How did the city evolve? By what mechanisms did it endure? I will first sketch what can be reconstructed for the seventh century when the city fell under Muslim rule and then identify some of the primarily Muslim features which affected it over the following fourteen centuries.

Much is still mysterious about how Jerusalem became a Muslim city in or around 637 C.E. and it is unlikely that the truth will ever be known. Actually, what really happened is not as important for an understanding of the city's role in traditional Islamic art than what was imagined. What follows is a reconstruction of events and attitudes as they seem to me to have occurred. The city surrendered by the Greek patriarch Sophronius was a Roman military camp adapted to the ruins of Herodian Jerusalem and transformed into a Christian city after the conversion of Constantine the Great in the first half of the fourth century. Two themes dominated its life and its monuments: the commemoration of a holy history centred primarily on the Passion of Jesus and the expectation of the last day and the arrival of the Kingdom of God on earth. Churches, among which the most important was the complex of the Holy Sepulchre, were dedicated primarily to the life of Jesus, but relics in the treasuries of churches and locally made or locally sold objects of all sorts recalled all scriptural personages from Adam to Christ. Eschatology was mostly evoked through the many cemeteries which adjoined the walled city, and through the holy places on the Mount of Olives celebrating the Ascension of Christ and His eventual return. Jews were officially banned from the city and could only come once a year to lament the destruction of the Temple whose ruins, mixed with whatever was left of a few pagan constructions, occupied a large abandoned space in the southeastern corner of the city.

It was this space loaded with memories and filled with standing or ruined buildings that was taken over by the newly arrived Muslims, perhaps even the caliph ʿUmar himself, as their own restricted place. This space was then called *bayt al-maqdis* ("House of the holy place"), from which eventually came *al-Quds*, "the holy one," as the name of Jerusalem in Arabic. It is only several centuries later, after 1200, that the space acquired its present name of *al-Haram al-Sharif*, "the noble sanctuary." The Muslims prayed there, probably in the southern part of the area, where they soon built a simple hypostyle mosque. Most immigrating Muslim Arabs settled to the south and the west of the Haram area. Some may even have come to live in other parts of the city, for ethnically or religiously defined quarters had not yet appeared in most Near Eastern cities. At some point, probably around 700, two large buildings were built to the south and the southwest of the Haram, whose foundations have been cleared some time in the seventies of the twentieth century. There is much debate around the function of these buildings, which may have been palaces for the caliphs, administrative buildings (the *dar al-ʿimarah* of texts), or settlements for incoming families, or any combination of these functions. Whatever they were, whether they were even completed or not, and whatever the span of time in which they were used, these buildings were within the boundaries of the walled city and in direct contact through a variety of passageways with the Haram.

But what utterly transformed the city's character and gave it its first Islamic complexion was the building of the Dome of the Rock. It was set over a rocky outcropping on the top of what was then known as Mount Moriah. The outcropping, with a partly artificially hewn cavern in it and a neatly cut hole more or less in the centre, had certainly had an earlier religious purpose for which only hypotheses can be provided. Already for several centuries before the Muslim takeover it had been associated by Jewish piety with the destroyed Temple. The new building over the rock was commissioned by the Umayyad caliph ʿAbd al-Malik and either begun or completed in 691 (there is some scholarly debate on how to interpret the date). It consists of a tall cylindrical rotunda covered with a large dome on a high drum and surrounded by an octagonal ring of two ambulatories set on twelve piers and twenty-eight columns. There are four doors into the building, one at each of the cardinal points, and no element of size or decoration privileges one door over the others. The outer walls are quite thin, more like a screen around a restricted place than a load-bearing wall. Above large panels of marble, mosaics used to cover large parts of the outside of the building; they were replaced in the sixteenth century with beautiful Ottoman tiles well restored in the middle of the twentieth century. The interior decoration of the building has been fairly well preserved in its original shape and consisted of large marble panels in the lower part of the walls and a spectacular display of mosaics (some 1200 square metres) on the upper part of the arcades and all over the drum. It is likely that the marble panels were chosen for the quality of the natural designs on them and the mosaics, while using a vocabulary current throughout the Mediterranean Late Antiquity, exhibit many unique features in the choices made and in the manner of their composition.

Several different explanations have been proposed for the construction of the Dome of the Rock. Already in the Middle Ages, some saw it as an attempt by ʿAbd al-Malik to have Jerusalem replace Mecca as the focal point of the *hajj*, the yearly pilgrimage so central to the Muslim faith. It is indeed true that much in the plan and location of the building can be explained by the liturgy of the *tawaf*, circumambulation, so dramatically essential to the practice of the pilgrimage. Then, it was argued in more recent times that it was a monument celebrating the victory of Islam over Christianity in the Christian city *par excellence*; this would have been done through the restoration to holiness of an old Jewish sacred place disregarded by the Christians. The idea was expressed through the representation of Byzantine and Iranian imperial jewellery hung like trophies in the middle of the mosaic vegetation in the octagonal arcade and through the choice for the decoration of the building of many of the Christological passages of the Qur'an ending with an exhortation to the People of the Book, Jews and Christians, to accept the new revelation. Other scholars have taken their cue from the imaginative representation of vegetation on the mosaics and from the inscription on the eastern gate of the building to claim that the building celebrated the forthcoming divine Judgement followed by reward or punishment, for these events to come were always associated with Jerusalem. In popular piety, it is under the small dome located just to the East of the Dome of the Rock and known as the Dome of the Chain that judgements will be meted out to all men and women. The main monument would be like a vision of the mansions described in the Qur'an as located in the eternal garden and, in a way that is totally unique in the history of architecture, it would have been a monument commemorating an event that has not happened yet. It is possible that this vision of the future may have reflected the rich legends associated with the king-prophet Solomon, whose temple and especially palace were thought to have been located in this area. And, finally, it is even possible, on the basis of an early Tradition later rejected by Muslim theologians, that the building commemorates the Rock from which God departed the earth after having created it.

These explanations all fit with memories (location of the temple and of Solomon's palace), events (Ibn al-Zubayr's revolt against the Umayyads and control over Mecca, victory over the great empires of Late Antiquity), and beliefs (eschatology and the immediacy of the end of time), which were current in the late seventh century. The impact of these memories, events, and beliefs slowly faded away and, little by little, a more specifically Muslim holiness took over the Haram and in many ways Jerusalem as a whole. At a lower level, this Muslim holy history brought in stories about Adam, Abraham, Jesus, Zakariyah, and Jacob, even Joseph, and associated them with various places in the city or on the Haram. But the most important and most profound association was with the prophet Muhammad. The Dome of the Rock became the place where he prayed after his Night-Journey (*isra'*) from Mecca and before his Ascension (*mi'raj*) into heaven. The mysterious verse 17:1 from the Scripture which mentions a *masjid al-aqsa* (the "farthest sanctuary") was associated with Jerusalem, the Haram was covered with memorials of various moments in the Prophet's arrival and ascension, and the early congregational mosque became the Aqsa

mosque with, in a mosaic of the early eleventh century, the appropriate
Qur'anic passage reproduced in the centre of the building. The process
by which this new set of associations were made is not well known.
It probably began quite early at a folk level and it became officially
expressed in the transformation of Jerusalem and of the Haram in the
early eleventh century, under the Fatimid dynasty of Egypt. It is during
these ninth through eleventh centuries that the Aqsa Mosque acquired
its largest shape and that holy men and pilgrims came to the city from
all over the Muslim world.

The Haram, not yet called by that name, was the centre of Muslim
Jerusalem, with new colonnades completed on its western and northern
sides, with new gates described by travellers, one of which was even
decorated with mosaics and inscribed with the name of a Fatimid caliph.
The city had shrunk in size, as much of its Byzantine extension to the
south had been abandoned in the early eleventh century, and it acquired
more or less its present dimensions. Unique in the whole world, it was
a holy city for Jews and Christians as well as for Muslims. The latter
controlled it physically, at some point reconstructing a large fortress-
citadel on the city's west side. Occasionally, as during the reign of the
caliph al-Hakim, there were persecutions of Christians and Jews and
the Holy Sepulchre was sacked and partly destroyed. But such instances
were relatively rare and all systems of belief coexisted in what appears
to have been relative harmony, due, for the most part, to a remarkable
ignorance of each other.

It is this relatively peaceful and harmonious city with its holy places
and its pilgrims from everywhere that is described by the Persian Isma'ili
traveller and philosopher Nasir-i Khosro in what is one of the rarest
medieval accounts that can be followed on the ground. Many of its
monuments are still standing and the Jewish accounts from the Geniza
or the Christian accounts by travellers seem to confirm the existence
of a city of three religions that lived independently of each other and
with a minimal number of contacts, but without significant conflicts
most of the time.

In 1099, coming from western Europe, the Crusaders took Jerusalem,
killed or exiled most of its inhabitants, and set up there the capital of
a Latin Kingdom. The kingdom did not last more than a century and
a half, if one counts the decades of symbiotic Christian-Muslim rule,
which followed Saladin's re-conquest of the city in 1183. But its impact
was enormous on the fabric of the city in that it modified the structures
by which the city operated. Much was destroyed, but the great monu-

ments of the Haram were preserved, because of their largely fictional association with the Temple of Solomon and the "Temple of God" to which, in medieval Christian theology, Mary was brought as a child before bringing her own child there and in which Jesus preached later. The Knights Templars were the masters of the Haram and reused its spaces for their purposes. For instance, they used the underground halls at the southern end of the sanctuary as stables and thus gave rise to the identification of these halls as the Stables of Solomon. The church of Ste. Anne in the northeastern sector of the city is the best, much restored, example of these activities. A great deal of the later city was built over the ruins of the immense building programmes of the Crusaders and few parts of the city do not have Romanesque or Gothic fragments embedded in later masonries.

As early as after 1183, but especially after 1260 and the defeat of the Mongol armies coming from the east, the rule of the Mamluks was established over Egypt, Palestine, and Syria and remained until 1517. During these two and a half centuries, Jerusalem became an extraordinary showpiece of late medieval Islamic architecture. The full reasons for this development are not altogether clear. There is no doubt that the wealth of the Mamluk realm was considerable. Cairo, Damascus, Aleppo, and even smaller cities like Hama or Tripoli were covered with new buildings of high architectural quality. It is also true that, away from the tumultuous changes, which characterized the Turco-Iranian world to the north and to the east or the revolutionary changes of Italian and Spanish Mediterranean Europe, the Mamluk world cultivated a highly original political and cultural structure which sponsored a very unique kind of social piety. It was a piety of service, as *madrasahs*, centres for religious learning and for the formation of judicial elites, *khanqahs* or *ribats*, dwelling places for holy men and women, hospitals, schools for children, libraries, public fountains, and so on were endowed by the ruling princes or wealthy members of the ruling class. The ways in which these establishments operated and answered concrete local social needs have not been elucidated so far. It does indeed seem strange that more than fifty such establishments for public welfare and teaching would have been preserved or recorded in a small and politically secondary city like Jerusalem. But, a third reason for the development of a monumental architecture under the Mamluks, Jerusalem fulfilled for the rulers in Cairo, and to a smaller degree for their viceroys in Damascus, a double role. It was a holy city with all the associations made and honed during the first centuries of Muslim rule and it was more accessible than

Mecca and Medina, thus guaranteeing that its monuments were better known and their patrons properly respected. But Jerusalem was also an isolated city without significant economic role which became a city of exile, the place where Mamluks who lost their place at court could be sent away from the power struggles of the capital. By supervising and endowing the building of schools and of other social institutions, they worked in Jerusalem for their faith and could quietly try to rebuild and consolidate their political power elsewhere. The result of this unusual combination favouring architectural investment was a true exhibition of buildings facing the western and northern sides of the Haram, at times moving on to the Haram itself as with the splendid fountain of Qaytbay, or lining up some of the streets leading to the Haram. The most successful of these buildings are the Ashrafiyah Madrasah (1482) facing the Haram, the Tankiziya Madrasah (1328–9) on the main street leading up to the sanctuary, the Khan al-Sultan (1386–7 with many later additions and modifications), the Suq al-Qattanin (market of the Cotton-Merchants) with a splendid monumental portal facing the Haram and dated 1336–7, and then a covered street of shops, two bathing establishments, and a caravanserai, all of which are still there but in poor state of repair. If one adds a number of small Muslim religious quality of buildings scattered in other parts of the city and a restored citadel on the west side which served as the secular anchor of the city counterbalancing the religious Haram al-Sharif (its name was by then fully accepted), it becomes evident that Jerusalem was, within its small space, a sort of miniaturized exemplar of a late Mamluk Islamic city in the Near East. It may have lacked the grand monuments of Cairo, but its compact assemblage of many buildings next to each other, all constructed in beautiful Palestinian stone, illustrates far better the very special formal mix that characterized Mamluk architecture. Elaborate gates, brilliant designs for wall masonries, courtyards with one or more vaulted *iwan*s, domes or half-domes on *muqarnas* squinches, multicoloured *mihrab*s, occasional pendentives, friezes with severe vegetal ornaments, or inscriptions in elegant monumental cursive Arabic writing; nearly all of these features appear on almost all Mamluk buildings. They usually reflect the more creative practices of Cairo or Damascus, but in a quality of execution and with local features that have transformed Jerusalem into a true museum of architecture. One should add that these Mamluk centuries were also important as being the time of self-reflection about the city. Its main religious associations were clearly fixed and the *Uns al-jalil fi ta'rikh al-quds wa al-khalil* by the local learned man

Mujir al-Din is a sort of summary of the holy and secular history and meaning of the city to a pious Sunni Muslim.

And in this deeply Muslim city Christians and Jews had their place. The Holy Sepulchre was in Christian hands, but it was a Muslim who regulated its operation because of the conflicts between Greek and Latin ecclesiastical authorities (essentially Franciscan monks during these centuries) and because of the necessity to incorporate the presence of less numerous and less powerful Christian groups like the Copts, the Armenians, the Syrian monophysites, eventually the Ethiopians, who formed, however, the bulk of the Christian population of the city. On either side of the Holy Sepulchre, there was (and still is) a small mosque whose minaret was built higher than the dome of the Christian sanctuary, thus expressing the Muslim domination of the area. Muslim power was also visible in the ways in which Muslims took over the Christian sanctuary on Mount Zion, which had been rebuilt under the Crusaders. Christian pilgrims during these centuries were mostly from within the Muslim world and there are only a few accounts by westerners describing, at times quite vividly, the difficulties involved in expressing one's faith in Jerusalem. Jews from many different places had by then settled in the southern part of the city around two synagogues and the Jewish mode of worshiping by the western wall of the Haram began to develop its pre-modern forms.

The Mamluk period ended in 1517, when the Ottoman sultans took over Syria, Palestine, the Arabian Peninsula, and Egypt. The most significant urban activity was undertaken by Suleyman the Magnificent (ruled 1520–1566) who, as a new Solomon, lavished particular attention on Jerusalem. The sanctuaries of the Haram were restored, the Dome of the Rock acquired its external cover of brilliantly colourful tiles, the Aqsa mosque was restored several times, and especially the walls of the city were restored to acquire the monumentality they still possess today. Little by little an Ottoman administrative structure was established with its offices scattered around the city and with the introduction of modern institutions like hospices, hostels, and a new commercial centre. Christian communities continued to fight with each other and it took a long time, after a fire, which in 1808 destroyed the dome of the Holy Sepulchre, to develop a system of joint management between sects which could operate with a minimum of confrontations. In the nineteenth century a new Christian presence was established with the growth of Protestant, Catholic, and Orthodox missions associated with secular states. As a result a Lutheran and a Catholic tower rose in the Christian quarter of the city, which were higher than the Muslim minarets that had dominated the early church of the Holy Sepulchre. Jewish settlers also increased in number with Ottoman rule, first migrating into the southern part of the Old City, near the synagogues, later in the nineteenth century moving sometimes to the west of the Old City. There and to the north, a suburban world of settlers, individuals or institutions, began to grow and foreshadow the enormous changes of the twentieth century.

All these changes, whose history is only slowly beginning to emerge, made Jerusalem into an Ottoman city, something quite different from the medieval Muslim city—for it was ruled by a secular authority protecting and maintaining a holy place. But these changes did not affect the physical appearance of the walled city except for the slow deterioration of its architectural fabric.

During the twentieth century, major Islamic monuments like the Dome of the Rock, the Aqsa Mosque, the Ashrafiya, the Khalidi Library, the citadel, and some of the gates to the city were restored and repaired, usually quite successfully. A new mosque was created under the southeastern corner of the Haram, in what used to be known as the Stables of Solomon. This construction has been very much criticized, partly for valid reasons, but it did succeed in meeting the needs of an expanded Muslim community. The Holy Sepulchre is still the scene of conflicts between Christian communities in which local Christian groups are more vocal than they had been for a century or so. A modern and totally rebuilt Jewish quarter in the southern section of the city has incorporated into its fabric the results of major excavations and has succeeded in staying within the aesthetic bounds imposed by the medieval and Ottoman cities. But the southern, western, and northern sides of the city have changed entirely and the image of a walled city on top of natural ridges with which I began this essay is gone forever.

Bibliography

There is a huge bibliography on the history and archaeology of Jerusalem in many languages. For a rapid survey, see the article "al-Kuds," by S. D. Goitein and O. Grabar in *The Encyclopaedia of Islam*. For written sources, the most complete survey of traditional sources is in G. Le Strange, *Palestine under the Moslems* (London, 1980 [repr. Beirut 1965]; New York, 2002). Since then the most important sources are the *fada'il* or "praises": Muhammad b. Ahmad al-Wasiti, *Fada'il al-Bayt al-Muqaddas*, ed. Isaac Hasson (Jerusalem, 1979) and al-Musharraf b. al-Muraja', *Fada'il Bayt al-Muqaddas wa al-Khalil* (Shfaram, 1995). The old classic is Abd al-Rahman al-'Ulaymi known as Mujir al-Din, *al-Uns al-jalil fi ta'rikh al-Quds wa al-Khalil* (latest edition Amman, 1973). All inscriptions are available through Max van Berchem, *Matériaux pour un Corpus Inscriptionum Arabicarum*, 3 vols. (Reprint, Geneva, 2001). Recent surveys of the city's history and monuments with good additional bibliographies are O. Grabar, *The Shape of the Holy* (Princeton, 1996); M. Burgoyne, *Mamluk Jerusalem* (Buckhurst Hill, 1987); S. Auld and R. Hillenbrand, *Ottoman Jerusalem* (London, 2000); A. Elad, *Medieval Jerusalem and Islamic Worship* (Leiden, 1995); A. Kaplony, *The Haram of Jerusalem* (Stuttgart, 2002). See also the series edited by Julian Raby and Jeremy Johns, *Bayt al-Maqdis* (Oxford, 1992 and 1999) and M. Ben-Dov, *Historical Atlas of Jerusalem* (New York, 2002) and the thoughtful article by C. Mekeel-Matteson, "The Meaning of the Dome of the Rock," *The Islamic Quarterly* 43 (1999).

ALEPPO: FROM THE OTTOMAN METROPOLIS TO THE SYRIAN CITY

Jean-Claude David

Aleppo which, following the Muslim conquest, became a "great city" once more, has to this day maintained an upward demographic curve, a few periods of crisis excepted. It remained for almost four centuries within the Ottoman Empire, under a domination at once foreign and close. For a good part of this period it was, with regard to population and economic activity, the third city of the Empire after Istanbul and Cairo. Such continuity doubtless characterizes a metropolis, a city with multiple bents, extended areas of influence, and diverse and complementary territories; one which has not, in consequence, been affected in any lasting or general manner by periodic uncertainty. Its upward curve has been far from undifferentiated; it has rather been sustained by periods of intense activity in the sixteenth and eighteenth centuries, reflected in building work, spatial extension, growing density of the urban fabric, intensification of commercial exchanges, and the accumulation of financial means that also fed the Ottoman tax revenues. At other times, during part of the seventeenth century, for instance, the city passed through crisis: numerous indicators, like activity in establishing great waqfs and constructing "public" monuments, were negative;[1] there was, rather, continued construction of buildings that were more modest and designed especially for the sphere of private activity: large dwelling houses (where it is possible to date these) and textile *qisariyyas*.[2] Even in times of crisis the metropolis continued to

---

[1] André Raymond notes a "significant gap in building during the seventeenth century, with 35 monuments built in the sixteenth century, 39 in the eighteenth and only 21 in the seventeenth, with a total absence of significant building for 45 years between 1602 and 1671." See André Raymond, "Réseaux urbains et mouvements populaires à Alep (fin du XVIIIᵉ–début du XIXᵉ siècles)," *Arab Historical Review for Ottoman Studies* (Zaghouan) 3–4 (1991): 278–79.

[2] The *qisariyyas*, sets of textile workshops arranged over two floors around large court-yards, are numerous in the northern suburbs, former Christian quarters. Curiously, they are often accessible not through the main streets that are a part of the public spaces, but from quarter alleyways, sometimes also, through cul-de-sacs that may give access

develop: André Raymond[3] notes a considerable rise in the seventeenth century population, comparing the consul D'Arvieux's calculation, in 1683, of 13,854 homes (i.e., an estimated 115,000 inhabitants) with 9,049 homes following the 1584 census (i.e., an estimated 75,000 inhabitants). The increase noted over a century is 53%.

Aleppo was an Ottoman city. It had its part in a project for developing the sultan's power, being integrated within a particular model of territorial and political organization. Ottoman centralization was fundamentally different from French monarchical and subsequent Jacobin centralism. Diversity of identities was a constituent element of the Empire: co-existence was on an organized basis, and inclinations to openness and to exchange were generally favoured. The way of life in Aleppo was not so very different from that in Istanbul or Damascus; Istanbul disseminated its influence throughout the Empire, though without seeking uniformity. In addition to the political and military systems that were the practical expression of domination and dependence in the region, there was a common city-dwelling identity which went beyond regional identities, and which was enriched from all the regions. In this context, national identity or identities did not exist, even in embryonic form, before the nineteenth century.

More than Damascus, the old and future capital of Syria, Aleppo was characterized by diversity, by tolerance and by a cross-fertilization of cultures; its inclination to all forms of exchange went beyond that of most other cities in the Empire, and marked out its destiny. Aleppo was the earliest and most extensively used point of passage, the one most subtly invested by the rising western powers in their movement towards the East—well before Beirut or Alexandria. Part of its centre was fashioned to fulfil this role as place of call. Far from the sea, the suq of Aleppo was both port and gateway.

At the end of the Ottoman period, Damascus became the focal point for Syrian national identity, with the birth of a nation state enclosed within narrow borders. Aleppo lost its status of metropolis, which was taken over by Damascus when it became capital.

---

to habitations too. Hence, these activities seem to be linked to the domestic sphere, as though they had preserved something from old localizations within houses.

[3] Raymond, "Réseaux urbains," 279–80.

Following the historical synthesis on Ottoman Aleppo advanced by A. Raymond,[4] published more than ten years ago, the explosion of written sources has taken the predominant form of new commentaries on old knowledge.[5] One of the objectives of this present work is, perhaps, a simple statement about the status of the metropolis of Aleppo, about what gave it this status, and about the material signs and distinguishing spatial marks of this status.

1. *Topography of Aleppo in the Sixteenth Century: The Mamluk Heritage*

At the beginning of the fifteenth century, the commercial routes between Persia and the Mediterranean via the Black Sea, the Taurus, and Lesser Armenia, controlled by the Genoese, were declining in favour of a more southerly route, via Aleppo, that essentially benefited the Venetians. The ships of Venice anchored regularly in the ports of the Syrian coast, and Aleppo became a highly important centre for the trade in silk. Sauvaget explained this flourishing, and all of Aleppo's periods of prosperity, by the Mediterranean trade with Europe, by the role of Aleppo in redistributing western products in the East—Flemish cloths and Italian velvets—and by the "return to Europe, through Tripoli, of bales of cotton and raw silk, and of certain eastern luxury fabrics."[6] Property investment started up once more, with two important foundations to the north of the suqs, each comprising a large khan and sets of shops. A final foundation, comprising a large khan and two suqs, was established just before the Ottoman conquest, by the last Mamluk governor, Kha'irbak. These waqfs of the Mamluk governors were built on a large scale: while lacking the dimensions and complexity of Ottoman foundations, they prefigured these latter.

The spatial development of Aleppo was accompanied by further displacement of activities and services, with a view to facing the growing complexity of the city, the new requirements of the quality of life, and the development of relations between the ruling power and

---

[4] A. Raymond, "Alep à l'époque ottomane (XVIe–XIXe siècles)," in "Alep et la Syrie du Nord," *REMMM* (Aix-en-Provence) 62 (1991).

[5] The research of Bernard Heyberger, generally from the archives of Catholic congregations, is among the most innovative.

[6] J. Sauvaget, *Alep. Essai sur le développement d'une grande ville syrienne, des origines au milieu du XIXe siècle* (Paris, 1941), 165.

society. Sauvaget has expressed the essence of these activities in his historical maps.[7] Between the citadel to the north, the Qinnasrin Gate hippodrome to the south-west, and the Iraq Gate hippodrome to the south-east, were concentrated the places of power. The construction of the Palace of Justice, the main seat of the civil and judicial administration, to the south of the citadel, completed by al-Malik al-Zahir Ghazi at the beginning of the thirteenth century, was a founding act which, over eight centuries, firmly established the importance of the location.[8] The services linked to the Mamluk cavalry were essentially concentrated in the triangle close to the palace and hippodromes to the south of the citadel.

The development of quarters was carried out to the east, beyond the Ayyubid enclosure. The new mosques, where the governors led prayer rather than in the Great Mosque, marked the new space: the mosque of Altunbugha in 1318, of Ashiqtimur in 1374, of Ylbogha al-Nasiri around 1385. In 801/1399, the construction of the mosque of Aqbugha al-Utrush began in front of the Horse Market, not far from the Palace of Justice. Its waqfs included a *qisariyya*, some forty shops in several suqs nearby, the straw merchants' suq, the suq for the makers of packsaddles to the east of the mosque (and also shops in the *Mdineh*, the city's economic heart); the importance of these commercial foundations prefigured urbanization by means of waqf, a system extensively used during the Ottoman period, and also confirmed the value of the site to the south of the citadel. Around 1428, the new surrounding wall to the east was completed: it took in the suburbs to the east of the city. The old wall, on which the old citadel had been set, was torn down. Less than a century before the Ottoman conquest, this particular feature had become established: the city surrounded the citadel on all sides.

Other suburbs developed, notably to the north, outside Bab al-Nasr and Bab al-Faraj; by the end of the Mamluk period, they had become

---

[7] Sauvaget, *Alep.*

[8] The old palace, in a very bad state, was destroyed by the 1822 earthquake and replaced a few years later by a new serail to the north of the citadel, built during the Egyptian occupation, between 1830 and 1840. The latter would, in its turn, be replaced by the serail planned by the Ottoman administration and built under the French Mandate to the south of the citadel in the 1930s. Soon a new administrative building would house the municipal services and the serail (prefecture), in the western extension of the city centre, outside the old quarters.

distinguished by a number of mosques, baths and monumental fountains at the crossings of main streets, thus determining the centres of quarters that would be developed at a later date. In the course of the fifteenth century, Christians who had come out from the city within the walls or immigrants began to develop the quarter that took the name of Judayda, the new, or Saliba, cited by Ibn al-Shihna in 1421, around churches which had no doubt been old monasteries outside the walls. From the beginning, there had been one or two Armenian churches, while Greek Orthodox, Syriac, and Maronite churches, attested during the Ottoman period, were without doubt old, too. These quarters, chiefly inhabited by Christians, were being developed up to the second half of the nineteenth century.

Exchanges with the West, via the Mediterranean, have been regarded as the essential vector of Aleppo's prosperity, but historians have failed to correctly assess the importance of its commerce with its region, with Egypt and the rest of the Middle East, which was certainly very active. We may also note that the city had been developing from the beginning of the fourteenth century, before the change in commercial itineraries pointed out by Sauvaget. The large mosques built by the Mamluk governors stood comparison with those of Ottoman governors, with regard to their dimensions, monumentality, richness of decoration, and beauty of their minarets, but with a different aesthetic. The birth and flourishing of a true Christian quarter, along with other processes of developing the urban space, orientations and new balances, that seem to have characterized the Ottoman city, thus have their origins in the last century of the Mamluk period, but assume their full meaning from the sixteenth century on.

Continuation of Mamluk urban rationales following the Ottoman conquest, 1530–1540

After 1516, the development of places of power and certain services to the south of the citadel continued: the first large Ottoman waqf, that of the governor Khusru Basha, planned by the Sultan's architect Sinan and built between 1537 and 1546, was at the foot of the citadel (there still remains a beautiful mosque, very Ottoman, with its annexes and the Khan al-Shuna). This waqf extended over more than four hectares, gathering around the mosque a *qisariyya* of more than 50 shops (no doubt the Khan al-Shuna), a khan of 95 shops, a substantial suq and numerous other shops. This large-scale establishment, poorly linked to the *Mdineh* suqs and not energized by the old specialized activities of the Mamluk era, was perhaps not profitable on a lasting basis.

The large waqf establishments that succeeded one another throughout the sixteenth century were in the *Mdineh*, the City, near the Great Mosque. They were designed for commercial and craft activities at the service of a city essentially civil, no longer an advanced bastion close to the northern frontier of the Mamluk Empire; a city little motivated by military preoccupations, by cavalry and arms, but rather by trade: the old hippodromes were progressively invaded by urbanization, while the quarters to the south of the citadel fell into decline.[9] This investment activity in the centre contrasted strongly with the former preferences of the Mamluk governors who had long established their waqfs to the south of the citadel. It also stood in opposition to an older rationale, still meaningful in the time of the Ottomans: that of the concentration of commercial activities—khans and suqs—along with services, near the gates of the surrounding wall.

Ottoman re-orientations after 1550: large waqfs and specialized quarters

The demand for space for commercial activities was strong at this time; and three large Ottoman establishments followed that of Khusru Basha to answer this demand. They were aligned to the south of the suqs, from east to west, and occupied a virtual totality of spaces: perhaps old waqfs that had escheated following the Ottoman conquest.[10] Muhammad Basha Duqakin Zada, *wali* of Aleppo from 1551 to 1553 and a relative of the Sultan, ordered the building of a substantial complex around the 'Adiliyya mosque (1555). It comprised four suqs (157 shops) and three large khans. The 1574 waqf of Ibrahim Khan Zada Muhammad Basha comprised the Khan al-Jumruk (0.6 hectares, 129

---

[9] Aleppo served as a base for the Sultan's expeditions to Persia, and, as such, was passed through by armies or even served as a stationing point.

[10] J. Sauvaget and R. Mantran, *Règlements fiscaux ottomans, les provinces syriennes* (1951). On pages 113 and 114, in the part concerning the *vilayet of Aleppo*, there are mentioned, among other taxation areas, those imposed on seven khans and hammams, Mamluk foundations. On p. 114, note 3, the authors submit the following hypothesis: "It is quite probably in respect of its being escheated property that this building, like those mentioned in § 20–23, 35, 39, found itself being the property of the Treasury."

premises), two monumental suqs parallel to the façade of the khan[11] and hundreds of other commercial premises in Aleppo and other parts of the Empire. The last large establishment, further to the west, set up in 1583 by Bahram Basha (governor in 1580) comprised a beautiful mosque, of a style fairly characteristic of Aleppo in its details, a suq and a monumental *qisariyya* (extending over half a hectare with the mosque), and a very large *hammam* in Judayda together with a suq and a *qisariyya*. This large Ottoman foundation, the last in the *Mdineh*, was also the first in a suburb, on the edge of the Christian quarters that were in full spate of development.[12]

During the sixteenth century, further enterprises for laying out space and improving living conditions were undertaken: a functional assemblage designed to take in tanneries (dar Dabbagha), and bringing together premises on two levels with 53 rooms on the ground floor and 58 rooms on the first floor, 170 metres long and 40 metres wide, was built outside the city, in front of the Antioch Gate, near the river Quwayq. It was part of the waqf of Ibrahim Khan Zada Muhammad Basha.[13] These industries, previously located to the north of the Great Mosque, were, thus, set at a distance from the residential quarters. The majority of dyers and coppersmiths also left the city within the walls to settle in the suburbs to the north of Bab al-Nasr. In the seventeenth and eighteenth centuries, *qisariyya*s grouping weaving workshops and other premises for textile activity were established in large numbers in the Christian quarters. The great soap factories, chiefly developed in the eighteenth century and counted by Rousseau at the beginning of the nineteenth (most are still in existence), were often situated within the surrounding wall, near the gates or on the main axes leading to the gates, rather than in the suburbs. These choices of location, subtly differentiated, did not result from any scientific planning. They, nonetheless, applied means of producing space that answered efficiently to the diversity of the city's needs.

If most places of trade were in the suqs and khans of the *Mdineh* in the heart of the city, the suburbs, which more than doubled the

---

[11] 125 elements are cited in the act of foundation, 34 of them in Aleppo (representing 937 premises for commercial and industrial use).

[12] A. Raymond, "Les grands waqfs et l'organisation de l'espace urbain à Alep et au Caire à l'époque ottomane (XVIᵉ–XVIIᵉ siècles)," *BEO* (Damascus) 31 (1979).

[13] A. Raymond, "Le déplacement des tanneries à Alep, au Caire et à Tunis à l'époque ottomane: un indicateur de croissance urbaine," *REMMM* (Aix-en-Provence) 55–56 (1990).

city's surface area during the Ottoman period, were also a place for manufacturing activities, or for premises designed for the storage and commercialization of agricultural and livestock produce. These suburbs received new populations which provided cheap labour or professional skills. They were essential places, marked by diverse activity and heterogeneous population, in accordance with the metropolitan status to which Aleppo laid claim.[14]

The specialized suburbs: consolidation of development in the northern suburbs, Christian and mixed

We might measure the importance of Christian communities by the considerable topographic development of their quarters in the northern suburbs,[15] and notably by the importance of "allotting" operations through the dividing up of space into strips of uniform width, which were then re-divided more or less regularly on a perpendicular basis to produce lots that were generally square. These allocations covered close to 10 hectares in four assemblages.[16] Partially dated by the houses found there (around 1600 for the Wakil house), they may go back to the sixteenth century[17] and may have been progressively inhabited. They were especially inhabited by Christians: Armenians, Maronites, and Melchites.[18] These quasi-allotments, numerous on the peripheries of the northern suburbs, are rare or absent in other suburbs and in the city within the walls.

---

[14] It would be interesting to specify the comparative functions of large suburbs in Aleppo and Damascus. Those of the latter, to the north and mainly to the south, corresponded to various activities, sometimes religious and commercial simultaneously, like the Midan, site for the formation of the Pilgrimage caravan.

[15] A. Raymond, *La ville arabe, Alep, à l'époque ottomane (XVIe–XVIIIe siècles)* (Damascus, 1998).

[16] J.-C. David, "Urbanisation spontanée et planification; le faubourg ancien nord d'Alep (XVe–XVIIIe siècles)," *Les cahiers de la recherche architecturale* 10–11 (1982): 62–73.

[17] According to the Aleppo historian K. al-Ghazzi, the Zuqaq al-Arba'in quarter was founded during the time of Sultan Selim the Conquerer (1512–1520) in order to settle forty Christian families.

[18] It seems that Sultan Murad IV, passing through Aleppo in 1616, authorized the Armenians considerably to enlarge their old cathedral. The dynamism of Christian communities in Aleppo, and the power of the notables and their good relations with the authorities, were also manifested in these enlargements and partial reconstructions of churches.

Other operations may be detected on the peripheries of suburbs: these were the *hawsh* or domestic *qisariyya*s, assemblages of collective dwellings, which also appear to have been planned by an authority. These large courtyards surrounded by dwelling rooms were no doubt designed initially for "single immigrant workers." Many Christians perhaps found their first arrival point in the city in this habitat of the poorest.

The large waqfs as means of producing public space in the Christian quarters

Another measure in the development of these quarters may be found in the activity of establishing waqfs, especially Muslim waqfs, on the edge of majority Christian quarters. The structure of these suburbs, a fanning out of roads exiting from the Bab al-Nasr gate, was consolidated by the founding, around 1490, of a water supply system to service monumental fountains, mosques and baths: the network of public spaces and services characteristic of Muslim space. Christians generally settled in the interstices and in the hearts of blocks, behind the first row of building, and in spaces still barely urbanized further to the west, around churches, and to the east. The position at the heart of blocks, away from public space, was secure and favourable to the discretion recommended to non-Muslims.

The first large Ottoman waqf in the quarter was that of Bahram Basha, mentioned above; founded in 1583, its main part was in the *Mdineh*, but its foundation in Judayda comprised one of the largest *hammam*s of the city. A complement to this first foundation was established in 1653, as a waqf, by the governor Ipshir Basha.[19] A number of eighteenth-century waqfs (Taha Zada, Jabiri, and so on) also comprised establishments in the northern suburb, which were generally suqs and *qisariyya*s, assemblages of weaving workshops and other workshops related to textiles. Taken together, these establishments constituted a genuine centre, with a fountain, a public bath, a very large and very beautiful café, other more modest cafés, hundreds of shops, warehouses, khans for storing food produce and textile fibres, dyeing works, mills, weaving *qisariyya*s, and a very small mosque. Both, powerful symbol and functional option, these waqfs, whose investment properties were

---

[19] Raymond, "Les grands waqfs"; J. C. David (in collaboration with B. Chauffert-Yvart), *Le waqf d'Ipchir Pacha, 1063/1653. Étude d'urbanisme historique* (Institut Français d'Études Arabes de Damas, 1982).

essentially used by the Christians of Aleppo, saw their revenues assigned
to the Holy Places of Mecca and Medina.

Christians had no direct power to produce public spaces; this was a
privilege of Islam in Muslim cities. Nevertheless, the economic weight
of their group and the relations of some of their notables with the
ruling power was manifested in the waqf established for their use.
Even so, the simple search for profitability might justify the implantation of these waqfs close to the Christian quarters, with their young,
productive and dynamically consuming society.[20] The prosperity of the
Christians was also reflected in the building of hundreds of houses in
the seventeenth and eighteenth centuries, relatively small, but accomplished in a single wave by the newly rich; luxurious and comfortable,
and more practical than old houses of Muslim families, which were
so huge and disparate.

*Development of the eastern suburbs, Bab al-Nayrab and Banqusa: the urban
space of "non-city-dwellers"*

One of the characteristics common to the cities in the interior of
Syria—Aleppo, Homs, and Hama[21]—was the existence of complex
quarters, developed by "non-city-dwellers" and generally located to the
east of cities, directly linked to the tracks of the steppe and the deserts.
In Hama, this quarter is, to this day, called *Hadir*, a term designating
the camp of nomads, a place of settlement fixed but not necessarily
permanent. Quarters of contact with the rural world, these also received
in the Ottoman era Turkmen, Kurds, janissaries, and so on. It was,
thus, a mixture or a juxtaposition of heterogeneous elements.

At the end of the eighteenth century, the corps of janissaries, originally defined by a military function, seems to have constituted a group
of around ten thousand individuals in Aleppo. Historians of this period
agree in considering their recruitment to have been mainly from among
populations of non-Arab immigrants, Bedouins, and peasants within
the city. "These were recently settled populations... relatively poor, and

---

[20] J.-C. David, "L'espace des chrétiens à Alep. Ségrégation et mixité; stratégies
communautaires (1750–1950)," in "Villes au Levant," *REMMM* (Aix-en-Provence)
55–56 (1990).
[21] The suburb of Midan in Damascus, a suburb of "rural folk" within the city,
was different from those of other cities, less marked perhaps by the intensification of
populations of Bedouin origin, nomads who had become sedentary.

who might be attracted by the possibilities provided by military service as a means of existence and as a means of social rise."[22] Belonging to a janissary group might in fact appear as a means of changing status and integrating better within the city.[23] The janissaries maintained close links with their groups of origin, with the tribes and their hierarchies, with professions: as such, they were relatively structured and capable of producing leaders—notables chosen, often, not from the military hierarchy but rather from the tribal hierarchies.[24] In periods of unrest in the nineteenth century, certain personages originating from these quarters, and claiming to be from the janissary group, played a role that went beyond their group. They worked together with the central power or rose against it, in the context of temporary alliances with other groups, notably the Sharifs. These alliances were sometimes effective, but they remained unstable and circumstantial.[25] The very strong anchoring of these powers within a space and within a group was doubtless one cause of their inability to combine with others on a lasting basis, so as to engender city-dwelling powers.

Investment in property and waqfs in the eastern suburbs: mobilization of local resources

The oldest parts of these quarters contained houses dating back to the beginning of the Ottoman period, their typology was eminently that of city-dwellers. On average, however, the habitat was poorer than in most other quarters.[26] The map showing the respective prices of houses

---

[22] Raymond, "Réseaux urbains," p. 99.

[23] The janissary quarters were in the richest part of these suburbs, the most open to the city thanks to the diversity of their activities and facilities. The Banqusa axis, where they gathered more than elsewhere, was also characterized by the existence of some waqf assets linked to the great foundations of notables in the eighteenth century. The quarters to the two sides of this axis in the eastern suburbs were the only ones to have Christian populations (dispersed) in the eighteenth and up to the end of the nineteenth century.

[24] J. C. David, "Les territoires des groupes à Alep à l'époque ottomane. Cohésion urbaine et formes d'exclusion," in "Biens communs, patrimoine collectif et gestion communautaire dans les sociétés musulmanes," *REMMM* (Aix-en-Provence) 79–80 (1996).

[25] The powers able to emerge in the eastern quarters of Aleppo were also founded on exterior groups: in 1850, rioters from the eastern quarters sought help from villagers and tribes when the situation turned to their disadvantage.

[26] As in other quarters, this habitat was socially contrasted, with houses sometimes quite extensive, and capable of having a monumental *iwan*. No *qa'a* with a cruciform

in the middle of the eighteenth century, prepared by A. Marcus[27] from judicial court registers, confirms the architectural indices.

The margins to the north of Banqusa were noteworthy for the considerable predominance of the *hawsh*, a popular collective habitat, specifically a group of ten or so large courtyards (each, on average, 50 metres × 25 metres) covering in all close to a hectare and a half.[28] We may detect other, smaller *hawsh* in a number of the quarters in this zone. The habitat in the outermost peripheries, notably the al-Safa quarter to the north (doubtless developed in the nineteenth century), was formed of large irregular courtyards surrounded by dwelling rooms and buildings for agricultural or pastoral use. To the east of Bab Nayrab, the diversity of habitat was also marked: small individual houses without courtyards in the quarter of the *qurbat* (gypsies), doubtless built at the beginning of the nineteenth century, houses with large courtyards belonging to the people of Sukhna and other semi-rural quarters; *hawsh* of small dimensions; large enclosures of rural usage; a habitat more typical of city-dwelling—of craftsmen and traders but also of notables, often dating back to rebuilding carried out at the end of the nineteenth century and the beginning of the twentieth.[29]

Apart from a certain poverty of habitat, and, sometimes, a markedly rural character, these suburbs were characterized by relative scarcity of collective facilities. The *hammams*, instead of being spread around the quarters, were especially located near the gates of the surrounding wall, notably Bab al-Hadid, where there were three large baths.[30] The number of fountains and other facilities, small mosques, *zawiya*s, etc.,

---

plan—a space characteristic of the richest houses from the sixteenth to the eighteenth centuries—has yet been noted there.

[27] A. Marcus, *The Middle East on the Eve of Modernity: Aleppo in the Eighteenth Century* (New York: Columbia U.P., 1989), figure 9.1.

[28] The *hawsh*, which were built in regular parcels, seem to have resulted from a concerted intervention, private or public. It is difficult to date them since their architectural content has been profoundly modified. It is probable, though, that they were built in the eighteenth century. They were re-divided at a later date and transformed into a family habitat of small dimensions, with a private courtyard, which set, in the centre of the old courtyard, an irregular collective space containing the well.

[29] These quarters were largely destroyed by urbanism operations in the years 1980–1982.

[30] The northern suburbs contained seven baths, far better distributed within the space. The lack of collective facilities in the eastern districts would be corrected, belatedly, by the building of new baths around 1900. See J.-C. David and D. Hubert, "Le dépérissement du hammam dans la ville: le cas d'Alep," *Les cahiers de la recherche architecturale* 10–11 (1982): 62–73.

dating back to the Mamluk era or to the beginning of the Ottoman era, was lower than for the quarters within the walls, and the network of water channels was less dense, comparable to that of the peripheral quarters of the northern suburb.

If waqf properties were important in these suburbs, the share of the large waqfs of the sixteenth- and seventeenth-century governors was zero—in contrast to the situation in the Christian suburbs. The waqfs of notables in the eighteenth century concerned few quarters: in the 1763 waqf of al-Hajj Musa al-Amiri, out of a total of 136 properties just 3 (a shop and two dye works) were located in the north-eastern suburb, and none in the rest of the eastern suburbs, while some 35 properties were located in the northern suburbs.[31] Some property from the Ahmad Pasha Taha Zada waqf (1753–1765)—shops, café, *qisariyya*, oven, houses, and so on—was located on the principal axis of Banqusa and close by.

Diversity of community, social marginality, the importance of local power, the mode of production and original characters of the urban space—all these expressed a strong deficit vis-à-vis city-dwelling, or rather, perhaps, city-dwelling of a specific kind. The marginality of the eastern suburbs was a concrete expression of the lack of interest taken by city-dwelling notables and of the existence of a category of notables distinctive to these suburbs. If there was a certain social and spatial mobility between these suburbs and the quarters within the walls, it is difficult to measure and designate. In the eighteenth century, Aleppo notables, especially the learned and the merchants, often said they were originally from other cities in Syria, in Iraq (especially Basra, Baghdad, and Mosul), in Anatolia, Egypt, the Maghreb—not from the popular quarters of Aleppo and still less from its suburbs. Most claimed to have been notables already in their city of origin.[32]

Like other "city-dwellers," the inhabitants of the eastern suburbs of Aleppo had a remarkable aptitude for maintaining relations with the world outside, but, in contrast to other groups—which belonged, at one and the same time, to a city, and more broadly to the world of city-dwelling, and to all the cities of Islam—the openness to the outside world of the inhabitants of these suburbs was a corollary of their

---

[31] J. Tate, *Une waqfiyya du XVIIIe siècle à Alep* (Damascus, 1990), p. 83 ff.
[32] M. L. Meriwether, *The Notable Families of Aleppo, 1770–1830: Networks and Social Structures*, thesis (University of Pennsylvania, 1981; U.M.I., printed 1988).

weak integration with the city, given that their outside anchorage was essentially non-urban. The majority preserved a double adherence: on the one hand adherence to their origin, generally tribal, and, on the other, a wish to integrate with the city.

2. *Domestic Spaces and Quarters:*
Familial Proximity, Social Hierarchies of Space

Domestic architecture evolved not simply to adapt to fashion, but rather in response to evolution in the way of life, in power relationships between groups, in family strategies, and in the way these became inscribed within space.

Local or regional dynamics, whose scope needs to be specified, may explain a certain independence vis-à-vis cultural and artistic currents, and political and social currents, disseminated from the centre. Cairo had very little influence on Mamluk Aleppo, though it influenced Damascus a great deal more, while Istanbul had relatively little influence on Ottoman Aleppo and Damascus. Certain mosques and other architectural features provide an exception.

New domestic architecture and the evolution of society

The average surface area of habitations decreased between the sixteenth and the end of the eighteenth century: the almost constant increase in population during this period[33] was absorbed at once by spatial development and densification. Architectural or legal sources (records of court acts), especially for the seventeenth and eighteenth centuries, mention numerous cases of sub-division, with or without rebuilding, following inheritance.[34]

From the sixteenth century on, rooms were spread systematically around an enclosed courtyard, rather than being organized in pavilions, in an open garden, in the way once preferred for palaces. Texts and architectural testimonies from the Mamluk era, and from the beginning of the Ottoman era, imply that some palaces continued with this

---

[33] A. Raymond, "The Population of Aleppo in the Sixteenth and Seventeenth Centuries according to Ottoman Census Documents," *IJMES* 16 (1984).

[34] A. Abdel Nour, *Introduction à l'histoire urbaine de la Syrie ottomane* (Beirut, 1982).

very flexible organization, combining large rooms with a centred plan (*qaʿas*), *iwans* and pools, and service rooms, in an enclosed garden.[35] The Janbulad palace, built in Aleppo in the sixteenth century on the remains of Mamluk palaces, and the Azem palace built in Damascus in the eighteenth century, doubtless on the site of far older palaces, both in quarters within the walls near the centre, clearly reproduce this idea of pavilions within a garden, evolving incompletely towards an organization around a number of courtyards, or subtly combining the two systems.

Another, very different organization of space coexisted with the pavilion system in the Mamluk era, for the palaces of emirs in Aleppo and Damascus. This arrangement, no doubt relatively exceptional for Syria, seems to have been inspired by forms and practices omnipresent in Mamluk Cairo. Dwelling rooms were elevated above a ground floor for services and especially for stables; some Cairo houses might be developed on more than two levels. The geometric and functional relation underlined in Aleppo and in Ottoman Syria, through the north-south axis formed by the succession of *iwan*-pool-mass of vegetation, could not be established within these palaces.[36] Such an organization was doubtless a response to the considerable importance of Mamluk cavalry as a base for power, and to the consequent presence of numerous horses and stables in urban palaces.[37] The Ottoman army was indeed no stranger to cavalry: horses did not disappear from the city, but their presence became more discreet.

In the majority of houses, excepting only the most modest, these two systems were replaced by a new, dominant combination, based on the pre-eminence of the *iwan*, a spatial and symbolic central place, the heart of a north-south axis organizing the yard. In this minimal space,

---

[35] J.-C. David, "L'espace des chrétiens"; idem, "Une grande maison de la fin du XVIᵉᵐᵉ siècle à Alep," *BEO* (Damascus) 50 (1998).

[36] There is only one example known of a monumental *qaʿa* in Aleppo built in the Ottoman period, no doubt at the beginning of the seventeenth century, on a substantial subfoundation designed for domestic services, especially kitchen and annexes, but not for stables as in Cairo or in the palaces of the Mamluk emirs. It is to be found in the Maʿarrawi house in the Bab Qinnasrin quarter.

[37] J.-C. Garcin underlines the change in domestic architectural forms in Cairo linked to the change in power and society with the fall of the Mamluks and the installation of Ottoman power. This change is manifested in a far more considerable development of spaces at ground level. See J.-C. Garcin, *Palais et maisons du Caire. L'Époque mamelouke, XIIIᵉ–XVᵉ siècles* [collective work] (Paris: CNRS, 1982), 146–216, especially pp. 214–215.

vegetation and water were reduced to an almost symbolic existence. The four sides of the courtyard were rarely all occupied by rooms. The façades, built in different eras, were rarely homogeneous; this was a house evolving and adapting to the needs of families.

The palace (serail, *qunaq*), the place of the ruling power, was a familial space, something not peculiar to the Arab-Muslim and eastern cultural context: palaces and chateaux of the same period in France were also domestic spaces. Architectural solutions and practices permitted this co-existence of public and domestic functions to be manageable: large houses always comprised a more developed part for the family and reception spaces whose development was proportional to the importance of the public function undertaken by the master of the house. The house with two courtyards, haremlik and selamlik, *juwwani* and *barrani*, was a circumstantial adaptation rather than the product of a preliminary conception and a preconceived plan.

Waqfs and familial spaces: the notables mark out their territory

Important personages of the eighteenth century, no doubt the richest of their time, such as Hajj Musa al-Amiri, Ahmad Basha Taha Zada, and 'Uthman Basha, are well known.[38] Their property and their foundations in waqf are largely preserved. Their houses corresponded to the type developed over the two previous centuries, but took on a "bourgeois" character: one is struck by their relative modesty, lack of elevation, reduced dimensions for the *iwan*, absence of the T-shaped *qa'a*, the generalization of smaller, more intimate rectangular rooms, richly decorated with painted panels and with coloured marble in the *'ataba*—a kind of threshold inside a room, determined by a difference in level of some forty centimetres. Houses built by Christians during the same period were also characterized by reduced dimensions, by richness of decoration, and by their comfort. Small private *hammam*s appeared. Water reservoirs, sinks, and kitchens were generalized. It would seem that some elements, such as the typical arcature windows of consular habitations in the khans, were borrowed from western architecture.

Hajj Musa al-Amiri, Ahmad Basha Taha Zada, 'Uthman Basha were large urban proprietors and landowners and could carry out official functions or commercial activities. They founded considerable waqfs,

---

[38] Tate, *Une waqfiyya*; Meriwether, *Notable Families*; Marcus, *Middle East*.

very different from those built by governors two centuries before, closely bound up with their domestic space, near their familial space, which was also the place where they exercised their power. All three built assemblages over a surface area comparable to that of the large waqfs of the governors, but less monumental. They combined quarter, local, and family rationales with economic rationales and the requirements of profitability. The investors of the Amiri family and its entourage were essentially located in the Suwayqat ʿAli, in the *Mdineh* and in the northern suburbs, three anchors of economic activity, power networks and familial strategies.[39]

New social hierarchy in the quarters

Contrasted social hierarchies marked the urban space, something quite different from the classic organization based on the dependence relation between a patron on the one hand and clients on the other, within a single neighbourhood, or a hierarchy within a family or tribe, as was doubtless the case during earlier periods or elsewhere. Some of the names of streets and central quarters, cited by Ibn al-ʿAjami or Ibn al-Shihna, and of architectural vestiges, pointed to a spread of emirs' palaces through all the quarters within the walls, including the *Mdineh*, with more modest houses close by. In the Ottoman period, some palaces of notables remained dispersed (Kawakibi in Jallum, Ghouri near Kaltawiyya, etc.), but those of the new notables were concentrated in quarters near the places of power and economic activity. The organization that imposed itself in the Ottoman city was founded on an assembly of the richest close to the centre and the thrusting out of the poor to the peripheries.[40] At the turn of the nineteenth century, according to M. L. Meriwether[41] on the basis of judicial court registers, the 30 notable families located there lived in only 16 of the city's 104 quarters; 75% of them lived in 7 of these quarters, of which 6 were located to the north of the suqs and the Great Mosque.

Rich Christian families lived in the Christian suburbs, which showed a similar scheme: generally, the houses of notables were near

---

[39] J.-C. David (in collaboration with F. Baker, T. Grandin, M. Hreitani), *La Suwayqat ʿAli à Alep* (Publication de l'Institut Français d'Études Arabes de Damas, 1998).
[40] J.-C. David, "Alep, dégradations et tentatives actuelles de réadaptation des structures urbaines traditionnelles," *BEO* (Damascus) 28 (1977).
[41] Meriwether, *Notable Families*.

churches, while the collective habitats of poorer people were on the peripheries.

The marginalization of certain groups—non-city-dwellers living in the city, rural people, people from tribes, janissaries, soldiers outside barracks, and single immigrants—has already been mentioned. They lived in the suburbs to the east and north-east where were also found those professional activities that were more or less despised: those related to the rural world, those having to do with animals, along with services for the organization and equipment of caravans.

For other excluded people of a particular type—western strangers not permitted to live within the quarters, consuls, European merchants, missionaries—a solution was contrived especially in Aleppo: namely, their grouping within the khans, along with any kind of merchandise.

3. *The Presence of Westerners and the Involvement of Local Groups: The 1850 Riots*

Consuls, missionaries and Aleppo Catholics

The nineteenth century was marked by the growing rise of the West vis-à-vis the Near East, which accompanied the rise of nationalisms within the Ottoman Empire and was cemented by colonial ascendancies. The presence of westerners was nothing new: commercial relations and the protection of eastern Christians had since the Middle Ages legitimized the permanent presence of Venetians, Genoese, then of French, British, and Flemish, especially in Aleppo. Commercial exchanges between Aleppo and France had been one of the main vectors of western presence in the region.

The activity of consuls and missionaries in Aleppo is known from the studies of Sauvaget. B. Heyberger has studied the process and consequences of Catholic proselytism in Aleppo, especially in connection with the reports and couriers sent by religious officials to their superiors and with other archive documents of congregations.[42] The dates and

---

[42] B. Heyberger, especially: "Les chrétiens d'Alep à travers les récits des conversions des missionnaires carmes déchaux (1657–1681), *Mélanges de l'École française de Rome* (Rome) 100 (1988); "Un nouveau modèle de conscience individuelle et de comportement social: les confréries d'Alep (XVIIIe–XIXe siècles)," in *Actes du premier symposium syro-arabicum*, Kaslik, September 1995, *Paroles de l'Orient* 21 (1996); "Réforme catholique

places of implantation of the different missionary orders in Aleppo are well known, as are the behaviour of Christians and the way their thinking developed. The Franciscans had had a permanent mission in Aleppo since 1560, and the Jesuits came in 1627. Other orders had also missions in Aleppo: Capuchins, Carmelites, etc. Likewise well known are the controversies, underlined by Sauvaget, between the Ottoman administration and Aleppo Christians, especially women attracted by the activities of missionaries who went to the chapels and monasteries in the khans of the *Mdineh*. The impetus of conversion was irresistible, despite the opposition of eastern hierarchies, the Ottoman administration, and sometimes consuls.[43] Members of the Catholic communities often became clients, employees, co-workers, and privileged associates of westerners, especially of the French.[44] Even before the end of the seventeenth century, the Franciscans and Jesuits had won an important section of the "Syrians" (Jacobites), Armenians, and Greeks over to Catholicism.[45] The conversion of the Jacobites was the work of the French consul, François Picquet.[46] The official act of conversion to Catholicism of the Armenian Patriarch goes back to 29 May 1690. The political and commercial importance of this religious act is clearly evident, since, for the occasion, the Patriarch addressed a letter to the King of France, Louis XIV. The 1724 schism marked the "return" of the majority of "Greeks" to Catholicism.

By the beginning of the nineteenth century, Christians allied to Rome had become a very substantial majority among the Christian population in Aleppo. Conflicts, often violent, between the new communities and the old (the only ones recognized by the Ottoman administration) disrupted established balances, especially those defining the status and space of Christians who were protected in a Muslim city. Among the Catholic majority were the most powerful Christian families of Aleppo.

---

et union des Églises orientales (XVIe–XVIIIe siècles)," *Homo religiosus. Autour de Jean Delumeau* (Paris, 1997).

[43] "The consuls protested constantly against the imprudences of the religious...In 1732, the consul left the Franciscan church, on the Day of Corpus Christi, so great was the number of Syrian women admitted to the service, despite the orders of the pasha." Sauvaget, *Alep*, note 778.

[44] The Jews also played this role. Hence, in 1660, the first dragoman of the French consulate was a Jew. (According to D'Arvieux, quoted by Sauvaget, *Alep*, note 763.)

[45] Sauvaget, *Alep*, 207–208.

[46] François Picquet had done as much for the conversion of eastern Christians to Catholicism as he did for the development of French trade, before continuing with his apostolate as Bishop of Babylon.

Some aspects of the ways of life involved showed that this conversion to Catholicism was far from constituting westernization, and that there was no profound development in ways of thinking.

The 1850 riots: were the Christians scapegoats?

Urban riots broke out in Aleppo throughout the Ottoman period. In the second half of the eighteenth century, popular uprisings expressed oppositions unable to translate themselves into effective power. Janissaries and Sharifs were the main actors.[47] During the first decades of the nineteenth century, unrest became less frequent and more profound, longer and more murderous, and did not essentially target the Ottoman authorities.

The occupation of Syria and Palestine by Ibrahim Pasha, son of the Viceroy of Egypt, which lasted for about ten years, marks the period in question: it was between 1830 and 1840, under Egyptian rule, attracted by modernism and profoundly marked by the West, that the first administrative reforms were attempted and applied, with conscription and the levying of new taxes, while new places of power were established: a "modern" serail to the north of the citadel, where the governor lived and exercised his functions, a large barracks on a height outside the city, clearly designed to control more than defend it. During the same period, the authorities recognized Catholic bishops as representatives of their communities and allowed them to build and rebuild their churches; this allowed Catholic communities to raise extensive and wealthy places of worship.

The 1850 riots began in the eastern suburbs, in the quarters of former janissaries, members of certain tribes, and those close to the rural world. Rioters reached the centre and the places of power, looked for interlocutors to voice their grievances, and tried to make contact with the governor, who slipped away. After roaming the city and its suburbs, the rioters entered the Christian quarters, looted houses, destroyed what property they could not carry away with them, and looted and burned churches. The number of fatalities was limited to a few. Jews were not troubled, nor were those Christians who found protection amongst

---

[47] Raymond, "Réseaux urbains," 93–104; J. P. Thieck, "Décentralisation ottomane et affirmation urbaine à Alep," *Mouvements communautaires et espaces urbains au Machreq* (Beirut, 1985).

their Muslim neighbours. After several days of riots, the Ottoman authorities gained control of the situation: the rioters were thrust back to their quarters or outside the city, repression was violent and resulted in numerous deaths among the insurgents. Christians were to receive indemnities for the damages incurred; the churches were to be rebuilt on a more monumental scale...

The events of 1850 were a popular reaction incited by ringleaders; the weakening or disappearance of the janissaries and the suppression of the system of corporations, two pillars in the organization of society, had doubtless led to a diffused discontent that was reflected in the refusal to accept conscription and direct taxation, modernist reforms inspired by the West. The citizens of Aleppo rose against a set of measures taken by the state to redefine its relations with the population, at the expense of traditional intermediary groups.[48]

Resentment against the Christians was also linked to the enrichment and arrogance of some of these. Chroniclers of the 1850 events tell of the hatred felt by rioters for the Catholic Greek Patriarch Maximos Mazloum. The cathedral of the Catholic Greeks, and that of the Catholic Syriacs, were more systematically looted, while the Armenian churches were not touched. However, the episcopal palace of the Orthodox Greeks was burned down.[49] For all that, the attack on Christians was surprisingly controlled: systematic looting and violence, with no intention to harm human life.

The European omnipresence was noteworthy; consuls and foreigners, settled in the khans of the *Mdineh*, were not, it seems, threatened by the rioters. The suqs were not looted, and most events took place in the suburbs. Rich Christians, some bishops and their entourages, and a portion of the Christian population, took refuge in the khans with the consuls, especially Edmond De Lesseps. There, too, some of the leaders of the riot would seek protection when the time of reprisal came.

The British consul Barker regarded victory for the Ottoman forces as certain, thanks to the new cannons provided by the British and the military assistance of refugee Hungarian and Polish officers who

---

[48] M. Ma'oz, "Syrian Urban Politics in the Tanzimat. Period between 1840 and 1861," *Bulletin of Oriental and African Studies* 29, no. 2 (1966); B. Masters, "The 1850 events of Aleppo: an Aftershock of Syria's Incorporation into the Capitalist World System," *IJMES* (Cambridge U.P.) 22, no. 1 (1990).

[49] Rioters demanded that Christians should not have Muslim servants or slaves, and that they should be subject to distinctive marks on their clothing.

were commanding the Ottoman troops. There seemed to be intense diplomatic activity, and the combined swiftness and effectiveness of Istanbul's reaction was certainly a consequence of the pressure exerted by the Great Powers: the Sultan sent to Aleppo a governor favourable to the Christians.

The Ottoman State, even though playing a multiple game, seemed to have come down on the side of the Christians and the Great Powers. This open or underlying presence of Europeans protecting Christians was one of the causes of the conflict before it was one of the factors for resolving it.

The Christians played an important role in Aleppo, one tightly defined and controlled, with commerce and crafts generally flourishing, thus, allowing their communities to function in a balanced way, between notables, merchants, financiers, and a large population of workers, traders and craftsmen, the last especially in textiles. After a short period at the outset of the nineteenth century, when dynamism was maintained thanks largely to the Ottoman internal market,[50] commercial trends began to reverse, and exports from Aleppo to the West, still in surplus at the beginning of the century, began to show a deficit. Christians already working with western merchants became their privileged intermediaries on the spot, and their representatives, redistributing, throughout the eastern part of the Ottoman Empire—including Cairo where Syrian Christians were numerous—products imported from the West. In this context, local Christians might be considered by their Muslim counterparts as having chosen the side of foreigners against that of their closest relatives. The wealth of their community, manifested in sumptuous public processions, like the one that marked the arrival of Maximos Mazloum in Aleppo, might be regarded as an insult to the poverty and precarious daily life of the majority of the population, including some Christians. By their refusal to pay tribute to the rioters they became the objective allies of the Ottoman power and hence jointly responsible for unacceptable changes. Present on the spot and socially close by virtue of their way of life and thought, they were the ideal victims for a kind of insurrection that was traditional in its form, but new in its object and scale. Were they not, above all,

---

[50] Eugen Wirth, "Alep dans la première moitié du XIXe siècle. Un exemple de stabilité et de dynamique dans l'économie ottomane tardive," in "Alep et la Syrie du Nord," *REMMM* (Aix-en-Provence) 62 (1991).

scapegoats, through whom the rioters were stigmatizing the Ottoman power, vector of change and modernization, along with the interests of the westerners instigating these changes? It was easier to attack Christians than to attack, directly, the real presence of the West, in the consulates and monasteries grouped in the khans of the *Mdineh*.

Was the westernization of Christians, propounded by Bruce Masters,[51] not superficial? In the context of an economic situation still negative in Aleppo in 1850, and an accelerated climate of development in Beirut, Syrian Catholics, especially from Aleppo, emigrated in large numbers. The role of citadel for Catholicism in the Middle East tended to switch from Aleppo to Lebanon, where there were seminaries, schools, monasteries, and so on. Different groups of the Christian population of Aleppo were differently affected by modernization; if the notables were attracted by western ways regarding entertainment, leisure, and furniture, that concerned only a very small number of individuals, and such passing fancies did not deeply impact their traditional practices. Other Christians were more affected by the activities of religious institutions, the influence of fraternities, third orders, charitable organizations—institutions more akin to Muslim fraternities in their impact on popular circles. Books, pious images, supports for private devotions, were disseminated from Europe. The first printing press in the Arab world was set up in Aleppo in 1706 for the Greek Catholics. Manifestations of mysticism, the cult of the Sacred Heart, chapels, etc., spread. The tragic episode of the mystic Hindiyya was significant:[52] When still being in Aleppo, Hindiyya 'Ujaymi, member of a family of Christian notables close to ecclesiastical circles, underwent the ferments of mental transformation that led her to mysticism. A while later, 1746 in the Lebanese mountains at Antoura and 1750 at the Bkerke convent, she became mother superior, and it was there that female religionists from Aleppo and from the Lebanese mountains—Melchites and Maronites, protégés of the Jesuits and of the Maronite Episcopate—confronted each another. These confrontations indicated very strongly the disagreements and incompatibilities between western Catholicism and eastern Catholic Christianity.

---

[51] Masters, "The 1850 Events."
[52] B. Heyberger, *Hindiyya Mystique et criminelle 1720–1798* (Paris, 2001).

4. Conclusion: 1868, New Urban Forms, New Territories, New Society

Perhaps Muslims sought the wrong target when they attacked the Christians in 1850. They were attacking the symbol more than the reality; but the Christians, in explicitly rejecting certain tokens bound up with Ottoman principles and mechanisms for the co-habitation of communities, were one step ahead in the ongoing process of modernization.

In 1868, a governorate of the desert was created, joining, in 1870, with that of Deir-al-Zor to constitute a sanjak comprising the totality of the Syrian valley of the Euphrates, the Djezire, and the north of the Syrian desert. When security was provided, it was possible to move between Aleppo and Baghdad by the road along the right bank. The permanent settlement of nomads grew apace, and with it the cultivation of land. The Aleppo notables began to invest in these regions with a view to establishing a more modern, speculative, exporting agriculture based on cotton and cereals. The new Aleppo spaces spread progressively towards the Euphrates and the Djezire.[53]

Between 1900 and 1910, roads were built and coaches, replacing caravans, moved between Aleppo and Baghdad towards Urfa and Mosul. The main markets of Aleppo remained those of a broad region integrated within the eastern knot of the Ottoman Empire, with Central and Eastern Anatolia to the north, Mosul and Baghdad to the east, and Egypt to the south. The continental polarization of the city's activities was confirmed.

The rail link between Aleppo and Beirut dates from 1906. Alexandretta, the traditional outlet for Aleppo on the Mediterranean, did not become accessible by rail until 1914. Aleppo traffic was very swiftly oriented towards Beirut,[54] a well-equipped and dynamic port, and this led to a decrease in the tonnage embarked and disembarked in Alexandretta between 1906 and the war. Northern Syria, around Aleppo, began to be integrated within a Syro-Lebanese rationale and consolidated its links between Damascus and Beirut. It was no longer a matter of access to a Mediterranean port but of far more fundamental regional choices.

---

[53] J.-C. David, "Bab al-Faraj à Alep: un nouveau *centre-ville* pour de nouveaux territoires extérieurs, pour une nouvelle société?" *Cahiers de Recherche GREMMO Monde arabe contemporain* (Lyon) 5 (1996).

[54] Despite some technical inconveniences, and moving from the normal roadway to metric gauge track for the stage from Rayak to Beirut.

1868 was also the year a municipal organism was created in Aleppo, within the framework of a general re-organization of the Ottoman administration. It marked the start of the construction of the first "modern" quarter, Aziziye, with orthogonal regular roadways and large houses without central courtyards, open to the exterior, essentially built by Christian notables. A little later, other quarters would be built by Muslims and Jews. Economic prosperity, affecting a broader society, favoured modernization, at least in some circles.

A new city centre began to be developed from 1882, answering to the needs of services and of space for new means of transportation, new travellers, and new regional links. Aleppo regained prosperity and a new function, that of regional capital, of centre for the re-organization of part of the Ottoman territory—a function that prepared it for withdrawal. It was the moment when the first sketches were made for a territorial organization that would eventually lead to the formation of Syria. The last decades of the Ottoman period saw the establishment of mechanisms, spaces, and services, to which the French Mandate would add little.[55] Christians played their part in nationalist struggles and in the construction of a Syrian society in which non-Muslims were full citizens and no longer only the protégés of Islam; it was in this way that the role of communities became an issue.

Bibliography

A. Abdel Nour, *Introduction à l'histoire urbaine de la Syrie ottomane* (Beirut, 1982).
J. G. Barbié du Bocage, "Description de la ville de Hhaleb," in *Recueil de Voyages et de Mémoires*, Société de Géographie, vol. 2 (Paris, 1825).
H. Bodman, *Political Factions in Aleppo, 1760–1826* (Chapel Hill, 1963).
J. Cornand, "L'artisanat du textile à Alep," *BEO* (Damascus) 36 (1984).
J.-C. David, "Alep, dégradations et tentatives actuelles de réadaptation des structures urbaines traditionnelles," *BEO* (Damascus) 28 (1977).
———, "Urbanisation spontanée et planification; le faubourg ancien nord d'Alep (XVᵉ–XVIIIᵉ siècles)," *Les cahiers de la recherche architecturale* 10–11 (1982).
——— (in collaboration with D. Hubert), "Le dépérissement du hammam dans la ville: le cas d'Alep," *Les cahiers de la recherche architecturale* 10–11 (1982).
——— (in collaboration with B. Chauffert-Yvart), *Le waqf d'Ipchir Pacha, 1063/1653. Étude d'urbanisme historique* (Institut Français d'Études Arabes à Damas, 1982).
——— and J. Tate, "Une waqfiya à l'épreuve de l'archéologie: la maison d'al-Hagg Hassan Galabi," *BEO* (Damascus) 36 (1986).

---

[55] David, "Les territoires des groupes."

——, "L'espace des chrétiens à Alep. Ségrégation et mixité; stratégies communautaires (1750–1950)," in "Villes au Levant," *REMMM* (Aix-en-Provence) 55–56 (1990).

——, "Domaines et limites de l'architecture d'Empire dans une capitale proviniciale, Alep," in "Alep," *REMMM* (Aix-en-Provence) 62 (1991).

——, "L'habitat permanent des grands commerçants dans les khans d'Alep: processus de formation locale et adaptation d'un modèle extérieur," in *Les villes dans l'Empire Ottoman: activités et sociétés*, ed. d. Panzac, vol. 2 (Aix-en-Provence: IREMAM-CNRS, 1994).

——, "Les territoires des groupes à Alep à l'époque ottomane. Cohésion urbaine et formes d'exclusion," in "Biens communs, patrimoine collectif et gestion communautaire dans les sociétés musulmanes," *REMMM* (Aix-en-Provence) 79–80 (1996).

——, "Bab al-Faraj à Alep: un nouveau *centre-ville* pour de nouveaux territoires extérieurs, pour une nouvelle société?" *Cahiers de Recherche GREMMO Monde arabe contemporain* (Lyon) 5 (1996).

—— (in collaboration with F. Baker, T. Grandin, M. Hreitani), *La Suwayqat 'Ali à Alep* (Publication de l'Institut Français d'Études Arabes de Damas, 1998).

——, "Une grande maison de la fin du XVIème siècle à Alep," *BEO* (Damascus) 50 (1998).

K. Fukasawa, *Toileries et commerce au Levant* (Marseille: CNRS, 1987).

H. Gaube and E. Wirth, *Aleppo Historische und geographische Beiträge zur baulichen Gestaltung, zur sozialen Organisation* (Wiesbaden, 1984).

K. al-Ghazzi, *Nahr al-Dhahab*, 3 vols. (Aleppo, 1342 A.H.).

B. Heyberger, "Les chrétiens d'Alep à travers les récits des conversions des missionnaires carmes déchaux (1657–1681)," *Mélanges de l'École française de Rome* (Rome) 100 (1988).

——, *Les chrétiens du Proche-Orient* (Rome: École Française, 1994).

——, "Un nouveau modèle de conscience individuelle et de comportement social: les confréries d'Alep (XVIIe–XIXe siècles)," in "Actes du premier symposium syroarabicum, Kaslik, September 1995," *Paroles de l'Orient* 21 (1996).

——, "Réforme catholique et union des Églises orientales (XVIe–XVIIe siècles)," in *Homo religiosus. Autour de Jean Delumeau* (Paris: Fayard, 1997).

——, *Hindiyya Mystique et criminelle 1720–1798* (Paris, 2001).

M. Ma'oz, "Syrian Urban Politics in the Tanzimat Period between 1840 and 1861," *Bulletin of Oriental and African Studies* 29, no. 2 (1966).

A. Marcus, *The Middle East on the Eve of Modernity, Aleppo in the Eighteenth Century* (New York: Columbia U.P., 1989).

B. Masters, *The Origins of Western Economic Dominance in the Middle East, Mercantilism and the Islamic economy in Aleppo, 1600–1750* (New York: University Press, 1988).

——, "The 1850 events of Aleppo: an Aftershock of Syria's Incorporation into the Capitalist World System," *IJMES* (Cambridge U.P.) 22, no. 1 (1990).

M. Meriwether, *The Notable Families of Aleppo, 1770–1830: Networks and Social Structures*, thesis (University of Pennsylvania, 1981; U. M. I., printed 1988).

A. Raymond, "Les grands waqfs et l'organisation de l'espace urbain à Alep et au Caire à l'époque ottomane (XVIe–XVIIe siècles)," *BEO* (Damascus) 31 (1979).

——, "The Population of Aleppo in the Sixteenth and Seventeenth Centuries according to Ottoman Census Documents," *IJMES* 16 (1984).

——, *Grandes villes ottomanes à l'époque ottomane* (Paris, 1985).

——, "Le déplacement des tanneries à Alep, au Caire et à Tunis à l'époque ottomane: un indicateur de croissance urbaine," *REMMM* (Aix-en-Provence) 55–56 (1990).

——, "Réseaux urbains et mouvements populaires à Alep (fin du XVIIIe–début du XIXe siècles)," *Arab Historical Review for Ottoman Studies* (Zaghouan) 3–4 (1991): 93–104.

——, "Alep à l'époque ottomane (XVIe–XIXe siècles)," in "Alep et la Syrie du Nord," *REMMM* (Aix-en-Provence) 62 (1991): 93–109.

———, "Groupes sociaux et géographie urbaine à Alep au XVIIIᵉ siècle," in *The Syrian Land in the 18th and 19th Century*, ed. T. Philipp (Stuttgart, 1992), 93–104.

———, *La ville arabe, Alep, à l'époque ottomane (XVIᵉ–XVIIIᵉ siècles)* (Damascus, 1998).

A. Russel, *The Natural History of Aleppo*, 2 vols. (London, 1794).

J. Sauvaget, *"Les Perles Choisies" d'Ibn ach-Chihna. Matériaux pour servir à l'histoire de la ville d'Alep* (Damascus, 1933).

———, *Alep. Essai sur le développement d'une grande ville syrienne des origines au milieu du XIXᵉ siècle*) (Paris, 1941).

———, *Les Trésor d'Or de Sibt Ibn al-ʿAjami* (Beirut, 1950).

J. Tate, *Une waqfiyya du XVIIIᵉ siècle à Alep* (Damascus, 1990).

J. P. Thieck, "Décentralisation ottomane et affirmation urbaine à Alep," in *Mouvements communautaires et espaces urbains au Machreq* (Beirut, 1985).

C. F. Volney, *Voyage en Egypte et en Syrie, pendant les années 1783, 1784 et 1785* (Paris, 1825).

Eugen Wirth, "Villes islamiques, villes arabes, villes orientales? Une problématique face au changement," in *La ville arabe dans l'islam. Histoire et mutation*, ed. Abdelwahab Bouhdiba and Dominique Chevallier (Tunis, 1982).

———, "Alep dans la première moitié du XIXᵉ siècle. Un exemple de stabilité et de dynamique dans l'économie ottomane tardive," in "Alep et la Syrie du Nord," *REMMM* (Aix-en-Provence) 62 (1991).

———, "Esquisse d'une conception de la ville islamique. Vie privée dans l'Orient islamique par opposition à vie publique dans l'Antiquité et l'Occident," *Géographie et cultures* (Paris) 5 (1993).

AT THE OTTOMAN EMPIRE'S INDUSTRIOUS CORE: THE STORY OF BURSA

Suraiya Faroqhi

From Princely Town to—Secret—Imperial City

Among the numerous cities of the Ottoman Empire, Bursa occupies a special place. This was the first major city that the Ottomans conquered, in 1326, perhaps still during the lifetime of the eponymous ruler Osman Gazi.[1] For today's visitor, it is remarkable for its fourteenth- and fifteenth-century buildings, particularly mosques, theological schools, and mausoleums. Their size and sophistication have few parallels in the Ottoman lands before Mehmed the Conqueror extinguished what remained of the Byzantine empire and refashioned Constantinople as Istanbul, founding the first of the capital's great imperial mosque complexes.

Until the late fourteenth century, when the rulers' residence was moved to the Balkan town of Edirne, close to the Balkan frontier, this was also an important centre of the expanding Ottoman principality. A palace was constructed on the citadel hill, of which, after earthquake damage and centuries of neglect, nothing remains today. Yet it would not be appropriate to describe Bursa as *the* capital, at least not during the reign of Sultan Orhan. For Ibn Battuta who visited the city in person described the sultan as possessing almost one hundred fortresses that he regularly inspected; he thus never spent even a single month in one and the same locality.[2] Bursa's links to the Ottoman court continued even after the sultans had come to spend most of their time in Edirne and Istanbul; for even though they might have met their end elsewhere, princes and princesses of the Ottoman dynasty throughout the sixteenth

---

[1] For basic information compare the articles "Bursa" and "harir" in the *Encyclopaedia of Islam* (from now *EI*), vol. 1, both by Halil Inalcik.

[2] Ibn Battuta, *Voyages d'Ibn Batoutah*, ed. and trans. by C. Defrémery and R. Sanguinetti, 5 vols. (Paris, 1854), 2: 322. The descriptions of many visitors to Bursa in the course of the centuries, of varying length and sophistication, have now been made conveniently available in English: Heath Lowry, *Ottoman Bursa in Travel Accounts* (Bloomington, IN, 2003).

century were often buried in the funerary complex linked to the name of Sultan Murad II (r. 1421–1451). In addition, the nearby Uludağ (in the sixteenth century: Keşişdağı) mountains were sometimes visited by the rulers' hunting parties. Thus, Bursa remained something of an imperial city at least to the end of the sixteenth century; and for yet a hundred years longer, its juridical and theological schools provided access to the highest offices in the judicial and teaching hierarchies.[3]

Outside Linkages: Serving the Ottoman Court, Serving the Capital, Serving the World Market

To the historian of economy, society, and culture Bursa is remarkable mainly because it was a major centre of trade and crafts, especially in the textile sector, and continued to play that role down to the end of the Ottoman Empire and beyond. The city's links to the palace and its commercial and artisan activity were at least at the beginning two sides of the same coin, for many goods produced in Bursa were consumed at the sultan's court and thus had to be transported to Istanbul, easily reached by boat even in the fifteenth or sixteenth century.

This means that we can see Bursa, in spite of its substantial size, as one of the "service towns" which so often developed around any great city the world over.[4] It has even been claimed that a major urban centre in the early modern period typically demonstrated its greatness by bending other towns to its will. It is well known that Istanbul had a relatively limited number of such towns at its disposal. We might name Rodosçuk/Tekirdağ where grain from outside the region could be stored until needed, İzmit (İznikmid) where, at least in the sixteenth century, mills manufactured the flour that fed the inhabitants of the capital, and especially Eyüp where a famous sanctuary provided legitimacy to newly enthroned sultans who, from the seventeenth century onwards, made a point of visiting the place where a companion of the Prophet was buried.[5] But Bursa was without any doubt the most important of these

---

[3] From the 1700s onwards, only the medreses of Istanbul provided access to top-level careers; see Madeline Zilfi, *The Politics of Piety, The Ottoman Ulema in the Classical Age* (Minneapolis, 1988), 60.

[4] Fernand Braudel, *Civilisation matérielle, économie et capitalisme*, 3 vols. (Paris, 1979), 1: 444.

[5] Nicolas Vatin, "Aux origines du pèlerinage à Eyüp des sultans ottomans," *Turcica* 27 (1995): 91–100.

"subordinate" settlements, and if Istanbul had not been so close, the city doubtless would have been a provincial centre in its own right.

But as things stood, it makes sense to consider Bursa's large population as a consequence of commerce and industries that could not have grown to the size that they did, if it had not been for a wealthy and demanding consumers' market only a short distance away. That the largest city of Anatolia by far was so dependent on the Ottoman capital in turn reflects the high degree of centralization that the sultan's government imposed on its core provinces.[6] In the more remote territories, particularly Egypt, it was often easier for merchants to escape the heavy hand of the central administration; thus Bursa's economic life, while in one sense it benefited from the closeness of a rich clientele, also suffered a significant disavantage, as the activities of its craftsmen and traders were supervised more closely than in Cairo or Aleppo.[7]

This link to the Istanbul market also explains why only in Bursa during the late fifteenth and early sixteenth centuries do we find an important number of slaves active not just as servants in great houses, but employed in commerce and crafts.[8] In principle, merchants might have expected to incur losses, if they entrusted their goods that were permitted to travel yet impatient for the opportunity to return home. However the employment of slaves in long-distance trade was not unknown, nonetheless; many masters must therefore have devised means of ensuring the loyalty of their men. Especially the widespread practice of manumission after some years of service and the opportunity to become traders themselves must have convinced quite a few servitors that their chances in Bursa were better than if they risked their lives in attempting to return to "Frengistan" or India. Moreover, some men in this position may well have suspected that after long years had elapsed, they might be less than welcome to relatives and business partners in the home country.[9]

Where skilled trades were concerned, recruiting slaves as part of the workforce also was a risky and expensive undertaking. After all,

---

[6] Daniel Goffman, *Izmir and the Levantine World, 1550–1650* (Seattle, 1990), 138–140.

[7] Nelly Hanna, *Making Big Money in 1600: The Life and Times of Isma'il Abu Taqiyya, Egyptian Merchant* (Syracuse, 1998).

[8] Halil Sahillioğlu, "Slaves in the Social and Economic Life of Bursa in the late 15th and early 16th Centuries," *Turcica* 17 (1985): 43–112, reprinted in idem, *Studies on Ottoman Economic and Social History* (Istanbul, 1999), 105–174.

[9] Frengistan was a generic term used for the lands of the Latin West. For Indian slaves in Bursa, see Sahillioğlu, "Slaves," reprint, 134.

slaves had to be housed and fed until they had overcome the shock
of separation from home and relatives, learned Turkish at least on a
minimal level and acquired the skills needed by masters and mistresses.
Costs were further increased by the fact that some of the slaves doubtless died after they had already occasioned considerable expenses, but
before their owners were able to profit from their labour; or else they
proved incapable of learning the intricate techniques needed to weave
a sophisticated piece of cloth on the simple looms available in the
early modern period. All this means that sixteenth-century Bursa looms
produced for an up-market clientele for whose members "price was no
object," and such a type of customer could only have been found in
significant numbers in and around the Ottoman court.

It appears, however, that from the seventeenth century onwards Bursa
textiles became less luxurious, and efforts to sell were less exclusively
directed at sultans, viziers and other personages at the apex of the
Ottoman state apparatus. Considerable uncertainty remains, because
it is often difficult to securely date fabrics, and it is possible that some
textiles that we date to the sixteenth century may in fact be of later
time. But it does appear that after a considerable lapse before and after
1600 the Bursa industry recovered to some extent: but now poor free
people were employed and moreover a substantial share of the raw silk
needed was produced locally, so that costs were reduced.[10] It was probably due to the availability of alternative raw material that Bursa's silk
manufactures survived the almost total cessation of Iranian silk imports,
after the wars that accompanied the fall of the Safavid dynasty led to
a major crisis in silk production. That fabrics were now directed at a
more modest, non-courtly, but still well-to-do clientele can be gathered
from eighteenth-century inheritance inventories; for now, silk apparel
in local women's clothing chests was much more in evidence than it
had been for instance in the 1480s.[11] Moreover silk was not the only

---

[10] Haim Gerber, *Economy and Society in an Ottoman City: Bursa, 1600–1700* (Jerusalem, 1988), 10–11 provides estimates concerning the declining number of slaves in
seventeenth-century Bursa. On the economic rationale of replacing slaves with poor
free people see Suraiya Faroqhi, "Bursa at the Crossroads: Iranian Silk, European Competition and the Local Economy 1470–1700," in *Making a Living in the Ottoman Lands* by
S. Farouqui (Istanbul, 1995), 113–148.

[11] Suraiya Faroqhi, "Female costumes in late fifteenth century Bursa," in *Stories of
Ottoman Men and Women: Establishing Status Establishing Control* by S. Faroqhi (Istanbul, 2002),
63–74.

textile fibre worked by Bursa artisans; to the contrary, cotton had come to the forefront, both on its own and mixed with silk.[12] As a working hypothesis, we can therefore posit that after 1600 Bursa served less the Ottoman court than the inhabitants of the capital and also the now considerably increased local market.

The next "turning point" in the city's economic fortunes came only in the 1830s, when the silk industrialists of Lyons and Great Britain, now fully set on a course of factory-based expansion, "discovered" the mulberry groves surrounding Bursa as a source of raw material. This led to the construction of factories in which a largely female labour force reeled and twisted silk thread adapted to the weaving of damasks, jacquards, and other fancy cloths that now could be produced on the mechanized looms of Lyons.[13] Weaving became a secondary activity and, as a result, Bursa's emerging textile factories no longer served Istanbul but rather the world market, or in more concrete terms, the French silk industry and, to some extent, other European manufacturers as well. This state of affairs continued, with some modifications, down to 1914, when the export market collapsed due to World War I. After 1923, the government of the newly established Turkish Republic certainly sponsored attempts to revive the silk industry, with a degree of success where domestic consumption was concerned. But a variety of domestic and international impediments made it all but impossible for Bursa silk to gain a major share in the export market.[14] Given this situation our story of Ottoman Bursa and its textile crafts and industries will end in 1914.

Commercial Infrastructures

"Through a glass darkly" we can observe the city of Bursa as it appeared to an Ottoman official in charge of recording taxpayers and taxable resources in the year 1487, the "darkness" being a consequence of the fact that the earliest register is incomplete and the descriptions of only 43

---

[12] Cotton production had been significant throughout, but only in the eighteenth century did documentation become more abundant.

[13] Leila T. Erder, "The Making of Industrial Bursa," unpublished Ph.D. thesis, Princeton Univ., 1976.

[14] Fahri Dalsar, *Türk Sanayi ve Ticaret Tarihinde Bursa'da İpekçilik* (Istanbul, 1960).

town quarters (*mahalle*) have come down to us.[15] Yet we know that there
was a total of 174 such quarters, inhabited by 6457 taxpaying heads
of households, as, luckily for us, this information has been recorded on
one of the surviving folios. However, we have no idea of the average
size of a late medieval Bursa household; if, as a very rough estimate,
we assume a household coefficient of 5, we arrive at about 32,000
inhabitants; yet this figure does not include the households headed
by widows, the garrison and the various tax-exempt representatives
of officialdom doubtless resident in the city. It has become customary
to assume that these people may have made up about twenty percent
of any large Ottoman city. Presumably Bursa thus had about forty
thousand inhabitants, somewhat less than half the population of late
fifteenth-century Istanbul.[16]

The list of taxable resources appended to this early count is fairly
standard, indicating that Bursa possessed the markets and workshops
that one would expect in any sizeable Ottoman city, such as a special
grain market, public weighing scales, and a workshop for the manufacture of fat (*şem'hane*). More noteworthy is the fact that Bursa was
equipped with a mint, that the *tamga* (stamp) tax was levied upon local
textiles, and that there were specialized weighing scales for the red dye
known as gum-lac and also for pepper; this means that Bursa was linked
to the great international trade network in south-east Asian drugs and
spices.[17] It is unfortunate that this early register does not include the
incomes accruing to the great sultans' foundations of the city, so that
our information on Bursa's late fifteenth-century commercial structures
remains woefully incomplete.

Some information on the city's commercial and artisan history in the
late 1400s can, however, be derived retrospectively from early sixteenth
century records. While it is of course possible that some urban revenue
sources were acquired after the deaths of the donors but before the
compilation of the relevant registers in the 1520s, this was probably

---

[15] Ömer Lûtfi Barkan with Enver Meriçli, *Hüdavendigâr Livası Tahrir Defteri I* (no more
publ.) (Ankara, 1988), introduction p. 66 and document section, p. 1. From a note in
the document section p. 35 it is apparent that there had once existed a register dating
from the reign of Murad I, but this has not survived. For estimates of Bursa population
based on a somewhat later register, see Lowry, *Ottoman Bursa*, 2–4.

[16] Compare the article "Istanbul," in *EI*, vol. 4, by Halil Inalcik.

[17] Halil Inalcik, "Bursa and the Commerce of the Levant," *Journal of the Economic and
Social History of the Orient* 3 (1960): 131–147. See also Barkan with Meriçli, *Hüdavendigâr*,
document section p. 10, note 179.

the exception rather than the rule. All sultanic foundations possessed extensive sources of income assigned to them by their royal donors. Many shops, urban khans and public weighing scales (*kapan*) were owned by these institutions which thus came to foster trade while at the same time deriving income from merchants and craftsmen who paid rents and fees whenever they used foundation-held properties.

Almost all the major mosque complexes established by early Otto-man rulers and their relatives possessed khans and shops. Thus, the Great Mosque (Ulu Cami), begun in 1396 and completed in 1400, was surrounded by khans and a covered market. Though located outside the citadel walls, this area developed into the city's commercial centre certainly after Mehmed I (r. 1412–1421) had built the "Market of the Cavaliers" (Sipahiler Çarşısı), if not earlier.[18] The mosque boasted 67 shops.[19] Given the still rather limited commercial activities of the early fourteenth century, the foundation of Orhan Gazi (r. 1326–1352) derived most of its income from land. Yet even so, the institution possessed 214 shops, urban real estate on which tanneries had been built and also the khan known as the Bezzaziye.[20] Murad I Hüdavendigâr (r. 1352–1389) had donated several villages to his pious foundation, but in addition, ample urban revenues. The latter included Bursa's weighing scales for fruit, probably located in a building where slaves were also offered for sale. A workshop for the manufacture of millet beer (*bozahane*) and some shops were also in evidence.[21] Bayezid I Yıldırım's (r. 1389–1402) son-in-law, the dervish sheik Emir Sultan, had established in his own right an all but royal foundation, which included the "Khan of the Grain Market," 25 shops and a tannery; in addition, this foundation, just like those established by the early sultans, was landlord to a con-siderable number of Bursa's inhabitants.[22] Finally Sultan Bayezid II (r. 1481–1512), whose major foundation was already located in Istanbul and not in Bursa, had assigned this institution two *caravansaries* located in the older centre, the so-called Eski-Yeni and the Yeni Han. Thus,

---

[18] For detailed information on the buildings compare Albert Gabriel, *Une capitale turque, Brousse-Bursa*, 2 vols. (Paris, 1958), see also Godfrey Goodwin, *A History of Otto-man Architecture* (London, 1971), 86.

[19] Barkan with Meriçli, *Hüdavendigâr*, document section p. 49.

[20] Barkan with Meriçli, *Hüdavendigâr*, document section p. 25.

[21] Barkan with Meriçli, *Hüdavendigâr*, document section p. 38; I do not know how else to interpret the expression *kapan-ı esir ve meyve*.

[22] Barkan with Meriçli, *Hüdavendigâr*, document section p. 43.

the commercial activity of Bursa around 1500 even served to finance charities in the Ottoman sultans' new capital.

From the *post-mortem* inventories of a number of moneyed men who died in Bursa at the end of the fifteenth century, it is possible to reconstruct the business environment of the city's khans.[23] The wealthiest personages of whom we possess information do not seem to have travelled themselves, but rather invested as senior partners in businesses managed by other people; this would conform to a general pattern, well studied and widespread throughout the Mediterranean world.[24] Some Bursa businessmen active in the silk trade may well have employed workers even in the late 1400s; if true, this would indicate that in this city the putting-out business had a long history. Slave owning was rather common among these men, and quite a few of them were themselves "sons of Abdullah," that is, in all probability, recent converts to Islam. Thus, it is quite likely that here we are in the presence of some of those select slaves mentioned earlier who were groomed for later manumission and entry into their former owners' businesses.

In pre-industrial and early industrial societies, textiles tend to form a key sector. Fabrics thus occupied the position of iron and steel from the mid-nineteenth century onwards and continuing well into the twentieth, of chemical industries after about 1890, electrical equipment between the 1930s and 1970s, and computer industries after that date. It comes, therefore, as no surprise that the production of Bursa was largely oriented towards textiles. Woollens were of minor importance, although some weaving of rugs and kelims certainly was practiced. But the principal raw materials worked in the city were silk and cotton, which could also be mixed to form a relatively cheap fabric known as *kutni*; dyed in suitably dark colours, this was considered suitable for the skirts of non-Muslim women.[25] As a large share of the necessary raw materials needed to be brought in from some distance away and the fabrics woven in Bursa were consumed both within and outside the Ottoman Empire, it comes as no surprise that quite a few merchants were involved in the trade in textiles and textile fibres.

---

[23] Suraiya Faroqhi, "The Business of Trade: Bursa Merchants of the 1480s," in *Making a Living*, 193–216.
[24] Murat Çizakça, *A Comparative Evolution of Business Partnerships: The Islamic World and Europe, with Specific Reference to the Ottoman Archives* (Leiden, 1996), 66–77.
[25] Ahmed Refik, *Onuncu Asr-ı hicrîde İstanbul Hayatı (1495–1591)* (Istanbul, 1988), 48.

Silk Trade and Silk Cloth: Coping with the Vagaries of Supply and Demand

Trading meant the coming and going of people from outside the Empire's borders including, for instance, in the second half of the fifteenth century, the presence of Florentine merchants.[26] Just as importantly, links were formed with eastern countries, and these closely involved the manufacture of silk fabrics: already in the years around 1400, so the Bavarian captive Hans Schiltberger informs us, raw silk from Shirwan was being brought to Bursa for this purpose.[27] However, it is possible that the (re)nascent Bursa silk industry actually could build on a tradition going back to the thirteenth century when Iznik, then known as Nicaea, was temporarily the seat of Michael Palaiologos who in 1261 regained Constantinople and established the rule of the last Byzantine imperial dynasty. For while silk weaving disappeared from Latin Constantinople after 1204, silk workshops were founded in Nicaea to serve Michael Palaiologos and his entourage; these were last mentioned in 1290.[28] Whether in the years around 1326 some of the—possibly—surviving weavers found customers at the Bursa court of Orhan Gazi, remains an open question.

Be that as it may, presumably it was the demand of the Ottoman rulers and their servitors that made silk weaving possible around 1400. Admittedly, information on this craft, as on the city's social and economic life in general, only becomes more abundant with the 1480s. For from this time, the local *qadi* registers have been preserved and, albeit with minor interruptions, they are available for as long as the Ottoman Empire existed. Contracts and disputes connected in one way or another with the local silk manufacture are not at all rare, and have long been mined for information by economic and social historians.[29]

In the fifteenth and sixteenth centuries raw silk woven in Bursa was imported by caravan from Iran; merchants typically crossed the Ottoman borders in Erzurum or Diyarbakır, and after paying their tolls either traversed Anatolia from the southeast to the northwest or

---

[26] See most recently Lowry, *Ottoman Bursa*, 20–22; for a sampling of original documents compare Dalsar, *Bursa'da İpekçilik*, 214.

[27] Johannes Schiltberger, *Als Sklave im Osmanischen Reich und bei den Tataren 1394–1427*, ed. and trans. by Ulrich Schlemmer (Stuttgart, 1983), 106.

[28] I owe this information to a public lecture by Professor David Jacobi (Munich, February 2004), to whom I am most grateful.

[29] Dalsar, *Bursa'da İpekçilik*, passim, Inalcik, "Bursa and the Commerce of the Levant."

reached Bursa on the northern caravan route passing through Tokat
and Amasya. Until Shah Ismail, the founder of the Safavid dynasty,
and the Ottoman Sultan Selim I (r. 1512–1520) went to war, Muslim
merchants from western Iran often organized the importation of raw
silk to Bursa. But around 1512, by prohibiting the import trade, Selim
I attempted to deprive his rival of revenue, and perhaps also to limit
contacts of Ottoman merchants with the Shah's subjects now considered
to be damnable heretics. Merchants incautious enough to venture onto
Ottoman territory were imprisoned and their wares confiscated. For a
short time, traders used the detour over the Mamluk trading mart of
Aleppo; but that route also became impassable after the Ottoman conquest of the Mamluk sultanate in 1516–17.[30] Certainly, when Süleyman
the Magnificent ascended the Ottoman throne in 1520 he released the
imprisoned merchants and their goods, having been advised that holding
them was illegal according to Islamic law. We may also presume that
the unemployment suffered by Süleyman's own Bursa subjects, with
the concomitant losses sustained by the Ottoman treasury, contributed
to this decision.

Apparently after this mishap, Muslim Iranians came less frequently
to Bursa, where, as Shiites on Sunni territory, they may now have felt
less than secure. Instead, the importation of raw silk was now largely
in the hands of Armenians from Iran who could not be suspected of
being sheiks of the Safavid order in disguise, an *idée fixe* of mid-sixteenth-
century Ottoman administrators whenever Muslim travellers from
Iran were concerned. This *de facto* situation became "official" around
1600, when Shah Abbas (r. 1587–1629) made the trade in silk a royal
monopoly and decided that Armenian merchants recently resettled
from northern Iran into a suburb of Isfahan (New Julfa) were the most
suitable agents to handle the exportation of his silk.[31] Whenever Shah
Abbas was at war with the Ottomans, he attempted to reroute his silk
through English merchants, who were expected to transport it by sea,
thus, once again depriving his rival of important revenues from customs
duties, weighing dues and stamp taxes. However, it turned out that in

---

[30] Dalsar, *Bursa'da İpekçilik*, 131–136.
[31] Ina Baghdiantz McCabe, *The Shah's Silk for Europe's Silver: The Eurasian Trade of
the Julfa Armenians in Safavid Iran and India (1530–1750)* (Atlanta, 1999); Rudolph P.
Matthee, *The Politics of Trade in Safavid Iran: Silk for Silver 1600–1730* (Cambridge, 1999);
Edmund Herzig, "The Rise of the Julfa Merchants in the Late Sixteenth Century," in
Safavid Persia: The History and Politics of an Islamic Society, ed. Charles Melville (London,
1996), 305–322.

years when the Shah had a great deal of silk to sell, English merchants were unable or unwilling to invest the money needed for buying up large quantities of silk. In peacetime, by contrast, not much could be gained from foregoing sales in Bursa's lively market, and trade soon reverted to its previous channels.

On the other hand, silk weaving expanded in sixteenth-century Europe, in London's Spitalfields as well as in Italy and other places. While silkworm breeding also became more widespread as a result, particularly in certain Italian regions, the demand for Iranian silk clearly rose. English merchants of the Levant Company now made their principal profits by distributing Middle Eastern raw silk among the various silk-weaving enterprises of Europe. This growing demand could only lead to an increase of the prices of raw material Bursa weavers were obliged to pay.[32] A secondary but not insignificant factor were the rebellions of mercenary soldiers seeking entry into the regularly established military corps, the so-called Celali uprisings, that shook Anatolia during the last quarter of the sixteenth and the first years of the seventeenth century. Often enough the roads were impassable, and the limited quantities of silk that did get through must have been more costly as a result. Moreover, in 1603 certain groups of rebels were active in the immediate vicinity of Bursa, and the central administration undertook veritable campaigns against them; the resulting destruction must have also increased the costs of local silk producers.[33]

Bursa silk weavers were especially affected by this turbulence, as they could not easily increase their prices in response.[34] This resulted in a case of veritable price scissors, due to the fact that a sizeable amount of the manufacturers' work was destined for the Ottoman palace, and the latter had the political power to insist on low prices in defiance of market conditions. In addition, an alternative was available to the sultan's court: as has recently emerged, there were workshops in Venice that produced Ottoman-style designs for the Ottoman market which only textile experts could distinguish from the originals. In addition to those pieces that arrived by means of trade, the Ottomans also received Venetian silk fabrics as diplomatic gifts. Recipients of such presents

---

[32] Murat Çizakça, "Price History and the Bursa Silk Industry: A Study in Ottoman Industrial Decline, 1550–1650," in *The Ottoman Empire and the World Economy*, ed. Huri Islamoğlu-Inan (reprint, Cambridge and Paris, 1987), 247–261.

[33] Mustafa Akdağ, *Celâlî İsyanları 1550–1603* (Ankara, 1963), 220.

[34] Çizakça, "Price History," 251–255.

included not only dignitaries established in Istanbul, but also the rather numerous Ottoman envoys who came to Venice in the sixteenth and earlier seventeenth centuries; it is quite possible that some of the presents received by the latter were ultimately sold in the Istanbul market.[35] As a result, the palace could always turn, or at least threaten to turn, to these outside suppliers.[36] And to make the situation of the weavers yet more difficult, the financial crisis of the late sixteenth century ate into the disposable incomes of Ottoman bureaucrats, so that increasing prices meant losing non-palace customers as well.

However, contrary to what has often been assumed, this crisis did not lead to the demise of Bursa's silk weaving. After the worst of the Celali rebellions had receded into the past, silk manufacture seems to have resumed. The author of a careful monograph on seventeenth-century Bursa has come to the conclusion that there was no evidence of a major crisis in this sector.[37] As we have seen, Bursa manufacturers survived the crisis by switching to cheaper free labour, and they also began to use more locally produced raw silk. As one piece of evidence for this latter tendency, there is the extension of mulberry groves in the vicinity of the city, as documented in numerous *post-mortem* inventories.[38] Admittedly, mulberries are edible, so that not every grove is incontrovertible evidence of silk cultivation. But equipment for the manufacture of silk thread also has left traces in the *qadi* registers of the 1600s, so that we can be certain of the continued activity of Bursa's silk manufacturers. Moreover, as seventeenth-century European merchants did not show any great interest in locally produced raw silk or silk thread, textile producers could to some extent counterbalance the price increase in imported Iranian silks.[39]

It is not at present possible to specify what fabrics were made out of locally grown raw silk and for which types the Iranian variety continued to be preferred. We may speculate that for the heavy silks favoured by the palace, the imported variety was more commonly used. However,

---

[35] Maria Pia Pedani Fabris, *In nome del Gran Signore, Inviati ottomani a Venezia dalla caduta di Costantinopoli alla guerra di Candia* (Venice, 1994), *passim*.

[36] Louise W. Mackie, "Ottoman Kaftans with an Italian Identity," in *Ottoman Costumes: From Textile to Identity*, ed. Suraiya Faroqhi and Christoph Neumann (Istanbul, 2004).

[37] Gerber, *Bursa*, 32 even considers the period 1650–1680 as a boom period.

[38] Gerber, *Bursa*, 81ff.

[39] Murat Çizakça, "Incorporation of the Middle East into the European World Economy," *Review* 8, no. 3 (1985): 353–378.

it is possible that within a few years textile researchers may be able to determine the localities in which surviving silk samples have been grown, and once these techniques can be applied to Bursa silk cloths, it will become possible to answer our question.[40]

Product Regulation and Its Limits: of Guildsmen and Non-Guild (Women) Workers

As was customary in Ottoman cities, a substantial share of the silk weavers were organized in craft guilds.[41] These organizations protected the interests of the masters who alone could be members, for instance by limiting the number of workshops that could be opened in the city. Guildsmen also determined when apprentices had completed their terms of instruction, a decision that presumably was made with the current market situation in mind. When disputes could be arbitrated within the guild, we normally do not hear about them. But when such disagreements were taken to the *qadi*, and the latter requested the aid of experienced masters in determining guild usage, a record was made by the scribes serving this official.

Day to day regulation of the artisans' affairs was in the hands of the market superintendent (*muhtasib*); he saw to it that guildsmen adhered to the prices decreed either by the *qadi* or agreed within the guild itself. A register of such administered prices from the year 1502 contains precious indications concerning the kinds of silk cloth woven in Bursa at the turn of the century, and also of the abuses of which dyers, weavers or other craftsmen and merchants involved in the silk trade were typically accused. The text refers to velvet (*kadife*), heavy silk cloth or brocade (*kemha*) and a light silk fabric known as *vale*. As these fabrics were divided up into numerous sub-categories, the weaving industry must have been highly sophisticated.[42] Moreover as this text pertains to a period usually considered to be very prosperous as far as the silk trade is concerned, it becomes evident that the manufacture

---

[40] Oral information given by Charlotte Jirousek, director of the textile museum of Cornell University, Ithaca, NY; many thanks for her help.

[41] Gerber, *Bursa*, 61.

[42] Ömer Lütfi Barkan, "Bazı Büyük Şehirlerde Eşya ve Yiyecek Fiyatlarının Tesbit ve Teftişi Hususlarını Tanzim Eden Kanunlar" *Tarih Vesikaları* 1, no. 5 (1942): 326–340; 2, no. 7 (1942): 15–40; 2, no. 9 (1942): 168–177. See particularly 2, no. 7: 28–31.

of cloths considered defective by some customers was not, as might easily be assumed, uniquely characteristic of periods of industrial difficulty. The craftsmen accused of dyeing their velvet in a cheap and shoddy fashion attempted to justify their actions by putting the blame on certain traders who had cornered the market in dyestuffs and only sold at high prices, so that they themselves could no longer afford the older and more expensive methods. Other complaints concerned silk cloths that had been woven too loosely, in other words the weavers had skimped on the raw material; in a similar fashion, gold and silver wire was spun too thin and therefore the quality of the finished brocades had suffered.

However, this did not mean that all changes to fabric quality were considered pernicious. For while it was admitted that some weavers of the so-called *gülistani kemha* produced a quality that was lighter than that marketed by their colleagues, the "experienced masters" opined that both varieties were demanded by customers and the lighter quality thus was not to be banned.

While only guild masters had a say when it came to the regulation of silk manufacture, they were by no means the only producers. Apart from the slaves that they might employ, who obviously had no decision-making power, there were the apprentices, of whom the same thing could be said. In addition, although they did not often own silk-cloth weaving looms, women formed an important part of the labour force.[43] Some of them might be weavers, as evidenced by a reference to a young girl who was meant to learn how to weave the light silk known as *vale*.[44] Even more significant was the role of females in the reeling and twisting of silk thread. In a rather early register, put together in 1530, reference was made to a certain Hacı Mehmed, who may have been either a merchant or a tax collector and who had given out state-owned silk to a local woman to be reeled.[45] In 1678, it emerged that of about three hundred pieces of silk-reeling and twisting equipment (*mancınık*)

---

[43] At least is the conclusion that we might draw from a text in the Bursa *qadi* registers, dated to 1586, that enumerates the owners of looms who had suffered heavy losses due to the current Ottoman-Safavid war; for there was no woman among them: Dalsar, *Bursa'da İpekçilik*, p. 335. However, from Haim Gerber, "Social and Economic Position of Women in an Ottoman City, Bursa 1600–1700," *International Journal of Middle East Studies* 12 (1980): 231–244 we do learn of a (probable) woman trader who owned silk-weaving looms.

[44] Dalsar, *Bursa'da İpekçilik*, 320.

[45] Dalsar, *Bursa'da İpekçilik*, 396.

about one half was owned by women; this would mean that the latter were independent agents of albeit very modest means, and not mere appendages to the enterprises of their husbands.[46] Other women manufactured silken braid that was then sown onto garments, and possessed the right to market their products wherever they pleased and without paying dues, much to the chagrin of the Bursa silk merchants.[47] Unfortunately, we do not know whether there were women silk embroiderers who established workshops of their own; to date, such persons are only known to have existed in seventeenth-century Istanbul.[48]

All this meant that the dominance of guild masters notwithstanding, non-guild labour was numerically important in the silk industry. Quite probably merchants could involve themselves in the various stages of silk cloth manufacture, and there seems to have been a certain amount of competition between artisans operating workshops and traders who instituted a kind of putting-out system, giving out silk to be worked by non-guild members who might be women and perhaps village dwellers as well. Thus, in 1677 a text in the *qadi* registers mentions certain non-Muslim silk twisters who were recorded as resident in Bursa and also sold their product in this city, but did the twisting, or else had it done, in the nearby township of Kite.[49] It is true that the craftsmen themselves pushed in the direction of a closely regulated production process in which "traditional" skills were highly valued, but as we have seen, merchants and non-guild labour tended, at least to some degree, to push in the opposite direction.

As a result it does not seem fair to say, as has often been done, that Bursa guildsmen were incapable of adjusting to market conditions: upon occasion, they might be perfectly willing to produce cheap fabrics such as *kutni* or admit that lower-quality silks might have a legitimate place next to more expensive items. Certainly, it does appear that the Ottoman palace was a factor making for industrial conservatism, as standards in this milieu changed very slowly. But on the other hand, the palace seems to have played a less determinant role as a purchaser after 1600 than appears to have been true in earlier periods, and some

---

[46] Gerber, "Women," 237.
[47] Gerber, "Women," 237.
[48] For Orthodox women who ran embroidery workshops see Angelos Delivorrias, *A Guide to the Benaki Museum* (Athens, 2000), 137–140; given my ignorance of Greek I have not been able to track down whatever research may have been done on this subject.
[49] Dalsar, *Bursa'da İpekçilik*, 388.

weavers do seem to have explored alternative outlets. We will follow
their lead.

Bursa Silks in the Hands of Non-Imperial Customers

In the sixteenth century we first encounter liturgical vestments that
had been manufactured in Bursa and were used in Orthodox Church
services performed by Ottoman subjects. Unfortunately, with the limited
number of sources presently at our disposal, we cannot say whether
the Christian churches had been important customers of high-quality
silk cloth already in earlier times, or whether sixteenth-century Bursa
producers had really managed to open up a new market. From the
historian's point of view, certain silk cloths used by Orthodox Christians
moreover present the advantage of being dated. Certainly, the date
given refers to the dedication to a church or monastery and not to the
date of manufacture, but at least such inscriptions provide us with a
secure *terminus ante quem*.

This applies for instance to an Ottoman garment with a gold chry-
santhemum and cloud-band design that was dedicated in 1629 to the
St. John Prodromos monastery in Serrai (Serres) after having belonged
to Neophytos, metropolitan of Iznik (Nicaea).[50] In this case it is hard
to determine whether the fabric was first made for some other use
and then "recycled" by Neophytos, or whether it was custom-made.
For it was not unknown for Bursa silk fabrics to be manufactured
directly for ecclesiastical purposes; in the Benaki Museum in Athens
there survives a sixteenth-century silk fabric of Bursa manufacture
with the repeating design of a "victory-bearing" image of the Virgin
Mary between angels, woven into the fabric.[51] In addition, we are left
to wonder where the embroiderers who produced liturgical veils and
other textiles for church use obtained their silver, gold and silk yarns; if
based in Istanbul, as some of them were, Bursa artisans were a possible
resource.

Other non-royal customers for Bursa silks were the wealthy Polish
noblemen who in the seventeenth century adopted a clothing style

---

[50] Delivorrias, *Benaki Museum*, 136; for a brief reference to this collection see Dalsar,
Bursa'da İpekçilik, 74.
[51] Delivorrias, *Benaki Museum*, 137.

strongly inspired by Ottoman models and purchased rich silk fabrics for this purpose. Some of these items ultimately were used as grave-clothes, and have been retrieved in the course of archaeological excavations.[52] Others were once again recycled, this time as vestments for Catholic priests, and while dates of dedication were rarely provided in this context, the heyday of the Sarmatian style was in the seventeenth century and it is assumed that many of the silk fabrics preserved in Poland also date from this period. This market for Bursa silks among Polish nobles and gentlemen should have constituted a genuine alternative to local textile producers; or, to put it differently, when we hypothesize that the manufacture of silk fabrics recovered after 1600 we can show where some of these items must have gone, if indeed the Ottoman palace purchased less than it had done in the sixteenth century.

Eighteenth-Century Exuberance in the Silk Industry

The infatuation of Polish gentlemen with the Sarmatian style seems to have died down in the eighteenth century, yet once again Bursa craftsmen appear to have found themselves new markets. For when we study Bursa probate inventories of the 1730s, it is immediately obvious that townspeople, especially the female half of the population, now owned many more textiles, both of silk and of cotton, than had been true in earlier periods.[53] While in the late fifteenth century the number of dresses, shirts, and veils possessed even by better-off women was usually very modest, clothing chests of the 1730s often yielded several silk dresses, to say nothing of numerous cushion covers, curtains, and bed-quilts.[54] Moreover, it must be kept in mind that husbands and wives could both be the proprietors of home textiles, but we normally

---

[52] *War and Peace: Ottoman-Polish Relations in the 15th–19th Centuries* (Istanbul, 1999), 237.

[53] Lowry, *Ottoman Bursa*, 66–70 provides evidence from travelers' accounts concerning the prosperity of Bursa silk and its orientation towards the home market.

[54] Faroqhi, "Female costumes." For eighteenth-century inventories compare, for example, the register B 160 located in the National Library, Ankara. Of course, we have no way of knowing whether the disposal of a deceased person's clothing was different in the 1700s from what it had been two and a half centuries earlier. Perhaps in early Ottoman times such pieces were often given away before death, so that they were no longer in the house when the scribes came around to make their lists. But maybe such a custom, if indeed it existed, also meant that textiles were rarer and therefore more highly valued in the late fifteenth century.

possess the inventory of only one person. Thus, we can hypothesize that the better-off families of the eighteenth century possessed quite a store of silk textiles, perhaps about twice the amount shown in the relevant inventory.

Presumably the silks owned by Bursa's inhabitants were not necessarily of the highest grade—but then a recent study has shown that even the Ottoman palace in its most prosperous days bought silks of vastly differing qualities.[55] In the middle of the eighteenth century, there were quite a few complaints concerning the quality of silk threads made in Bursa that were considered too light for the proper manufacture of *kutnı* and other fabrics.[56] It was claimed that, due to this defect, the trade of the city was suffering and, from the central administration's point of view, this was a problem because it led to a decrease in taxes. But perhaps the lighter *kutnı* was easier to sell in the local market? In any event, the *post-mortem* inventory of a moderately prosperous *kutnı* manufacturer, dated May 1790, contains dyed cotton and linen yarns, in addition to two different qualities of silk.[57] Apparently, *kutnı* came in many different varieties: our register distinguishes *elvan* (coloured?), *göz* (with an eye-shaped design?), flowered and white.

The deceased owner of these textiles, a Greek described as the son of Constantine, had entrusted most of his products to three other Greeks; either the latter had manufactured *kutnı* on behalf of their master and had not as yet had a chance to deliver, or else they had been ordered to sell fabrics on account of the son of Constantine. From the list of the deceased's debtors it is possible to discern a rather wide network of contacts in the artisan world. For, contrary to the normal practice of scribes in *qadis*' offices, the person responsible for this particular register has included the trades of many of the debtors. The son of Constantine had business relations with Muslims, a few Armenians and, of course, with members of his own community: among them there were quilt-makers, dyers, shoemakers, tailors, and even an imam. Unfortunately, it is impossible to determine who had delivered goods to the deceased—this is probable in the case of the cleaners of cotton

---

[55] Mackie, "Ottoman kaftans."
[56] Dalsar, *Bursa'da İpekçilik*, 349–353.
[57] Bursa sicili B 243, fols. 10a–11a, located in the National Library, Ankara.

also mentioned in the inventory—and who had quite simply borrowed money.[58]

Less prosperous was the silk weaver Ebubekir b Abdullah who ran a business that produced the silken wraps known as *futa* (1787).[59] Apparently, this man did not own any looms himself, but since he left 18 pieces of *futa* as yet incomplete, we can posit that Ebubekir had entered into putting-out arrangements of some kind. His shop contained an unspecified number of wraps and above all different qualities of raw silk: *paybürek, harir-i şehri, pot,* and others.[60] As the amount of cotton yarn on the premises was minute, we can assume that Ebubekir's wraps were in fact made of silk, perhaps with just a tiny decoration in contrasting cotton yarn. How our craftsman sold his output is an open question, but the one debt owed to his estate may have been due to deliveries made to him and not yet paid for.

All this should be taken to mean that Bursa's eighteenth-century manufacturers coped with the interruption of the supply of Iranian silk that resulted from the wars that shook Iran during the last decade of Safavid rule and beyond.[61] This was due to the extensive cultivation of mulberry trees and silkworms which seems to have been sufficient for the needs of local weavers. For a single year, namely 1775, the names of traders in Bursa silks can be read off from an account of the local tax officials who recorded mainly sales of silk but also of cotton textiles.[62] Numerous Muslims, Armenians, Greeks, and Jews at the time were doing business in this sector; unfortunately, the scribes did not record where these merchants ultimately took their wares.

---

[58] Money-lending had been an important source of income for well-off inhabitants of Bursa in the 1730s, and continued to be significant at the century's end: Suraiya Faroqhi, "A Builder as Slave Owner and Rural Moneylender: Hacı Abdullah of Bursa, Campaign mimar," reprint in *Stories of Ottoman Men and Women: Establishing Status Establishing Control* (Istanbul, 2002), 95–112.

[59] See Mine Esiner Özen, "Türkçede Kumaş Adları", *Tarih Dergisi* 33 (1980–82): 291–340, see p. 314 for a list of the different varieties of *futa*.

[60] For a listing of the qualities of silk available in Bursa, unfortunately around 1600 and not around 1800, compare the dissertation by Murat Çizakça, "Sixteenth–seventeenth Century Inflation and the Bursa Silk Industry: A Pattern for Ottoman Industrial Decline?" Ph.D. dissertation, University of Pennsylvania, available through University Microfilms, 1978, 39–97.

[61] Neşe Erim, "Trade, Traders and the State in Eighteenth Century Erzurum," *New Perspectives on Turkey* 5–6 (1991): 123–150.

[62] Başbakanlık Arşivi-Osmanlı Arşivi, Istanbul, section Bab-ı defteri-Bursa Mukataası No 24377.

Apart from local manufactures, the then prosperous silk industry of the island of Chios also depended at least in part on raw silk grown in Bursa, as the island's own supply of raw silk was insufficient for local needs. Manufacturers of the well-known sashes (*kuşak*) that even the mid-eighteenth-century Ottoman palace passed out to its pages on the occasion of religious festivities, thus, depended upon a supply of Bursa raw material.[63] On the other hand, the exportation of raw silk to Europe seems to have been rather limited in the eighteenth century, and the Italian scholar Domenico Sestini, on the occasion of his visit to Bursa in 1779, confirmed that while some export existed, it was minor when compared to local consumption.[64] After all, English merchants were at the time, albeit temporarily, withdrawing from the Levant trade, as Bengali and Chinese silks proved more lucrative, and the head of the one and only French firm active in Bursa failed to convince anybody back home that the institution of even a vice-consulate was worthwhile.[65] This may have been due to the fact that Bursa silks were not much esteemed by contemporary French manufacturers: thus the firm of Garavaque & Cusson, well-established in Izmir, wrote to their correspondents in Marseille in 1769 that they had cancelled an exchange deal of French woollens against Bursa silk because of the anticipated loss on the latter.[66] Thus, it would seem that throughout the 1700s local manufacturers did not need to fear serious foreign competitors when it came to their sources of raw material.[67]

But it is perhaps even more remarkable that in the early nineteenth century, the Austrian consular official and notable Ottoman scholar, Joseph von Hammer, found on his visit to Bursa that the local silk manufacture was still prosperous—and he was certainly no all-out admirer of things Ottoman.[68] Presumably, von Hammer's impressions

---

[63] On fabrics with the stamp (*damga*) of Chios compare Hülya Tezcan, "Döşemede Tarih: Sakız Adasının Osmanlı İpeklileri," *Ev Tekstili Dergisi* 2, no. 7 (1995): 10–15. This publication being difficult to locate, I am indebted to the author for providing me with a photocopy of her article.

[64] Domenico Sestini, *Voyage dans la Grèce Asiatique, à la péninsule de Cyzique, à Brousse et à Nicée, avec des détails sur l'histoire naturelle de ces contrées* (London and Paris, 1789), 194.

[65] This was one of the brothers Auzet, also encountered by Sestini: Sestini, *Voyage dans la Grèce Asiatique*, 87 and elsewhere.

[66] Chambre de Commerce de Marseille, Fonds Roux, LIX/743, September 1769.

[67] On the basis of the travel reports he has studied, Lowry has come to a very similar conclusion: Lowry, *Ottoman Bursa*, 55–62.

[68] Joseph von Hammer-[Purgstall], *Umblick auf einer Reise von Constantinopel nach Brussa...* (Budapest, 1818), 69–70.

dated from before the great economic crisis that followed the collapse
of the Napoleonic regime in 1814–15, when bad harvests and the
end of the war-related boom in the grain sector probably affected the
Bursa textile economy as well. Von Hammer relayed an estimate that
100,000 pieces of silk fabrics left the city each year. This included velvet
for cushions, *burundschik* (today: *bürümcük*) for vests and shirts and also
kutni that this author described as a silk fabric, and not as a silk-cotton
mixture, as is normally assumed. Von Hammer was appreciative of
the fanciful designs that ornamented the cushion covers, but especially
of the striped semi-transparent *bürümcük* that in his eyes singularly
enhanced female beauty.

An Item Long-Established but only Documented in the 1700s: Bursa Cotton Fabrics

While much less evidence survives on the manufacture of cottons, this
industry, which in fact continues to exist in Bursa down to the present
day, must also be taken into account when evaluating the city's role
as an industrial centre. In this context the fabric known as *beledi* is of
some interest, apparently a relatively low-grade material.[69] Ubiquitous
according to the inheritance lists of the time, *beledi* was made in most
cases out of cotton, but occasionally also silk. Whether it was sometimes a silk-cotton mixture is difficult to determine. The relevant craft
prospered in eighteenth-century Bursa; and once again, the inventory
of a manufacturer and trader in this fabric provides some evidence
on the manner in which *beledi* was made.[70] In contrast to the prosperous son of Constantine, the *beledici* Halil b Halil, whose inventory was
dated to 1786, must have been wretchedly poor. Apart from his loom
and auxiliary implements, his shop held 25 cushions made of *beledi*,
presumably finished but as yet unsold; and the nine shirts on record
must also have been intended for sale. Halil b Halil's basic raw material was evidently white yarn, probably of cotton; for purposes of
decoration, he owned a small quantity of red yarn and a bit more of
a type simply described as "dyed." As he was not owed any money and

---

[69] Esiner Özen, "Türkçede Kumaş Adları," 304 describes *beledi* as a cotton textile
without any reference to Bursa as a manufacturing centre.
[70] Bursa sicili B 232, fol. 6b, located in the National Library, Ankara.

did not leave any debts either, we may assume that our *beledici* was an ordinary artisan who sold the goods he had himself produced, perhaps with some help from his family.

However customers searching for cotton and a few other fabrics could find a much better selection if they went to one of the large *bezzaz* shops that offered an impressive variety of such items from different parts of the Ottoman Empire. Such a shop was in fact documented in 1787, after the death of its owner Hacı Salih b Ahmed. The *post-mortem* inventory, valued at over 1700 *guruş*, contained a veritable checklist of cotton textiles, often characterized by the name of the place from which they had come or from which the design had once originated. Hacı Salih's inventory included what seem to have been "ready-to-wear" turbans (*sarık*) wrapped six-, eight- or tenfold, at least if that is the proper interpretation of the terms *altılı, sekizli*, and *onlu*.

From Aleppo there came the fabric known as *alaca*, which might be of cotton or else of silk, in addition to silk wraps and sashes.[71] The Anatolian cotton town of Denizli and its surroundings, such as Ağras and Karacasu, were also well represented, among other things by a coarse fabric known as *yemeni*.[72] There were quite a few cottons that seem to have come from Bor, a small town of southern Anatolia that in earlier times had not been noted for its textiles. In addition, there were fabrics described as "flowered" without any further qualifications; presumably these were pieces from the Bursa region itself that were well known to the compilers of the register and therefore did not need any further description.

Once again, Hacı Salih's business connections can be read off from the list of debts owed to his estate, as well as from the unpaid debts left behind by this merchant. A sizeable share of his 113 debtors, who taken together owed over 4000 *guruş*, lived in the Bursa region, particularly in the villages or minuscule towns of Kestel, Karaman, and Kite. Therefore, it is possible that these were also the places in which Hacı Salih had his cottons woven. We may imagine that regular supplies for the shop were ensured by lending money to the weavers so that they would be obligated to deliver when needed. In addition, Hacı Salih

---

[71] Esiner Özen, "Türkçede Kumaş Adları," 300.

[72] On the importance of the "lake district" of southwestern Anatolia as a centre for cotton manufacture, see Suraiya Faroqhi, "Notes on the Production of Cotton Cloth in Sixteenth and Seventeenth-Century Anatolia," *Journal of European Economic History* (Rome) 8, no. 2 (1979): 405–417.

owed money to his suppliers: to a merchant who had brought in goods from Aleppo and to three others who had supplied *yemeni* fabrics for linings (*astar*) and the coarse material known as *bogası*, also favoured for underclothes and linings. Once again, as no places of origin have been mentioned, it is probable that these items had been brought into town from the immediate hinterland. All this activity is, moreover, consonant with Von Hammer's remark that blue and green "linen" was worked into handsome wraps for the bath; however, in the latter source, there is a slight error, as our documents have shown such items to have been made mostly of cotton. These references are especially remarkable since we must keep in mind that the last quarter of the eighteenth century and the beginning of the nineteenth constituted a period of serious economic difficulty throughout the Ottoman lands. Bursa seems to have escaped rather more lightly than other places.

The Final Years of an Ottoman Textile Centre: Incorporation into the World Economy

This concordance between Ottoman and non-Ottoman sources shows that down to the beginning years of the nineteenth century, Bursa was a centre producing textiles principally for the domestic market, and only in a secondary sense a source of raw or semi-finished material for European factories. However this situation changed after the end of the Napoleonic wars, and thus begins the third phase in the history of Bursa as an Ottoman textile-manufacturing centre: when after the 1820s local demand for silk cloth ceased to expand, some weavers turned to reeling in order to make a livelihood.[73] Not that silk cloth production came to an end, at least not during the 1800s. But the ready availability of machine-made English cotton yarn meant that from mid-century onwards, cotton replaced silk in many textiles being woven in Bursa.

---

[73] The nineteenth-century fate of Bursa silks has been admirably discussed by Donald Quataert in his seminal study *Ottoman Manufacturing in the Age of the Industrial Revolution* (Cambridge, 1993), 107–133. Compare also his earlier article "The Silk Industry of Bursa, 1880–1914," in *The Ottoman Empire and the World Economy*, ed. Huri Islamoğlu-Inan (reprint Cambridge and Paris, 1987), 284–299. As these studies are readily available, the present account, which depends mainly on Quataert's work, can be very brief.

On the other hand, demand for silk in Europe expanded once even members of the petty bourgeoisie could afford a "Sunday best" silk dress. Moreover, an epidemic affecting silk worms hit Bursa later than it did southern Europe, so that, for a short time during the 1850s, Bursa silk growers were able to benefit from record-high prices before, in turn, their own worms were struck by the disease. These price increases had the side-effect that growers found it more profitable to export than to supply local weavers. However, once the know-how needed to develop disease-free populations of silkworms, developed by Louis Pasteur, had become established in Bursa as well, local production of silk textiles resumed.[74] Even so, the export of raw silk remained dominant, largely as a result of the Ottoman state-bankruptcy of 1875, which placed significant Bursa revenues in the hands of the Ottoman Debt Administration (Dette Ottomane) in which French interests prevailed.[75] Thus, "integration into the world economy" dominated by European capital did make Bursa producers vulnerable to fluctuations in world demand, while in earlier centuries, they had been concerned mainly with sultanic and later with Ottoman urban customers. But, contrary to what has often been assumed, producing reeled silk for the factories of Europe did not mean the total demise of local manufactures. If the latter did not share in the phenomenal expansion that characterized factory output, at least they managed to hold their own by producing for local markets that Ottoman manufacturers, though often working with old-fashioned handlooms, yet serviced much better than their European competitors.

In a sense, we can say that Bursa industries existed as long as the Ottoman Empire did, as it was World War I that spelled the empire's end, and, at least for the time being, that of the Bursa industry as well. Under wartime conditions export markets collapsed. At the same time, non-Muslim employers, who had achieved a dominant position under the sponsorship of the Dette Ottomane for the most part left the city and hard-to-replace mulberry groves were destroyed as the result of fighting, and probably also because of the overall scarcity of fuel. In addition, female factory workers of the early 1900s had been largely Greek and Armenian, with only a limited Muslim presence, and most

---

[74] Quataert, *Ottoman Manufacturing*, 115.
[75] Erder, "Industrial Bursa," 121–131.

of these women also left the area, especially during the Greco-Turkish population exchange of 1923. Certainly, with official encouragement, silk production revived in a limited way during the following years. Bursa even became a centre of factory-based textile production specializing in cottons and synthetics; but that is part of a different, post-Ottoman story.[76]

---

[76] Erder, "Industrial Bursa," 136.

THE OTTOMAN TRIPOLI: A MEDITERRANEAN MEDINA

Ludovico Micara

It is not an easy task to isolate a specific historical period as Ottoman in the history of the urban development of Tripoli. Cities indeed grow on themselves, reusing and transforming the traces inherited from the past, unless a natural or artificial event breaks the continuity of their development, producing early endings and new beginnings. This can be observed in a clearer way in the cities of the Islamic world where the urban fabric is organized in a way that overcomes any crisis, no matter how severe.

In the case of Tripoli the disastrous Spanish occupation and the resulting urban decay that affected the city for a period of about forty years (1510–1551) strongly modified the urban topography, deleting important traces of its ancient past.[1] Such destructions, nevertheless, have not been able to block the process of formation of the urban fabric and, on the contrary, stimulated the development of the city.

During the Ottoman period and particularly under the reign of the Karamanli dynasty the present image of the Medina of Tripoli was consolidated.

The achievement of a strong urban image was the result of different building activities that concerned great religious, collective, and commercial institutions, together with the careful design of the defensive

---

[1] The common identification of the *cardo* of the Roman Tripoli, Oea, with the long street called Sciara Arba'a Arsat and Sciara Jama el-Druj is questionable. The direction of this road is, in fact, different from the orientation of the openings of the Arch of Marcus Aurelius that was the very centre, *umbilicum*, of the Roman city; whereas the supposed *decumanus* is perfectly in axis with the main openings of the same arch. Moreover the cross streets of the *cardo* are not orthogonal to it, but are oriented in the same way as the *decumanus*. We may speculate therefore, in lack of more advanced archaeological researches, that the destructions caused by the Spanish troops and the Knights of Saint John in the urban area to the west of the Castle, (see the following footnotes 11 and 12), together with the demolitions made by the Ottomans in order to conquer again the city, produced the obstruction of the ancient *cardo* and its shifting westwards. Darghut Pasha, who built also the Jama Darghut Mosque and its connecting street that is the only orthogonal to the new *cardo*, probably determined its direction. Apparently his palace was also in the same neighbourhood.

walls, bastions, and the castle, as well as the creation of particularly refined houses and residential spaces. The establishment of good relations and active collaboration between the Islamic ruling community and the dependent Jewish and Christian communities also enriched the urban image.

The specific features of the urban fabric of Tripoli are due to a process of assimilation of models belonging to other urban cultures of the Mediterranean world. This explains the particular way the houses open, through windows, balconies, and terraces, towards the street, unlike in other Islamic *medinas*, as well as the polarization of the urban routes on the waterfront that was clearly a Roman heritage.

The Making of a Mediterranean City

In the articulated structure of the plan of Tripoli, we can distinguish a series of urban patterns that can be referred to specific historical periods of the city. The orthogonal grid of the streets recalls the order of the classic Roman layout based on *cardo* and *decumanus*; the irregular and curvilinear passages generate the dead-end alleys of the Arab-Islamic city; and the polygonal geometry of the walls are typical of the sixteenth century system of fortification. These urban patterns reveal, diachronically, the different moments of the complex formation and evolution of the city and, synchronically, suggest the composite character of the Mediterranean urban culture, through the overlapping historical traces.

In this sense, the Medina of Tripoli constitutes a typical case. In fact, since the beginning of the seventeenth century, under the Karamanli dynasty, the different communities were strongly integrated. This resulted in a less rigid division between the quarters where the walls were demolished.[2] The composite organic urban fabric corresponded, until the beginning of the twentieth century, to the cohabitation and integration between Moslems, Hebrews, Maltese, Sicilians, Nigerians, and Sudanese, each specialized in different arts and crafts.

Another element that underlines the Mediterranean character of Tripoli is the careful choice of the site. In fact, the Phoenicians settled in Uiat, later Oea, the ancient Tripoli, in a place that ensured a deep

---

[2] P. Cuneo, *Storia dell'Urbanistica. Il mondo islamico* (Roma-Bari: Laterza, 1986), 393.

harbour, well protected by a promontory to the northeast, and guarded to the west by a low hill. Oea was also the terminal of the caravan roads that, originating from the internal areas of Libya, crossed a vast and fertile oasis, entering the city from the west and southeast. The site having good access to the sea, as well as permitting easy commercial and agricultural exchanges with the hinterland, allowed Oea to survive Sabratha and Lepci (Leptis Magna), the other two cities founded by the Phoenicians on the same coast. The city inherited also the name Tripolis, meaning the confederation of the three urban centres that were united in different vicissitudes since the domination of the Carthaginians.[3] The Roman pattern of Oea confirmed geometrically the direction of the pre-existing roads. One of these, running parallel to the coast from southeast to northwest, became the *cardo*, and the other, leading to the port from southwest to northeast, established the direction of the two principal *decumani*. The crossing between the *cardo* and the northern *decumanus* constituted the principal public centre of the settlement, marked by the arch erected in 163 A.D. in the honour of the Emperors Marcus Aurelius Antonius and Lucius Verus. The arch, financed by the *curator muneris* C. Calpurnius Celsus, was a *tetrapylon*, facing the above-mentioned crossing directions. The span of the arches along the road leading to the port is larger than the other revealing the primary role of sea trade in Tripolis-Oea.

Extensive walls protected the city only from the land,[4] as the sea, *Mare Nostrum*, was friendly to the Romans. There was also a fortress

---

[3] D. E. L. Haynes, *An Archæological and Historical Guide to the Pre-Islamic Antiquities of Tripolitania*, Antiquities Museums and Archives of Tripoli (Tripoli, 1965); E. Rossi, *Storia di Tripoli e della Tripolitania dalla conquista araba al 1911*, (Rome: Istituto per l'Oriente, 1968); A. Hutt, and G. Michell, "The Old City of Tripoli", in *Islamic Art and Architecture in Libya*, World of Islam Festival and Architectural Association (London, 1976); M. Warfelli, "The Old City of Tripoli", *Art and Achaeology Research Papers* (*AARP*), April 1976, 2–18; G. Messana, "La Medina di Tripoli", *Quaderni dell'Istituto di Cultura di Tripoli* 1 (1979), 6–36; F. Cabasi, "Profilo storico urbanistico e sociale della Medina o Città vecchia di Tripoli", *Quaderni dell'Istituto di Cultura di Tripoli* 1 (1979), 37–44; Abdalla Ahmed Abdalla Elmahmudi, *The Islamic Cities in Libya: Planning and Architecture* (Frankfurt am Main: Peter Lang, 1997); V. Christides, G. Oman, C. E. Bosworth, "Tarabulus al-Gharb", in *Encyclopaedia Islamica*, 2nd edition, 212–214. For the western sources on Tripoli and Libya see S. Bono, "Storiografia e fonti occidentali sulla Libia (1510–1911)", *Quaderni dell'Istituto Italiano di Cultura di Tripoli* (Rome), new series, 2 (1982).

[4] The complex history of the wall fortifications of Tripoli has been studied by S. Aurigemma, "Le fortificazioni della città di Tripoli", in *Notiziario Archeologico del Ministero delle Colonie*, II, fasc. I–II, 1916, 217–300. Of the same author see also: S. Aurigemma, "Per la storia delle fortificazioni di Tripoli", *Rivista delle Colonie Italiane* 3, no. 5 (1929),

guarding the gate of the city to the southeast, which stood on the site where the Castle is today.

The pre-existing Roman pattern, well evidenced in the contemporary topography, has been a constant feature in the urban history of Tripoli. In fact, it was noticed by Abu Mohammad Abdullah at-Tijani, in the occasion of his travel to the holy lands of Islam in 1307–8 A.D. In his travel accounts, *Rihlah*, he relates "the streets of the city were clean, and larger than other places, extending from one end to the other of the city and intersected as a chessboard, and easy to go through."[5]

The structuring role of the *cardo* and *decumani* is evident in the urban history of Tripoli, as their intersections constitute the two main public centres in the Roman and Arab-Islamic periods. The Tetrapylon and the Arba'a Arsat, both named after their four-pillar structures, were the landmarks highlighting the area between the *cardo* and the port, where the archaeological Roman remains, *spolia*, were reused in the main Islamic collective institutions, mosques (*jami'*, pl. *jawami'*), markets (*suq*, pl. *aswaq*), caravanserais (*funduq*, pl. *fanadiq*) and baths (*hammam*, pl. *hammamat*).

In 643 A.D./22 A.H. Tripoli was conquered by Arabs headed by Amr Ibn al-As, who entered the city from the sea, probably from the northwest, where, as mentioned, there were no fortifications. Tarabulus, or Atrabulus, became an Arab *medina* until 1510 A.D., except for the period between 1146 and 1158, when the Normans who had already conquered Sicily and Malta established there a garrison. It was probably in these nine centuries that the western part of the Medina developed. Here, as in many Arab-Islamic cities, the layout of the streets followed an irregular pattern. The urban plots do not correspond to constant measures, a multiple of the size of a *domus* as in the Roman cities, but became larger and with complex shapes, requiring the use of dead-end alleys in order to reach their internal areas. The ancient walls of the Medina, called by at-Tijani the white city, al-Baida,[6] were demolished by Amr Ibn al-As. These were later rebuilt and extended along the seashore, starting from the Castle. The new walls had at least three gates,

---

460–73; "Le fortificazioni di Tripoli in antiche vedute del seicento e del settecento", *Rivista delle Colonie Italiane* 3, no. 11 (1929): 1104–1128; 3, no. 12 (1929): 1217–1237.

    [5] At-Tijani, *Rihlah*, in E. Rossi, op. cit., 76.

    [6] "When we approached Tripoli, the brilliant whiteness of the city with the reflection of the sun nearly blinded us. Therefore I realized why it is called al-Bayda [The White City]", in M. Warfelli, op. cit., 2.

Bab Hawwara (probably the Bab al-Mensha of today), Bab al-Ashdar (today Bab Zenata), and Bab al-Bahr, the gate on the sea shore, from which one could enjoy the splendid view of the port, admired by at-Tijani as "beautiful and vast," and of the ships "that were aligned as racing horses in their stalls."[7] These fortifications were also completed by a second wall and moat.[8]

The city in this period focused on its hinterland rather than the sea. Consequently the second *decumanus* gained significance and its intersection with the *cardo* became the public centre of the city. The intersection was highlighted and architecturally defined by Arba'a Arsat, recalling the Tetrapylon by Marcus Aurelius. On the corners of the crossing, four remains of roman columns with beautiful capitals were used to support the arches spanning the streets.

On the 25th of July 1510, the Spanish, led by Count Pedro Navarro, occupied Tripoli after overcoming the resistance of its inhabitants. The political situation in the Mediterranean Sea was totally different. In 1453, Constantinople fell to the Ottomans who threatened Europe. The resistance and reaction to the Moslems started from Spain where Ferdinand of Aragon and Isabelle of Castile defeated in 1492 the last Arab king of Granada. In 1502, the Arabs were expelled from Spain and frequent expeditions and incursions were sent to conquer the North African ports and cities (Oran, Bougie, Algiers, Tunis, and Tripoli).

After conquering Tripoli, Pedro Navarro describes the city as follows, "This city is larger than what I thought, and although those who admired it spoke well about it, I can see that they were saying only half the truth; and among all the cities I have seen in the world, I do not find any that is comparable to it, both for its fortifications and for its cleanliness. It seems rather an imperial city...."[9] We learn from a certain Battistino de Tonsis who participated in the conquest that "the city of Tripoli is on a flat land, in quadrangular shape and a mile in circuit. It has a double wall with a narrow and deep moat. The first wall is small and low, the second one is very tall and of appropriate thickness, with towers and ramparts that are strong and bulky. From the sea, it is walled almost on three sides, with a great and good port that contains 400 ships and rowing vessels. This has been the reason

---

[7] At-Tijani, *Rihlah*, in E. Rossi, op. cit., 77.
[8] S. Aurigemma, op. cit., 246.
[9] E. Rossi, op. cit., 112.

for the loss of the city. It is said to be inhabited by more than then
thousand Moors and some Jewish people, five thousand of whom were
imprisoned. The remaining people died except the few who escaped
from the walls near the Jewish quarter."[10]

In 1530 Charles the Fifth gave Tripoli, together with the islands of
Malta and Gozo, to the Knights of Saint John who had been expelled by
Suleyman the Magnificent from Rhodes. But in 1551 Sinan Pasha con-
quered the city again with the help of the corsair admiral Darghut.

A new imprudent assault of the Spanish fleet was successfully repelled
in 1560. Tripoli remained under Ottoman rule, at times exercised
through autonomous local dynasties as the Karamanli, until the Italian
occupation of Libya in 1911.

Information regarding the conditions of Tripoli during the Spanish
rule is rather scant.

Leo the African, a Muslim thus baptized after being captured and
converted to Christianity, visited the city in 1518 reporting that Tripoli
"was ruined after its conquest by Christians. Nevertheless, they reinforced the castle with solid walls and an important artillery."[11] It is possible therefore to presume that, due to such events, the general level of
the streets rose[12] and the old castle was transformed into a fortress with
bastions, following the new theories of military art that were spread by
Charles the Fifth all over the Mediterranean world.

Two views, printed in 1559 and 1567,[13] show the situation of the
castle and the walls of Tripoli.

In the 1559 view, clearly based on more recent information compared
with the apparently later view of 1567, a new fortress is represented,
besides the castle reinforced with the bastions. Darghut Pasha built the
fortress, called St. Peter, at the north-eastern corner of the Medina, in
order to protect the harbour, in 1559, "when he expected to be attacked
by the Spanish army."[14] In the same view another fortress, Castellejo,

[10] E. Rossi, op. cit., 113.

[11] Jean-Léon l'Africain, *Description de l'Afrique*, (Paris: Librairie d'Amérique et d'Orient
Adrien Maisonneuve, 1981), vol. 2: 406.

[12] S. Aurigemma, op. cit., 263.

[13] G. Fumagalli, "La più antica pianta di Tripoli", *Accademie e biblioteche d'Italia* 6, no. 1
(August 1932): 28–40; S. Aurigemma, "A proposito di un'antica pianta di Tripoli",
Rivista delle Colonie italiane, 1933.

[14] *Histoire chronologique du Royaume de Tripoly de Barbarie*, man. cod. nn. 12.219, 12.220,
Bibliothèque Nationale, Parigi, 1685; in S. Aurigemma, "Per la storia delle fortificazioni di Tripoli", op. cit., 466. The author of the manuscript, anonymous according
to Aurigemma, is, in the opinion of E. Rossi, the Provençal surgeon Girard.

later Burg el-Mandrik, is represented, that was built on the rocks protecting the entrance to the harbour on the northern side.

In the 1567 view entitled "The real plan of the port, the city, the fortress and the site where Tripoli of Barbaria is placed" the city appears in ruins, confirming the testimony of Leo the African about the destructions carried out by the Spanish troops.

The Ottoman City

On the fifth of August 1551 the Ottoman fleet, headed by Sinan Pasha, with the help of the Darghut's pirate ships and Murad Agha's Arab warriors, coming from the nearby Tajura, besieged the Castle of Tripoli that surrendered on the fourteenth of August, opening its gates to the Turks allowing the lasting Ottoman domination of the city.[15]

Murad Agha, the founder of the mosque of Tajura, and the corsair Darghut, both playing a leading role in the conquest of the city, were the first governors, Pashas, of Tripoli. Their first and most urgent work carried out was to repair and reinforce the defensive system of the city. Darghut Pasha, ruling from 1556, established the definitive plan of the walls, demolishing the part, on the southwestern side of the city, that connected the Burg el-Karma fortress with the sea.

The new plan leaves out the "sperone" (spur) and "speroncello" (little spur) that, according to the above-mentioned views, formed the corner between the southwestern and the northwestern walls. A new straight tract of walls between the entrance gate to the middle *decumanus*, Bab Zenata, and the sea is, thus, created transforming the primary trapezoidal shape of the enceinte into the today almost pentagonal one. The building of the fortification Burg et-Trab (earthen fortress), later called Burg el-Fanar (lighthouse fortress), on the hill that overlooks the northern coast, and of the St. Peter or Darghut fortress, in the northeastern corner of the city, is also a work of Darghut.

In the same area of the Medina, to the south of the Marcus Aurelius arch, Darghut had created also his new palace and a new congregational

---

[15] On the history of the Ottoman Tripoli besides E. Rossi, op. cit., see C. Bergna, *Tripoli dal 1510 al 1850* (Tripoli, 1925); C. Féraud, *Annales Tripolitaines* (Tunis and Paris, 1927).

mosque,[16] Jama Sidi Darghut. Given that the Jama al-Naqah, the ancient cathedral mosque,[17] had been seriously damaged during the Spanish occupation, he reused the remains of a chapel built by the Knights of Malta for this purpose.

In 1604 Iskandar Pasha, builds near the Sidi Darghut Mosque the homonymous *hammam*, confirming a new urban focus, created by the two first Ottoman governors of the Medina, halfway between the Marcus Aurelius Arch and the crossing Arba'a Arsat. The ancient cathedral mosque Jama'a al Naqa'a will later be restored and opened to the public in 1610 by the governor Safar Dey. He combined both the military and political authority as the head of the Turkish troops, the Janissaries, and as *pasha*, notwithstanding the formal presence of the Pasha sent from Istanbul as the real representative of the Ottoman administration.

In fact, until the Karamanli took the power as an autonomous dynasty, recognized by Constantinople, the administrative system of the African provinces (Algiers, Tunis, Tripoli) was based on *pashaliq*, that is, a region subject to the authority of a *pasha* directly appointed by the central Ottoman government.

The Pasha had in his employment a Janissary army corps (*ojaq*, "heart" in Turkish, a word that in a wider sense replaces the term *pashaliq*) consisting of Levantines, Christians separated from their families, militarily educated and converted to Muslim religion. The Janissary army corps had its own hierarchy and was headed by high officers, *bey*, charged with the command, and officers responsible for the troops wages, *dey*, literally paternal uncle. The common affairs of the Janissary army corps were discussed in a council, called Diwan, headed by an *agha*. The relationship between *pasha*, *bey*, and *dey* varies

---

[16] The new mosque and palace of Darghut are clearly recognizable in the 1559 view. The mosque is also represented in some engraving of the late seventeenth century, among which the 1675 view in the *Atlas maritimus* by John Seller and the 1696 view in *Les Forces de l'Europe* by De Fer.

[17] The Jama al-Naqah, "Mosque of the camel", also reported by At-Tijani in his *Rihlah*, was probably built by order of the Fatimid Caliph al-Muizz, who visited Tripoli during his transfer from Tunisia to Egypt in 971–72. According to a reliable tradition the Caliph, enthusiastically received by the Tripoli's population, presented the city with a camel of his caravan, in order to enlarge and to embellish the principal mosque with the proceeds of the sale of his precious load. See G. Messana, *l'Architettura Musulmana della Libia* (Castelfranco Veneto, 1972), 108–110; A. M. El-Ballush, *A History of Libyan Mosque Architecture During the Ottoman and Karamanli Period: 1551–1911. Evolution, Development and Typology* (Tripoli, 1984), 58–60.

considerably in relation to the power or decay of the Ottoman Empire or the emerging of local and military leaderships. With it varies the level of autonomy[18] or subordination to the Sublime Gate of the province, frequently compared, in the European sources, to the rank of Regency or Kingdom.

After obtaining the government of Tripoli and the title of *pasha* from Murad the Fourth, Muhammad al-Saqizli, third *dey* of the Regency, became for the first time the only authority of the country. Consequently he and his successor Uthman al-Saqizli were able to guarantee a period (1633–1672) of relative peace and prosperity. Under their government piracy developed considerably. New warships, steering between the shores of Spain and Italy, led to the capture of many Christian captives, the ransom of which contributed considerably to the improvement of the public finance. At the same time the steady interior political situation encouraged European states, like France, Holland, England, Venice, and Sicily, to sign commercial treaties with Tripoli and to open consulates inside the Medina.

Besides performing the activity of commercial agencies, the consulates were entrusted with the task of negotiating the ransom of the Christian slaves and establishing agreements for the protection of merchant ships from piracy, through expensive tributes paid to the Regency.

A specific quarter, characterized by the presence of the European consular seats with their warehouses began to take form in the neighbourhoods of the harbour. New markets, *aswaq*, and warehouses, *fanadiq*, were realized along the ancient *cardo* that became the Bazar Street. The Suq at-Turk and the Suq er-Rba or the Moors' Market, near the Castle, contributed to create the most dense commercial area of the Medina, integrating the already existing system of the *aswaq*.

---

[18] The role plaid by *élites* expressed from autochthonous urban communities as regards the Ottoman rule, with its centralized and bureaucratic government machinery, is very important, particularly in the case of medium and small cities faraway from the capital, to understand the different levels of autonomy of the urban local power. On this subject, essential for many Islamic Mediterranean towns, see A. Raymond, "Les caractéristiques d'une ville arabe 'moyenne' au XVIIIᵉ siècle: le cas de Constantine", *Les Cahiers de Tunisie* 34, nos. 137–138 (1986): 175–196. The subject of the comparative autonomy of Islamic cities-state during the Medieval period has been discussed, in the case of Tripoli, by M. Brett, "The City-State in Medieval Ifriqiya: The Case of Tripoli", *Les Cahiers de Tunisie* 34 nos. 137–138 (1986): 69–94. More generally see M. Kisaichi, "The Maghrib", in *Islamic Urban Studies: Historical Review and Perspectives*, ed. by M. Haneda and T. Miura (London and New York: Kegan Paul International, 1994).

Uthman Pasha reinforced the urban focus created by Darghut by building the new monumental *madrasa* called after him in 1654. The magnificent *madrasa* was endowed with many *waqfs*[19] including the Funduq al-Kabir, at the northern end of Suq at-Turk, and the Hammam al-Kabir, on the southern *decumanus* west of Arba'a Arsat.

The extraordinary engraving by John Seller[20] depicts, in 1675, the overall image of the city, already described in details by the Provençal surgeon Girard,[21] imprisoned in Tripoli from 1668 to 1676. The above engraving, considered exact by Girard,[22] reveals a well-defined and almost complete urban structure. The pentagonal plan of the walls, with their bastions and gates, encloses an urban area represented in a very realistic way. It is possible to recognize the *cardo* and the two principal *decumani* that identify along the strip parallel to the sea a regular and wide grid of streets, recalling the ancient Roman plan. West of the *cardo*, in the higher part of the image, the streets lose gradually their regularity becoming curvilinear to follow progressively the polygonal geometry of the walls. The urban fabric represented in the engraving is clearly the compact and continuous one of the Arab-Islamic *medina*. The terraces and domed roofs identify houses, minor religious buildings, warehouses, and laboratories. The houses, mainly two floors high, open towards the street through doors and windows, highlighting the close relationship with the exterior urban space that is a feature of the Mediterranean cities rather than the Islamic *medinas*.

The elevation drawn by Seller depicts a powerful system of walls, bastions, towers, and batteries of canons that characterize the exterior image of the city. The castle has an inedited appearance, recognizable through the northern and eastern façades which are today neglected. Beyond the horizontal outline of the fortifications characteristic of numerous cities on the Mediterranean shores after the Spanish rule, three tall minarets, emerging from rows of swollen domes, reveal unequivocally the cultural and religious identity of the city. The minarets

---

[19] On the institution of *waqf* and on its fundamental role in the development of the Ottoman cities see R. van Leeuwen, *Waqfs and Urban Structures: The Case of Ottoman Damascus* (Leiden-Boston-Köln: Brill, 1999), 33–92.

[20] "A Mapp of the Citie and Port of Tripoli in Barbary" and "A Prospect of the City of Tripoli in Barbary", in J. Seller, *Atlas Maritimus, or the Sea-Atlas: Being A Book of Maritime Charts. Describing The Sea-Coasts, Capes Headlands, ... of the World.* (London, 1675); see S. Aurigemma, "Per la storia delle fortificazioni di Tripoli", op. cit.

[21] *Histoire Chronologique...*, op. cit.; in E. Rossi, op. cit., XIX, 191–194.

[22] E. Rossi, op. cit., 192, footnote 76.

are the landmarks of the most significant mosques of the seventeenth century. The Sidi Salem built at end of fifteenth century and restored in 1670 is located on the slope of the hill culminating in the Fortress of the Lighthouse. The new cathedral mosque, built by Darghut Pasha in 1556 on the eastern edge of the Medina, is near the sea. The Jama Kharruba, probably built before the Turkish conquest and restored in the second half of the seventeenth century, is close to the castle.

The above minarets,[23] together with that of the Jama Mahmud Khaznadar (1680), not represented in the elevation drawn by Seller, have all cylindrical structures, which was a seventeenth century feature.[24] After this period the plan of the minarets started to become octagonal with taller shafts, as can be seen in the mosques of Shai'b al-Ayn (1699), al-Karamanli (1738), and Gurji (1834).

The *silhouettes* of the three solid and pointed minarets in the drawing of Seller thus imprint a recognizable feature of the urban skyline and powerfully seal the end of the period of Pashas and Deys.

At the death of Uthman Pasha (1672) these offices were separated. The *pasha* continued to hold only nominally the position of the head of the administration. After a troubled period of struggles for power between the local governors, Muhammad al-Imam Sha'ib al-Ayn (the white eyelash man), *agha* of the Janissaries' army corps, succeeded in restoring order in the administration, achieving the acknowledgment also of the title of *pasha* as well as *dey* from the Ottoman Sultan Mustafa II. In this new period of prosperity the Pasha erected the Shai'b al-Ayn mosque, the second major mosque after the Darghut, while high government officers such as *khaznadar* (treasurer), *qapudan* (admiral of the fleet), *beylerbey*, and *dey* (Janissaries' commander) were building other new mosques.

The City of the Karamanlis

The troubled period of the Turkish-Ottoman rule, administrated by *pasha*s and *dey*s and their recurrent controversies and fights with the

---

[23] Darghut (1604), Sidi Salem (1670) and Jama Kharruba (second half of seventeenth century).

[24] A. M. El-Ballush, op. cit., 152, 173.

autochthonous people ceased when the Karamanli[25] family came to power. They were of Turkish origin but related to the Arab-Berber people who were the dominant group in Tripoli and its region. Notwithstanding their acknowledgment of the authority of the Sultans in Constantinople, the Karamanlis ruled as a true autonomous and hereditary dynasty. They somehow forerun the formation of other local dynasties at the end of eighteenth and the beginning of nineteenth centuries in such countries of the Ottoman Empire as Albania and Egypt.

The founder of the dynasty, Ahmed Pasha Karamanli, got rid of the cumbersome presence of the Janissaries with a massacre similar to the one committed a century later by Mohammed Ali Pasha of Egypt against the Mameluks. The advent of Ahmed Pasha initiated a long period of peace. The unconstrained commercial politics towards the European States that aimed at gaining money and profitable friendship agreements through the ever-present threat of the piracy would bring to Tripoli embassies and delegations. They established regular consulates in some of the important houses of the Medina, located in the north-eastern urban area facing the harbour.

The major building activities of the long rule of Ahmed Pasha (1714–1745) regarded the aqueduct supplying water to the castle and the city,[26] the *suq*s, *funduq*s and, above all, the mosque, *madrasa*, and mausoleum, *turba*, completed in 1738 and integrated in the new architectural complex facing the western side of the castle.

In the urban evolution that shifted the main public spaces of the Medina from North to South, along the ancient *cardo*, a new pole takes form at the south end close to Bab el-Mensha. The new pole is constituted by the castle, repaired and enriched with new apartments (*maqsura*) and the royal mosque endowed, through the *waqf* legal institute, with the *madrasa* and the new *aswaq* and *fanadiq*.

---

[25] On the history of Tripoli under the Karamanli dynasty, besides E. Rossi, op. cit., see N. Slousch, "La Tripolitaine sous la domination des Karamanli", *Revue du Monde Musulman* 4 (1908): 58–84, 211–232, 433–453; R. Vadala, "Essai sur l'histoire des Karamanli Pachas de Tripolitaine de 1714 à 1835", *Revue de l'Histoire des Colonies Françaises* 7 (1919): 177–288; R. Micacchi, *La Tripolitania sotto il dominio dei Caramànli* (Verbania: A. Airoldi, 1936); R. Mantran, s.v. "Karamanli", *Encyclopaedia Islamica*, 2nd edition.

[26] See the plan drawn in 1766 by Antonino Borg, *Piano del porto di Tripoli e fortificazione*, in *Piano di tutta la costa delli stati soggetti al Gran signor nel Mediterraneo…*, 1768–1770. An image of the aqueduct in ruins is reproduced in R. Tully, *Narrative of a ten years residence at Tripoli in Africa* (London, 1816).

Under the reign of the successors of Ahmed, Mohammed Pasha (1745–1754), Ali Pasha (1754–1793), Ahmed Pasha the Second (1795), and Yusuf Pasha (1795–1832) the multiracial and multireligious character of the Medina develops very fast. The Jews already constituted a remarkable and active minority.[27]

According to a contemporary account,[28] in 1783 the Jews amounted to 3.000 persons in a population of 14.000 souls. The Christian community, not considerably numerous, consisted of the European consuls with their retinue and some merchants, including Genoese and natives of Leghorn. Only later, at the beginning of the nineteenth century, the Maltese appeared, due to the increasing role of England in the Mediterranean world.[29]

Under the rule of Yusuf the relationships with the nations that faced or had interests in the Mediterranean Sea assumed greater importance. However, there were mainly conflicting relationships with such nations as the Reign of Naples,[30] the Reign of Sardinia[31] and the United States of America,[32] because of the piracy sponsored by Karamanlis. Hence the need to reinforce the sea-defence of the city arose. The Admiral, Minister of the Navy and Commandant of the Customs, Mustafa Gurji, "the Georgian", carried out a new fortress, al-Burj al-Jadid, at the end of the harbour, near the Burj al-Mandrik, the old Spanish Castellejo. The new fortress fulfilled the system of the sea-defence that on the oriental coast consisted of the Spanish Fort, Burj al-Ahmar, the

---

[27] "The Tripoli's Jewish community, dispersed after the Spanish army conquered the city, re-formed again in the second half of sixteenth century absorbing new elements from Jebel Nefusa, Garian, Zliten, Spain, and Leghorn. They lived secluded in their quarter called *hara* and had a *qa'id* as a leader for the relationship with the government; gradually they gained the direction of the commerce as well as particular industry as the metalworking," E. Rossi, op. cit., 236, footnote 61; N. Slousch, *Un voyage d'études juives en Afrique* (Paris, 1909); for the usages and customs of the Libyan Jews see M. Cohen, *Gli Ebrei in Libia* ([Roma 1930] Firenze, 1994).

[28] The 1784 manuscript *Giornale istorico* of the Venetian merchant Marino Doxerà, in E. Rossi, op. cit., 248. See, besides, F. Corò, "Una relazione veneta su Tripoli nel '700", *Rivista delle Colonie Italiane* 6, no. 12 (December 1930): 1092–1102.

[29] The Congress of Vienna in 1814 entrusted England with the possession of Malta.

[30] G. Paladino, "La spedizione della Marina napoletana a Tripoli nel 1828", *Rivista delle Colonie Italiane* 3 (1929): 909–924, 1003–1014.

[31] G. Ferrari, *La spedizione della Marina sarda a Tripoli nel 1825* (Rome, 1912), off-print from *Memorie Storiche Militari*, 1912.

[32] Col. E. De Agostini, "Una spedizione americana in Cirenaica nel 1805", *Rivista delle Colonie Italiane* 2, no. 5 (October–December 1928): 721–732; 3, no. 1 (January 1929): 41–56.

Slaughterhouse Fort, Burj al-Mazgarah, and the Castle itself; while on
the northern coast the defensive system was based on the Vine Fort, or
Burj al-Farrarah and the Light-house Fort, or Burj al-Fanar also called
Burj et-Trab (Earth Fort). Mustafa Gurji was also the founder of the
homonymous mosque built in 1834 near the Marcus Aurelius Arch.

In 1832 Yusuf Pasha Karamanli abdicated in favour of his son Ali.
The new political situation characterized by the fight between France
and England for the supremacy in the Mediterranean Sea (in 1830 the
French occupied Algiers) led to a decision of the Sultan of Constantinople to dismiss Ali Pasha and govern directly Tripoli.

On the fourth of August 1838, Yusuf Pasha died in his urban house
near Arba'a Arsat and was buried in the family *turba*. Thus an important
and prosperous period for Tripoli came to an end also symbolically.
The new Turkish governor of the city, together with the officers and
all the urban population rendered the last funeral honours to Yusuf:
"at the time of *zuhr* (midday) the *muezzin* climbed the minarets and for
about an hour eulogies (*tamjīd*) were recited. The slaves were set free
and prisoners released from jail. The consuls hoisted the national flags
at half-mast with a great satisfaction of all the population."[33]

Tripoli, a Mediterranean Medina

The Ottoman administration of Tripoli (1835–1911)[34] did not produce big transformations in the city, as it was engaged in fighting, on
one hand, the continuous rebellions led by local aristocracies, and on
the other hand, the commercial interests of foreign embassies and
consulates.

Pellissier de Reynaud, the Consul of France in Tripoli from 1850 to
1852, depicts the Medina as "a small city with ten or twelve thousand
inhabitants, clean enough except for the Jewish quarter. The city was
surrounded by walls that were in a bad condition."[35]

---

[33] E. Rossi, op. cit., 291.
[34] E. Rossi, op. cit.; F. Corò, *Settantasei anni di dominazione turca in Libia (1835–1911)*
(Tripoli, 1937); A. J. Cachia, *Libya under the Second Ottoman Occupation (1835–1911)*
(Tripoli, 1945); R. Micacchi, "La Tripolitania dal 1835 al 1858", *Rivista delle Colonie*
11 (1937): 816–832, 974–989.
[35] E. Pellissier de Reynaud, "La Régence de Tripoli", *Revue des Deux Mondes* 12, no.
4 (1855) in E. Rossi, op. cit., 313.

The commercial activity of Tripoli and its harbour increased for a short time, after the Turkish Pashas repressed the riots of the Arab populations, headed by Ghumah (1858). In fact, they occupied and pacified the inner country and the oases in the Fezzan, Ghadames, Murzuk, and Ghat, which were defended by imposing Turkish fortresses. In this period, esparto grass that naturally grows in the arid habitat of the western Libya and was used for producing baskets, ropes, cloth, and paper, constituted an important resource of the Libyan commerce and exportation. The value of esparto, after which a square[36] and a specific pier in the harbour were named, corresponded to about half of the total goods exported from Tripolitania that included olive oil, wheat, wool, and such Sudanese products as ostrich feathers, ivory, and gold dust. Other handicraft and extractive industrial products, in particular salt, were residual exported items.

According to a 1300 H. (1882–1883 A.D.) almanac,[37] "there are 25000 inhabitants, among which, 4.000 Jewish and 3.000 foreigners in the capital of the province, *vilayet*, of Tripoli. Tripoli the Western was the most densely populated and the largest city of the *vilayet*."[38]

A wall with four gates surrounded the town: the gates Bab el-Khandaq and Bab el-Mensha were located on the southern side; Bab el-Jedid was to the west and Bab el-Bahr to the north. Tripoli had six quarters that were called "Homat Garian, Homat el-Beladia, Kasha el-Sogar, Bab el-Bahr, Harat el-Kebir, Harat el-Seghir."[39] According to Cabasi, these appeared separated by void spaces.[40] The subdivision of Tripoli in quarters, *homa*, was evidence of the variety of tribal and religious groups. The *homa*s inhabited by the Jewish community were called *hara*, "Hara es Sghira (the smaller one) and Hara el Kbira (the larger one), even though the former was larger than the latter, but was inhabited by people in more modest social conditions."[41]

The particular character of a quarter was due not only to its different inhabitants, but also to its location in the Medina. "Bab el-Bahr had purely marine features; Homet Gharian and Cushet es-Sefar were mainly related to the caravan traffic; Homet Baladia had a merchant

---

[36] F. Corò, op. cit., 92.
[37] C. Piazza, "La Vilayet di Tripoli d'Occidente nel 1300 dell'Egira secondo un almanacco", *Studi Senesi* 108 (3rd series, 45), no. 1 (1996): 139–173.
[38] Ibid., 150.
[39] Ibid., 151.
[40] F. Cabasi, op. cit., 41.
[41] Ibid.

and intermediary character, with 'managerial' tendencies, as we may say today, due to its direct connection with the Castle as the seat of government. It is remarkable that the building typology of the quarters clearly reflected their functional diversity. The Bab el-Bahr houses were and still are not as spacious as those located in the centre-eastern ones, because the fisherman did not need storages. Fish, being a perishable good, had to be sold on the same day, whereas in the merchant district the house was composed of dwelling place, warehouse and shop, in order to allow the conservation of goods that were seasonal, scarce, or needed to be stored until their price would rise in harder times. Moreover, the merchants needed space for a horse or calash. These were lodged in the *sqifa* or entrance-hall that was used as carriage house, stable or even waiting room for the clients. The *sqifa* was, therefore, very large and the social position of its owner could be assumed by its features."[42]

The above mentioned almanac records also a series of buildings within the walls among which there are "the Castle..., the clock tower, ten mosques, seven synagogues, four churches, 23 schools, two hospitals, three drugstores; four public baths or *hammam*, 2.470 houses, 1.100 shops, 50 warehouses, 50 taverns, 72 mills, 33 bakeries, three industrial factories and about fifty different buildings. Outside the walls there were two barracks which, together with the Castle, were used as the quarters of the troops, the military hospital, 120 small shrines, two schools, 2.000 houses, 2.500 gardens, 260 warehouses, about sixty taverns, 27 mills and some other buildings."[43]

The above list is interesting as it points out to the predominance of the walled town as compared to the built-up area in the oasis. Nevertheless," houses and shops that have been built in last years outside the city walls show that the oasis is considerably growing."[44]

The collective institutions belonging to the different communities forming the urban population are located in the Medina. Besides the Muslim community, the Jewish and Christian communities emerge with their numerous synagogues and churches.

The number of schools bears witness to the new concern of the Ottoman administration in introducing educational reforms (*rüsdiyye*) that

---

[42] Ibid.
[43] C. Piazza, op. cit., 150.
[44] Ibid.

were implemented in the entire area of the Empire despite the *ulama*'s opposition. "In Tripoli the Western the reforms started in 1276/1859 by creating the first professional (later technical) school and were completed in 1297/1879 with the opening of the primary schools. In 1300 H., according to the almanac, there were fifteen public schools one of which was a technical one and fourteen were primary and elementary schools.... The distribution of the schools in the city is known: seven in Hawmat al-Baladiyyah, one of which was a school for girls with a teacher and fifty pupils; two in Hawmat al-Gharyan; three in the Kiln suburb; two in Bab el-Bahr. Besides the public schools (*sultani*) there were others. The Koran-schools assured the education of the young before and against the *rüsdiyye* policy in Tripoli and its *vilayet*. The madrasa of Darghut and the *makatib* run by the learned and holy men were famous. There were also the Jewish community-school in Hara el Kbira and 'foreign schools' such as the French run by the 'Frères', the 'girl's school' of the 'Sisters of Charity' and the 'Italian' school of the 'Marulli Sisters'."[45]

It is interesting to compare the information on Tripoli resulting from the almanac with the data of the census on 3rd of July 1911, on the eve of the Italian occupation of Libya. "The city of Tripoli had 29.869 inhabitants, 19.409 of whom were Muslims, 6.460 Jews, and about 4.000 Europeans, including the Maltese."[46] Regarding the buildings, there were "about 2.750 houses, 1.309 shops, 35 *funduqs*, 72 cafés, 95 taverns, 3 hotels, 5 inns, 2 cinemas, 1 Arab theatre, 1 military steam mill, 45 mills moved by camels, 43 bakeries, 4 soap factories, 3 leather tanneries, 33 mosques, 22 synagogues, 1 catholic church, 1 orthodox church, 21 *marabut*s, 5 among *zawiya*s, *refayye*s, *arussiyye*s, *medaniyye*s, 5 Italian schools, 2 French schools, 3 Muslim religious schools, 1 Turkish military college, 2 Jewish schools, 21 Arab schools for boys where Koran was taught, 2 Muslim schools for girls similar to those for boys, 1 Muslim high school where Koran was taught, 6 Turkish primary and secondary schools, 1 Christian hospital, 1 Italian surgery, 5 drugstores, 3 *hammam*s, 1 Turkish town hospital, 1 military hospital."[47]

---

[45] Ibid., 152–153. The almanac does not mention the Royal Italian School of Tripoli, opened in 1883 and directed by Felice Rostagno; ibid., 173, footnotes 114 and 115. See also E. Rossi, "La colonia italiana a Tripoli nel secolo XIX", *Rivista delle Colonie Italiane*, 4 (1930), p. 1065; A. Del Boca, *Gli Italiani in Libia* (1986; Rome-Bari, 1993), 47.

[46] F. Corò, op. cit., 92.

[47] Ibid.

The plan of Tripoli outlined by Fehmi Bey in 1910[48] registers exactly the population and building increase that was larger in the Jewish quarters of the northwestern corner of the Medina. The urban area inside the walls was entirely filled with houses. The gardens and cemeteries, close to mosques and shrines, and the open spaces separating the quarters no longer exist. The extant gardens contiguous to the walls in the 1910 plan[49] belong to the Muslim, Christian, Orthodox, and Jewish cemeteries.

The synagogues increased together with the Jew population. Their considerable presence is recorded in 1912 in the first Italian Master Plan of the city.[50] Many new small mosques or shrines were also present inside the quarters. The Marcus Aurelius arch, almost fully enclosed in the urban fabric, was used as a cinema, one of the two registered in the 1911 census. While many schools of different kind are a new presence in the network of the collective institutions.

On the eve of the Italian occupation of Tripoli in 1911, the main public spaces and institutions, representing the different periods of urban growth, were concentrated along the strip of land between the ancient *cardo* and the harbour. The Roman Marcus Aurelius *tetrapylon*, the early Islamic Jama al-Naqah, the medieval Arbaʿa Arsat Crossing, the Spanish and the Knights of Malta fortified castle, the early Ottoman Darghut Pasha and Muhammad Pasha mosques, the Karamanli Ahmed Pasha mosque in the *aswaq* and *fanadiq* quarter, and finally the eighteenth and nineteenth-centuries consulates and the embassies quarter all reveal the unending occurrence of major historical events on the same urban axis.

While this strip is easily recognizable in the Medina, a more detailed plan[51] is needed in order to understand how these buildings were

---

[48] In S. Aurigemma, *Le fortificazioni della città di Tripoli*, op. cit., pl. VII.

[49] "There was just a small space called Genan El-Ferik, near the Esparto square, arranged as a public garden; such space was reduced in 1902 when were built nearby the new Turkish barracks, where the military club found a place after the Italian occupation", F. Corò, op. cit., 92.

[50] On the transition from the Ottoman to the Italian city see M. Talamona, "Città europea e città araba in Tripolitania", in *L'architettura italiana d'oltremare (1870–1940)*, Catalogue of the Homonymous Exhibition, a cura di G. Gresleri, (Venezia, 1993), 257–277; L. Micara, "Città storica e architettura moderna in Libia. Il caso di Tripoli", in *Architettura moderna mediterranea*, ed. G. Strappa and A. B. Menghini (Bari, 2003), 81–96.

[51] The here-published plan is the up-to-date scientific result, on the subject of the Medina of Tripoli, of "The Italian Mission for the Study of the Architectural and

inseparable from their urban context. We are dealing indeed with a compact urban fabric, characterised mainly by its physical, structural and functional continuity.[52] Here the cutting of a void produces, due to a domino-effect, further voids all around, spreading the pathology into the surroundings.[53]

The mosque, a public meeting place for the occasion of the ritual collective prayer, is connected through its entrances to the pattern of streets leading to other public spaces and to the residential *enclaves*. The Jama al Naqah, since centuries congregational mosque of the Medina,

---

Urban Heritage of the Islamic Period in Libya". The work of the Mission, carried out in accordance with the Department of Libyan Antiquities and with the Organizational and Administrative Project of the Old Town of Tripoli, aims at the study of the buildings, the urban structure and the transformations of the Medina in order to identify the suitable strategies for its recovery and conservation. The plan, as the eighteenth century G. B. Nolli plan of Rome, includes in the same drawing at the 1/500 scale the plans of all the public buildings (*jawami, masagid, madaris, zawaya, aswaq, fanadiq, hammamat,* etc.) and of the houses that has been possible to survey. The computerized processing of the drawing allows recording all the changes and variations of the plan, in order to realize a basic document for a permanent observatory of the urban transformations of the Medina. For a bibliography on the Mission's activity see: P. Cuneo, "The Italian Architectural Mission for the Islamic Period (1989–1994)", *Libya Antiqua,* new series, 1 (1995): 170–4, tavv. 81–84; P. Cuneo, K. Abdelhadi, P. Barucco, E. Benedetti, and B. Pinna Caboni, "The Italian Architectural Mission for the Islamic Period: 1995 Report", *Libya Antiqua,* new series, 2 (1996): 204–210, tavv. 91–94; L. Micara, "Missione italiana per lo studio dei monumenti architettonici di periodo islamico. Relazione sull'attività del 1996", *Libya Antiqua,* new series, 3 (1997); L. Micara, "Missione italiana per lo studio dell'architettura di periodo islamico", in Ministero degli Affari Esteri, *Missioni archeologiche italiane* (Rome: "L'Erma" di Bretschneider, 1998); L. Micara, "Missione italiana per lo studio dell'architettura e della città di periodo islamico in Libia. Relazione sull'attività del 1997", *Libya Antiqua,* new series, 4 (1998): 259–268; L. Micara, "Scenari dell'abitare contemporaneo: Tripoli medina mediterranea", *Piano Progetto Città, Rivista dei Dipartimenti di Architettura e Urbanistica di Pescara,* nos. 20–21 (2003).

[52] The model of the Medina produced on the occasion of the International Seminar *The Mediterranean Medina,* organized by L. Micara and A. Petruccioli in the Faculty of Architecture of Pescara and in the Michetti Museum of Francavilla al Mare, highlights the continuous and compact character of the urban fabric. The model, in scale 1/500, recreates the topographical situation of the Medina in 1911, on the eve of the transformations performed during the Italian colonial period. It is the result of the investigations carried out by the "The Italian Mission for the Study of the Architectural and Urban Heritage of the Islamic Period in Libya" on the historical cartography of the Medina of Tripoli.

[53] This phenomenon is particularly evident today in the western area of the Medina, mainly inhabited by Jewish people, that was in poor conditions since the colonial period. When in June 1967 the Jews left definitely Libya, after the Six Days war, they, abandoning their houses, caused a progressive decay in that area of the city. It is today necessary to plan urgent recovery strategies in order to halt a process that already reached macroscopic dimensions, threatening the identity loss of a large portion of the Medina.

is bordered by *aswaq* and *fanadiq*, as is that of the Ahmad Pasha al-Karamanli mosque. This feature is due to the *waqf* institution, consisting in the endowment of real properties by the founder to the mosque, the revenues of which are devolved for the maintenance and support of the building. At times, a *hammam* or *madrasa* are closely linked as *waqf* properties with the mosque, creating large religious, commercial and educational units.[54]

In these urban complexes, the commercial routes are the endings of the territorial system of the caravan routes. These enter the Medina mainly from the south, through the Bab el-Mensha and Bab el-Hurria gates, or from the west, through Bab el-Jedid and Bab Zenata. In the central part of the city these routes develop a continuous network of covered or open alleys, sided by shops specialized according to the goods sold.

However, in the peripheral quarters the scattered system of minor or neighbourhood mosques (*masjid*, pl. *masajid*) become the nucleus around which the urban fabric is organized.

At times, larger houses produce particularly interesting urban fabrics. This is the case of Arba'a Arsat Crossing that is physically created by four houses belonging to wealthy families of the city, such as Karamanli, Gurji, and Mohsen. These houses integrate in fact covered *aswaq* bordered by shops and enhance the image of an emerging urban focus.

At times the houses attract special activities and become, thereby, places of particular interest. Such were the houses of rich merchants dealing in land or maritime-trade in Shara' Sidi Amura and Cushet es-Sefar, the house of Pasha in Shara Jama al-Drug that served as Islamic court and the houses turned into French and English Consulates near the Marcus Aurelius Arch.

The Medina of Tripoli is not just another replica of the Arab-Islamic city with its peculiar collective institutions. This urban system was developed on a pre-existing Roman town and was built by different populations such as Arab-Berber, European, and Jewish. Therefore, notwithstanding the prevailing use of courtyards, the buildings open on the public street through particular architectural elements such as arcades, portals, windows, terraces, and balconies are not always pro-

---

[54] Even though the bibliography on such subjects, related to the cities in the Islamic world, is very extensive, see, on the architecture of the collective institutions, L. Micara, *Architettura e spazi dell'Islam. Le istituzioni collettive e la vita urbana* (Rome: Carucci, 1985).

tected by *mashrabiyya*. For this reason it is possible to speak of Tripoli as a Mediterranean *medina*. This definition suggests a legacy of values of urban life and space common to the cities that face the Mediterranean Sea as the privileged space of relations and exchanges, despite other cultural and religious differences.

The peculiar history of the city, particularly in the Ottoman and Karamanli period, favoured the formation of special building types that, deriving from the Islamic tradition, resulted in significant hybridizations.

The accounts of Abu Muhammad Abdallah at-Tijani in his *Rihlah* (travel) to Tripoli in the years 1306–1308 does not add reliable information on the architectural form and type of its mosques. He says that Tripoli was a flourishing city, "where the mosques were so numerous that they exceeded the number of the houses."[55] Tijani mentions among these the al-Sha'ab mosque in the eastern part of the city and the congregational mosque, *jami*, located near the Madrasa al-Mustansiriyya, not far from the Marcus Aurelius Arch, both of which are no longer existing. He describes the latter mosque as large with lofty columns. It had a great hexagonal shaped minaret that was presumably supported by columns.[56] At-Tijani also mentions a mosque near the walls, between Bab al-Bahr and Bab al-Akhdar. It can be speculated that At-Tijani is referring to the Jama al-Naqah, or Camel Mosque, still standing in the same place. It should be remarked that Safar Dey had rebuilt this mosque in 1610, after its demolition during the Spanish occupation.

The mosque has a square hall (18 × 18,50 m.), composed of 49 smaller modules (2,60 × 2,60 m.) covered with domes. These are supported by 36 columns made of archaeological remains. The modules of the bay opposite to the *mihrab*, being rectangular in plan, are the only ones covered with barrel vaults. Four arcades, each formed by seven cross vaults, surround the courtyard that is similar in its dimensions to the hall.

The repetitive architectural system of the hypostyle hall, consisting in a series of modules covered with domes, is the constant feature in the mosques of the Medina of Tripoli.[57] This type differs substantially

---

[55] At-Tijani, "Rihlah", in Ali Mas'ud El-Ballush, op. cit., 58.
[56] A. M. El-Ballush, op. cit., 59.
[57] G. Messana, *L'Architettura musulmana della Libia*, (Castelfranco Veneto, 1972); M. Warfelli, op. cit.; Ali Mas'ud El-Ballush, op. cit. In the greater mosques the hypostyle interior space is enriched with women's galleries on the side facing the *mihrab*, or on

from the central space of the Ottoman mosque covered with a single great cupola.

The size and the proportions of the hypostyle hall varies: from the 9 domes of Jama al-Kharruba and Jama al-Druj, to the 16 of Jama Muhammad Pasha, to the 27, later 32,[58] of the Jama Darghut Pasha, to the 25 of Jama Ahmed Pasha al-Karamanli,[59] and to the 16 domes of Jama Mustafa Bey Gurji.[60]

In the two latter mosques, the architectural type is further elaborated to define a complex made of different elements that consist of a square mosque facing southeast, a madrasa with its courtyard, a *turba* or mausoleum, a minaret with an octagonal or dodecagonal[61] terrace, an ablution fountain, and latrines. Since the northwest-southeast orientation of the mosque does not correspond to the north-south Roman layout of the street, irregular connection spaces are created between the borders of the complex and the central religious building. These consist in three trapezoidal courtyards that, as scholars speculate, were prescribed by the Hanafite ritual.

The shifting between the orientations of the plan of the mosque, defined by the direction of the Mecca, and that of the street façades of the buildings is a constant feature in the architecture of the Islamic countries. This occurs when the mosques are built in an already established and consolidated urban fabric. The need for an architectural solution was evidenced first in 1125 in the al-Aqmar mosque in Cairo.[62] The different spatial solutions for the entrances vary from the simple ones elaborated for the al-Aqmar mosque to the more complex ones of the Safavid mosques facing the Meydan i-Shah in Isfahan.[63] In Tripoli the solution is clear and neat. It is a precise answer to a more general

---

the three sides encompassing, with the *qibla* one, the square central plan. A wooden and decorated gallery, called *dikka* (A. M. El-Ballush, op. cit.) or *sedda* (G. Messana, *L'Architettura Musulmana della Libia*, op. cit.), received the founder of the mosque with his family, above the main entrance looking the *mihrab*.

[58] After the restoration in 1947 of the central part of the T plan.

[59] S. Aurigemma, "La moschea di Ahmad al-Qaramanli in Tripoli", *Dedalo* 7 (1927): 492–513.

[60] S. Aurigemma, "La moschea di Gurji in Tripoli", *Africa Italiana*, 1927–1928, 257–285.

[61] That is the case of the Gurji mosque.

[62] K. A. C. Creswell, *Muslim Architecture in Egypt* (Oxford, 1952), 241–246; V. Meinecke-Berg, "Outline of the Urban Development of Cairo", *Art and Archaeology Research Papers, AARP* (London), 1980, 8–13.

[63] About this subject see L. Micara, *Architetture e spazi dell'Islam*, op. cit., 30–36.

problem concerning the evolution of the architectural typology of the mosque and its urban setting in the fabric of an Ottoman city.

The institutional solution of condensing different public spaces in a complex is as clear as the architectural one. The complex is here articulated according to a geometrically controlled plan that introduced order in the spontaneous creation of different functions and public spaces around the main hypostyle space of the ancient cathedral-mosques.

Other building types such as the *aswaq, fanadiq, hammamat,* or *madaris* reveal a similar process of assimilation of elements deriving from the Arab-Islamic civilization in forms deeply related to the particular environment, spatial sensitivity and building tradition of the Medina of Tripoli. This can be also read in the Othman Pasha Madrasa.

The houses of the Medina are particularly interesting in this regard. The aggregation of plots and courtyards of large and uniform size recalls the compact and regular fabric of the Roman city.[64] The old houses of today's Medina of Tripoli, mainly from seventeenth and eighteenth centuries, are organized around a square courtyard, surrounded by arcades and covered balconies that can be reached from the street through an indirect entrance. Marble, sandstone, or wooden columns support the arcades on the sides of the courtyard on the ground floor, and the galleries on the upper floor. Four rooms are built on the sides of the courtyard, where frequently a small water basin and always a well are placed.

In the larger houses the rooms are planned with a lofty central chamber, *dar el-gbu,* made of a great arch or covered with a barrel vault, flanked by two symmetrical side rooms. The latter spaces are arranged in two levels, whose lower one is a storage, while the upper floor, about one metre and half above the ground floor, is a gallery, *sedda,* screened with curtains, used as a niche for sleeping.

The main stairs leading from the courtyard to the upper galleries are located in the wall facing the entrance. These are the cases of the Karamanli house that was turned into the English Consulate or the Pasha house used formerly as the Islamic court of law. Here the staircases have a T form, where the first flight is orthogonal to the wall, reaching a landing from which two opposite flights of stairs run parallel to the wall.

---

[64] P. Romanelli, "Vecchie case arabe di Tripoli", *Architettura e Arti Decorative* 3, no. 5 (January 1924): 193–211.

This refined architectural solution is used at times in the *fanadiq* of the Medina.

The high quality of the residential architecture, the clear layout of the sober yet decorated spaces and the smart contrast between the solid basement walls and the light wooden structures suggest the rich values of the domestic life in the Medina. These values emerge notwithstanding the state of decay of the buildings that are today overcrowded by immigrants.

The investigation on the residential situation of the Medina reveals not only the presence of more or less important houses related to a traditionally Arab way of life, but also the widespread interest towards housing typologies, mainly built by Italian and Maltese entrepreneurs and workers, that open through windows and balconies toward the street. These residential typologies are frequently adopted in the marginal urban areas to solve the problem of the increasing density of population in the Medina, integrating in the same building an apartment that opens only towards the street and another that opens only towards the interior courtyard.

A Mediterranean air, suggesting the assimilation of various foreign influences, emerges from the different ways of the urban life. It seems to represent a basic code for the understanding and interpretation of the complexity of the Ottoman Medina of Tripoli.

ALGIERS IN THE OTTOMAN PERIOD: THE CITY AND ITS POPULATION

Federico Cresti*

Introduction

Amongst the topics concerning Algiers in the Ottoman period over which historians and researchers still debate, often taking up widely differing positions, undoubtedly one of the most interesting concerns its population. Indeed, in the last few decades many scholars have dealt with this topic; and it is one which is important for anyone interested in the city in the Muslim world during the Ottoman period. Furthermore, from a more general, historiographic viewpoint, it has significant implications for the collocation of Algiers within the framework of events in the Mediterranean between the sixteenth and nineteenth centuries, as well as for its importance as a territorial capital of the Ottoman Regency.

On this occasion I shall return to research begun several years ago, part of the results of which have already been published,[1] though there is still ample room for further hypotheses. My purpose here is to state precisely the terms of the debate, to review in detail the present state of research and, as far as possible, to add some further, little known, elements.

It might be useful to recall some geographical and historical facts that constitute a frame of reference and form the basis for any other considerations on the printed sources or on the archival documents available. First of all, the size of the city in the Ottoman period.

* COSMICA—Centro per gli studi sul mondo islamico contemporaneo e l'Africa, Università di Catania (Centre for Studies on the Contemporary Islamic World and Africa, University of Catania, Italy). This article is based on the text of a lecture given at the international conference "Alger: Lumières sur la ville" held in Algiers, 4–6 May 2002.

[1] See especially F. Cresti, "Quelques réflexions sur la population et la structure sociale d'Alger à la période turque (XVIᵉ–XIXᵉ siècles)," *Cahiers de Tunisie* 34, nos. 137–138 (1986): 161–164; id., "Gli schiavi cristiani ad Algeri in età ottomana: considerazioni sulle fonti e questioni storiografiche," *Quaderni storici* 36, no. 107 (2001): 415–435.

It is well known that after Khayr al-dīn "Barbarossa" seized power
and recognised the Sultan of Constantinople as his sovereign (1518)
the fortifications of the city were adapted to the new defence requirements and their perimeter enlarged.[2] Even though we do not know the
exact size of the al-Jazā'ir of Banī Mazghanna, the defensive walls of
the Ottoman period covered a larger surface area than those of the
preceding period. Moreover, the city was given new port structures,
which in the following decades would make landing easier, giving rise
to a period of prosperity, based mainly on an increase in privateering.
Within the perimeter of the walls the surface area of the city measured
at least 45 hectares.[3] We should recall that this area did not notably

---

[2] The chronicle of this episode recounts that Hasan Agha, the successor of Khayr
al-dîn as Governor of Algiers, had the walls rebuilt and the damaged parts repaired,
providing them with batteries of canons (R. Basset, *Documents musulmans sur le siège d'Alger
en 1541* [Paris and Oran, 1890], 20–21). The fortifications of the city had been repaired
several times in the past, if we are to believe Leo Africanus (who visited Algiers in
1515 during one of his journeys): in his *Description of Africa* he speaks of rebuilding the
city walls with the stones of Tamendfust (Jean-Léon l'Africain, *Description de l'Afrique*,
French translation by A. Epaulard [Paris, 1981], p. 352). Nevertheless the text does
not specify the period of the reconstruction. I have suggested elsewhere that this took
place in the Zayyânid period in the course of the fourteenth century (see F. Cresti,
"Note sullo sviluppo urbano di Algeri dalle origini al periodo turco," *Studi Magrebini*
[henceforth: *SM*] 12 [1980], 115). 'Arûj had already begun work on improving the
defence of the fortress ("the Kasbah, which in that period was the only fortress in
Algiers") according to the *Epitome de los reyes de Argel* by Diego de Haedo ("Histoire des
Rois d'Alger," French translation by H.-D. De Grammont, *Revue Africaine* [henceforth:
RA] 24, no. 139 [1880]: 58). The work on the fortifications continued throughout the
sixteenth century, and more episodically in the course of the following centuries.

[3] "Son développement, mesuré sur les remparts, est d'environ 3.000 m, sa superficie
de 415.000 mc" (Archives du Service Historique de l'Armée de Terre, Vincennes,
Génie, Algérie, art. 8, sec. 1, cart. 2, no. 1: *Mémoire sur la Place d'Alger par le Chef de
Bataillon Collas*, 1830 [henceforth: *Mémoire Collas*], 2); according to Rozet the city had
an extension of c. 53 hectares (P. Rozet, *Voyage dans la Régence d'Alger, ou description du
pays occupé par l'Armée française en Afrique* [...], 3 vols. [Paris, 1833], *passim*); according
to Lespès "la superficie de la ville turque [était] sans la citadelle de la Casbah, de 41
hect. 1" (R. Lespès, *Alger. Etude de Géographie et d'Histoire urbaines* [Paris, 1930], 524, note
3). In his first article on the subject Raymond takes up the data provided by Lespès
(A. Raymond, "Signes urbains et étude de la population des grandes villes arabes à
l'époque ottomane," *Bulletin d'Études Orientales*, no. 27 [1974]: 185) and later states that
its surface areas was 46 hectares (Id., *Grandes villes arabes à l'époque ottomane*, [Paris, 1985],
62); Klein maintains that its extension was 50 hectares and 53 ares for the *intra muros*
city, but that it was necessary to add a further 4 hectares and 9 ares for the Admiralty
(H. Klein, *Feuillets d'El-Djezaïr* [Algiers, 1937], 30). The data provided by Klein are
taken up by D. Lesbet in *La Casbah d'Alger* (Algiers and Talence, 1985), pp. 35 and 38;
F. Benatia (*Alger, agrégat ou cité* [Algiers, 1980], 24) gives an extension of c. 60 hectares for
the city in 1830. T. Shuval states that in its period of greatest expansion the Ottoman
city "s'était étendue sur 54 hectares 62 ares, dont l'espace bâti occupait 46 hectares"
(T. Shuval, *La ville d'Alger vers la fin du XVIIIe siècle. Population et cadre urbain* [Paris, 1998],

increase over the following decades, not because there was no need for more space on which to build, but for military reasons. We know that during the pashadom of ʿArab Ahmad (1573) the city had begun to expand to the south, outside Bāb Azūn, with the formation of a suburb that was later destroyed for defence reasons.[4]

The Importance of Immigration in the Early Ottoman Period

Scholars generally agree[5] over the reasons for an increase in the population of Algiers in the early Ottoman period, which was due mainly to the immigration of Muslims forced to leave the Iberian peninsula in the last phases of the Christian conquest. A phenomenon which had certainly begun before the arrival of the Turks, but was accentuated at the time of ʿArūj and Khayr al-dīn's capture of the city, or in any case in the first two decades of the sixteenth century. Diego de Haedo, who was in Algiers around 1580 and who later published a crucial work for our knowledge of the city in this period, writes:

> The fourth category of Moors [in Algiers] is made up of those who came here from the kingdoms of Granada, Aragon, Valencia and Catalonia, and who continue to come here today from Marseilles and other French ports whence it is easy to embark. They can be divided into two groups: the Mudejares who have left Granada and Andalusia, and the Tagarinos who come from the kingdoms of Aragon, Valencia and Catalonia. These Moors are white-skinned and well-proportioned, as are all those who come from Spain. They exercise a great number of different professions and every one of them is skilled in some craft: from those who make harquebus, gunpowder or saltpetre to locksmiths, carpenters and masons, tailors, shoemakers, potters, and so on. Many breed silk-worms or own shops in which all kinds of merchandise are sold [...] They dress like Turks [...] In Algiers there are about a thousand houses of these Andalusian Moors.[6]

---

41). The discrepancy between the above-mentioned figures (from 41.5 hectares to c. 60 hectares) is conspicuous. It would be useful to verify the different calculations in order to define more precisely the relation between the built space of the city and the surface area of the *intra muros* city.

[4] According to Haedo, who speaks of a suburb of 1,500 houses.

[5] See H.-D. De Grammont, *Histoire d'Alger sous la domination turque, 1515–1830* (Paris, 1887), *passim*; R. Lespès, op. cit., 105–106. Nevertheless, these authors base their information above all on Haedo's text.

[6] D. de Haedo, "Topographie et histoire générale d'Alger," French translation by Monnereau and Berbrugger, *RA* 14, no. 84 (1870): 495.

It is interesting to note that, according to Haedo, while occupying less than a twelfth of the houses (a total of 12,200 "small and large"),[7] the Andalusians made up a fifth or a sixth of the Moorish population of Algiers.[8] There is little else on Andalusian emigration to the city. For instance, again according to Haedo, in 1517 a military expedition leaving Algiers under the command of ʿArūj counted 500 Andalusian Moriscos among its ranks.[9] Nevertheless, the text does not tell us whether these included members of the families that had settled in Algiers. We must remember that the careers of ʿArūj and his brother Khayr al-dīn in the western Mediterranean included transportation to the North African coast of those Spanish Muslims who desired to leave the country. According to De Grammont (who cites as his source certain "oriental writers" without giving their names), "they carried more than 10,000 Moors across the sea."[10] In the *Ghazawāt ʿArūj wa Khayr al-dīn*, which is probably De Grammont's source, there are several episodes of this kind. Khayr al-dīn crossed the Spanish waters for three months "in order to help his brothers and take on board those whom he could wrest from

---

[7] D. de Haedo, "Topographie...," cit., 431. The number of houses proposed by Haedo is based on a seemingly easy calculation, which is nevertheless erroneous once the data in the text have been scrutinized. The calculation is further complicated by the fact that for some groups, for example the 'Azuagos' (*zwâwa*-s), the reference is to "families" and not "houses"; for unmarried men he speaks of "barracks" not houses; he often speaks of families who live in huts or in "rented rooms," and at least in one case he refers to precarious habitations made of straw leaning against the houses outside the city. If we add up the habitations that the author explicitly attributes to each of the categories of the urban population (4,100 for the Moors, 7,600 for the Turks, 150 for the Jews) we reach a figure of 11,850. Perusing Haedo's text, the population is determined by a sum that includes the occupants of 11,850 houses, 100 families and 200 or 300 (sometimes more) unmarried men, to which may be added "c. 25,000 Christian slaves" and a small number of free Christians.

[8] Among the four distinct groups comprising the Moors, Haedo considers that "those who were born in the city," the *Baldis*, occupy c. 2,500 houses, the *Azuagos* reach 100 families and 200 or 300 unmarried men, the other Kabyles occupy c. 600 houses, while the *Alarbes* do not own houses in the city, since they live "in the porticos of houses" or else in straw huts outside Bâb ʿAzûn (ivi, pp. 491–494). N. Saidouni ("Les morisques dans la province d'Alger "Dar-es-Soltan" pendant le XVIᵉ et XVIIᵉ siècles," in *L'expulsió dels moriscos. Conseqüències en el món islàmic i el món cristià*, Proceedings of the International Congress [Barcelona, 1984], 141) states that Algiers at the time of the exodus of the Moriscos was a city mainly inhabited by Andalusians; even this author bases his information on Haedo's text, stating that they made up about half of the population of Algiers.

[9] D. de Haedo, *Epitome...* cit., 62. See also R. Lespès, *op. cit., ibid.*

[10] H.-D. De Grammont, "Histoire...," cit., 3.

the Christian tyranny,"[11] though how many is not specified. Some years later his vessels sailed along the Spanish coasts in order to take on board Muslims who desired to move to Africa, and on this occasion "he embarked a large number who came to live in Algiers."[12]

Even later, between 1529 and 1535, the Algerian fleet made several crossings and "carried 70,000 souls to Algiers." This last figure is improbably large, since only a relatively small number of Spanish Moriscos set up residence in Algiers, which was not one of the cities where the majority settled. Most of those who landed in the central Maghreb went to live inland, or else in other cities along the coast, such as Sharshāll, which the *Ghazawāt* tells us underwent a kind of renascence thanks to the Andalusian Moors.[13]

Apart from this rather vague information, other categories of immigrants populated the city and it doesn't seem as though the Andalusian community was the most important in terms of its demographic increase in the sixteenth century. Actually, Haedo states that when he arrived in Algiers the Turks were those who made up the largest nucleus of the population. We should recall that by "Turks" Haedo meant all those "who were born or whose fathers were born in Turkey," but also all those "who can call themselves Turkish by profession": in other words, those recently converted to Islam, Christians (often former slaves) who had renounced their faith. They made up the majority of the population ("they, together with their children, are more numerous than the other inhabitants, Moors, Turks, Jews, since there is not a single Christian nation that has not provided Algiers with its contingent of

---

[11] Translation by J. M. Venture de Paradis, edited by S. Rang and F. Denis, *Fondation de la Régence d'Alger. Histoire des Barberousse* (Paris, 1837), 37. Venture de Paradis' translation was based on an eighteenth century Arabic manuscript; it has been considered "a very poor French translation of an 18th century Arabic version, which is actually just a summary and is not always faithful to the original" (Gallotta, *op. cit. infra*, 3); an Italian translation of a Spanish manuscript held in the Biblioteca Comunale in Palermo, which is in turn a translation of a copy of the *Ghazawāt* held in the Escurial in Madrid, was published by E. Pelaez at the end of the nineteenth century, in "Archivio Storico Siciliano," 1880–1887; a more recent edition of Pelaez' text is G. Bonaffini, *La vita e la storia di Ariadeno Barbarossa* (Palermo, 1993). A return to the source texts would now seem opportune. Some years ago G. Gallotta published a critical edition of one of the Turkish manuscripts of the *Ghazawāt* ("Il 'Ghazavāt-i Hayreddīn Pasha' di Seyyid Murād," *SM* 13, [1983]), but he has not published his translation of it.

[12] *Ibid.*, 152.

[13] *Ibid.*, 282, translated by Pelaez and edited by Bonaffini, cit., 167: "Ariadeno avea edificato il castello di Cherchelle ed avealo popolato di Mori Andalusi."

apostates"). Haedo gives them 6,000 houses, that is, a little less than half the population of the city.[14]

As for those "born in Turkey," the first nucleus was made up not only of the troops commanded by 'Arūj and Khayr al-dīn but also of 2,000 janissaries whom Sultan Selim II had sent to Algiers after his act of allegiance, and by Turkish volunteers who had arrived at the same time: altogether around 4,000 persons, as far as we can glean from the sources.[15] Adding up the various categories, the Turks, with 7,600 houses in all, constituted the most important part of the population. To complete the picture of "ethnic" groups listed by Haedo were the Jews, with 150 houses in two different neighbourhoods.

Leaving aside for the moment any reflections on the absolute value of Haedo's figures and confining ourselves to their relative value, the contribution of populations from other countries seems to peak around the end of the sixteenth century. If we consider that, before the Turks seized power, the urban population was probably comprised mainly of Haedo's category of "Baldis"—to which we can add the "Azuagos" and other "Kabyles" together with the Jews and a certain number of Andalusians—then we can deduce that during the sixteenth century the population of Algiers tripled with the arrival of immigrants, favoured by the new position of the city within the context of events in the Mediterranean in this period. If we add the Christian slaves, then the population of Algiers was perhaps quadrupled. Such an increase—three or four times the initial population over a period of about 100 years—seems to be a unique phenomenon for a city of "*ancien régime*." From an economic perspective it corresponds to "the prodigious growth of Algiers" thanks to the privateering described by Fernand Braudel.[16]

---

[14] Haedo, *Topographie*...cit., 497. This figure is probably exaggerated: the presence of a large number of "apostates" must have particularly impressed a religious man like Haedo. On the presence of converts to Islam in the militia in a later period, see T. Shuval, *op. cit.*, 60–62.

[15] According to an evaluation which is currently accepted (see H.-D. De Grammont, op. cit., 30–31) but absolutely uncertain: the *Ghazawāt*, for example, makes no reference to the arrival in Algiers of janissaries or other armed forces from Anatolia. Other authors speak of the arrival of 2,000 janissaries and 4,000 volunteers.

[16] "La course musulmane n'est pas moins prospère [...]. Ses centres sont nombreux, mais sa fortune se résume toute entière dans la prodigieuse croissance d'Alger" (F. Braudel, *La Méditerranée et le monde méditerranéen à l'époque de Philippe II*, 4 ed.–1 ed., [Paris, 1966]–2: 203). Braudel speaks of a "première et prodigieuse fortune d'Alger,"

Sources and Data on the Population

This enormous increase in its population would be acceptable, if we could ascribe a reduced size and a modest position to Algiers with respect to other central North African cities in the period prior to Ottoman rule. Yet what exactly do we know about the population of Algiers in this period? Very little indeed. In the twelfth century, al-Idrîsî describes it as a "very populous" city with a flourishing trade, though this tells us little about its true demographic size.[17] The first numerical calculation in the sources dates to the beginning of the sixteenth century, when Hasan al-Zayyati (aka Leo Africanus) gave it 4,000 hearths.[18] This figure, the accuracy of which we have no comparative means of judging,[19] certainly does not place Algiers amongst the most densely populated cities of the central Maghreb.[20] Its reduced demographic size in the first decades of Ottoman rule seems to be confirmed by Nicolas de Nicolay who was the first European to describe it in the sixteenth century.[21] Passing through Algiers in 1551, he gives it a population of 3,000 hearths, even fewer than Leo Africanus.

This is just a brief outline of the scanty information available to us for the pre-Ottoman period. If we concede a substantial increase in the number of inhabitants due to immigration (tripling or quadrupling in about 100 years), we are immediately faced with the problem of

---

from 1560 to 1570, and of a "seconde et toujours prodigieuse fortune d'Alger" from 1580 to 1620 (*ibid.*, 203–205).

[17] R. Dozy and M. De Goeje, ed. and trans., *Description de l'Afrique et de l'Espagne par Edrisi* (anastatic reprint of the 1866 edition; Leiden, 1968), 65. Other Muslim geographers in other periods, such as al-Bakrī and Pīrī Reʾīs, use the same locution in their descriptions of Algiers.

[18] Leo Africanus, *op. cit., ibidem.*

[19] Without trying to find "des solutions au problème irritant que pose l'interprétation de la notion de 'feu'" (A. Raymond, "Signes urbains...," cit., 192), we shall follow the currently accepted hypothesis that a "hearth" corresponds to a minimum of 4–5 persons. The problem remains, however, of the equivalence between "hearth" and housing unit, since living conditions were subject to variations, depending on the period and social class of the population. Far be it from me, however, to give "3(!) individus par famille" (T. Shuval, *op. cit.*, 43, note 25) for the average Jewish family in 1725, as attested by Laugier de Tassy. A typographical error in my article "Quelques réflexions...," cit., 162 tripled the 5,000 houses or families given by Laugier.

[20] Leo Africanus attributes 6,000 hearths to Wahrān, 8,000 to Qusantīna and Bijāya and 12,000 to Tilimsān [which according to the same author counted as many as 16,000 in its period of greatest prosperity]. In this case Algiers would be the fifth city of the region in terms of demographic importance.

[21] N. de Nicolay, *Les quatre premiers livres des navigations orientales* (Lyon, 1568), *passim.*

physical space. Did the enlargement of the defensive walls in the early Ottoman period triple or quadruple the surface area of the city *intra muros*? Certainly not, even though, as mentioned above, it is difficult to evaluate the extension of the city prior to this period.

If we accept Pasquali's conclusions[22]—whose analysis of the expansion of Algiers in the Berber and Ottoman period is based on an overly long list of hypotheses concerning the morphology of the site and on comparison with a medley of other urban sites—then the new space acquired by the city with the expansion of its walls would have been no more than about ten hectares. Another possibility is that the buildings in the pre-Ottoman city were concentrated within a limited area, with much of the space either uninhabited or used for the cultivation of crops.[23] A further hypothesis is that the pre-Ottoman city walls delimited a smaller perimeter than the one proposed by Pasquali and that they only enclosed the actual built environment—no more than twenty hectares at the most—in the low-lying area of the site, nearest the sea. This last hypothesis seems plausible,[24] even though we would need to interpret afresh the archaeological data and carry out new land surveys in order to prove it. All of which seems unlikely in the near future.

Whichever of these hypotheses is correct, the result of this demographic increase was the progressive occupation of all the space within the new city walls[25] and the gradual congestion of the built environment. This increase in the density of the buildings reached an extreme limit that shocked most Europeans who described the city in the sixteenth

---

[22] E. Pasquali, "L'évolution de la rue musulmane d'El-Djezaïr," *Documents Algériens*, Série culturelle, no. 75 (1955). In the absence of more convincing material proof, Pasquali's hypothesis of the city's extension in the Berber period seems very doubtful (see also E. Pasquali, "Alger aux époques phénicienne et romaine," *Documents Algériens*, Série culturelle, no. 62 (1952); M. Leglay, "À la recherche d'Icosium," *Antiquités Africaines*, no. 2 [1978]).

[23] This seem to be the hypothesis accepted by, amongst others, S. Missoum, "El desarrollo de la medina de Argel entro los siglos XVI y XVII y sus relaciones con los textos y practicas juridicas," in *L'urbanisme dans l'Occident musulman au Moyen âge: Aspects juridiques*, (actes recueillis et préparés par) Cressier, Fierro, and Van Staëvel (Madrid, 2000), 220, fig. 3.

[24] Not even the landed property sources examined by Devoulx, on the basis of which we may state with certainty that the Ottoman walls covered a larger surface area than the earlier city, are able to corroborate this hypothesis (see A. Devoulx, "Alger. Étude archéologique et topographique...," *RA* 115 [1876]: 71–74), whereby the *qasaba al-qadīma* (from the name used in the documents for the pre-Ottoman fortress, which according to Pasquali was within the city walls) would have been isolated with regard to the inhabited area.

[25] See A. Devoulx, "Alger...," cit., 73.

and seventeenth centuries. Returning once again to Haedo, it never-theless seems unlikely that the available space within the walls could have allowed for the construction of over 12,000 houses (in the sense of separate individual units) and so we may conclude that this figure is exaggerated.[26]

Arab and Turkish documentary sources from the seventeenth and eighteenth centuries contribute little to our knowledge of the demo-graphic size of Algiers, while European sources provide quite a lot of data, though this is mostly information which does not come from a direct knowledge of the city, but from compilations, or which does not correspond to the physical size of the city. Throughout most of the seventeenth century many European writers state that the number of houses in Algiers was even greater than Haedo's estimation: from c. 13,500 according to Jean-Baptiste Gramaye, who was a prisoner in Algiers in 1619, to 15,000 according to the Venetian Giovanni Battista Salvago and to François Pierre Dan who both sojourned there a few years later. These last figures were taken up by many geographers and writers who dealt with events in Algiers and North Africa in the Otto-man period.[27] Starting with the figure of 12,200 inhabitants provided by Haedo, Jean-Baptiste Gramaye estimates that in the last quarter of the sixteenth and the first two decades of the seventeenth century the number of houses in the city increased by 1,300. These would have

---

[26] It is important to stress the fact that Haedo does not consider Algiers a large city, since it "only has 12,200 houses, both large and small" ("Topographia..." cit., in *RA* 14 (1870): 431). A more acceptable point of comparison could be that of 6,800 houses in the French military census after the Conquest (see *infra*). Nevertheless, we do not know with any accuracy the evolution of housing typologies in the two and a half centuries circa that separate the two estimates. In his above-mentioned article S. Missoum states that the lack of space generated—towards the end of the seventeenth century—a new typology of dwellings, the " '*alwī*, casas de pequeñas dimensiones, sin *wast ad-dār* o patio, que se desarrollan en altura" (op. cit., 225; on this type of dwell-ing, described as *olie* o *oleah* by T. Shaw, who was in Algiers from 1720 to 1732—and who seems identify it with the *duwīra*, one of the types of lodging preferred by the janissaries according to Shuval—see also T. Shuval, op. cit., 97–98). Braudel speaks of the urban development of Algiers during the sixteenth century as that of a "ville neuve, poussée à l'américaine" (F. Braudel, op. cit., vol. 2: 194). The existence of pre-carious types of dwelling both inside and outside the city walls (*gourbis*, huts, *masures*), sporadically mentioned in the sources, is also difficult to evaluate, as is the number of "rented rooms" cited by Haedo.

[27] The figure of 15,000 houses is cited by Du Val (1665), Dapper (1668), Ogilby (1670), De La Croix (1688), Laugier de Tassy (1725) and Palermo (1784); that of 13,000 by De Rocoles (1660). Sanson d'Abbeville (1656) and Auvry (1662) propose between 12,000 and 15,000 houses.

been mainly houses built inside the walls by the former inhabitants of the *extra moenia* suburbs that had been destroyed in 1573, while a further wave of Andalusians, expelled from Spain in 1609, supposedly found asylum in Algiers in 300 new houses ("casas vel domus" writes Gramaye in Latin; that is, both shanties and proper houses).

From the last decades of the sixteenth century the population recorded by most of the European sources seems to rocket: 130,000 inhabitants according to Lanfreducci and Bosio (1587); 150,000 according to Salvago (1625), who describes the city as being "full as an egg"; the same figure according to Tollot (1731); and c. 117,000 according to Shaw (1738). The figure of 100,000 is the one that recurs most frequently. At least twelve European authors mention it in their writings, though we must remember that others mention lower figures: Botero (1595), Davity (1625) and Coppin (1686) cite 80,000 inhabitants, Lithgow (1615) 30,000. Later, Cano (c. 1750) speaks of 50,000 inhabitants, as do Venture de Paradis (1789) and Shaler (1815). According to Raynal (1788), there were fewer than 50,000, while, according to Dubois-Thainville (1809), there were between 75,000 and 80,000.

The discrepancies between the European authors' estimations correspond to the real difficulty of proposing figures that are not merely the result of subjective appraisals or that take up uncritically more reliable reports. It would seem that a first-hand knowledge of North African cities and the related literature which could provide better tools for evaluation does not generate greater objectivity. Gråberg, for example, who was Swedish consul in North African countries and who bases his observations on consolidated bibliographical research, gives the city a minimum of 70,000 inhabitants and c. 10,000 houses: as a point of comparison, we should recall that the first French military census, after taking the city, gives 24,200 inhabitants and c. 6,800 houses.[28]

---

[28] *Mémoire Collas*, 2. Lespès (op. cit., 140) cites the figure in this text from a copy held in the same archives ("art I, n. 11"), which is probably different from our copy (see note 3 above). We have not found the document cited by Lespès, who does not give figures for the population (see R. Lespès, op. cit., 140). The census to which Collas refers was ordered by General Clauzel in October 1830 (see Aumerat, "La propriété urbaine à Alger," *RA* 41 (1897): 321; see also Id., *La propriété urbaine et le bureau de bienfaisance musulmane d'Alger* [Algiers, 1900], 7). Since we still have not found any other original documents relating to this census, the *Mémoire Collas* remains the most reliable source. Later authors (Aumerat and Klein, for example, who in general do not cite their sources accurately) give a confused image of the data in this census and propose figures that vary from 8,000 to 4,000 dwellings. Lespès accurately cites the 6,800 dwellings mentioned in the *Mémoire Collas*.

The data from the available sources, almost all of which have been published,[29] highlight both the above-mentioned discrepancies and the widespread acceptance on the part of European writers of 100,000 or more inhabitants, especially up to the beginning of the eighteenth century.

Table I. The population of Algiers in the ottoman period according to the sources.

1516	Hasan al-Zayyāti/ Leo Africanus	4,000 hearths
1550	Nicolay	3,000 hearths
1578–1581	Haedo	12,200 houses
1587	Lanfreducci and Bosio	130,000 inhabitants
1588	Sanuto	4,000 hearths
1595	Botero	80,000 inhabitants
1605	Savary de Brèves	100,000 inhabitants
1615	Lithgow	30,000 inhabitants
1619	Gramaye	c. 13,500 houses
1621–1626	Mascarenhas	12,000 houses
1625	Salvago	150,000 inhabitants, 15,000 houses
1634	Dan	more than 100,000 inhabitants, c. 15,000 houses
1640–1642	Aranda	100,000 inhabitants
1656	Sanson d'Abbeville	12,000/15,000 houses
1660	Davity (ed. De Rocoles)	c. 13,000 houses
1662	Auvry	100,000 inhabitants, 13/15,000 houses
1665	Du Val	15,000 houses
1668	Dapper	c. 15,000 houses
1670	Ogilby	100,000 inhabitants, 15,000 houses
1674–1675	Arvieux	more than 100,000 inhabitants, 15,000 houses
1683	Manesson-Mallet	100,000 inhabitants
1685	Laugier de Tassy (ed. 1725)	100,000 inhabitants
1686	Coppin	c. 80,000 inhabitants
1688	De La Croix	15,000 houses
1700	Comelin	more than 100,000 inhabitants

---

[29] See F. Cresti, "Quelques réflexions..." op. cit., 155. The reference to the dates for the authors of the printed works who lived in Algiers is that of their stay, not the edition of their works. In this table some information has been added, for instance, regarding the text by João Mascarenhas, published in Lisbon in 1627, and the number of inhabitants proposed in the *Mémoire Collas* in 1830.

Table I (*cont.*)

1719	Gueudeville	100,000 inhabitants
1729	Vander Aa	c. 5,000 houses
1731	Tollot	150,000 inhabitants
1738	Shaw	c. 117,000 inhabitants
1750 c.	Juan Cano	50,000 inhabitants
1784	Palermo	more than 100,000 inhabitants, no fewer than 15,000 houses
1785–1788	Von Rehbinder	80,000 inhabitants
1788	Raynal	fewer than 50,000 inhabitants
1789	Venture de Paradis	c. 50,000 inhabitants, 5000 houses
1808	Boutin	73,000 inhabitants
1809	Dubois-Thainville	75,000/80,000 inhabitants
1815	Shaler	c. 50,000 inhabitants, c. 5,000 houses
1815–1817	Pananti	100,000 inhabitants
1830	Grâberg	70,000 inhabitants, c. 10,000 houses
[1830	Mémoire Collas	24,200 inhabitants, 6,800 houses]

Data from the European Sources: A Comparative Critical Approach

The European sources disclose a quite stable population throughout the seventeenth century; indeed all the authors except two give the city 100,000 inhabitants. Yet can we really imagine a population of 100,000 or more for a city the size of Algiers in the Ottoman period? This figure has been generally accepted by modern historians and geographers. In an analysis published in 1929 on the distribution of the population in the Kasbah, which in the colonial period corresponded roughly to the perimeter of the Ottoman city, René Lespès does not express surprise, considering the recorded density, "that 17th century authors could, without exaggeration, give an estimate of 100,000 or more inhabitants for Algiers."[30] More recently this figure has been questioned by André Raymond. In one of his studies on Arab cities in the Ottoman period we read:

> Much more modest [at the end of the eighteenth century] was a city like Algiers, the surface area of which was only 46 hectares and its population, estimated at 30,000 inhabitants in 1830, is generally considered much

---

[30] R. Lespès, *op. cit.*, 524. See also P. Boyer, "L'évolution démographique des populations musulmanes du Département d'Alger (1830/66–1948)," *RA* 98 (1954): 320 and 323.

lower than its population in the seventeenth century. The doubt arises especially for Algiers: the density [of its population] is extremely high, with 646 inhabitants per hectare (per 30,000 inhabitants in 1830), even more than the Qâhira district in Cairo. This may be explained by the "compression" of the city within its walls, the density of the buildings, their vertical structure, and finally the presence of prisons, in which the slaves were locked up at night and barracks crammed with thousands of janissaries and Christian slaves. Yet it is obvious that the estimated figures for earlier periods (one speaks commonly of 100,000 inhabitants in the seventeenth century) merit the soundest scepticism. A density of 2,000 inhabitants per hectare is only a recent phenomenon, in cities like Algiers and Cairo, for reasons linked to colonization or to the demographic explosion in the twentieth century.[31]

Raymond's comparative approach shows that, even with the lower estimate of 30,000 inhabitants, Algiers would have had a higher density than any other large city in the Arab world at the end of the eighteenth century, with 650 inhabitants per hectare.[32] Moreover, Raymond suggests that the figure of 50,000 proposed by Venture de Paradis at the end of the eighteenth century is closer to the truth.[33]

Venture de Paradis' account (who was in Algiers from 1788 to 1790) seems carefully thought out. Besides, with the French Consulate as an observation point, he would have had a clearer idea of the urban reality of Algiers, while with respect to other European writers he had the advantage of knowing Arabic and Turkish. He writes:

Algiers has the extension that a city of 25,000–30,000 inhabitants in France would have and I think that its actual population could be realistically estimated at 50,000 souls, taking into account the number of women who are always at home and so are never part of the crowd. Of these 50,000 we can count 6,000 Couloglis, 3,000 eastern Turks, 7,000 Jews, 2,000 slaves and other Christians and 32,000 Moors, amongst whom we include those who come from Biskra and have the same function here that people from Savoy and Auvergne have in Paris, the Zawâwa, those who come from M'zab and Jerba, etc.[34]

---

[31] A. Raymond, *Grandes villes arabes à l'époque ottomane* (Paris, 1985), 62–63.

[32] Cairo had an estimated density of 300 to 600 inhabitants per hectare, depending on the neighbourhood, Tunis 446, Aleppo 327, Damascus 288, Mossul 283 and Baghdad 265.

[33] T. Shuval (*op. cit.*, 41–44) shares Raymond's opinion. If we accept Venture de Paradis' estimate, then the city would have had a density of more than 1,000 inhabitants per hectare in the last decades of the eighteenth century.

[34] J. M. Venture de Paradis, *Alger au XVIIIe siècle*, ed. E. Fagnan (Algiers, 1898) [which contains in a single volume the work published by Fagnan in the *Revue Africaine* in the

We may note in passing that in the second half of the eighteenth century, while Venture de Paradis was writing his *Notes*, almost all the other European sources abandon the estimates of 100,000 or more inhabitants and propose lower figures, from 80,000 to even fewer than 50,000. Taking into account these figures, Venture de Paradis' estimates still seem plausible, though we need to make a few observations before accepting them.

The second half of the eighteenth century was certainly not the most prosperous time for the capital of the Ottoman Regency and, "to the extent that the parallel between the growth or decline of a population and economic progress or decline can be accepted as a valid hypothesis for research,"[35] we may assume a larger number of inhabitants during its period of greater prosperity. It is tempting to locate this period in the second quarter of the seventeenth century—a few years more than the period proposed by Braudel[36]—though no documentation gives us an exact evaluation of the population then. The figure of 100,000 inhabitants (or more) proposed by European authors who visited Algiers in this period (more than 100,000 according to Dan in 1634; 100,000 according to De Aranda in 1640–1642) is not really acceptable, not only in relation to the size of the city, but also because it clearly corresponds to the writers' desire to strike the reader with an exceptional image of the situation.[37]

---

years 1895–1897], 3. In another passage we encounter an interesting comment, which is nevertheless difficult to translate in numerical terms: "On pourrait peut-être juger de la population d'Alger par les moulins à farine qu'il y a dans la ville, moulins à meules tournées par des mules ou des chameaux; il y en a vingt-cinq tenus par les *Mozabis*, qui font au plus trente mesures chacun par jour" (*ibid.*).

[35] A. Raymond, "Signes urbains..." cit., 183.

[36] The effects of the "seconde prodigieuse fortune d'Alger" of which Braudel speaks [he dates the city's apogee between 1580 and 1620, *op. cit.*, vol. 2: 195] were still being felt. The mid seventeenth century corresponds, moreover, to the end of that "*trend* séculaire [du] long XVIᵉ siècle" [1650 would be its peak], which would effect the economic situation throughout the Mediterranean. The fame of the city's might was then at its apex. Salvago writes that contemporary opinion (his text was written in 1625) estimated the urban population at 300,000 inhabitants; after numerous calculations he reduces this by half, though he also states that, counting the dwellings in the surrounding countryside, the population would have been 200,000 (G. B. Salvago, *Africa ovvero Barbaria* [...], ed. A. Sacerdoti [Padua, 1937], 85).

[37] See F. Cresti, "Gli schiavi..." cit., 422.

A Gradual Demographic Decline

The inversion that appears in the vicissitudes of the city and its eco-nomic resources can be located towards the end of the third decade of the sixteenth century, even though from a demographic point of view this did not translate into an immediate decline. The year 1638 and the Battle of Valona seem acceptable as the symbolic moment of this inversion. Nevertheless, the consequences of this battle in which Turks and Venetians faced one another were not merely symbolic for Algiers: the city lost an important part of its ships and their crews, together with many Christian galley slaves.[38] The cost of rebuilding the fleet (which a few years later, in 1644, would again suffer heavy losses during the siege of Canea) forms a pair with the "technological" changes of the navigation: the galley system was gradually but definitively abandoned after Valona: "The maintenance of groups of slaves in the prisons no longer made any sense economically and [so] it was easy to pass from the concept of 'slave-energy' to that of 'slave merchandise'":[39] together with the need to swell the Regency coffers, this meant that the liberation of slaves increased during the following decades, leading to a clear preponderance of "outgoing" with respect to "incoming" slaves, in other words, a progressive decline in their number.

During these same years, especially in 1639, earthquakes, famine and other tragic events befell the population of the city. From 1650 the demographic crisis that struck the population after a series of devastating epidemics becomes apparent.[40] Yet the crisis was also a political one:

---

[38] See H. D. De Grammont, "Histoire..." cit., 187–188. According to De Gram-mont the losses were 16 galleys and 2 brigantines (almost half the galleys and a fourth of the Algierian naval fleet? See M. Belhamissi, *Marine et marins d'Alger 1518–1830* [Algiers, 1996], 1: 94), 1,500 dead and 3,634 slaves set free (according to S. Bono, *I corsari barbareschi* [Turin, 1964], 43–44, the losses were quickly recovered). See also P. Boyer, "Alger en 1645 d'après les notes du R. P. Hérault," in *Revue de l'Occident musulman et de la Méditerranée* [henceforth: *ROMM*], 17 (1974): 19–26, who considers this episode within the framework of a more general crisis.

[39] P. Boyer, *op. cit.*, 25.

[40] Epidemics were quite frequent in Algiers, occurring throughout the century (see M. W. Dols, "The second plague pandemic and its recurrences in the Middle East: 1347–1894," *JESHO* 22, no. 21 [1979]: *passim* and esp. tab. 4, p. 187); though according to the chronicles the years 1654–1657 and 1664 saw some of the worst, when most of the population (more than half, according to some documents from the period) perished (see H.-D. De Grammont, "Histoire..." cit., 203. See also F. Cresti, "Algeri nel XVII secolo. Documenti iconografici e fonti letterarie. I, 1600–1634," *SM*, 16 [1984]: 57; D. Panzac, *La peste dans l'empire ottoman, 1750–1850* [Leuven, 1985], 218–219). We should note, however, that some of the figures proposed by the documents concerning

until 1671 and the beginning of the Dey period, but also afterwards, there was a series of institutional upheavals. The military power of the city and its very safety were threatened, especially during the attacks and bombardments of the French fleet in the 1680s.[41] Greater political stability set in from the second decade of the next century and continued, more or less, until the end of the eighteenth century. Throughout the Regency the peace and economic revival that characterised the long period of the Dey government under Muhammad bin 'Uthmān (1766–1791) has lead André Raymond to state that this period "can be considered as a period of Algerian renaissance."[42] The revival of privateering (with the consequent economic recovery) and the peace treaties with a part of the Christian potentates led to a renewed wealth for Algiers. Nevertheless, while on the one hand the city saw an increase in its number of slaves, on the other it underwent naval attacks and was struck by periods of famine and a series of epidemics which closed the last years of Muhammad bin 'Uthmān's government.

Summing up the main features of the evolution of Algiers in the seventeenth century and the first three-quarters of the eighteenth: the arrival of immigrants during the expulsion of the Moriscos from Spain

---

the number of deaths seem exaggerated. The priest Gianola, chaplain to the Christian slaves at the time, states that during the 10 months of the pestilence in 1690 and 1691, 40,000 Turks and Moors and 1,000 slaves died (Archivio della Sacra Congregazione per l'Evangelizzazione dei Popoli, ex De Propaganda Fide [henceforth: APF], SC-Barbaria, vol. 3, f. 29: G. Gianola's letter from Algiers, 29.04.1691. For references to the documents in APF quoted below, especially in Tables 3 and 4, see F. Cresti, *Documenti sul Maghreb dal XVII al XIX secolo* [Perugia, 1988], *passim*). De Grammont states, without comment and without citing his sources, that the epidemic that broke out in 1698 killed between 25,000 and 40,000 people a year for four years (H.-D. De Grammont, "Histoire..." cit., 268–269). These figures are unacceptable, unless De Grammont is implicitly referring to the whole territory under the Regency.

[41] The bombardments in 1682, 1683, and 1688, which greatly damaged the buildings, don't seem to have taken many lives, since the population fled to the countryside (ibid., 256; see also F. Cresti, *Algeri nel XVII secolo...* cit., Part 2, 1635–1700, *SM* 17 [1985]: 45–52). From a demographic perspective none of the bombardments of Algiers had serious consequences, even though the documents give varying figures for the loss of lives. For example, in the most terrible in the city's history, those of the English fleet under Lord Exmouth on 28 August 1816—the fleet was able to take up a position very close to the city walls—the number of dead varies from 300 to 2,000. For a summary of the data, see D. Panzac, *Les corsaires barbaresques. La fin d'une épopée 1800–1820* (Paris, 1999), 240–241. See also A. Temimi, *Le bombardement d'Alger en 1816*, in Id., *Recherches et documents d'histoire maghrébine. L'Algérie, la Tunisie et la Tripolitaine. 1816–1871*, 2nd ed. (Tunis, 1980), 36–41.

[42] A. Raymond, "North Africa: Pre-colonial Period," in *The Cambridge History of Islam*, ed. P. M. Holt (Cambridge, 1970), 2: 278.

after 1609, together with an increase in the population generated by economic prosperity and the influx of slaves, swelled the population to its greatest number between 1625 and 1638. The space within the city became saturated, with a dense built environment inside the city walls made up of two and three, or even more, storey buildings.[43] The forms of precarious habitat of the most recent immigrants may have disappeared in this period. The end of the period of great wealth and a political crisis, together with natural calamities, led to an initial demographic decline, of uncertain proportions, towards the half of the seventeenth century. A gradual decline, with moments of acute crisis (during natural calamities such as earthquakes and epidemics), took place over the course of a century, with a hypothetical moment of revival from the mid-seventeenth century to 1797. At the end of this period the population count may be estimated at c. 50,000.

The documentary evidence concerning the effects of the earthquakes that struck the city in the seventeenth and eighteenth centuries is somewhat imprecise, since the known sources generally confine themselves to describing the material damage. For instance, there is a curious account of the effects of an earthquake on the height of the buildings in the report of an eighteenth century mission for the liberation of Christian slaves, in which we read that the French consul's house was "one of the most beautiful in Algiers: before the last quake [3 February 1716] it was three storeys high, while today it is only two."[44] We learn from the same source that this earthquake, which was followed by more tremors until June of the same year, badly damaged all the buildings in the city and that seven years later, despite repairs, many houses were still "destroyed or half-collapsed. [The quake] was so violent that most of the houses in the countryside were reduced to rubble and the whole city would have suffered the same fate had the houses not been so close together that they supported one another."[45]

The documents concerning the epidemics are not generally unanimous in their assessments. There was, however, a notable demographic

---

[43] Gramaye, who was a slave in Algiers in 1619, describes the houses with "duas, tres etiam plures contignationes" (I. B. Gramaye, *Africae illustratae libri decem*, Tornaci Nerviorum [Tournai] 1622, 3: 7). Dan speaks of houses "toutes fort serrées, et où demeurent quelques-fois dans un seul logement, cinq ou six mesnages" (F. P. Dan, *Histoire de Barbarie et de ses corsaires [...]*, 2nd ed. [Paris, 1649], 90).

[44] *Voyage pour la rédemption des captifs aux royaumes d'Alger et de Tunis, fait en 1720 par les PP. Comelin, de la Motte, Bernard [...]* (Paris, 1721), 14.

[45] *Ibid.*

crisis towards the end of the eighteenth century about which we have more precise information thanks to the sources and archival records: the plague of 1787–1788. While we have only vague estimates of the effects of earlier epidemics, in this case the sources give us a more precise vision of the loss of human life, and all the figures they give are very high. According to the writer Ahmad al-Sharīf al-Zahār who dedicated a few lines of his Chronicles (written a few decades later) to this event, up to 500 people a day died during the epidemic.[46] According to Raynal who was in Algiers during this period, amongst the dead counted at the city gates were 14,334 Muslims, 1,774 Jews and 613 free Christians and slaves.[47] The total of 16,721 dead is confirmed in a letter from the consul De Kercy who calculated, moreover, between 5,000 and 6,000 dead in the nearby countryside, while Von Rehbinder, who was in Algiers between 1785 and 1788, speaks of 15,829 victims in five months.[48] Finally, here is Venture de Paradis' account:

> 1787 was a mournful year for Algiers, the plague carried out a terrible massacre. Every day for four whole months 200, even 240, Muslims died, without counting Christians and Jews. In 1788 the pestilence struck again, though it was not so cruel. In two years almost 700 Christian slaves died. The plague of 1787 must have killed a third of the inhabitants.[49]

If we accept Venture de Paradis' estimation, together with that of the other eyewitnesses, the population of Algiers would have been slightly over 50,000 inhabitants before the plague, and c. 35,000 afterwards.

In the next forty years, from this event to the capture of Algiers by the French, the population would remain more or less constant. The absence of natural disasters and serious epidemics and a certain eco-

---

[46] Cit. in M. Belhamissi, "Une lettre inédite sur Alger au XVIIIᵉ siècle," *Archives Nationales* (Algiers), no. 6 (1977): 41.

[47] G. T. Raynal, *Histoire philosophique et politique des établissements et du commerce des Européens dans l'Afrique septentrionale*, 2 vols. (Paris, 1826), 2: 112, cit. in R. Lespès, *op. cit.*, 139.

[48] The passage in De Kercy is quoted by M. Belhamissi, *Une lettre...*cit., 40. The letter says that the epidemic ended around mid August 1787 after it had raged for at least 7 months. Von Rehbinder's account is quoted by Lespès (*op. cit.*, 139). De Grammont (*op. cit.*, 339) speaks of 17,048 victims, but without citing his sources.

[49] J. M. Venture de Paradis, *Alger...*cit., 52, note 1. T. Shuval's examination of the *post mortem* property inventories (*op. cit.*, 46–49) confirms the particular violence of this epidemic: starting with "des différences que l'on trouve entre le nombre moyen d'inventaires et celui des années de peste, le résultat s'élève à 14.600 [morts], ce qui représente environ 29% du nombre maximal de la population de la ville" (*ibid.*, 49).

nomic stability[50] allow us to discard the hypothesis of a marked period of demographic, indeed general, decline that is commonly accepted by colonial historiography. Yet we still need to use caution when affirming that the population remained constant between the end of the great epidemics and 1830, since the sum total of the population in Algiers before the French conquest is in any case the object of conflicting evaluations and hypotheses.

The most reliable, and the first "modern," piece of information concerning the population is the first census of 1830 in the above-cited document in the Vincennes military archives, the *Mémoire Collas*:

> The census ordered by the General in command gives these results:
> 1) Moors, a cross between ancient Mauritanians, who remained in the country after the various invasions, Spanish émigrés and Turks, for a total of 16,800
> 2) Jews expelled from Europe in the thirteenth century, c. 5,200
> 3) Negroes, freed slaves, or domestic servants of both sexes, 1,200
> 4) Indigenous Kabyle and Arab workers, together with Negroes, for a total of (their number is not known), c. 1,000.[51]

Thus, a total of 24,200 people, which nevertheless does not constitute the whole of the urban population at the end of the Ottoman period. Actually, both before and after the entry of the French troops on 5 July 1830, a part of the population which is difficult to estimate fled the city.[52] Moreover, members of the janissary militia (2,500 single and 1,000 married men according to the documents)[53] and their families

---

[50] The presence of slaves (see *infra*), which was fairly constant until 1816, indeed showing a notable increase between 1800 and 1815, could constitute an interesting gauge.

[51] *Mémoire Collas*, 3. In the manuscript the number of "Negroes" ("Environ 1,000") seems to have been added after and the total is not given. P. Rozet's observations (*op. cit.; passim*) on the "premier dénombrement, effectué au lendemain de notre arrivée," which are taken up by Lespès (*op. cit.*, 497), are misleading. After a long series of calculations and observations, Rozet gives the city 30,000 inhabitants before the French Occupation.

[52] See H. Khodja, *Le Miroir* (Paris, 1985), who recounts the departure by boat of many families "pour se sauver dans les pays des Kabyles et à Bougie" before the Occupation (199). Hamdan Khodja also describes the departure of the owners of houses requisitioned by the army (204) and the wealthy classes (195) after the Occupation. The first edition of the *Miroir* came out in 1833. According to Ch.-A. Julien (*Histoire de l'Algérie contemporaine*, vol. 1 [Paris, 1964], 55) tens of thousands of people left the city either by sea or via the road to Constantine in the days preceding the arrival of French troops.

[53] 2,500 janissaries embarked for Smirne in July; c. 1,000 married janissaries were expelled along with their families in August (see G. Gautherot, *La conquête d'Alger 1830*

were expelled along with other Turks on the orders of the expedition commander Bourmont.[54] About 1,000 families and 2,500 single men, and so certainly more than 5,000, indeed probably at least 7,000 people altogether.

If we add all those who fled the city and those who died during the military operations from the landing of French troops at Sidi Ferruch to the armistice, we can state with a fair degree of certainty that on the eve of the colonial conquest the population of Algiers counted well over 30,000 inhabitants. Two further documents seem to confirm this: the first (probably written by someone close to Bertrand Clauzel, the chief commander of the army, who had ordered the first census) states that the population "before the French invasion had risen to 40,000 souls,"[55] while the report of the commission of inquiry sent to Algiers three years after the conquest states that "Algiers counted 35 to 40 thousand souls before the siege."[56]

The Number of Slaves

In the demographic context of an *ancien régime* city in which, as we can assume, birth and mortality maintain the population at a more or less constant level, immigration becomes a decisive factor in any marked variation in the number of inhabitants. We have already examined and discussed the impact of Turkish and Andalusian immigration, as well as that of converts to Islam, on the sudden rise in the population during the early Ottoman period. It is more difficult, however, given the present state of our knowledge, to evaluate another decisive factor in the population of Algiers during its most controversial period: that

---

[Paris, 1929], 182–189. In view of their expulsion 965 married Turks registered with the police at the end of July; on 30 July "cinq cents et quelques Turcs paraissent avoir été embarqués, ainsi qu'un grand nombre de femmes et d'enfants"). Other authors speak of the expulsion of 4,000 janissaries (see R. Lespès, *op. cit.*, 497).

[54] See *Mémoire Collas*, p. 3: "depuis l'expulsion des Turcs par les Français, et l'émigration d'une partie des Maures, [la population] a beaucoup diminué."

[55] "Réfutation de l'ouvrage de Hamdan Khodja" (in *L'observateur des Tribunaux* 4, livr. 1, Paris, June 1834, in the appendix to H. Khodja, *op. cit.*, 281), "écrite par des amis de Clauzel (ou par Clauzel lui-même?)" according to A. Djeghloul (*ibid.*, 33). Did Clauzel or someone in his *entourage* have the necessary information to propose this figure? It's hard to say.

[56] See X. Yacono, "La Régence d'Alger en 1830 d'après l'enquête des commissions de 1833–1834," *ROMM* 1, no. 2 (1966): 244.

of the slaves, in the city's most auspicious days, from the end of the sixteenth to the mid seventeenth century.

This problem no longer presents itself for the later period, from 1736 to the French conquest, since in the last century of Ottoman rule the Arab-Turkish documentary sources give very precise indications. Below is a table of the figures found in the *Defter-i teschrifât*,[57] one of the Ottoman administrative registers studied by Albert Devoulx, keeper of the state archives in Arabic during the first decades of the colonial period.

For the period from 1787 to 1830, during which time we suggested that the population was fairly stable—between 30,000 and 40,000 inhabitants—the *Tachrifat* allows us to calculate the number of slaves on a total variable number as between a minimum of 1.5% and a maximum of 4.7%; thus an average of c. 3% of the population. Using the figures from the *Tachrifat*, this average would also be confirmed for a population of c. 50,000 inhabitants in 1780. The sharp drop registered in the number of slaves between 1786 and 1787 (a reduction of c. 60%, with the loss of 854 lives in one year, a number close to the c. 700 given by Venture de Paradis) was due to the epidemic that ravaged the city in those years (see above).

From 1816 the impact of the number of slaves on the total population was greatly reduced. Following Lord Exmouth's expedition, when he informed the Governor of Algiers of the abolition of slavery decreed by the Congress of Vienna and freed all Christian slaves, the number dropped to 0.5% of the urban population, with a residual presence of c. 150 slaves in 1830.

---

[57] A. de Voulx, *Tachrifat. Recueil de notes historiques sur l'administration de l'ancienne régence d'Alger*, Imprimerie du Gouvernement (Algiers, 1852) [henceforth: *Tachrifat*]. The documents translated into French (some of the Turkish documents were initially translated in Arabic) in this collection merit a scrupulous verification and a critical revision based on the original documents (see J. Deny, "Les registres de solde des Janissaires conservés à la Bibliothèque Nationale d'Alger," *RA* 61 [1920]: 21: "on ressent quelque inquiétude quand on songe que la brochure en question constitue en ce moment, malgré ses inexactitudes flagrantes, une source de documentation à caractère authentique"). In particular, in the list of the figures for the slaves in Devoulx's *Tachrifat* there are discrepancies, which are difficult to account for, between the general census (86) and the census by nationality for the period 1774–1816 (86–88): in both cases the sums do not give the same results, as they should.

Table II. Christian slaves in Algiers 1736–1816 (source: *Tachrifat*, p. 86).[58]

1736	1,063	1757	1561	1778	1,369		
1737	931	1758	1,571	1779	1,481	1798	1,168
1738	705	1759	1,753	1780	1,494	1799	1,019
1739	569	1760	1,941	1781	1,586	1800	860
1740	412	1761	1,993	1782	1,532	1801	545
1741	499	1762	1,902	1783	1,507	1802	772
1742	530	1763	1,900	1784	1,520	1803	946
1743	582	1764	1,920	1785	1,372	1804	901
1744	739	1765	*1,904/1,944	1786	1,426	1805	1,022
1745	741	1766	2,004	1787	572	1806	1,228
1746	783	1767	2,062	1788	574	1807	1,267
1747	821	1768	1,131	1789	659	1808	1,422
1748	1,003	1769	1,226	1790	715	1809	1,545
1749	950	1770	1,323	1791	762	1810	1,357
1750	1,063	1771	1,320	1792	832	1811	1,345
1751	1,773	1772	1,190	1793	755	1812	1,475
1752	609	1773	1,326	1794	*779	1813	1,656
1753	632	1774	1,376	1794	*896	1814	1,525
1754	591	1775	1,373	1795	730	1815	1,450
1755	564	1776	1,468	1796	659	1816	1,016
1756	694	1777	1,501	1797	546		

* The dates are those of the Christian era: in two instances the double figure is probably due to the discrepancy between the Gregorian and Islamic calendars.

---

[58] For the same period we possess data provided by European authors and sources given in the table below.

Table III. Christian slaves in Algiers according to european sources (1738–1830).

1738	T. Shaw	c. 2,000
1785	Von Rehbinder	2,000
1786–1787	Venture de Paradis	2,000
1788	Raynal	800
1788	Von Rehbinder	800
1788–1789	Venture de Paradis	500
1796	Alasia (APF)	700
1801	Vicherat (APF)	500
1805	Joussouy (APF)	1,200
1816	(in De Grammont)	1,642 freed by Lord Exmouth
1830	P. Rozet	122 freed at the time of the capture of Algiers
1830	(in De Grammont)	c. 150 freed as above

A comparison of the data in the European sources with those in the *Tachrifat* reveal a general over-estimation of the former, but also the very precise estimates of some authors, for example, the Roman Catholic priests (Alasia, Vicherat, Joussouy) sent to assist the slaves.

What can we say about the period prior to 1736? As far as the Arab and Turkish sources are concerned, only the *Ghazawāt* gives us figures, which it is nevertheless difficult to verify. An initial figure testifies to the presence of 7,000 slaves in Algiers (there was a slave revolt around 1532 which Khayr al-dīn put down).[59] Other passages state that this first substantial nucleus of slaves was not comprised of Christians captured by corsairs, but was the result of Spanish attacks against the city. The *Ghazawāt* cites in particular 3,036 Spaniards captured when the fleet commanded by Hugo de Moncada was sunk in 1519. A further expedition which arrived too late to help the Peñon's spanish garrison and was partially destroyed by Khayr al-dīn in 1529 provided the city with a total of 2,700 slaves.[60] Apart from this information, for the period prior to 1736 we only have the data supplied by European sources:

Table IV. Christian slaves in Algiers according to european sources (1578–1729).[61]

1578–1581	Haedo	almost 25,000
1587	Lanfreducci and Bosio	20,000
1598	Magini	almost 15,000
1619	Gramaye	more than 35,000
1621–1626	Mascarenhas	more than 16,000
1625	Salvago	25,000
1634	Dan	25,000
1640	Aranda	30,000/40,000
1644	Hérault	30,000/40,000
1660	Davity (ed. De Rocoles)	35,000
1662	Auvry (Miroir de la Charité)	30,000/40,000 "dans toute la Régence" more than 12,000 "à l'intérieur de la ville"
1665	Du Val	more than 40,000
1674	Arvieux	10,000/12,000
1676	The Present State of Algiers	18,000 of which 9,000 French

---

[59] G. Gallotta, entry on "Khayr al-dīn Pasha," in *Encyclopédie de l'Islam*, 2nd ed., vol. 5 (Leiden and Paris 1978), 1188.

[60] *Fondation de la régence...* cit., 1: 111, 228, 291. After those captured during Charles V's disastrous expedition in 1541, many more Spaniards were enslaved after another failed expedition against Mustagānim in 1558: according to Haedo on this occasion more than 12,000 prisoners were taken. Braudel, following Haedo's text, states that "à Alger toutes les maisons furent pleines de ces nouveaux captifs" (*op. cit.*, 2: 284).

[61] See F. Cresti, "Gli schiavi..." cit., table 1, p. 425, which integrates Id., "Quelques observations..." cit., table 2, p. 159.

Table IV (*cont.*)

1678	De Fercourt	20,000/30,000
1683	Manesson Mallet	35,000/40,000
1684	Pétis de la Croix	35,000 "dans le Royaume d'Alger"
1693	Lorance (APF)	4,000
1696	Lorance (APF)	1,600 "dans les Bagnes"
1698	Lorance (APF)	2,600
1700	Comelin	8,000/10,000
1701	Lorance (APF)	3,000
1719	Gueudeville (Atlas)	4,000
1729	Fau	9,000/10,000
1729	Vander Aa	more than 5,000

The highest figures (30,000, 35,000, 40,000) proposed by most of the sixteenth century authors, especially for the period from 1620 to 1680, do not seem acceptable, unless we were to admit that Algiers was nothing more than an enormous prison![62] Indeed, they presuppose a huge proportion of slaves with respect to the total population: 30% to 40%, if we accept the average of 100,000 proposed by the same authors, even more, if this average was lower when the city was at its most prosperous. A comparative analysis shows us that no other city in the Mediterranean in which the phenomenon of slavery was significant and for which we possess some relevant series of data reached similar levels. In Trapani (Sicily), a *rivelo* (census) of 1569 allows us to calculate that the slaves comprised 15% of the total population. According to some analyses, in Civitavecchia the slaves comprised 20% of the population in 1601, 10% in 1622 and 8% in 1642–43, while for Genoa the estimate is 3% at the end of the 16th century.[63] For Malta—"a kind of Christian equivalent of the privateering cities of North Africa"—the estimates vary, since the available data only refer to the total population: their results vary between 4.3% and 5% in 1590, with 3.5% as the highest figure in 1632 (9% of the population of La Valletta, where the

---

[62] Such was the situation around 1518 according to the *Ghazawāt*, in which we read that a slave revolt was feared since they had outnumbered the inhabitants. According to the same source, Khayr al-dīn decided to build three prisons in which the strongest slaves were chained up (ed. Rang-Denis, cit., 1: 115–116; ed. Bonaffini, cit., 118).

[63] See S. Bono, *Schiavi musulmani nell'Italia moderna* (Naples, 1999), 24 ff. Bono considers the 36% proposed for Leghorn in 1616 as very unlikely, or in any case, absolutely exceptional.

slaves were concentrated, since at that time the city had a population of 22,000).[64] Nevertheless, not even in this case does a comparative evaluation give us any certainty, even though it allows us to entertain some doubt over the validity of the figures proposed for Algiers.

Returning to the European sources in the table above, only the figures given by Yvon Lorance, apostolic vicar in Algiers from 1693 to 1705, though imprecise and merely indicative, seem plausible. The vicar was particularly active in helping Christian slaves and so he must have been able to estimate their number. Presumably the disparity in the numbers he gives over the years is due to his interest in this phenomenon in terms of quantity.[65] The data tell us, moreover, that towards the end of the seventeenth century the slaves living in the baths (the majority of whom probably belonged to the *beylik*) represented less than half the total number.

If Lorance's figures are close to the truth, then they are far from those of other European observers who speak of 20, 30, 40, even 50 thousand slaves for the years immediately preceding. No known event in the second half of the seventeenth century justifies such a sudden decrease in the number of slaves (from a minimum of 15,000 to more than 30,000 over a period of about 30 years). Most likely the number of slaves followed a diminishing curve due to their liberation in large numbers, the assaults against the city and the various epidemics, especially, if we consider that during the same period privateering continued uninterrupted.[66] Perhaps the figures given by D'Arvieux (10,000–12,000

---

[64] M. Fontenay, "Il mercato maltese degli schiavi al tempo dei Cavalieri di San Giovanni (1530–1798)," *Quaderni storici* 107 (2001): 394.

[65] The disparity in Lorance's figures (a total of 4,000 in 1693, 1,600 "dans les bagnes" in 1696, a total of 2,600 and 3,000 in 1698 and 1701 respectively) is not exceptional, though it is strange not to find any echo of the expedition against and capture of Tunis, which brought Algiers "une grande quantité d'esclaves" according to De Grammont (*Histoire*... cit., 265). Nevertheless in a letter to Rome, Lorance describes the triumph of the Algerian troops on their return from Tunis, which they had taken after the defeat of the *bey*'s army at the end of 1694 (APF, SC, Barbaria, vol. 3, f. 251: Lorance to PF, 2/3/1695). The "grande quantité" of slaves consisted only of 400 slaves once belonging to the *bey* Muhammad (T. Bachrouch, *Formation sociale barbaresque et pouvoir à Tunis au XVIIe siècle* [Tunis, 1977], 198).

[66] For the "incoming" slaves, De Grammont's information (300 slaves captured from French ships in 1681 and "plus de six mille matelot [anglais]" captured between 1668 and 1681; in "Histoire..." cit., 247) is doubtful, especially for the English, and it is also impossible to verify, since he does not cite his sources. Moreover, we know from the scant available figures, that after the attacks by the French fleet under Duquesne (1682 and 1683) and D'Estrées (1688), an initial truce led to the liberation of all the French slaves (c. 500; see H.-D. De Grammont, *Histoire*... cit., 250–251). One might

slaves in 1674) and Auvry in his *Miroir de la charité* (more than 12,000 within the city in 1662) are closer to the truth.[67] Supposing that the greatest number of slaves corresponds more or less to the demographic and economic apogee of the city, between 1625 and 1638, or in any case in the first decades of the seventeenth century, we can hypothesise that the slaves were more numerous in this period (perhaps several thousand more, c. 15,000?).[68]

A Numerically Important Minority: The Jews

Another category of the population for which we are in possession of data, especially from European sources, is the Jewish community, though the highest figures are not to be accepted without reservation, especially those given by Shaw (15,000), as well as the 5,000 houses inhabited by Jewish families given by Laugier de Tassy, both of which are highly unlikely. The only plausible reference is to be found in the census at the end of 1830, which records the presence of 5,200 Jews in Algiers. This figure should also correspond to their presence before the French Occupation, since the Jews did not leave the city after this event.

Table V. The jewish community in algiers according to european sources.

1533–1536	*Mémoire Simancas* (trans. De la Primaudaie)	300 families
1578–1581	Haedo	150 houses
1619	Gramaye	more than 8,000
1634	Dan	9,000–10,000
1660	Davity (ed. De Rocoles)	more than 8,000
1662	Auvry	8,000–9,000
1670	Ogilby	9,000–10,000
1674	D'Arvieux	10,000–12,000

be tempted to use De Grammont's ratio of 1:20 French slaves in relation to the total number ("Etudes algériennes. La course, l'esclavage et la rédemption à Alger," in *Revue Historique* 26, no. 1 [1885]: 37), though his estimate seems based on mere supposition. Finally, a letter from Algiers written by a missionary in 1691 speaks of the death of c. 1,000 slaves in a period of epidemics lasting almost 10 years (see F. Cresti, "Gli schiavi..." cit., 423–424).

[67] Michel Auvry was part of a slave-redemption operation organized by the French fathers of Notre-Dame de la Merci in 1662, that left Algiers with about a hundred freed slaves (see G. Turbet-Delof, *Bibliographie critique du Maghreb dans la littérature française 1532–1715* [Algiers, 1976], 167–168). D'Arvieux stayed in Algiers in 1674–1675.

[68] In a previous article I put forward the hypothesis, based on purely statistical calculations, of a figure comprising between 6,000 and 16,000 slaves at the most (see F. Cresti, "Gli schiavi..." cit., 431).

Table V (*cont.*)

1676	*The Present State of Algiers*	13,000 "native Jews"
1725	Laugier de Tassy	5,000 houses or families
1738	Shaw	15,000
1742	Tollot	5,000 families
1754 (before)	Ricaud (in Venture de Paradis)	7,000–8,000
1784	Palermo	5,000 families
1789	Venture de Paradis	7,000
1808	Boutin	10,000–12,000
1826	Shaler	5,000
1830	*Mémoire Collas*	c. 5,200
1830	Rozet	5,000

The demographic evolution of this part of the population is known in its broader spectrum.[69] The Jewish community was formed, or in any case enlarged, at the end of the thirteenth century, thanks to immigration from the Balearic Islands. In the following century, but also after the edict of 1492 which only left them the choice of exile or conversion, many arrived from Spain. Before the establishment of Ottoman rule many had already come from Italy, the Netherlands, France and England. Khayr al-dīn facilitated their settlement in Algiers, after which they played an important part in the city's economy, especially thanks to the trade and commerce generated by privateering.

Algiers experienced a final immigration of Jews from Europe in the eighteenth century with the arrival of entire families from Leghorn who quickly assumed a prominent commercial and political role in the life of the city, especially once they obtained the monopoly on the exportation of cereals. This period of prosperity ended in 1805, the year in which their houses were sacked and they were massacred after the assassination of Nephtali Busnach, the richest and most powerful Jewish merchant in the city. Using French documents in his reconstruction of events, De Grammont informs us that at least 50 Jews were murdered on this occasion, while another 200 escaped unharmed by seeking asylum in the French Consulate. De Grammont writes that "a

---

[69] See I. Bloch, *Inscriptions tumulaires des anciens cimetières israélites d'Alger* (Paris, 1888); J. Hanoune, *Aperçu sur les israélites algériens et sur la communauté d'Alger* (Alger, 1922); M. Eisenbeth, *Les Juifs en Algérie et en Tunisie à l'époque turque*, RA 96 (1952): 101–102, 343–384. See also the synthesis by Ch.-A. Julien, op. cit., 11–13.

very large number of survivors"[70] was immediately exiled by the *dey*
Mustapha. It is impossible to define precisely the reduction in the Jewish
population on this occasion, but if we rely once again on Venture de
Paradis' account who calculates their number at 7,000 in 1789, and if
we take for granted a certain degree of stability in the following years,
then the reduction over the last two decades of the Ottoman period
would be between 1,000 and 2,000 people.

A constant of the Ottoman period, cited by at least two authors with
a 200 years interval, Gramaye and Venture de Paradis, is the density
of the population in the Jewish neighbourhoods. The former claims to
have counted at least 300 people in one house, while the latter writes
that 7,000 Jews lived in only 180 houses, with an average, therefore,
of a little under 40 inhabitants per house.[71]

The Military Presence: The Janissaries

The European sources also give quite variable figures for the janissaries. The 11,897 recorded in 1745 in the pay-roll registers,[72] constitute
a precise figure for the second half of the eighteenth century. The
distinction between "men in the fighting services" (9,322) and "soldiers
out of the ranks" (2,575), used in the analysis of these registers, is of
little importance for our own, while their total number is considerable when compared to other known situations.[73] It is difficult to say
whether the number of janissaries recorded in this period is lower than
in earlier periods, though probably the highest number of troops was
in the first half of the seventeenth century. The construction of two

---

[70] H.-D. De Grammont, *Histoire*...cit., 361. In a Judeo-Arab lament quoted by
Bloch, the militia massacred 42 Jews in the synagogue and wounded many more. The
author states that the expulsion was only a threat, but that 300 families left for Tunis
and Leghorn in July of the same year (see M. Eisenbeth, *op. cit.*, 377).

[71] I. B. Gramaye, *op. cit.*, 13; Venture de Paradis, *op. cit.*, 3.

[72] J. Deny, *op. cit.*, 36. See also F. Cresti, "Quelques réflexions..." cit., 161.

[73] For example Cairo, where 6,461 janissaries were counted, out of a total of 15,916
soldiers, in the second half of the seventeenth century (see A. Raymond, *Égyptiens
et français au Caire 1798–1801* [Cairo: IFAO, 1998], 9). Nevertheless the situation in
Cairo, with a large number of Mameluke troops, was an exception in the Ottoman
Empire. Moreover, in one of his earliest works on the great Arab cities in the Ottoman
period, A. Raymond states that the janissaries in Algiers "étaient peut-être 20,000 au
XVIIe et encore 10,000 au XVIIIe siècle sur une population totale qui ne devait guère
dépasser 100.000 habitants" (A. Raymond, "La conquête ottomane et le développement des grandes villes ottomanes. Le cas du Caire, de Damas et d'Alep," *ROMM*,
no. 27 [1979]: 122).

military barracks in the Ottoman period, known by the Turkish names of *Odalar eski* and *Odalar yeni*, in 1627–28 and 1637 respectively, seems to confirm this hypothesis.[74]

The natural mortality rate, together with the mortality rate of those who died in armed combat, could open up great voids in the military ranks. According to a 1754 account, for instance, the number of troops was reduced to 4,000 men.[75] The census carried out on the orders of *dey* Muhammad Khaznaji in 1815 constitutes a further, quite reliable, datum: it demonstrates that the reduction in the number of troops was not filled by new recruits and reveals the presence of 4,000 men of whom 700 were not in active service.[76] These figures seem to be confirmed by the number of janissaries expelled after the French Occupation. Taken as a whole, they seem to indicate a constant decline in the armed forces from the mid eighteenth century onwards: the 8,533 new recruits between 1801 and 1829[77] (with an average of c. 300 per annum) were not sufficient to renew the military might of the city's most glorious days.

We might speculate that the decline in the number of janissaries was compensated for by the recruitment of local militia men, though the available sources are inaccurate and the data they provide disparate and hence unreliable. Grâberg, for instance, states that the Regency could, if needed, call on the services of at least 100,000 soldiers, and estimates that on the eve of the French expedition the city garrisons counted 4,000 to 5,000 Turks and 10,000 "Coloulis" and Moriscos. The author also mentions the presence of 2,000 cavalrymen and a new battalion of "natives" and slaves from central Africa recruited shortly before by the *dey*.[78]

---

[74] See G. Colin, *Corpus des inscriptions arabes et turques de l'Algérie* (Paris, 1901), *passim*; R. Meunier, "Les casernes des Janissaires d'El-Djézair," *Feuillets d'El-Djezaïr*, new series, no. 5 (July 1962): 5–6.

[75] A. Sacerdoti, "La mission à Alger du consul de Venise Nicolas Rosalem (1753–1754)," *RA* 96 (1952): 87. Following a sudden drop in numbers the sultan's permission was requested to recruit 500 janissaries in Anatolia. See also T. Shuval, *op. cit.*, 64–65.

[76] H.-D. De Grammont, "Histoire..." cit., 374. As Deny (*op. cit.*, 19–20) notes, the existence of pay-rolls, probably part of a larger series, casts doubt on De Grammont's statement that the *dey* Muhammad Khaznaji was killed "pour avoir ordonné le recensement de la Milice: l'on sait que cette opération cause toujours aux Orientaux une sorte de terreur superstitieuse" ("Histoire..." cit., *ibid.*).

[77] M. Colombe, "Contribution à l'étude du recrutement de l'Odjaq d'Alger," *RA* 87 (1943): 180.

[78] J. Grâberg di Hemsö, *Cenni geografici e statistici sulla Reggenza di Algeri* (Florence, 1830), 62. According to the Commission of 1833–1834: "les Turcs avaient à peine

Table VI. Troops and Janissaries in Algiers according to the sources.

1536	Perez de Idiacayz	2,000 Turks and 7,000–8,000 Andalusian Moors
1587	Lanfreducci and Bosio	25,000 soldiers, of which 6,000 janissaries
1605	De Brèves	10,000
1615	Lithgow	6,000
1619	Gramaye	6,000 families of veterans
1621–1626	Mascarenhas	7 barracks with 500–600 men each; 5,000–6,000 in the whole territory, of which 1,000–1,500 in Algiers
1625	Salvago	10,000
1634	Dan	22,000 militia men
1640–1642	De Aranda	12,000
1660	Davity (ed. De Rocoles)	6,000 families
1684	État présent du Royaume	14,000 janissaries
1686	Darcy (Plan d'Alger)	10,000–14,000 men
1719	Gueudeville	12,000
1731	Tollot	13,000–14,000 men (with the majority in Algiers)
1745	*Régistres de solde*	11,897
1754	Ricaud (cit. Venture de Paradis)	11,000–12,000
1754	Rosalem (ed. Sacerdoti)	4,000
1784	Palermo	3,000
1785 (*ante*)	Venture	7,000–8,000 altogether, of whom 3,000 in Algiers
1788	Raynal (cit. in Lespès)	10,000 men, of whom 6,000 Turks throughout the Regency
1808	Boutin	10,000(?) in the Regency ("15.000 hommes dont 5.000 Maures dans toute la Régence")
1815	De Grammont	4,000 (from the census of Muhammad Khaznaji)
1830	Grâberg di Hemsö	4,500 "Turks, Ostmanli"
1830	expelled after the French Occupation	3,500

3.000 hommes lorsque nous avons débarqué: le reste de l'armée du Dey se composait d'indigènes et même de Noirs qu'ils employaient de préférence dans certaines parties de la Régence" (X. Yacono, *op. cit.*, I, 1: 238).

As in the case of the slaves, the highest figures proposed for the troops in Algiers pose the problem of their division between the capital and the other garrisons in the Regency. The European documents do not often make this distinction. In the absence of more precise documentation, the importance of this division, which undoubtedly varied, escapes us. Mascarenhas who was in Algiers between 1621 and 1626 states that only between a third and a sixth of the janissaries were stationed in the city while the rest were stationed in garrisons inland. Venture de Paradis gives an estimate of 3,000 soldiers in the capital out of a total of 7,000 or 8,000 "Turcs levantins" throughout the Regency.[79]

Conclusions

So what can be said with a minimum of certainty about the demographic evolution of Algiers in the Ottoman period? Given the present state of our knowledge, the following summary seems possible:

a) In the period prior to Ottoman rule, even though Algiers was one of the main cities of the central Maghreb, it was quite small physically and demographically. The scarcity of inhabitants seems to be a constant in Algerian territory in the middle ages and the city had a modest population compared with larger cities, such as Fez or Tunis, but also less important cities such as Tilimsān and Qusantīna.

b) The sixteenth century saw the beginning of the development that would lead the city within a few decades to occupy a prime place, politically, economically and demographically, amongst the capital cities of the central Maghreb. This phenomenon was due to an increase in the population linked to international events (the expulsion of Muslims from the Iberian peninsula), political events (the gradual transformation of Algiers into the provincial capital of the Ottoman Empire and the influx of a Turkish military élite) and economic factors (especially the development of a system of production and distribution of wealth based largely on privateering). Privateering and a series of victorious battles against the Spaniards in the sixteenth century gave Algiers a large number of Christian slaves, a part of which was integrated with the urban population through conversion to Islam.

c) The absence of data makes it difficult to evaluate the attraction exercised by the Ottoman city on the population of the internal regions

---

[79] J. Mascarenhas, *op. cit.*, 102; J. M. Venture de Paradis, *op. cit.*, 3. T. Shuval (*op. cit.*, 54) estimates that about a quarter of the janissaries were "en permanence à l'extérieur de la ville" in the eighteenth century.

of Algeria, who remained a minority inside the city, according to the
rare sources on the subject.

d) As far as the built environment is concerned, this was extended in the
Ottoman period with the construction of a larger perimeter of walls in
the first half of the sixteenth century. Nevertheless, it seems that this
enclosed space was insufficient to hold the fresh wave of immigrants,
since a new suburb sprang up outside the walls. We don't have any
details about the demolition of this suburb, but we can imagine that
afterwards its population moved to within the city walls.

For the rest of the Ottoman period the city would remain enclosed
within its walls. The stability of its physical dimensions allows us to
presume that the demographic pressure was bearable and that there
was perhaps the political will to contain the population within limits
that were easier to control.

e) Concerning the immigrant population, we need to make a distinction
between different groups. Firstly between Muslims and non-Muslims,
and secondly between "eastern" and "western" Muslims. A final immigration of Spanish Muslims took place after 1609 with the expulsion
order against the *Moriscos*. Eastern Muslims were essentially composed
of Anatolian Turks who made up the backbone of the armed forces;
their recruitment was continuous, though variable, over this period,
and indeed in decline from the mid eighteenth century onwards.

As far as non-Muslims are concerned, we need to distinguish between
Christians and Jews. The latter were present prior to the Ottoman
period and their number increased from the beginning of the sixteenth
century thanks to the special terms granted them by the new rulers of
the city. Their number probably continued to increase with the arrival
of immigrants from Italy, though this process is difficult to define; that
is, until the beginning of the nineteenth century, when a part of this
minority group was expelled or fled the city after acts of violence and
massacres.

As far as Christians, especially Christian slaves, are concerned,
their number varies considerably, depending on the opportunities for
privateering and international, political and military events. The presence of slaves in the population of Algiers was continuous throughout
this period, and we can imagine that their number was higher during the city's most prosperous time and that it began to decline after
1638.

Finally, for the last 'imported' group, African slaves, information
is scarce and may be summed up in the 1,200 "freemen, slaves and
servants" recorded in the 1830 census.

f) Assuming a demographic growth parallel with an increase in economic
prosperity, political stability and military power, the population of
Algiers was at its apex in the first half of the seventeenth century.
We have chosen 1638 as the symbolic (but not just symbolic) date of
its apogee. Moreover, the presence of janissaries and slaves probably
reached its highest level in this period, too.

We can assume that the density of the buildings within the city walls was at a maximum in this period: a form of habitat had developed vertically which is one of the most original features of the city from an architectural and urban-morphological viewpoint, the different typologies of which are still imperfectly known.

g) In the mid sixteenth century there was a decrease in the population due to various factors, amongst which, in particular, a decrease in the number of slaves due to a reduction in privateering (caused by the losses of the Algerian fleet), changes in navigation techniques and an increase in the ransoming of slaves. This decline was more rapid during epidemics (especially in 1654–57 and 1664) and natural disasters. No documentation allows us to state that these losses were replaced by the local population.

h) The bombardments, especially of the French fleet in the 1680s, damaged some of the buildings in the capital, though they did not seriously affect the population. They did, however, weaken its political and economic situation with demographic consequences that are difficult to evaluate.

i) In the course of the next 100 years, until c. 1780, the main nucleus of the population remained fairly stable, with greater losses during natural disasters. The numbers of Christian slaves (accurately recorded from 1736) decreased and probably only comprised a maximum of 4% of the total population. There was a period of slight demographic increase, from 1757 to 1786, when their numbers stabilised around the highest figures of the century, due to several decades of economic growth and political stability.

j) The gradual political decline of the capital, as part of the general crisis of the Ottoman Empire, is also manifest in a reduction in the number of recruits in the Turkish militia. In the absence of more accurate data, we may surmise that this reduction was a progressive one. No documentation allows us to state, however, that it was compensated for by the recruitment of local auxiliaries, though this cannot be excluded.

k) If we accept the figures proposed by Venture de Paradis, then we can state that shortly before the plague of 1787 the population of Algiers was c. 50,000 inhabitants.

l) The years 1787 and 1788 represent a moment of sharp demographic decline: the population was reduced by a third (c. 35,000 inhabitants) due to a plague epidemic.

m) From the end of the eighteenth century until 1830 the population seems to have stabilised. Nevertheless, we cannot exclude a progressive tendency to decline, which it is difficult to evaluate accurately. There was a known decrease in the number of slaves and Jews over this last period.

n) Before the French Occupation, the population of Algiers had certainly reached over 30,000 inhabitants, perhaps even 35,000.

Many elements are still lacking that would help define more accurately the demographic evolution of Algiers in the Ottoman period, though, taken as a whole, the available data allow us to go beyond a simple "opinion de confiance"[80] and formulate an hypothesis that is perhaps close to the historical reality. Thus Algiers appears to have been an extraordinary phenomenon in the panorama of provincial Arab capitals in the Ottoman Empire, especially in terms of the density of its population: slightly more than 1,100 per hectare around 1780; even more at its demographic peak; between 650 and 750 before the French Conquest in 1830. The overcrowding, especially during the period in which its population was most numerous, must have created terrible living conditions, especially for the poorer strata of society. The spacious mansions, some of which have survived to the present day and so are better known to us, were certainly the exception not the norm.

As far as the documentary sources are concerned, the available data, especially from European sources, can be misleading. Often based on ideological prejudices or falsified for "promotional" reasons that have nothing to do with the quest for historical truth, they nevertheless offer many valid, albeit partial, elements which help enrich our knowledge. Clearly, as with all historical sources, they must be subjected to critical scrutiny. The documents in the Arab and Turkish archives call for a fresh examination which is indeed already underway and should with time provide some of the figures that have so far been lacking.

Finally, any discussion of the demographic evolution of Algiers under Ottoman rule, whether today or in the future, can be based solely on documents and written sources. Some years ago, I completed my first exposition of the subject, confirming that an analysis of the urban fabric of the extant Ottoman city would remedy, at least in part, the shortcomings of the written sources and allow us to understand better its evolution over more than three centuries, thereby making it possible to "establish on a sounder basis the different hypotheses [...] concerning the population and social structure of Algiers in the Turkish period."[81] Today, these hopes have been dashed. The piles of ruins and rubbish, the void left by demolished or collapsed buildings, the numerous projects of urban renewal, restoration and conservation, either never begun or

---

[80] This is the expression used by captain Boutin in his report (1808): see X. Yacono, "Peut-on évaluer la population de l'Algérie vers 1830?" *RA* 98 (1954), p. 277.

[81] F. Cresti, *Quelques réflexions*...cit., p. 164.

never completed, the shanty towns that have sprung up in the empty spaces of the old medina make the city seem on its deathbed, from which it is unlikely ever to be resuscitated. And so we will have lost an irreplaceable document for the history of Algiers in the Ottoman period: the Ottoman city itself.

(English translation by Lisa Adams)

Bibliographic and Archival Sources

Below is a list of the texts and archival sources of the authors mentioned in the article, especially in the tables, that are not always included in the notes.

Aranda E. de. *Relation de la captivité et liberté du sieur Emanuel de Aranda* [...]. Brussels, 1656.

Arvieux L. d'. Ed. J. B. Labat. *Mémoires du Chevalier d'Arvieux* [...]. Paris, 1735.

Auvry M. (anonymous but attributed to). *Le Miroir de la Charité Chrestienne ou Relation du voyage* [...]. Aix-en-Provence, 1663.

Botero G. *Delle relazioni universali* [...] *parte prima. Nella quale si da ragguaglio de' Continenti e dell'Isole fino al presente scoverte*. Rome, 1595.

Boutin V.-Y. Ed. G. Esquer. *Reconnaissance des villes, forts et batteries d'Alger par le chef de bataillon Boutin (1808), suivi des Mémoires sur Alger par les consuls De Kercy (1791) et Dubois-Thainville (1808)*. Collection de documents inédits sur l'histoire de l'Algérie. Paris, 1927.

Collas. *Mémoire sur la Place d'Alger par le Chef de Bataillon Collas 1830*, Archives du Service Historique de l'Armée de Terre. Vincennes: Génie, Algérie, art. 8, sec. 1, cart. 2, no. 1.

Comelin, De la Motte Bernard. *Voyage pour la rédemption des captifs aux royaumes d'Alger et de Tunis, fait en 1720 par les PP.* [...]. Paris, 1721.

Coppin J. *Le bouclier de l'Europe ou la Guerre sainte* [...]. Lyons, 1686.

Dan F. P. *Histoire de Barbarie et de ses corsaires* [...]. Paris, 1637.

Dapper O. *Naukeurige Beschrijvinge des Africaensche gewesten van Egypten, Barbaryen* [...]. Amsterdam, 1668. (French translation: *Description de l'Afrique* [...]. Amsterdam, 1686.)

Darcy. *Plan d'Alger tiré sur les lieux par le Sieur Darcy*, 1686. Bibliothèque Nationale de Paris, Cartes et Plans. 106–5–26.

Davity P. Ed. J. B. De Rocoles. *Description générale de l'Afrique seconde partie du monde* [...]. Paris, 1660.

De Fercourt Cl. Ed. M. Targe. *Relation de l'esclavage des Sieurs de Fercourt et Regnard, pris par les corsaires d'Alger sur mer* [...]. Toulouse, 1905.

De Kercy. Ed. G. Esquer. *Reconnaissance des villes, forts et batteries d'Alger...cit.* Paris, 1927.

Dubois-Thainville. Ed. G. Esquer. *Reconnaissance des villes, forts et batteries d'Alger...* cit. Paris, 1927.

Du Val P. *La carte générale et les cartes particulières des Costes de la Mer Méditerranée* [...]. Paris, 1665.

"État présent du Royaume d'Alger," anon. In *Le Mercure Galant*, July 1684, pp. 197–261.

Fau (le R. P. Fau religieux de Notre-Dame de la Mercy). Ed. M. Emerit. "Un astronome français à Alger en 1729." In *Revue Africaine* 1940, pp. 249–255.

Grâberg di Hemsö J. *Cenni geografici e statistici sulla Reggenza di Algeri.* Florence, 1830.

Gramaye I. B. *Africae illustratae libri decem* [...]. Tornaci Nerviorum, 1622.

Gueudeville de. *Atlas historique* [...]. Paris, 1719.

Haedo D. de. *Topographia, e Historia general de Argel* [...]. Valladolid, 1612. (French translation: Monnereau-Berbrugger, "Topographie et histoire générale d'Alger," in *Revue Africaine* 1870–1871.)

Hasan al-Zayyati/Giovan Leone Africano. *Descrittione dell'Africa e delle cose notabili che quivi sono.* Ed. G. B. Ramusio. *Delle navigationi et viaggi.* Venice, 1550. (French translation: A. Épaulard, *Description de l'Afrique,* Paris 1981.)

Hérault L. Ed. P. Boyer. "Continuation des mémoires des voyages du feu Père Hèrault en Barbarie pour la Rédemption qu'il a escrit luy mesme [...]." In *Revue de l'Occident musulman et de la Méditerranée* 18, 1975, pp. 29–74.

Juan Cano. cit. in H.-D. *De Grammont.* "Histoire..." cit., p. 240.

La Croix Ph. de. *Relation universelle de l'Afrique antique et moderne* [...]. Lyons, 1688.

Lanfreducci et Bosio. Ed. Ch. *Monchicourt and P. Grandchamp.* "Costa e discorsi di Barbaria." In *Revue Africaine,* LXVI, 1925, pp. 35–165.

Laugier de Tassy N. *Histoire du Royaume d'Alger avec l'état présent de son gouvernement.* Amsterdam, 1725.

Lithgow W. *The totall Discourse of the Rare Adventures and Paine full Peregrinations* [...]. London, 1614.

Magini G. A. *Geografia cioè Descrittione universale della Terra* [...]. Venice, 1598.

Manesson-Mallet A. *Description de l'Univers contenant les différents systèmes du monde* [...]. Paris, 1683.

Mascarenhas J. C. *Memoravel relaçao da perdita da nao Conçeiçao e Descripsao nova da cidade de Argel.* Lisbon, 1627. (French translation: P. Teyssier, *Esclave à Alger. Récit de captivité de João Mascarenhas 1621–1626.* Paris, 1993.)

Nicolay N. de. *Les quatre premiers livres des navigations et pérégrinations orientales de Nicolas de Nicolay* [...]. Lyons, 1568.

Ogilby J. *Africa being an accurate description of the regions of Aegypt, Barbary, Libya* [...]. London, 1670.

Palermo S. ("paid for by"). *Istoria e descrizione in compendio della città e regno di Algeri dalla sua fondazione fino a' giorni nostri* [...]. Naples, 1784.

Pananti F. *Avventure e osservazioni sopra le coste di Barbaria.* Florence, 1817. (French translation: De Blaquière. *Relation d'un séjour à Alger, contenant des observations sur l'état actuel de cette Régence* [...]. Paris, 1820.)

Perez de Idiacayz F. *Lettre de F. Perez de Idiacayz à sa Majesté l'Impératrice,* Bougie 29.3.1536 (Simancas, Estado, legajo 463). French translation in É. De la Primaudaie, cit., p. 463.

Pétis de la Croix F., fils. *Description abrégée de la ville d'Alger* [...]. Ed. M. Emerit, "Un mémoire sur Alger par Pétis de la Croix (1695)". In *Annales de l'Institut d'Études Orientales* 11, 1953, pp. 5–24.

Raynal G. T. *Histoire philosophique et politique des États barbaresques et du commerce des Européens dans l'Afrique septentrionale.* Paris, 1826.

Régistres de solde, Deny J. *Les régistres de solde des Janissaires conservés à la Bibliothèque Nationale d'Alger.* In *Revue Africaine,* 61, 1920, pp. 19–46, 212–260.

Ricaud. *Notes sur le mémoire de M. Ricaud, ingénieur au service de l'Espagne, et qui a été longtemps esclave à Alger, présenté par lui au ministère le 15 juin 1754,* in *Venture de Paradis,* cit., pp. 168–169.

Rosalem N. Ed. A. Sacerdoti, "La mission à Alger du consul de Venise Nicolas Rosalem (1753–1754)." In *Revue Africaine,* XCVI, 1952, pp. 64–104.

Rozet P. *Voyage dans la Régence d'Alger, ou description du pays occupé par l'Armée française en Afrique* [...]. Paris, 1833.

Salvago G. B. *Africa ovvero Barbaria*. Ed. A. Sacerdoti, *Africa ovvero Barbaria. Relazione al Doge di Venezia sulle reggenze di Algeri e di Tunisi del Dragomanno Gio. Batta Salvago*. Padua, 1937.

Sanuto L. *Geografia di M. Livio Sanuto distinta in XII libri*. Venice, 1588.

Sanson d'Abbeville N. *L'Afrique en plusieurs cartes nouvelles* [...]. Paris, 1656.

Savary de Brèves F. *Relation des voyages de Monsieur De Brèves* [...]. Paris, 1628; and *Description moderne de la Barbarie, Tunis et Alger selon les mémoires du voyage d'orient de Monsieur de Brèves* [...]. In P. Davity, *Les Estats, empires, royaumes et principautés du monde* [...]. Paris, 1625.

Shaler W. *Sketches of Algiers*. Boston, 1826. (French translation: X. Bianchi, *Esquisse de l'Etat d'Alger* [...]. Paris, 1830.)

Shaw T. *Travels or Observations relating to several parts of Barbary and the Levant*. Oxford, 1738. (French translation: J. MacCarthy. *Voyage dans la Régence d'Alger par le Docteur Shaw*. Paris, n.d.)

Simancas. *Mémoire sur les affaires d'Alger*. n.d. (Simancas, *Estado, legajo* 461), French translation: É. De la Primaudaie. *Histoire de l'occupation espagnole en Afrique (1506–1574)*. Algiers, 1875, p. 65.

The present State of Algiers. (anonymous). London, 1676.

Tollot. *Nouveau voyage fait au Levant ès-années 1731 et 1732. Contenant les descriptions d'Alger, 1731 par le sieur Tollot*. In *Revue Africaine*, XI, 1867, pp. 417–434.

Vander Aa P. (Ed.). *La galerie agréable du monde, où l'on voit* [...] *les principaux empires, roïaumes, republiques*. Leiden n.d. [1729].

Venture de Paradis J. M. Ed. E. Fagnan. *Alger au XVIIIe siècle par Venture de Paradis*. In *Revue Africaine*, 1895–1897. (separate ed., Algiers 1898.)

Von Rehbinder. *Nachrichten und Bemerkungen über den Algierischen Staat*. Altona, 1798–1800.

THE "CITADEL, TOWN, SUBURBS" MODEL AND MEDIEVAL KIRMAN

Lisa Golombek

Kirman, like many older cities in Iran, still looks like a medieval town. The broad highways that encircle the medieval kernel still conjure up images of a circumvallated city. Mud-brick houses line the rambling laneways inside it. Here and there a tiled dome peers over them. A noisy covered bazaar sporting some very fine decorative vaults stretches in a straight line across the old town like a belt, dividing it into northern and southern hemispheres. At the western end it opens into a large *maydan*. Beyond that the street patterns are modern as is the housing. At the eastern end it opens into the empty space of a traffic circle not far from the city's Friday mosque. Should we assume that the present boundaries of this medieval enclave coincide with the earliest Islamic town, or even that it overlies the original settlement? Was the main bazaar always where it now lies, cutting the city roughly into two equal halves? Kirman actually has two Friday Mosques lying in close proximity. What could explain this apparent duplication? Let us examine more closely what we glimpse today.

The Nineteenth Century

A study of old maps and aerial photographs confirms that what we see is pretty much the way Kirman looked in the nineteenth century, except for the broad streets and traffic circles. A city map was drawn by the Feodorov Brothers and recently published in a collection of maps of the Qajar period.[1] The map produced by Khanikoff in 1859 appears to be based on this work, as it simplifies many of the features.[2] The most useful map, and one which will provide us many clues about the history

---

[1] *Pictorial Documents of Iranian Cities in the Qajar Period*, 192.
[2] N. Khanikoff, *Mémoire sur la partie méridionale de l'Asie Centrale* (Paris, 1861).

of the city, is that of Percy Sykes, printed in 1902 (figure 12).[3] This map is almost identical to the Russian one but with many more details and toponyms. The Qajar city was studied by Paul English who used some of this material as well as maps of the city that preserved pre-Revolution toponomy. He did not attempt to dig further into Kirman's past, and his map of nineteenth-century Kirman contains a number of errors (such as switching the names of the two outcrops east of the city).[4] In order to probe further into the urban history of the city a collabora-tive project between the Iranian Cultural Heritage Organization, the Royal Ontario Museum of Toronto, and the University of Michigan was initiated in 2001. The ICHO undertook to record the disappear-ing urban fabric of the pre-vehicular Qajar city.[5] Dr. Sussan Babaie (University of Michigan) began a survey of the Safavid monuments, and I investigated the pre-Safavid city using historical texts, old maps, and aerial photographs. The preliminary results are presented here.

A map of the Qajar city has been reconstructed by the Daftar-i Bih-sazi-yi Baft-i Shahr, based on work by a group from Tehran Uni-versity (figure 1). Using old maps and collective memory, it shows the walled perimeter of the city and the pre-vehicular streets that have disappeared. Boundaries of old quarters and their names have been retrieved from the local population. For orientation purposes some of the major streets cut through the city in the early twentieth century are shown. A less accurate rendition of this map by Gholam Hosayn Bijari shows the location and names of the six gates in the Qajar walls (unpublished).

Using these resources, let us see what additional features become visible. Sykes' map shows a large enclosure on the west labelled "Ark" (i.e., citadel) which was built by the Qajar rulers. The Grand Bazaar (labelled Bazar-i Vakil on English's map) runs all the way across the city from the Ark to the "Masjid Gate." Here stands the Friday Mosque of the city, built in 1350, but it is not connected directly to the Grand Bazaar. The earliest surviving foundations leading directly off this bazaar are those of Ganj Ali Khan (1598), with its centrepiece

---

[3] P. Sykes, *Ten Thousand Miles in Persia or Eight Years in Iran* (New York, 1902), facing p. 188.
[4] P. English, *City and Village in Iran: Settlement and Economy in the Kirman Basin* (Madison, WI, 1966), figs. 11–12.
[5] Supervised by Ms Fariba Kermani, with Dr. Nozhat Ahmedi responsible for recording inscriptions and documents.

a *maydan*, surrounded by commercial institutions. Most of the other institutions entered from the bazaar date from the Qajar period. The section of the bazaar closest to the fourteenth-century Friday Mosque is believed to be contemporary with the Muzaffarid mosque and is still called the Bazar-i Muzaffariyah. A second mosque, also still standing, the Masjid-i Malik (late eleventh century), lies south of the Grand Bazaar. Outside the city walls lay other inhabited areas, including the large quarter on the northeast, labelled, "Mahala Gabr" (Quarter of the Zoroastrians) and a quarter by the same name north of the city, indicated as "Deserted." Several monuments are individually identified, as are some of the quarter names. The two outcrops east of the city are labelled "Kala Dukhtar" (Qal'eh Dukhtar, the westernmost) and "Kala Ardeshir" (Qal'eh Ardashir). Thus, the present Grand Bazaar looks much the same as it did in the Qajar period, and the limits of the "old city" still visible in aerial photographs from the 1950's correspond to those of the Qajar city (figure 2). A series of icehouses, some of which still stand and others being indicated on Sykes' map, lie outside these walls. In places where the city walls are no longer in evidence, the position of the icehouses can be used to indicate the course of the walls. A Safavid date has been suggested for some or all of these icehouses; so the Safavid city may have been roughly the same extent as that of the Qajars. One of these lies far from the walls near Qal'eh Dukhtar, which suggests that the Safavid city may have been slightly larger on the east than the Qajar city.

The configuration that we have described for the Qajar city poses several problems that lead us to ask whether the Qajar city indeed overlies the early Islamic settlement. One of the problems alluded to earlier is the very straightness of the bazaar. How was Ganj Ali Khan able to construct a through-street connecting his *maydan* with the four-teenth-century mosque at the eastern edge of the city? Was it already some kind of thoroughfare, monumentalized through the construction of a covered bazaar, or did Ganj Ali Khan have to destroy part of the residential fabric to build it?

A second question is raised by the duplication of Friday mosques. In addition to the Muzaffarid Friday Mosque, there is a second very large mosque, known as the Masjid-i Malik. It lies south of the bazaar about a ten-minute walk from the other mosque (figure 1: feature 2). It dates to the late eleventh century, and although most of it was rebuilt in the Qajar period and later, Saljuq elements survive, such as the corner minaret on the northeast, the carved brick inscriptions and decoration

on the qibla eyvan, the triple mihrabs on the roof (figure 9), and a
recently discovered stucco mihrab in the hall below.[6] The justification
for the construction of the Muzaffarid mosque only 270 years later is
difficult to understand because one Friday mosque should have sufficed
for a city this size. Normally, the mosque would have been kept in repair
by the local ruler. The two mosques are not sufficiently far apart to serve
different communities, nor do there appear to be sectarian differences.[7]
We shall suggest an explanation for this phenomenon later on.

We can now turn to the question of locating the early Islamic city.
Does it lie beneath the city as defined by the Qajar/Safavid walls and
the great covered bazaar, or was it elsewhere, affiliated in some way
with the ruins on the hilltops? According to the earliest descriptions
of Kirman, which we will examine shortly, the early city had one or
more strongholds (including one on an elevation), a fortification wall
and moat, four gates, and eventually, one or more suburbs. This configuration conforms to the generally accepted model for early Islamic
towns in Iran which comprised four basic elements, the walled town
(*shahristan*), the citadel or castle (*qal'eh, hisn…*), one or more suburbs
(*rabad*), and bazaars. Yet, when we look at what remains today, it is
impossible to see how this description fits the present remains, or even
what is shown on Sykes' map. While the Arabic and Persian histories
of early Kirman have been studied by scholars, there has been no
attempt to match these with the real topography of the city.[8] Only by
looking at the texts together with information revealed by maps such
as Sykes' and other clues to disappeared topographical features, can we
begin to lay out the boundaries and elements of this early city. What
we will discover is not only a city that fits the "model" perfectly but also
one for which the interaction of these urban elements (citadel, town,
suburbs) is clarified. They are all mentioned in the chronicles, so it is
possible to study even their evolving roles and ultimate fates. Existing

---

[6] E. Schroeder published a plan of the mosque in the *Survey of Persian Art*, ed. A. U.
Pope et al. (London, 1938), 1034; Antony Hutt, "Three Minarets in the Kirman
Region," in "Studies in Honour of Sir Mortimer Wheeler," *Journal of the Royal Asiatic
Society*, 1970, 172–180.
[7] For example, Bam had three Friday mosques: one in the bazaar, one in the citadel,
and one for the Kharijites. H. Gaube, *Iranian Cities* (New York, 1979), 106.
[8] For general history and geography of Kirman see A. K. S. Lambton, s.v. "Kirman,"
EI 2, 5:147–166; for an attempt to reconcile the historical sources with existing remains,
see G. Le Strange, *The Lands of the Eastern Caliphate* (Cambridge, 1905), 303–307.

monuments and their traces, geographical features, and toponymy help link this information to fixed points on the ground.

The Buyid Period

The most important Arabic source is the geography of al-Muqaddasi:[9]

> Bardasir [the former name of Kirman]: a capital city (*qasabah*), not of great size but fortified. It has the regional offices now, for the army is there. On its side is a large fort (*qal'eh*). In it are gardens. In it was dug a great and marvellous well, which is among the buildings of Abu Ali b. Ilyas. He has chosen this capital and resided there for twenty years.
>
> At the gate is a stronghold (*hisn*) and a moat traversed by bridges. It has four gates: the Mahan Gate, the Zarand Gate, the Khabis Gate, and the Mubarik Gate. Most of the drinking water comes from wells, and they also have a qanat. In the middle of the town (*balad*) there is another fort (*qal'eh*), and the graceful jami' is near it. Gardens surround the town (*balad*). The fort (*qal'eh*) is high up, and Ibn Ilyas would ascend to it on special mountain horses accustomed to climbing it and sleep in it every night. Canals irrigate their surrounding gardens.

This passage presents many problems because one is never sure of the antecedent for all of al-Muqaddasi's "its." However, if we begin by locating the stronghold/*hisn* with its four gates, the other features will fall into place. Each of the gates, with the exception of the "Mubarik" Gate, was located at the point where the road from the town for which it is named entered the walled *hisn*. If we follow the roads shown on Sykes' map (figure 12), they intersect at a point just west of Qal'eh Dukhtar. The Khabis Gate must be located on the north. Confirmation of the location of the Zarand Gate comes from an unexpected source. The Timurid historian Fasih al-Khvafi recorded events year by year. Under the year 752/1351–52, he tells us that the Muzaffarid ruler of Kirman founded a new Masjid-i Jami' "at" (*dar*) the Zarand Gate.[10] In the following year he says that the mosque "near" (*qarib*)

---

[9] Muhammad b. Ahmad al-Muqaddasi, *Ahsan al-taqasim fi ma'rifat al-aqalim*, ed. de Goeje (Leiden, 1906), 461–462; Eng. trans. B. A. Collins, *The Best Divisions for Knowledge of the Regions* (1994), 406–407. Al-Muqaddasi began writing his geography of the Islamic world in 985 in Shiraz, not far from Kirman (*EI* 2, 7:492b), and only twenty years after the governor Abu Ali b. Ilyas had carried out an extensive building program.

[10] Fasih Ahmad b. Jalal al-Din Muhammad Khvafi (known as Fasihi), *Mujmal-i Fasihi*, ed. Mahmud Farrukh (composed in 1442; Mashhad, 1341HS/1962), 3:79.

the Zarand Gate was completed.[11] It is not clear whether the mosque stood inside or outside the city wall, but as we do know the location of this mosque (which is currently the Friday Mosque of the city), we can be certain that the route from Zarand entered Bardasir/Kirman in the vicinity of this mosque. The references also imply that the Buyid walls were still in evidence in the Timurid period (or, at least, when the mosque was built). The Zarand Gate, therefore, falls on the west side of al-Muqaddasi's *hisn*. This would also confirm the antiquity of the western border of Mahalleh-yi Shahr, which I believe gives us the northwestern corner of the Buyid town (see below).

The position of the Mahan Gate must be on the south. We, thus, have three gates on three different sides, suggesting that the fourth gate is on the east. Perhaps *"mubarik"* ("blessed") refers to the cemeteries that have always lain to the east, and the earliest monument of Kirman (probably tenth century), the Jabal-i Sang mausoleum lies on the road from the city to the cemeteries.[12] We can tentatively draw a rectangle connecting these gates so that they each lie at the midpoint of the walls. It is evident from this exercise that the term *hisn* refers to something lying in the plains, not on a hill, and that it was more like a town than a fort. I am therefore identifying this element with its moat, four gates, and bridges, as the fortified enclosure of the town (*balad*). This conclusion is supported by the Saljuq historian Afdal al-Din Kirmani, who says that the town walls (*baru*) were built by Ibn Ilyas and that there are four gates, on one of which (Khabis) his name appears. He also built the moat (*khandaq*) and the three forts.[13]

Dealing with the forts is more problematic, but if we consider Afdal's information and some of the data culled from incidental references to the forts throughout his text, the situation becomes clearer. Al-Muqaddasi's report would seem to suggest two forts, one adjacent to the town and one within it. The adjacent fort had an extraordinary well, while the one in town served as a royal retreat. Afdal names Ibn Ilyas' three forts: Qal'eh Kuh (the Hill Fort), Qal'eh Kuhneh (the Old Fort), and Qal'eh Now (the New Fort).[14] He mentions the famous

---

[11] Ibid.

[12] Frequently published, the most recent discussion of its date by Bernard O'Kane, "The Gunbad-i Jabaliyya at Kirman and the Development of the Domed Octagon in Iran," in *Arab and Islamic Studies in Honor of Marsden Jones*, ed. T. Abdullah et al. (Cairo, 1997), 1–12.

[13] *Iqd*, 67.

[14] Ibid.

well and places it in the Hill Fort. We must trust his word because he was an eyewitness to the destruction of this Fort which, he says, was commonly known as the "Large Fort." In 1213 the Malik of Zuzan totally destroyed it and its notable well: "That wondrous well which had been cut into the rock, said to be 400 gaz deep (the outside of which I, Afdal, saw almost 8 gaz by 8 gaz length and width), divided into four parts and with four wheels set upon it, this well of such vast proportions and wonder they filled up and made void. The reason for the destruction of this fort was that the well was big and had several doors and storeys. Preserving and guarding it required too many men. Among the wonders of the fort was that its silvery doors were made of iron.... They brought this down (the hill) and had the men of the city, recruited for this, destroy it. Parts which remained were thrown away. As they were destroying this, in the walls a sort of arched vault appeared. When they took it down, two or three stone vessels were found. In these was a crown of gold and several gold and silver vessels, weighing 15 *mann* of gold and 27 *mann* of silver. They took these out and carried them to the treasury of the King. No one knew to which ruler or *kutwal* during the 300 years the treasure had belonged."[15] After its destruction, the well was employed as a prison, and one story tells of an escape engineered with the help of the water-drawer.[16]

Three facts suggest that the Hill Fort, or the castle "within" the city, sat atop Qal'eh Dukhtar. First, it is the closest elevation to the existing city. Second, Sykes' map indicates that there was a wall descending the hill onto the plains. The remains of a tower, perhaps part of a Gate, can still be seen at the bottom of the hill (figure 7).

While it was probably rebuilt many times, very large bricks in the lower courses suggest a pre-Safavid date. The third fact is the existence of a water source that appears to still be in use, now covered with modern housing. I am suggesting that this was the original "wondrous well."

I would like to identify the "Old Fort" with the ruins on Qal'eh Ardashir which Ibn Ilyas repaired and extended. One reference stating that the army encamped between the two forts, Qal'eh Kuh and Qal'eh Kuhneh, presumably in the open plain visible between Dukhtar and Ardashir, supports this identification because the space would

---

[15] *Muzaf*, 51.
[16] *Simt*, 43.

accommodate such a camp.[17] The "New Fort" may be a feature that has disappeared within the original city, or it may be the square fortification that once stood in the southwest corner of the Qajar perimeter (figure 1).[18] It is visible in aerial photographs of the early twentieth century, surrounded by a moat (figure 4). If this is correct, it was not tangent to the Buyid city and its Hill Fort but rather served to guard the entrance to the city from the west.

We now know something about the location and size of the Buyid city. We can say that it extended on the east at least as far as Qal'eh Dukhtar. Popular tradition places the earliest settlement in Mahalleh-i Shahr, the easternmost quarter of the Qajar city (figure 12). This area is too limited to have represented the entire "City," but if we follow the ruined walls shown on Sykes' map and join them to the western wall of Mahalleh-i Shahr, we create a rough rectangular form that permits us to properly place the four gates named by al-Muqaddasi. When we extended the routes labelled Zarand, Khabis, and Mahan on Sykes' map, they penetrated the walls of our hypothetical city, roughly at the midpoint of the west, north, and south sides. If we turn back to the aerial photograph (figure 2), we can see traces of a street pattern forming concentric circles following the northeastern quadrant of the hypothetical Buyid city.

Afdal gives us more details about what lay inside this city in his day in the course of his enumeration of buildings destroyed during the battles between two of the Saljuq princes Bahramshah and Arslanshah.[19] These were the Mint (*dar al-darb*), the Brokerage (*bayya' khaneh*), the Courthouse (*dar al-hukm*), the bath, the bazaar, and shops, suggesting a concentration of civic buildings in a single locale situated near the commercial centre. Perhaps these elements were even arranged around a large open space or *maydan*, although the sources never allude to a *maydan* in Saljuq Kirman. We shall see below that the principal residence of the Qavurtian Maliks was still in the city until the building of the royal suburb.

A final question about the early city concerns the Zoroastrians. Today there is still a street called "Ateshkadeh" (fire-temple) running east-west from the western border of Mahalleh-yi Shahr to the Masjid-i Pa

---

[17] MbI, 193.

[18] This possibility was suggested by G. Le Strange, 306, but he assumed that it stood where the Qajar citadel was built.

[19] MbI, 52–53.

Minar (793/1390). During my visit in 2001, local residents pointed to an empty lot nearby where they said a fire-temple stood until recently. If we are correct in placing the Buyid wall along the western edge of Mahalleh-yi Shahr, then the Zoroastrian quarter before the late Safavid period lay just outside the early city. We shall see that this area was to become a suburb at least as early as the late Saljuq period. It was not until the reign of Shah Sulayman (1667–94) that the Zoroastrians were required to move out of the city and settle north of the walls.[20] This is the area shown as ruined on Syke's map, situated north of the Qajar walls. The remains of the gate leading from this suburb into the city along the route from Zarand still bears the name "Darvazeh-yi Gabri," or the Gate of the Zoroastrians (Syke's map: "Gabr Gate"). During the Afghan plunder of 1720–21 and the destruction of the city by Aqa Muhammad Khan in 1794, the Zoroastrians moved east of the Qajar city, repopulating the original Buyid settlement.

The Saljuq Period

We have just alluded to the creation of suburbs and the possibility that the earliest suburb may have been built by the Zoroastrians. The main suburb, known as Rabad-i Dasht, or the Suburb of the Plains, was created by fiat. The anecdotal account of Afdal bears retelling. In 478/1085–86, with great determination the Saljuq Malik Turanshah went up on the roof of his house in the city and shot three arrows toward the qiblah. Where the first landed, he ordered the construction of a mosque. The second arrow's landing place was to be his tomb, and the third was to locate his "saray, a kushk, a khanaqah, and a ribat for sufis, all touching one another."[21] All of these royal institutions were to form a cluster as the nucleus of a new suburb, the Rabad, or more specifically, Rabad-i Dasht, the Suburb of the Plains.

What reasons lay behind this ambitious foundation? Why did the Malik decide to move his residence out of the city? The story goes as follows. Turanshah was such an avid builder that he attended to the activities and conversations of the tradesmen and craftsmen. When he saw a carpenter working in the Saray of the city with an apprentice

---

[20] Lambton, "Kirman," *EI* 2, 5:157.
[21] MbI, 20.

who resembled a Turk, he asked the carpenter, "Is this child the son of a Turk?" The carpenter responded, "This is a question which the Truthful One asks of you. The mother of this boy says he is from me. There is a Turkish soldier billeted in my house. Undoubtedly, he can give you an answer."[22] In the variation appearing in Ibn Shihab's retelling of Afdal's history the craftsman is a potter, and the king observes: "He (the child) is a Turk and you are a Tajik."[23]

Turanshah was greatly perturbed by these words and immediately ordered all of his army to leave the houses of residents in the city and move to the suburb, where "there was no building. People lived in the city (shahr)." The "amirs, vazirs, and military" who were living in the city were ordered to pitch tents and build shelters in the Rabad. "That very day all the Turks and Tajiks of the army pitched tents outside [the city] and built houses such that by evening prayer time no soldier or Turk remained in anyone's house. Construction outside the city began on that day..."[24] While this story may be apocryphal, it gave Turanshah a pretext to create a visible and impressive symbol of his regime. Note that the date of foundation, 1085, coincides with the building of the famous domes in the Jamiʿ of Isfahan by the Great Saljuq ruler Malikshah. The Saljuqs of Kirman were closely related to the ruling dynasty. Turanshah's father Qavurt was the eldest brother of Alp Arslan. He had even attempted to take over the sultanate after the death of his brother in 1072, but was defeated and finally killed by Malikshah, Alp Arslan's son. Turanshah may have seen the transformation of the Jamiʿ of Isfahan as a glorification of his uncle's branch of the family, and this could have spurred him on to emulate the act. On a broader level, the story invites comparison with the just kings of the past, and the anecdote about the shooting of arrows implies divine assistance in choice of sites, a motif that appears in many other foundation stories.

Nevertheless, the story is of the utmost importance in informing us about the pattern of urban growth for Kirman. This suburb and its palace, known as Saray-i Dasht, are frequently mentioned in the sources I have cited as the domain of events played out in the twelfth and thirteenth centuries.[25] The suburb is often contrasted with the City

---

[22] Ibid.
[23] BAVK, 18.
[24] Ibid.
[25] MbI, 70, 107, 113.

(*shahr*) as being resplendent but poorly defended, presumably because it had no fortification walls. This point is made by Afdal's account of the Ghuzz invasion toward the end of 569/1174. Of the magnificent palace he says: "the likeness of those royal rooms and dwellings, mansions, delightful places, orchards, and meadows has not been seen in the regions of Islam, with spacious courtyards and ceilings decorated with wondrous images and delicate paintings like the pages of the heavens decorated with stars. When dawn came, these fell into destruction. Everyone who wished pillaged that castle, removing its bricks." During this attack the Malik transferred his residence to the Saray of the City. The Ghuzz sacked the suburban palace, and residents of the suburb clambered to take refuge in the city.[26] Many died or left the city. The Ghuzz returned about ten years later and wrought further destruction to the mansions and houses in the suburb.[27] Some thirty years earlier when the aging Malik Arslanshah was overthrown by his son Muhammad in 1142, he was removed from this palace (Saray-yi Dasht) to the Hill Fort for safe-keeping.[28]

Two surviving features allow us to locate the royal suburb and possibly also the palace of the Malik. The first feature is the mosque, the Masjid-i Malik (or, as it is known today, the Masjid-i Imam), built by Turanshah, which still exists and which retains some of its Saljuq structure, as mentioned earlier.

The second piece of evidence helping us locate the Saljuq suburb here is the name of the quarter, "Shah-i Adil" (i.e., the Just King), which appears on Sykes' map. This was the popular title bestowed on Turanshah. Traces of the Saljuq suburb might still exist in the neighbourhood of the mosque. A visit to this site in 2001 revealed adjacent to the mosque on the south side a deep and extensive pit excavated for the construction of a new shopping centre. Along the roadway into the site, in the walls beneath the ruined Qajar houses, were tantalizing fragments of collapsed arches, perhaps the remains of the Saljuq period, or even the palace itself (figure 10). The layers of debris just below the Qajar houses were full of early seventeenth-century Safavid sherds, which will be important in our discussion of changes in the Safavid period.

---

[26] MbI, 114–115.
[27] MbI, 117.
[28] MbI, 28.

The Royal Suburb was not the only area developed by the Saljuqs although it may have been the earliest. Outside the Mahalleh-yi Shahr are two Saljuq monuments, the Khwajeh Atabek mausoleum[29] and the Masjid-i Bazar-i Shah. This mosque has recently been completely rebuilt but Eric Schroeder recorded Saljuq remains.[30] Both lie along the route to Zarand and demonstrate the importance of this highway at that time. If the Zoroastrian suburb originally lay here, these Muslim foundations indicate that the populations of this quarter had become integrated. Perhaps this was the "suburb of the Yazdis" and referred to Zoroastrians coming from Yazd. This suburb is mentioned as the location where Arslanshah's wife had founded a ribat.[31] For Kirman and the region the period of the Qavurtian Saljuqs (1041–1186) was a highpoint, and texts record many other institutions that have not survived. Much of this growth was turned back by invasions of the Ghuzz in 1174 and following years.

Prosperity was restored by Malik Dinar (d. 591/1195), but his successor depleted the treasury and Kirman was once again ravaged by warring parties. Malik Dinar built at least two public edifices that survive: the Masjid-i Malik Dinar (located between the Masjid-i Malik and the Ganj Ali Khan Hammam) and the cistern known as Hawz-i Malik (located along the route leading from the Masjid-i Jami' to the Masjid-i Bazar-i Shah). Both foundations are completely restored and no trace of the original buildings was detected in our visit of 2001. Malik Dinar's son resided for a time at the New Fort, the location of which is not known.[32] In 605/1213 Qiwam al-Din Mu'ayyid al-Mulk, Malik of Zuzan, took Kirman and destroyed the Hill Fort (see above).

The Qutlugh-Khanid Period

Under Mongol tutelage Kirman revived. Many new foundations were erected by the Qutlugh-Khans (c. 1224–1305). Tradition holds that the monument now designated as the Qubbah-yi Sabz ("the Green Dome"),

---

[29] This anonymous tomb tower, octagonal on the exterior but square on the interior, is notable for its brick patterns with stucco overlay and glazed terracotta inserts (A. Hutt and L. Harrow, *Islamic Architecture: Iran*, 1 [London, 1977], pl. 70–71).

[30] *Survey of Persian Art*, fig. 368.

[31] MbI, 27.

[32] MbI, 190–191.

located in the northwest quadrant of the Qajar city, represents the remains of a grand memorial complex erected by the dynasty's founder, Qutlugh Khan Baraq Hajib (d. 632/1235). He had converted to Islam only several years before his death[33] and built a madrasah, perhaps to mark the occasion. The *Simt al-ʿula* reports that Baraq Hajib was buried in his madrasah in the quarter known as Turkabad, which was "outside the city."[34] The location of this suburb is given on Paul English's map of nineteenth-century Kirman as the northwest quadrant, presumably based on the tradition cited above. The problem with this identification is that, unlike the case of the Masjid-i Malik, the monument now standing there and known as the Qubbah-yi Sabz, cannot be used to confirm the location of the suburb because it does not, in its present state, fit with the facts. It is an *eyvan*, not a dome chamber, although one could surmise that the *eyvan* was the entrance to the madrasah and the domed mausoleum has disappeared. However, the mosaic faience decoration of the *eyvan* is stylistically datable to a period much later than the Qutlugh-Khans. A photograph of a dome chamber identified as the Qubbah-yi Sabz of Kirman appears in Sykes' book,[35] but even this monument, no trace of which remained after an earthquake in 1896, could not belong to so early a date and is more likely to be of the fifteenth century.[36] Nevertheless, the name does occur on Syke's map (as a "Ruin") and the identification of the ruins with the Turkabad quarter is also made by Vaziri (1874). We shall tentatively assume that this toponym refers to a foundation of the Qutlugh-Khans and that the northwest suburb of the city was built up by them.

---

[33] W. Barthold-[J. A. Boyle], s.v. "Buraq Hadjib," *EI* 2, 1:1311.

[34] *Simt*, 26.

[35] Op. cit., facing p. 264; Sykes' transmits information read to him from an inscription on the monument naming architects and giving the date 640/1242 (194). This date falls within the correct period but is the foundation date of neither of the two major Qutlugh-Khan madrasahs.

[36] According to Vaziri (149), the madrasah had a lofty domed mausoleum in which he was buried. "It is now standing and is called Qubbah-yi Sabz." The dome appearing in Sykes' photograph resembles the double-domes on high drums, which begin in the mid-fourteenth century and are common in the Timurid period and later. This type of dome appears at the earliest in the mid-fourteenth century Do Minar Dardasht of Isfahan. No building of this sort can be found today at the site popularly known by this name. Vaziri comments that according to another source (Mirza ʿAbd al-Muʾmin), this is the tomb of Khwajeh ʿAbd al-Rashid, a contemporary of Shah Sulayman and therefore datable to the mid-seventeenth century. Perhaps this building replaced the original madrasah.

A second memorial complex which enjoyed greater fame than that of the dynasty's founder was erected by his daughter. In 656/1258 'Ismat al-Dunya Qutlugh Turkan Khatun built a madrasah (the Qutbiyah or 'Ismatiyah) with a mausoleum for her husband Sultan Qutb al-Din, who died in 656/1258.[37] She ruled Kirman for twenty years following his death and founded many other institutions, including a Friday Mosque, which was located in the old Buyid city near the New Gate (a post-Buyid gate, presumably).[38] The madrasah attracted many famous scholars.[39] Several other family members were buried in the dome chamber (*gunbad*) of the Qutbiyah Madrasah.[40] It is not clear whether this foundation adjoined that of her father in Turkabad or lay in a completely different place. According to the *Simt al-'ula*, this madrasah was located *dar S*R*H-yi shahr*, a designation difficult to interpret. As Turkan Khatun's Friday Mosque lay near the New Gate, perhaps her funerary complex was also there.

As the suburbs grew, new avenues of communication appeared. Syke's map shows a through-street running from the vicinity of the Darvazeh-yi Gabri in a southwesterly direction. It abuts the Ganj Ali Khan Maydan on its east side and continues southward from its western side down to the southern gate of the city (Rigabad Gate). The southern section is still a bazaar, known as Bazar-i Mahmud, as it runs parallel to the east walls of the disappeared Qal'eh Mahmud (possibly the New Fort mentioned by Afdal). The north branch would appear to date from the foundation of the Turkabad quarter, and the south branch may go back to the Saljuq period as it would have serviced the royal quarter (Rabad-i Dasht). The designation "Bazar-i Mahmud" pre-dates Ganj Ali Khan's creation of the *maydan* as it is mentioned in his *vaqfiyyah*.[41] This combined route suggests that the main commercial flow in the late

---

[37] *Simt*, 37, gives her titles; on the numerous charitable works undertaken by Turkan Khatun, particularly the Madrasah Qutbiyah and the Friday Mosque at the New Gate, see *Simt*, 39–43; see note 4 on existing monument by Bastani Parizi in Vaziri, 155, n. 4, and citation from the Geography of Hafiz-i Abru, giving the date of the Friday Mosque as 666/1267–68 (467–468), but not providing any further clues as to its location.

[38] See previous note.

[39] *Simt*, 43–44.

[40] *Simt*, 54 (referring to the burial of Turkan Khatun there); for burial of Padishah Khatun, her daughter, see p. 77, where she was taken to the "green roof" (*saqf-i akhdar*) and buried "on the women's side" (*dar janb-i banat*). This designation is very interesting because male members of the family were also buried in the mausoleum [Muhammad Shah, d. 703/1303–04] (95).

[41] I am grateful to Sussan Babaie for this information.

thirteenth century was north-south rather than east-west, as it became in the Safavid period.

Struggles for the throne in Kirman toward the end of the thirteenth century once again threw the region into disarray. For Kirman the maintenance of its commercial and manufacturing facilities always came first. Reorganizing the mint and brokerage houses is specifically mentioned as one of the major steps in recovery, and when continuous assault on the town from within and without ensued, it was the "markets, workshops, and residential quarters" that suffered.[42] So great was the destruction at this time that "not a branch was left on a tree."[43] Famine further reduced the ability of the town to resist. Perhaps it was at this time that the Saljuq mosque of Turanshah and his royal suburb fell into ruin and the next ruler declined to rebuild it. Instead the Muzaffarid prince constructed his own Friday Mosque some fifty years later and this has remained the city's main mosque.[44] This would explain the peculiar duplication of functions in having two Friday Mosques, one of the questions we raised in the beginning.

The Muzaffarid and Timurid Periods

We turn now to the construction of this mosque and its impact on the further urban development of the city. By the middle of the fourteenth century Kirman had at least three commercial arteries. One had been created during an early period along the route leading into the Buyid town from the direction of Zarand. Another connected the Turkabad quarter with the Saljuq suburb, as just described. A third route may have run through the middle of the Buyid city, connecting the Zarand gate on the west to the route to the cemeteries on the east. The easternmost part of today's bazaar is believed to date back to the foundation of the Muzaffarid mosque, but we do not know if it extended the full length of the bazaar today. The choice of location may be seen as a

---

[42] *Simt*, 83.

[43] *Simt*, 86–87.

[44] D. Wilber, *The Architecture of Islamic Iran: the Il Khanid Period* (Princeton, N.J., 1955), 182, inscriptions date the portal and vestibule to 750/1350, but much of the tilework is restoration; L. Golombek, "The Safavid Ceramic Insdustry at Kirman," *Iran* 41 (2003): 263–266, the *mihrab* and *qiblah* wall contain work dating from this period and the sixteenth century, and the façade on court was revetted with blue-and-white underglaze tiles and *cuerda seca* tiles in the mid-seventeenth century.

confirmation that the real city now lay outside the Buyid walls and
that this mosque was positioned to serve both the old city and the two
major suburbs on the west.

Little is known about Kirman in the Timurid period, and no archaeological evidence has come to light except for a small number of sherds
from the city and on Qal'eh Dukhtar.

The Safavid Period

Some construction took place during the sixteenth century, particularly,
additions to the Muzaffarid mosque, but the next major moment came
during the reign of Shah Abbas, when Ganj Ali Khan was sent to
Kirman as governor (1596–1622). The route initiated by the Muzaffarid bazaar became the central spine of Safavid Kirman. It reached
a climax in the Maydan of Ganj Ali Khan and its surrounding public
monuments. This ensemble has been compared with the creation of
the Maydan-i Shah in Isfahan by Shah Abbas, which no doubt inspired
the governor of Kirman.[45] The provincial version is on a much smaller
scale and is more oriented to the promotion of commerce. According
to the Safavid historian Mashizi, "During the rule of the [Ganj Ali]
Khan the town became extremely prosperous. Various peoples intent
on mercantile service came to Kirman. Day by day the quantity
mounted...."[46] Despite its scale, the complex is executed at a high
artistic level comparable to the work done at Isfahan. The south border
of the Maydan coincides with the north arcades of the bazaar (figures
1, 3). On the east lies the facade of a magnificent caravansary, which
contains a gem of a royal chapel in the corner of the entrance block.
On the north of the Maydan is the domed hall of the mint (today it
has been restored as a numismatics museum), and in the southwest
corner is a monumental *chahar-su*. South of the bazaar lies a splendid
bathhouse (restored as a museum).

---

[45] R. Hillenbrand, Chap. 15 (b) "Safavid Architecture," in *The Cambridge History of
Iran: The Timurid and Safavid Periods*, vol. 6, ed. P. Jackson (Cambridge, 1986), p. 793 ("...a
Maidan-i Shah in miniature?"); recently the subject of a lecture presented at Harvard
University by Sussan Babaie, who is undertaking an in-depth study of this complex.
[46] Mir Muhammad Sa'id Mashizi, *Tazkirah-yi Safaviyyah-yi Kirman*, ed. Muhammad
Ibrahim Bastani Parizi (Tehran, 1349HS/1970–71), 276.

We have already referred to the fact that routes from the north and south connected to the Maydan. The route from the Friday Mosque now funnelled the population into this new commercial centre. Together with this foundation Ganj Ali Khan promoted the reconstruction of older quarters, particularly those lying near this centre. Mashizi describes several areas that underwent development. Only one of these areas is easy to identify: "Most of the people from south of the Masjid-i Jami' Muzaffari are desirous to build houses and establish places near the Mazar of the Malik Turanshah Saljuqi who is known as Malik Adil. Since the construction of that quarter became so beautiful, it was known as Husnabad. Today it is extremely flourishing."[47] People still living in the quarters of the old city between Qal'eh Dukhtar and the Muzaffarid Friday Mosque moved into the old Saljuq suburbs and restored them. Most likely they found it attractive because of its proximity to the governor's own residence. The Safavid occupation of this quarter was confirmed by the finding here of hundreds of very fine early seventeenth-century sherds (figure 11).[48] Most were underglaze-painted with cobalt and black outlines following Chinese models. Some were painted in cobalt only, and a very few monochrome with slip decoration were found. Almost no sherds datable to the second half of the century came from this area, although elsewhere in the city all types of Safavid wares were retrieved with the exception of lusterware.[49] Evidence for pottery production in this area includes a clay trivet, found among the sherds, and possibly a kiln. The distribution of Safavid sherds collected throughout the city confirms that the Safavid city included all of the Qajar area represented in Syke's map and possibly more (figure 12). Areas beyond the Qajar walls have not yet been studied. It is likely that the Safavid city extended beyond the Qajar walls to the east and included parts of the Buyid town because there is an icehouse just north of Qal'eh Dukhtar.

Let us return to the two problems raised earlier having to do with the straightness of the bazaar and the duplication of mosques. The explanations would appear to lie in the course of events, not in any

---

[47] Ibid.

[48] L. Golombek, "The Safavid Ceramic Industry at Kirman," *Iran* 41 (2003): 253–270; R. B. Mason, "Petrography of Pottery from Kirman," *Iran* 41 (2003): 271–278.

[49] Safavid lustre ware, at least those tested, came from Mashhad (R. B. Mason and L. Golombek, "The Petrography of Safavid Ceramics," *Journal of Archaeological Science* 30, no. 2 (February 2003): 251–261.

hypothetical model for an Islamic city. Just as Shah Abbas knitted together the north and south banks of the river that runs through Isfahan, Ganj Ali Khan used the bazaar to integrate the two suburban masses on the north and south. The difference is that at Isfahan the old city was incorporated into the new. With only a slight shift to the south the seat of government remained in the same place. In Kirman a new wall was built to encircle the renovated parts of the city, but in so doing it cut off most of the original tenth-century town. The adjacent hilltop castle also faded from view, never to play an active role again.

A fragmentary stone slab stored in the Friday Mosque bears a titillating inscription that may explain what happened. It says that the "Muzaffarid Jami'" which once lay "outside the city of Kirman, and which has been brought into a state of repair, is now in the midst of the inhabited city (*dar vasat-i ma'murah'yi shahr*)."[50] The inscription is not dated but seems to belong to the Qajar period when a new hall (*shabistan*) was added to the mosque. Thus, by the Qajar period what had once been the "city," the *shahr*, became a suburb, and the former suburbs, now enclosed by a wall, became the city. The Qajars embellished Kirman with many new foundations, lining the great bazaar with colourful spacious madrasahs, mosques, caravansaries, and bathhouses. It was they who extended the bazaar further west to join the Maydan-i Ark and its Citadel and also "straightened" the bazaar on the east. Perhaps the bazaar had once connected directly to the Muzaffarid mosque and was not so straight.

This study makes the point that, while models are useful in understanding urban development in the Islamic world, they do not fully explain the course of development in individual cases. The set of historical circumstances peculiar to an individual city convey the dynamics of it growth.

---

[50] Cited in the *Merat al-Buldan*, 4:118 (also cited by Bastani-Parizi, 193, n. 3 from preceding page, but not cited in full; recorded by Kirman Project in 2001).

Abbreviations

[BAVK]

Afdal al-Din Kirmani, Ahmad b. Hamid. *Badayiʿ al-azman fi vaqayiʿ Kirman* [*Tarikh-i Afdal ya badayiʿ al-azman fi vaqayiʿ Kirman*]. Reconstructed text by Mahdi Bayani. Tehran, 1326H/1927. (Origins of the city to the period of Malik Dinar, continued by *Iqd*.)

This is the key work for the Saljuq period. The original has not survived but it has been reconstructed from several works that included parts of it almost verbatim. The most important of these are Ibn Shihab Yazdi and Muhammad b. Ibrahim.

[*EI 2*]

Encyclopaedia of Islam, new edition.

[*Iqd*]

Afdal al-Din Kirmani, Ahmad b. Hamid. *ʿIqd al-ʿula liʾl-mawqif al-aʿla*. Edited by Ali Muhammad Amiri Naʿini. Tehran, 1311HS/1932. (Covers the period 584–591/1188–1195.)

[MbI]

Muhammad b. Ibrahim. *Tarikh-i Salajuqiyah-yi Kirman*, ed. M. T. Houtsma [*Histoire des Seljoucides du Kermân; texte perse* . . .]. Lugduni-Batavorum, 1886. (Includes all of the works of Afdal as well as glosses relating to his own time, the period of Ganj Ali Khan; 1025/1616.) Extensively cited in Vaziri (see below).

[*Muzaf*]

Afdal al-Din Kirmani, Ahmad b. Hamid. *Muzaf ila badayiʿ al-azman fi vaqayiʿ-i Kirman*. Edited by ʿAbbas Iqbal. Tehran, 1331H/1952. (Covers the years 602–612.)

[*Simt*]

Nasir al-Din Munshi Kirmani Yazdi al-asl. *Simt al-ʿula liʾl-hazrat al-ʿulya*, ed. ʿAbbas Iqbal. Tehran, 1328HS. (A history of the Qara-Khitays of Kirman, written 715–716/1315–16.)

[Vaziri]

Ahmad Ali Khan Vaziri Kirmani. *Salariyyah* (begun in 1291 as a comprehensive history of Kirman). Edited by Muhammad Ibrahim Bastani Parizi with extensive notes and discussion of historical sources for the history of Kirman. Tehran, 1961.

ISTANBUL 1620–1750: CHANGE AND TRADITION

Maurice Cerasi

This paper deals with the change in architecture and urban culture, before the reference to Western models had yet become explicit and dominant. We might define that period also as that which followed the Sultan Ahmet Mosque, during which the last drops of classical Ottoman culture and urban mentality were squeezed out of the spirit and techniques of the period of Soliman the Magnificent and his son and of their architect Sinan, and which ended before the planning of the Baroque Nuruosmaniye, or again, as that which includes the mid-seventeenth century urban events and achievements described by the historian Naima and the chronicler Evliya. It was before architects like Mehmed Tahir and Simyon Kalfa, though continuing the Ottoman typological tradition, gave a wholly new turn to façades, volumes, and urban space. In the period I am examining, the classical manner was still sought and change came subtly, setting gradually the stage for the Baroque or Rococo Istanbul of the second half of the eighteenth century.[1]

---

[1] I have widely used the following reference works: Ahmet Refik Altınay, *Hicri Onikinci asırda İstanbul Hayatı* (İstanbul, 1930); Ahmet Refik Altınay, *Hicri Onüçüncü asırda İstanbul Hayatı* (Istanbul, 1932); Oktay Aslanapa, *Osmanlı Devri Mimarisi* (Istanbul: İnkilap Kitabevi, 1986); *Dünden bugüne Istanbul ansiklopedisi* (Istanbul: T.C. Kültür Bakanlığı ve Tarih Vakfı, 1993–); *Eminönü camileri* (Istanbul: Türkiye Diyanet Vakfı Eminönü Şubesi, 1987); Evliya Celebi, *Narrative of travels in Europe, Asia, and Africa, in the seventeenth century*, translated from the Turkish by the Ritter Joseph von Hammer (London: Parbury, Allen, and Co. 1834–50); *Fatih camileri ve diğer tarihi eserler* (Istanbul: T.C. Diyanet İşleri Başkanlığı Fatih Müftülüğü, 1991); *The Garden of the Mosques: Hafız Hüseyin al-Ayvansarayi's Guide to the Muslim Monuments of Ottoman Istanbul*, ed. Howard Crane (Leiden: Brill, 2000); Godfrey Goodwin, *A History of Ottoman Architecture* (London: Thames and Hudson, 1971); Cornelius Gurlitt, *Der Baukunst von Konstantinopel* (Berlin: Wasmuth, 1912); Joseph Freiherr von Hammer-Purgstall, *Constantinopolis und der Bosporos/Örtlich und geschichtlich beschrieben von Jos. von Hammer; mit...dem Plane der Stadt Constantinopel und einer Karte des Bosporos* ([Budapest]Pesth: Hartleben's Verlag, 1822); Halil İnalcık, s.v. "Istanbul," in *Encyclopédie de l'Islam* (Leiden: Brill, 1978); Doğan Kuban, *Istanbul, an Urban History: Byzantion, Constantinopolis, Istanbul* (Istanbul: Economic and Social History Foundation of Turkey, 1996); Robert Mantran, *Istanbul dans la seconde moitié du XVIIᵉ siécle* (Paris: Adr. Maisonneuve, 1962); Wolfgang Müller-Wiener, *Bildlexikon zur Topographie Istanbuls* (Tubingen: Wasmuth, 1977); Mustafa Naima, *Annals of the Turkish Empire from 1591 to*

Was that a period of transition? Istanbul, like all great world cities, had no specific and limited periods of transition. After all, its story was, throughout its evolution, one of continuous transition. It did have some periods in which indecision seemed to reign and the coming new ages were not easy to perceive, and yet, if some sectors of its making stagnated, others were preparing a subdued change which would reveal itself explosive a few decades later. The changes and developments of the 1620–1750 period have had much less weight on Istanbul than the very strong Ottoman basis laid in the preceding century and a half, but it would be impossible to understand Baroque Istanbul without the gradual break which preceded it.

The Making of the Ottoman City

The decadence of Byzantine Constantinople had been a two centuries long process.[2] Its once very large population had dwindled to fifty, sixty thousand, and its vast walled-in area contained what looked like a series of semi-rural villages, interspersed by convents, churches, palaces, many in ruin. Across the Golden Horn, Italian Galata was almost a city apart.

When Mehmed II conquered the decrepit and under-populated Constantinople in 1453, it took him almost two decades to decide, if and how to make of it a brilliant and ambitiously universal capital. Then followed two decades of frenetic building consolidated by his heirs who handed over to Süleyman the Magnificent a city totally Islamic-Ottoman in its form and culture, if not in its population. The Sultan moved his court a few years later from Edirne (Adrianople), some two hundred and fifty kilometres northwest. In the following twenty-five years he established the Ottoman and Islamic basis of the

---

1659 of the Christian Era (London: Oriental Translation Fund, 1832); Zeynep Nayır, Osmanlı Mimarlığında Sultan Ahmet ve Sonrası (Istanbul: İTÜ Mimarlık Fakültesi Baskı Atölyesi, 1975); Gülru Necipoglu, Architecture, Ceremonial, and Power: The Topkapı Palace in the Fifteenth and Sixteenth Centuries (Cambridge, MA, and London: MIT Press, 1991); İnci Nurcan, "18. Yüzyılda İstanbul Camilerine Batı Etkisiyle Gelen Yenilikler," Vakıflar Dergisi 19 (1985): 223–36; Mehmed Zeki Pakalın, Osmanlı Tarih Deyimleri ve Terimleri Sözlüğü (Istanbul: M.E.B., 1946); Mouradja d'Ohsson, Tableau Général de l'Empire Othoman, divisé en deux parties, dont l'une comprend la Législation Mahométane; l'Autre, l'Histoire de l'Empire Othoman, vol. 1, vol. 3 (Paris, 1790; 1820); Tahsin Öz, Istanbul Camileri (Ankara, 1962).

² Roughly from the 1260 Crusader invasion to the 1453 Ottoman conquest.

city, transferring population, both Islamic and Christian, from other towns of his reign, reinforcing the central market district (*çarşı*) with a commercial hall (*bedesten*) and new shops, and building a very large walled-in palace on the site of the Forum Taurii (but later abandoning it for the new Topkapı palace on the promontory that had been the Late Roman forum). During the repopulation of the city, the settlement of dozens—sometimes hundreds—of families homogeneously grouped around a religious building, mosque, church, or synagogue was a more or less planned process. The unit would take the name of a *mahalle*, an administrative unit, but also an urban, topological, and social place identity. He imposed on his principal pashas and courtiers the donation of some 184 mosques (*cami*) and prayer-halls (*mescit*), 24 theological and scientific teaching institutions (medrese), 32 Turkish baths (*hammam*), 10 further *bedesten*s, and *han*s (court type commercial building with cells and porticos). His own main contribution to the city was the 1470 Fatih *imaret*, a huge precinct containing mosque, medreses, schools, and other social institutions. Placed to the northwest of the ancient centre, it became the focus of the Islamic core of the city, both for the population of the surrounding quarters and for the diverse urban and architectural evolution of the whole area. An important move by Fatih was the establishment—with a mausoleum built in 1459 and in 1462–70 a large mosque—of the holy site of Eyüp, a kilometre out of the city walls along the Golden Horn, out of which would grow one of the most important outer quarters of Istanbul.[3]

From Fatih's *imaret* on, up to the late eighteenth century, all Istanbul community utilities would be based on a principle common to all Islamic cities, that of pious foundations (*vakıf*, Turkish for waqf). For centuries the triad *imaret-mahalle*-sepulchre (*imaret* donated by a leader, *mahalle* settled by homogeneous groups, and symbolic legitimation of possession of land and place through the burial of hero or leader) gave identity and form to Istanbul. In time, their size, modality, and psychological impact would change and give colour to each period and part of the city, but the fundamental ideological and mental processes of town building did not vary. As in all Islamic towns, the term 'public' is misleading for Ottoman Istanbul. Structures which needed specific

---

[3] The site was supposed to be the burial ground of Ebu Eyyub al-Ansari, Mahomet's companion in arms and standard bearer, fallen during the first Islamic siege of Constantinople in 672.

buildings of pious nature—mosques and prayer halls, medreses, but also schools for children (*sibyan mektebi*) and libraries, and kitchen for the poor and hospitals, which in Islamic ideology had all a direct connection to religion—would be mostly donated by individual members of society, some from the sultan's finances. Almost always, the foundation act would provide income for the pious structures from rural or urban tenures. These last would include *han*s, *hammam*s, shops, which in turn would enrich the city. Christian and Jewish minorities, too, would have their own services. Even primary services such as fountains, bridges would be delivered by the foundations, either free of charge or on payment. Water, a vital resource for city life, was brought through the voluntary munificent action of pashas and sultans.[4] Aqueducts were invariably addressed at the great ensembles whose necessities they satisfied and on their way through the town provided water for the fountains of the various quarters. They took the name of the pious foundation and hence of the primary donator of the ensemble. Those complex water systems would therefore be called *Fatih suyolları, Köprülü suyolları,* and so on. Many large endowments would contain various functions in different buildings which would form an ensemble (called *külliye* in modern times), sometimes, but not always, enclosed within a well-defined architectural organism with courts and precinct walls. Of course, based as it was on individual generosity, the system would not provide all the public services a post-medieval urban community needed. For example, hospitals, mostly built in the fifteenth and sixteenth century, gave seventeenth century Istanbul and its half-million population no more than two hundred individual cells, setting an example of excellence in quality but not in quantity, if compared with western cities which had by then very large hospitals with huge and uncomfortable naves to house thousands of patients.

In the years following the reign of Fatih, Beyazit II (1481–1512) concentrated his first building efforts on his provincial *imaret* in Edirne and Amasya, and it is only during his last years as a sultan that he had the Beyazit mosque and complex built near the market district; Selim I (1512–20) was too busy with his military campaigns: the mosque

---

[4] The term "Sultan" followed by the name (for example Sultan Ibrahim) indicates the ruler. The term Sultan preceded by the name (for example Kösem Sultan) refers to the sultana mother of a Sultan, otherwise Valide (mother) Sultan.

named after him was actually built in 1522 by his son Süleyman I (the Magnificent).

Süleyman and his heirs, Selim II and Murad III, put to work Sinan and his disciples to enrich that basic and solid structure laid by Fatih, giving it magnificence through architecture and demographic consistency through a policy of immigration and deportation. Their buildings were all over Istanbul, in its main suburbs—Eyüp, Galata, Üsküdar—and in the surrounding territories: palaces, religious ensembles, bridges, and aqueducts. Almost nothing has remained of the palaces. Most mescit have been disfigured. And yet, the well-known silhouette of Istanbul and something more than the mere outlines of its extra-muros expansion date from the 1540–1580 period. Most of the monuments of that period set the typological and linguistic apparatus of the central plan domed space of the typical Istanbul mosque, its symbolic triangular composition, closely framed by one or two minarets, and its sequel of accessory functional building types and mausoleums. It also refined the *modus operandi* of architectural patronage, enhancing the role of Valide Sultans (Queen Mothers). One peculiar characteristic of the Süleyman I period (d. 1566) was that the sultan mosques had been built off the main axis on hills dominating the Golden Horn, as if trying to avoid a direct contact with the commercial and social fabric of the city. One feels that they did try to create new central places, whereas the earlier Fatih and Beyazit ensembles were on the main axis and influenced directly the central urban development.

Not much was donated to the city by Süleyman's successors. Selim II (1566–74) built his mosque, Sinan's senile masterpiece, in Edirne. Murat III (1574–1595) donated his Muradiye to the town of Manisa, one of the two Anatolian seats of crown princes. On the contrary, Ahmet I (1603–1617) forced his finances (and political consensus) to add a crowning masterpiece to the Istanbul promontory: the so-called Blue Mosque completed in 1617.[5] It was distant from the commercial cores and its effect on urban development was more spectacular than functional. Its accessory elements—*türbe* (mausoleum), *arasta* (vault-covered commercial street), schools, etc.—are, however, less compact than precedent sultan

---

[5] See Nayır, *Osmanlı*; Zeynep Ahunbay, art. "Sultan Ahmed Külliyesi," in *Dünden bugüne İstanbul ansiklopedisi* (İstanbul: T.C. Kültür Bakanlığı ve Tarih Vakfı, 1993–), 7:55–61; Howard Crane, *Risale-i-Mi'mariyye: An Early Seventeenth Century Ottoman Treatise on Architecture* (Leiden and New York: Brill, 1987); Aslanapa *Osmanlı*, 325–334.

ensembles and show a certain dispersion and lack of symmetry which reflects the increasing complexity of the city.

Crisis or Change?

From the standpoint of conservative historiography when it breaks down the flux of events into wars, economic expansion, international treaties, power intrigues, and lists of great names, the seventeenth and eighteenth centuries of Ottoman history would certainly be called a period of crisis. It is a long period of unlucky wars and of shrinking frontiers and finances, of rebellion in Anatolia, and of court intrigues. The conservative and military-oriented mentality of the Ottoman ruling class harped on the loss of the Golden Age, seeing in its own political and organizational setbacks the fall of a civilization. It has yet to be proved, however, that political crisis, military insipience, and restrictive public finance brings immediately artistic and cultural pauperism. It was not the case of Istanbul, no more than that of Genoa and Venice, which enacted their most brilliant way of life when their political and financial fortunes were setting.

True, great *selatin* (pertaining to the sultan) monumental works were rare. But, as we shall see, endowments of medium and modest size by pashas and court ladies transformed the street scene and many aspects of town life. Medreses and schools for children became diffuse; most Istanbul libraries were founded in this period.[6] Water distribution systems were reformed, reservoirs built, fountains decupled. Population grew. Town markets increased their importance and size, stone masonry *han*s became a staple feature of Istanbul. Increase in prices and lack of materials was a constant worry for merchants and craftsmen and for the authorities, and yet, commerce prospered. True, the great palaces of the fifteenth and sixteenth century grandees were falling down or were less numerous. But on the other hand, elegant and enjoyable timber mansions on beautiful seaside sites (*yalıs*) were ever more numerous. Ever larger groups of people took part in a brilliant and (almost) careless

---

[6] See: Behçet Ünsal, "Türk Vakfı İstanbul Kütüphanelerinin Mimarî Yöntemi," *Vakıflar Dergisi* 18 (1984): 95–124.

life. There was no real misery or poverty in urban life. The common people's life was modest and austere but not without grace.

After Ahmet I's death followed a decade of unrest. Mustafa I (1617–18, 1622–23) and Osman II (1618–22) did not leave their mark on the city except for the infill of a stretch of sea and beach of what would be called from then on the pleasure gardens of Dolmabahçe (Filled in Gardens) at the southwestern tip of the Bosphorus. Murad IV (1623–1640) enjoyed a fairly long reign but was busy campaigning. His only important buildings are the 1635 Revan and 1638 Baghdad kiosks (köşk in Turkish) within the Topkapı Palace grounds to celebrate his eastern victories. During his reign, his mother, Kösem Sultan (wife of Ahmet I, mother also of Ibrahim, grandmother of Mehmed IV) patroned the 1640 Çinili Cami in Üsküdar, and the vizier Bayram Pasha built his medrese near Haseki.

Ibrahim (1641–48) is generally held to have been emotionally disturbed. His love for wine, women, and feasting was legendary. Court intrigues were at their peak during his reign. His only important building was the 1643 Sepet Köşk on the northwestern seaside of the Topkapı promontory facing the Bosphorus. In the same period Kemankeş Mustafa Pasha built his medrese on the Divan Yolu (1641).

One noteworthy factor for urban history in the second half of the seventeenth century was the preference of many sultans for Edirne. The people of Istanbul noted and resented the frequent absence of the sultans from the city. Mehmed IV (1648–1687), called 'The Hunter' because of his passion for hunting and campaigning, mistrusted and hated the city. Ahmet II (1691–95) managed to keep himself in the Edirne court and never came to Istanbul. Much the same can be said of Mustafa II (1695–1703), enthroned and dethroned in Edirne, who used to leave it only for his frequent military campaigns in the West, and went as far as to have all Divan meetings in that city. He also had his mother (the Valide) brought there from Istanbul in great pomp. Even Ahmet III, who reverted the trend and returned with his court to Istanbul (one month after his accession to the throne in Edirne!), absented himself for one whole year in 1718, partly because his war headquarters were in Edirne, and partly because of the great Istanbul fire. As the Grand Viziers in charge usually accompanied the sultan, but also because of their frequent deposition, Istanbul was often in the hands of the kaymakams (the official substitute of the grand vizier for the city affairs). For a town in which the court had a great part in town spending and town crafts, this had an enormous effect both psychological and economical. In 1687 and 1703 during the so-called "Edirne events" the population and janissaries gave vent to their resentment and eventually forced the court permanently back to Istanbul.

A sense of crisis affected the spirit of the town people certainly also for other and more general causes. Anatolian rebellions (the Celali movement and the mutiny of local pashas), wars on the Austrian and Russian fronts, Cossack incursions on the Black Sea deep into the northern inlets of the Bosphorus, the Venetian blockade of the Dardanelles could not but increase the sense of insecurity of the population, already harassed by the undisciplined and rebellious attitudes of janissary and *sipahi* (select cavalry troops). Uprisings and change of humours, superstitions, and dangerous gossip were diffuse. The state's budgetary problems, as well as the abundance of gold in the Western Mediterranean, brought deeply felt inflation.

Despite his aversion to the city and his long sojourn in Edirne, Mehmed IV's reign (1648–1687) was relatively rich in building activity. In the forties, his grandmother Kösem Sultan had transformed the Cerrah Pasha palace in the commercial heart of the city between the Bazaar and Eminönü into Istanbul's largest *han*, the Valide Han. The greatest monumental mosque of the period, the Eminönü Yeni Valide, completed in 1663, can hardly be considered typical of the classical period in its setting and accessorial buildings, though the external aspect and interior space of the mosque proper were not much different from those of the earlier sultan mosques. Started in 1597 under the patronage of the Venetian Safiye Sultan, mother of Murad III, by the architect Davut Agha, Sinan's disciple, the construction was stopped after a few years and remained standing till 1660, with only the ground floor window level completed. It was taken up that year by Mehmed IV's mother, Turhan Sultan, another Venetian, and inaugurated in 1663. The new architect was Mustafa Agha but the design was unvaried and reflected that of the late Classical period. The building programme of the ensemble had however changed: the original medreses were abolished. Instead a double market (*çifte çarşı*), *türbe, darülkurra* (Koran commentary classes), primary school, two *sebils*, and a *sultan kasrı* (a royal pavilion giving access to the sultan's gallery—*hünkâr mahfili*—in the mosque) with view on the sea were introduced.[7] Thus, with its impor-

---

[7] See *Istanbul Yeni Cami ve Hünkar Kasrı* (Istanbul: Vakıflar Genel Müdürlüğü, [undated]) for its *vakıfname* (foundation act) and functional programme. See also: Doğan Kuban,

tant commercial auxiliary buildings and its Sultan apartments, it gave a new perspective to the commercial heart of the city and anticipated new developments.

On the Divan Yolu medrese and mausoleum building which had been very important at the end of the sixteenth century (Koca Sinan complex of 1593, Gazanfer Ağa medrese and *türbe* of 1596), and beginning of seventeenth (Ekmekçizade and Kuyucu Murat complexes, both around 1610), Kemankeş Mustafa (1641), was taken up again with the Köprülü (1661) and Kara Mustafa (1683) medrese and mausoleum complexes,[8] and Köprülü's Vezir *han*. Also on the main axis were the Amcazade Hüseyin Pasha complex (around 1699) and the Feyzullah Efendi library and medrese (1700). Other medrese-*sebil*-and-mausoleum complexes would later be added: those of Çorlulu Ali Pasha (1708), Damat Ibrahim Pasha (1720), Seyyit Hasan Pasha (1740).

Another outstanding achievement of the period was the 1668 new Topkapı Palace harem quarters built after the 1665 fire had destroyed the old ones. In 1679 work was started on the sultan's Beşiktaş seaside palace. Turhan Sultan had her Eyüp seaside palace built in 1683, perhaps the first outstanding construction which would start the fashion of court ladies building their main or secondary mansions in that holy quarter.

Absentee sultans and court intrigues, military defeats and political instability should have discouraged, one would think, urban development. It was not so. As we shall see, the seventeenth century is a century of powerful pashas, whose *vakıfs*, mausoleums, and medreses leave a stronger mark on the city fabric than the imperial works of the same period. True, intrigues and political strife brought an impressive amount of demotion and decapitation of many of pashas, and a frequent turnover of grand-viziers. But it is to them that we can attribute the most important donations. In a context of frequent change and clamorous falls, two names, whose activism preludes to the reforming spirit which would set in much later, stand out for their political influence and for their contribution to the city between 1660 and 1730. They are those of the Köprülü dynasty and of Damat Ibrahim Pasha (Nevşehirli),

---

s.v. "Yeni Cami Külliyesi," in *Dünden bugüne Istanbul ansiklopedisi* (Istanbul: T.C. Kültür Bakanlığı ve Tarih Vakfı, 1993–), 7:464–67.

[8] Kuran sees the origin of this new form of the *türbe-medrese* complex in Sinan's Eyüp Sokullu complex taken up by Davut Agha and other Sinan disciples. Aptullah Kuran, *Sinan: The Grand Old Master of Ottoman Architecture* (Washington and Istanbul: AKA Press, 1987), 132.

whose tenure was only a decade long and yet deeply influenced imperial policies and the city.

The Köprülüs reigned for over thirty years with three grand viziers:
Mehmed Köprülü, the first and most eminent, his son Fazıl Ahmet,
Kara Mustafa Pasha, and Amcazade Hüseyin Pasha, a relative.
Despite the diverse historical evaluation of the various members of the
dynasty—ranging from that of the founder Mehmed as a reformer of
the state machine, to the condemnation of the calamitous ambitions
of Kara Mustafa Pasha who attempted the siege of Vienna and was
executed for its failure—they were all involved in the Ottoman political
system's difficult march out of the chaos of the first and central decades
of the seventeenth century. They were also remarkable patrons of most
of the important buildings of that period. Of course, their achievements
and failures (military defeats and weak diplomacy which could not
exploit military victories) have to be judged within the context of the
dwindling powers of the Ottoman state in world politics and military
balance. They were part of a class that perceived success and setbacks
in military terms and as a matter of central state authority, and acted
sympathetically in a milieu which produced a historical criticism of the
state of things. It is interesting to note that, despite the political-military
outlook and contempt of commerce and trade which dominated the
Ottoman ruling class, their contribution to *han* building was consistent.[9]
Their religious and funerary foundations were small-scale and modest if compared to the commercial buildings that had acquired urban
momentum and dimensional extension. They were benevolent witnesses,
if not supporters, of what we might call the 'bourgeois development'
of the Istanbul architectural scene with its small- and medium-sized
but accurately designed housing, its large stone *han*s, and the religious
complexes well integrated in the street scene. Two buildings of the last
Vizier of the dynasty, Amcazade Hüseyin Pasha, his small *yalı* pavilion
on the Bosphorus and his medrese and mausoleum complex in Saraçhane, are significant examples of the new Istanbul scene.

Ahmed III's reign (1703–1730) was one of change, but also of the
consolidation of previously latent trends. It brought such architectural achievements as the Üsküdar Yeni Valide mosque, the Ankaravi

---

[9] Aslanapa *Osmanlı Devri*, 354–62, writes that the second half of the seventeenth
century is the epoch of the Köprülü both politically and in their patronage of architecture, perhaps more remarkable in Anatolia than in Istanbul. Many a *taş han* (stone
or stone and brick *han*) was built in that period.

medrese,[10] the great Simkeşhane Han donated by the Sultan's mother, the Çorlulu Ali Pasha complex on the Divan Yolu, the first Saadabad pleasure grounds and kiosks, the Palace library, and the small and delicious room called Yemiş Odası (Room of Fruits) in the Topkapı Palace, many fountains, of which the most important are the Topkapı Bab-I-Hümayun and Üsküdar Ahmet III *sebils*, and all the works commissioned by Nevşehirli Damat Ibrahim Pasha which include a long list of restoration works, of which more should be said.

Damat Ibrahim Pasha's ambition as an individual, his cultural overtures, his friendship with Ahmet III and his influence on policies even before he became Sadrazam in 1720, make of him a case quite apart. He certainly is one of the main protagonists, if not *the* protagonist, of that brilliant period of Ottoman art and way of life called the Tulip period. Much has been written on the taste for ephemeral joys of life and of environment, on the stupendous floral ornamentation of fountains, on light and well-lit pavilions, on the admiration for Western garden art and the attempts at imitating it, on the introduction of the first serious printing establishment. It has been often held that the new tendency to look to the West for examples was the outstanding factor of this nearly twenty year long interlude that ended with a violent reaction of rebellious sectors of the population, leading to the execution of Damat Ibrahim. I would emphasize, however, this period's continuity both with the past and its prolongation into the middle decades of the eighteenth century. Was not the apparent hiatus at both ends of those decades overrated? Floral art was a peculiarity of late seventeenth century Edirne where the court had established itself for many decades.[11] The interest for Western art and customs was no stronger and not less patronized than the interest for Persian art and ways: it was a period of reviving intellectual curiosity. The translations encouraged by Ibrahim Pasha can be seen both ways: as the expression of the interest for things Turkish: a strong way of addressing the enrichment of the common and popular cultural fabric in letters, in miniature, in architecture monumental and residential, of absorbing alien elements into the diverse local *koiné* and reducing the previous distance between elite and popular expression, between previously somehow despised

---

[10] Aslanapa, *Osmanlı Devri*, 370.
[11] A. Süheyl Ünver, "Türk Sanat Tarihinde Edirnekâri Lâke İşleri ve Sanatkârları," *Vakıflar Dergisi* 6 (1965): 15–20.

local models and prestigious Persian and Western models. A striking example is the absorption, before, during and after the Tulip Period, of timber town-house architectural ways into masonry monumental architecture in certain parts (in the *hünkar mahfili* of imperial mosques, in certain school and library buildings, in *han*s...). This corresponded also to novel refinements in house architecture and pavilions, taking up composition techniques from classical Ottoman monumental architecture (for example in window composition), from Persian pavilions (high porches and wood columns, symmetry), and even from the Far East and China (as in the case of elaborate cantilever eaves of *sebils* and richer houses).

There is a very subdued and conservative treatment of mosque, minaret, and medrese, in the 1710 Çorlulu Ali Pasha and 1720 Damat Ibrahim complexes, whereas the precinct walls and the *sebils*, that is, the street-front elements are flamboyant, innovative, and ornate, outweighing the functional core of the ensembles, hardly perceivable from the public spaces. In both complexes the introversion and simplicity of the layout and of the inner court's architectural elements have a very graceful effect and shift the accent to the street scene.

Fundamentally peace-loving, Ahmet III and his vizier Ibrahim set the basis for the long (1717–1737) peace with Austria, the Ottoman Empire's main antagonist in the preceding decades, but could not avoid wars with Persia and Russia. Nevertheless, Damat Ibrahim's impressive activism allowed him to impose a felicitous programme of restoration and new building. His restoration of the city walls, of Leander's Tower (Kız Kulesi), of the Byzantine Tekfur Saray, of Galata Saray, the rebirth of the arcade street type in Şehzade, point to an incipient historicism, typical of conservative Ottoman intellectuals. In this case, however, it appears to open the way to pride in local traditions and to the reappraisal of ancient techniques. In the course of time, such empirical historicism developed into an interesting aspect of later eighteenth and nineteenth century architecture in the Central and Eastern regions of the Empire, marking a revival of some Byzantine and Classical Ottoman models and techniques in Istanbul, of Seljuk, Armenian and Late Roman re-visitations in Eastern Anatolia and Syria, and of Mamluq taste in Syria and Egypt.

The only large monumental mosque of the whole period I am examining, after that of the 1663 Eminönü Yeni Cami, is another Valide work, the 1708 Valide-i Cedit (or Yeni Valide) mosque in Üsküdar. Its layout is traditional, and yet it sets a number of innovations which will be taken up in a more coherent and organic form in the third large mosque of the whole period, the 1733 Hekimoglu Ali Pasha mosque: a very vertical volume of the mosque, free-standing in a garden-like court, rich aggregation of accessory elements (school, *sebil*, apartments…) on the precinct walls, high basement of prayer hall with monumental flight of stairs leading to the entrance porch.

Outstanding monuments of Mahmut I's (1730–1754) reign are the already mentioned Hekimoğlu Ali Pasha complex, the Seyyit Hasan Pasha medrese and *han* (completed around 1745), the Cağaloğlu Hacı Beşir Ağa complex (1744–45), the monumental Tophane *sebil* (1732), all containing Baroque-Rococo elements and fragments in their ornamentation, but still keeping faith to the architectural principles of the Ahmet III period. Finally, the start of the great Nuruosmaniye complex in 1750, which would be completed after Mahmut's death, opens a new chapter in the history of Istanbul architecture and town building.

The Development of City Life

The city expanded all through the seventeenth and eighteenth centuries. Üsküdar, Eyüp, Beşiktaş, Tophane all on the coastline, were very large town parts, no mere suburbs, having all their markets and public utilities. Galata spilled out of its walls into the Pera orchards. Istanbul became basically a city of parts—the port, the bazaar, the large religious precincts, Eyüp and its cemeteries, the external boroughs,…—some connected by the Divan axis and others by the sea. In 1680, a survey of naval facilities had registered an enormous growth in those activities. By 1668 the city depended on urban sea transportation needing 1444 oar-boats (*kayık, perame*), many owned by pious foundations for their revenue, to connect its sprawl.[12] Within the urban fabric, the streets were narrow and meandering, though the cliché of the Islamic cul-de-sac structure does not apply well. They were also ill kept. Travellers and chroniclers considered only one thoroughfare, the so-called Divan Yolu, as being of some consequence.[13] It starts near the Topkapı Palace

---

[12] See Cengiz Orhonlu, *Osmanlı İmparatorluğunda Şehircilik ve Ulaşım Üzerine Araştırmalar* (Izmir: Ticaret Matbaacılık, 1984), 85–87.

[13] D'Ohsson *Tableau Général*, 2:175, writes: "*Dans la Capitale il n'y a qu'une seule rue remarquable par sa largeur et par son étendue; c'est le Divan-yoli: elle s'étend depuis le Sérail jusqu'à la porte Edirné-Capoussy…*"; see also Cosimo Comidas da Carbognano, *Descrizione topografica*

running roughly along the ancient Mese, coasting the busy central markets, the Fatih ensemble and outs at the Edirne gate, Its width varied from 3,6 to 6 metres and could be travelled through in a litter born by four mules.[14] Towards the end of the seventeenth century emerged a new important urban direction: the Bab-ı-Ali-Bazaar line. Since 1654, when the Grand Vizier Halil Pasha's *konak* near the Alay köşk had been confiscated,[15] it had become on and off for the next decades the seat of the Grand Vizier in charge. From the first decades of the eighteenth century it became the permanent seat of the government, acquiring in the meantime more bureaucratic services. There was, therefore, a conspicuous shift of activities from the Topkapı Palace to Bab-ı-Ali (which took on the name of Sublime Porte), hence a partial shift in ceremonial symbolism and a tangible shift in effective urban traffic to and from the city's centre and main routes. The two axes converged on the throbbing heart of the city, which was the *çarşı* (Bazaar) rather than the Divan Yolu.

After the end of the great building sites of the Classical period, building activities did not stop, but went on at a smaller and more diffuse scale with commercial architecture, better quality (and sometimes brilliant) housing. The trend to put the accent on civic and commercial structures was already noteworthy in the two great complexes planned in early seventeenth century, those of Yeni Valide and Sultan Ahmet, with their covered commercial streets and imperial apartments so similar to Istanbul houses as they would later emerge.

A change in the character of the *vakıf* complexes is quite evident in the second half of the seventeenth century, growing even more marked in the following century. They are smaller in size, better integrated in the current fabric of the city, more oriented to individual piety, with a greater interest for the founder's sepulchre and his family cemetery. The sixteenth and seventeenth century pashas were substantial medrese endowers. Their *külliye* are mainly centred on that institution. The emergence of the medrese as the main element of the complex dates from the end of the sixteenth century. As a matter of fact, after the

---

dello stato presente di Constantinopoli, Bassano: 1794, 51: "...*riesce bella ed agevole, quella dicesi Divan-Iolu, la quale dal Serraglio conduce alla porta di Adrianopoli.*"

[14] D'Ohsson *Tableau Général*, 2:304; see also Pitton de Tournefort, *Relation d'un voyage du Levant, fait par ordre du Roy* (Lyon, 1717), 2:183.

[15] Robert Mantran, *La Vie Quotidienne à Constantinople aux temps de Soliman le Magnifique et de ses successeurs (XVI° et XVII° siécles)* (Paris: Hachette, 1965), 36–41.

1496 Atik Ali medrese in Çemberlitaş dominated by the mosque of the complex and the Edirnekapı Atik Ali Pasha complex (1499) whose medrese was not dominant though large, the other main *külliye* of the axis were centred on their medrese, though some did have small mosques or prayer halls.[16]

In the last decades of the seventeenth and all through the eighteenth there was a substantial increase in the building of *sibyan* schools and libraries.[17] Many were freestanding, not incorporated in *külliye*. From 1697, when the Amcazade Hüseyin Ağa medrese and *türbe* complex presented a school protruding on the street side, they contributed greatly to the architectural street scene. Important examples are the 1723 Kaptan Ibrahim in Beyazit and the Ismail Efendi in Çarşamba, 1728 Elhaç Süleyman Efendi, and 1732 Res'ülkittab Ismail Efendi. They all have a slightly projecting first floor classroom and shops or elaborate fountains and *sebils* at street level. Libraries like those of Ahmet III in the Topkapı palace and the Vefa Atif Efendi library also were innovative. The dervish *tekke* (more like assembly centres than convents), despite their standing contrast with the medrese based ilmiyye class, were important social centres, rather inconspicuous and merging with the surrounding natural and residential fabric. They incessantly increased in number and mostly were extra-muros or in residential areas.[18]

In Ottoman Istanbul the palace was the beginning and end of all city life. Acclamations and rebellions were addressed to it. The state, the institutions of the town and the ruler's dwelling (and ruling pashas' dwellings) politically and institutionally penetrated each other, but were separated as buildings and space. Topkapı can be seen only from the sea at a distance: a mirage of tall trees, low-roofed pavilions and a wall.

---

[16] See Mübahat S. Kütükoğlu, "1869'da faal Istanbul Medreseleri," *Tarih Enstitüsü Dergisi*, 1977, 277–85. Sixty-three of the 166 medrese standing in Istanbul and Üsküdar at the end of the nineteenth century face the thoroughfare or are in its immediate hinterland.

[17] Özgönül Aksoy, *Osmanlı devri Istanbul sibyan mektepleri üzerine bir inceleme* [published thesis] (Istanbul: İstanbul Teknik Üniversitesi, 1968). *Sibyan* schools appear to be fairly diffuse throughout the entire historical peninsula.

[18] See: M. Baha Tanman, s.v. "Tekkeler," in *Dünden bugüne Istanbul ansiklopedisi* (Istanbul: T.C. Kültür Bakanlığı ve Tarih Vakfı, 1993–), 7:236–40; (Zakir Şükrü Efendi) *Die Istanbuler Derwisch-Konvente und ihre Scheiche (Mecmu'a-i tekaya)/Zâkir Sükrî Efendi; nach dem Typoskript von Mehmet Serhan Taysi*, ed. Klaus Kreiser (Freiburg im Breisgau: Schwarz, 1980). See also: Bilgin Turnalı and Esin Yücel, "İstanbul'daki bazı tekkelerin yerlerine dair bir araştırma," *Vakıflar Dergisi* 18 (1984): 141–63; *The Dervish Lodge: Architecture, Art, and Sufism in Ottoman Turkey*, ed. Raymond Lifchez (Berkeley: University of California Press, c. 1992).

Nonetheless, the power of its tentacles could be felt in almost all points of the city. It was an invisible crown. The control of prices, of building activities, of norms was decided within it. Tens of thousands of people worked for, thrived on and lived near the palace (palaces).[19] But it was also a fragmented crown: dozens of pashas and some religious leaders had set minor decisional centres in their own palaces: each one was a small court. Evliya recounts that the *saray* and *konaks* of the chief authorities were concentrated in two areas, the first across the DivanYolu in the tract between Ayasofya and Beyazıt, the second in the district of Süleymaniye-Şehzade-Vefa, a few were in Ahırkapı-Kadırga by the Marmara shore. Up to the seventeenth century grand palaces in masonry, each with hundreds of rooms, punctuated the city image, as did, and for two centuries would continue doing, the grand *hans*.[20] By the eighteenth century almost all had disappeared. The major pashas still ruled on public affairs in their own household, but they lived and held court in rambling timber structures, very large, but surrounded by architecturally and typologically very similar housing that could vary in size from two-rooms-in-two-floors minuscule houses to prosperous *konak*s with dozens, and in some rare case, hundreds of rooms. The quality and detailing could vary from the haphazard and careless to the masterly and precious, but fundamentally the basic technology and the semantic principles were the same.

Commercial Development, Lady Patrons and Residential Architecture

Commercial growth, the closer link of monumental architecture with the active parts of the city, and the role of court ladies as patrons, were fundamental factors of Istanbul's physical and architectural evolution in that period.

Of course, activities connected to court and state were an important segment of Istanbul's urban economy, but 'bourgeois' development (though certainly inappropriate in the Ottoman context, the term is the

---

[19] See Necdet Sakaoğlu, "Saray ve Istanbul," in *Aptullah Kuran İçin Yazılar: Essays in honour of Aptullah Kuran*, ed. Ç. Kafesçioğlu and L. Thyss-Şenocak (Istanbul: Yapı Kredi Kültür Sanat Yayınları, 1999), 277–86.

[20] See Melchior Lorich's panorama view of Istanbul. Sinan's opus includes 26 palaces, of which 7 on the Bosphorus and Marmara sea, 6 near the Hippodrome, 3 near Beyazit-Vefa.

only one available) of small and medium tradesmen and bureaucrats (*esnaf, memur* etc.) and more substantial merchants and owners of *hans*, *hammams*, warehouses, as well as people working for and living on *vakıf* activities and services account for housing development.[21] Many circumstances point to the seventeenth century for the birth of the traditional Ottoman house type as we come to know it from eighteenth century Western graphic sources and from a few standing examples. Though at first it was apparently restricted to the better off, later it became diffuse to most social classes as part of a general trend to the enjoyment of space and nature. The typical house had no more than a masonry ground floor and an upper residential floor in timber, with large or numerous windows. It was easy to build and replace, allowing both the fast decay and the easy updating of the urban fabric.[22] On the other hand, the emergence of a rich Greek merchant class in the course of the eighteenth century left a conspicuous typological heritage through their stone masonry houses, a link between public stone architecture and private residential timber architecture.[23]

It is significant that up to the seventeenth century building activities were either controlled by the Imperial *has* architects or by simple anonymous craftsmen, and that in the seventeenth century emerge the so-called town architects in provincial towns.[24] Although this category is not mentioned in Istanbul, a marked refinement of housing and non-imperial and non-*vakıf buildings* denote a new organization of the arts which reflects the rise of upper and upper-middle classes and their increasing patronage of non-monumental building activities.

The concentration of commercial activity and storage and of the crafts had always been very intense near the Golden Horn and the

---

[21] See Bahaeddin Yediyıldız, *Institution du Vaqf au XVIIIème Siècle en Turquie—étude historique* (Ankara, 1985). If so extensive in the eighteenth century, they must have been present, even if in a lesser degree, also during the last decades of the seventeenth.

[22] See Sedad Hakkı Eldem, *Türk evi: Osmanlı dönemi—Turkish houses: Ottoman period* (Istanbul: Türkiye Anıt Çevre Turizm Değerlerini Koruma Vakfı, 1984–), and Doğan Kuban, *The Turkish Hayat House* (Istanbul: Muhittin Salih Eren, 1995). See also chapter 8 of Maurice Cerasi, *La Città del Levante: Civiltà urbana e architettura sotto gli Ottomani nei secoli XVIII–XIX* (Milano: Jaca Book, 1988); Turkish translation: Maurice Cerasi, *Osmanlı Kenti: Osmanlı İmparatorluğunda 18. ve 19. Yüzyıllarda Kent Uygarlığı ve Mimarisi* (İstanbul: Yapı Kredi Kültür Sanat Yayınları, 1999).

[23] See: Haluk Sezgin, "Les Maisons en Pierre de Fener," in *ΑΡΜΟΣ, Armos: Volume in Honour of Professor N. K. Moutsopoulos* (Thessaloniki: Arsitotle University of Salonicco, School of Architecture, 1991), tomos Γ 1597–1629.

[24] See: Orhonlu, *Osmanlı*, 1–6, 9–26.

Mahmut Pasha district, climbing up to the Grand Bazaar. This last, and its surroundings up to Beyazıt, absorbed the more valuable commercial activities requiring lesser storage space. From the *bedesten* (the central commercial building of the Bazaar) three streets proceeded (and still proceed) up towards Şehzade and Sarraçhane (the market east of Fatih), and down to Mahmud Pasha, and the Golden Horn.[25] The central Bazaar area contained some 4000 shops in the Bazaar proper, in the *han*s and in the surrounding streets. Shops dealing in foodstuffs and books were in the exterior of the bazaar. The whole *çarşı* had narrow but regular streets, sometimes covered with pergola and wooden overhangs. After mid seventeenth century most of this district would be vaulted over in masonry, and would hence be called the Covered Bazaar (Kapalı Çarşı). The Beyazit area had a high concentration of public entertainment activities.[26] All these areas and the outer boroughs of Eyüp, Üsküdar, and Beşiktaş acquired further weight with the development of their market districts and the great number of *han*s—a most characteristic Ottoman aggregation of workshops, warehousing and business in cell-like rooms around arcaded two-floor courts—new, rebuilt, or enlarged. Evliya Çelebi mentions 556 *han*s extant in his time.[27] *Han*s were predominant in the area between Kapalıçarşı and the port: Büyük Valide Han (second quarter of the seventeenth century), Vezir Han (around 1660–70), Simkeşhane (around 1710), Hasan Pasha Han (around 1740) are of this period.

Despite the absentee sultans, the court's decision makers contributed to that expansion. The decisive role of the Valide and Grand Viziers in policy-making was very evident in the seventeenth century, when court intrigues affected the choice of grand viziers and even of the members of the Ottoman dynasty to accede to the throne. The ensuing balance of power greatly affected patterns of patronage: court ladies and powerful pasha families emerged as the main architectural patrons, particularly up to the first decades of the eighteenth century. The importance of the lady sultans and of the *valide*s in all periods is well known. Most sultans showed great devotion to their mothers,

---

[25] Mantran *Istanbul* (38–39, 414–15, 452–467) has widely analyzed the dislocation of commerce and other urban functions in the town in the sixteenth and seventeenth centuries.

[26] Ibid., 499: according to Evliya the entertainment activities employed 15.000 people.

[27] Evliya Celebi, *Narrative*.

many of whom were truly kingmakers. As in the case of Saliha Sultan, mother of Mahmud I, the sultan might even go out from his palace to meet his mother in pomp; the *valide* funerals could sometimes be a state affair. But of course, the long rule of Kösem Sultan[28] and Turhan Sultan, their mutual enmity, and their half-century-long hold on politics could be the product only of the seventeenth century.

Though that hold was slackened in the eighteenth century, lady patronage still continued as before and the role of the *kızlarağası* (the chief eunuch, overlord of the inner palace and in close touch with the influential court ladies) was as great as ever in city politics, giving him substantial power on *vakıf* assignments and patronage.[29]

Such patronage probably had some effect on the character of the new buildings. Did the decision-making of the female members of the court bring about a less austere, more domestic-oriented architecture, and a marked taste for naturalistic ornamentation and potentially non-symmetrical composition? I doubt that a causal link between lady patronage and the specific architectural character of their donations will ever be proved. It is true that a general tendency to soften the monumental, symmetrical and domineering affirmations of precedent Ottoman non-residential architecture had developed. But, after all, this is true of almost all the architectural expression of the age, whatever the gender of the patrons.

Sea, Land, and Water Architecture

On the whole, Istanbul was a semi-rural city with the conspicuous voids of orchards, promenades, and suburban cemeteries. This was the outcome of devastating fires and of dispersed endowments, but it also reflected the Ottoman propensity for an open urban fabric intermingled with natural elements and space.[30] The many leisure grounds (mesire)

---

[28] Kösem was murdered in 1651, consequently allowing Turhan Sultan to assume fully only then the role of Valide, though her son, Mehmet IV, still a boy, had been sultan since 1648.

[29] Mantran *Istanbul*, 173. One later example is Kızlarağası Beşir Agha, patron of the eponymous 1745 *külliye* near Bab-ı-ali. He had great influence in decisions regarding *vakıf* endowments and was a vizier-maker and un-doer.

[30] For open space in Ottoman towns see Maurice Cerasi, "Open Space, Water and Trees in Ottoman urban Culture," *Environmental Design: Journal of the Islamic Environmental Design Centre* 2 (1985).

along the Golden Horn and the Bosphorus or on hilltops were no more
than wide meadows with a few pavilions, sparse fountains, and small
raised platforms, or sometimes, with none at all of these accessories.
Called promenades or walks by foreign observers, they were neither
because Ottoman people did not go out to mix socially or to be seen,
but sat down in groups, for picnics or for the view of landscape and
fireworks. Even the many meydans were more like fairgrounds and
small town greens in the West than like squares or piazzas. Only two
had some urban relevance: the ancient Hippodrome now called At
Meydanı (the horse grounds) and the Sipahi Meydanı (the cavalryman's
green) no more than the infill of the ancient galleon port, both being
used mostly for riding sports, meetings and big processions, or as leisure
grounds. The open spaces of the large religious complexes were the
real architectural squares of the city, and, with the main commercial
spaces, the effective meeting places for the citizenry. But in the eighteenth
century the outer courts of the large mosques took on more and more
the aspect of gardens, rather than of urban piazzas: the court of the
1734 Hekimoglu complex is a typical example of this development.

With their beautiful cypresses and the views they offered, the extra
muros cemeteries (except the bleak and unadorned Jewish cemeteries)
easily became leisure grounds of a sort. Eyüp, a saintly town of mausoleums, mosques, dervish convents, and cemeteries had by the seventeenth
century become a leisure town where the people of Istanbul went to buy
toys, to eat, and to promenade. The Bosphorus, and partly the Golden
Horn, became gradually the background for hundreds of seaside mansions (yalıs). The Golden Horn with its Arsenal was simultaneously port
and thoroughfare and warehouse for the city and had an enormous
impact both functionally, creating centrality, and psychologically, for
the perception of urban form and life it enhanced.

From Fatih Mehmed to Süleyman I important aqueducts had been
added to the still efficient remains of the Roman and Byzantine water
supply system. The Halkalı and Kırkçeşme water ducts and some of
the other underground aqueducts which supplied most of the *külliye*[31]
ran along the crest lines of the main Istanbul hills, just as the Divan

---

[31] The principal aqueducts running on the crest line are the Mahmutpaşa, Köprülü,
Beylik, Süleymaniye, Bayezit, Fatih, Sultan Ahmet, Nurosmaniye, Mihrimah aqueducts.
See: Kâzım Çeçen, *İstanbul'un vakıf sularından Halkalı suları* (İstanbul: Istanbul Su ve
Kanalizasyon İdaresi Genel Müdürlüğü, 1991); Kâzım Çeçen, *II. Bayezid suyolu haritaları*
(İstanbul: İstanbul Su ve Kanalizasyon İdaresi Genel Müdürlüğü, 1997).

axis does. Water consumption was so high that hammam-building had to be discouraged. That is why not many hammams were built after the sixteenth century. Most of the Istanbul Ottoman supply system still functioning in the beginning of the twentieth century had been established by 1750. All the aqueducts constructed in the 1620–1750 period were aimed at supplying the larger *vakıf* ensembles. The 1672 Köprülü aqueduct was built and maintained by the foundation of the same name. However, many public fountains, and sometimes hammams and even private mansions were allowed to connect to those aqueducts.

Fountains and *sebil*s became emergent fixtures of the street scene. Slightly less than a thousand historical Istanbul fountains and over forty *sebil* have been registered in various lists.[32] It is a moot question whether the extension of the water supply system preceded urban development, or if it followed the demand. There is no doubt, however, that the impressive buildup of Üsküdar, Beşiktaş, Pera in the eighteenth century and the construction of the main water supply lines and accessories were contemporaneous. Both Ahmet III and Mahmut I were enthusiastic endowers of fountains, *sebil*, and water reservoirs. Around 1620 was built the first bent (water dam) in the Belgrade forest north of Istanbul. Others were to follow: by 1722 there were seven bends in the same area. Their contribution was not purely logistic. They were used also as leisure grounds for the court and the town elite, and became an important proof of the Ottoman capacity to create an architectural environmental in natural surroundings.

The Aesthetics of Urban Space, Symbolism of the Dead and the Pomp

Pomp and magnificence of retinues was a constant of Imperial Istanbul. The most impressive and perhaps most involving of the state processions, was the weeklong parade (*alay*) of troops and pashas outing for military campaigns in the West. The parade-like march developed along the five kilometres of the Edirnekapı-Topkapı route. Another stately *alay* procession was the five-six hour cavalcade of the Sultan before or

---

[32] See: İbrahim Hilmi Tanışık, *Istanbul çeşmeleri* (Istanbul: Maarif Matbaası, 1943–45); Affan Egemen, *Istanbul'un çeşme ve sebilleri: resimleri ve kitabeleri ile 1165 çeşme ve sebil* (Istanbul: Aritan Yayinevi, [1993]); İzzet Kumbaracılar, *Istanbul sebilleri* (Istanbul: Devlet Basımevi, 1938); Ömer Faruk Şerifoğlu, *Su güzeli: İstanbul sebilleri* (Istanbul: Istanbul Büyükşehir Belediyesi Kültür İşleri Daire Başkanlığı, 1995).

after the sword-girdling ceremony in Eyüp Ansar's mausoleum in Eyüp outside the city walls.[33] Courtly feasts, and not only the most important ones, gave occasion to processions with *nahıl* (an ornamental tree shaped or pyramid-like gift and sweetmeat packed structure) between the New and Old Palaces, and the illumination and decoration (*donanma*) of houses and public buildings must have been a frequent event.

Once or twice in a century, a Sultan would organize an imperial festival, which would involve the whole town population for weeks with feasts, fireworks, and parades. In 1675, one had been held in Edirne. After 1582, although marriage festivals for the bridals of princesses were held in 1646, 1695, 1708, 1709, 1724, 1740, only one really important and grand festival was held in Istanbul towards the end of the period we are discussing.[34] In October 1720, a great procession ran through the city centre after the fifteen-day festival in various outskirts of the town for the circumcision of Ahmet III's sons. The *alay* assembled in Eski Saray, and in its progression to the Topkapı Palace, first moved West through Vezneciler up to Saraçhane Başı, past the janissary quarters, plied left to Aksaray through the Horhor residential quarter where it inverted its direction and turned eastwards by the Laleli fountain, the Old Mint and the Valide Hamam, and, finally, paraded under the Sultan's window in the Nakkaşhane.[35]

In the brilliant Vehbi Surname album, the procession itself is perceived as being monumental, not its theatre. The splendid garb and haughty bearing of the participants, the sometimes over ten metre high *nahıl*, were more carefully designed than the architectural background in which they moved. This is one of the keys for understanding the Ottoman use and perception of urban space. More care was lavished on the ephemeral structures in those occasions than on the permanent aspect of public space. Processions, interesting and picturesque in themselves, did not seem to require magnificent backgrounds. In no case, with the rare exception of the short-lived experiment in arcaded streets by Nevşehirli Damat Ibrahim Pasha, have Ottoman builders and patrons tried to revive the grand Roman and early Byzantine Mese tradition.

---

[33] See, for example: Sakaoğlu *Saray*, and İsmail Hakkı Uzunçarşılı, *Osmanlı Devletinin Saray teşkilatı* (Ankara: 1984).

[34] See: Stefan Yerasimos, "The Imperial Procession: Recreating a world's order," and Doğan Kuban, "The miniatures of Surname-i Vehbi," both in *Surname: Sultan Ahmed the III's Festival of 1720* (Bern: Ertuğ Editions, 2000).

[35] An excellent facsimile of the Surname with transcript and translations can be found in *Surname: Sultan Ahmed...* mentioned in note 34.

In the second half of the seventeenth century only Edirne had had such imperial processions. Instead, the city was offered the daily show of the retinues of the important pashas and processions for funerals and weddings. In the image of pashas and members of the Divan plying at least twice a week between the Palace and their konaks (which were, remember, office and residence, centre for their clans, each a palace in its own rights) we have a paradigm of power. Naima, the outstanding late seventeenth century chronicler,[36] tells of the retinues moving in and around the Divan Yolu and palace not only on ceremonial occasions but also for political meetings and conspiracies. In 1644, the newly appointed Kethüda Bey, Murad Ağa, revived the old tradition of the double *alkış* (acclamation) of his followers dedicated to the chief Kethüda on his return from the Divan, first, moving out of the Topkapı Palace, and later by the Süleymaniye mosque, the same *alkış* claque having run before him to repeat their exploit. Not dominated by Imperial monuments (Şehzade, Beyazit were exceptions), the view of the DivanYolu was crowded with the pashas' tombs and schools and libraries and *hazire* (small urban burial grounds within a *külliye*).

Tombs and mausoleums were an important psychological and politically effective component of Ottoman mentality. Not all, but quite a few, of the Sultan tombs were on the western part of the Divan axis: Mehmed II (d. 1481) at Fatih, Beyazit II (d. 1512) at Beyazit, Selim II (d. 1574), Murat III (d. 1595), Mustafa I (d. 1623) and Ibrahim (d. 1648) in Ayasofya, Ahmet I (d. 1617), Osman II (d. 1622) and Murad IV (d. 1640) in the Sultan Ahmet complex nearby. But from 1648 to 1789 almost all Sultans (except Süleyman II and Ahmed II, both buried in the Süleymaniye complex) kept away from it, and, seemed to prefer burial near centrally located mosques within important commercial areas (mainly in the Eminönü Valide Camii and in Laleli). In the daily scene, the pasha mausoleums and *hazire* of the Divan Yolu were far more important. A grand vizier might be demoted (almost all were) and even be decapitated (quite a few were), his *konak*s and *yalı*s confiscated, and yet his mausoleum and the tombs of his sons and family would be there to remain and mark the urban scene. The *türbe* of the Pashas were not isolated. They were located within their medium-sized and even smallish endowments, enriched by small urban cemeteries (*hazire*) and fountains.

---

[36] Naima, *Annals*.

The Aftermath of the Transition

In the eighteenth century, the *vakıf* 'public utilities'—*sibyan* schools, libraries, *sebil*, and fountains, *tekke*—increased in number and were more diffuse, though smaller and less costly than in the past. Minor elements such as fountains and portals acquired a hitherto unknown importance. The fenestrated *hazire* walls, so placid and regular in preceding centuries, brought a great variety and inventiveness in the form and details of individual openings. The *hazire* walls and epitaph placing show great refinement aimed at obtaining maximum visibility and transparency from the street. The breaking up of the *vakıf* complexes into smaller parts and the increasing relevance of accessory elements, in that context of plural composition techniques, became an asset rather than a problem and was addressed in ever finer ways.

The eighteenth century also brought a more subtle formal linkage of urban elements and a certain degree of integration between monument and town life. Some late seventeenth century examples such as that of Amcazade Hüseyin Pasha had already expressed the need to unify and diminish the reciprocal contrasts of the *külliye* elements. It is a more fluent composition, a softening of the formal transition from one distinct element to the other. The richer forms of each element, such as the larger cantilever arches and the generous openings of the enclosure walls of cemetery and *türbe*, prepared the way for the urban perspective, which Ottoman Baroque later brought.[37] The sense of continuity of space, not in mere linguistic development, but also experimented as a type, was that of the already mentioned Damat Ibrahim Pasha's arcaded street (the so-called Direklerarası) near Şehzade, and, three decades later, of the shop arcades on the northwestern margin of the Nur-u-Osmaniye complex. The idea—unfortunately unique—could have been Western influenced. Yet, the scale and the form of the constitutive elements of the arcades recall rather modest Byzantine examples and the central arcade of seventh-century Anjar, the only arcaded town centre in Islam.

The commercial areas of the city expanded in apparent contrast with the gradual fall in the town's economical role in the Mediterranean. Housing grew more and more refined in composition and building

---

[37] See: Maurice Cerasi, "Un Barocco di Città: trasformazioni linguistiche e tipologiche nel Settecento ad Istanbul," *Quaderni di Storia dell'Architettura* 3 (2000): 81–102.

technique. Western technology and Western taste filtered into every aspect of life, but up to the second quarter of the nineteenth century, Ottoman urban civilization kept its identity as it had been set in the long period of change from the twenties of the seventeenth century to the fifties of the eighteenth century.

BUKHARA AND SAMARKAND

Attilio Petruccioli

1. *The urban organism*

Like any city, Bukhara and Samarkand are living organisms that are constantly undergoing processes of change and being enriched by them. For this reason they cannot be analysed as totalities in a general manner, but must be broken down into their three component parts: i) the building fabric, which includes the basic (residential) fabric and specialised (public and commercial) fabric; ii) movement, consisting of the routes and their hierarchical relationship to the building fabric, and iii) the nodes, or focal points, and poles, including not only monuments, but also moments of discontinuity in the building fabric, such as squares, gateways and fords. At the same time, it is important to recognise how each of these components is interconnected, how the building fabric is related to the routes, the routes to the nodes and the nodes to the building fabric. Starting with the plan of the city we shall analyse and classify these three components, then focus on the monuments individually.

2. *Urban Fabric and Monuments*

The building fabric of modern Bukhara and Samarkand dates from the beginning of the sixteenth century to 1868 under the suzerainty of the Uzbek Khan dynasty. Anything built prior to this must be analysed retrospectively through the traces left in the urban layout by a typological process. This procedure applies above all to the three great periods that shaped the history of these cities: the pre-Islamic era, and in particular the Hellenistic layout of the Bukharian shahristan, the Samanid period, and the Timurid period.

In his essay, Heinz Gaube describes ninth century Bukhara in terms of the position of its gateways and main streets.[1] The picture painted by contemporary literature is that of a city which had spread beyond the *shahristan* into the outskirts of the *rabad* known as Hisar-i Nau, to the west beyond the *registan* and to the south beyond the Shahrud canal. To the north the city stretched to the tomb of the Samanids, some 500 metres beyond the present wall. At some point during the Samanid period the city's defences must have been relaxed in favour of this fairly sparse fabric, which is not unlike an urban garden. The markets and commercial activities were concentrated to the south of the *shahristan*, where the caravans arrived, beyond the Narshakh-i Dar Bazar gate.

The *shahristan* is characterised by two different types of urban fabric in terms of orientation and density: (1) more homogeneous and densely grouped courtyard houses, with facades based on a 12–15 metre module and (2) more sparsely grouped monuments, the dimensions of which conform to a higher numerical module and which show up in the plan of the city with the consistent thickness of their walls. This sequence of large buildings with courtyards, connected to shops and domed crossroads by a network of smaller modules, is similar to the great bazaars of Isfahan or Kashan in neighbouring Iran.

The *shahristan* comprises five horizontal main routes and nine vertical secondary routes. As demonstrated by Bol'shakov's[2] (1973) simple line drawing of the urban layout and his analysis of the alignment of the walls, the layout of the *shahristan* and part of the *rabad* to the south of the bazaar gate generally follows the orientation of the cardinal points *secundum coelum*.

Even though it is difficult to say whether this layout relates to the old Hellenistic/Kushan fabric, or whether the oblong and rectangular houses hypothesised by Bol'shakov are related to the alignment of the walls, the continuity of the foundations would seem to point to the

[1] A. Gangler, H. Gaube, and A. Petruccioli, *Bukhara. The Eastern Dome of Islam* (Stuttgart and London, 2004). General texts on urban studies are: P. Cuneo, *Storia dell'urbanistica. Il mondo islamico* (Bari, 1986); I. I. Notkin, "Arkhitektura Srednej Azii XIII–XIV v," in *Vseobshaja istoria arkhitektury*, no. 5 (Moscow, 1996); A. B. Prochazka, *Bukhara* (Prague, 1993); A. Petruccioli, ed., *Bukhara: The Myth and the Architecture* (Cambridge, MA, 1999). On the social structure of Bukhara see: O. A. Sukhareva, *Kvartal'naia obshchina pozdnefeodal'nogogorodo Bukhary* (Moscow, 1976).

[2] A. M. Belenitskii, I. B. Bentovich, and O. G. Bol'shakov, *Srednevekovyi gorod Srednei Azii* (Leningrad, 1973).

pre-Islamic period. Of course, the walls may have been re-aligned at a later date, a process that would have been possible only if the *shahristan* had been totally destroyed and abandoned after the Arab conquest. Yet historical records speak of a peaceful partition between the Samanids and the local population. It seems even less likely that the city was re-planned after the Chinggis khanates (fourteenth century), since we would find traces of it in the historical records.

Less extensive than the *shahristan*, but equally important, is the building fabric comprising the two Timurid monuments of the Kalyan mosque and the Ulugh Beg madrasa, as well as the monuments of the bazaar, such as the Abdullah Khan Timcheh. Corresponding to the extensive grid published by Ginzburg in 1931,[3] the rotation of these monuments (by about 10° to the southwest) acts as a magnet for the surrounding building fabric situated to the south of the Kalyan mosque and the area to the east of the Abdullah Khan Timcheh, comprising the Maulana Sharif mosque, the Bazar-i Gul mosque, the Turkman madrasa and the Mirza Turdi caravanserai. The sparse specialised building fabric is aligned with the same rotation as the Tursunjan madrasa. Though located in the centre of the Dihqan district, which is aligned with the cardinal axes, the Maulana Sharif madrasa is aligned with the Timurid fabric. Also typical of this tension within the urban layout is the Mirza Turdi caravanserai, which is aligned on three sides with the Kushan fabric and on the fourth side with the Timurid fabric.

Built in the first half of the sixteenth century, together with the Hauz, the Khwajah Zaynuddin mosque, the *khanaqah* and the district by the same name have a rotation to the southwest which is far too pronounced to be associated with the Timurid fabric. They constitute an autonomous part of the urban fabric created by the oblique line of the street between the Banu Sa'ad gate and the Samanid bridge over the Shahrud.

The *guzar* (neighbourhood) mosques of the *shahristan*,[4] the prayer halls and small primary schools (*maktabs*), the small warehouses and medium-sized community buildings that have arisen over the tomb (*mazar*) of a Sufi saint, are all aligned with the cardinal axis; in other words, with the old pre-Islamic building fabric. All the Timurid mosques, on the other hand, are aligned with the Kalyan mosque, thus contradicting

---

[3] Belenitskii, Bentovich, and Bol'shakov, op. cit.
[4] Gangler, Gaube, Petruccioli, op. cit., 117–125.

the idea that the *mihrab* should ideally point towards Mecca. Indeed, the establishment of the *qibla* and hence the orientation of religious buildings was a dynamic process, depending as much on dynastic directives as on the periodic recalculation made by astronomers.[5]

A convincing explanation can be found in a comparison with Samarkand, the Timurid capital south of the Afrasiyab plateau, where the building fabric is designed with two different orientations. The first is to the northeast of the *registan*, where all the *guzar* mosques orient the *mihrab* to the west along the cardinal axes. The rest of the city, and other monuments, such as the Bibi Khanum mosque, are aligned with the *registan* with an approximately 10° rotation to the southwest, though the Gur-i Amir, which is situated over an older religious site, deviates from this alignment. There are thus two alignments: the first corresponding to the extension beyond the Afrasiyab walls and dating to the Samanid period, or even earlier, is oriented along the cardinal axis *secundum coelum*; the second concerns the three buildings of the *registan* (of which the Ulugh Beg mosque may be dated to 1417 and the Bibi Khanum mosque slightly earlier, to 1399–1404) and a large part of the Timurid city.

Timur imposed his vision on this fairly regular Samanid fabric, which was probably confined to the eastern grid, with its commercial centre proceeding in a line from the *registan* to the Afrasiyab gate. Construction was carried out in two phases: a series of building stages, prior to the monuments, with an approximately 10° rotation to the southwest/northeast, followed by a series of radial axes, centring on the *registan*, that cut through the old Samanid building fabric.[6]

The role of these radial axes is easily recognisable in the triangular and trapezoidal plots along their perimeter. In Bukhara something similar occurred: here a Timurid building fabric was superimposed on a pre-Islamic one oriented *secundum coelum*—the sole difference being that the axis of the *decumanus* was the widening of an earlier route, which runs parallel to the building plots in such a way that it does not interfere with the alignment of the building fabric, thus ensuring that

---

[5] M. Bonine, "The Sacred Direction and City Structure: a Preliminary Analysis of the Islamic City," *Muqarnas* 7 (1990): 50–72. See also the *Encyclopaedia of Islam*, 2nd ed. (Leiden, 1965).

[6] M. Bernardini, "The Ceremonial Function of Markets in the Timurid City," *Environmental Design: Journal of the Islamic Environmental Design Research Centre*, ed. by A. Petruccioli, 1–2 (1991): 90–97.

these plots remained regular. The similarity with Samarkand does not end here, since in both cases the main axis begins from the *registan*, in Samarkand towards the Afrasiyab (now Tashkent street), in Bukhara towards the eastern gate of the *shahristan*. On these two similar routes stand respectively the great Bibi Khanum mosque and the Kalyan mosque (the plan of the latter dating from the Timurid period). The change in alignment here appears to be part of Timur's dynastic project for re-planning the city in the image of the ruler, thus leaving an indelible mark on the urban fabric with its imposing structures and the richness of its polychrome decoration.

The urban form of Samarkand is the result of a series of later transformations in the plan of the pre-existing spontaneous organism. The site occupied today by the city does not correspond to the site of the first anthropic settlement of the area. The ancient capital of the Satraps, Marakand, was, in fact, located on the northern slopes of the Afrasiyab plateau—a system of natural land elevations that is defined by precise orographic boundaries and controls the plain to the south. After the attacks carried out by the Mongols in 1220 and the subsequent devastation of the city, Marakand was abandoned.

The pre-Timurid city of Samarkand, thus, reveals a structure that suggests the superimposition of several urban systems, of which one, probably planned in the Qarakhanid period,[7] was superimposed on the first built fabric outside the walls of Marakand.

We can understand the sequence of growth and transformation from the information we have on the development of the earlier capital. The core of its foundation was located on the northernmost border of the Afrasiyab plateau, which is inaccessible from the north, because of the presence of a very steep cliff, and only approachable from the west. Connections with Bactria, capital of the neighbouring satrapy, were assured by a route which, leading south, skirted the edge of the plateau from the west. This layout, probably the most ancient, goes from north to south through the present fabric of Samarkand and borders a natural canal—beyond which, to the west, the Timurid fortress (*qal'eh*)

---

[7] G. Andriani, D. Catania, F. Gigotti, L. Guastamacchia, L. Pisano, C. Rubini, and P. Traversa, "Samarkand: the Planned City. A Hypothesis of Structure through the Reading of the Historical Fabric. The Karakhanid Design and Timurid Restoration," in *The Planned City*, Atti del Convegno Internazionale (Trani, 2003). See also: L. Pisano, C. Rubini, and P. Traversa, "Samarkand: A Case Study of Urban Restoration and Renewal," in *The Mediterranean Medina*, Atti del Seminario Internazionale (Pescara, 2004).

would have been located—that probably ran slightly to the east of the site occupied today by the Ruhabad mausoleum. The most ancient settlements are spontaneously grouped along this route, while their building fabric is articulated in an east-west direction. Two can still be recognised: the first is next to the area occupied by the *registan* and extends to the east of the matrix route; the second is laid out around the Gur-i Amir and extends to the west.

Beginning with its first nucleus, the expansion of Marakand was toward the south, taking advantage of the slight natural slope of the plateau on which it was founded. New defensive walls were built to the south,[8] and one entered the city through a gate along a new route parallel to the earlier one. This route breaks away from the older one at a ford which was probably located outside the limits of the Timurid city. From here, it curves in a northeast direction and runs parallel to the earlier one, beside another watercourse.

In the fabric of Samarkand we can still clearly read the presence of this plan, which like the earlier one, extends in a north-south direction. It traverses the whole territory of what would be the future city, skirting the zone of the *registan* and that of the Bibi Khanum mosque, and reaching the southern gate of Marakand. The route fords another canal, traces of which are still legible in the urban fabric of Samarkand, in correspondence with the *chaharsu* located in the present zone of the *registan*. From here going north, it passes the zone next to the Bibi Khanum mosque, on the side of the *qibla*, and then proceeds toward the Afrasiyab gate.

As in the above case, the natural and artificial canals in the territory underwent a process of transformation too. Over time, the canals parallel to the matrix routes were filled in, thereby creating new urban routes. In the urban form of Samarkand we can see how to the east of this important communication axis the matrix routes are rotated by 90° and are laid out in an east-west direction up to the natural limit established by the Djakerdize canal.

Their direction coincides with that of the orientation of a now destroyed Qarakhanid madrasa, the remains of which have been uncovered in the area of the Shah-i Zindeh, next to the Quthama ibn

---

[8] Belenitskii, Bentovich, and Bol'shakov, op. cit.

'Abbas mausoleum.[9] These buildings are rotated by about 10° to the southeast. The distance between the northernmost and southernmost routes is such that the *chaharsu* built in the eighteenth century and hence the ford, on which the building rests, falls on the central line of the route adjoining them. The two internal matrix routes seem to converge toward this ford.

The northernmost matrix route is marked by a node at the point where there may once have been a gate giving access to a new foundation. It then forks off from this nodal point, thereby generating another route, and continues in a northwest direction toward Bukhara, crossing the area later occupied by the Bibi Khanum mosque. The southernmost matrix route proceeds in the direction of Shahrisabz to the point where it would later converge with another new route that went as far as the gate in the Timurid walls. So we can read a square structure with precisely defined boundaries, each side measuring about 985 metres. It is therefore possible to hypothesise a planning stage, most likely Qarakhanid, some time after the space available for building on the Afrasiyab became completely congested and before the destruction and definitive abandonment of Marakand, following the Mongol sack (19 March 1220).

In the Timurid period this system underwent profound transformations. Timur took possession of a pre-existing urban structure, the radial route system of which was already legible in the hierarchy of nodes around which the spontaneous fabric of the Marakand *rabad* was organised. Through the opening of new routes the city received its present radial structure centred on the *registan*. Timur decreed the construction of a new processional and commercial axis[10] that went as far as the facade of the new Bibi Khanum mosque, commissioned by him. We have a first-hand account of this route and the demolitions necessary to construct it in the memoirs of Ruy Gonzalez de Clavijo,[11]

---

[9] N. B. Nemtseva, *Ansambl' Shah-i Zinda, Zodcestvo uzbekistana* (Tashkent, 1970). On the Tamgach Bogra-Khan madrasa, see N. B. Nemtseva, "Medrese Tamgach Bogra-Khan v Samarkande," *Afrasiab*, no. 3 (1974).

[10] S. E. Ratija, *Mečet' Bibi Chanym* (Moscow, 1950), 14, plate 6.

[11] F. L. Estrada, ed., *Ruy Gonzales de Clavijo: Embajada a Tamorlán. Estudio y edición de un manuscrito del siglo XV*, critical edition, (Madrid: C.S.I.C., 1943). For a French edition, see Ruy Gonzales de Clavijo, *La route de Samarkand au temps de Tamerlan* (Imprimerie Nationale, 1990); republished as *Route de Samarkand au temps de Tamerlan (1403–1406). Relation du Voyage de l'Embassade de Castille à la cour de Timour Beg* (Imprierie Nationale, 2002). For an English translation of Clavijo's memoirs, see C. R. Markham, *Narrative*

chamberlain to the King of Castille and León, who came to the city on behalf of Henry III on 8 September 1404. From this central nucleus the capital of the realm would be the object of profound transformations over the centuries, reaching its present spatial order only in the seventeenth century when the last of the madrasas defining this space, the Tilla Kari, was built.

The congregational Bibi Khanum mosque was built with an approximately 8° rotation to the southwest, analogous to what happened for the Ruhabad mausoleum and Ulugh Beg madrasa. The other buildings that define the *registan* today, the madrasas of Tilla Kari (fifteenth–sixteenth century) and Shir Dor (1619–1636), rotate in the same direction by about 10°, while the rotation of the Gur-i Amir complex is even more marked (about 20° to the southwest).

A second route in the new urban layout which proceeds from the zone of the *registan chaharsu* and confirms the radial nature of the new plan cuts through the pre-existing fabric diagonally in a southeast direction, reaching the gate that led to Shahrisabz, a settlement of the Barlas tribe from which Timur descended. Starting from the *registan*, once again, a route to the west passed over the Gatfar bridge to the new Timurid citadel. In a southwest direction, another radial route reached the site of the Gur-i Amir, a religious complex with multiple functions, and the tomb of Timur and his descendants.

The new city commissioned by Timur is thus superimposed on the Samanid and Qarakhanid layout, and dis-articulates it. At the same time the centralized configuration of its plan underlines its role as capital of the empire and centre of the world. Similar to the circular plan of al-Mansur in ancient Baghdad, the gates of Samarkand connect the city to a world in which it recognised its roots and into which it extended and sought to impose its political and military control: to the northeast, into the lands of the Mongols from whom Timur claimed descent; to the southeast, to the Barlas tribe's city of origin; to the southwest, to the regions formerly controlled by the Arab Caliphs; and to the west, to Bukhara, ancient capital of Transoxiana.

of the Embassy of Ruy Gonzalez de Clavijo to the Court of Timour at Samarcand, A.D. 1403–06 (London: Hakluyt Society, 1859).

3. *Routes and Building Fabric*

In Bukhara a long, low-lying ridge starts in the east and rises up to the citadel (*arq*) and the city (*sharistan*) and then flattens into a low promontory. Through the piedmont to the north runs the Zarafshan canal, to the south the Shahrud canal, which meet outside the city to the west of the *registan*. From the very beginning this topography determined the layout of the routes which, with a few exceptions, are still in use today:

1. The east-west route cuts through the *shahristan* from the Kalabadh or Nau gate and climbs up to the citadel through the eastern gate known as the Guriyan. This is the oldest route which undoubtedly predates any settlement on the *shahristan*. An alternative route starts from the Banu Asad gate and runs towards the Talipal gate on the outskirts of the city in the direction of ancient Khorezm (Khiva).
2. The north-south track, dropping down through the 70 metre wide valley between the citadel and the *shahristan* and crossing the east-west route, is also very old. Still discernible in many of the old forgotten streets of the Khwajah Zaynuddin district, the track used to run past the Tursunjan madrasa and ford the Shahrud canal near the modern school complex, finally rejoining Karakul street at the smaller Ghaziyan madrasa.
3. The north-south route leaves the northern gate of the *shahristan* and, crossing the *decumanus*, threads through the Taq-i Zargaran, the Taq-i Tilpak Furushan to the south of the old Samanid Dar Bazar gate and the Taq-i Sarrafan (the steep-banked ford-track). Between the Taq-i Zargaran and the Taq-i Sarrafan, it passes through the fabric of residential and commercial buildings, before curving through the southern suburb (*rabad*); finally, skirting the Rashid Hauz, it reaches the Riu or Sallakhana gate.
4. The commercial zone of Bukhara is a cluster of routes spreading out from the Taq-i Tilpak Furushan:
    4.1. The horizontal route at the foot of the southern embankment of the *shahristan*, now Mirza Sachak street, runs past the Tursunjan madrasa, before turning abruptly north along the sharp bend of the Shahrud and entering the *registan* beneath the Taq-i Ordfurushan. Immediately to the north of Mirza Saciak street, 50 metres along the *shahristan* canal, between the Taq-i Tilpak Furushan and the Tursunjan madrasa once lay the Mullah

Amir district. This was an orthogonal fabric of residential and
specialised buildings on a grid plan which included the Mullah
Amir mosque, the Tim-i Jam'eh Furushan, the Miri baths and
the Latif Mirak Timcheh. The bazaar was closed off at either
end by a gate.

4.2. The southwest route leading to the Karakul gate and the Khorasan area and the Shaybanid Gaukushan religious complex
ends at the canal by the Khorasan minaret. This route can only
be explained by the presence of an old ford near the minaret,
which, as shown on Bol'shakov's plan of nineteenth century
Bukhara, is marked as the Khandaq bridge.[12]

4.3. A link road towards the south, connecting the Taq-i Tilpak Furushan with a ford near the Russian Bank, was clearly determined
later by the gradual shift towards the focal point of the Taq-i
Sarrafan.

4.4. The route following a north-south direction (no. 3), and tangential to the Maghoki Attari mosque.

4.5. The secondary route from the southeastern corner of the pre-
Timurid city re-enters the *shahristan* from the eastern gate.

The importance of the ford near the Gaukushan minaret is
borne out by the directional axis pointing to it, comprising the
route (no. 4.2) that bisects Karakul street and the fork that skirts
either side of the Turk-i Jandi cemetery, as well as by one of
the local streets that turns abruptly to the north. The Russian
Bank ford is defined by the cluster of streets that converge on
this point: Karakul street where the two Shaybanid madrasas,
the two Ghaziyan madrasas and the *rabad* around the Hauz, no
longer visible, are situated; the street leading to the Namazgah,
now known as the Namazganskaya Ulitsa, which skirts the
Turk-i Jandi cemetery; the route now lost in the outlying area
behind the cemetery; and the east-west route on the southern
bank of the Shahrud that skirts round the Lab-i Hauz to the
Karsh gate. Now known as Glavnaia Ulitsa, this route is now
the main access for vehicles entering the city from the east.
The cluster of streets by the Russian Bank ford is met by a
counter-radial which proceeds from the Gaukushan ford to
the south of the Taq-i Sarrafan through the densely populated

---

[12] Belenitskii, Bentovich, and Bol'shakov, op. cit.

suburban areas, following a pattern reminiscent of the Borgo
Longobardo in Bologna.

5. The north-south route runs from the Samarkand gate to the Lab-i
   Hauz behind the Nadir Divanbegi, where the cinema is today. Along
   its length are the Shah Yakhshi mosque and cemetery, the Maulana
   Mirzayan mosque and the Pay Astana mosque and madrasa.

6. Finally, the wide urban infrastructure of the Khiyaban boulevard.

4. *Poles and Urban Focal Points*

A city is like a chessboard with hundreds of players. One player makes
a move and suddenly everything is at the mercy of change and movement. With this image in mind, we can define a node as a focal point
in the exchange of movement. It is not so much the piece that counts,
nor the point itself, but the force acting on the position in relation
to the other pieces at a given moment, which we could define as the
nodality of the focal point. Typical nodes, or focal points, are fords
or gates, intersections of two routes at a crossroads, or *chaharsu*, and
the purely visual intersection of two geometrical axes, like an obelisk.
Nodes can also comprise building complexes in the prime sites of the
city. A pole, on the other hand, can be seen as something more than a
node—a point that overwhelms the immediate surroundings—affecting,
as it were, the entire urban chessboard.

In the centre of Bukhara there are six fords across the Shahrud,
five *taqat* (two of which are no longer extant) and at least four large
architectural complexes that we can identify as nodes. Some of the
fords are no longer important: the track (1) that once ran down the
little valley between the citadel and the *shahristan* must have already
disappeared during the Samanid period because it does not show up on
the nineteenth century plan. To the east of this is a diagonal route (2)
that once ran from the southeastern Banu Saʿad gate of the *shahristan*
to the ford over the Khasaka bridge. Still important, however, is the old
pedestrian crossing (3) by the Gaukushan minaret which determined
the sixteenth century Gaukushan complex and which Bol'shakov associates with the Khandaq bridge. Its importance is underlined by the
irregular shape of the monuments, such as the coffin-like shape of the
Gaukushan caravanserai and the trapezoid of the madrasa, suggesting
the predominance of the routes. One side of the ʿAbdarrahman Aʿlam
madrasa is shorn off in relation to the Shahrud canal, while the irregular

polygon of the 'Abdullah Jan caravanserai can be explained by streets that must have led back up to the bazaar gate in the Samanid period. In this period it must have been the most important ford.

Only towards the end of the sixteenth century, with the re-planning of the commercial district under way, did the ford near the Russian Bank (4), along with the network of streets from the south, grow in importance, similar to the ford in front of the Taq-i Sarrafan (5), which, thanks to the bridge, became the gateway to the Shaybanid commercial centre,[13] thus diverting the north-south route of the Taq-i Tilpak Furushan so that it passed in front of the newly renovated facade of the Maghoki Attari mosque.

As demonstrated by the town plan of Shahrisabz commissioned by Timur, and the plan of Herat (1404) commissioned by his son Shahrukh, the *taqat* are architectonic poles that mark the intersection between two or more bazaar streets. The emphatic hierarchical composition of brick vaulted and domed chambers seems to reproduce in plan the complexity of the urban fabric.

Today, three *taqat* remain in Bukhara. The oldest is the Taq-i Zargaran, or Jewellers' Dome; a Timurid building that stands at the intersection of the *cardo* and the *decumanus* of the *shahristan*. The Taq-i Tilpak Furushan, or Hatters' Dome, is just below the old bazaar gate at the intersection between a network of streets coming from the south and the *cardo* from the north. The Taq-i Sarrafan, or Money Changers' Dome, stands at the intersection between the Riw gate and the southern bank of the Shahrud.

A series of interrelated brick-vaulted arcades when seen in elevation, the *taqat* are rotational structures that mirror the complexity of the urban fabric on an architectonic scale. The 44 metre wide Taq-i Zargaran is divided into two parts: a central section similar in layout to the Shahrisabz *chaharsu*, with two cardinal axes that correspond to the four *pishtaq* entrances, and two half axes on the diagonal of the quadrant. The centre is circumscribed by a walkway with vaults over the artisan shops, or *dukkan*, and is dominated by a dome 14 metres in diameter on an octagonal base. The base rests on a cylindrical drum with windows and multi-serial shield-shaped pendentives in the form of a grid casing of 32 intersecting arches.

---

[13] E. Nekrasova, *Die Basare Bucharas vom 16. bis zum fruehen 20. Jahrhundert: das Antlitz einer Handelsstadt im Wandel* (Berlin, 1999).

Before 1930, four busy streets used to run through the Taq-i Zargaran, creating one huge internal space, without a front or facade. The dome and side vaults were once part of a building fabric which was continuous with the houses to the north, the rice caravanserai to the west and the Indian caravanserai to the east, but after the senseless demolition of the surrounding building fabric during the Soviet era, it now looks like a traffic island. According to G. Pugachenkova,[14] this *taq* was probably built during the Timurid era, but if we are to believe Hafiz Tanish, a sixteenth century chronicler,[15] it was re-built in 1569–1570 on the site of the Chaharsu Bukhari, another magnificent building.

The effect of a continuous route through a covered space can still be seen in the short gallery that runs north of the Taq-i Tilpak Furushan, dated 1570–1571.[16] This *taq* consists of a centralised structure on a hexagonal plan along three axes that split into six different half-axes and a gallery facing the north-south axis of the bazaar. The north axis penetrates the centre of the *taq* without traversing it, before coming up against a closed space and refracting by 120° along two diagonals that correspond to two old extra-urban routes.

With its many geometrical and constructional irregularities the *taq* appears to be an attempt to dignify the old intersection of five streets all running at different angles. The *taq* is dominated by a dome 14.5 metres in diameter that rises from a 12–sided drum on a hexagonal plan. From the excavations carried out, Filimonov has suggested that in the Samanid era there was a hexagonal shaped pavilion to the north of the bazaar gate/*taq* with a portal facing south. According to Nekrasova,[17] a bridge would have connected the two buildings.

The Taq-i Sarrafan, dated 1534–1535,[18] is a square crossing aligned along the cardinal axes, with a slight rotation of 45°; the latter axis also defines the corner niches overlooking the Guzar mosque, the *chay khana* and two moneychanger's shops. The Taq-i Sarrafan is covered by a tall, bulbous dome with a lantern, resting on four large intersecting arches, which were rebuilt in the nineteenth century. The arches

---

[14] G. A. Pugachenkova, *Arkhitekturnoe nasledie Timura* (Taskent, 1976).

[15] B. A. Ahmedov, *Istoriko-geograficheskaja literatura Srednei Azii XVI–XVII vv. Pis'mennye pamjatniki* (Tashkent, 1965).

[16] G. P. Juraeva, "Bukhoroda kadimgi khamom wa sugorish inshoot lari," *Sharqshunolik*, 1994.

[17] Nekrasova, op. cit., 1999, (plate 4).

[18] V. Filimonov and E. Nekrasova, "L'ensemble architectural de Taq-e Sarrafan à Boukhara," in "Boukhara la noble," *Cahiers d'Asie Centrale* 5–6 (1998): 95–124.

are also maintained on the outer curve of the dome as a decorative motif common in Bukharian oases; see for example the roofing of the Bahauddin *khanaqah*.

The two *taqat* which no longer survive, the Taq-i Ordfurushan (Dome of the Pomegranate Sellers) and the Taq-i Tirigama, are not structures with a complete central rotation, since they once covered a T-junction, as can be seen from Rempel's reconstruction (1982). The first is a replica of the Taq-i Sarrafan, while the second is very similar to the Taq-i Zargaran. According to Jureva,[19] there was also a third *taq*, known as the Chaharsu-i Dunba Furushan (Dome of the Fat Sellers). All five *taqat* were positioned in one neat line of communication, like the beads of a rosary, though for some unknown reason the two *registan taqat* were never directly connected.

5. *Nodality and Polarity*

The concepts of nodality and polarity define the quantity and quality of nodal and polar zones, whereas those of anti-nodality and anti-polarity define anti-nodal and anti-polar zones. The organisation of nodal zones involves not just the physical organisation of space, or building type, but also their functions. Nodal functions and services occupy the centre, or nodal zones, while anti-nodal functions occupy the margins, or anti-nodal, zones. Property value constitutes another important factor of differentiation. As can be seen with the convents of medieval Europe or the Sufi complexes in Islamic cities, the low cost of anti-polar zones tends to favour not just the spread of production centres but also religious centres. Surrounded by functions that do not disturb the sanctity of the place, the Friday mosque occupies the geometric centre of the bazaars in Islamic cities. Dyers, tanneries and butcher shops, on the other hand, are placed outside the city centre. Unless it was intended by Timur as a marker between the old and new city, the Bibi Khanum mosque in Samarkand, with its somewhat eccentric position near the Afrasiyab gate, seems to be an exception to this rule.

In the ancient city of Bukhara the north-south route, which used to run through the little valley between the two hills of the citadel and

---

[19] Jureva, op. cit., 87.

the *shahristan*, had a polar function. This is confirmed by the eastern gate of the citadel, no longer extant, and the four or more gates that until the nineteenth century pierced the western wall of the *shahristan*, as well as the possible presence of a much smaller fort to the east of the citadel, where the Shah-i Zindeh prison is now located. This route is polarised in the quadrilateral of the viaduct leading to the citadel, the *decumanus*, the citadel walls and the *shahristan* walls opposite the Banu Sa'ad gate. The area continued to be central to the city right up to the invasion of Ghengis Khan. Three Friday mosques were built here between 770 and 1068: the Fadl b. Yahya (770), the Hamid Nuh (951) and the Shams al-Mulk (1068).

Until the eighteenth century anti-polar zones were situated to the north and east of the *shahristan* and to the south of the canal.[20] The necropolis to the east of the bazaar gate suggests evidence for this. Even today, dangerous or 'unclean' activities, such as the production and sale of building materials, are located just beyond the northern gate of the *shahristan*. The horse bazaar, on the other hand, is situated opposite the Rashid caravanserai to the south of the Taq-i Sarrafan.

The records between 840 and the twelfth century speak of a new suburb (*rabad*) enclosed by a double wall, whether defensive or simply delimiting. Bol'shakov and Davidovich[21] posit the existence of one or even two concentric circles of walls around the city. From the previous examples, however, polarity and anti-polarity seem to us historically relative. There is always a continuous exchange of roles between nodes and anti-nodes, poles and anti-poles. The outskirts of a city are continually subsumed by the centre, as anti-polar functions give way to new centralised activities. A transition of this kind occurred in Bukhara in the ninth century, when the *registan* and the area immediately to the south of the bazaar gate became the focal point of the Samanid city. In the thirteenth century, the square of the *registan* was full of administrative and palatial buildings which were later replaced by commercial and religious buildings.

Anti-polar zones were then pushed beyond the Shahrud, as can be seen in the first ring of small cemeteries: Khwajah Charshamba Qazaq, Turk-i Jandi, Khwajah Bulgar, Shah Yakhshi and Khwajah Nur Abad.

---

[20] Nekrasova, op. cit., map 1.
[21] Belenitskii, Bentovich, and Bol'shakov, op. cit. See also E. A. Davidovic, *Istoria deneznogo obrashchenija srednevokovoj Srednei Azii* (Moscow, 1983).

Bol'shakov posits a second circle of concentric walls about 400 metres from the city moat, and it is probably for this reason that the *shahristan* declined in importance. Many of the gates disappeared and the track itself became blocked by houses. The external street that runs parallel to the Shahrud, connecting the two poles of Samanid Bukhara—the bazaar gate and the *registan*—thus became increasingly important. In 1121 the Friday mosque[22] was built under Arslan Khan on the large, at that time open, square to the east of the Taq-i Zargaran, thereby restoring a central position to the *shahristan*.

This tendency to anti-polar/polar exchange is confirmed by Timurid building projects at the beginning of the fifteenth century, as the main axes of the *shahristan* were revitalised and key monuments were erected along the *decumanus*, a tendency underlined by the geometry of the centrally planned Taq-i Zargaran. The *registan* remained important, though it gradually changed roles, as it became surrounded by a ring of great monuments—various guild mosques, hospitals (*dar al-shifa'*) and other religious buildings—which were, anti-clockwise from the citadel gate: the Dar al-Shifa' madrasa, Usto Ruki *khanaqah*, Bolo Hauz *khanaqah* and madrasa (the only surviving madrasa), Shodimbi madrasa, Khwajah Nicol madrasa and Poyanda Atalik mosque. Photographs from the nineteenth century show an open space, delimited by the high walls of the citadel and large religious buildings, crowded with market stalls by the citadel gate, a sign that the *registan* never lost its original function as a caravan station.

Timurid Bukhara is defined by its routes (street axes) and nodes (monuments). The point of intersection between the two main axes (religious east-west and commercial north-south) is based on a common model, the most notable example of which is the urban layout of Herat. These axes function as continuous trajectories, tangential to the public architecture. The east-west religious axis goes from the Banu Asad gate to the Nau gate. Along this route stand the Mir-i Arab madrasa, the Kalyan mosque and the Ulugh Beg madrasa, and at one time the Badalbeki Nau and the 'Abdashshukur and Abdulaziz madrasas. The colossal monuments, on the other hand, cluster around visually striking "signs" and an earlier building fabric, which is of a serial, repetitive kind and on a smaller scale.

---

[22] Nekrasova, op. cit. (plate 1).

The Timurid project testifies to an "analogous" city—to use Aldo Rossi's term—planned and partly realised by one generation, and gradually revised by successive generations. In spite of an economic recession in the early sixteenth century, the aspirations of Ubaidullah Khan and his successor, Abdullah Khan, and later of the Juybari sheikhs, were to create a multi-polar city. Following a Timurid project, a continuous bazaar was conceived from the *registan* to the Dar Bazar, with two perpendicular axes lined with specialised buildings, though separated from the Taq-i Zargaran. The first urban nodes were created with a closed square halfway along the *decumanus*, starting with the surviving twelfth century Kalyan minaret, then the Ghaziyan complex to the south along Karakul street and the Gaukushan complex (comprising a madrasa, congregational mosque and pool) built in 1562–1579.

The Gaukushan complex is a textbook case in the transformation of the polarities of a city. Previously the area near the canal comprised a slaughterhouse (Gaukushan means "He Who Slaughters Cattle"), windmills and other artisan activities: in other words, it was an area of marginal importance with an anti-polar function. At the same time, the area of the Turk-i Jandi cemetery, anti-polar by definition, took on a polar function, as confirmed by the presence of the new Green bazaar serving the two Jewish districts, forming a *chaharsu*, to the south of the cemetery.

The zone north of the *shahristan* and the empty zone still further west, such as the ring of cemeteries—Chashma Ayyub, Wadar Khwajeh Gunjar, Imam-i Imla, Ishau-i Ustaz, Zindeh-Fil Ahmad-i Jami, Bahadur Bi to the west; Khalifeh Husayn and Khwajah Sasaran to the east; Aq Mazar and Khwajah Namadpush outside the eastern wall; and finally the Shaykh Jalal and Shah 'Arab along the trajectory to Karakul—remained marginal, or anti-polar, throughout the sixteenth century. From this time onward the camel market was situated outside the Namazgah gate, thereby marking the outer limits of the city.

Each new phase in the growth of the city sets up a mechanism of inversion of its nodes and poles. The building fabric continues to blend and unite with the adjacent fabric, while anti-nodal zones remain, until a new centre determines a new set of relations—a thesis borne out in Bukhara by the great building projects of the last decades of the sixteenth and beginning of the seventeenth century. The urban organism reached a phase of maturity with the completion of the buildings along the route of the *shahristan* bazaar and the Lab-i Hauz. These two axes between the three nodes of the *registan*, Taq-i Zargaran and Taq-i

Sarrafan were completed with the construction of many monuments, such as the Abdullah Khan Timcheh, the Abdulaziz Khan madrasa and the many caravanserais, such as the Indian caravanserai. There was a definitive move eastwards to the important pole of the Russian Bank ford, and the Gaukushan complex was, thus, reduced to a neighbourhood centre.

At the end of the sixteenth century the new pole of the Lab-i Hauz—comprising the Kukeldash madrasa (1568–1569), the Nadir Divanbegi *khanaqah* (1620) and the Nadir Divanbegi madrasa/caravanserai (1622–1623), built around a 46 × 36 metre pool with a bank of stone steps—came into prominence. As with the great religious complexes, the growth of this polar zone was connected to the rise of Sufism. The *khanaqahs* in Transoxiana (Mawarannahr) which were formerly hostels and teaching centres for travelling Sufis—isolated spaces, reflected in the fence surrounding the Khalifa Khudaidad *khanaqah*—now became great meeting places and secular schools organised around the *samat*, or *zikrkhana*, the central hall of Sufi ceremonies, and the pivot of urban planning on a monumental scale.

In this phase two urban projects incorporated the periphery into the city. The city walls were extended to the west during the reign of Abdulaziz Khan I (1540–1549), using the remains of the old Samanid walls to the north and west. The Juybari district to the south of the city was added during the reign of Abdullah Khan II (1557–1598). Along the tree-lined Khiyaban boulevard running north-south between the Sirgaram and Karakul radials, the open space of the demolished west wall was turned into a strip of orchards and suburban gardens that were later built over. Thus, from the seventeenth century there were the two above-mentioned centres, while the poles—the Ghaziyan madrasa and the *kosh* complex of the Abdullah Khan and Mader-i madrasas on Shursuran street, the Gaukushan and the Hauz-i Nau—remained mere neighbourhood centres.

As products of the dialectical exchange between pole and anti-pole in the development of Bukhara, the main squares grew out of the space in front of the neighbourhood mosques. In present day Bukhara one generally finds two or more monumental buildings situated in closed or semi-closed squares. Compared to Iran, and particularly eastern Iran, where squares are generally associated with the Shiite Moharram Festival (or Passion Plays) commemorating the martyrdom of Husayn, in Bukhara and Samarkand, where Sunni Islam predominates, the squares remained a vital part of everyday life.

Some of these squares can be defined as *kosh*, a layout unique to Central Asia from the mid-sixteenth century. The *kosh* consists of two large buildings—a mosque/madrasa or madrasa/madrasa—which face each other along the street, leaving enough space for the creation of a square. The prototype is the layout of the Kalyan mosque and Mir-i Arab madrasa, commissioned by Ubaidullah Khan in 1536. The choice of the site was determined—together with the former mosque—by the Arslan Khan minaret built in 1127. The facade of the Kalyan mosque (1514) and the large madrasa opposite, both on a more monumental scale, are an expression of the limitless power of the prince. The *kosh*, which is rectangular in plan, is closed-off to the north by a row of houses (now a hybrid modern bazaar) and to the south by the isolated volumes of the 'Abdarrahman A'lam madrasa baths and the cylindrical shaft of the Arslan Khan minaret.

The minaret—45.6 metres high, 9 metres in diameter at the base and 6 at the summit—is surmounted by a 16–sided polygon on projecting rows of masonry arranged as stalactites (*sharaf*) and overlaid with intricate brickwork. Together with the ogival roof of the baths, the minaret creates a play of light and shadow over the square. The facades of the two public buildings mirror each other in many ways. With their jointly aligned *pishtaqat*, polygonal plans and multiple niches and entrances, the facades create two great apses in the architecture of the square. The facade of the Mir-i Arab madrasa is more sculpted, comprising two storeys of deep loggias. The Kalyan mosque mirrors it in a series of wide, shallow niches on one storey. The differing height and size of mosque, madrasa, minaret, and baths, together with their contained lateral extension, imbue the space of the square with a dynamic tension.

A little further to the east is the *kosh* comprising the Ulugh Beg madrasa (1417) and the Abdulaziz Khan madrasa (1651–1652) on the *decumanus*. Here the space is rendered less dynamic by the incomplete east-west axis which was later formalised in a small square. The facade of the Ulugh Beg madrasa is aligned with the street, while the Abdulaziz Khan facade stands several metres back—further confirmation that the Timurids did not intend to build a square, which must therefore be attributed, together with the *kosh*, to the Uzbek Khan dynasty.

The most important characteristic of the *kosh* is not the longitudinal axes shared by the two buildings, but the fact that their facades mirror one another. This iron rule may be observed in the *kosh* comprising the Abdullah Khan (1588–1590) and Mader-i Khan (1566–1567) madrasas where, in order to maintain the line of the Abdullah Khan facade, the Mader-i Khan facade is rotated. This rotation creates a deformation in the depth and shape of the interior spaces, which is also partially absorbed by thickening the walls. The Abdullah Khan madrasa lies perpendicular to the street, thereby rotating the position of the prayer room inside the *miansaray* with an interesting spatial effect. In the *kosh* comprising the two Ghaziyan madrasas,[23] the smaller madrasa is enveloped in a serial layout of rooms, which recovers the street alignment by turning the complex into an irregular pentagon. In so doing, it preserves the regular form of the rectangular inner courtyard and the hall with three aisles.

The great urban pole of the Lab-i Hauz, a square separated from traffic, which skirts it, derives its layout from the Kalyan mosque *kosh* and Samarkand *registan*. This is reflected in the position of the three buildings in relation to the tangential routes, as well as in the loggia facades, dominated by the large-scale *pishtaq* entrance. In Samarkand, on the other hand, the three high walls of the facades, together with the stone pavement, recreate the sensation of being on a magnificent indoor stage.

Such a space is the result of the progressive transformation of the city centre towards a more monumental character. Between 1417 and 1420, Ulugh Beg built the first madrasa close to a pre-existing *khanaqah* and caravanserai, both of which would be substituted between 1619 and 1635 by a second madrasa, Shir Dor, facing the first. And so the first *kosh* was created. A few years later the Tilla Kari madrasa (1646–1647), surrounded by the urban fabric that left only one facade free, would give the *registan* its present form.

In Bukhara this effect is completely lost in the Lab-i Hauz due to the opening up of the space. Here the axis of the Kukeldash madrasa has been shifted to the east—probably because of pre-existing structures on the northeast side, including the Nazar Elchi madrasa—while the presence of the Hauz and the garden enclosed by the madrasas, where one can still see mulberry trees planted as long ago as 1475, multiply the visual axes, rendering the complex (comprised of two independent buildings) more marginal. The earlier anti-polar function

---

[23] L. I. Rempel, *Dalekoe i blizkoe. Bukharskie zapisi. Stranitsy zhini, byta, stoitel'nogo dela, remesla Staroi Bukhary* (Tashkent, 1982), 141. See also: V. A. Lavrov, *Gradostroitel'naja kul'tura Srednej Azii* (Moscow, 1950).

of the area is confirmed by the fact that the northwest and southeast corners of the Divanbegi madrasa have been cut off, thus indicating two pre-existing routes converging on the Shahrud at the point where Bol'shakov locates the old Suveuk bridge which, not surprisingly, coincides with the extension of the longitudinal axis of the Kukeldash madrasa. Today the Kukeldash madrasa blocks an earlier curvilinear route coming from the north, which used to lead to the ford.[24] This route is still partly legible today, for example, in the missing corner of the Domillo Shir madrasa.

Other complexes with a *hauz* at the centre include the Khiyaban Hauz in western Bukhara with a madrasa and mosque of the same name, the Jafar Khwajeh Hauz in eastern Bukhara, and finally the Hauz-i Nau with the Abdulaziz I mosque (1540–1550) and the Juybari Kalyan madrasa.[25] Today the latter *hauz* is buried under the street, making it impossible to recognise the square.

To summarise, from the end of the fourteenth century medieval Bukhara underwent a radical transformation under the Timurids in terms of its main axes and the strategic position of its large-scale monuments. In the sixteenth century these construction works were extended by the Uzbek khanate into hierarchically equivalent poles that generally confirm the main nodal points of the earlier Timurid city without establishing any absolute ascendancy of one point over another. In the last decades of the sixteenth century, however, the polar zones became more specialised and a hierarchy was established in which the two poles of the *registan* and the Lab-i Hauz predominated.

The term "square" may seem slightly ambiguous. The Bukharian *kosh* and squares are very different from Italian Renaissance squares, for example. From the Timurid period specialized buildings became progressively more focalised, thereby creating a symmetrical axis which was also a route axis starting from the *iwan* (entrance portal) of the monuments. This might suggest a strong dependence on urban morphology, as with an entrance aligned to a street, yet this is not the case. If a monumental *pishtaq* entrance gives onto a street, as in the case of the Ulugh Beg madrasa, it acts simply as a facade, not as an urban backdrop. If, on the other hand, access is mediated by a square,

---

[24] Rempel, op. cit., 111.

[25] B. Babajanov, "Arhitekturnye pamjatniki v sredneve-kovyh pis'mennykh istochni-kakh na arhitekturnikh pamjatnikakh—Uzbekistana," *Arhitektura i stroitelstvo Uzbekistana* (Tashkent), no. 7 (1991).

as in the case of the Kalyan mosque, it is completely dissociated from the route, in contrast to Italy and other European countries where, in general, an urban route is ideally aligned with the symmetrical axis of a building.

In European architectural history, a change in route determines whether a door is opened or blocked off, especially in Italian patrician palaces. And a door always means a street, whether open or closed, in the surrounding urban fabric. In Central Asia, on the other hand, the memory of an earlier residential building fabric often persists. In Islamic cities, this fabric is organised in so-called endogamous clusters, which always interpose a mediating space, or a kind of decompression chamber, between public street and private zone. A gate sometimes closes off the private lanes that converge on covered public spaces.[26]

Another difference from the medieval Italian city is that the Islamic city is governed by a rigid system of zoning, which separates residential areas from production areas and public activities. Thus, the specialised fabric has a non-spatial relationship with the residential fabric and both tend to operate as closed systems independent of one another.

In the case of the Kalyan mosque, for example, the *decumanus* (the pivot of Timurid urban renewal) runs tangentially to the 130 metre long side of the building. The facade has two regular entrances for the faithful. The *pishtaq*, on the other hand, is aligned with the *mihrab*, and opens onto the small square, rotating 90° degrees in relation to the route. The same can be said for the *pishtaq* of the Mir-i Arab madrasa opposite, though in this case the function of the madrasa requires a more inward-looking building with only one access. In the *kosh* comprising the Abdulaziz Khan and Mader-i Khan madrasas, where the symmetrical axis is perpendicular to the street, the two facades are seen in oblique perspective. Thus the internal axes of the monuments do not coincide with those of the urban routes.

In the case of the Maghoki Kurpa mosque (1637), situated at a junction of the main street running from the Taq-i Tilpak Furushan towards the *registan* to the west and the Gaukushan complex, the ambiguity of the urban collocation of the building is repeated inside. Here the symmetrical longitudinal axis does not coincide with the route axis;

────────────

[26] See M. I. Filanovic, "Traites principaux de l'urbanisme dans le Mavarannahr et le Turkestan à la fin du XVème et au XVIème siècle," in "L'heritage timuride," ed. by M. Szuppe, *Cahiers d'Asie Centrale* 3–4 (1997): 169–182.

the *pishtaq* entrance is only to the lower hall, while for the upper one there are two side doors.

The buildings comprising the monumental Gaukushan complex, the Khwajeh Kalan mosque and madrasa and the small madrasa known as ʿAbdarrahman Aʿlam are aligned neither with the route, which widens into the small square of the *hauz*, nor with each other. This entire pole seems determined by the topography of the site: the trapezoidal form of the Gaukushan madrasa is determined by the forking streets on which it lies, as is the coffin shape of the Gaukushan caravanserai behind it. One side of the ʿAbdarrahman Aʿlam madrasa is shorn off by the Shahrud, and even the little *hamman* is situated between the two converging routes.

In the Lab-i Hauz the main route parallel to the canal runs tangentially to the complex. For this reason the facades of the Divanbegi *khanaqah* and madrasa are seen in oblique perspective, while the *pishtaq* of the Kukeldash madrasa is too far away to establish a direct relation with the route.

The only exception seems to be the rural Chorbakr complex (1560–1563) where the street is almost, though not quite, aligned with the mosque entrance. The mosque itself is part of a larger monumental complex in the form of a C, with the *khanaqah* and *musallah* in the open. The mid-point of the axis is marked by the squat minaret which is not aligned with the route giving access to the complex.[27]

In the course of the 150 years that mark the most important changes in the architecture and urban morphology of Bukhara, the madrasas (Koranic schools) greatly influenced the character of public spaces. The inner, private space of the courtyard, like a kind of ivory tower impermeable to the secular world, gradually opened up to the outside world and the city. Just two examples: the Mir-i Arab madrasa is enclosed by three high, impenetrable walls onto which minor buildings were slowly added, while a century later the Kukeldash madrasa opened its three sides to the city, which were pierced by loggias on several floors. The gradual conquest of street and public space depends not only on the changing form of education and the pursuit of knowledge, but also on two related factors: the anti-polar location of the new madrasas and the introduction of loggias in the facades.

---

[27] G. A. Pugachenkova and L. I. Rempel, *Vydaiushchiesia pamiatniki arkhitktury Uzbekistana* (Tashkent, 1958), 341.

The placing of loggias on all sides of a building is possible once it occupies a whole block and is surrounded by streets and squares. Loggias become balconies, and during festivals and processions they were probably decorated and thus had an active role in the urban spectacle.[28] In rural areas, on the other hand, the passage from an introverted to an extroverted architecture was more gradual. In the monumental complex of the Chorbakr, and especially the Bahauddin *khanaqah*, the system of cells giving onto a courtyard and connected by a long service gallery is turned inside out: blind service corridors are placed on the inside and the cells face outwards (though they are still within the religious compound): Despite the important precedent of the Ulugh Beg madrasa facade (1417), the phenomenon became widespread in Bukhara only after 1560, with the Khiyaban, Bazar-i Gusfand, Muhammad Yar Attalik, and Kukeldash madrasas, and from here it spread to the rest of Central Asia.

6. *Specialized Buildings*

The study of monuments in terms of typological processes is based on the definition of building types as the organic summation of the construction features of buildings in a given place and time and relies on the axiom that, independent of their size, all specialised buildings in a city are related and that the spirit of place influences any changes made to them. A small *guzar* mosque, with a simple flat roof, will have been built according to the same construction module (or one of its multiples) as the Kalyan mosque with its many domes. Further confirmation of this similarity is to be found in the construction systems: the load-bearing walls both of dwellings and *guzar* mosques are a filled frame, a wooden structure packed with sun-baked bricks (*guvalyak*).

The construction module, together with a predilection for certain techniques and materials, is part of the specific cultural heritage of a social group and only changes, if that group is uprooted from its original context. The typological processes of specialised buildings, in a large and ancient city like Bukhara, resemble a huge tree with many branches but only one trunk. Starting from the shoots we can reconstruct their ramifications and growth.

---

[28] Bernardini, op. cit.

Specialised buildings invariably derive from basic, or residential, building processes.[29] If the dwelling is a response to the need for shelter, the monument is a response to the need of a social group to represent its collective values. The monument, in turn, derives from the reorganisation of the basic fabric in terms of specialised spaces and a more hierarchical composition. There are many small settlements in the oases around Bukhara which are simply an agglomerate of houses without even a prayer hall; and when there is a prayer hall, it is indistinguishable from a dwelling. Yet it would be impossible to imagine a city composed of specialised building fabric alone.

We shall now examine the typological processes of small to medium size monuments—namely those monuments on a neighbourhood scale—represented by the three Tables 10, 12, and 18. The minimum common denominator of specialised buildings in Bukhara is a square construction module of about 3.30 metres, corresponding to six *gaz*, with four walls, pierced by a single door and covered by a wooden roof with mono-directional beams. It may be simply a room in a house, or a bay, forming part of a composition of similar structures that go to make up an isotropic plan adaptable to commercial or religious purposes.

7. *A Typological Reading of the Major Monuments of Bukhara*

So far we have dealt with the relation between minor buildings and their derivation from the dwelling, and our analysis has implied a strong local influence. When dealing with large-scale monuments, however, we must bear in mind that external cultural influences play a more central role. Above all, large monuments require more audacious techniques, for example, in their vaulting and decoration. So we have to imagine groups of specialized craftsmen, which formed itinerant corporations or guilds, like the Shirazis. In this context, the aesthetic aspirations of a whole society, including the lower classes, count less than the patronage of the aristocracy and high clergy, who preferred the latest trends in architecture coming from the capital and the court. While it is true that from the sixteenth century Bukhara became the main cultural centre of Central Asia, and from 1560 to 1590 we can even speak of

---

[29] G. Caniggia and G. L. Maffei, *Composizione architettonica e tipologia edilizia. Lettura dell'edilizia di base* (Venice: Marsilio Editore, 1979), 105–108.

a Bukharian School, for two centuries prior to this the cultural centre was Samarkand. Moreover, Timurid cultural horizons were vast, and so artistic influences must be sought throughout the Empire.

Architecture is a spatial and structural organism, the spatial axes of which may be read as a synthesis of the various psychological, ritual and practical interests of the user. The organisation and distribution of collective architectonic space is traceable to four type-models based on four increasingly organic degrees of axial plan, from the linear to the polar: mono-directional; bi-directional; tri-directional (with a vertical axis); and multi-directional (with a vertical axis). Each model may be analysed using the basic geometrical principles of the plan, the correlation between the various axes in section and perspective, the laws of internal unity relating to the spatial definition of each element, and the arrangement of the internal and external volumes.

Buildings without a predominant axis and with an open plan belong to the first category; for example, many of the baths in Bukhara. These consist of freely assembled groups of architectonic elements on a square or polygonal plan, with a strong internal geometry and double symmetry; in sequence, they function as vestibule, massage room (*khadim khana*), hot room (*garm khana*), and cold room (*khunak khana*). The baths next to the Taq-i Sarafan have eight different rooms—round, rectangular, square, pentagonal, hexagonal, and octagonal—arranged around a central room on a cruciform plan.[30] According to Juraeva,[31] the waqf documents cite the following baths in sixteenth century Bukhara: Khiyaban, Tirkashduzan Rigistan, Zargaran, Mochi Chapazi, Shoki Minoi, Gaukushan, Ghaziyan, Kappa, Juybari, Sar-i Bazar-i Rigistan, Khwajeh, Gharibiya, Kafser, Furushan.

To this category also belong mono-directional buildings with courtyards, characterised by a single entrance, or iwan, a uniform section and rows of cells (*hujrah*) on all four sides. The load bearing structure is no longer the column but the wall and the space is barrel-vaulted. There are no outstanding architectonic elements; at most, there is an entrance portal or a cut-off inside corner (hinting at an octagonal plan, and hence more organic), as in the ʿAbdarrahman Aʿlam madrasa, Miskin madrasa and Gaukushan madrasa. Most of the caravanserais belong

---

[30] M. I. Filanovic and U. Alimov, "K obnaruzeniju Srednevekovoj bani v Tashkente," *Istorija material'noj kultury uzbekistana* (Tashkent), no. 22 (1988): 179–182.

[31] G. P. Juraeva, "Bukhoroda kadimgi khamom wa sugorish inshootlari," *Sharqshunolisk*, no. 5 (1994): 85.

to this category; for example, the Gura Bek and Kuliota caravanserai, the latter next to the Taq-i Tilpak Furushan. In the Indian caravanserai the courtyard lacks an *iwan* but has a sophisticated arrangement of passages, running at 45° from the corners and serving as access to cruciform rooms. Compared to more organic structures, such as the miansaray, the serial plans of this building category can be more easily deformed by removing modules, yet without serious damage to the internal function; see, for example, the plans of the Rashid caravanserai and the Nadir Divanbegi madrasa/caravanserai.

To the second category belong those buildings with bi-directional axes in plan. The longitudinal axis is normally indicated by two internal *iwan*s, which correspond to the *pishtaq* and the niche of the *mihrab* on the building exterior. The plan is composite: the main, or front, side differs from the others in their repetitive arrangement of modules, and is organised like a *miansaray* in its transverse sequence of entrance hall (*dihliz*), funerary or prayer hall (*gurkhana*) and winter auditorium, which together form a transept. So the definition of space of the longitudinal axis predominates over the cross axis. The angles are specialised, both in terms of their use for collective social functions and the rotation by 45° of the corner spaces and entrances. The corner rooms are domed, unlike the row modules, which are vaulted. In section, the hierarchy of volumes is articulated by portals and domes which are much higher than the main body of the building.

The third category consists of buildings with bi-directional axes in plan and a vertical axis. This is typical of cruciform plans and is common in Persian architecture with a four-*iwan* scheme. The two axes of the plan are almost equal, though the transverse counter-axis is normally weaker. These buildings have a typical nodal conformation in the intersection of axes and plan. The nodal elements of *iwan* and *miansaray*, the niche of the *mihrab*, the *darshkhana* (teaching hall) in front of the *mihrab*, the vertical axes along the longitudinal axis (the 'virtual' intersections and the rotational or cross-vaulted structures) all dominate over the serial arrangement of vaulted galleries, as in the Kalyan mosque. The great sixteenth century congregational mosques and madrasas, such as the Mir-i Arab, belong to this category.

The fourth category consists of buildings with pluri-directional axes, in other words, those that rotate around a vertical axis, such as large centrally planned buildings, in which the central dome dominates over a surrounding group of smaller domes. The axes of the plan, including the diagonals, are at least four, though they are not necessarily equal.

The general definition of space, on the other hand, is uniform, in that even the most complex spatial and constructive volumes tend to gravitate around the vertical axis, which deflects upwards any horizontal thrust. We have already mentioned the conflicting tensions, in the *guzar* kiosk mosques, created between the direction of the *qibla* and the direction of the heavens.

The plan may be open or closed: in the first case it has a radial structure, in the second an encircling structure. The Bukharian *taqat* already mentioned are exemplary in their geometrical clarity: the Taq-i Tilpak is an open polar structure, as is th e Timcheh Abdullah Khan Taq; the Taq-i Zargaran is open at the core but closed in its general layout; the Bahauddin *khanaqah* is a closed structure.

In Table 5 a selection of monuments in Bukhara has been classified using a grid: the different degrees (or categories) are represented on the X axis, while examples on the Y axis are arranged according to progressive levels of spatial complexity, following the principles of typological processes.[32]

The Amir A'lam Khan madrasa (no. 1) is composed of three interconnected elements. The present entrance (rebuilt during the Stalin era) connects the centrally planned baths with a ribbed dome to the eighteenth century madrasa, which consists of serial modules on two storeys, with a corner rotated by 45° and served by a small gallery.

The small Gaukushan madrasa (no. 3) and the following example (no. 4) share the same feature of a cut-off corner in order to facilitate access, thereby creating an octagonal courtyard. The precedent is established here for many later madrasas: on three sides of the building there is only one floor, with rows of students' rooms, while the facade with the *pishtaq* is double the height of the rest. The smaller Ghaziyan madrasa also belongs to this category.

The Maghoki Kurpa mosque (no. 6) is a complex structure of superimposed basilicas with three naves of twelve domed modules each and an east-west longitudinal axis accentuated by the tall *pishtaq*, which reaches the top of the facade, the domed *mihrab* and the high quality of the vaulting decoration in the central nave, especially on the dome of the *darshkhana*. The hall is surrounded by a gallery and the *qibla* wall has been deepened in order to accommodate service rooms. The two-

---

[32] Caniggia and Maffei, op. cit.; see also: L. Y. Mankovskaya, *Tipologicheskij osnovi sodchestva Srednei Azii IX nachalo XXV* (Tashkent, 1980).

sided galleries are open to the north and south, where the light floods in through great arches, but is then filtered through smaller apertures into the prayer hall. The layout suggests that the building was originally not just a mosque but also a *khanaqah* and that there were rooms in the side galleries. Part of the facade wall is deep enough to contain the *pishtaq* and the entrance to the upper hall. The symmetrical axis of the upper hall is an ideal one and thus does not correspond to the route axis, while the entrance to the lower hall is at the base of the *pishtaq* through an axial staircase. The third cell from the entrance, where the *darshkhana* is situated, has a double-calotte dome on a tall drum, setting up a potential counter-axis, which does not, however, affect the side facades. The whole layout is similar to the Maghoki Attari mosque.[33]

The Maghoki Attari mosque is the result of three successive layers of construction over the ancient Moon Temple. In 1940, the archaeologist Shishkin[34] discovered an eleventh century mosque with four columns on the present site. It is known that there was a twelfth century mosque with six columns, already in ruins in the fifteenth century, on the same site. The actual plan corresponds to this version and consists of three aisles with a total of twelve bays. In 1546–47 the mosque was rebuilt to correspond to the new layout of the bazaar. Along the longitudinal axis a new door with a *pishtaq* was opened to the east on an upper level and two stilted double-calotte domes were added to give a sense of hierarchy to the whole. The southern door, on a lower level, corresponding to the original twelfth century entrance, opens onto a monumental portal decorated with a geometrical pattern in brick (*girikh*). The ambiguity of the structure is due to the various modifications: the *mihrab* and sixteenth century door correspond to the main axis, but the presence of two doors facing each other on the longer sides creates a transverse counter-axis. The complementary nature of the axes and the articulation of the mosque in elevation mark this as an example of the second category.

Morphologically, the Ulugh Beg madrasa (no. 8), dated 1417, created a model for later developments by experimenting with original spatial and distributive systems for the first time, such as the *miansaray* on the facade and a central entrance hall leading to the auditorium and

---

[33] L. Y. Mankovskaya, *Bukhara: A Museum in the Open* (Tashkent, 1991), 80.

[34] V. A. Shishkin, "Arheologicheskie raboty v mecheti Magak-i Attari v Buhare," *Trudy Instituta Istorii i Arheologii Bukhara* (Tashkent), no. 7 (1955): 56–57.

mosque. Only the courtyard (22.5 × 24.5 metres) is well-proportioned, however, and is surrounded by an arcade of two-storey cell blocks (*hujrah*) on three sides, which are set back on the second storey to make room for a service gallery. The main north-south axis is indicated by two portals inside and an apse to the north that protrudes from the main body of the building and, thus, deepens the *iwan*. The corner rooms are still of a serial type, without any attempt at a more organic solution. The main axis is indicated on the facade by a monumental crowned *pishtaq*, almost 20 metres high, double the height of the main body of the building. This is a simple technique developed in Timurid architecture in order to enhance the monumental effect of even small buildings. The central entrance is doubled, while a vestibule encircles the *iwan* along two galleries. If this layout serves to leave the southern *iwan* free for teaching purposes, it nevertheless creates a dichotomy between the route axis and the structural axis that renders an objective reading of the building difficult. The two vaulted halls of the *miansaray*, together with the entrance *dikhliz* behind the *pishtaq*, create a counter-axis, aligned with the *mihrab*, that reinforces the whole front of the building. The street facade, dominated by a portal with typical fifteenth century decoration and framed by two cylindrical corner towers (*guldasta*), has a representational role. The series of loggias on the facade give it the appearance of a civic building. An inscription on the facade states that it is the work of the architect Ismail Bini Tahir Bin Mahmud Isfahani.[35] Ulugh Beg commissioned two copies of the madrasa, one in Samarkand, the other in Ghujdivan. (For a comparison of the plans, see Golombek and Wilber 1990, vol. II, plate 7, p. 88).[36]

Almost 150 years later, in 1651–52, Abdulaziz Khan II completed the layout of the *kosh* with a madrasa (no. 14). The transverse *iwan*s dominate the courtyard and their protruding form counterbalances the force of the *miansaray*. This is a typical composition with a longitudinal axis, which, nevertheless, has unconventional features: behind the courtyard portals are corridors leading to cells on two floors, while the outer perimeter is articulated by apses and *guldastas*. The cells deserve attention for their spatial complexity: each cell has a room, anti-room, fireplace, niches, mezzanine, dais for the bed and decorated vaulting.

---

[35] V. A. Levina, "O reznoy derevyannoi dveri medrese Ulugbegav Bukhare," *Trudi SAGUAGU*, no. 49 (1953): 161–169.

[36] L. Golombek and D. Wilber, *The Timurid Architecture in Iran and Turan*, 2 vols. (Princeton, 1990).

The library above the *dikhliz* on the first floor is unusual, while the entrance has the same cruciform plan as the Ulugh Begh madrasa that forces the visitor to go round the *iwan*s, using the galleries at the side. The architect of the madrasa was Muhammad Salih. Three other madrasas were commissioned by Abdulaziz Khan II: the Mirukon madrasa (1650–52), the Khiyaban madrasa (1654–55) and the Bazar-i Gusfand madrasa (1665–70).

The Bibi Khanum mosque in Samarkand near the Iron Gate has a surface area of 167 × 109 metres. The mosque, built to celebrate the triumph of Timur in India, faced a madrasa, now destroyed, standing on the site of the Saray Mulk Khanum mausoleum. The plan of the mosque is a traditional four-*iwan* courtyard. The longitudinal axis is marked by the 30 metre high double *pishtaq* (entrance and interior). It anticipates the deep *iwan* that leads to the domed room with a *mihrab*. Two minor cells, domed and square in plan, are marked by the transverse axis of the mosque. The four internal *iwan*s were connected by a continuous arcade (*riwaq*), 4 modules deep on three sides and 9 modules deep towards the *qibla*. Four minarets mark the four external corners.

Though perhaps not as impressive as the Bibi Khanum in Samarkand, the Kalyan mosque (no. 15), with its 130 × 81 metre plan and 30-metre high dome, is the most important landmark in Bukhara. The traditional layout with a 77 × 40 metre courtyard and four *iwan*s is not, however, an altogether organic solution. The longitudinal axis predominates, emphasised by a sequence of architectonic elements: the entrance *pishtaq* and internal *iwan*s linked by a gallery, and the dome opposite with an *iwan* in front and a deep apse for the *mihrab*. Each of these nodes with its vertical axis rhythmically punctuates the trajectory. The layout of the two *iwan*s facing each other in the courtyard (a motif taken from the Timurid Aqsaray Palace at Shahrisabz), the central pavilion (*taratkhana*) for ablutions and even the isolated tree on a low platform lead the visitor's eyes and movements along the longitudinal axis, which is the only real structural element in the whole composition. Indeed, the two *iwan*s in the middle of the long sides hint at a weak counter-axis, which does not affect the outer perimeter, while the two doors opening onto the street suggest two further counter-axes, which do not affect the courtyard facade. With its 200 or so vaulted bays that create a continuous, rhythmic space, punctuated by architectonic nodes, the plan of the Kalyan mosque is a metaphor for the urban fabric with its houses and monuments. The quadripartite plan, possibly inspired by the Friday mosque at Herat, shows the same refined contrast between the marked nodality of the *iwan*s and the serial arrangement of colonnaded galleries, with the difference that in the Kalyan mosque the *iwan*s are deeper and the entrances are at the side, thereby accentuating the cross axis.

Typical of large-scale Timurid architecture, and commensurate with its imperial aspirations, the dome towers disproportionately high above the roof of the colonnaded galleries rather than harmonising with the scale of the surrounding buildings. It rests on the gallery of the deep prayer hall, which is divided into three different sections: transitional *iwan*, *darshkhana*, and apsidal *mihrab*. The scheme is very like that of the Gauhar Shad at Herat. The dome follows the Timurid scheme of a double calotte on a tall drum, a simple solution allowing the rounded surface of the dome to dominate the urban fabric, but with the defect of seeming extremely heavy. The inner dome rests on an octahedron of pendentive arches and is surmounted by a blue-tiled, elongated dome, which, in turn, rests on the tall tiled drum.[37]

The Mir-i Arab madrasa (no. 16), dated 1536, has a layout of four *iwan*s and rows of cells on two storeys, typical of the third category. The four *iwan*s (all alike) generate two axes that intersect in the middle of the courtyard, creating a strong vertical thrust. The *iwan*s and the buttressing, together with the two stilted domes of the *miansaray*, dominate the skyline. This is the most striking part of the monument, with the extraordinary, novel solution of domes over the tomb and mosque resting on four intersecting arches with secondary ribs in alabaster that prop up the projecting 'arms' of the arches. The interstices are filled with herringbone brickwork in the form of shield-shaped pendentives. The frame of the intersecting arches forms a grid, while the corners between the main arches are clad in sections of vaulting and decorated with *muqarnas*.

Structurally, the dome is the usual double calotte on a tall drum, except that in section the inner dome is open and lit from above by windows in the drum. This novel invention revolutionises the interior space, which is now brighter and so more suitable for complex relief decoration.

---

[37] M. Yusupova and G. A. Pugachenkova, "Material and Spiritual Culture," in *Bukhara: An Oriental Gem* (Tashkent, 1997), 90.

If we compare this solution with the similar one of the Kukeldash madrasa *miansaray*, we note that while the first is an ingenious adaptation of a Timurid structure, the second is an invention *ex novo*: here the section of the dome that rests on the diagonal intersecting arches is transformed into a kind of lighting contraption and the squat dome rises from the drum like a diaphanous lantern. For Voronina[38] the Mir-i Arab madrasa surpasses Timurid architecture in that its architects have managed to conjoin the grandeur of massive buildings with a stylistic terseness and a technical skill in lightening the sense of mass.

The Kukeldash madrasa (no. 17), with its 86 × 69 metre surface area and 130 student cells, is the largest madrasa in Bukhara. The focal point of the general layout of two *iwan*s and rows of cells on two storeys is the complex *miansaray* which is almost a building in itself. The corners in the courtyard rotate the rooms by 45°, thus making them autonomous—by far the most organic solution.

The Abdullah Khan madrasa (no. 18), dated 1589–90, has a quadripartite plan with sections of the main body of the building protruding from the outer perimeter. The most striking innovation is the double-lit hall on the central axis of the courtyard, called the Abdullah Khan *fanusi* (*fanusi* means "lantern"). This hall leads to the twenty cells and is covered by a dome on a drum pierced by windows.[39] To the same category belong the Tursunjan madrasa, with a quadripartite courtyard and corner rooms rotated by 45°, the Gaukushan mosque and the Abdulaziz Khan madrasa.

The Abdullah Khan Timcheh is a polar structure typical of the more organic fourth category. Its plan incorporates two central axes and two diagonal axes at 45° to the main ones. A gallery runs around the central octagon of the dome, connecting various shops and corner rooms rotated by 45°. The Bahauddin Nakshbandi *khanaqah* also has a central, polar plan with double axes. The two perpendicular axes, emphasised by monumental double-height *pishtaqat* on the facade and four shorter *iwan*s on the interior, the mighty masonry walls that support the ribbed dome on eight crossed ribs and even the four cut-off corners of the facade suggest a very strong mirror-symmetry dominated by the vertical axis of the dome. In effect, the building was begun with

[38] V. L. Voronina, *Architectural Monuments of Middle Asia: Bukhara, Samarkand* (Leningrad, 1969).

[39] L. Y. Mankovskaya, *Bukhara: A Museum in the Open* (Tashkent, 1991), 74.

a single-axis plan, like the Fayzabad *khanaqah* (1598–1599), which has only two rows of parallel cells, turned toward the exterior. During the following century it was considerably rearranged and made completely symmetrical on the four sides through the introduction of the balanced counter-axis and two further rows of perpendicular cells. The only evidence in plan of the former layout is to be seen in the four mono-directional corner rooms.

(English translation by Lisa Adams)
Otherwise stated all surveys and drawings by the author

SHIRAZ: THE CITY OF GARDENS AND POETS

Mahvash Alemi

This paper initially provides a comprehensive plan of Shiraz in the Safavid period, based on the newly found documentary evidences, and subsequently examines the relation between royal and sepulchre gardens and the city as revealed by this plan. This relation is compared with the garden city created in the same period in Isfahan, in order to find the common features and highlight the specific characteristics of Shiraz.

The custom of Persian kings to move from *Yeylaq to Qeshlaq*, hunting along the way, has resulted in the creation of a network of royal gardens that dotted the main roads leading to places of interest. As the urban history of the Iranian plateau shows, the capital was also often moved from a city to the other, due to strategic reasons, related to the nomadic origins of the royal power. Thus, royal gardens were built in time in different cities. During the rule of the Safavid dynasty the capital changed from Tabriz, to Qazvin, and then to Isfahan. The study of the relation between royal gardens and the cities in Qazvin and Isfahan has identified certain common features. In both capitals, the choice of establishing the royal court had given place to the creation of a garden city at the side of the urban centres. It is therefore interesting to understand how gardens were related to the urban centres in those cities that were not capital, and to see whether this relation changed only because of the natural context or also due to other social and historical factors, among them the presence of the royal court.

Shiraz of the Safavid period is, in this sense, a relevant case study. It was neither the capital, nor just a hunting resort but the capital of the province of Fars. The city, the largest town of the southern Zagros region, was of particular strategic and commercial interest, lying along the main roads of communication, leading from Isfahan to the Persian Gulf, and also due to the European presence in the area. The plain around the city was covered with numerous sepulchre gardens besides pleasure gardens that belonged to local governors or royalty.

The European travellers of the Safavid period give an idea of the relation between the urban and natural landscape of Shiraz and its gardens through their descriptions and views of the city. However this

relation can be better depicted and read in a graphical plan. Given that
a Safavid plan of Shiraz and its suburbs is not available to this date,
this paper first provides a plan drawn through the synthesis of previous studies,[1] the accounts of the European travellers,[2] and unexplored
graphical and textual documents, mainly in Engelbert Kaempfer's
manuscripts in the British Library. Only after the principal royal and
sepulchre gardens are located and drawn on the plan, it is possible
to compare their relation to the city with that of Safavid Isfahan and
discuss the common features as well as the differences.

Plan of Safavid Shiraz

The oldest plan of Shiraz is a drawing by Carsten Niebuhr in 1765[3]
(figure 1) that shows the walled city and part of the surrounding plain.[4]

---

[1] The history of the city has been studied by:
  Laurence Lockhart, *Famous Cities of Iran* (Middlesex, 1939);
  Fredy Bemont, *Les Villes de L'Iran* (Paris, 1973);
  Karamatollah Afsar, *tarikh-e baft-e qadimi-ye Shiraz* (Tehran, 1374/1995) [shortened
  as Afsar];
  Manuchehr Daneshpajuh, *Shiraz* (Tehran, 1377/1998) [shortened as Danesh-
  pajuh].
  The gardens of Shiraz have been studied by:
  Donald Newton Wilber, *Persian Gardens and Garden Pavilions* (Washington, 1979);
  Alireza Arianpur, *Pajuheshi dar shenakht-e baghhaye iran va baghhaye tarikh-ye shiraz*
  (Tehran, 1365) [shortened as Ariyanpur].
[2] The main Safavid travellers accounts that have been used in this article are:
  Pietro della Valle, Biblioteca Apostolica Vaticana, Ms. Ottob. Lat. 3382 [abbrevi-
  ated Della Valle];
  Jean Chardin, *Voyages*, vol. 9 [abbreviated Chardin];
  Jean Baptiste Tavernier, *Les six voyages en Turquie, & en Perse*, vol. 2: 307–19;
  Cornelis de Bruyn, *Voyages de Corneille le Bruyn par la Moscovie, en Perse et aux Indes
  Orientales*, 5 vols. (Paris, 1725) [shortened as Le Bruyn];
  British Library, Ms. Sloane 2846, *Comentarios de Don Garcia de Silva de sus Embaxada
  que de parte del Rey de Espana Don Philippe III Rizo al Rey Xà Abas de Persia. Ano de
  1618* [shortened as Comentarios];
  Don Garcia de Silva y Figueroa, *L'ambassade de D. Garcias de Silva Figueroa en Perse*
  [shortened as Figueroa];
  Engelbert Kaempfer, British Library, Sloane Manuscripts.
[3] Carsten Niebuhr, *Voyages en Arabie et en d'autres pays circonvoisins* (Amsterdam, 1776),
  vol. 2, tab. 35 [shortened as Niebuhr].
[4] Niebuhr, 138: "*je n'ai pas pu faire le plan exact de cette ville. Cependant le lecteure pourra
  se former une idée suffisante de la grandeur et de la situation de cette ville, par la Table XXXV. La
  situation et les noms des portes y sont exactement indiquées. Prés d'A il y a là cy devant si belle porte
  de la ville Tandsji All akbar, et B, marque la situation du tombeau de Hadsji Hafès. Sarbach est
  la factoire des Anglois. Prés d'a, b, c l'on vois les ruines des factoires d'autrefois des Francois, des*

It recalls the ancient circular form that was characteristic of the cities in Fars (Darab, Firuzabad, and Bishapur).[5] The gates indicated on this plan are Bagh-e Shah and Isfahan to the northwest and northeast, Saadi to the east, Qassab[6] to the southeast,[7] Shah Daii to the southwest, and Kazerun to the west.[8] The roads starting from these gates and leading to Isfahan, Baba Kuhi, and Shaykh Saadi are labelled. The river Khorram Darre, or Khoshk, and three watercourses leading to Bagh-e Shah gate, and to the Sarbagh quarter are marked. Along the road to Isfahan, the gate at Tang-e Allah-o Akbar (A), the tomb of Hafez (B), and the Mir Hamze mausoleum and cemetery are shown. To the south, the Khatun Qiyamat mausoleum and the Shah Daii cemetery are represented. Inside the walls, the mosques of Seyyed ol-Hoseyn and Shah-e Cheragh are marked. Sarbagh,[9] where the Armenians had a chapel in the "Commercial Agency of the English," as well as a, b, c the ruins of the agencies of the French, the Dutch, and the Portuguese are identified.[10] In a view by Niebuhr, from the north other landmarks can be distinguished, among which are the bridges, close to the Isfahan and Saadi gates, Khatun Qiyamat, the Gunpowder warehouse, Seyyed al Hoseyn, Bibi Dokhtaran, Madrese, Shah-e Cheragh, and the house of the Beglerbeg, brother of Karim Khan.[11]

Hollandois et des Portugais; Aussi la situation de quelque Mosquées est marquée sur le plan, mais de ces dernières on voit d'avantages sur le table XXXVI dont j'ai fait le plan dans l'édifice prés du tombeau de Hadsji Hafes."

[5] Abol Abbas Moin-ed-Din Ahmad ibn Shahab ed-Din Abi al-Kheyr Zarkub Shirazi, *Shirazname*, ed. Esmail Va'ez Javadi (Tehran, 1350/1971) [abbreviated as Shirazname], 34.

[6] This gate is called Koshtargah, in the plan by Mirza Hasan Shirazi. Pascal Coste in fact calls it "abbatoir." Pietro della Valle refers to it as Fasa gate. According to Chardin, the gate to the south was called "la porte de Phess, du nom d'une petite ville à la quelle elle conduit."

[7] Chardin mistakenly mentions this gate to the west *"la porte de Brebis (Gusfand), a cause d'un marché de betail qui est tout contre."*

[8] Chardin mistakenly mentions this gate to the east, instead of west.

[9] Herbert Chick, *A Chronicle of the Carmelites in Persia* (London, 1939), 1071: The Discaled Carmelites had a hospice and residence at Shiraz from 6th August, 1623 till 1738—some 115 years—with religious in regular residence except for the two periods August 1631 to November 1634 and from early 1644 to March 1654, i.e. some thirteen years out of those 115 years. The first and more spacious site was used for thirty-three years, the second for eighty-two years.

[10] Kaempfer, British Library, Ms. Sloane 2912, fol. 41, refers to Mahalle Sarbagh, the Armenians, and the different companies.

[11] Niebuhr, 93: *"Le palais du Beglerbeg n'est bati que nouvellement par son maitre actuel, et se trouve sur une grande place, qui est semée. L'édifice anterieure ne fait gueres plus de parade que la belle maison d'un bon Bourgeois; derriére cet édifice anterieure se trouve le corps de logis, avec*

Niebuhr's plan coincides substantially with the historical section of
the city distinguishable in the 1946 plan of Shiraz (figure 2).[12] The
latter is the best available background for drawing a topographically
reliable restored plan, as it shows the city and its surroundings at the
beginning of the Pahlavi dynasty, when the trend of cutting streets for
allowing cars within the old fabric had just started. The 1946 plan still
shows the historical section of the city, characterized by the fabric of
the narrow streets, with the exception of the Karim Khan and Lotfali
Khan streets that were just being cut through.[13] It is therefore possible
to draw the walls and the other landmarks shown by Niebuhr on this
plan. The shape of the walls seems fairly correct as, once overlapped
on the 1946 plan, it matches with the existing streets. On the contrary,
the road to Isfahan through Tang-e Allah-o Akbar is drawn to the east
rather than northeast and is probably mistakenly traced along the road
to Isfahan through Neyriz.

Karim Khan Zand rebuilt the walls after his capital was established
in Shiraz in 1765.[14] At the time, Shiraz was mostly in ruins, not only
because of the damage inflicted during the Afghan retirement, in
1729, and pursuit by Quli Khan (afterwards Nader Shah), but also as
a consequence of the floods that destroyed the northern quarters close
to the riverbed.[15] The accounts of the Carmelitan friars reveal that the
limits of the city were reduced in this occasion.[16]

The gates in the Safavid period were nine; their names were Estakhr
(Isfahan), Saadat (Gazorgah), close to Saadi, Manzar (between Saadi
and Fasa), Fasa (also called Gusfand, Qassabkhane, and Kovar), Naw
(or Khatun Qiyamat), Salm (or Shah Daii), Kazerun (or Shushtar),
Beyza (between Bagh-e Shah and Kazerun), and Murdastan (Bagh-e
Shah or Darak Musa or Ahani).

---

une cour, où il y a un grand réservoir et des jets d'eau. On nous mena dans une grande salle, qui
étoit toute ouverte du coté de cette cour." He adds "Apres l'audience...nous conduisit par tout le
palais...après cela nous fumes conduit dans le harem, ou l'apartement des femmes, qui n'étoit pas
encore entièrement prés...Le Beglerbeg dormoit sous une forte garde, dans une Tour ronde, qu'il fait
batir sur le derrière de la maison."

[12] Sazeman-e Havapeymai va Naqshebardari, *1946 plan of Shiraz*, scale 1:10000,
1326 A.H.

[13] Afsar, 285–287.

[14] Afsar, 197.

[15] Herbert Chick, 1068.

[16] Herbert Chick, 614. "*in the narrowing (of the limits) of the town that House of ours was
razed to its foundations.*"

The Urban Fabric Inside the Walls

Niebuhr's plan does not show the urban fabric inside the walls. A later plan drawn by Chirikov in 1850 shows the urban fabric,[17] though it contains manifest mistakes regarding the location of the Masjed-e Naw and Shah-e Cheragh complex. The city fabric is as well readable in a drawing by Wilber that represents the historical centre of Shiraz in 1935.[18] By matching these documents to the 1946 plan of the city, it has been possible to restore the missing historical urban fabric, where new streets were cut through. The toponymes of the quarters, *mahalle*, can be retraced from the plan published by Afsar.[19]

The historical urban fabric was characterized by courthouses accessed through narrow sinuous streets, except in the northern quadrant between the Bazaar and Bagh-e Shah gate that was the area of the governmental complex developed in the Safavid and rebuilt in the Zand period. Longer streets connected the main gates creating an organic grid, based on two directions. The northwest-southeast direction was defined by the topographic lines which were parallel to the rivers Khorram Darre and Qarebagh.[20] Perpendicular to the former direction were the streets following the watercourses running from the mountains on the north and northeast that entered the city at Isfahan and Saadi gates.[21]

Among the main structural elements of the city was a bazaar that connected the Isfahan gate to the core of the city and can be distinguished morphologically in two pieces. Its northern section is characterized by a geometrical layout with a crossing of four galleries, *chaharsu*, near the governmental complex; while its southern section has an organic layout ending in the Masjed-e Jame, Masjed-e Naw, and Shah Cheragh religious complex.

Pietro della Valle who arrived in the city in 1618 from the Isfahan gate mentioned the bazaar, close to a square, *meydan*, that was the

---

[17] Plan of Shiraz drawn by Prescuryakov and Ogranovich directed by Chirikov published in: *Pictorial Documents of Iranian Cities in the Qajar Period*, edited by M. Mehryar, Sh.S. Fatullayev, F.F. Tehrani and B. Qadiri, (Tehran, 2000).

[18] Donald Wilber, "Shiraz 1935," *Journal of Persian Studies*, 1935, 125–129 [abbreviated as Wilber].

[19] Afsar, pages not numbered, before the Introduction.

[20] Afsar 6–8: the river Khorramdarre starts in the mountain Babakuhi and runs to Maharlu depression, while the Qarabagh river starts at the source Pir-e Bonab.

[21] Afsar, 18–20.

vestibule to the house of Emamqoli Khan,[22] the governor of Shiraz. The Meydan, like the one in Isfahan, was surrounded by arcades and there was a high loggia, *naqarakhane*, where music was played.[23] Chardin is more precise regarding the location of that Meydan. He writes that Davud Khan, brother of Emamqoli Khan, had built a bazaar during the reign of Shah Abbas at the crossing of four galleries above which was a great cupola.[24] One of the galleries ended in a *meydan* that was the vestibule to the house of the governor, the other ended in the Multani Caravansaray. The Divankhane of Emamqoli Khan, where the English Ambassador Sir Dodmore Cotton was received in 1627 A.D./ 1036 A.H., was probably in the place where Karim khan built his later. The best caravansaray of the bazaar was called *qaysariyye*.[25] The section of the bazaar built by Davud Khan was the northern one, characterized by its geometric layout. It was restored during the Zand period and is shown in a 1931 view by Fred Richards.[26] This bazaar is still extant, although the Lotfali Khan Street cuts it in two parts near the crossing.

Della Valle mentions also a new *madrase* that was built during the Safavid period, at Tel Shater Ali.[27] This was the Madrase Emamqoli

---

[22] Emamqoli Khan was the son of the famous *ghulam* of the Shah's household, Allah Verdi Khan, succeeded to his father as *beglerbegi* of Fars in 1022/1613 A.D.

[23] Della Valle, "*Vidi poco lontano dalla casa nostra di là dal bazar, il palazzo dove risiede il chan che inanzi ha un meidan o piazza quadralunga circondata tutta di mura con archi assai politi et incontro in faccia alla porta una loggia alta dove suonan la sera le Raccase, come nella piazza di Spahan e quivi si riducono i soldati e genti del chan a corteggiare. In Sciras non c'é altra piazza che questa detta di sopra, e un'altra che vidi più sotto, che io sappia.*" "*Dentro alla porta poi dopo haver camminato molto una seconda meidan e bazar, entrammo un gran bazar coperto.*" *vidi anco tornando a casa un altro bazar coperto presso al palazzo del chan sotto alla loggia dove si suonano le racasse, qual palazzo mi parse il meglio fatto e di migliore fabrica su tutti gli altri della città.*"

[24] Chardin, 9:177: "*le Bazar de Daoud Kan, du nom de celui qui l'a fait bâtir, qui étoit frère du fameux Imam Kouli Kan...Il consiste en quatre Galléries, toutes de pareille symétrie, remplies de boutiques de part e d'autres, dont chacune à un petit magasin derrière et une chambre au dessus. Le centre, où le milieu, de ces quatre Galléries, dont les voûtes sont fort hautes et eercées à distances en soupirail, pour donner tout le jour qu il faut, est une place ronde couverte d'un grand Dôme. Les bouts se rendent, l'un à la place qui est au devant de la maison du Gouverneur, l'autre au Caravanserai des Multani, qui sont les Indiens, ainsi nommez de Multan, grandes villes des Indes sur les frontières de la Perse du cotez du Nord; les deux autres en d'autres endroits....*"

[25] Afsar, on page 156, mentions that the *qaysariyya*, although ruined, was still extant 40 years ago in the Mahalle Bazar Morgh. It had on one side the *bazar-e mesgarha*, and to the west was another caravansaray. The Masged-e Ma'reke Khane was later constructed in its place.

[26] Fred Richards, *A Persian Journey* (London, 1931), 128.

[27] Pietro della Valle, Biblioteca Vaticana, Ms. Ottoboni Latino 3382, fol. 154: "*Vidi un loco che chiamano Tel Sciater Ali con le Medressè nuova, è stata fabricata dove prima impiccavano i mal fattori inanzi alla qual fabrica in un poco di largo che cè, hoggi i Ciarlatani fanno i lor giuochi.*"

Khan,[28] mentioned also by Chardin[29] and le Bruyn, to the southeast of Tel Shater Ali, today called Tel Hassir Bafan. This Madrase had a great portal with two minarets and is distinguishable in the view by Chardin (figure 3). According to della Valle, the principal mausoleum was Sadat Mir Mohammad.[30] Chardin mentions it among the twenty principal tombs and mausoleums[31] and gives a list of nine mosques that were greater and more sumptuous than the others: Meydan-e Shah, Dervazek, Derkeme, Dar-e Ahani, Shahzade, Barekat, Hagi Nassir, Nou, and Jamé.

The palace built by Emamqoli Khan inside the walls of Shiraz was according to Chardin close to a great hospital, the Dar ol-Shafa.[32] We may speculate that the grounds of this palace were at the site where, later, Karim Khan made his garden, Bagh-e Nazar.[33] Curzon gives a

---

[28] Madrese Emamqoli Khan no. 93 on Wilber's plan, Afsar, 126: According to *Farsname Naseri*, 139, in the year 1022, a year after Emamqoli Khan was appointed Governor of Shiraz, he ordered to build a Madrase with more than a hundred rooms, "*hojre ye fowqani va tahtani va zawaya va karyas va madrese va chahartaq boland*," and it had, on four sides, a Chaharbagh; the rooms faced both the Chahabagh and the Madrase. The latter is today called Madrase-ye Khan and lies between the Mahalle Bazar Morgh and Eshaq Beyk; the Lotfalikhan Street runs to its south. A bare land, to the north, and the Meydan-e Alafha, to the east are the only remains of the above *chaharbagh*.

[29] Chardin, 9:180: "*C'est la même chose des collèges qui sont au nombre de 12 lesquels tombent en ruines. Le principale est celui que on appelle Collège du Prince ou des Gouverneurs, dont le portail est fort large, et fort élevé avec deux tours hautes aux cotez, mais dont partie est tombée en ruine. Le corps de logis est double et a deux étages autour d'une grande cour plus longue que large, à l'entour de la quelles sont les apartmenes des étudiants consistants chacun en un bas et un étage double. Le milieu de la Cour est orné d'un grand bassin d'eau.*"

[30] Pietro della Valle, Biblioteca Vaticana, Ms. Ottoboni Latino 3382, fol. 154: "*Vidi la meschita principale che chiamano Sadat cioè li Syti Seidi perché forse alcuni seidi della setta di Mohhammed da loro onorati per santi ci dicono esser sepolti....Non è gran fabrica ma per casa loro ben fatta e polita di non mala architettura con cupola e minare, fabricata in isola in mezzo d'un cortile circondata pur di mura con archi in ordine d'architettura non malo e da i paesani questo loco è tenuto molto in devotione.*"

[31] Chardin, 9:176: "*Shah Cheragh, Chahzade Zolfaqar, Chah Hagi, Chah Hagi Hafez, Chah Khezr (le roi Elie), Chah Rustem, Chah Dawlat, Malekeldar, Chah Parioun, Baba Lour, Baba Kuhi, Behtariun, Sheykh Mohammad Sabbaq, Sheykh Salec Alamdar, Chehel Makan, Sheykh Saadi, Seyyed Haji Gharb, Mir Mohammad, Shazade Mansour, Seyyed Alaeddin, Hossein.*"

[32] Chardin, 9:180: "*le Palais d'Imam Couli Can, autrefois Gouverneur de cette Ville, & de sa Province & de plusieurs autres Pais au delà. Ce palais étale dans ses ruines beaucoup de grandeur, & de magnificence...En faisant le tour de ces Palais on se trouve sur les masures d'un grand Hôpital. Les Persans appellent les Hôpitaux dar el Shafa...*"

[33] Niebuhr, 95: "*Entre les jardins de Schiras, je n'en trouvois de remarquables, que celui la seulement, que Kerim Khan avoit fait planter.... Au milieu d'un jardin, il y a un haut édifice octangulaire, avec un toit Chinois et deux hautes ailes. La salle de l'édifice principal est aussi octangulaire et passe par les deux étages. Au haut tout autour il y a une gallérie, et dans les coins il y a en haut et en bas, de petits cabinets. Les vitres de la fenêtre ne sont que petites, et la plus part de verres peint. Les murailles en bas sont couvertes de Marbre de Tauris. Le reste étoit couvert d'ornemens et de fleurs, en partie dorées et en partie peintes avec des vives couleurs. Même au dehors à l'édifice principal, on*"

detailed description of the palace of Karim Khan that is still, partly, existing in which he clarifies that the Meydan in front of the palace was related to the *chaharsu* of the bazaar, exactly as it was reported in the accounts of the travellers of the Safavid period.[34] Olivier refers to a superb palace among the buildings built by Karim Khan that was in the middle of a great square garden, Bagh-e Nazar, where in a pavilion, Kola Farangi, the body of Vakil was supposed to rest some day.[35]

Le Bruyn depicts the mosques and other places of interest in a view drawn from the northeastern mountains, close to the tomb of Shaykh Saadi.[36] It should be remarked that one of the main features of Shiraz was that there were numerous tombs and mausoleums inside the walls and in the *extra moenia* cemeteries. Wilber remarks that the overwhelming number of mosques, madrasas, shrines, and tombs in Shiraz was witness to the priority of Islam in the local life of the city. This was due to historical reasons. The area of Shiraz, at the crossing of important routes that connected Sassanian and Achaemenid sites, had been of

---

trouve des figures humaines en peinture. Dans la grande salle, aussi bien qu'au devant, il y a des jets d'eau; dans chacune des deux ailes, il y a sur le second étage une grande salle ouverte d'un coté. L'un des cotés d'une des ailes et contre la muraille du jardin, et a une grande cour quarrée, aussi entourée d'une bonne muraille, dans laquelle il y a des éspèces de voûtes, ou de petites demeures, qui servent de casernes, lors que le Vekil passe icy quelque temps. De l'autre coté de la cour, il y a un batiment étroit et élevé, sous lequel, à ce qu'on disoit, se placent les musiciens, comme les tambours, les tympanistes et les hautboiste."

[34] George N. Curzon, *Persia and the Persian Question Persia* (1st ed. 1892; London, 1966), 2:99: "*One face of the palace fronts the principal Meidan... On its northern side is a large building, now occupied by the Indo European and Persian Telegraph establishments, but formerly the diwan khaneh, or audience-chamber of the palace of Kerim Khan. An arched gateway opens from the square on to a fine garden containing a hauz or tank, at whose upper end, on a platform, the face of which is adorned with sculptured bas-reliefs in marble, is the large recessed chamber, now filled with official bureaux and counters, that once held the twisted marble columns and the Takht-i-Marmor, or marble Throne, previously described as standing in the talar or throne room at Tehran, whither they were removed a hundred years ago by Agha Mohammad. From the Meidan access is gained to the Bazar-i Vekil... It is crossed by a shorter transept, 120 yards long, a rotunda or circular domed place marking the point of intersection.*"

[35] Olivier Guillame Antoine: Voyages dans l'empire Othoman, l'Egypte, "*dans le genre européen, ou le corps de Vekil devait reposer un jour.*"

[36] Le Bruyn, 294, 414: 1) Khatun Qiyamat; 2) Sheykh Seyyed ud Din; 3) Seyyed Ala'ud-Din Hoseyn; 4) Sheykh Nurbakhsh; 5) Sadat Mir Mohammad; 6) Shah Cheragh; 7) Masjed-e Naw. Madrese Emamqoli Khan can be seen between the two latter monuments; 8) Bibi Dokhtaran, great building where there are a few tombs; 9) Seyyed Mir Ali Hamze, was close to the bridge, called Pol-e Shahzade, outside the walls of the city; 10) Chaharbagh; 11) Ziya ud-Din or Shayadan village, on the river, where there is a bridge that is 65 paces long; 12) River Rudkhane; 13) Semé verdoneck (verdoyant, *Kuh-e sabz pushan*), or the small mountains; 14) Kuh-e Siyakh, the higher mountains; 15) Ferdaws, or paradise.

interest to pre-Islamic kings who had built numerous castles and palaces in the area, witnessed also in the remains of Qale Fahandar and Masjed-e Madar-Soleyman. It was in fact close to important sites such as Persepolis, where Nawruz was celebrated and also to Naqsh-e Rostam and Pasargadae where they would visit the tombs of their ancestors at the beginning of spring.

The Qale Fahandar constituted for Zoroastrians an important point of resistance to Arab Moslems. In fact, many of the warriors (*mujahid*) of Islam were killed and their tombs built in Shiraz, among which were those of Shaykh Dawlat ebn-Ebrahim and Shaykh Manzar ebn-e Qeys, after which the gates Dawlat and Manzar were named. The Moslem Arabs made Estakhr their seat and as they were not secure there, they chose Shiraz after some time as their centre. Mohammad ebn-e Yussef is said to have built the city in 74 A.H. because he had dreamt of a round space close to Estakhr that would become the passage (*qadamgah*) of thousands of sufis.[37]

After the conquest of the major cities in Fars by the Arab Moslems, some of the people accepted Islam but others continued to practice the religion of their ancestors. Zoroastrians were still numerous in the area in the fourth century A.H. and this was so common that, as Moqadassi remarks, they did not wear special signs.

The fall of the Omayyad Khalifs with the help of Iranian Shiites led to the advent of Ma'mun, the Abbassid Khalif, who, aiming at their support, had decided that Emam Reza would be his successor. But when he changed his mind and endowed the reign of Khorasan to Taher ebn-e Hoseyn, he ordered not only Emam Reza's martyrdom but also that of his brothers and nephews who departed to join him in Khorasan, many of whom were buried in Shiraz.

The successive rise of different local dynasties that reigned in Fars, Khorasan, Gilan, Sistan, and other regions, during the Abbasid rule, was mostly based on the rebellion of Zoroastrian or Shiite people who looked forward to the independence of Iran from the Khalifs of Baghdad. As Shiraz had been spared by the Mongol invaders, many of the tombs of the important shaykhs survived.[38] The ancient rituals of remembering the *farvashi* of death at the beginning of Spring, when people would visit the tombs of their ancestors and distribute

---

[37] Afsar, 35.
[38] Jean Aubin, "Le mécénat Timouride a Chiraz," *Studia Islamica* 8 (1957).

food to the poor, as well as the feasts of Nawruz and Qorban, were maintained throughout the Islamic centuries also by many of the local governors such as the Shiite Rokn od Dawle Deylami. Although the Turkish based governors were Sunnite, the ancient rituals survived even during their reign.

With the advent of Safavids in the tenth century, the ancient rituals were still more enforced. Most of the existing tombs were rebuilt and developed as a consequence to the empowerment of Shiites. The most important mausoleums mentioned in the accounts of the travellers of the Safavid Period were in fact built on the tombs of the brothers of Emam Reza, venerated by the Shiites. Among these was the mausoleum of Ahmad, son of Musa Kazem, brother of Emam Reza, built in 791 HQ and restored by Shah Esmail, the founder of the Safavid dynasty, in 912 A.H. This mausoleum, which is today the most popular of Shiraz, was known in the Safavid period by the name Shah-e Cheragh. The mausoleum of Seyyed Mir Mohammad,[39] son of Musa Kazem, built in 1070 A.H., was connected to Shah-e Cheragh in the last century. The tomb of Seyyed Alaeddin Hoseyn,[40] another brother of Emam Reza, was found in the Qatlagh garden and a cupola was erected above it, during the Atabakan period. During the reign of Shah Esmail, Soltan Khalil Zolqadar, the governor of Shiraz, added other structures to this mausoleum by the year 923 A.H. The mausoleum of Ali ebn-e Hamze,[41] another son of Musa Kazem, was known in the Safavid period as Shah Mir Hamze and was in a great cemetery called Javanabad that extended to the site of the present Honarestan and Bagh-e Melli. The tomb of Emamzade Ebrahim, another son of Musa Kazem, was close to the old cemetery Dar-ol salm.

It is remarkable that there were loggias for playing music, *naqara khane*, close to the Shah Mir Hamze and Shah-e Cheragh mausoleums. The ancient practice of *naqara kubi* was common at sunrise and sunset. But it is also depicted in the reliefs at Taq-e Bostan, during the

---

[39] Buq'ah Seyyed Mir Mohammad, was built in no. 2 on Wilber's plan.

[40] Buq'ah Seyyed Alaeddin Hoseyn, no. 3 on Wilber's plan. Danesh Pajuh, 105.

[41] Seyyed Mir Ali Hamze, no. 5 on Wilber's plan. See Daneshpajuh, 139: This mausoleum, built close the old bridge that led to the Isfahan gate, was the burial of Ali ibn Hamze ibn Musa al Kazem. The original building was built in the reign of Azad od-Dawle Deylami.

hunting session of the king.[42] The Safavid kings used to play *chawgan* in the Meydan to the sound of *naqara kubi*. Apparently, the Deylami kings were the first who used it in combination with Islamic rituals. Its presence on the front of mausoleums that carried the inscription of *Shah* reveals a contamination between royalty and divinity in the Shii rituals, as in the ancient ones.

The Suburban Gardens

Chardin and le Bruyn picture the urban centre of Shiraz surrounded by suburban gardens that were related to the sources of water in the northern and western mountains, as well as in the area that extended along the river in the Jafarabad plain to the north of the river Khoshk. This was probably the *baghestan*, literally place of gardens, mentioned in *Zafarname*.[43] Here Timur's army fought against that of Shah Mansur whose tomb, known as Shahzade Mansur,[44] is still extant within the walls in the Shayadan *mahalle*, between the Isfahan and Saadat gates.

A sketch by Kaempfer[45] shows the northern mountains of Shiraz and the *baghestan*, with the bridge Shah Rostam[46] in the foreground. The monuments and gardens shown from west to east are the following:

a) Sebedun; b) Baba Kuhi; c) its great cypress; at the foot of the Baba Kuhi mountain the vineyards, *hortulum*, and garden Takht-e Qaradje or Hortus Ferdaws; d) the dome of Shah Mir Hamze mausoleum that rises above its surrounding gardens; e) the garden to the east of the *baghestan*, with its wall in the foreground, is Chaharbagh; Haft Tanan sepulchre garden is shown below the gorge Tang-e Allah -o- Akbar; f) Sepulchrum; g) *Pyr-e bendbas*; on the Chehel Maqam or 40 Dervish mountain are: h) *Chah-e Ghadir*; i) *Qadamgah-e Khezr*; . . .; m) *sepulchrum*

---

[42] Yahya Zaka, *"Ain-e naqarakubi dar Iran-va piscine-ye an,"* *Honar va Mardom*, year 15, no. 180 (Tehran, 2536/1977): 29–49.

[43] Mawlana Sharaf-ed-Din Ali Yazdi, *Zafarname*, ed. Mohammad Abbassi, vol. 1 (Tehran, 1336AH), 434.

[44] Kaempfer, British Library, Ms. Sloane 2912, fol. 41.

[45] Kaempfer, British Library, Ms. Sloane 2912, fol. 45.

[46] Afsar, 94. This bridge mentioned by Kaempfer was named after the mausoleum of Sheykh Rostam ibn Abdollah Khorasani (died in 741) built in the Jafarabad plain.

(Saadi) is shown between the two eastern mountains; n) *horty*...; k) the ruins of *Qale-ye Benderga* or Fahandar are shown above the far eastern mountain, also called Kuh-e Sheykh Saadi; below these is Berme Delek; p) *tentoria depruntiater*; shown in a small sketch; q) *Mare Sallum*, that is Derja Nemek; r) *Karsang i.e. imagi...magnum formes rupe* also called Masjed-e Madar-e Soleyman...Khezr-e Zendeh...[47]

A feature that should be remarked is that almost all the places shown by Kaempfer had some sort of popular sacred character. Such were Baba Kuhi and its great cypress, the gorge Tang-e Allah -o- Akbar, the Chehel Maqam, the Chah-e Ghadir or Morteza Ali, the Qadamgah-e Khezr, and the Masjed-e Madar-e Soleyman. The sacred character of mountains, water sources, and trees were related to ancient Mesopotamian and Ariyan beliefs which were common to the people living in southern and eastern Iran and had survived in the local traditions. The sacred mountain, Rahmat, where the ancient Achaemenid kings had built their tombs is only a few kilometres away.

The sketch by Kaempfer regards the same landmarks and gardens shown later by le Bruyn, confirming that these were the most important ones throughout the Safavid period, as they were mentioned also by Pietro della Valle, Tavernier, and Chardin. But the above gardens were mostly in ruins in 1765, when Niebuhr travelled to Shiraz, and are not shown in his plan.[48]

To better perceive the structural elements of this landscape we should refer to later plans. Pascal Coste has drawn in 1840 a general plan entitled "Plaine de Chiraz," in which the city is shown in a plain surrounded by mountains to the north, west, and south and two rivers running eastwards to the salt lake Maharlu. The northern mountains are called Baba Kuhi, Kuh-e Chehel Maqam, and Kuh-e Saadi or Fahandar, the western one was called Kuh-e Darak or Qalat, and the southern ones were called Se Chenar, Siakh, or Qeble. At the foot of the mountains, where water sources were abundant, were the gardens.

---

[47] Kaempfer, British Library, Ms. Sloane 2912, fols. 39 and 39v: Kaempfer draws detailed views of the latter ancient ruins, known as Masjed-e Madar-e Soleyman and Qadamgah-e Khezr.

[48] Niebuhr, 97: "*de plusieurs batimens, qui étoient autrefois hors de cette porte, et près des montagnes d'environs, on ne voient plus rien que de tristes restes; et de tout le faubourg, qui a été entre icy et Schiras, il n'y a aussi plus rien que deux mosques.*"

The plan by Coste (figure 4),[49] together with the one by Chirikov and that by Sykes, of the neighbourhood of Shiraz (figure 5),[50] allow to speculate on the location of the main suburban gardens, mentioned in the accounts of travellers in the Safavid period, and to better understand their relation to the urban centre.[51] The principal suburban gardens belonged to governors or were built around the tombs of preachers (*sheykh*), devouts to mysticism (*sufi* and *aref*), descendants of Muhammad (*seyyed*), judges (*qazi*), philosophers (*hakim*) and poets. These were related to the city through the following connections: Raste-ye Mossala; Meydan-e Saadat; the road connecting to Saadiyye and Bagh-e Delgosha; the avenue leading to Bagh-e Takht; the Khiyaban connecting the Safavid palace of Emamqoli Khan to his suburban garden. What were the features of each of these connections?

Raste-ye Mosalla

Since ancient times, the road to Estakhr and Isfahan, from the northern gate bearing the same names, passed through the gorge between the mountains Baba Kuhi and Chehel Maqam called Tang-e Allah o Akbar. It was described by all the travellers in the Safavid period as *khiyaban*, or avenue, called also *raste* because of its straight layout, along which were laid numerous pleasure gardens and tomb gardens. *Khiyaban* was referred to as a public promenade used for picnics on the occasion of feasts which were, since ancient times, related to royal tombs or gardens.[52] The plain to the west of this avenue was called Mosalla and that to the east Jafarabad. These were irrigated by the qanat systems called Ab-e Rokny and Ab-e Zangy founded respectively by Rokn od-Dawle Deylami, and Atabak Zangy.

On the sixteenth of October 1621, Pietro della Valle described the main features of this avenue as being straight and long with gardens on its sides decorated with different buildings. After he had walked

---

[49] Pascal Coste, Voyage en Perse pendant les anées 1840–42. Perse Moderne (Paris, 1843–54) pl. 55.

[50] Sir Percy Sykes, *A History of Persia*, 2nd ed. (London, 1921), vol. 2: the plan shows the fights between the Indian Troops and the South Persia Rifles in 1918.

[51] See also: British Library, shelfmark 51140 (8), Map of southern Persia by haji Mirza Hasan Shirazi, known as Fssai, intended as a companion to Farsname ye Naseri (1293 HQ).

[52] Jallal Matini, "Khiyaban," *Irannameh* 1(1982): 57–99.

more than half the length of the avenue, he reached a great tank. This
tank was 80 paces long and 50 wide. The avenue was enlarged on the
sides of the tank, to make space for the passage, forming a square surrounded by a wall with arches and windows. On the western side, close
to the square, he mentions an old mosque built by a Kalantar, which
was the Shah Mir Hamze mausoleum.[53] Chardin's description of this
Raste casts light on some features shared with the famous Khiyaban-e
Chaharbagh in Isfahan: it was flanked by gardens, with great entrance
portals surmounted by pavilions, one in front of the other.[54] Le Bruyn
explicitly compares the Raste to Khiyaban-e Chaharbagh in Isfahan and
adds that it was in ruins.[55] He mentions the great basin at a distance
of 1500 paces from the gate at Tang Allah-o Akbar and refers to the
mausoleum of Shah Mir Hamze as a mosque, which had a front of
100 paces and was situated close to the bridge called Pol-e Shahzade.
A drawing by le Bruyn depicts the avenue looking towards the Tang of
Allah-o Akbar, with the Shah Mir Hamze mosque in the foreground.

Kaempfer adds to the above descriptions a drawing (figure 6),[56]
showing the plan of the section of the avenue with the great basin,
called *Daryacha Qorbungah*. The epithet *Daryacha*, lake, was a metaphor

---

[53] Pietro della Valle, Biblioteca Apostolica Vaticana, Ms. Ottob. Lat. 3382, fol. 154:
"*passato questo arco, si trova subito una strada lunga, larga, dritta, eguale e bellissima, con giardini
da una parte e dall'altra, ornati tutti da fabbriche diverse, che è la più bella cosa che sta in Shiraz.
Camminammo più della metà di questa strada fin dove si trova una grandissima peschiera d'acqua,
il cui vano è largo ottanta, e largo cinquanta passi dei miei; e perché occupa assai più loco, che la
larghezza della strada gli è fatto più strada larga attorno, con circuito di mura con archi e fenestre
in guisa d'una piazza seguitando poi, più a basso, la strada dritta come prima fin alla porta della
città. Vicino a questa peschiera fuor di strada alquanto a man sinistra presso a una meschita vecchia
e piccola che chiamano del Kalantar, per un Kalantar che la fabricò e c'è sepolto nella contrada della
Mussellè.*"

[54] Chardin, 9:176, "*La porte de la ville mène en une Rue qui est le plus bel endroit, étant long et
droite, large de cinquante pas, bordée de deux cotez de jardins de deux cens pas de face, dont les entrées
sont de grands Portails fait en demi dôme, avec des Pavillons au dessus vis à vis l'un de l'autre.*"

[55] Le Bruyn, 294: "*Après avoir passé cette porte, qui est grande & fort élevée, on trouve une
allée, nommée Teng- all-agber, bordée de bâtiments, à droite & à gauche, comme le Chiaer-baeg à
Isfahan; mais presque tous en ruine, de même que les jardins, qui sont encore remplis de beaux cyprès
& d'arbres fruitiers.*"

[56] Kaempfer, British Library, Ms. Sloane, 2912, fol. 34v, "Derjacza Kurbunga" *Der
erste theil dieser Allee heiset (:a ista plaga loci:) Rastai Musallà, gehed bis zu einer grossen 4draten
tang, 80 passum quadratum, so wegen ihrer grose mit dem nahmen eines kleinen meeres sat hyperbol-
icè beehert und deryache ye kurbunga genand wird. Worumb auch beyder seiten die Garten Mauren
eingezogen dem wegen um diese tange vollen raum zu geben! Die andere continuation dieses weges bis
zu der bruck furt von dem grosen spendiden beg . . . tempel der nahmen Rasty Scha Mir Hamsy sat zu
den seiten, tempels, gantz und wohn . . . unter denen sich Scha Mir Hamsy begrebnis velut lenta solent
inter viburna cupressi, sic hoc inter cypressos palatium, hervorthut ist ein solches gebau, tempel, area
vor geben, Nagarachony, tekiyè, alles zierlich mit weisen lateribus und vielen orten gegittert, aufgebauet.*

commonly used for great basins in this period. Kaempfer refers to the
section of the avenue from the gate Allah-o Akbar up to the square
with the great basin as *Raste-ye Mosalla*, and from this square to the
bridge as *Rasta-ye Shah Mir Hamze*, after the splendid mausoleum that
was on its eastern side. The name *Qorbungah* for the basin recalls the
place of martyrdom of Shah Mir Hamze, who was killed together
with his brothers in Shiraz.[57] Here, during the feast of *Eid-e Qorbun*,
animals were sacrificed.

The garden shown along the Raste, in front of the Daryache Qorbungah, belonged to Vizir Imani Beyk.[58] Kaempfer is the only traveller
who draws the plan of this garden in detail, showing:

> An entrance building, *emarat-e sardar* (a), that had a semi-octagonal layout,
> from which an avenue, *khiyaban*, led to a basin in front of a porch, *talar* (b);
> the main *khiyaban* of the garden, decorated with a water channel, two sets
> of 12 water jets, interspersed with a second basin, crossed a perpendicular
> one that led to a great basin (d) in front of the *haram* building (c).

An interesting element in the design of this garden is the *talar* (b), which
was composed of sixteen columns supporting the ceiling and was *not*
composed with a masonry building, as we find in the same period in
Isfahan. The poet Abdi Beyk refers to the use of such free standing
*talar*s in the gardens of Shah Tahmasb in Safavid Qazvin.[59]

A comparison between the entrance building, *emarat-e sardar*, of this
garden and that of the Bagh-e Bolbol in Isfahan confirms that there
were common features also in their architectural solutions.

In the representation of the plain of Shiraz, Pascal Coste shows
two pleasure gardens along the sides of this *khiyaban* that correspond
to the location of Bagh-e No and the present Bagh-e Jahan Nama.[60]
A view of Bagh-e No,[61] by Eugene Flandin, depicts an octagonal basin

---

*Wohin die leute ad orationes confluiren und unter dieses Grosen heiligen protextion tekiyè mizanent
i.e. ihre ruhe und sitz nehmen.*

[57] Afsar, 282, maintains that Qorbungah was the cemetery around the Bagh-e no,
where there was a great vault called Mosalla. The index of the Russian plan has the
name Qorbungah too.

[58] Kaempfer, British Library, Ms. Sloane 2912, fol. 34 "Vizir Imambek."

[59] Markazi Library, University of Tehran, Abdi Beyk, Ms. no. 2425.

[60] British Library, *Album of 58 views of Persia mostly made during the Ouseley Embassy of
Tehran (1810–12)*, shelfmark WD3274 fol. 44. A view an octagonal pavilion in masonry
surrounded, on the ground floor, by a wooden arcade is in the Album of D'Arcy, that
could be the pavilion of Jahan Nama.

[61] Eugéne Flandin and Pascal Coste, *Voyage en Perse pendant les années 1840 et 1842:
Perse Moderne* (Paris, 1843–54), pl. 85.

in front of the *talar* of its building that corresponds to descriptions of the works carried out in gardens of the Qajar period. This garden was built on the site of a Safavid garden about which we have no other documents.

To the east of the Raste were the tomb gardens, defined also as *tek-kiye*, Chehel Tan (40 bodies), Haft Tan (7 bodies), and Hafeziyye. When della Valle went back to Shiraz, in July 1622, he visited the sepulchre of the great poet Khwaje Hafez, located in a garden in the Mosalla quarter.[62] A drawing by Kaempfer shows the features of this garden in the Safavid period, prior to its twentieth century modifications (figure 7).[63] It should be remarked that all the travellers to Shiraz refer not only to the tomb of Hafez, but also to that of the other great poet, Saadi. Hafez is the most popular poet in Iran and most people know his poems by heart. Kaempfer highlights in his manuscript one of the reasons for his popularity, mentioning the fact that his poems are used as oracles. The garden was surrounded by a series of vaulted niches. A greater *eyvan* distinguished with letter (a) was the place where the holy Qur'an was read. It was planted mainly with cypress trees.[64]

Meydan-e Saadat and the Garden Chaharbagh

The Shayadan neighbourhood, outside the Saadat gate[65] was a cluster of gardens that is a *baghestan*. Among these gardens, there was a greater one near the bridge Shah Rostam, called by le Bruyn and Kaempfer Chaharbagh. Chardin who was in Shiraz before them draws a formally defined square, outside the Saadat gate, that constituted the vestibule to a great garden, situated in the same place as the above-mentioned Chaharbagh. This was probably the Meydan-e Saadat referred to in the chronicles as the place in which Amir Sheykh Abu Ashaq had built a

---

[62] At times Mossala is said to the area on both sides of the raste and not only to the western side In fact the tomb of Hafez that is to the east of the Raste is considered in the Mosalla quarter by Della Valle. "andai a veder vicino alla casa dove ero allogiato pur nel vicinato della Mussalà una meschita e cubbet (qobbe), che sta in un gran giardino adorno di molta fabrica dove è sepolto Chogia Hafez Poeta famoso tra Persiani."

[63] Kaempfer, British Library, Ms. Sloane 2912, fol. 37v.

[64] Kaempfer also reveals a curious method used by Persians who write the dates in verses, where the letters corresponding to specific numbers add up to the year of the event mentioned, that was in this case the year of death of the poet Hafez.

[65] This gate was between Isfahan and Saadi gates on the plan by Niebuhr and was also called Fahandar.

palace.[66] It was probably in the same site that previously a palace was built by Jalaleddin Shah Masud.[67]

The Meydan-e Saadat was destroyed because of a severe inundation in 1668, which could be the reason why neither Kaempfer nor le Bruyn mention it.[68] The Bagh-e Meydan referred to in *Zafarname* could be the same Chaharbagh.[69]

However, at the beginning of the Safavid period the Chaharbagh garden was extant. According to Herbert, the Ambassador Sir Dodmore Cotton had stayed there in 1627/1036 A.H., during the governorship of Emamqoli Khan, in a palace called Ali Khan which was a royal house surrounded by an immense garden to the east of Shiraz, the location of which corresponds to the above-mentioned Chaharbagh as shown in Chardin's view.

The Road to Saadiyye and Delgosha

Another structural element of the landscape of the northern plain of Shiraz was the road that led to Neyriz along which ran the water from the Saadi Qanat. It was also called Qanat-e Bandar or Fahandar after the ancient fortress built by Fahandar close to this site. Above this was also the fountain called Chah-e Mortaz Ali on the mountain Chehel Maqam where there was a small source of mineral water. A watercourse started in the strait between the Saadi and Chehel Maqam mountains to the east of the city and appeared in a basin known as Hawz-e Mahi, close to Saadi's tomb, standing somewhat apart from the gardens scattered in rich profusion in the plain below. After passing through some mills and irrigating Bagh-e Delgosha, the waters of the qanat entered the city from the Saadi or Gazorgah Gate.[70]

---

[66] Afsar, 103–104.

[67] Shirazname, 102–112.

[68] Niebuhr, "*Le tombeau du célèbre Poète de la Perse Hasjdse Hafês, étoit autrefois dans le faubourg de Schiras, aujourd'hui il est à un quart de lieu de la porte de la ville; et sur tout le chemin l'on rencontre plus un seul édifice, outre un grande mosquée, Schach Mir Hamza, indiquée sur la vue Table XXXVI... on trouve aussi près de ce lieu de prière (Musalla) une petite eau courante, qui prend son cours par un grand réservoir, et se divise ensuite dans les campagnes des environs. De la grande quantité de cyprès d'une grandeur extraordinaire, qui se trouvoient autrefois icy, la plus grande partie est abattue du temps des troubles intestines.*"

[69] Zafarname, 439.

[70] E. G. Browne, *A Year Amongst the Persians* (Cambridge, 1926), 304. See Danesh-pajuh, 203.

A view drawn by le Bruyn of the northeastern valley shows the sepulchre of Sheykh Saadi, Bagh-e Delgosha defined as the house of the
governor, and the above-mentioned Chaharbagh garden.[71] Pietro della
Valle[72] describes the sepulchre of Saadi behind which was a gathering
place of sufis *khaneqah* that he defines as a *madrasa*, and mentions the
basin full of fish also depicted by le Bruyn.[73]

Close to Saadi's tomb and along the watercourse running from the
Qanat-e Fahandar to Saadi gate there was a great garden that belonged
to the Kalantar Murtesa Quli Khan and was called Bagh-e Delgosha.
Kaempfer has drawn the plan of this garden showing its layout, before
the modifications in the nineteenth century (figure 8).[74] It was composed
of three walled spaces:

> The walled garden (G) with the great watercourse (k), that led to the
> basin (i), in front of the principal *talar* (h), of the *emarat* that opened into
> the second walled space that was a wine and chenar garden (E) with
> three *emarat*-s (f f f). There was a small basin in front of each of the
> four-*eyvan*-s of its central *emarat* (f); a third *emarat* (f) was along the wall
> of this garden, and a door (d) led to the courtyard (B) where the *haram*

---

[71] Le Bruyn, page 423. In the drawing by Le Bruyn the following places are
marked: "*1. Le chemin qui conduit à Isfahan; 2. une petit chapelle consacrée à la soeur d' Ali;
3. la Chappelle d'Elie; 4. Le Jardin de Chiaer-baeg; 5. Le Tombeau de Zeig-zady; 6. La maison
du Gouverneur; 7. Les Ruines des anciennes fortresses; 8. La riviere, où s'arrêtent les caravanes, en
allant & en revenant.*"

[72] Pietro della Valle, Biblioteca Apostolica Vaticana, Ms. Ottob. Lat. 3382, *fol.* 154:
"*10 luglio andai a vedere la sepoltura di Sceich Saadi poeta famoso Persiano, che sta un miglio o
poco più fuor della città di Sciraz…E' una fabrica grande, cioè una meschita scoperta in mezzo
alla quale è piantato un grand albero di cipresso, e sotto un'altra fabrica a man destra entrando che
è come una cappella grande contigua a detta meschita son la sepoltura del detto sceich al cospetto: la
tomba è di marmo di sopra perché era gia scoperta, hora è coperta con un coperchio di legno a guisa
d'una cassa et a dritta tutta da capo a piedi è incasso con molti epigrafi…e dietro alla sepoltura
del Sceich c'è una Medresse o loco di studio…inanzi all'entrata della meschita grande ma in terreno
più basso dove si scende per certi scalini c'è una peschiera rotonda d'acqua corrente, qual acqua dopo
haver piena detta peschiera corre in faccia a drittura con un grosso rivo sopra le sponde del quale di
qua e di la son fabricate con poco architettura certe botteghe che in altri tempi ci si faceva bazar ma
hora son disabitate e mezze distrutte.*"

[73] Le Bruyn, 418: "*On trouve aussi un autre édifice démoli dans la Plaine, & le Tombeau d'un
des premiers Poètes de la Perse nommée Siegzady, qui vivoit il y a environ 400 ans…On trouve, à
côté de ce Tombeau, un grand bassin octogone, dont l'eau est tiéde & remplie de poisson. Ce Bassin
est entouré d'une muraille basse, & l'eau qui en coule, du côté de la Ville, par-dessous un bâtiment,
forme plusieurs autres fontaines, qui se répandent ensuite au travers des Prairies…*"

[74] Kaempfer, British Library, Ms. Sloane, 2912, fol. 36v: "*Der Kelantar Wohn ist meo
judicio der aller beste in Chiras, w…von dem curieusen holdseeligen manne nicht nur alles costbar
extruirt, sondern auffscurieusen holdseeligen manne nicht nur alles costbar extruirt, sondern auffs
curieusenste unter halten wird*".

with the rooms (c) "camera gynaecei" were found and to which access was also provided through the portal (a).

Kaempfer adds another graphical source showing the above *emarat*, which was between the first and the second garden, described as "Asylgarten" or *khalvat khane* (figure 9).[75] It is interesting that the only building still in Bagh-e Delgosha has a similar elevation with a central *talar* surmounted by a room with a pitched roof. The structures to the side were, however, different. There were two rooms on each floor, while today there is only one, with a terrace on the upper floor on the sides of the central body. This garden was according to Kaempfer the best in Shiraz.

A specific Shirazi taste is revealed in the elevation of this *emarat*. Its *eyvan* does not follow the vaulted type that was common in the royal gardens of Isfahan, but is composed of two columns supporting a flat ceiling. A type that is used also in later Zand and Qajar buildings in Shiraz.

Bagh-e Delgosha was existing in the Timurid period and Sharafeddin Ali Yazdi mentions that Timur gathered in Herat the engineers and builders from east and west and built a garden with the same name, in the prairie called Kan-e Gol, according to the model of the garden he had stayed at in Shiraz.[76]

The features of the road that connected this garden to the city are not described and its plan does not follow a straight line. It does not however seem to have been a *khiyaban* as the Raste-ye Mosalla.

Avenue to Bagh-e Takht-e Qaradje

At the foot of the Baba Kuhi Mountain there was a great terraced garden called Bagh-e Takht-e Qaradje[77] that was created by Atabak Qaradje, close to the source of water on Baba Kuhi Mountain. Jean Aubin writes, Mirza Eskandar, son of Omar Shaykh, reigned in Fars

---

[75] Kaempfer, British Library, Ms. Sloane, 2912, fol. 36v: *"Der Kelantar Wohn ist meo judicio der aller beste in Chiras, w...von dem curieusen holdseeligen manne nicht nur alles costbar extruirt, sondern auffscurieusen holdseeligen manne nicht nur alles costbar extruirt, sondern auffs curieusenste unter halten wird"*.

[76] Zafarname, 2:13–15.

[77] Kaempfer, British Library, Ms. Sloane 2912, fol. 38: gives a description of this garden; see also *Shirazname*, 64.

from 1409 to 1414. In Shiraz he built the qale Jalali. His residence was
Takht-e Qaradje, situated to the north of the city. Antonio Tenreiro,
who visited it in 1524, says that its walls were two leagues around and
enclosed a marble palace, decorated with stucco motifs and coloured
faience, trees of all sorts, roses, avenues bordered by cypresses so great
that in the middle of the day it was in shadow, a great piece of water
in the centre of which was a richly decorated pavilion. When Niebuhr
visited the city this garden was in ruins.[78] It was later restored by Agha
Mohammad Khan Qajar and became famous as Bagh-e Takht-e Qajar.
Wilber has produced a plan of the latter garden in his book.[79] A beautiful view of Shiraz, in the album of D'Arcy in the British Library, shows
the city in the Qajar period, with the *haram* building of this garden in
the foreground on the mountain, overlooking an immense garden that
surrounded a great basin in the plain below (figure 10).[80]

However, a view by Hofsted van Essen shows (figure 11)[81] the above
garden as it was before the modifications in the Qajar period. The *talar*
in front of the great vaulted *eyvan* of the building, erected above the
upper terrace or *takht*, had a semi-octagonal plan. The terraced levels
between the lower garden and the *takht* were in ruins. The caption under
the view reads "Castel Fardous." Kaempfer informs us that the Takht-e
Qaradje was also called Bagh-e Ferdaws.[82] Tavernier who admires the

---

[78] Niebuhr, 135: "*Une demi lieue au nord de Schiras, devant une haute montagne, se trouve
un petit rocher, dont on a une fort belle vue vers la ville et vers la grande et fertile plaine, et dans le
lointain l'on voit les hautes montagnes. La situation de ce petit rocher a donc beaucoup de rapport avec
la situation de celui, sur lequel le Palais de Persepolis est batis. Un Mahometan avoit bati icy un
palais; mais si leger que l'on ne trouve plus rien de tout le batiment, que le pied d'une petit colonne et
on diroit, qu'il là cherché a Tschil Minar car il est du meme marbre dur et noir, dont faites les ruines
de Persepolis, au lieu que le rocher près de Schiras est une pierre blanche et pas dure. La montée à
cet edifice etoit une plaine penchente, soutenue d'une muraille de chaque coté.... Du coté de la pleine
campagne, et pour ainsi dire, sous l'edifice principal, l'architecte a taillé le rocher en forme de degrés,
et il a conduit une petite eau courante sous l'edifice, de sorte qu'il y avoit icy une jolie cascade; mais
celle cy n'est déja plus d'aucune utilité, puisque la source a repris son ancien cours. Pas loin de là
dans la plaine, l'on voit encore un grand reservoir, et il y a aussi des traces de jets d'eau.... Au bas
du rocher, on voit encore des voutes à moitié enforcées, qui selon toute apparence ont été des ecuries,
et des logemens pour des domestiques. Un peu plus haut sur la montagne, on trouve le tombeau d'un
pretendu saint Baba Queée, que les Mahometans vont visiter très souvent.*"

[79] Donald Wilber, *Persian Gardens and Garden Pavilions*, 2nd ed. (1962; Washington,
DC, 1979).

[80] British Library, *Album of 58 views of Persia mostly made during the Ouseley Embassy of
Tehran (1810–12)*, shelfmark *WD3274, fol. 37*.

[81] Kaempfer, British Library, Ms. Add. 14758, fol. 7.

[82] Kaempfer, British Library, Ms. Sloane 2912, fol. 34v: Kaempfer locates this
garden below the Baba Kuhi and defines it as "*Bagi Ferdos, ab tachta Karadjeb...Konig
Karadjeb.*"

remaining beauty of the building that overlooked the great basin adds that its gardens were planted with cypresses and those in Shiraz were "*les plus beaux du monde.*"[83] The descriptions by Don Garcias de Sylva y Figueroa, a Castilian noble dispatched as Ambassador by King Philip III who arrived to Shiraz in 1617,[84] and Le Bruyn[85] correspond to the view of Hofsted van Essen.

It is probable that Don Garcias de Sylva y Figueroa who was staying at Bagh-e Shah arrived at this garden through a road located in the same place that is indicated in Sykes' plan. Nevertheless, no other document shows an avenue in this place before Sykes. The plan by Coste shows a road coming from Shushtar that passed on the verge of the gardens at the foot of Baba kuhi and joined the Raste near Shah Mir Hamze. As we have no news of a bridge on the river Khoshk, at this point, it is possible that the avenue shown by Sykes is a recent one and that during the Safavid period it was this road that connected the hillside gardens to the city.

According to *Zafarname*, it was near Takht-e Qaradje that the *amir*s and *kalantar*s kissed the ground in the sign of submission to the army of Timur.[86] He created a garden with the same name on top of a mountain near Samarqand, recalling the model of the one he had stayed at in Shiraz.[87]

---

[83] Tavernier, 313.

[84] Figueroa, 129: "*au pied de cette montagne du coté par ou l'on vient de la maison ou l'Ambassadeur logeoit il y a un grand jardin d'arbre fruictiers & d' allées de cyprés et d'ormes, au bout duquel l'on voit un estang, qui est si grand, qu' il a cent trente pas en carré e plus d'une toise et demie de profondeur. L'eau, dont il y remply, descend d'un fort grand rocher, qui n'est qu' a vingt pas de là, sur lequel est une tres -vielle maison, dont la muraille est revestue du plus belle ouvrage de marqueterie qui se puisse voir; il en reste une partie debout, mais la pluspart en est ruinée. Elle a un petite portique,et au delà un grand quarré, ayant une fontaine, et à chaque costez deux chambres, dont l'une est mediocrement grande, et l'autre fort petite…Le portique et les fenêtres de la maison, donnent sur le grand éstang, sur le jardin et sur la ville, et forme une parfaitement belle vue de tous costez. Et encore que par le derriere regarde la montagne, l'on y puisse monter à cheval depuis le jardin et l'estang, parce que le roc y est fort uny jusqu' à la hauteur de trois piques, l'on monte neanmoins jusqu'à la moitié du chemin par un escalier taillé dans le roc mesme, et là il y a une grajde fontaine sous une vôute, d'où l'eau descend dans l'estang, et de là, parce qu' il n' y a plus de degré l'on monte jusqu' en haut par la mesme roc, iusq'à la maison…qui est une grande cour…*"

[85] Le Bruyn, "*On trouve, au pied de la Montagne, sur un petit rocher, les ruines d'un joly édifice, avec un grand bassin sans eau, et un grand jardin, remply de cyprès et d'autres arbres, avec de belles allées plantées au niveau; et au bout de celle du milieu, les ruines d'un autre édifice, qui répondoit au premier: ce Jardin étoit ceint d'une muraille de terre, mais il étoit en friche en ce tems- là, sans que personne en prit soin. Ce joly lieu se nomme Ferradous, ou le Paradis: il y a 200 ans qu 'il étoit habité par un Roy appellé Karagia.*"

[86] Zafarname, 1:316–320.

[87] Zafarname, 2:18.

Chardin mentions the Bagh-e Ferdaws as a garden close to Takht-e Padsha Kachal.[88] The latter garden is also mentioned by Tavernier.[89] It was laid out according to the same model of a terraced garden as Takht-e Qaradje and was probably created by Alyas Beyk Zolqadar who was famous as Kachal Beyk[90] and had ruled in Shiraz during the reign of Shah Esmail, the founder of the Safavid dynasty.

Coste shows in the Plaine de Chiras, Bagh-e No, Takht-e Qaradje and two other gardens at the foot of the mountain to the west of the Raste. One of these could be the place of the Takht-e Padshah Kachal which has probably changed name later.

The creation of a *takht* or *soffe* at the foot of a hill had its archetype in the Takht-e Jamshid. It was created by the Achaemenid kings for the celebration of the spring feast of *nawruz*. The rituals of this feast comprised sacrifices of cows and horses, visits to the tombs of ancestors in nearby sites, and illumination of their tombs. Takht-e Jamshid was, according to Mehrdad Bahar, a stone garden, created at the foot of a sacred mountain as the house of Gods. The mountain Baba Kuhi was also sacred and contained sacred water sources; it was, therefore, fit for creating the royal garden.

Khiyaban to Bagh-e Shah

Don Garcia de Silva y Figueroa gives a description of his arrival in Shiraz that is relevant for the placement of Bagh-e Shah and the *khiyaban* which linked this royal garden to the city. He entered Shiraz through Fasa Gate, to the southeast, crossed some winding streets and arrived at a Meydan where Allahverdi Khan was building a great mosque.[91]

---

[88] Chardin, 186: "*entre le midi et l'occident on decouvre diverse ruine, come d'un grand parc: celle de plusieurs hermitages et particulierement on en trouve qui sont remplies des marbre figurès ... Les persans appellent ces belle ruine tact padcha ketchel, le palais du rois teigneux, de quoi je n ai pu aprendre la raison. Il y a un grand jardin tout proche qu'il nomment Bag Ferdous, Le Jardin du Paradis et à demi lieue au de là une maison de plaisance, dont les murailles sont revetues de marqueterie d'un ouvrage merveilleux. Au milieu du jardin, il y a un quarré d'eau du cent trent pas de face et de neuf piés de profondeurs. On voit avec étonnement au coté occidental de ce palais, des vases de marbre noir très dur et très poli d'un prodigeuse grandeur. C'est entièrement la meme pierre et la meme ciseau q'au Persepolis.*"

[89] Tavernier, 317.

[90] Afsar, 122.

[91] Comentarios, fol. 72v: "*una plaça o terrero grande en que se stava acabando de fabricar una sumptuosissima mesquita que Alaverdecan dexo commencada toda de piedra blanca.*"

Hence, passing through a greater Meydan where the house of the Sultan was found he went through other similar streets to the opposite gate that was called "Darvaza Aheni," and looked to west-north-west. From this gate a large avenue of almost "2000 pasos long and 90 wide" led to a house of the king where the ambassador was lodged. The avenue was level, sided by walls of great orchards, with two leisure pavilions, also belonging to the king, at two thirds of the street, one in front of the other. This place was used for exercises on horses and at equal distances there were six[92] columns in white marble, two by two, that were used as goals for polo, *chawgan*.[93] Also, Tavernier described to the northwest of the city, an avenue that ended at a garden named Bagh-e Shah where three sets of columns, *mil*, were installed.[94] Four *mil*s were still extant in the 1990s: two were on the sides of the British Consulate (the location of which is shown on Sykes' plan),[95] and two at the northern end of Rudaki Street, after which the place was called *do mil*, that is "two columns."[96]

Chardin also mentions the Bagh-e Shah[97] and shows it in his view, outside the gate known also as Darak Musa in the Safavid period.

The Darvaze Ahani (literally, Iron gate), mentioned by Figueroa was, therefore, the same Bagh-e Shah gate on Niebuhr's plan. It is also found in the account of Cornelis Le Bruyn who, after describing the Raste-ye Mosalla, mentions another road across the river leading to the Ahani Gate.[98] It is possible that this "other road" was not the continuation of

---

[92] It is unusual to have six poles, as the game is played between two teams and two goals are needed.

[93] Comentarios, fol. 72v: "Portodla largura de la calle a espacios yquale ay en medio della dos en dos seys colonas de piedra de marmox blanco de dos pies de gruesso cada una y de altura de media pica apartadas una de otra quinze odiez y seys pasos sixuiendo de metas para los que andar a cavallo corriendo en los dichos exercicios."

[94] Tavernier, 309.

[95] This plan was drawn to show the line of the Indian troops and South Persia Rifles during the investment of Shiraz in 1918, as recorded by Brigadier-General Sir Percy Sykes, *A History of Persia* (London, 1921), "*We occupied a belt of walled gardens to the North West of Shiraz, which gave protection from all but distant Rifle fire... Between this cantonment and the city was open ground, perhaps half a mile wide. There was also a gap of perhaps a quarter of a mile between it and the garden quarter. The Consulate and Telegraph office were situated in the cantonment.*"

[96] Afsar, 166. The latter columns were later transferred to the entrance to Golestan St.

[97] Chardin, 182: "*Entre tous ces beaux et grands jardins on admire le Jardin Royale qui est un quarée d'environs mille pas detour. Les Grenadiers, l'orange et le citronier y sont en pleine terre... on y trouve aussi toutes les espèces d'arbres fruitiers de l'Europe....*"

[98] Le Bruyn, "*L'allée de Teng-alla-agber commence à ce Pont, & a 30 pas de large. On va de-là, par un autre chemin de la même étendue, à une des plus anciennes Portes de la Ville, nommée*

the Raste-ye Mosalla which ended at Isfahan gate, but led to Darvaze Ahani from outside the walls.[99] Thus, the Ahani gate should not be mistaken with the Isfahan gate. Chardin refers to both gates, *"au Nord, la porte d'Anamin* (Ahani) *et aussi la porte d'Ispahan."*

Pietro della Valle refers to the space in front of this royal garden, where the English stayed, as a "piazza," *meydan*, that was used as horse market and was the greatest he had seen in Shiraz.[100] Le Bruyn calls the "beautiful avenue" that connected Bagh-e Shah to the palace of Emamqoli khan in the city, *kuche bagh*. It should be remarked that this expression is commonly used for narrow streets delimited by garden walls, and it is rather in contrast with the width of the avenue that he measured as 95 paces wide and 966 long.[101]

These descriptions are supported by the only Safavid graphical document of the entrance of the garden of Emamqoli Khan, drawn by Kaempfer, where the poles for *chawgan* are shown in the foreground, but the length of the avenue leading to the garden was, according to Kaempfer, "700 ps" (figure 12).[102]

In the "Plaine de Chiras" by Pascal Coste, a rectangular space is shown outside the western gate that is labelled as "hippodrome."[103] A view of Shiraz by Flandin shows the space outside the gate of the city in the Qajar period. The only element visible of the hippodrome, along which the gardens were already destroyed, is the pole for the *qabaq-andazi* and the columns for *chawgan*. The Mamassani tower depicted in this view is also shown, close to the river, in Coste's "Plaine de Chiras," as

---

Dervaze Hanie, ou Porte de Fer, Laquelle est forte endommagée, & sert presentement de Bazar; elle est voutée & a 80 pas de long. Il y a plusieurs caractères turcs sur les murs de cette porte, & les débris d'une Tour au-dessus. On entre de là dans une grande rue, à la gauche de laquelle il y a un cimitiére, & un Jardin ruiné à droite, avec plusieurs édifices. Cette rue s'étend jusques au coeur de la Ville, qui a une petite lieue de tour."

[99] E. G. Browne, *A Year Amongst the Persians* (Cambridge, 1926).

[100] Pietro della Valle, Biblioteca Apostolica Vaticana, Ms. Ottob. Lat. 3382, fol. 154: *"Vidi un'altra piazza che è la più grande che io habbia veduto in Sciras, quale lo chiamano il bazar o mercato dei cavalli. Quivi è una casa del re con un gran giardino, che tra le fabriche di Sciras è delle migliori, dove hoggi hanno alloggiati gli Inglesi che quivi in Sciras tengono sempre casa e gente."*

[101] Le Bruyn, 421: *"On trouve, hors de la porte de Dervasi Bagh Zjia, au Nord-Ouest, la belle Allée de Kot-Zjia-Baeg (Kucheh Bagh), qui s'étend jusques au Jardin du Roy, qui a 95 pas de large sur 966 de long."*

[102] Kaempfer, British Library, Ms. Sloane 2912, fol. 35.

[103] Pascal Coste, *Voyage en Perse pendant les années 1840 et 1842. Perse Moderne* (Paris, 1843–54), pl. 84.

well as, in Sykes' plan. This landmark, together with a street that still bears the name Bagh-e Shah, is significant for locating the garden.[104]

Tavernier mentions the garden and its avenue, planted with cypress trees that led from the entrance building to another one, to the left of which was a great basin made of stones. He observed that the garden had a beauty that would not be remarkable in France. It was full of fruit trees, rosaries, and jasmines, but all without symmetry and alignment.[105] Nevertheless, this was what a garden was to Persians. In fact, le Bruyn, who happened to be there on the 22nd of March, during the feast of Nawruz, remarks that people from every corner had chosen the place for their pleasure and its avenues were as crowded as a marketplace.[106]

Kaempfer is the only traveller who has drawn the layout of Emamqoli Khan's garden and the two elevations "facies binae" of its pavilion (figure 13).[107] The plan of Bagh-e Shah shows:

> an entrance building defined as *Vestibulum* or *portal amouret* (h) from where a Khiyaban lined with cypress trees (c.c.c.) leads to an octagonal *amouret* (a), to the left of which lies a great basin (b) measuring "90 ps. quadrati." In front of the entrance building there were two columns for the game of *chawgan* (i i).

Many of these features correspond to the description that the Spanish Ambassador gives of the above garden in the entrance building of which he was lodged.[108] The garden was made of many walks creating

---

[104] In a modern plan of Shiraz, along the Boulevard Karimkhan Zand between the Falake Setad and Falake Tamasha, the fourth crossing street, parallel to Moshir Fatemi, is called Bagh-e Shah. The next street, Molla Sadra was later changed to Namazi. See also Ariyanpur, 148.

[105] Tavernier, 310: "*mais tout cela est confus, sans aucun alignement ni symétrie.*"

[106] Le Bruyn, 421: "*Après avoir traversé le Vestibule de la Loge, qui est au bout de ce jardin, on entre dans un autre belle Allée, bordée de cyprés, qui a 620 pas de long & 20 de large, & est remplie de fleurs au milieu. On y trouve une belle maison, entourée d'un beau Canal; & deux Fontaines, à chaque coin du bâtiment, qui mêlent leur eaux à celle du Canal. Cette maison est spacieuse, & a au milieu un grand salon, couvert d'un dôme, remply de niches en dehors. Avant d'entrer dans cette maison, on voit à gauche un bassin quarré, dont les angles ont 85 pas de long. Cette belle Allée est bordée, de part & d'autre, de 72 beau cyprés, dont il y en avoit 22 paumes de circonférence. Il y a une autre Allée, bordée de cyprès & de senez, derriere la maison, de l'etendue des autres. Ce Jardin se nomme Baeg Siae, ou le Jardin Royal. Je m'y trouvay le 22 de Mars, Fête de Nouw-roes, pendant laquelle on s'y rend de tous côtez pour se divertir, de sorte que les Allées en ressembloient à une Foire.*"

[107] Kaempfer, British Library, Ms. Sloane 2912, fol. 35v.

[108] Don Garcia de Silva y Figueroa, *L'ambassade de D. Garcias de Silva Figueroa en Perse,* 109–112: "*...la porte du Palais Royal, auquel aboutissoit cette grande & belle rue...en cette endroit-là l'on montoit, par deux marches, sur une petite terrasse, plus elevée que le reste de la rue...A l'entrée & au portique du Palais, au milieu de cette terrasse, il y avoit un estang ocatgone...La maison où*

a grid of plots full of fruit trees, the main walk, being over "900 paces long and 30 wide,"[109] lined with cypress and plane trees, led from the entrance building to the pavilion in the middle of the garden used as *haram*. The pavilion was built on a raised platform that was 40 feet larger and flanked on each side with ten small octagonal basins linked by a small water channel.[110] From here a perpendicular walk led to a basin in which boats were kept for the pleasure of the women.

A miniature depicting Emamqoli Khan in a boat surrounded by servants[111] recalls the passage in the account of Don Garcia de Silva y Figueroa where he describes the basin in front of the *haram* building, saying that it was elevated on three sides and that its water could be reached through a set of steps in the shape of a theatre, wherein the ladies could take the pleasure of boating.[112]

---

l'Ambassadeur logeoit, & le jardin, dont elle estoit accompagnée, est un ouvrage du grand Ismael Sop. hi.... Elle est bastie comme une tour, & est à trois estages, où l'on monte par de petite escaliers etroits à vis.... Au seconde estage...il y a un beau salon...au milieu duquel est un dôme voûté, qui couvre toute la salle...Entre les balcons, dont cette Maison de plaisance est ceinte, il y a deux qui sont plus grands que les autres. L'un est sur la porte de la Maison, & donne sur la rue...la muraille, qui fait le frontespice de la Maison, n'est point droite, mais oblique & de travers, ayant aux deux costez deux galeries plus petites...L'autre gallerie ou balcon, opposé a celuy dont nous venons de parler, est sur la porte, par laquelle on entre dans le jardin, & donne sur le jardin de la mesme facon que l'autre...& ayant de chaque costé une gallerie plus petite, lesquelles aussi bien que le balcon sont vis a vis d'une belle allée de gros cyprés & de planes...Chacune de ces deux grandes galleries a trois portes, sur une mesme lignes...Et du centre de la mesme sale...l'on découvroit pas seulement la rue & l'alee, mais l'on voyoit aussi le bout jusqu' à la porte de la Ville, & à celle de l'Arame, ou du Serrail qui est au milieu, & comme au centre du jardin..."

[109] Figueroa, 112.

[110] Figueroa, 113: *"Au bout de cette allée est l'Arame, ou le Serrail...qui est une maison bastie de la mesme forme & structure que l'autre; mais elle n'est pas si grande ny si haute;...Ce Serrail est basty sur une terrasse, qui est élevée du reste du jardin de sept pieds, & massonnée de grosses briques carrées, & elle est si grande, qu' outre ce que les fondaments du batiment occupent, elle a encore quarante pieds de large de chaque costé, & en cet espace dix petits estangs octangulaires, qui ont environ une demy toise de profondeur. Ils se communiquent leurs eaux, qui sont fort belles & claires, par de petits ruisseaux, qui passent des une aux autres, & ont environ un demy pied de large & de profoud."*

[111] A miniature in the British Library, Ms. Sloane, Add. 7801, fol. 49: copy of *Jarunnama*, reproduced in Barbara Schmitz, "On a Special Hat Introduced During the Reign of Shah Abbas the Great," *Iran* 22 (1984): 103–112, depicts Emamqoli Khan in a boat surrounded by servants.

[112] Figueroa, 115–116: *"A soixante ou soixante & dix pas du Serrail, ou Arame...il y a un grand & bel Estang, auquel on monte par quatre ou cinq degrez, & à l'entour il y a un passage de brique carrées, comme celuy qui ceinte le bastiment, de plus de vingt pieds de large; & l'Estang qui est carré, en ayant plus de cent entre les deux angles de chaque flanc, qui sont revetus de marbre, & plus de trois toises de profondeurs, fournit une tres belle promenade. De trois en trois pieds il y a un degré, qui en a autant de large, fait en forme de theatre, par lequel l'on descend à l'eau, dans laquelle il y a deux grandes barques, pour la promenade & le divertissement des Dames, quand il y en a dans le Serrail.... Cet Estang estoit élevé de la terre de quatre ou cinq degrez, mais ce n'estoit que de trois costez, & dechargeoit, par un ruisseau de plus de trois pieds de large & d'un & demy de profondeur...Et*

Pir-e Bonab and Bagh-e Vahsh

To the southwest of Shiraz, at a natural source of water, there was a hermitage called "Peer Bouno" or Pyr-e Bonab (*bonab* means source of water) where a few dervishes stayed. Tavernier underlines the fact that the dervishes chose the most agreeable places for their retreats. It may be recalled that water sources were sacred places and the most appropriate place for creating a garden which was since ancient times considered as the house of gods. Therefore, when Emamqoli Khan created along the watercourse a great enclosure for a park where he had gathered numerous animals, we may speculate that he was repeating the ancient ritual of creating a *pairidaeza* similar to the one depicted at Taq-e Bostan where the Sassanid king was hunting. The garden created by Emamqoli Khan was known as Bagh-e Vahsh and was already in ruins when Tavernier visited it.[113] Pascal Coste, in his "Plaine de Chiras", shows a garden on this site. It was connected to the city through a road that led to Darvaza Kazerun.

Comparison of the relation between the gardens and the city in Shiraz and Isfahan

The plan of Shiraz and its surroundings shows that the gardens outside the urban fabric were created near the natural water sources or where qanats appeared on the surface. The whole plain was dotted with gardens. In particular on the slopes of the hills which bound it towards the west, there was a compact mass of them extending towards northwest to Masjed-e Bardi. The location of the gardens was, therefore, closely related to the natural conformation of the oval plain surrounded by mountains on three sides and the watercourses that ran towards the lower eastern side forming the lake Maharlu.

---

cette mesme eau, apres avoir traverse l'estang, en sort par un autre ruisseau, vis à vis du premier, & *de la mesme facon, dans laquel elle entre en descendant jusq'au niveau du jardin, par une ouverture* *que l'on a fait dans le marbre, dont l'estang est revetu, de la largeur du ruisseau...taillée en forme* *de coquilles; en sorte que l'eau qui y passe, forme en ce petit espace, plusieurs belle & agreables veues,* *comme dans un tres parfait cristal."*
[113] Tavernier, 317.

Shiraz had with the capital Isfahan in common that the most important garden sites were connected to the city through *khiyaban*s and *meydan*s.

The Raste-ye Mossala was, as already remarked, explicitly compared by the European travellers to the Khiyaban-e Chaharbagh in Isfahan (figure 14).[114] Both avenues were flanked by gardens; their entrance buildings were situated symmetrically with rooms on the upper floor looking towards the avenues. Their straight layout and considerable width was also a common feature. If we compare this Raste to any other connection in the old city, we can understand the strength of its design. In fact, the European travellers underline clearly this feature in their views of Shiraz. This is a feature that was particularly appreciated by the Europeans, as in the same period promenades were becoming popular in Rome, Naples, and Paris.

However, there were substantial differences between the Khiyaban in Shiraz and that of Isfahan. In Isfahan the decision of choosing the city as the capital gave place to the creation of a garden city to the south of the Selgiuchid one. The Khiyaban-e Chaharbagh constituted the backbone of this addition. It connected the palace of Shah Abbas to the royal suburban garden across the river. Along this promenade, that was a true elongated garden with different basins and plane trees *chenar*, the emirs and dignitaries of the court created their own gardens.

It defined not only the orientation of the gardens flanking its sides, but generated the grid of perpendicular streets in the adjacent quarters. The water channels, *madi*, that ran parallel to the river Zayande and perpendicular to the promenade also delineated this grid. The Khiyaban in Shiraz did not have the same impact. In fact it was created along the existing road between Shiraz and Isfahan, where in time sepulchre gardens had developed and a few pleasure gardens were added. But the Raste could not have the same structural role of the Khiyaban-e Chaharbagh in Isfahan. It is true that traces of the gardens and *tekiyye*s on the sides of both avenues have survived to the present time due to the great size of the properties, but obviously the impact of the Khiyaban on the urban form was stronger in Isfahan than in Shiraz. Besides, the gardens flanking the Raste of Shiraz were situated along the watercourse and did not create a similar extended impact except for the area of the *baghestan*, along the river Khoshk. The plan of Safavid Shiraz clearly

---

[114] Mahvash Alemi, Plan of Safavid Isfahan.

reveals the structure of the connections between the main garden sites and the city. Gardens were created close to water sources at the foot of the mountains that surrounded the plain on three sides and along the river Khoshk. The result was a landscape that conveys a more natural order in comparison to the grid of the garden city of Isfahan.

Moreover, the gardens around Shiraz, although numerous, were not comparable to the royal addition of Isfahan where the system of royal and court gardens constituted a true garden city conceived altogether. In Shiraz, the gardens of governors were created in different sites along different watercourses. The western avenue that led towards Bagh-e Shah was, though on a much smaller scale, the only avenue comparable to the model of Khiyaban-e Chaharbagh in Isfahan which ended at the Royal garden Bagh-e Hezar Jarib.

Another common feature mentioned by the travellers was that a *meydan*, like the one in front of the royal palace, *dawlatkhane*, in Isfahan, was created in Shiraz as the vestibule to the palace of Emamqoli Khan. Furthermore, in Shiraz there were arcades along the sides of the Meydan and a high loggia where music was played. It was also related to the mosque and the Bazaar, but there is no news of *chawgan* being played there. The space for these exercises was instead provided in front of the vestibule of the royal garden, Bagh-e Shah, where Kaempfer shows the poles for polo.

On the contrary, the Meydan in Isfahan was the setting for such royal rituals as *chawgan* and *qabaq andazi*. These rituals of imperial grandeur referred to established models and traditions that were mostly defined in ancient times. Safavids had restored many of the ancient rituals, particularly those related to a royalty that was conferred by divine will. The king playing *chawgan* in the Meydan manifested his power and bravery. These rituals, symbols of sovereignty and divinity, were significantly influential in the planning and architecture of Isfahan. There was, therefore, in this sense a substantial diversity between the Meydan in Shiraz and the one in Isfahan.

In a few words, although the *khiyaban*s and *meydan*s connecting the suburban gardens and the city of Shiraz were similar in their physical features to some aspects of the ones in Isfahan, nevertheless, these spaces did not play the same symbolic role; just as the governor who ruled in Shiraz was appointed by the king and could in no way compete with his sovereignty and divinity.

Shiraz had, however, its own specific features. The views of the city reveal that one of the main features of its landscape was the overwhelming presence of cypresses in the gardens of Shiraz. The *sarv-e naz* of Shiraz was famous in Iran. It was not only used in the sepulchre gardens but also in the pleasure gardens along the main walks. There were also vineyards from which the famous wine of Shiraz was produced as well as roseries from which rosewater was extracted.

But the most important feature of Shiraz was that people visited and still visit the sepulchre gardens of the poets, shaykhs, sufis, *arefs*, *seyyeds*, *qazis*, *hakims* in the baghestan to the north of the city, as well as the many shrines inside the city walls, not only because they loved and venerated the poets or saints but because these rituals were intertwined with entertainment, eating, and drinking. In many of these gardens the poor were given food, and these visits helped their desires to come true.

Shiraz had the epithet of Dar-ol Elm, that is, "the abode of knowledge," because it was the home of numerous shaykhs, philosophers, and mainly of the two great poets, Saadi and Hafez, who were buried there.

It was mostly these sepulchre gardens that added to its fame as the city of *gol o bolbol*, that is, the city of "roses and nightingales," or, in other words, the city of gardens and poets.

MUGHAL AGRA: A RIVERFRONT GARDEN CITY

Ebba Koch

Introduction

The contribution of the Mughals to the "Islamic city" is as yet not sufficiently understood, the attention of scholars having been focused on Shah Jahan's Shahjahanabad laid out from 1639 onwards in the area of Delhi, the old capital of the sultans.[1] (Gaborieau in this volume.) It is suggested here that Agra, the first capital of the Mughal empire, represented the most original urban planning achievement of the Mughals, in a consistently developed scheme, which has the riverfront garden as a modular unit.

Agra, the city of the Taj Mahal, was founded long before the Lodi Sultans made it their seat of government in 1505.[2] Twenty years later, in 1526, when the Mughals established themselves in Hindustan, Agra became the first capital of the Mughal empire and acquired during this period its distinctive character as a riverfront garden city. The Mughals, coming from Central Asia via Kabul were used to reside in formally planned gardens. Babur, the founder of the Mughal dynasty, and his followers, began to lay out gardens "on the model of Khurasani edifices" along the available water source at Agra, the large slow flowing river Yamuna, Jamna, or Jawn, as the Mughals called it.[3] The Timurid

---

[1] See e.g. S. P. Blake, *Shahjahanabad: The Sovereign City in Mughal India 1639–1739*, Cambridge South Asian Studies 49 (Cambridge, New York, Melbourne: Cambridge University Press, 1991).

[2] There are only a few works on pre-Mughal and Mughal Agra; see in particular S. Muhammad Latif, *Agra: Historical and Descriptive* (1896; rpt. Lahore: Sandhu Printers, 1981); H. R. Nevill, *Agra: A Gazetteer* (Allahabad: Superintendent Government Press, United Provinces, 1921); Abdul Aziz, "The City of Agra at the Beginning of Shah Jahan's Reign," in "A History of the Reign of Shah Jahan," *Journal of Indian History* 7 (1928): 128–147; Mahdi Husain, "Agra before the Mughals," *The Journal of the United Provinces Historical Society* 15, no. 2 (1942): 80–87; I. P. Gupta, *Urban Glimpses of Mughal India: Agra: The Imperial Capital, 16th & 18th Centuries* (Delhi: Discovery Publishing House, 1986).

[3] Babur, *Babur-Nama (Memoirs of Babur)*, trans. from the original Turki text of Zahiru'd-din Muhammad Babur Padshah Ghazi by A. S. Beveridge (1921; rpt. New Delhi: Oriental Books Reprint, 1970), 531–533; Zayn Khan, *Tabaqat-i Baburi*, English trans. Sayyid Hasan Askari, annotated by B. P. Ambastha (Delhi: Idarah-i Adabiyat-i Delli, 1982), 160 ff.

concept of a formally planned garden was creatively adapted to a riverfront situation.

At the beginning of the seventeenth century, Mughal Agra was "a wonder of the age—as much a centre of the arteries of trade both by land and water as a meeting-place of saints, sages and scholars from all Asia...a veritable lodestar for artistic workmanship, literary talent and spiritual worth."[4] The English observer John Jourdain who saw it in 1611 considered "This Cittie of Agra," as "one of the biggest in the world" and "by reporte farre greater then Grand Cairo."[5] The German traveller Johann Albrecht von Mandelslo judged it in 1638 "at least twice as big as Ispahan"[6]; its population was then estimated to 700,000.[7]

The nucleus of Agra was formed of gardens lining the river Jamna on both sides; the remaining city encircled the waterfront scheme in the west. The gardens constituted the residences of the imperial family and the highest-ranked nobles, some of the sites had been transformed into funerary gardens. It has not been fully understood by previous scholars that the centre of the city had, thus, a suburban character;[8] and that the waterfront garden represented the microscopic module of this urban landscape. No individual or prominent site was chosen for the Taj Mahal, it was integrated into the riverfront scheme. The city reflected the concept of the garden as primordial residence of the Mughal dynasty and in a wider ideological sense served as a symbol of the bloom of Hindustan under the just rule of Shah Jahan.

---

[4] Abdul Aziz, "City of Agra," 129.

[5] *The Journal of John Jourdain 1608–1617*, ed. William Foster (Cambridge: Hakluyt Society, 1905), 162.

[6] *The Voyages and Travels of J. Albert [sic] de Mandelslo into the East Indies*, English trans. John Davies of Kidwelly, 2nd ed. (London: J. Starkey, 1669), 35; quoted in Abdul Aziz, "City of Agra," 136.

[7] Abdul Aziz, "City of Agra," 138; Gupta, *Urban Glimpses*, 31.

[8] See e.g. Gupta, *Urban Glimpses*, 15, 19–20, 69, also his maps 1 and 2 should be used with caution. I began to analyze the riverfront scheme in several publications for which see note 30 below. The fullest treatment is provided in Chapter I of my *The Complete Taj Mahal and the Riverfront Gardens of Agra* (London: Thames and Hudson, 2006) 29–81.

1. *The components of the urban scheme*

The Mughal garden (figure 1)

Babur, and this is well known, informs us in his autobiography about his attempts to introduce the Persian Timurid garden tradition of his native Central Asia into Hindustan.[9] Babur calls his first garden at Agra, laid out in 1526, a *chahar bagh*, like some of his earlier gardens in present-day Afghanistan. In its strictest interpretation the much-discussed term *chahar bagh*, or its abbreviated form *charbagh*, designates a cross-axial four-part garden. Babur, however, uses the term in its widest sense, for large architecturally planned gardens with intersecting, raised, paved walkways, platforms, and pools.

After Babur the Mughals did not use the term *chahar bagh* very much; in Shahjahani sources it is employed metaphorically, for the earth or the terrestrial, "the *chahar bagh* of the world,"[10] and a garden was usually called just *bagh*, garden. Still, though they did not use the term, the Mughals built the grandest and most consistently planned *chahar baghs* in the entire history of garden architecture. We can identify three formal variants of the Mughal *chahar bagh* or *charbagh*:

1) In its ideal form the Mughal *charbagh* consists of a square, which is divided by cross-axial paved walkways (*khiyaban*)[11] into four equal parts. The symbolically highly charged centre is usually occupied by a garden pavilion (*'imarat, nashiman*) but a pool (*hawz*) is also possible.

---

[9] See note 3.

[10] "For insightful persons, it is clear that the gestures of the *padshahs* of pure spirits, who are like water to the *chahar bagh* of the world, and the acts of the *shahinshahs* of bright hearts, who are like the sun for the sky of world rulership, are not at all devoid of wisdom." My trans. with the help of Dr. S. M. Yunus Jaffery, from Muhammad Salih Kanbo, *'Amal-i Salih or Shah Jahan-nama*, Persian text rev. and ed. Wahid Qurayshi based on the Calcutta edition of 1912–46 by Ghulam Yazdani, 2nd ed., 3 vols. (Lahore: Majlis-i Taraqqi-yi Adab, 1967–72), vol. 1 (1967): 270.

[11] In the use of the Mughal terms I follow the practice of Shahjahani authors, in particular the official historian 'Abd al-Hamid Lahawri, *Badshah-nama*, Persian text ed. M. Kabir al-Din Ahmad and M. 'Abd al-Rahim (Calcutta: Asiatic Society of Bengal, 1867–72), or the self-appointed chronicler Kanbo, *'Amal-i Salih*, who give us the most detailed and consistent architectural terminology in their descriptions of the emperor's building projects. See Ebba Koch, *Mughal Architecture: An Outline of Its History and Development, 1526–1858* (1991; 2nd ed. New Delhi: Oxford University Press, 2002), 96, 143. On Shah Jahan's historians see Stephan Conerman, *Historiographie als Sinnstiftung: Indo-persische Geschichtsschreibung während der Mogulzeit, 932–1118/1516–1707* (Wiesbaden: Reichert Verlag, 2002), in particular 101–109, and 125–126.

The walkways may contain sunk channels (*nahr*), and, at the points where the walkways meet the garden wall, may be placed real or false gateways (*darwaza*). The quadrants of the garden may in turn be subdivided so that multiples of the squares are created. The garden is enclosed by a wall (*diwar*) with towers or tower pavilions (*burj*) at its corners.

2) The second type is the terrace garden which the Mughals had developed in Kashmir by introducing the Central Asian concept of a garden laid out on a hill slope into the mountainous landscape of the valley. The main buildings are arrayed on ascending terraces (*martaba*) along the central axis formed by a water channel (*nahr*) which collects the waters of a spring. The garden is also walled in. The terrace garden represents a *charbagh* in the loose sense of the word. The individual terraces may, however, be given the canonical four-part form.

3) The third Mughal garden type is the waterfront garden.[12] It represents a variant of the *charbagh* invented by the Mughals for the specific geographical conditions of Hindustan, that is the Indo-Gangetic plain. Here the main water source was not a lively spring on a mountain slope but a large slow-flowing river, from which the desired running water had to be brought into the garden by means of water lifts. Accordingly, the Mughals conceived a garden type to take advantage of the waterfront situation; the main building was not placed in the centre of the garden as in the classical Mughal *charbagh*, but was arranged on an oblong open terrace (*kursi*) along the riverfront. Usually the terrace had subterranean rooms below the main building and stairs providing access from above to a landing. This shift towards the riverfront which went hand in hand with the opening of the garden provided the main pavilions with the climatic advantages of running water. It generated also a carefully composed front to those who saw the garden from a boat or across the river. The waterfront structures could be viewed from both sides: from inside, the buildings provided an equally satisfying backdrop for the garden.

The waterfront garden became the favourite plan of the residential gardens of Agra and reached its grandest expression in the Taj

---

[12] Ebba Koch, "The Mughal Waterfront Garden," in "Gardens in the Time of the Great Muslim Empires: Theory and Design," ed. Attilio Petruccioli, *Muqarnas* Supplements, vol. 7 (Leiden, New York, Cologne: Brill, 1997), 140–160; rpt. in Ebba Koch, *Mughal Art and Imperial Ideology* (New Delhi: Oxford University Press, 2001), 183–202.

Mahal. After having been idealized and monumentalized in the Taj Mahal the waterfront garden became an imperial prerogative; at Shah Jahan's new city, Shahjahanabad (1639–48), it was used almost exclusively for the gardens and courtyards of the emperor's riverfront palace, the Red Fort. The nobles had to build within the city.

Plantation

While we are informed in detail about the architectural features of Mughal gardens, the sources tell us less about what was planted and where. Gardens were expected to be not only beautiful but also useful; they were planted with decorative and good smelling trees, flowers, and bushes, and also with fruit trees. The fruit harvest from the Taj Mahal garden, for instance, continued from Mughal times into the British period.[13]

The garden pavilion

The favourite Mughal garden pavilion was a centrally planned building; in Persian it was called *hasht bihisht* which means Eight Paradises. The design comprised nine parts, a domed chamber in the centre, rectangular open halls in the middle of the sides, and square rooms, often domed and two-storied, at the corners. The central chamber is connected to the axial halls in a cross-axial pattern (+). In the radially planned versions of this scheme another cross axis (x) is introduced through additional diagonal passages which link the corner rooms to the main domed chamber. The term *hasht bihisht* refers to the eight rooms, surrounding the hall in the centre.

In sixteenth and early seventeenth century Mughal architecture the design was the most popular form for pavilions as well as mausolea which were seen as a funerary form of a garden pavilion.[14] Later in the seventeenth century, in the architecture of Jahangir and Shah Jahan central plans were increasingly abandoned for residential pavilions and replaced by structures showing large halls flanked by side rooms. This form appears in the riverfront pavilions of Agra. The *hasht bihisht* continued however to be used for tombs, several mausolea of riverfront Agra are built on this plan. The *hasht bihisht* tomb is usually set in the

---

[13] Koch, *The Complete Taj Mahal*, 101, 139, 233.
[14] Koch, *Mughal Architecture*, 45–50.

middle of a funerary *charbagh*, but in the Taj Mahal it appears most grandly on the terrace of a riverfront garden.

Tower pavilions (burj)

Elaborate tower pavilions were and still are a characteristic feature of the waterfront scheme of Mughal Agra. They have their origin in for-tificatory architecture and were adapted to function as garden pavilions in that their (upper) stories were opened with arched niches or pillared galleries which surrounded an inner octagonal chamber. The top was formed by a *chhatri*, a pillared and domed kiosk. In a characteristic Shahjahani waterfront garden the towers accentuated the beginning of the enclosure walls which surrounded a garden on its three landward sides. In this way they framed the open riverfront terrace, in the centre of which stood the main garden pavilion.

Agra's riverfront presented itself as a sequence of such elevational modules, of a pavilion or house flanked by towers (figure 2).

2. Urban development

When Babur took Agra in May 1526 he initiated a remodelling of its urban landscape. For him, as a Timurid, gardens were the preferred type of residence and since none, or none to his taste, were available at Agra, his first enterprise was to create a garden in the city.[15] Babur deplored the lack of running springs and streams, which he consid-ered indispensable for such a project and found it difficult to reconcile himself to the idea of having to make with a large slow-flowing river, the Jamna and its surrounding terrain.[16] Overcoming his scruples, he founded the primordial Mughal garden of Agra, the Charbagh, also

---

[15] T. W. Lentz, "Memory and Ideology in the Timurid Garden," and Anthony Welch, "Gardens That Babur Did Not Like: Landscape, Water, and Architecture for the Sultans of Delhi," both in *Mughal Gardens: Sources, Places, Representations, and Prospects*, ed. J. L. Wescoat and Joachim Wolschke-Bulmahn (Washington, D.C.: Dumbarton Oaks Research Library and Collection, 1996), 31–58 and 59–94. Welch traces the Sultanate gardens only up to the fourteenth century and does not include the gardens of the Lodis, the immediate precursors of Babur.

[16] Babur, *Babur-Nama*, 531–532, cf. Babur, *The Baburnama: Memoirs of Babur, Prince and Emperor*, trans., ed., and annot. Wheeler M. Thackston (New York: Oxford University Press; Washington D.C.: Smithsonian Institution, 1996), 359–360.

called Bagh-i Hasht Bihisht, on the left bank of the Jamna, opposite to the fort of the Lodi's and the existing city.[17] His followers also laid out gardens "on the model of Khurasani edifices," as Babur's companion Zayn Khan tells us.[18] The people of Agra nicknamed the stretch with the new gardens "Kabul" which shows that they considered the development of the left bank of the river as new and foreign.[19]

Babur's activation of the riverfront set, thus, a new accent of urban planning in Hindustan, and it was also to have a decisive impact on the design of Mughal gardens of the plains. It led to the creation of the waterfront garden, as a module of the waterfront city (figure 3). [20]

The development of Agra as a riverbank city was taken up again by Akbar (r. 1556–1605). Humayun had chosen Delhi as his residence and planned to build a new city there but the plan was abandoned because of his exile in Iran. In 1558, Akbar moved the court again to Agra and the city grew in size, wealth, and power. His historian Abu'l Fazl tells us that "abodes (*manazil*) were distributed to the grandees" and that "on either side [of the river] the servants of fortune's threshold [i.e. the court] erected pleasant houses and made charming gardens."[21] Under Jahangir the riverfront scheme was fully developed. In the 1620s the Dutch trader Francisco Pelsaert observed that

> The breadth of the city is by no means so great as the length, because everyone has tried to be close to the riverbank, and consequently the waterfront is occupied by the costly palaces of all the famous lords, which make it appear very gay and magnificent.[22]

In Pelsaert's eyes "the luxuriance of the groves all round makes it resemble a royal park rather than a city." He lists 33 gardens with their names; about a third of them were created or remodelled during Jahangir's reign.

---

[17] Scholars like Abdul Aziz, "City of Agra," 132–135, and Gupta, *Urban Glimpses*, 12, have followed Abu'l Fazl who says that the fort of the Lodis was on the eastern side of the river which is clearly a mistake, because Babur tells us that he set out from the Lodi fort, where he had first taken up residence, across the river to find a place for his garden, and the gardens of his followers.

[18] Zayn Khan, *Tabaqat-i Baburi*, trans. Sayed Hasan Askari [in English], annot. B. P. Ambastha (Delhi: Idarah-i Adabiyat-i Delli, 1982), 160f.

[19] Babur, *Babur-Nama*, 532.

[20] For this and the following, see Koch, "Waterfront Garden."

[21] Shaykh Abu'l Fazl 'Allami, *Akbar-nama*, trans. H. Beveridge [English trans. in 3 vols.] (1902–39; 2nd rpt. Delhi: Ess Ess Publications, 1979), 2: 117–118, 187–188.

[22] *Jahangir's India: The Remonstrantie of Francisco Pelsaert*, trans. W. H. Moreland and P. Geyl (1925; rpt. Delhi: Idarah-i Adabiyat-i Delli, 1972), 2ff.

562 EBBA KOCH

Shah Jahan, after his accession, renamed Agra Akbarabad, "the city of Akbar,"[23] in honour of his revered grandfather. In his time the strictly planned riverfront garden or waterfront garden became the most widely used residential form. The impression that Agra made on contemporaries is put in flowery words by Shah Jahan's historian Muhammad Salih Kanbo:

> On either side of that sea [the Jamna] full of pleasantness, buildings and gardens (*'imarat-ha wa bagh-ha*) of paradisiacal space are placed together in such a handsome close way that the sigh of the beholder from the heart-attracting entertainment of each of them gathers the flowers of bounty of the month of [spring] Urdi Bihisht. Because of the riverfront buildings (*'imarat-ha-yi sahil*) and the flower gardens in front [of the landward side] of all, it appears that garden is linked to garden and garden plot (*chaman*) to garden plot [and, thus,] the desire to stroll in the garden of Paradise is completely erased from the page of memory... In particular, the spacious buildings (*'imarat-i wazi'*) and wonderful pavilions (*nashiman-ha-yi badi'*) of the princes of exalted origin and other famous *amirs*... give a display of the garden of Rizwan (the gatekeeper of Paradise) and the palaces of the garden of Paradise.[24]

The French traveller de Thevenot, who visited India in 1666–67 confirms that the river front scheme formed the centre of the city:

> This Palace [the Agra Fort] is accompanied with five and twenty or thirty very large ones, all in a line, which belong to the Princes and other great Lords of Court; and all together afford a most delightful prospect to those who are on the other side of the River, which would be a great deal more agreeable, were it not for the long Garden-walls, which contribute much to the rendering the Town so long as it is. There are upon the same line several less Palaces and other Buildings. All being desirous to enjoy the lovely prospect and convenience of the Water of the Gemna [Jamna, Yamuna], endeavored to purchase ground on that side, which is the cause that the Town is very long but narrow, and excepting some fair Streets that are in it, all the rest are very narrow, and without Symmetry.[25]

[23] Muhammad Amin Qazwini or Amina-i Qazwini, *Padshah-nama*, Persian MS., British Library, Oriental and India Office Collections (henceforth quoted as BL OIOC), Or. 173 fol. 143a/refoliated 144a; Lahawri, *Badshah-nama*, vol. 1, pt. 2: 156; Aziz Ahmad, "City of Agra," 136.
[24] Muhammad Salih Kanbo, *Bahar-i Sukhan*, Persian MS., BL, OIOC, Or. 178, fols. 248a and b, as trans. in Koch, "Waterfront Garden," 143, rpt. Koch, *Mughal Art and Imperial Ideology*, 194–195.
[25] *The Travels of Monsieur de Thevenot, The Third Part: Containing the Relation of Indostan, the New Moguls, and of Other People and Countries of the Indies* (London, 1687), 34.

Comparable urban schemes were developed in the capitals of the other two great Muslim empires. In Ottoman Istanbul royal and non-royal suburban garden villas lined the Bosporus. In seventeenth-century Safavid Isfahan garden residences were built on the banks of the Zayanda river. However, in its tight, systematic, and uniform planning—in which we recognize a peculiar Mughal logic—Agra differs from these more informal waterfront schemes. In the other great Mughal capital Lahore the waterfront scheme was only realized partially, and, at Shahjahanabad it was abandoned.

Also, Mughal Agra is different because the suburban riverfront scheme formed here the nucleus of the city; the bulk of the remaining urban fabric was situated to its west. This has not been recognized by previous scholars who considered only the right bank as part of the city and the left bank as suburbia.[26] Shah Jahan did indeed also undertake initiatives to develop the remainder of Agra. In 1637, he ordered the construction of a bazaar (now lost) on the plan of a large irregular octagon (a form which the Mughals called *muthamman Baghdadi*) as an organizing link between the palace fortress, the Agra fort, and the new Jami' Masjid (1643–48) to its west, sponsored by his daughter Jahanara. The octagonal piazza enclosed by the bazaar wings (all now lost) was to serve as a *jilaw khana* for the court; the absence of such an assembly square was now, in a time of greater awareness for ceremony being criticized as one of the shortcomings of the Agra palace, and eventually served as one of the official reasons for the foundation of the new city of Shahjahanabad.[27] The mosque was built instead of an earlier one whose foundation had already been laid on the bank of the Jamna, but the construction had been halted when the new project of the Taj Mahal got precedence.[28] This pause led to the change of the site for the mosque. Perhaps it was felt that an isolated religious structure would not fit into the residential waterfront garden scheme, or else the mosque which forms part of the river front group of the Taj Mahal was to remain without competition. To widen the streets leading to the new Jami' Masjid a great number of houses were demolished.[29]

---

[26] Gupta, *Urban Glimpses*, 19, 24, 69.
[27] Lahawri, *Badshah-nama*, vol. 1, pt. 2: 251–252; 'Inayat Khan, *Shah Jahan Nama*, English trans. A. R. Fuller, rev. and ed. Wayne E. Begley and Z. A. Desai (New Delhi: Oxford University Press, 1990), 205–206.
[28] Kanbo, *'Amal-i Salih*, vol. 2: 193.
[29] Kanbo, as in previous note.

But still, even after the project was completed, the emphasis of the city was on the riverfront scheme. Observers like Thevenot who was at Agra after the octagonal bazaar and the mosque had been completed, found nothing noteworthy to report beyond the river.

Agra presented itself as a riverfront city like London or Paris but expressed in its own Mughal way. Bands of garden palaces flanked by towers, set in gardens with flowers and trees, lined both banks of the Jamna. The gardens were linked by boats and a boat trip on the river along the elegantly arranged garden fronts was a truly spectacular experience.

3. *Reconstruction of the riverfront scheme*

Today only a few gardens remain of Mughal Agra. Most of them stand isolated from each other, having lost their original urban context. But for a few exceptions they are largely ruined, and depending on their situation, used for cultivation or built in and over by later structures of the encroaching city.

The waterfront garden scheme of the city can, however, be reconstructed with the help of Mughal and European records and a large map on cloth in the Maharaja Sawai Man Singh II Museum in the palace of Jaipur.[30] It was prepared in the 1720s when the Mughal emperor Muhammad Shah (r. 1719–48) made Maharaja Sawai Jai Singh of Jaipur (1699–1743) governor of the Agra province who in turn appointed Rai Shivadasa his deputy at the city.[31] Maharaja Sawai

---

[30] Cat. no. 126. The plan is painted on cloth and measures 294 × 272 cm. I have studied it since the mid-1980s; see Ebba Koch, "The Zahara Bagh (Bagh-i Jahanara) at Agra," *Environmental Design* 2 (1986): 30–37; eadem, "The Mughal Waterfront Garden"; M. C. Beach, E. Koch, and W. Thackston, *King of the World: The Padshahnama: An Imperial Mughal Manuscript from the Royal Library, Windsor Castle* (London: Azimuth Editions; Washington, D.C.: Arthur M. Sackler Gallery, Smithsonian Institution, 1997), cat. no. 29, pp. 185–187, cat. no. 45, pp. 209–210, fig. 132. I thank Dr. B. M. Jawalia, Keeper of Manuscripts, for assisting me in reading the inscriptions of the plan in July 1985 and February 1986, and Dr Aśok Kumar Das, then Director of the Maharaja Sawai Man Singh II Museum, Jaipur for the permission to study and to publish it.

[31] Lalah Sil Chand, *Tafrih al-'Imarat*, compiled for James Stephen Lushington, Acting Collector, Agra, 1825–26, BL OIOC Persian MS. Or 6371, copied for James Davidson, Sessions Judge, Agra, 1836–37, BL, OIOC Persian MS. I.O.L. 2450, fol. 97b lists the riverfront garden of Rai Shivadasa; see also V. S. Bhatnagar, *Life and Times of Sawai Jai Singh, 1688–1743* (Delhi: Impex India, 1974), 162–163; Chandramani Singh, "Early 18th-Century Painted City Maps on Cloth," *Facets of Indian Art* (London: Victoria and

Jai Singh was then planning and building his own new city at Jaipur,[32] and, obviously for comparative studies, he instructed Rai Shivadasa to prepare maps of the old capital of the Mughal empire and plans of prominent buildings.

The Jaipur map is the basis for a reconstruction of Mughal Agra; it shows schematic representations of its gardens and buildings. The artist of the map considered the waterfront garden so characteristic of the urban landscape that he even showed centrally planned *charbaghs* in this way, such as the tomb garden of I'timad al-Dawla. The names are given in Devanagari script, often with corrupted spellings, using the Persian word *bagh* (garden) for the residential gardens on the left bank of the Jamna, and the Arabic term *haveli* (courtyard house) for the (garden) residences on the right bank, the side of the city. There was a differentiation in the types of riverfront residence, the left bank had a more suburban character than the right bank, where the *haveli*s, which had a more built in character, dominated. The Arabic words *rawza* (garden) or *makbara* (tomb) are employed for funerary gardens. Most of the gardens of the map carry the names of members of the imperial family and of the highest ranked *amirs* of Jahangir and Shah Jahan. The left bank of the river was occupied but for a few exceptions by gardens of the emperor and the imperial women; the right side towards the city was allotted to the princes and the nobles. Gardens as well as *haveli*s constituted the residences of the princes and nobles when the court was at Agra.

4. *The impact of landownership on the architectural patronage of the Mughal nobility*

Mughal nobles, or "rankholders" (*mansabdars*), were subjected to significant limits in their rights to own property and bequeath it to their heirs. They had no base in land and derived power mainly from their rank (*mansab*), determining their military strength for which they depended

Albert Museum, 1986), 185–192, 190, 192; S. Gole, *Indian Maps and Plans: From the Earliest Times to the Advent of European Surveys* (New Delhi: Manohar, 1989), 200–201.
[32] Bhatnagar, *Life and Times of Sawai Jai Singh*, 331; Singh "City Maps on Cloth," 190–192; G. N. Bahura and C. Singh, *Catalogue of Historical Documents in Kapad—Dwara, Jaipur, Part II: Maps and Plans* (Jaipur, 1990), 11; V. Sachdev and G. Tillotson, *Building Jaipur: The Making of an Indian City* (New Delhi: Oxford University Press, 2002).

entirely on the emperor. As a rule, they were allowed to own land only on a temporary basis, this is true even of members of the imperial family. The Indian Rajputs who participated in the administration were in a better position than the Muslim nobility; they could usually keep their ancestral lands and raise large palaces on them. The escheat practice had a certain dampening effect on non-imperial architectural patronage; this was noted by European observers, among them Sir Thomas Roe, envoy of James I of England to the Mughal court from 1615–1619, who remarked that "His [the Mughal emperor's] great men build not for want of inheritance."[33] After the death of its temporary holder, a palace or a garden would usually be integrated into the imperial estate (*sarkar-i khassa sharifa*). If the emperor did not keep it for himself, the property would be given to another member of the imperial family, or to another noble. The new owner would then refashion the building and/or the garden. The palace or the garden of a Mughal noble could, thus, go through a chain, a *silsila*, of owners.

In contrast Rajputs were allowed to own heritable property. The piece of land, which Shah Jahan wanted for the construction of the Taj Mahal, had been in the possession of the Khachwaha rajas of Amber since Raja Man Singh (died 1614). The Khachwaha clan had been the first Rajput house to cooperate with the Mughals under Akbar. Shah Jahan made it a point to acquire the land legally correct from Man Singh's grandson Mirza Raja Jai Singh (died 1667) by giving him in exchange four other mansions from the crown estate at Agra.[34] A tomb was exempt from these regulations, and, thus, it became the favoured building type of the Muslim nobility or officeholders, besides structures for the common good, such as caravanserais, baths and mosques, with which a patron could make him or herself a name and assure Divine rewards in the next world. Francisco Pelsaert, the senior factor of the Dutch East India Company who was at Agra from 1621 to 1627, did not fail to notice the peculiarities of the architectural patronage of the Mughal nobles and informed his readers that "Here the great lords far surpass ours in magnificence, for their gardens serve for their

---

[33] Sir Thomas Roe, *The Embassy of Sir Thomas Roe to India, 1615–19*, ed. William Foster (1899; rpt. rev. ed. London: Oxford University Press, 1926; rpt. New Delhi: Munshiram Manoharlal, 1990), 105.

[34] Lahawri, *Badshah-nama* 1, 402–403; trans. W. E. Begley and Z. A. Desai, *Taj Mahal: The Illumined Tomb: An Anthology of Seventeenth-Century Mughal and European Documentary Sources* (Cambridge, MA: The Aga Khan Program for Islamic Architecture), 41–44, 168–171.

enjoyment while they are alive, and after death for their tombs, which during their lifetime they build with great magnificence in the middle of the garden."[35]

It appears that when Shah Jahan transferred the seat of government, in 1648, to his new capital Shahjahanabad at Delhi, the usual escheat practice of taking back gardens from nobles and granting them to new temporary holders was abandoned at Agra. The greater part of the gardens of Agra seem to have remained in the families of their last owners, or retained at least their names. Also, several nobles had built their tombs in their gardens and, thus, their families kept possession of the land, which otherwise after the death of its temporary holder would have fallen back to the crown. This changed the residential character of Agra's urban landscape. The largest funerary accent had been set by the construction of the Taj Mahal on a previous residential estate. The Jaipur map which was prepared in the 1720s still gives a fairly close image of Agra at the time of Shah Jahan and is supported by sources of the later eighteenth and nineteenth centuries.

5. *Forty-five gardens of riverfront Agra according to the Jaipur plan (figure 4)*

 1 Bagh-i Shah Nawaz Khan
 2 Buland Bagh
 3 Bagh-i Nur Afshan (today Ram Bagh)
 4 Bagh-i Jahanara (today Zahara or Zahra Bagh)
 5 Nameless Garden
 6 Rawza of Afzal Khan (today Chini-ka Rawza)
 7 Bagh-i Khwaja Muhammad Zakarya or Bagh Wazir Khan
 8 Bagh-i Sultan Parwiz
 9 Maqbara (Tomb) of I'timad al-Dawla
10 Bagh-i Musawi Khan Sadr
11 Bagh Padshahi (Imperial Garden)
12 Moti Bagh Padshahi
13 [Bagh] Padshahi
14 Lal Bagh Padshahi
15 Second Charbagh Padshahi

---

[35] Pelsaert, *Jahangir's India*, 5.

16 Charbagh Padshahi (Babur's first garden at Agra, called Chahar
    Bagh or Bagh-i Hasht Bihisht)
17 Bagh-i Mahtab Padshahi (today Mahtab Bagh)
18 Haveli of Khan Dawran
19 Haveli of Agah Khan
20 Rawza of Shah Jahan (Taj Mahal)
21 Bagh-i Khan ʿAlam
22 Haveli of Asalat Khan
23 Haveli of Mahabat Khan
24 Haveli of Hoshdar Khan
25 Haveli of Aʿzam Khan
26 Haveli of Mughal Khan
27 Haveli of Islam Khan
28 Padshahi Qilaʿ (Agra Fort)
29 Haveli of Dara Shikoh
30 Haveli of Khan Jahan Lodi
31 Haveli of Hafiz Khidmatgar (two enclosures)
32 Haveli of Asaf Khan
33 Haveli of ʿAlamgir
34 Haveli of ʿAlamgir
35 Masjid-i Mubarak Manzil
36 Haveli of Shayista Khan
37 Haveli of Jaʿfar Khan
38 Rawza of Shayista Khan
39 Haveli of Wazir Khan
40 Haveli of Muqim Khan
41 Haveli of Khalil Khan
42 Bagh-i Rai Shiv Das
43 Bagh-i Hakim Kazim ʿAli
44 Rawza of Jaʿfar Khan
45 Chhatri (memorial pavilion) of Jaswant Singh (beyond the end of
    the map)

Only the gardens, which are preserved, at least to some extent, will be
discussed here (compare figure 4 with figure 5).[36]

---

[36] For a fuller treatment see chapter 1 in my *The Complete Taj Mahal*.

The left bank gardens

The left bank of the Jamna preserves the character of the original urban landscape of Mughal Agra as a riverfront garden city to the largest extent; it was the area which Babur and his followers developed first with their garden foundations. The eastern stretch is occupied nowadays by surviving Mughal gardens as well as by commercial nurseries, and the northern stretch, after the bend of the Jamna is occupied by agricultural fields. At the riverfront and within the plantation remains of the old Mughal gardens can be traced. The numbering of the gardens refers to the map of figure 4.

4.2   Buland Bagh ("High Garden") (partly preserved)

The garden is attributed by tradition to Buland Khan, or Sarbuland Khan, an otherwise unknown *khwajasara* or eunuch of Jahangir. A high riverfront tower known as Battis Khamba is the most prominent remains of the largely ruined Buland Bagh which serves today as a nursery. A similar tower appears in a riverfront view which shows probably Agra and appears as background of a painting called *Nobleman with Musicians*, late seventeenth century, in the collection of Howard Hodgkin (figure 6).

4.2a   Utilitarian Complex (preserved but ruinous)

Between the Buland Bagh and the Ram Bagh are the remains of an oblong architectural complex which is not designated on the Jaipur plan. It consists of an open street flanked on both sides by rows of squarish cells (*hujra*) preceded by an arcaded porch (*iwan*). On the east and west sides are gates. This type of architecture was used for bazaars, and in this function it must have served the adjoining gardens.

4.3   Bagh-i Nur Afshan (Light Scattering Garden) or Ram Bagh (preserved)

The garden is now known as Ram Bagh or Aram Bagh but its original name was Bagh-i Nur Afshan and it features under this name on the Jaipur plan and in the nineteenth century descriptions of Agra.[37] The

---

[37] Sil Chand, *Tafrih al-'Imarat*, fols. 119b–129b; Raja Ram, *Tamirat Agra*, written in Persian "a few years" before the mutiny [1857–58] and trans. by S. Abu Muhammad under the title "The Gardens of Agra," *Journal of the United Provinces Historical Society*

component "Nur" (light) in the name of the garden is typical of foundations of Jahangir and his queen Nur Jahan; it alludes, as he himself
tells us, to Jahangir's honorific title Nur al-Din (Light of Religion) and
the title he gave to his wife, Nur Jahan (Light of the World).[38]

The architecture of the Bagh Nur Afshan clearly dates from Jahangir's
time and testifies to the patronage of Nur Jahan as an outstanding
garden builder; her other creation at Agra is the mausoleum of I'timad
al-Dawla (9) where her parents are buried.

The Nur Afshan garden is the earliest preserved Mughal garden of
Agra and it may have been laid out on the foundations of an even
older garden, built by Babur. The garden displays the earliest surviving waterfront scheme of Agra, of a terraced area lining the river, and
a garden on the landward side, although the configuration is still
vaguely expressed and does not show the strictly planned symmetrical
form of the later Shahjahani examples. No detailed documentation has
ever been published of the garden, sketch plans of the general layout go
back to a British plan of 1923 indicating its plantation with fruit trees.[39]
I have prepared a plan of its pavilions in 1986,[40] and an overall plan
in 2002.[41]

The garden buildings on the river front terrace consist of two narrow
oblong pavilions with their shorter front towards the river; they form an
open court with a sunken pool between them. The walls and intricately
patterned plaster vaults of both pavilions were originally covered with

---

4, no. 1 (1928): 17, he attributes the buildings wrongly to Raja Jawahir Singh of
Bharatpur; A. C. L. Carlleyle, "Agra," in *Archaeological Survey of India Report* (1871–72):
199; A. Führer, *The Monumental Antiquities and Inscriptions in the North-Western Provinces and
Oudh*, Archaeological Survey of India, New Imperial Series 12 1891; (rpt. Varanasi and
Delhi: Indological Book House, 1969), 53. For this and a description of the garden see
Ebba Koch, "Notes on the Painted and Sculptured Decoration of Nur Jahan's Pavilions
in the Ram Bagh (Bagh-i Nur Afshan) at Agra," *Facets of Indian Art*, A symposium held
at the Victoria and Albert Museum on 26, 27, 28 April and 1 May 1982, ed. Robert
Skelton, Andrew Topsfield, Susan Stronge, Rosemary Crill, and Graham Parlett (London:
Victoria and Albert Museum, 1986), 51–65, and Koch, *The Complete Taj Mahal* 37–40.

[38] Jahangir, *Tuzuk-i Jahangiri or Memoirs of Jahangir*, English trans. Alexander Rogers,
ed. Henry Beveridge (1909–14; rpt. Delhi: Munshiram Manoharal, 1968 [2 vols. in
one]), 1:269–270; 2:75–76, 151, 192, 226.

[39] *A Complete Set of Site Plans of the Major Gardens of the United Provinces, Supplement to
the Report on the Working and Administration of the United Provinces Government Gardens for the
year 1923–24* (Allahabad: Superintendent Government Press, United Provinces, 1924),
Pl. vi.

[40] I have surveyed the garden since 1978; for the plan of the pavilions, see Koch,
"Notes on Painted and Sculptured Decoration," 52.

[41] See Koch, *The Complete Taj Mahal*, fig. 34.

representations of animals, human figures, winged beings and birds, including a *simurgh*, all related to Solomonic imagery and similar to the decoration of the Lahore fort.[42]

Below in the basement is a large underground chamber (*tahkhana*) for the hot summer months. Most of the riverfront pavilions of Agra had such underground rooms in the terrace on which they stood. To the north is another platform below which is a much larger *tahkhana*, containing a set of rooms including a bath or *hammam*.

At the riverfront are wells which provided the water supply for the garden, and its ends are accentuated with corner tower pavilions topped by *chhatris*.

The large garden is still cared for by the Archaeological Survey of India and, together with the tomb of Iʿtimad al-Dawla and the Taj Mahal, belongs to the most intensely restored gardens of the city.

4.4   *Bagh-i Jahanara or Zahra (Zahara) Bagh (preserved in fragments) (figure 2)*

The garden was not founded by a daughter of Babur, as previously assumed, but by Mumtaz Mahal, Shah Jahan's queen.[43] It is the only architectural foundation which can be connected to her patronage.[44] After her death in 1631 it passed to her daughter Jahanara, and, in the course of time, the name Bagh-i Jahanara or Jahanara Bagh—still in use in the nineteenth century—was changed by popular pronunciation to Zehra, Zahra or Zahara Bagh. Jahanara turned her inheritance into the most splendid garden palace of Agra, if we are to believe Shah Jahan's court poet Abu Talib Kalim who gave it special space in his descriptive praise-poem of the city. Several of his verses provide information about the layout, the plantation, and the founder:

> A boat trip will remove the sorrow from your heart
> Pass by the garden of Jahanara!

---

[42] Ebba Koch, "Jahangir and the Angels: Recently Discovered Wall Paintings under European Influence in the Fort of Lahore," in *India and the West*, ed. J. Deppert (New Delhi: Manohar, 1983), 173–195, rpt. in Koch, *Mughal Art and Imperial Ideology*, 12–37.

[43] Abu Talib Kalim, *Diwan*, Persian text ed. Partaw Bayzaʾi (Tehran: Khayam, 1336 AH/1957), 350–351; Lahawri, *Badshah-nama*, 2: 99, says it was founded by Shah Jahan when a prince and given to Mumtaz after his accession.

[44] Ebba Koch, "The Zahara Bagh (Bagh-i Jahanara) at Agra," *Environmental Design* 2 (1986): 30–37; Koch, *Mughal Architecture*, 117; Koch, *The Complete Taj Mahal*, 41–42.

In this paradise is an alluring palace (*qasr*)
That the sight gets impatient to behold it.

On three [of its] sides is the flower garden, and in front there is the river
Every wave of which is the curl of a delightful ringlet.

When the exalted lady of the world, the Bilqis of the age
Went to paradise from the assembly of Solomon [Shah Jahan]

That very paradise which she had made to flourish [the garden]
She gave to her own world adorning child [play on the name Jahanara,
world adornment]

The eldest beloved daughter of the king, the exalted veiled lady,
The cherished reminder of Her Majesty, the Queen.[45]

The garden was not only frequented by the imperial family but Shah
Jahan received there also the court and foreign dignitaries. In May 1638,
the emperor invited the Persian ambassador Yadgar Beg to the Bagh-i
Jahanara, and in the evening ordered illuminations and fireworks which
were displayed on the bank of the Jamna below the pavilion (*'imarat*).[46]
Shah Jahan's son Prince Awrangzeb—who was to become the successor
of his father—visited his sister Jahanara in her garden when he stopped
in 1652 at Agra to inspect the condition of the Taj Mahal.[47]

Today, only fragments of the garden remain, it is not protected by
the Archaeological Survey of India. The layout followed the waterfront
design with the main building on a terrace overlooking the river.[48] The
pavilion can be identified on an old photograph taken by John Murray
in the early 1850s.[49] The southwestern front corner tower of the Bagh
Jahanara is the best-preserved element of the garden and represents a
splendid example of the garden towers of Agra (figure 7).

---

[45] Selected verses from the *mathnawi*, "Praise of Akbarabad and the Bagh-i Jahanara,"
from Abu Talim Kalim, *Diwan*, 346–351.

[46] Lahawri, *Badshah-nama*, 2:99.

[47] Aurangzeb's letter mentioning his visit has been translated by W. E. Begley and
Z. A. Desai, *Taj Mahal*, 175–177; they did not identify the garden of Jahanara.

[48] I have surveyed the garden repeatedly since 1978, and with R. A. Barraud took
measurements of the remaining structures in February 2001 and March 2003 from
which the survey plan was prepared.

[49] See Koch, *The Complete Taj Mahal*, figs. 39, 40.

4.6 *Rawza or Tomb of Afzal Khan, now called Chini-ka-Rawza ("Chinese Tomb") (building preserved) (figure 2)*

The tomb was built by Mulla Shukrullah Shirazi, entitled ʿAllami Afzal Khan Shirazi who served under Jahangir and under Shah Jahan held the office of *diwan-i kul* (also called *wazir*, that is finance minister). Afzal Khan died in 1639 at Lahore, and his body was brought to Agra to be buried in the tomb he is reported to have built during his lifetime.[50] The noble was the brother of Amanat Khan who composed the calligraphic inscriptions of the Taj Mahal, and who had come with him to India; it is likely that he created also the inscriptions of his brother's tomb who are, however, only preserved in fragments.

The tomb which has lost its original garden setting derives its popular name from its facing with mosaic of glazed tiles in the manner of Lahore and is a truly exotic element in the Mughal architecture of Agra.[51] The cubical tomb is set on a platform with now closed vaulted chambers and is erected on a *hasht bihisht plan*, with large *pishtaqs* (monumental arched niches in rectangular frames) in the centre of each side. The Chini-ka Rawza has been repeatedly restored, in particular the outer tile facing and the inner painted decoration which have lost much of their original character.[52]

4.7 *Bagh-i Khwaja Muhammad Zakarya or Bagh-i Wazir Khan (riverfront buildings preserved but ruined) (figures 8, 2)*

The identity of the garden cannot be established with certainty but probably it was the garden of Hakim ʿAlim-al-Din Wazir Khan,[53] a

---

[50] Athar Ali, *The Apparatus of Empire: Award of Ranks, Offices and Titles to the Mughal Nobility* (1574–1658) (Delhi: Oxford University Press, 1985), 167 S2326; Samsam al-Dawla Shah Nawaz Khan, *Maʾathir ul-Umara*, Persian text ed. ʿAbd al-Rahim and M. Ashraf ʿAli, 3 vols. (Calcutta: Asiatic Society, 1887–96); English trans. H. Beveridge, revised by Baini Prashad (1911–64; rpt. Patna: Janaki Prakasham, 1979), 1:149–153.

[51] The architecture of the tomb is described by E. W. Smith, *Moghul Colour Decoration of Agra*, Archaeological Survey of India, New Imperial Series 30 (Allahabad: Superintendent Government Press, North-Western Provinces and Oudh, 1901), 3–17 with special emphasis on its decoration, which was to inspire contemporary design.

[52] For a more detailed discussion of the tomb see Koch, *The Complete Taj Mahal*, 43–45.

[53] On the Jaipur map it is designated as Bagh-i Khwaja Muhammad Zakarya, who was a noble of Jahangir, but the nineteenth century records indicate it as that of Wazir Khan; so does as Gupta, *Urban Glimpses*, maps 1 and 2. Wazir Khan succeeded perhaps Khwaja Muhammad Zakarya in the ownership of the garden.

physician and distinguished noble of Shah Jahan who died in 1641.[54]

The surviving garden buildings, though ruined, still represent the best-preserved waterfront garden ensemble of a non-imperial patron of Shah Jahan's time at Agra. Characteristic is the pavilion in the centre of the riverfront over a sub chamber, a *tahkhana*, flanked by two towers at the end of the terrace. All buildings are faced with red sandstone.

4.8   *Bagh Sultan Parwiz (only tomb preserved)*

Sultan Parwiz was the son of Jahangir and, thus, Shah Jahan's brother and the father of Nadira Banu Begam who was married to Prince Dara Shikoh, the eldest son of Shah Jahan. Francisco Pelsaert, the Dutch trader lists his garden in 1626 on the left bank of the Jamna in his description of riverfront Agra.[55] Sultan Parwiz died in 1626 at Burhanpur of which he was governor,[56] and his body was brought to Agra and buried in the garden he had built.[57] His family was ordered to court and allowed to continue to reside in the garden because Shah Jahan's official historian Lahawri mentions the residence of Sultan Parwiz in November 1632 when, as part of the engagement ceremony of Dara Shikoh and Nadira Banu, presents were sent along the riverfront to the widowed mother of the bride.[58]

The site of the garden lies to the north of the tomb of I'timad al-Dawla; it is partly covered by nurseries and the residential colony of Moti Bagh. The main surviving building of the Mughal garden is a tomb structure, locally known as Parwiz Khan-ka-Maqbara, the tomb of Parwiz Khan; it is situated between the river and the Aligarh Road, to the west of the police station. The garden or *haveli* of Sultan Parwiz is mentioned only in the early nineteenth century records,[59] but not in the later descriptions of Agra. Today the tomb is not generally known and not protected by the Archaeological Survey. The cube shaped domed tomb stands on a substructure with vaulted rooms, arranged on a *hasht*

---

[54] Shah Nawaz Khan, *Ma'athir ul-Umara*, 2:981–983; Athar Ali, *Apparatus of Empire*, 97 S67, 105 S325, 117 S698, 175 S2599, 177 S 2653.
[55] Pelsaert, *Jahangirs India*, 5; cf. Raja Ram, "Gardens of Agra," 16.
[56] Athar Ali, *Apparatus of Empire*, 87 J1471.
[57] Beni Prasad, *The History of Jahangir* (London: Oxford University Press, 1922), 428.
[58] Beach, Koch, and Thackston, *King of the World*, cat. nos. 21–22, 23–24.
[59] Sil Chand, *Tafrih al-'Imarat*, fol. 109b; Raja Ram, "Gardens of Agra," 16.

bihisht plan.[60] Originally, the entire tomb, including its substructure, had a painted decoration which survives only in fragments. It is datable to the second quarter of the seventeenth century.

4.9 *Tomb of I'timad al-Dawla (well preserved)*

The mausoleum was built between 1622 and 1628 by Nur Jahan, Jahangir's powerful wife, for her parents. Her father Ghiyath Beg Tehrani, entitled I'timad al-Dawla, was *wazir* (finance minister) of the Mughal empire under Jahangir.[61]

The tomb which his daughter Nur Jahan built for him reflects her elegant taste, for her many talents included also a pronounced interest in architecture.

Like most of the funerary gardens of Agra—with the exception of the Taj Mahal—that of I'timad al-Dawla does not follow the water-front design but instead the classical fourfold *charbagh*, with the tomb structure at its centre at the crossing of the *khiyaban*s, the walkways.[62] A concession to the waterfront scheme is that the pavilion in the middle of the riverfront, which served as a gate towards the river, is treated with particular elaboration. The riverfront terrace has staircases lead-ing down to basement rooms, and the riverfront towers are enlarged by well chambers and ramps for water lifts. The *hasht bihisht* plan of the tomb pavilion in the centre has the simplicity of a magic square, enriched with towers at the four corners. The entire outside of the building is faced with marble inlaid with different-coloured stones.[63] The inlay work anticipates the even more refined inlay of the Taj Mahal. The date 37 AH which corresponds to 1626–27 A.D. is found

---

[60] For a plan see Koch, *The Complete Taj Mahal*, fig. 52.

[61] Jahangir, *Tuzuk-i Jahangiri*, 2:222; Shah Nawaz Khan, *Ma'athir ul-Umara*, 2:1072–1079 who includes into the account of the life of Ghiyath Beg also that of his daughter Nur Jahan; Athar Ali, *Apparatus of Empire*, 78 J1194.

[62] C. B. Asher, *Architecture of Mughal India*, The New Cambridge History of India 1. 4 (Cambridge, New York, Oakleigh: Cambridge University Press, 1992), 130–133; For a new detailed photographic documentation, unfortunately with a wrong plan (which shows the tomb of Maryam al-Zamani at Sikandra), see Amina Okada (text) and Jean-Louis Nou (photographs), *Un joyau de l'Inde moghole: Le mausolée d'Itimad ud-Daulah* (Milan: Continents Editions, 2003). For a fuller treatment and a new plan see Koch, *The Complete Taj Mahal*, 48–53, fig. 57.

[63] E. W. Smith, *Moghul Colour Decoration of Agra*, 18–19; in his characteristic approach he saw the tomb mainly as a carrier of ornamental design.

together with the name of the calligrapher ʿAbd-al-Nabi al-Qarshi on an inscriptional panel of the southwest corner tower. The date 1036 AH/1627–28 A.D. appears inside the upper chamber on the first panel from west of the north wall.

In British times the river front pavilion was adapted as visitor's bungalow for the European residents of Agra who would occasionally stay there for a change of air.[64]

4.10, 4.11, 4.12, 4.13, 4.14, 4.15, 4.16

After the Bagh Musawi Khan Sadr, which is not preserved (10) followed a series of imperial gardens situated around the bend of the Jamna and lining the following straight stretch up to the Mahtab Bagh opposite the Taj Mahal. Today the area has been built over up to the Iron Bridge by a modern residential colony, the remainder is used for cultivation.

4.16   *Chahar Bagh Padshahi or Bagh-i Hasht Bihisht (not preserved)*

This was Babur's first garden at Agra, discussed at the beginning. Only a few wells remain in the area which was occupied by the garden.

4.17   *Mahtab Bagh (partly preserved)*

The garden was built by Shah Jahan. It is of the same width as the garden of the Taj Mahal and situated exactly opposite it which has given rise to the speculation that Shah Jahan intended to built his own tomb here as a counter image in black marble of the mausoleum of his wife, linked to it with a bridge over the river. This story was reported by the French traveller Tavernier who was at Agra in the 1660s and has never died since then.[65] Excavations carried out by the Archaeological Survey of India in the 1990s have brought no evidence to light to substantiate this assumption. The garden historian Elizabeth Moynihan has suggested that the Mahtab Bagh was conceived as a place to view the Taj Mahal; its reflection being captured by a large pool placed in the centre of its now ruined riverfront terrace.[66] What

---

[64] Carlleyle, "Agra," 141.

[65] Jean-Baptiste Tavernier, *Travels in India*, English trans. V. Ball, ed. William Crooke (1925; rpt. New Delhi: Oriental Books Reprint Corporation, 1977) vol. 1, 91.

[66] E. B. Moynihan, *The Moonlight Garden: New Discoveries at the Taj Mahal* (Washington,

speaks for her hypothesis is that the main building of the riverfront garden design has been replaced by a large pool, a feature, which does not occur elsewhere.

The gardens of the right bank up to the Agra Fort

4.18   Haveli of Khan Dawran (ruined and built over)

The founder of the complex was Khan Dawran Bahadur Nusrat Jang, one of Shah Jahan's great commanders who distinguished himself in the emperor's Deccan campaigns.[67] He was, however, feared and hated for his cruelty and was killed in July 1645 by a Brahmin boy from Kashmir whom he had taken into his service and converted to Islam.[68]

Khan Dawran's residence on the riverbank is referred to as *haveli*, a building type with one or more enclosed courtyards and, thus, a more solid construction than a *bagh* where individual pavilions were set into a garden. Still, the river front *havelis* of Agra followed the design of the waterfront garden in that the main structure was placed so as to overlook the Jamna. What is left of the Haveli of Khan Dawran has been built over by the Taj Tannery and visitors are not welcome.

4.20   Rawza-i Shah Jahan (Taj Mahal) (well preserved) (figures 9, 10)

The Taj Mahal formed part of the riverfront garden scheme of Agra; it expresses the waterfront garden in its most monumental and ideal form.[69] The mausoleum and its flanking buildings stand on a large terrace with a decorated façade towards the river, a *charbagh* appears on the landward side. The waterfront scheme determines not only the shape of the funerary garden of the Taj, it is also a key element in the planning of the entire Taj complex; to the south of the garden is a

---

D.C.: Arthur M. Sackler Gallery, Smithsonian Institution; Seattle and London: University of Washington Press, 2000), for the reflected image of the Taj see 31, 40. See also Koch, *The Complete Taj Mahal*, 56–57.

[67] Beach, Koch, and Thackston, *King of The World*, cat. nos. 10, 18, 19, 31, 32, 35, 36, 40, 43.

[68] 'Inayat Khan, *Shah Jahan Nama*, 325; Shah Nawaz Khan, *Ma'athir ul-Umara*, 1:778–783.

[69] Here, the monument is only discussed as a "module" of the waterfront city. For the first full treatment of its history and the architecture, see Koch, *The Complete Taj Mahal*.

large rectangle (figure 9, C) whose central square forms the forecourt of the Taj, called *jilawkhana* by ʿAbd al-Hamid Lahawri and Muhammad Salih Kanbo, the historians of Shah Jahan.

The *jilawkhana* square (figure 9, 11) is framed on both of its shorter sides by two smaller courtyard enclosures. An open bazaar street (figures 9, 12 a, 12b) divides these courtyards and provides the main access to the *jilawkhana*, and beyond that, through a monumental gate (figure 9, 9) to the tomb garden. The northern pair of courtyards contained the residential quarters for the tomb attendants, the *khawasspura*s (figures 9, 10a, 10b). The southern pair contained subsidiary tomb gardens of lesser wives of Shah Jahan (figure 9, 13a, 13b). These tomb enclosures echo the design of the main tomb garden on a smaller scale because they follow the characteristic waterfront scheme of a cross axial *charbagh* combined with an oblong terrace on which stands the tomb structure and its flanking buildings (the latter are no more preserved but for one). In these miniature replicas of the main garden the waterfront scheme is transferred onto a landlocked situation. Not only that, the waterfront garden is also used as a ordering scheme for the entire subsidiary complex of the Taj, because south of the *jilawkhana* there was another courtyard complex with a cross axial arrangement (figure 9, D) (now largely lost). It was formed by open bazaar streets crossing each other (figures 9, 12c, 12d, 12e, 12f), which corresponded to the walkways of the garden, and four squarish *saraʾi*s, that is caravanserais or inns (figure 9, 16a, 16b, 16c, 16d), taking the place of the four garden plots. We meet here with a unique and highly creative transferral of a *charbagh* design onto a complex of utilitarian civic architecture. The configuration of the rectangular unit containing the *jilawkhana* and the cross axial unit to its south echoed the waterfront scheme of the Taj garden. The entire complex of the Taj Mahal, consisted, thus, formally of two units following the waterfront design, that of the Taj garden, a true waterfront garden, and that of the landlocked variant of the subsidiary units.

To the west of the Taj Mahal are its waterworks with a large aqueduct that brought water from the Jamna into the garden (figure 9, E).

4.21   *Bagh-i Khan-i ʿAlam (partly preserved) (figure 11)*

The garden is situated immediately to the west of the waterworks; it belonged to Mirza Barkhurdar, a Timurid (Turani) noble to whom Jahangir in 1609 gave the title Khan-i ʿAlam; two years later the

Khan was sent as ambassador to the court of Shah ʿAbbas of Iran. Khan ʿAlam served also Shah Jahan in his early reign, but in 1632 he retired because of old age and "he spent the remainder of his days with tranquility and comfort" at Agra, presumably in his garden near the Taj Mahal.[70]

The garden followed the scheme of the residential Mughal gardens of Agra with the main garden building on a terrace overlooking the river and the garden on the landward side. The riverfront building is preserved but ruinous. Like several of the gardens of Agra, the Bagh-i Khan ʿAlam was used as a burial of the owner of the garden, but here the main garden building was not replaced with a mausoleum as in the case of Chini-ka Rawza (6), Iʿtimad al-Dawla (9), or Jaʿfar Khan (44), but a platform with cenotaphs was raised on the central axis, south of the riverfront building.

The Garden of Khan ʿAlam is today used as a nursery by the Horticultural Department of the Archaeological Survey of India.

4.28   *Agra Fort (well preserved)*

Besides the Taj Mahal the great fort of the Mughal emperors sets the main accent in the riverfront landscape of Agra. Like the mausoleum it took the position of a garden in the urban scheme, and furthermore, its palace garden and main courts followed in their layout the waterfront garden design.

History
The large fortress palace was erected by the Mughals in place of an older mud-brick fort of the Lodis. Akbar began to build it in 1564 as his main seat of government and gave it the splendid fortifications in red sandstone. The fort was altered by Akbar's successors, in particular by Shah Jahan who reconstructed the three main palace courtyards between 1628 and 1637, with facings of white marble and polished stucco, characteristic of his buildings.[71] The fort remained the main

---

[70] Pelsaert, *Jahangir's India*, 4; Shah Nawaz Khan, *Maʾathir ul-Umara*, 1:389–392; Sil Chand, *Tafrih al-ʿImarat*, fol. 77b; Raja Ram, "The Gardens of Agra," 21; Athar, *Apparatus of Empire*, 117 S702 and previous references.

[71] Koch, *Mughal Architecture*, 53–55, 106–109; Asher, *Architecture of Mughal India*, 49–51, 111–113, 182–89.

Mughal residence, until Shah Jahan moved his court to Shahjahanabad in Delhi. The British established their garrison in the fort when they conquered Agra in 1803 and the greater part of it is still under military administration, because after India's independence in 1947 it remained with the Indian army. Many of the Mughal structures were built over or pulled down and replaced by barracks, but the main palace court-yards are preserved and represent a unique ensemble of sixteenth and seventeenth century Indian and Islamic palace architecture. In 1923–24 the Archaeological Survey of India fenced off the archaeological area comprising the palaces and Shah Jahan's Moti Masjid from the military area and made it accessible to visitors through the Amar Singh Gate which was opened to them on 25th February 1924.[72] In 1982 the Agra Fort became, together with the Taj Mahal, a UNESCO World Heritage Site.

The three main palace courtyards of Shah Jahan reflect the water-front garden design. The courtyard of the Diwan-i 'Amm was the heart of the palace, it was reconstructed by Shah Jahan from 1628 to 1637, together with the two courtyards to its east, of which the one to the north is today called Machchhi Bhawan and the one to the south Anguri Bagh with the riverfront buildings which are called Khass Mahal. All three courtyards are organized in a similar way and follow the scheme of the riverfront gardens of Agra: three of their sides are formed by narrow wings of one or two stories; on the fourth, the eastern side, are individual buildings elevated on terraces; they served the main ceremonial functions of the court and the personal use of Shah Jahan and his women. To the south of the Anguri Bagh are two further courtyard complexes of a more compact form, dating from Akbar's period, they are called Jahangiri Mahal and Akbari Mahal.

Diwan-'Amm

From the east wing of the courtyard of the Diwan-i 'Amm projects the great pillared audience hall, the Dawlat Khana-i Khass-u- 'Amm (lit. Palace Building for the Special Ones and for the Wider Public), commonly referred to as the Hall of Private and Public Audience, briefly called Diwan-i 'Amm.[73]

---

[72] *Archaeological Survey of India, Annual Report* (1923–24), 8.
[73] Ebba Koch, "Diwan-i 'Amm and Chihil Sutun: The Audience Halls of Shah Jahan," *Muqarnas* 11 (1994): 143–165; rpt. in Koch, *Mughal Art and Imperial Ideology*, 229–54.

Machchhi Bhawan

The present name of this courtyard Machchhi Bhawan (Fish House) was attached to it at a later date; in Shah Jahan's time it had no special name and was referred to as Ground Floor Courtyard of the Hall of Private Audience, the Dawlat Khana-i Khass, briefly Diwan-i Khass.[74] This is a large pavilion faced with white marble which stands on the south side of the riverfront terrace of the courtyard. Opposite, on the other side of the terrace, is Shah Jahan's bath, a suite of vaulted rooms, with its facing and its forehall missing.[75] The wings of the Machchhi Bhawan housed the treasury, and in the courtyard the emperor would view his hunting animals, his hounds, hawks, and cheetahs, and watch his horses working out. It was also used for animal fights.

Khass Mahal and Anguri Bagh

The garden courtyard is now called Anguri Bagh (Grape Garden), Lahawri refers to it only as the "Garden" (bagh), and in Shah Jahan's time it was the only garden within the imperial palace complex.[76] The design of the classical waterfront garden of Agra is here transposed onto a palace courtyard enclosed on three sides by double storied wings. On the riverfront terrace stands the Khass Mahal, a group of three imperial marble buildings which forms a distinct group from inside as well as when seen from outside: the Khwabgah or Imperial Sleeping Pavilion in the centre is flanked on the left side (north) by the Bangla-i Darshan or Imperial Viewing Pavilion, a pavilion with a curved gilded roof, and on the right side (south) by its mirror image, the Bangla of Jahanara, the pavilion of Shah Jahan's daughter.

The highly valued closeness to the river determines the position of the semi- official area of the Machchhi Bhawan and the most inaccessible area, the private courtyards used by the emperor and the imperial women, the Anguri Bagh, and to the south of it the older Jahangiri Mahal and Akbari Mahal, dating from Akbar's period. Screens closed the open spaces towards the river but even so, the buildings were highly

---

[74] Lahawri refers to it as "*sahn-i ruyi zamin*" and "*sahn-i pa'in*." Lahawri, *Badshah-nama*, vol. 1, pt. 2: 238; trans. Nur Bakhsh "The Agra Fort and Its Buildings," *Archaeological Survey of India: Annual Report* (1903–04), 177–179.

[75] Ebba Koch, "The Lost Colonnade of Shah Jahan's Bath in the Red Fort of Agra," *The Burlington Magazine* 124, no. 951 (1982): 331–339; rpt. Koch, *Mughal Art and Imperial Ideology*, 255–268.

[76] Lahawri, *Badshah-nama*, vol. 1, pt. 2: 240, trans. Nur Bakhsh, "Agra Fort," 180–181.

visible from the outside and, thus, contradicted general notions of the public and the private sphere in Muslim culture. The most widely accessible area for the reception of the court, the Diwan-i ʿAmm, was situated within the palace. The emperor kept the privileged riverfront to himself, to his family and to his women. The concept of the riverfront garden determined the layout of the palace.

The garden residences to the north of the fort

So far it is uncertain how much remains of the garden residences lining the riverbank between the fort and the Rawza of Jaʿfar Khan (44) because the area has been absorbed by the city of Agra and is densely built over. The most visible remains along the Yamuna Kinara Road are, at about three quarters of a kilometre (half a mile) north of the fort in the part of the city called Belanganj, two towers topped by *chhatris* in Shahjahani style at a distance of 40 metres from each other. The towers are locally known as Khuni Burj (Blood Tower) and formed the riverfront corners of a complex called locally Puttariya Mahal.[77] Beyond, set back from the road is Awrangzeb's Mubarak Manzil turned by the British into the Customs House, and, where the road turns towards west, stands a large ruined building now known as "Library of Dara Shikoh."

4.29   *Haveli of Dara Shikoh (not preserved)*

Dara Shikoh's was Shah Jahan's favourite son and designated heir, who lost however his life in 1659 through the hand of his younger brother Awrangzeb.[78] His *haveli* at Agra is not preserved but its location can be determined.[79] According to the Agra Gazetteer of 1921 the remains of the *haveli* were taken down in 1881 to make space for the Town Hall.[80] This building is still standing, c. 250 metres north of the fort, set back

---

[77] Kind information of Mr Naveen Chand, the present owner of Mubarak Manzil (for which see below 33, 34, 35), on 12 March 2004.

[78] Bikrama Jit Hasrat, *Dara Shikuh: Life and Works* (New Delhi: Munshiram Manoharlal Publishers Pvt. Ltd., 1982).

[79] For a fuller treatment see Koch, *The Complete Taj Mahal*, 72–73.

[80] H. R. Nevill, *Agra: a Gazeteer*, District Gazetteers of the United Provinces of Agra and Oudh, vol. 8 (Allahabad: Superintendent Government Press, United Provinces 1921), 198.

from the Yamuna Kinara Road. A tablet on its west façade describes it in English and Persian as Municipal Hall with the date 1882. Later it was converted into a school.

4.33, 4.34, 4.35 *Complexes of Awrangzeb*

33 and 34 are inscribed on the Jaipur plan as Haveli 'Alamgir, 35 as Masjid Mubarak Manzil.

The history of the site of Awrangzeb's *haveli* is a telling example of changing landownership in the Mughal system. We can trace its owners back to the sixteenth century. In the reign of Akbar the riverfront property belonged to Khan-i Khanan (Commander in Chief) Bairam Khan Turkoman, the guardian and wakil of Akbar. After Bairam Khan's fall from power, Akbar gave his title and office, as well as his residence at Agra, in December 1560 to Mun'im Khan.[81] Upon his death in 1575, the property went again to the crown. When Jahangir came to the throne, he granted it to his eldest son Khusraw, together with one *lakh* of rupees, to rebuild it.[82] After Khusraw's untimely death for which his brother Shah Jahan was responsible, the building seems to have gone to him because De Laet does not list a house of Khusraw but that of "prince Sultan Khrom [Khurram was the given name of Shah-Jahan]" as the fourth north of the fort, that is almost in the position of the Jaipur plan.[83] In February 1628 Shah Jahan stayed in his princehood residence, which was then entitled *dawlat khana*—imperial palace—for twelve days in order to await the auspicious hour (calculated by his astrologers as the fourteenth of the month) for his formal entry into the fort for his accession ceremony.[84] In March 1633, Prince Shah Shuja', Shah Jahan's second son, resided there on the occasion of his wedding.[85] The emperor, however, continued to use it. When the plague broke out in Agra later in the year, he moved there in June 1633 "because of its spaciousness, closeness to the water and purity of air,"

---

[81] Abu'l Fazl, *Akbar-nama*, vol. 2, 187–88; Ram Kishore Pandey, *Life and Achievements of Muhammad Bairam Khan Turkoman* (Bareilly: Prakash Book Depot, 1978), 260.

[82] Jahangir, *Tuzuk-i Jahangiri*, 1:12.

[83] Joannes De Laet, *The Empire of the Great Mogol*, trans. J. S. Hoyland, annot. S. N. Banerjee (Delhi: Idarah-i Adabiyat-i Delli, 1975), 38–39.

[84] Muhammed Amin Qazwini, *Padshah-nama*, fol. 121a/refoliated 122a; Lahawri, *Badshah-nama*, vol. 1, pt. 1: 86–87; Kanbo, *'Amal-i Salih*, 1:186–187; 'Inayat Khan, *Shah Jahan Nama*, 15.

[85] Lahawri, *Badshah-nama*, vol. 1, pt. 1: 463.

to avoid becoming infected in the palace.[86] The position of the *haveli* north of the fort is confirmed through the description of an historical elephant-fight which took place during that time, it started in front of the princehood palace and moved down the Jamna to the fort.[87] Eventually the building came to Awrangzeb because, on the occasion of his wedding in May 1637, Lahawri mentions that Shah Jahan had it granted to him "after his accession."[88]

The Jaipur plan shows two enclosures entitled as Haveli of ʿAlamgir and north of them another enclosure inscribed as Masjid-i Mubarak Manzil (Mosque of the Blessed House). What survived of the complex is a building which has been known since the nineteenth century variously as the Mubarak Manzil, Custom House, Permit Kothi, and now as Tara Niwas. It was used from 1810 to 1877 as the Custom House or the Head Office of the Salt Department in Agra, and in 1817 it was largely modified, with a second storey added to it. A plan of Agra prepared by the British administration in 1868–69 shows the Custom House at the head of the pontoon bridge.[89] The building was sold by the British government on 28 June 1878 in a public auction for a sum of 17,000 Gold Mohurs to Seth Hira Lal from a family known as the Seths of Mathura.[90] In 1902 the Muslim community of Agra brought it to the notice of Lord Curzon and claimed it as a place of worship but since no evidence of mosque architecture could be found, their petition was denied.[91] A year later, A. C. Polwhele, Executive Engineer, Agra reported that the Mubarak Manzil was used as the East Indian Railway goods depot and that, with the permission of the then owner, Seth Chuni Lal, the son of Hira Lal, a marble tablet had been fixed

---

[86] Kanbo, *ʿAmal-Salih*, 1:460.

[87] Beach, Koch, and Thackston, *King of the World*, cat. no. 29, in particular Koch, 185–187.

[88] Lahawri, *Badshah nama*, vol. 1, pt. 2: 268; Beach, Koch, and Thackston, *King of the World*, in particular Koch, 187, n. 10.

[89] BL OIOC, Map x/1381/1–15, Koch, *The Complete Taj Mahal*, fig. 28. I thank Jerry Losty, then Head of Prints, Drawings and Photographs Section of the British Library for drawing my attention to this map and for generously sharing his knowledge about Agra under the British.

[90] I identified the Mubarak Manzil on 12 March 2004 with the help of its present owner Naveen Chand, a direct descendant of Seth Hira Lal, who kindly provided details of the acquisition of the building and its history and allowed a brief survey of the architecture. On the Mubarak Manzil see also Sil Chand, *Tafrih al-ʿImarat*, fols. 92b–93a; Raja Ram, "Gardens of Agra," 20; S. Muhammad Latif, *Agra*, Historical and Descriptive (1896; rpt. Lahore: Sandhu Printers 1981), 200–202, Nevill, *Agra*, 198; and Koch, *The Complete Taj Mahal*, 74–75.

[91] Curzon Papers: Indian Archaeology 1899–1905, BL OIOC, Mss Eur F111/621, 170–171.

on it, with an inscription which reproduced the local tradition about the building having been erected by Awrangzeb after the battle of Samugarh in June 1659.[92] The original Mughal building is still standing, encased in the construction of 1817; it had the shape of a flat-roofed pillared hall with faceted columns and multi-lobed arches, typical of Shah Jahani architecture, and shows towers topped by small domes at its four corners.

4.39 *Haveli of Wazir Khan (partly preserved?)*

Hakim Alim al-Din Wazir Khan was perhaps also the owner of this garden on the left bank of the Jamna. It was possible for a high ranking noble to have a *haveli* as well as a garden at Agra, especially for Wazir Khan since he was twice governor of Agra, in the years 1628–31, and 1640–41. A drawing in the Maharaja Sawai Man Singh II Museum in the palace of Jaipur, datable to the eighteenth century, shows Wazir Khan's Haveli right opposite the tomb of I'timad-ud-Dawla.[93] The situation of the *haveli* corresponds to that of a large building at the bend of the Yamuna Kinara Road towards west, now known as Sheron Wali Kothi or "Library of Dara Shikoh." It is built over a Mughal structure of which an arcade with faceted Shahjahani columns and multi-lobed arches is still visible on the riverfront. A marble tablet at its gate identifies it as "Rai Bahadur Seth Suraj Bhan ki Haveli"; it still belongs to a branch of the Seths of Mathura, descending from Suraj Bhan.[94]

4.44 *Rawza of Ja'far Khan (preserved)*

Ja'far Khan's wife Farzana Begam was the sister of Mumtaz Mahal.[95] In addition to his close ties to the imperial family Ja'far Khan distinguished himself by devoted service.

---

[92] *Annual Progress Report, Agra: Gazetteer of the Archaeological Surveyor United Provinces and Punjab* (1903–04), 23. The battle took in fact place on 29 May 1658.

[93] Map no. 128, so far unpublished. It gives the name of the *haveli* and the garden in Devanagari script. On the Jaipur plan the Haveli of Wazir Khan is placed further upstream but that this plan is shifting the gardens north of the Agra Fort too much towards north is also evident from the situation of the Rawza Ja'far Khan (44) which should be opposite the Ram Bagh [Bagh-i Nur Afshan] (3) and not further upstream.

[94] Personal communication of Mr. Naveen Chand, present owner of the Mubarak Manzil on 12 March 2004.

[95] Beach, Koch, and Thackston, *King of the World*, 183–184.

The Rawza of Ja'far Khan is situated immediately to the north of
the bridge of the Bypass of National Highway No 2 at the riverbank,
opposite the Ram Bagh or Bagh-i Nur Afshan (3).[96] The tomb, a
square flat-roofed building, stands in the middle of what was once a
large, walled-in garden with towers at each corner.[97] It is now used as
a government storeroom.

The river bank up from the Rawza of Ja'far Khan is no more
included on the Jaipur plan. Sil Chand gives the name of the area as
Rajwara, the stretch contained the residences of Rajput nobles who
served in the Mughal administration.[98] Today, the name Rajwara is held
by a village in which stands the Chhatri of Jaswant Singh.

4.45   *Chhatri of Jaswant Singh (well preserved)*

Jaswant Singh Rathor of Jodhpur was confirmed by Shah Jahan as his
father's heir and raja in 1638–39, and since he came from one of the
noblest families of India, the emperor treated him with many favours.
He died probably in 1678.[99]

Jaswant Singh's *chhatri* or memorial structure[100] stood originally
in a rectangular enclosure with towers at its corners of which only
the ornamental wall on the riverfront survives. The *chhatri* is built of
red sandstone and has the shape of a flat-roofed *baradari* (lit. "having
twelve doors"), that is, a pavilion with three openings on each side. Its
ornate retrospective sandstone style reaches back to the architecture of
Fatehpur Sikri of the 1570s. The Chhatri of Jaswant Singh is protected
by the Archaeological Survey of India and is kept in a good state of
preservation, though in squalid surroundings.

---

[96] The position of the Rawza of Ja'far Khan on the Jaipur plan, where it is placed
further upstream, is not correct.

[97] Führer, *Monumental Antiquities and Inscriptions*, 67.

[98] Sil Chand, *Tafrih al-'Imarat*, fols. 98b–99a; See also Gupta, *Urban Glimpses*, 19.

[99] Shah Nawaz Khan, *Ma'athir ul-Umara*, 1:754; Athar Ali, *Apparatus of Empire*, 163
S2201, 278 S5917, 322 S7342.

[100] Sil Chand, *Tafrih al-'Imarat*, f. 99a; Führer, *The Monumental Antiquities and Description*,
67; Raja Ram, "The Gardens of Garden," 23.

6. *The waterfront city is abandoned by the Mughal nobility and taken over by the people of Agra.*

The river Jamna which is one of the great holy rivers of India was the essence of the unique concept of the Mughal waterfront city of Agra. It formed the artery which bound all gardens together, a large water avenue (*khiyaban*), as the poet Kalim saw it,[101] on which one could move by boat from one residence or tomb to the other.

Agra began to decline when Shah Jahan moved his court to his newly built city Shahjahanabad (Delhi) in 1648. It even had to cede its title Dar al-Khilafa (Seat of the Caliphate) to Shahjahanabad and got a substitute title, namely Mustaqarr al-Khilafa (Settled Abode of the Caliphate).[102] Also the "democratic" character of the city, where the nobles could build their houses on both sides of the river next to the imperial gardens, was abolished. Only the east and northeast side of Shahjahanabad lined the Jamna, and the riverfront was taken by the imperial fortress palace and the residences of the emperor's son Dara Shikoh and a few selected nobles. The majority of the nobles and even the emperor's favourite daughter Princess Jahanara had to build their gardens and *haveli*s inside the new city. The riverfront garden scheme had become an imperial prerogative (figure 12).[103]

The neglect of Agra by the ruling elite increased when Awrangzeb imprisoned his father there in the fort until he died in 1666. Agra became the city of the deposed emperor. When the riverfront city was abandoned by the ruling elite, it was taken over by the inhabitants of Agra. The gardens served as recreational spots from which the waters of the river could be accessed. The river and its banks became the centre of the civic life at Agra. It led to the emergence of an outstanding swimming culture in which people of all walks of life participated, young and old, rich and poor. It culminated in an annual swimming festival, the Triveni, held jointly by both communities at the Rawza of

---

[101] Abu Talib Kalim, *Padshah-nama*, Persian MS. BL OIOC Ethé 1570, fols. 115 a–b.

[102] Ebba Koch, "The Delhi of the Mughals prior to Shahjahanabad as Reflected in the Patterns of Imperial Visits," in *Art and Culture: Felicitation Volume in Honour of Professor S. Nurul Hasan*, ed. A. J. Qaisar and S. P. Verma (Jaipur: Publication Scheme, 1993), 11; rpt. in Koch, *Mughal Art and Imperial Ideology*, 171.

[103] Koch, "Mughal Waterfront Garden," rpt. in Koch, *Mughal Art and Imperial Ideology*, 183–202.

Ja'far Khan, the Hindus celebrating Krishna and the Muslims Khwaja Khizr, who, according to Muslim lore, found the water of life.[104]

After the British takeover in 1803, the people of Agra still celebrated the swimming festival of Triveni but the gardens lining the banks of the Jamna continued to disintegrate. Eventually the British became, though with good intentions, instrumental in the destruction of large parts of the riverfront scheme.[105]

In the twentieth century, the original urban landscape of Mughal Agra was largely forgotten and absorbed by the ever-expanding city. The water level of the Jamna, now officially called Yamuna, has been reduced by dams built upstream to draw water for irrigation, and what remains to flow through Agra, is heavily polluted by untreated sewage and industrial wastes.[106] The bank of the Jamna has become from the most privileged site the least privileged one. It is used as a latrine and for garbage disposal and for the illicit entertainment of gambling.

---

[104] A similar festival called Pairaki was held at Mathura, north of Agra, the centre of the Krishna cult. See F. S. Growse, *Mathura: District Memoir* (1882; rpt. New Delhi: Asian Educational Services, 1979), 181. See also Koch, *The Complete Taj Mahal*, 33.

[105] See Koch, chapter 5, *The Complete Taj Mahal*, 60.

[106] *Taj Mahal Agra: Site Management Plan*, of the Taj Mahal Conservation Collaborative (Delhi, 2003) compiled by A. Lopez, 19.

NINETEENTH-CENTURY HYDERABAD: RE-SCRIPTING URBAN HERITAGE

Alison Mackenzie Shah

In the nineteenth century, the Indian city of Hyderabad was easily identified as a city of the Islamic world. Arab, Abyssinian, Pathan, and Turkic military men, Sufis and Maulvis, and Shia and Sunni Muslim courtiers from north and south India all migrated to the capital of the Asaf Jah state, seeking the patronage of the city's Mughal successor dynasty, the Nizams. From organization of space to ritual calendar, and from Mughal court dress to Persian language, the practices and ideals of Hyderabad's rulers and their diverse Muslim community shaped city life. If the city was Islamic in cultural practices, to the increasingly powerful political authority in nineteenth-century South Asia, the British, the character of the urban form became a way to display the cultural deficiencies of that identity—the very lack of an overall urban plan confirmed for British authorities a medieval outlook in urban life.

The British saw colonial cities as planned and their inhabitants orderly; Indian ones they saw as haphazard, and this dichotomy served visually to define places with political traditions and societal values that needed to be brought into a colonial modernity.[1] This division of cities into oppositional categories of modern-colonial and traditional-native is as old as the joining of urban planning with the colonizing project, yet, due to the nature of textual archives on cities, analyses of urban design in the colonial era are still usually examined in terms of European processes, based in Public Works Departments, and European goals such as sanitation and social control.[2] Thus, cities like Hyderabad,

---

[1] See V. Oldenberg, *The Making of Colonial Lucknow 1865–1877* (Princeton, 1984).

[2] For examples within urban history, see Narayani Gupta, "Military Security and Urban Development: A Case Study of Delhi 1852–1912," *Modern Asian Studies* 5, no. 1 (1971): 61–77; Ira Klein, "Urban Development and Death: Bombay City 1870–1914," *Modern Asian Studies* 20, no. 3 (1986): 725–54; Susan Neild, "Colonial Urbanism: The Development of Madras City in the 18th and 19th Centuries," *Modern Asian Studies* 13, no. 2 (1979): 217–46; Norma Evenson, *The Indian Metropolis: A View Toward the West* (New Haven, 1989). Some recent studies have begun to work outside of urban

when they "modernized" in the twentieth century with "European" ways of planning, appear at best derivative.[3] An alternative methodology that focuses on the architectural patronage of a mid-nineteenth-century Hyderabadi ruler, the fifth Nizam, Afzal ud Daulah, provides a visual archive of materials, rather than an urban vision, linked to the pre-colonial past.

Afzal ud Daulah, Patronage, and Political Change

For a twelve-year period between 1857–1869, Nawab Mir Tahniat Ali Khan, Afzal ud Daulah, Asaf Jah V ruled from the city of Hyderabad over a Deccan state of the same name. He was the fifth ruler of a Mughal successor dynasty known as the Asaf Jahs—or more colloquially "the Nizams," based on their Mughal title Nizam ul Mulk—who had made Hyderabad city their capital in the 1770s. Afzal ud Daulah is primarily known from his portrayal in mid-nineteenth-century British publications as a crucial ally from an ever-faithful dynasty, though personally a ruler of "superstitious" and petulant character.[4] This article seeks to reconstruct the dynamics of his relationship with the British. The question of alliance, the character of a superstitious worldview and its relation to Islam and Indo-Islamic ritual are brought to light in this Nizam's own construction of his identity from the mid-nineteenth-century, published, as it were, in the urban form: a monumental design for all to read.

Afzal ud Daulah's reign coincided with South Asia's major transition in colonial governance, as British rule was transferred from the East India Company to the British Crown in the aftermath of the 1857

---

planning, most notably, J. C. Masselos, "Appropriating Urban Space: Social Constructs of Bombay in the Time of the Raj," *South Asia* 14, no. 1 (1991): 44–67.

[3] See Metcalf, *An Imperial Vision: Indian Architecture and Britain's Raj* (Berkeley: University of California Press, 1989) and G. H. R. Tillotson, "Vincent J. Esch and the Architecture of Hyderabad 1914–1936," *South Asian Studies* 9 (1993): 29–46.

[4] Sir Richard Temple, *Journals Kept in Hyderabad, Kashmir, Sikkim, and Nepal* (reprint New Delhi, 1977), 72. The superstitious aspect refers to his support of *faqirs*, and his petulance was noted in part because of his opposition to the modernizing genius Minister Salar Jung who dismantled the Nizam's government and replaced it with a bureaucratic system. General Fraser, *Our Faithful Ally, the Nizam: being an historical sketch of events showing the value of the Nizam'a alliance to the British government in India and his services during the mutinies* (London, 1865).

rebellions. The borders of British India were designated permanent; there would be no further expansion. Those areas outside direct colonial rule, however, entered into new formal relations with the British Crown. Thus, in the ostensibly sovereign Hyderabad, 1857 brought about significant political change, and new treaties confirmed the first real political security for the Asaf Jah dynasty since the British arrived in India in the eighteenth century. A guarantee against annexation into British India was finally assured by designating the Nizam as head of a newly defined political category, the Princely State. While nominally independent, British officials—backed up by the local presence of their largest military force in southern India—nonetheless continued to play significant advisory roles in Hyderabad affairs. Political security was tied to support of the new British Raj.

Not only was the fifth Nizam the first nineteenth-century Hyderabadi ruler to be politically secure, he was also the first to have a full treasury at his disposal. While years of debt to bankers left his predecessors selling off their *jagirs* as well as their jewels, the fifth Nizam was finally solvent.[5] With his new position as Nizam of the fiscally healthy Princely State of Hyderabad, Deccan, Afzal ud Daulah made the first major royal intervention into the city form in over fifty years, inscribing a new political identity into the urban fabric. In 1858, he rehabilitated the monumental arches, the Char Kamans, built in 1595 as part of the city's foundation. Between 1859 and 1861, he sponsored the construction of a bridge with a majestic landmark gate into the city, the Afzal Darwaza.[6] He added a monumental mosque at the northern end of the new bridge, the Afzal Gunj Mosque, apparently completed in 1868.[7] And he is credited with the rehabilitation of a palace complex,

---

[5] Fraser records on "October 5, 1861, Nizam holds darbar in khilwat and British resident present gifts on behalf of queen, including cancellation of debt of Rs. 50 lakhs, and the return of districts of Raichore and Dharaseo. Gifts of Rs. 30,000 were also presented to Shamsul Umra and Salar Jung" (Fraser, 315).

[6] "In June 1861 [Zilhijja 1277], a bazaar in the vicinity of, and bridge over, the Moosey River were completed at Hyderabad under the orders of the Nizam's government, at a cost of Rs. 130,814. The present Nizam [Afzal ud Daulah, Nizam 5] inaugurated his reign by ordering the above works to be executed." (occurs Fraser, 321). No mention of it in Nizam's official chronicles.

[7] Attributed, consistently. There is no external evidence to confirm the date, but it is possible that there is an inscription plaque now covered by the contemporary addition of a two-storey concrete structure enclosing the courtyard, which unfortunately abuts and covers the mosque's original front façade. Cost of patronage is said to be Rs. 100,000, one *lakh*.

the Chowmahallah, though precisely when during his twelve-year reign this occurred is difficult to establish.[8]

There is no contemporary evidence from the Nizam records of the intent behind the construction of these buildings.[9] But in an age in which architecture was widely discussed in terms of its symbolic power, it is not surprising that the palace and mosque received attention in later nineteenth-century sources. Afzal ud Daulah's palace, the Chowmahallah, was lauded as a copy of the Shah's palace in Iran, and his mosque, the Afzal Gunj Masjid, was said to be a remarkable copy of a mosque patronized by Hyderabad's early modern Muslim dynasty, the Qutb Shahs (1518–1687).[10] In both instances, these are half-truths at best. The buildings share features with buildings from other times and places, but are in no way copies. Such statements assume that the mid-nineteenth-century Nizam had little creative energy, and that "Islamic" vision had to be centred in other centuries and other states.[11] It is time to reconsider not only the buildings themselves, but also the lens through which they have been examined.

I suggest that the fifth Nizam's buildings manipulate the city's architectural heritage, and as such they are highly conscious of cultural memories encoded in the urban form. Because Afzal ud Daulah ruled at a time of political transition, he emphasized symbolically potent sites in the urban form that had come to represent earlier key moments in the political history of this Deccan state. The Char Kamans, built in 1595, marked the foundation of the city, presenting the urban vision of the non-Mughal, Deccan Qutb Shah dynasty. The Chowmahallah

---

[8] The naming of the *mahals* on the south, Afzal Mahal, and the north, Tahniat Mahal of the complex commemorate the fifth Nizam, Mir Tahniat Ali Khan, Afzal ud Daulah, Asaf Jah V. This lends support to the primary evidence of his role as patron, which is derived from a text by S. Bilgrami, *Historical and Descriptive Sketch of His Highness the Nizam's Dominions* (Bombay, 1883–84) that claims he renovated the palace.

[9] There is also no evidence that any contemporary British official had any role in these patronage projects. And given the concern of the British Raj in urban design and symbols of power, any agency on behalf of local British Residents would have been recorded. Recorded examples of British involvement include a commitment to having the Golconda Tombs rehabbed and their constant urging for improved sanitation in the old city.

[10] On Chowmahallah, "Char Mahal," in *Glimpses of the Nizam's dominions: being an exhaustive photographic history of the Hyderabad state, Deccan, India. With nearly 600 superbly reproduced views, with descriptive text prepared from material personally collected by A. Claude Campbell* (Bombay, 1898); on Afzal Mosque, Syed Bilgrami, *Historical and Descriptive Sketch*, 581.

[11] His palace was also likened to something out of the Arabian nights (ibid.).

palace is one of the oldest palaces owned by the founders of the Asaf Jahi dynasty, and speaks to the establishment of the dynasty in the city. The individual pavilions that Afzal ud Daulah refashioned in the Chowmahallah interpret designs derived from the British Residency, a historic monument built at the turn of the nineteenth century that at once proclaimed the establishment of British power and the end of complete sovereignty for the Asaf Jahs. The Afzal Gunj mosque was a new construction, but it was designed as a historic revival of an early modern Qutb Shahi mosque set within a contemporary Asaf Jahi complex design, and like his other projects it plays upon the power of historic monuments to represent collective identities. These forms had served as icons of separate and successive authorities that had held power in the Deccan: the Qutb Shahs, the Asaf Jahs, and the looming threat of the British. Afzal ud Daulah's patronage reinterpreted their symbolism, conflating previously separate identities and selecting monuments that re-presented a historical plot structure of origins and key historical transitions that led logically to his new identity as a Prince of the State of Hyderabad.

In constructing a new political identity that tempered British power while increasing his own, the control over the past was one of the fifth Nizam's most important strategies. But to understand the scope of the work of this princely patron, Afzal ud Daulah's projects need to be seen not as separate monuments, but as an integrated, innovative urban design. Afzal ud Daulah's new works recalibrated the authority symbolized by cultural heritage into a new statement on Asaf Jahi political identity that shifted his allegiance away from the Mughals toward a new claim for roots in the Deccan. At the same time, his placement of these buildings into a new linear sequence re-framed sites that had symbolized competing authorities in British and Hyderabad diplomacy in the early nineteenth century. His design of three key building projects reconfigured urban space, aimed to codify a future political hierarchy of authority in Hyderabad with the Nizam positioned clearly at the top. Afzal ud Daulah's manipulation of space and form worked together to re-present both the British Resident and the Nizam's Minister—who had established himself as a powerful intermediary between these two opposing political authorities, as tied to the royal centre of the Nizam in a number of different ways. In so doing, the design displayed a new history for a new political identity. The ritual relations between buildings expressed in narrative form his new identity by the way historic sites were organized into new ritual paths for British-Asaf Jahi diplomacy.

His architectural patronage used both processes and symbols that were clearly linked to traditions in the Islamic world and were imagined on an urban scale. And when analyzed together, in their urban context, I argue that they were intended to present an urban design that changed a proto-colonial Mughlai city into a new Princely State capital.

The Nizams, the British, and Politics of Mughal Identity before 1857

Early nineteenth-century Hyderabad looked from a bird's eye view like a proto-colonial city (figure 1). Though the city was not colonized, a cantonment was set up on the northern outskirts of the city after the signing of the Subsidiary Alliance guaranteeing British troops for Hyderabad's "protection" in 1798.[12] And between 1803–08, a monumental official palace that served as the British administrative centre was constructed on the edge of the walled native city. What the cantonment marked in military terms, the Residency confirmed politically; the city had entered into a shared political system of Resident and ruler that characterized India's nineteenth-century colonial periphery.[13] In its image and its function, the Residency was an icon of the founding of British authority in Hyderabad (figure 2). With its enormous staircase leading to a neoclassical portico, the exterior closely resembled the central building of the Calcutta Viceroy's palace, Government House, which in turn was based on the Kedleston palace in England.[14] In imperial terms, the commemorative character of this architectural sequence of like British-derived monuments was a powerful political act that brought the cultural heritage of the eighteenth-century English landed aristocracy to the trail of expansion of British power in India.[15] And as if to confirm its connection to the cultural geography of British India, the Residency building faced north, looking out toward the British-led troops stationed in the new Secunderabad cantonment and, more generally, north toward the seat of British power, Calcutta.

---

[12] See Sarojini Regani, *Nizam British Relations, 1724–1857* (Hyderabad, 1963) for treaties.

[13] This is like other Residencies such as Lucknow.

[14] Nilssen, *European Architecture in India, 1750–1850* (New York, 1968), 101–104.

[15] Ibid. "[I]t is certainly not by accident that the Residency in Hyderabad both in detail and in its general architectural features recalled his newly completed Government House in Calcutta," 113–114.

The Residency's symbolism in the establishment of a foreign government was widely understood in Hyderabad.[16] But it was, of course, part of a competing system of Asaf Jahi political power. The patronage of this monument had exemplified the negotiation of local political authority in Hyderabad that the singularity of the building's foreign style belied. Russell, a British architect working in Calcutta had designed it, but the Nizam's Minister had suggested a grand English design, and as the *Notes on the Hyderabad Residency* confirm, the building was "built and furnished by the [third] Nizam's government at its own expense and in a very costly manner, the outlay on the building alone having, it is stated, amounted to the enormous sum of twenty lakhs of rupees."[17] This exchange marks a nineteenth-century innovation in Mughlai *nazr* practices to reflect the new political climate. Courtiers traditionally offered military service to the Nizams, who in return bestowed on them the cultural appurtenances required for them to participate in their courts. In this case the British offered a military alliance that took power away from the Nizam, and the Nizam in return provided a cultural form totally distinct from courtly ceremonial for the British to participate in his government. Mughlai ritual may have helped broker the unwelcome alliance, but the ambiguity of its meaning between form and context was further highlighted through diplomatic processions and *darbars*.

While visually serving as a monument to British power in the region, the Residency was increasingly scripted into a larger narrative of local identity through its placement in the city, through ritual and geography. Because it faced north and Hyderabad city was to the south, visitors exited and entered the complex from what would be considered the rear of the building (figure 3).[18] Entering the complex on the side that faced the river Musi meant that in order to get to the *darbar* hall, one had to proceed past the *zenana*, the kitchen, and offices of the tailors and washermen.[19] The Nizam's court was based on the Mughal traditions of axiality and gazes, in which formal entrances and approaches

---

[16] The Residency and its suburb in Chaderghat developed as a district for bankers and other immigrants who sought British support and patronage.

[17] Anon., *Notes on the Hyderabad Residency* (no date), 5.

[18] Government House in Calcutta also faces north, most likely out of climactic concerns. (Nilssen, 1968, 114–15). This was commemorated by the large gateway "borrowed" from the one at Government House, ornamented with British lions, and built at the rear entrance of the Residency garden.

[19] S. Nilssen, *European Architecture in India*, 115.

were key features in the exercise of political authority.[20] Through the relationship of form and location, the struggles for political control between the British and the Nizams could be fought in cultural as well as explicitly political battles.

In the early nineteenth century, the Nizams themselves did not construct any new monument of their own to counter the British presence; instead, they focused on ritual enactments of power in the urban form. Their walled city's identity had changed; its entire domain had become a physically and culturally identifiable part of the larger urban geography, as the city grew in a significantly different direction on the northern Chaderghat Bank.[21] The walled city became increasingly bound to the court through cultural constructions of religious and political time. The third and fourth Nizams held their *darbars*, at which there were *nazr* presentations and conferment of titles, at times of the festivals of the Indo-Islamic religious calendar: *'Id ul fitr*, *'Id uz zuha*, *Nouruz*, and the Hindu festival of *Basant*.[22] They held an annual secular state parade in the old city, the Langar Procession, on the fifth of Muharram, tying into the Shia processions commemorating the battle of Kerbala five days later.[23] Through this merging of state and religious calendars, they joined the cultural rhythms of old city life with ceremonial enactments of royal authority.[24] While it successfully wove

---

[20] Gulru Negopoglu, "Framing the Gaze in Ottoman, Safavid, and Mughal Palaces," *Ars Orientalis* 23 (1993): 303–26. Continuity of Mughal practice is seen through organization of palaces in Hyderabad under Mughal governors in the Golconda Fort, the Nau Mahal, and in the old city *jilukhana* complex of the Nizam, as well as through continuation of Mughal *darbars* and their formal organization of space.

[21] Alison Mackenzie Shah, "Mapping Space, Mapping Identity: Imagining Hyderabad's Walled City in the nineteenth-century," *Marg* 56, no. 1 (2004): 50–60.

[22] This is based on Mughal as well as Deccan court festivals and includes the major Muslim ids as well as the Persian Nauruz and the Hindu Basant (spring) festival. See S. Naqvi, *Muslim Religious Institutions and their Role under the Qutb Shahs* (Hyderabad, 1993). These festivals had been celebrated under different rulers and dynasties, but the nineteenth-century Nizams were the first to tie them to the ceremonial of rule.

[23] This is a festival derived from a Qutb Shahi vow made to an *alam*, but the conducting of the parade for the "salamati of the Gaddi [throne]" was an Asaf Jahi invention. See Alison Mackenzie Shah, "Constructing a Capital on the Edge of Empire: Politics and Urban Patraonge in the Nizams' Hyderabad, 1750–1950," Ph.D. Dissertation (University of Pennsylvania, 2005); for a definition of "Langar," see Central Records Office, *Chronology of Modern Hyderabad, from 1720–1890* (Hyderabad, 1954), Glossary, 8–9.

[24] The Nizams celebrated the four major *darbars* of the year during which *nazr* was presented to the Nizam, and titles presented to the courtiers on the following *'Ids*: *'Id uz zuha*, *'Id ul fitr*, *Nouruz*, and following the Qutb Shahs and Mughals before them, the Hindu festival of spring *Basant*, at which time Hindu courtiers presented *nazr* ("Darbar," *Chronology* Glossary, 3).

the court into urban life, it also helped to draw the boundaries of the Nizam's power in physical geography, since the processions and festivals were essentially tied to an Islamic calendar. The walls of the city and the south bank of the River began to suggest the cultural borders of the Nizam's dwindling domain.

As the presence and power of the British in the early nineteenth-century Deccan increased, the Nizams defensively focused on Mughal political ceremony to diminish symbolically the British presence through the scripting of diplomacy within the city's greater urban geography. The third (1803–1829) and fourth (1829–1857) Nizams ritually held *darbars* and audiences with the Resident in various city palaces, such as Manjli Begum's Haveli, Khwabgah palace, Ragmala palace, Roshan mahal, and other *mahals* situated in and around the royal centre, in the palaces of the city's nobles, as well as in the Purani Haveli, a palace that was purchased in the old Shia quarter near Mir Alam's house[25] (figure 1, #5). They often left the walled city and held audiences in their private gardens in the city's suburbs, but rarely did they leave the city to visit the Chaderghat Residency—that was a task they left primarily to their diplomatic agent, the Minister.

The Mughal connection was activated not only by audience, but also in procession. The third Nizam used to leave the city via the Delhi Darwaza (figure 4) for political ceremonies—for receiving *farmans* from Delhi, for visiting the Residency and for escorting a new Resident to the Nizam's palace.[26] The Delhi Darwaza was a gate at a significant distance from the Residency, and required fording the Musi on the backs of elephants[27] (figure 1, #6). The path was overtly indirect, and seemingly chosen primarily for its symbolic orientation to Mughal Delhi. The threshold of the city—that critical transition space that separated the old city of the Nizam from the British suburb of Chaderghat—was negotiated through Delhi, bringing to bear the symbolic power of the northern Mughal capital, not the local British officials in the nearby district. And after visiting the Residency, the Nizam continued on to his private estates beyond the Residency in the ring of royal hunting

---

[25] *Chronology*, for example, 165, 169, 194, 241, 242, 243, 246, 247.
[26] *Chronology*, 117, 122, 176.
[27] "Delhi Darwaza," *Chronology*, 117/20 May, 1808. This naming of a gate as Delhi Darwaza was an urban feature common to fortified cities, and provided orientation for cities across the subcontinent toward the imperial capital at Delhi. The Chaderghat access to the River and the Nizam's procession from the east appears in an aquatint from R. M. Grindlay's *Scenery, Costumes, and Architecture* (London, 1826–1830).

and garden properties that surrounded the city.[28] The Nizam never accorded the British Residency the status of a destination; it was only a way station within a larger cultural geography of royal possessions of a Mughal successor dynasty.

The Residency remained a site of ambiguous political symbolism. The third Nizam (1803–1829) only visited the Residency once. When he did, the interaction was as complicated a statement of power as the process of its construction had been. The Nizam was offered as *nazr* by the British the items with which to conduct a *darbar* in the Mughal style, with jewels, and gold brocaded clothing. The Nizam offered nothing in return to the Resident or British officers present; instead, he took the jewels presented to him and then conferred them as status-bearing gifts on his attendant courtiers. The nature of the power relationships between the Nizam and the British was suggested by the sources for cultural authority presented to the courtiers by the Nizam, but the ritual ceremony did not reach out to include the British officials.

The fourth Nizam (1829–1857) contributed more significantly to the ceremonial relationship of power between palace and Residency. After years of the British fording the shallow river on horseback to get to the city for meetings with Ministers and agents, the fourth Nizam granted permission in 1831 for a bridge connecting the Residency's rear gate to the Musi's south bank, outside the walls to the east of the city (figure 1, #2). This solidified the Residency's political orientation. The bridge provided a practical route to Hyderabad, linking the British centre directly to the south bank of the river, but not directly into the walled city. The path required British officials enter the city through the Chaderghat gate, passing through the city's residential quarters with the plain high exterior walls of the city's palaces and small neighbourhood shops lining the road. There was no grand processional avenue of political partnership; the Chaderghat bridge route was closer to a servants' entrance to the Nizam's urban household.

As an icon of the permanence of British power in Hyderabad, the Residency proved an unwelcome monument whose identity the Nizams had to manipulate in order to construct their own authority in the uncertain political climate of the early nineteenth century. Not

---

[28] *Chronology*, 117. 19/20 May 1808 records the visit of the third Nizam to the Residency and the scribe makes clear that the ending point for the visitation is the Nizam's continuing journey on to Nizam Imad Bagh.

surprisingly, the Nizams' political and financial frustrations continued to be played out on the building, which fell into increasing disrepair. Substantial repairs were made in 1826, but the Residents grew disgruntled at having to beg the Nizams for money to fix their palace. In 1833, it was proposed to the Nizam that the Chaderghat Residency be abandoned for "a less pretentious Residency at a greater distance from the City."[29] A more modest bungalow was constructed at the northern edge of Hussain Sagar Lake in Bolarum, for administrative purposes. The abandoned Chaderghat Residency, however, remained an important part of the growing city and represented the promise of British rule of the district, which provided its own money, taxes and troops for protection of a developing community of British, Parsi, and Marwari bankers whose loans were financing—or perhaps more accurately, bankrupting—the Nizam government. With European-style Public Gardens added in the 1840s, and St. George's church completed in the 1860s, the suburb developed a completely different fabric, both built and social, from the heart of Hyderabad, the old walled city on the south of the river.

The two sides of the river increasingly represented different cultural districts and different political authorities. The political rituals that linked the royal palace and the Residency in the first half of the nineteenth century were primarily intended to obfuscate the relationship of dependence between the Nizam and the British, and in this nexus, the role of the Nizam's Diwan as political intermediary became crucial. While the position of Minister was not hereditary, the extended family of Mir Alam held the position of Diwan throughout most of the nineteenth century.[30] The Ministers carried out the duties of their office from their palace, the Diwan Deodhi, establishing a third core of power in this nineteenth-century political system (figure 1, #3). This meant that, like the British and their Residency, a single site became associated with the intermediary position.

---

[29] *Notes on the Hyderabad Residency*, 3. "The reasons that he gave for this proposal were the expense of maintaining the present building, that its proximity to the City afforded facilities for intriguers and corrupt servants and exposed it to danger from the lawless soldiery of the City: he further considered it undesirable that the Resident should live so near His Highness' Court that constant references were possible between the two."

[30] Mir Alam (diwan 1804–1808); his son in law, Munir ul Mulk (1809–1832); his son Siraj ul Mulk (1846–1848, 1851–1853); his nephew, Mir Turab Ali Khan, Salar Jung I (1853–1883); his son, Mir Laik Ali Khan, Salar Jung II (1884–1886); his son, Mir Yusuf Ali Khan, Salar Jung III (1912–1914).

Throughout the early nineteenth century, the palace's visual form was shaped to claim a central position in the power negotiations between Hyderabad's ruler and its Resident. The 1830s Minister, Munir ul Mulk, who struggled against other Hyderabadi agents to establish the Diwan as the sole conduit between Resident and Ruler, designed some unusually creative pavilions. These include the famous *chini khana* hall (figure 5) in which the walls and ceiling were covered in imported English cups and saucers, an *aina khana* (figure 6) filled with imported plate-glass mirrors. By the 1840s, the role of intermediary was firmly in his family's hands and the role of the Diwan Deodhi as a power centre clearly established. The halls, in their display of traditional old-city architectural forms filled with British goods, spoke to the current political identity of the colonial periphery. By placing goods imported by British firms into Hyderabadi pavilions, they materially represented the ways Nizam's authority was being filled with British advice through the Minister.

As the British Residents had retreated from the Chaderghat Residency and the Nizam was almost completely bankrupt, this site vied for potential as the new centre of Hyderabadi power. Munir ul Mulk's Diwan Deodhi thus suggested a power centre for the walled city that competed with the Nizam's *darbar* halls. Its imagery and its lack of *darbar* ceremony complicated the strong arguments of political continuity that the Nizams were making through Mughal space and ritual and suggested the cultural and spatial politics that characterized the three-way power struggle that shaped the city in the first half of the nineteenth century.

By mid-nineteenth century, the city then had a set of monuments that represented the negotiations of power between Nizam, Resident and their intermediary Ministers that together symbolized the limits of Asaf Jahi political authority. The city with its Indo-Persian court on one hand and the Minister's Diwan Deodhi on the other, and the Chaderghat suburb and its non-Muslim merchant banker immigrants, all had visually unrelated anchors representing the political power struggles imposed by the arrival of the British Residency. Not only were the loci of power dependent on different cultural heritages, but they were also ritually disconnected since the Nizam and the Resident each had a different path between the sites.

The River Musi provided an easy physical boundary that maintained the cultural distinctness between the Islamic old city and the new suburb that was growing up under British Residency patronage.

Both local British officers and Hyderabadi courtiers believed that the Nizam would eventually fall prey to British annexation, as other states did in the Indian subcontinent. As one local British observer noted in 1825, "[a]n alliance with us [the British] on the subsidiary system leads inevitably to the ultimate destruction of the state which embraces it."[31] However, the ritual processions between the sites scripted a narrative for the Nizams that was intended to lessen the Residency's status as symbol of the establishment of new authority. While the British received no status through their paths to the Nizam's city, the procession to the Residency contained important commemorations that tied the Nizams to Mughal Delhi, in the path across the river through the Delhi gate and the Mughlai *darbars* held in the Residency when the Nizam did visit. And because the Residency did not receive the status of end point, the political rituals that linked these sites in the first half of the nineteenth century continued to ceremonially obscure the importance of the British and deny the Residency a role as the symbol of foundation of British power, turning it instead toward another site for the Nizam's *darbar*. The fact that by the 1840s the building had been abandoned and was intentionally brought to a state of decay visually belied any perception that the foundation of British power was the beginning of a strong and rising political power.

Afzal ud Daulah and the Princely State

In 1857, when Afzal ud Daulah ascended the throne to become the fifth Nizam, Hyderabad's political geography reflected the discomfort which the unwanted alliance with the British caused his predecessors. With the symbols of urban authority such as the announcement of the Mughal emperor's name in the *khutbah*, the Mughal emperor's name on the coins, and the continuation of Mughal court ritual in the palace, the Nizams held on to many of the symbols of power from the early modern heritage which had become culturally embedded into this rapidly changing landscape of power. In 1858, after the British deposed the last Mughal emperor and sent him into exile in Burma, the authority that the Nizams had enacted through ceremonial dependent on

---

[31] H. Russell, in *A Sketch of the Proceedings connected with Certain Pecuniary Transactions of Mssrs. Palmer and Co. with the Government of His Highness the Nizam* (London, 1825), 18.

Mughal cultural heritage required rethinking.[32] Nizam Afzal ud Daulah
responded with visual statements that expressed a new iconography of
modern Deccan power in Indo-Islamic terms. The State's sovereignty
was granted only over internal affairs, and was based on its continued
support of the British Crown. Afzal ud Daulah's vision used the urban
heritage to express both the nature of the necessary partnership with
the British Crown and the character of Asaf Jahi independence. His
argument was displayed in a cultural discourse that relied on Persianate
palace design, a mosque, and a combination of building technologies
that confidently defined a new Asaf Jahi identity.

The fifth Nizam's focus on palace and mosque are almost standard,
certainly predictable monuments for Muslim rulers to declare political power to those they rule and to their peers. Yet together with the
bridge they made a powerful and locally rooted urban construction
of the ruler's image and affirmed the status of the capital city as the
symbol of the Nizam's identity. The palace, mosque, and bridge not
only declared a new future for the dynasty, it also suggested a new
past, adding new monuments that at once changed the heritage of the
dynasty and rescripted the roles of the earlier monuments of political
authority by contextualizing and connecting them in new ways.[33] And
at the same time, they united the greater city—the walled centre and
its northern suburbs—more clearly under the Nizam, and his Indo-
Islamic cultural authority, by constructing sites that transferred symbols
of power from one side of the river into the other (figure 7).

The building of a new bridge came first. Despite the growth to the
north, the walled city had been self-contained, with its main north–south
avenue ending at the river's bank, and the northern suburbs were
connected to the city only through the Chaderghat bridge on the east
and the old bridge, the Purana Pul, far to the west. Afzal ud Daulah's
first project was to extend the city's central avenue into the northern

---

[32] And the British were quick to adopt and adapt Mughal cultural heritage for their
new imperial identity. B. Cohn, "Representing Authority in Victorian India," in *The
Invention of Tradition*, ed. Hobsbawm and Ranger (Cambridge, 1983), 165–210.
[33] The Chowmahallah Palace and the development of the Afzal Jung Mosque
complex were also tied directly into patronage trends that had shaped the city in its
modern incarnation as seat of power for a tenuously empowered dynasty. Previously,
patronage had been piecemeal, but Afzal brought the planned complex and narratives
through space and ritual movement together in a relationship of urban parts: the city
was imagined under his patronage as an entity.

suburbs. In so doing, he aligned the original double cross layout of the early modern planned city to the south of the river with the development of the city in the nineteenth century on the northern bank (figure 7, #3). The extension of the city's main north–south avenue shifted the urban geography from an older Indo-Islamic centre and a new separate district characterized by occupation and opposition to the Nizam government into a synthetic, even natural, integration of the two phases of urban development (figure 8). The extension of the avenue into a bridge required breaking a new gate into the city's wall. The new monumental Afzal gate (figure 9) at the south end of the bridge became the transition between walled city with its centuries of Indo-Islamic heritage and the new suburb with its decidedly un-Mughal, un-Islamic character. Afzal ud Daulah's concomitant establishment of a grain market, the Afzal Gunj, on the north side of the bridge encouraged the development a commercial node that would secure economic activity there, such that the expansion from the old city through this new path would be seamless.

If the bridge laid claim for the Nizam over both city and the northern suburb, it also resonated into a new symbolic identity for the Residency. On the one hand, the bridge codified, spatially, the peripheral nature of the British centre, which was now located at some distance from the top of the new bridge, and the urban heart. But if the bridge secured a peripheral status for the Residency in Hyderabad urban life, it also integrated the Chaderghat Residency more clearly into the political geography. In the late 1860s, the Chaderghat Residency experienced a renaissance as a ceremonial centre for British authority. While the Residents still resided in Bolarum, they revived the ceremonial role of the grand Palladian palace, perhaps because of their own growing interests in cultural expressions of power appropriate to an Imperial power.[34] While the British officials may have made the decision to return to the Residency, the bridge created the diplomatic path between the Nizams' palace and the Residency that remained central to political ceremony well into the twentieth century. The bridge ritually tightened the relationship between ruler and Resident, and focused them more clearly on the State of Hyderabad. Both British and Asaf Jahi officials

---

[34] In 1868, Resident Temple wrote that a ball was held "in the upper story of the house [Residency], furbished up for the occasion after many years of disuse" (Temple, *Journals*, 139).

passed through the Afzal gate, rather than the Delhi gate or the Chaderghat bridge. And, visitors from the Chaderghat Residency were now
funnelled to the centre of the city through a single, formal avenue.

The Nizam's path between the two sites symbolized the shared
identity of the two powers.[35] Ceremonially, through the change in the
ritual path linking the two sites, Delhi disappeared from the history
and identity of the dynasty, and through his bridge and gate Afzal ud
Dualah became the link between the two districts of his Princely State
capital. The Nizam's new road from the bridge also provided access
to the formal front of the Residency's *darbar* hall, ending the approach
from the rear, riverside entrance. The Residency still looked out toward
Calcutta, but Afzal ud Daulah had now effectively connected its front façade
directly to the city (and in turn to a new palace) with a new curving road,
such that Calcutta and Hyderabad were no longer symbolically oppositional.

Within the walls, the Nizam's use of the wide axial north–south
boulevard in the centre of the city as an access route for official political interaction highlighted a new claim of the cultural origins of the
ruler through Hyderabad's oldest urban monuments. The Nizams
had always been the rulers of a Deccan kingdom, but they had found
more utility in constructing their identity as Mughal vassals. The fifth
Nizam's legitimacy was now severed from the defunct Mughal north.
His capital, however, had been founded as the capital of a previous
Deccan dynasty, the Qutb Shahs, who ruled Hyderabad for a century
before being conquered by the Mughal armies in 1687. Their identities
were significantly different. Though both were Muslim dynasties, the
Qutb Shahs were Shia and the Nizams, like the Mughals, were Sunni.
In a twist of historical imagination, however, the Nizam shifted his
identity from alignment with the conquering Mughal armies, under
whom his ancestor Asaf Jah I had come to Hyderabad, to affiliation
with the Deccan Qutb Shahs.

The effect of the axial road being joined to the north with the new
bridge provided a stronger tie between the suburb and the city itself.
Entering the walled city on this spacious boulevard, one could gaze
down a grand avenue that displayed a sequence of lofty monuments

---

[35] Resident Temple in his *Report on the Administration of the Government of His Highness
the Nizam in the Deccan* (Calcutta, 1868) noted many of the requests made to the Nizam's
government for changes to the city, but nothing about connecting the Residency formally
to the city was ever mentioned. See particularly Chapter 7: Material Improvements.

from days of Hyderabad's role as the early modern Deccan capital (figure 7, #5, #6). Visitors crossed the bridge and turned onto the main avenue gazing at the approach to the majestic Char Kamans, the four monumental stone arches that marked out the intersection of four avenues in the original planned city, newly renovated by Afzal ud Dualah in 1858 (figure 10). After passing through those arches, they continued past the Jami Masjid (1001H) before coming to the Charminar, Hyderabad's most famous monument, also from its foundation in 1591 and marking the second intersection of the city's original double cross plan (figure 11). Passing by the Charminar, the official visitors turned west toward the Nizam's royal centre. In their use of soaring arches and minarets, these monuments declared Indo-Islamic heritage both religious and secular, an urban identity that was greater than the individual monuments. With the placement of these historic monuments between the Afzal gate and the Nizam's new palace, they united the walled city into a single stage of Indo-Islamic Deccan history, bringing the city's distant past to serve a Princely Asaf Jahi dynastic identity.

The destination at the south end of this political path was Afzal ud Daulah's new palace complex. The Chowmahallah palace's name reflects its four (*chahar/chau*) pavilions (*mahal*) that face each other around a rectangular tank. This Persianate form was adapted to Hyderabadi taste under the early modern Shia Qutb Shahi dynasty, which sought out connections to Iran as a way to counter the Mughal presence in the north. And it is the general Persian-style layout that led the British author Campbell to state that it was "a copy" of the Qajar Shah's palace.[36] The refashioning of the Chowmahallah, however, had nothing to do with Iran, and had everything to do with the political identity of the Asaf Jahi dynasty. The Chowmahallah was the palace in which the Asaf Jahs housed French troops in 1750 with whose support the establishment of the British in Hyderabad was actively opposed.[37] At the end of the eighteenth century, a powder keg exploded and destroyed one of the pavilions, marking the last time that the complex is mentioned in local histories or chronicles until 1849, when a disturbance is recorded taking place outside its gate, and a private audience is granted there

---

[36] "Chowmahallah" Campbell, 1898.
[37] Sarkar, "Haidarabad and Golkonda in 1750 as Seen Through French Eyes," *Islamic Culture* (April, 1936): 234–247.

to Resident Colonel Fraser.[38] Returning to this neglected site for the primary power centre was a way to replot the early history of the Asaf Jahs in Hyderabad as well as that of the British.

The location of the Chowmahallah affirmed the idea of a core royal district yet presented a broader interpretation of royal identity than the earlier palaces of the Nizams. It is situated directly to the south of the Nizams' eighteenth century palaces, behind the throne hall (figure 7, #7). This location—unlike the Nizams' Purani Haveli palace—enabled the lengthy procession along the central boulevard past all the grand monuments of Deccan Muslim political authority. And, as it is just behind the *qiblah* wall of the Mecca Masjid, the city's main congregational mosque in whose courtyard the Nizams are buried, it expanded the district in which all of the activities of the royal family could take place, from ascending the throne, to the announcement of authority in the *khutbah*, the *darbar*, to burial, to *'urs* ceremony, generation after generation.

This district had been identified ceremonially by its Mughlai character, but the refashioning of the Chowmahallah shifted the emphasis of Mughal heritage in royal identity to something both more antique and more contemporary. Unlike the previous Mughal layout of palace complexes in this area, which were linear successions of courtyards ending with single pavilions, the old Hyderabadi Persianate form of four pavilions facing one another enabled the Nizam to represent different collective identities through their visual heritages and join them into a unified formal relationship. The Chowmahallah functions as two sets of complementary pavilions, facing each other in responses, or *jawab*s. The single-story pavilions on the east and west, the Mihtab Mahal and the Aftab Mahal respectively, are in plan and in scale mirror images of one another. In ornament, however, they suggest the separate characters of the sun, *aftab*, and moon, *mihtab*, whose names they bear. The central hall of the western Aftab Mahal is ornamented with a composite of Europeanate features: ionic columns and Palladian mouldings that speak to the localizing of British heritage in the city. The central hall of the eastern Mihtab Mahal is composed of lobed arches, sitting atop double baluster columns in a style that old city palaces of

---

[38] *Chronology*, 237/11 Sept. 1849. The Chowmahallah was an old palace but apparently not a centre of political ceremony. There is no mention of the palace as a complex in the first half of the nineteenth century, though possibly we do not recognize some of the earlier names of the individual *mahals* before they were rebuilt/renamed.

the Nizam's Muslim and Hindu courtiers employed. Both palaces are finished in plaster rather than constructed with the traditional Hyderabadi teak, emphasizing a material tied to both the British Residency and the public Islamic heritage in the city as a symbol of new power. The plaster-faced pavilions were not only innovative constructions in terms of their materials, but the decision to represent two separate ornamental styles in these facing pavilions suggested the integration of the imported British design into the modern Deccan identity.[39] The contrasting pavilions linked into complementary identities as sun and moon, suggested that the Nizam was the ruler of two different communities, which like day and night, join to make a complete form. This idea of necessary opposition is expressed in these smaller pavilions that mark the sides of the complex. The choices made in the southern Afzal Mahal and the northern Tahniat Mahal, which are not mirror images in name or in form, require further analysis.

At the south end of the Chowmahallah is the largest pavilion, aptly named the Afzal Mahal. It is a grand double-story pillared hall, whose referent is quite clearly the British Residency at Chaderghat (figure 12). Facing the Afzal Mahal at the north end of the complex is the Tahniat Mahal, (Mir Tahniat Ali Khan being another title of the fifth Nizam) a scaled-down adaptation of the Afzal Mahal, using the ornament of the southern palace in a more modestly proportioned Hyderabadi pavilion (figure 13). The Afzal Mahal, with its portico displaying six towering Corinthian columns, its interior *darbar* hall ornamented with Palladian detail in carved plasterwork and with a gallery encircling the room on the second floor, evokes the Residency not so much in its exterior silhouette, whose Palladian pediment was completely removed from Deccan aesthetics, as in its interior space.[40] The space for political

---

[39] Unfortunately, there is not much evidence for what sort of actions took place in each *mahal*. In the late nineteenth-century, the Tahniat Mahal was used for formal entertainment of visitors, in the twentieth century, the Aftab mahal was used for administration, and photographs confirm that the Mihtab mahal was used for formal *darbars*. That does not suggest much about the mid-nineteenth century, however. The layout of four palaces for a site of political authority suggests that there were different communities with whom the Nizam had to negotiate his power and the variety of styles of the halls does leave open the possibility for highlighting one identity over another. This was certainly the case in the late nineteenth century when the sixth Nizam highlighted a Sufistic *darbar* identity by holding *darbars* in the Mughlai hall, which had the same form as the *samakhanas* of his *pir*.

[40] The Chowmahallah is still the property of the Nizams' Trust and measured drawings are not permitted within its precincts.

ritual of the *darbar* was both more politically potent and more easily blended with local architectural heritage.

For Afzal ud Daulah's predecessors, the Chaderghat Residency had clearly proved a complicated monument, considering the passive aggression enacted upon it by the earlier Nizams. It had represented the foreignness of the British and their power outside the city, looming outside the walled centre as if poised to take over the state. Its abandonment in the 1830s, on the other hand, had suggested that ceremony was to be absent from authority. The Afzal Mahal actively reclaimed the image of the British Residency in Chaderghat as a piece of royal heritage by setting it within a grammar of Deccani Persianate architecture.[41] Thus, he at once took over the visual definition of British authority, diminished the foreign-ness of the power represented by the original Palladian building, and made the Residents' cultural heritage the central feature of this Deccan Indo-Islamic Princely identity. The fifth Nizam's new palace retuned the memory of his dynastic origins further back into a general Deccan origin, blurring the transitions between Qutb Shah and Mughal successor dynasty through the development of a new part of the royal core, and including British heritage in his symbol of power. At the same time, the complex, through the interdependence of British and Mughal visual forms, placed the English architecture in a more collaborative position than its previous role as a oppositional symbol of British colonial origins. This relatively simple act of refashioning a Persianate palace symbolically reshaped an entire dynastic history.

---

[41] Not only did Afzal ud Daulah place imported British architecture in symmetrical arrangement with the Hyderabadi pavilions to formulate a new Asaf Jahi collective identity, but he also layered the English heritage on top of the history of the French in the Deccan. The Afzal Mahal is built on the location that the French commander de Bussy, the nemesis of the eighteenth-century British East India Company, had used for his quarters. See Sarkar, "Through French Eyes." While the nature of "support" had certainly changed—from providing military service in the mid-eighteenth-century to precluding complete sovereignty in the mid-nineteenth-century, the history of the Chowmahallah opened up a founding moment of British authority by returning to the site associated with French heritage. The fact that the northern pavilion had been blown up in a gunpowder explosion at the end of the eighteenth-century, and apparently not rehabilitated until Afzal's reign would provide evidence for a continued memory of the site as associated with the French military presence, though its specifics cultural dynamics are now lost. While history suggests that the origins of the Princely State began with the establishment of the British, the origins of the Nizam dynasty go back significantly further and include the French.

The Chowmahallah has been reinterpreted so far only as the self-contained complex it has been imagined to be, but I argue it should also be read in relation to the Nizam's larger urban design. The new bridge and its new access route between the Residency and the Chowmahallah expanded the palace's reach and enabled the Nizam to claim for the Afzal Mahal a *jawab* in the distant Chaderghat Residency. The Afzal Mahal and the Residency do not exactly face each other, since they both look north, but the new Afzal Gunj bridge now linked to a curving road that led north and then east to the front façade of the Residency. Thus, leaving the neo-classical *darbar* hall of Chowmahallah's Afzal Mahal, with its six Corinthian pillars, one would proceed in a diplomatic procession to the "mirror" neoclassical darbar hall with its six Corinthian pillars at the Chaderghat Residency (figure 7, #1, #7). In this sense, the Tahniat Mahal can be read as simply a smaller step to complete the palace courtyard in a much larger urban design. Through the road and its diplomatic end points, the iconic power of the Residency was shifted from marker of the establishment of British authority in Hyderabad to a piece of the collective identity of Hyderabad State.

Through their landmarks the two sectors of the city entered into dialogue and through the bridge they were becoming more clearly intertwined. The path from the bridge now effectively displayed historic Indo-Islamic monuments and more recent British monuments that bolstered the depth of the Nizam's legitimacy and the currency of his authority. But his legitimacy and authority were also was tied directly to that third player in Asaf Jahi negotiations of power: the Minister. Afzal ud Daulah had an extremely powerful Minister, Salar Jung, whom the Nizam tried hard to bend to his royal will, but whose independence and "modern" ways gained him recognition as far as London. Salar Jung's Diwan Deodhi palace was located at the top of the avenue that now reached across to Chaderghat with the Afzal Gate and new bridge, sitting on the road almost midway between the Residency and the Nizam's new palace (figure 7, #4). As the fifth Nizam had used this linear urban design to re-plot the heritage of his dynastic identity, he also used it manipulate the site of the Minister's power, spatially scripting a future role of the Minister for his new State. Since the Subsidiary Alliance established the British permanently in their city at the end of the eighteenth century, the Nizams had been struggling against their ministers for full political control. Resident after Resident noted that the

Nizams did not trust their Ministers and felt that their Ministers were attempting to usurp their authority.[42] The Nizam's struggle to contain this Minister was well known. Salar Jung had to get his royal patron's permission in order even to leave the city.[43] This commitment of royal control was symbolically inscribed into the urban form: from the north, the Resident had to pass through the Afzal Darwaza in order to reach Salar Jung's palace—and Salar Jung had to pass through that gate to leave the city. Within this new urban design, the Minister was not to be an independent player any longer in a three-way system. If the Nizam was to be joined to the British for his political position, he suggested through his new access road that the Minister was to be more clearly dependent upon him.

Yet the Nizam's urban design was not an unassailable way to claim power and its features left it open to the very kind of contestation that the Nizam continually sought to contain. From another perspective, the location of the new bridge beside the palace gate also meant that the Minister possessed the Nizam: the British could not enter the city without receiving an escort from the Minister. And Salar Jung posted guards on the new bridge to ensure this was so.[44] And a year after the bridge was completed the Minister visually confirmed the status of his palace as a new point of mediation between two political powers, adding a "spacious banquet house" called the Naya Makan to his palace complex.[45] The Naya Makan, which was outfitted in the British style— but not the Residency style—had furnishings such as chairs and tables as well as an enclosed room.[46] The Naya Makan replaced the *aina khana* as the site for receiving British visitors and enabled the British to maintain their practices of sitting on chairs and not removing their shoes for the first time within the Nizams' cultural world of the old city.[47] Over time this pavilion became the sole transition space, where the British were entertained and where they (and later other European visitors) were

---

[42] Temple, *Journals*, 108.

[43] Bilgrami, *Historical and Descriptive Sketch*, 174.

[44] Ibid., 552.

[45] M. A. Nayeem, *Splendour of Hyderabad: Last Phase of an Oriental Culture* (Bombay, 1987), 98.

[46] Temple, *Journals*, 92. He describes it as very spacious and had been constructed and furnished in the English fashion.

[47] Temple mentions dinner at Salar Jung's palace given by the Nizam's government for one hundred and fifty people. The "courtyards were brilliantly lit" and "dinner was in the English style and the band of the Reformed Troops playing the while after dinner." (Temple, *Journals*, 100).

required to go to receive elephants for visiting the city and procession to the Nizam's palace. And the author of an 1880s book on Hyderabad was impressed by the decoration of this hall with "a complete set of portraits (half-lengths) in oil of all the former Residents at the Court of Haidarabad down to Sir Stuart Bayley, who left in April last year [1882]."[48] From the furniture to the decoration, this hall did not blend British and Hyderabadi cultures as the Diwan Deodhi's earlier pavilions had, but overtly separated them, making his domain a specifically desirable place for British official visits. The visual setting shows that the Minister's independence was now based on maintaining the differences between two opposing political powers; the cultural traditions of political ceremony of each allowed him to highlight their differences.

The design of the Diwan Deodhi confirms the importance of architecture and procession in mid-nineteenth-century Hyderabad for claiming a past appropriate for a new political identity. It also points to the fact that the real battles for the future of royal authority were taking place between the Nizam and the Minister Salar Jung.[49] Salar Jung's claim to authority was based a different construction of the Princely State, one that had its origins not in the distant past of the Indo-Islamic heritage but in the arrival of the British Residents in Hyderabad. Unlike the Afzal Mahal, which actively worked with urban heritage, the Diwan Deodhi's Naya Makan was clearly not tied to a historic site in the city, and its name, the New House, proclaimed the Minister's independence from the cultural symbiosis of power represented in the Residency and the Nizam's Chowmahallah palace.

By placing monumental forms of British style on the southern side of the River, the Nizam's and the Minister's complexes had blurred the bifurcation of the city into British and Asaf Jahi districts. While these sites were accessible only to the political elite, Afzal ud Daulah's final patronage project, the Afzal Gunj Masjid in 1868, placed a monumental symbol of the Nizam's Indo-Islamic authority on the northern bank of the Musi (figure 7, #2). Situated on the southern periphery of the primarily non-Muslim cultural district of Chaderghat, it was a landmark visible to all. This mosque, elevated on a one-storey platform with elaborate entry gates and a substantial courtyard, was larger than

---

[48] Bilgrami, *Historical and Descriptive Sketch*, 558.
[49] See particularly V. K. Bawa, *The Nizam between the Mughals and British: Hyderabad under Salar Jung I* (New Delhi, 1986) for Salar Jung's role in bureaucratizing the Nizam's government and ending the power of the court.

any but the Mecca mosque, the grandest congregational mosque in the old city. In its style, grandeur, and location, the Afzal Gunj mosque staked a claim for the Nizam's old city culture in the area previously defined by its non-Muslim society and urban fabric.

As an historic revival of a Qutb Shahi building, the mosque provided an image both historic and pristine, constructing a sense of depth to the new ruler's political lineage and visually articulating continuity with the local artistic and cultural heritage displayed in the monuments that ornamented the road on the other side of the river (figure 14). In its materials, engineering, as well as its ornament, the mosque was a masterpiece of Qutb Shahi monumental mosque architecture. The dramatic, incised plaster ornament marking the stages of the minarets with their domical caps recalled those of the mosques lining the main street of the *karwan-e sahu* suburb near the Golconda fort (figure 15). From a distance, with the sight of the intricately carved minarets and the highly ornamented registers of the parapet punctuated by small domical capped finials, a passerby might be led to think that it was indeed a Qutb Shahi mosque and that the area was one of the older settlements of the city. When the *khutbah* was recited in the name of the Deccan ruler, the architectural ambiance of the Afzal Gunj mosque provided deep local resonance. Yet key features in the mosque's design confirmed its contemporary patron.

While the mosque silhouette itself did not stray significantly from the models of early modern monumental prototypes, it did not perpetuate Shia symbolism in the use of a five bay façade.[50] This was to be a Qutb Shahi mosque, but without the Shia symbolism. In addition to that alteration, the complex, with its second-storey platform courtyard, and with shop stalls carved into niches in the façade's perimeter below, was a nineteenth-century Hyderabadi design. Qutb Shahi period monumental mosques were constructed in the centre of caravanserais, from which the rental income from long distance merchants staying in the rooms provided income to support the upkeep of the building and maintenance of its staff. Under the hundred years of Asaf Jahi rule, only two small congregational mosques had been built. These differed significantly in their elevations, each looking for a way of representing a nineteenth-century identity, but both employed the double story

---

[50] The Shia *panjtan* is often symbolically highlighted in Deccan architecture by patterns of five.

complex design that suited the old city demands of limited space (figure 16). Visually this design raised the elevation of the landmark silhouette of the mosque dramatically, and technically it was impressive since it required significant engineering skill to situate the mosque's tank on a second-storey plinth. In Hyderabad's suburbs, there was no demand for this two-storey adaptation: land was not scarce as it was in the old city. Supporting shops could just as practically have lined the street front on either side of the mosque, but the Afzal Gunj Masjid followed the model of the earlier Mir Alam Mandi Masjid and the grander Chowk Masjid (figure 17).

The decision to design such a complex, I argue, was political. The Nizam created a complex simultaneously old and new, and provided a codification of the stacked mosque elevation model as reflecting an Asaf Jahi royal identity. The design of the exterior front façade of the complex was where the innovative arguments took place. Here was presented for the first time a specifically Asaf Jahi royal image through the use of *jharokha* balconies on either side of the simple arched entry gates. This is the same pattern that is displayed on the entrance to the *jilukhana* hall, which leads to the royal throne hall. The finials on the entry pavilions' roofs complement those on the mosque's roof, and through these seemingly extraneous buildings, the separate images of Qutb Shahi and Asaf Jahi are blended. And by choosing to subtly alter an historic style for the mosque building, rather than to create a contemporary or innovative one, he brought Shia and Sunni royal patronage visions together as generally Hyderabadi Muslim. The Afzal Mosque visually fused the two Deccan dynasties, Qutb Shah and Asaf Jah, obfuscating the Mughal history in their regionally defined identity.

While ostensibly constructed to point the faithful toward the *qibla* and the sacred centre in Mecca, the mosque obviously served a local political culture as well. By fashioning a hybrid design and by constructing the site on the diplomatic ritual path, the patronage of a mosque took on a particularly potent meaning. As an institution of political authority, it served the purpose of commemorating the ruler in the *khutbah* to his Muslim subjects. As a landmark on the path of diplomatic ritual it made a statement about the heritage of Islamic authority in the city in relation to the British. Islam had been the banner behind which the anti-British rebels had gathered 1839 and again in 1857 (in Hyderabad's contribution to the regional rebellions of that year). In the mosques in the city, *maulvis* had organized men against the British, and according to urban lore the green flag of Islam had even been hoisted over the

Residency at one point in 1857. The mosque symbolically countered
the power of the Residency, and competed against its role as the sole
landmark and anchor for a separate district. Since the mosque marked
the connection directly north from the old city, Islamic heritage and
orientation provided its own anchor for the future growth of this suburb
of the Asaf Jahi capital.

Conclusion

Afzal ud Daulah died a few months after his mosque was completed,
so he never had a chance to display his integrated vision through
rituals and diplomatic ceremony. His projects nonetheless shaped the
dynamics of political ritual for the duration of the British Indian and
Asaf Jahi governments and still continue to encourage the perception
of a seamless link between the Qutb Shahs and Asaf Jahs. The fifth
Nizam, whose rule traversed the major transition in political authority,
was the first of his dynasty to undertake major public patronage projects in the city. His urban design rewrote the history of the Asaf Jahs
through select historic sites and the creation of new paths for political
interaction. Afzal ud Daulah's three projects worked together as an
urban design, the route between them forming a ritual path to unify
the form of the city with an axis of political power, while the individual
pieces marked the construction of a new identity spelled out in both
historical depth and political currency. These monuments had expressed
commitments to different heritages and cultural authorities as well as
political power, but the projects of the fifth Nizam brought these sites
into a clear spatial relationship by changing the symbolic contexts in
which they were set. And, I have suggested, through them, the Nizam
displayed a new presentation of Asaf Jahi origins.

In nineteenth-century British India, historic architectural styles served
political ends, and the definition and control of urban space were also
perceived as a powerful political act. The architecture that Afzal ud
Daulah left us offers evidence to explore how he defined his own status. Looking at the urban environment of the monuments shows how
three building projects created a complex construction of power in
a new urban geography. Analyzing his bridge, palace, and mosque
together as interdependent political statements based in Indo-Islamic
heritage suggest that the imperial periphery was actively engaged in
the same processes as the colonial heartland, though working toward
significantly different cultural and political ends.

SANA'A

Ronald Lewcock, Arief Setiawan

Sana'a survived into modern times with its medieval features and its old way of life still flourishing. The Imams of Yemen had prevented access to the country from the late seventeenth century onwards, broken only by a brief period of Ottoman occupation. After a civil war in the 1960s, it became possible for the old city to be studied by a group of international scholars before any significant modernization had occurred.

A visit to the functioning medieval city in the early seventies

Shimmering above the morning mists, the minarets of Sana'a rose over the central plateau. At close quarters the ancient medieval city could be seen to be surrounded by a wall. Sana'a was very tiny in pre-Islamic times and the form approaching visitors saw now was mostly built on virgin land. Ancient Sana'a—and the trade route that passed through it—was defended by a citadel, of which the upper fortifications were separated from the old city on higher ground (figures 2 and 3). This position enabled the citadel to control the city easily. The lowest part of the citadel itself was the original city, according to legend, and later contained the barracks. Some of the walls of the fortifications date from the eighth century.

There were seven gates giving access to the old city of Sana'a. Originally, some of these were protected by bastions arranged so that the approaches to the gates took a bent form. Since a *wadi* runs through the city, dividing it into two parts, the defensive wall had to cross it twice, with arches allowing the floodwaters to pass through it (figure 1).

The congregational, or Friday, mosque was built at the instructions of the prophet Mohammad himself, according to early historians of Islam; it is possible that he knew the city because he had traded there, for he was reported to have instructed his representative exactly where to build the mosque in the garden of the Persian governor. It seems likely that a substantial part of original building has survived to modern times on the southern and western sides. It is a rectangular building with blank stone walls punctured by only a few doors (figure 4). On the northern, *qibla*, side, the mosque was subsequently expanded in the eleventh century A.D. and the *mihrab* reconstructed. The eastern *riwaq* was rebuilt in the eleventh century. Throughout the building there are reused materials from pre-Islamic pagan temples and Christian churches, including columns, the latter sometimes placed upside down. The mosque has two minarets, one narrow and one broad, with corresponding calls for prayer, high-pitched and low-pitched—fascinating to hear across the city five times a day. In the centre is a courtyard containing a treasury in which the ancient copies of the Koran and public records were kept.

Next to the mosque were the shops of the scribes and the bookbinders, and then the market itself was entered. Unlike all the areas around it, which had high buildings, the market was low (figure 5).

The scene in the market was very colourful, with bright casual awnings, and even more brilliant clothing worn by the people. This was a society which believed that men should dress as colourfully as the women. The men actually appeared brighter, for the women were shrouded in shawls to protect their modesty.

A typical shop was one in which a range of goods was provided and several activities took place, although the shop itself was the size of a cupboard. That was characteristic of the market stalls. There was a box for a water pipe, with a flexible tube for smoking coming from it and a safe. Artifacts were manufactured inside the shop, in spite of its small size.

Some activities could not be carried on in the small shops. Heavy duty work involving high temperatures, industrial forges, and so on, was carried out in workshops behind shops.

Another characteristic of the market was that it managed its own affairs and security. A sheikh, a headman, was appointed over every residential neighbourhood in the city, and there was likewise a sheikh of the market, nominated by the shopkeepers and appointed by the governor.

Another characteristic of the market was that it was wealthy—it needed policing. Indeed the goldsmiths and silversmiths served as the bankers in such Islamic cities. Protecting the wealth of the market from robbery in the night became a serious issue. It was achieved, first, by not allowing residential accommodation within the market area. Hence the whole market remained single-storied. The only vertical projections were watchtowers for policing and a central control station (figure 5).

The carriage of goods was an important part of the wealth of medieval Sana'a. It was a trading city, dealing in spices, grain, salt and manufactured goods. The trade was carried on using camel and donkey trains. Storage for the goods and stables for the animals was provided around the edge of town in open-air caravanserais (the Persian term for them). But around the edge of the market there were also covered caravanserais.

On the arrival of a caravan, the camels or donkeys were stabled inside and the goods were unloaded and put away for storage, sale, and possibly reshipment. Above, accommodation was provided for the merchants and the drovers. As the merchants were fairly prosperous the accommodations not only had kitchens and dining rooms but also contained public hot baths and small mosques. There were two such hotels above the stables in the caravanserai illustrated, each designed around a courtyard; they were comfortable and provided a high level of amenity. Caravanserais like these were the characteristic medieval complexes of trade in the larger Islamic cities.

A second kind of hotel building existed at the edges of the market area, one built at ground level, so that it could also contain a coffee bar and a restaurant (figures 8 and 9). At the bar was a counter from which the coffee was served as well as sherbet and other drinks; it appeared remarkably like a Pompeian or even a modern café. On the floor above, bedrooms surrounded the courtyard. This kind of hotel accommodation was very like that of a medieval European hotel; Shakespeare's plays were first performed in courtyards of similar inns in Britain with galleries around them.

Also around the market, at the edges where buildings were allowed to be higher, the market provided for free accommodation for the poor. Because of this there were no homeless in Sana'a streets. Students were also permitted to live there, as were mothers and children without support.

Another building type around the edge of the market in Sana'a was the factory. The most characteristic kind of factory was a mill for grinding salt and grain. Salt in those areas was ground from rock salt found in the desert, and the mills were also used for grinding all sorts of grains. From some of these grains, like sesame, oil was obtained. To provide power in turning the mills, animals, donkeys or camels were used. In order to maintain their balance in the endless walk around the grinding stone the animals were blinkered.

Outside the city: other market activities, which were not considered desirable inside the walls, took place at the gates. The two most characteristic of these were the sale of meat and fuel. Because meat and fish were regarded as potential pollutants they were not sold in the market but at the gates of the city. And the same was true of fuel, not only because it might be potentially dangerous but also because fuel included not only wood but also animal dung.

An even more important activity took place outside the city. This was the communal dawn prayer of the festivals of the Muslim calendar. A decision was made at the time of the Prophet that the prayer for the two *'Id* would not take place inside the built-up areas of towns or cities; instead, it would be held outside, for reasons that are discussed below. The open-air prayer space (*musala*) had at first only one wall, which was traverse to the direction of Mecca, towards which the congregation prayed, the minimum requirement for a place of prayer. If there were four walls around the prayer space, a symbol, a niche (a *mihrab*) marked the *qibla* wall, and thus indicated clearly the direction of prayer.

People came to the *id* prayers heavily armed because of tribal feuds. With the topic of tribalism we reach to a key point about traditional Islam cities—and about Sana'a. Islam brought the urban civilization of the past together with the people of the countryside in a way that had not occurred before. Country people came into the city to pray at least twice a year from hundreds of miles around. The interactions between city dwellers and country dwellers was much more constant in Islam than it had been in earlier societies. And the most characteristic feature of country people was that they belonged to clans and tribes. Because of its conquests, Islam became incalculably rich within a generation of the death of the prophet. A huge number of people who had been in the country settled in the cities, and the growth of towns and cities was phenomenal within that period. Yet the country people retained their tribal allegiances for many generations—in some cases until the present day. This is an important factor in understanding the form of Islamic cities. Tribalism had often been a central element in the governing of communities in antiquity.[1] Tribal allegiances were generally based on blood-ties. Fundamentally, it was most common for everybody in a specific tribe to believe that they shared an ancestor,

---

[1] Cf. the tribes of Israel, and the role of tribalism in the political structure of the city states of ancient Greece.

no matter how ancient or even legendary. But there was a closer kind of bond—the clan, when people shared a common ancestor within recent memory. The clan would usually number about two hundred to five hundred people. The tribe might number up to ten thousand. And almost the whole population of the countryside would be made up of these types of division. Each clan paid respect and obedience to its leader. And similarly each tribe had an elected chief, a sheikh, whom everybody obeyed implicitly. The social structure was thus hierarchical. The most efficient form of central government was clearly to utilize the power of the tribal chiefs. That was the way Islam administered many territories with relative ease, including those around Sana'a. But a recurring issue with tribalism—as with families—was that it was very easy for feuds to develop. Individuals bore grudges; in tribal societies they might bear grudges for hundreds of years. Revenge thus became a central part of tribal tradition, and dealing with it a central problem in administration.

An example of this problem in Sana'a is that people arrived at the annual communal prayers armed to protect themselves from others who might have decided to enact revenge for an ancient clan or tribal grievance. Policemen had to be stationed at the morning 'Id prayers to protect the whole community from any tribal fighting that broke out. Hence the reason why the 'Id prayers were held in the open countryside and not in the city.

Following the above argument, it would be reasonable to ask: how were rural tribesmen who came into the city controlled? On an ordinary shopping day, tribesmen from the country who wanted to go to the market and take part in trading inside were controlled in two ways: first, their arms were removed at the gates by the guards of the city and stored there until their return; secondly, if any tribesmen in the city market began to make trouble, the shopkeepers were responsible to prevent it, and serious penalties were enacted against them, if tribal fighting took place.

The effect of the rivalries between tribes were also evident in the form taken by the city. The urban area inside the walls was divided into neighbourhood quarters, each of which originally represented a particular tribe or group of alliances. Each neighbourhood quarter enjoyed a considerable autonomy. And in order to reduce the risk of tribal dispute and fighting, ancient laws restricted the access to any quarter of large groups of outsiders.

If we examine plans (figure 2) or aerial photos (figure 10) of old Sanaʿa carefully, we will see that there are wide patches of open space scattered all over the city. These spaces are the market gardens or *bustan*. Each *bustan* has grown up on what was originally vacant land that kept the quarters apart. From it, the clay and earth needed for the initial buildings were extracted. Afterwards the open space was developed for market gardening.

One of the problems in a city like Sanaʿa was how to maintain order between dusk and dawn. Rivalries between the tribal inhabitants of the different quarters were common. Social control was partly solved by the practice of curfew. Curfew was sounded traditionally with a gong or a bell, later with cannon fire, at eight o'clock in the evening and at six in the morning. During that time the inhabitants had to stay within the boundaries of their own neighbourhood quarters, and were not allowed to venture onto the primary streets. This was not such a hardship as it might appear to have been, as within each quarter a secondary street acted as the central thoroughfare of the neighbourhood; on it there were local mosques and shrines, public baths, some local shops, and workshops. From the secondary streets narrow tertiary streets led to the houses.

One of the first impressions of the view of Sanaʿa was the great height of its houses. As in the other parts of Southern Arabia, the dwellings took the form of tower houses (figure 11). The tower house type emerged from the necessity to conserve valuable land so as to retain as much as possible for agriculture. Although it is known from early accounts that tower houses had existed in Sanaʿa from early times (Serjeant/Lewcock, 487–496) most of those surviving today were less than three hundred years old.

The dwellings in old Sanaʿa reached from five to nine stories in height (figure 12). They were generally rectangular in plan, and densely packed along the sides of the streets.

The materials of the houses were stone and brickwork. The stone lower level reaches to approximately 30 ft. above the ground. After that height, the material changed to baked brick. For structural reasons the walls gradually diminished in thickness throughout the height of the buildings.

The façades of the dwellings tended to be symmetrical. They were adorned with rich decoration; ornament framed the windows and openings. Strips of decorative brickwork indicated the transition from stonewall to the brickwork above. Whitewash added articulation to the façade.

A house was typically organized around a stair shaft, which acted as a hollow column providing strength to the house (figure 13). The ground level of the house contained the entrance hall, from which the stairs were reached, as well as stables for animals, such as camels and donkeys. The family used the first level above, often a mezzanine, as storage for grain and fruits.

Above this was the level to which strangers are admitted. A large room served for enacting business and for welcoming (male) guests. The largest room in the living levels above that was the *diwan* (figure 15). The whole clan might gather here to mark important events in the life of the family, such as childbirth and death. The remainder of the living functions were loosely arranged. Sitting, dining, and sleeping might take place in any of these rooms at different times of the day. There was minimal use of furniture in the rooms, which carpeted and lined with wool-stuffed cushions around the walls. Traditionally, Sanaʿa houses had gypsum in the windows instead of glass. At the top of the house there was an entertaining room on the roof to take the advantage of the views and the cool air.

On each of the living levels there was also a bathroom containing a toilet. Each bathroom generally had a stone floor (figure 17). Water for bathing was stored in a large earthenware pot outside the bathroom door and transferred for use into smaller pitchers. Bathing was done by showering, standing on two raised stones set in the floor and pouring water over the head from the pitcher placed on the circular stone in front of the bather.

The solid waste from the toilet dropped down a vertical shaft into a small masonry box underneath. The urine flowed across the floor and down the outside of the external wall. The floor and the toilet were then washed and the drain on the outside wall would naturally be cleaned by the same water. This system was praised by medieval travellers from other countries as being extraordinary clean. The solid waste—just like night soil in our world until a century or so ago—was gathered at intervals and taken to the public hot baths for burning. The ash from this fuel became a sterile fertilizer for the market gardens that separated the quarters. Vegetables grown there were sold to supply the houses, thus completing a neat ecological cycle.

The water supply for the city was provided in a number of ways. At many street corners there was a double cistern in which water for human use was separated from that for animal use (figure 18). Water was brought to those cisterns from wells; many sources of power were used to raise the water, usually camels or donkeys.

A more sophisticated system was to provide large cisterns for water in the hills around the city. Springs and streams were gathered into each cistern, from which water was channelled to the town. Such cisterns could be 12 miles, 20 miles, or even 40 miles outside the town. The Romans had channelled the water in this way using open aqueducts. But in the hot dry air of Arabia evaporation was such a problem that the channels had to run underground. They were called *ghayls* in Arabic (*kanat* in Persian) and a number brought water into medieval Sana'a.

Analysis: the form of the city

The lower citadel was the heart of the pre-Islamic city, with the later Persian and Ethiopian population immediately to the west of it, south of the open space known as Maidan Sana'a. In the centre of the later area was erected the Jewish synagogue, which survived into early Islamic times, and opposite it, the great Christian cathedral was built, with a martyrion at the east end to commemorate Christ's legendary sojourn in the city during the flight from the massacre of the innocents. On the west side of the early city was Ghumdan, at first the palace of the king and in later times of the governor; it is now a hill of ruins. To the north of it the market developed outside the gates, in the position it still occupies but now swallowed up within the later expansion.

The significance of the conversion of the city to Islam was the development around this nucleus of a completely different form of city. First, during the lifetime of the prophet and under the direction of his companions, the great mosque was erected in the garden of Ghumdan. Next, Muslim tribesmen came to settle the north and west, enclosing the mosque, which was outside the former gates. The non-converted Jews, Christians, and Persians were thus surrounded on two sides, and the city extended far to the north and west.

The new Muslim settlement neighbourhoods were apparently spontaneous and unplanned, and depended for their cohesion on tribal affinities—a pattern that served as the model for expansion of the city thereafter.

It is interesting to note that the new areas of growth of Islamic Sana'a do not appear to have been surrounded by a defensive wall until the late eighth or early ninth century. Expansion had been restricted to the east, as here lay the ancient citadel, continually renewed and strengthened to control trade up through the highlands. Extension of

the city to the west continued, so that by the time of the conquest of
South Arabia by the family of Salah al-Din in the twelfth century the
city had crossed the *wadi* which had formerly protected it to the west. A
new palace of their governor, together with the camp of their invading
army, was now built on the other side of this *wadi* bed from the rest,
with new walls to enclose it within the confines of the city.

As they were built, all the new quarters were separated from each
other by large open spaces. These served as protection against disturbances between the clans and tribes and provided the building materials
of earth and clay. Eventually they became market gardens to provide
vegetables and fruit to the quarters. A number of these gardens survive
to this day.

The expansion of the city led to the steady extension of the surrounding walls. But this process came to an end when Ottoman armies
of Suleiman the Magnificent fought their way up to the highlands from
the coast and occupied Sana'a. Their governors controlled the city
from the citadel—turning the castle-guns on the city, they built a fine
tree-lined boulevard from the Maidan outside the castle to northern
gate, on which were situated a new Friday mosque, splendid Ottoman baths, military schools and coffee houses. Upon the recapture
of Sana'a by the Yemeni rulers, the former extent of the city within
its wall became fixed. A new palace for the Yemeni rulers was built
outside at the western edge, and the garden villas, which had grown
up further west were enclosed by a separate wall to create a distinctive
area known as Bir al-Azab.

Here, in the late seventeenth century, the Jews, who had been forced
to evacuate their homes in the old city in the wake of the first anti-
Semitic riots, were allowed to settle in a district known as al-Qa'.

Conclusion

The old city of Sana'a, thus, functioned as a completely self-sustain-
able social and economic system. The constant social interaction was
physically matched by the reuse of materials and a cycle of growth,
consumption, and the reuse of edible crops as fertilizer. City life was
rendered relatively harmonious—given the warlike nature of tribal
society—by the division of the city into quarters, each under its own
sheikh, by strict laws governing the carrying of arms, and by the
prohibition of groups crossing over from one quarter to another. The

market gardens ensured the availability of food in time of siege, and provided open natural space within the city for children to play and for the enjoyment of adults. Above all, in the city there was communal life in the mosque, the market, the bath, in the gatherings during the quiet afternoons in the big houses and, throughout the year, religious festivals, dawn prayers, funeral processions to the cemeteries outside the walls, and dancing in the streets to celebrate marriages.

Bibliography

Abdel-Rahm, M. "Governmental Institutions." In *The Islamic City*, edited by Serjeant et al., 90–103. Paris: UNESCO, 1980.

Akbar, Jamal A. *Crisis in the Built Environment: the Case of the Muslim City*. Leiden: E. J. Brill, 1988.

Belkacem, Y. "Bioclamatic Patterns and Human Aspects of Urban Form in the Islamic City." In *The Arab City*, edited by El-Sadek Serageldin et al., 1–12. Riyadh: The Arab Institute, 1982.

Elisseeff, N. "Physical Lay-out." In *The Islamic City*, edited by Serjeant et al., 52–64. Paris: UNESCO, 1980.

Lapidus, I. M. "Muslim Cities and Muslim Societies." In *Middle Eastern Cities*, edited by I. M. Lapidus et al., 47–79. Berkeley and Los Angeles: University of California Press, 1969.

Lewcock, Ronald. *The Old Walled City of San'a'*. Paris: UNESCO, 1986.

———. "Towns and Buildings in Arabia, North Yemen." *Architectural Association Quarterly* 8 May (1976): 3–19.

Serjeant, R. B., and Ronald Lewcock. *San'a': An Arabian Islamic City*. London, 1983.

HARAR: THE FOURTH HOLY CITY OF ISLAM

Serge Santelli

It seems that Muslim shaykhs had been known in Harar prior to and during the time of Amda Seyon, the Christian Emperor of Abyssinia (1314–1344). The oldest document referring to the city's existence is the chronicle of his victories over the Muslim Kingdom of Adal which, although being independent, was part of the Abyssinian Empire. Upon his death, the Sultanates of Hadiya, Fatajar, Dawaro, and Ifat—of which Harar was a part—were reduced to the rank of simple provinces governed by a Muslim prince who was a vassal of the Negus.

After the reign of Amda Seyon, Harar became an important foothold for Islam which included the important port of Zayla on the Red Sea. At the end of the fourteenth century, the Sultan of Adal transferred the capital to Ouahal where he prepared a holy war that lasted thirty years. The entire region was then re-conquered by the Christians who, in 1425, occupied the port of Zayla. In 1515, the Christian emperor defeated and killed the Emir of Harar, Mahfuz, and pursued his routed troops. But a coalition of Muslim peoples grouped and based in the Harar region under the authority of Imam Ahmad b. Ibrahim al-Ghazi (1506–43), known as Gran (who had killed the Sultan Abu Bakr to re-establish the authority of the Quran and the Tradition in his own country), was then to rise up and fight against Christians.

It was during his reign that the capital of the Sultanate was transferred to Harar in 1520. Gragn, known as the "first conqueror" of the city, was killed in 1543. Upon Gran's death, the province of Harar and its capital remained the preferred fiefdom of his companions, his family, and his followers. Nur b. al-Mujahid headed the movement and was named Emir and successor to Gran in 1552. He was the veritable chief of Harar and made of the city a citadel with ramparts. It was his tomb—at the centre of the city—that consecrated the place as a holy city, closed to non-Muslims up until the conquest of the region by Menelik in 1887.

After his death, the withdrawal of the Muslim community led—especially in Harar—to a deepening of the Muslim faith and practice in populations which for the most part had been only superficially

Islamized. There existed in Harar a number of *madrasa* and some *qadi*. Throughout the decades following the death of Nur b. Mujahid the composition of an entire body of religious literature can be witnessed that was to profoundly anchor the practice of Quranic obligations and the cult of certain local saints. This action was carried out under the influence of brotherhoods, notably that of the Qadiriyya, which was introduced in Harar as of the end of the fifteenth century and was influential well beyond the borders of the Emirate as far as southwest Ethiopia. For a long time, up until the nineteenth century, this was the sole brotherhood in Ethiopia, and it was basically a brotherhood of a teaching vocation.

The Independence of Harar

As of 1567, the Oromo people who had by now settled in the whole South of Ethiopia and along the eastern slopes of the plateau occupied the entire region of Harar, devastating it. Amir Nur tried to resist, but he died from the plague, following a famine in 1567–8. The city then saw its territory shrink as well as its trade routes. Nevertheless, a majority of the Oromo people converted to Islam, which allowed for the development of its markets and trade. Harar was the first area in Ethiopia to cultivate the coffee trees and at the end of the seventeenth century the city and its outlying countryside were the first exporters of Ethiopian coffee, transported from the port of Zayla on the Red Sea.

The Sultanate, of which Harar was still a part, once burdened down by the famine and the Oromo incursions, moved its centre to Aussa in 1577. The second half of the sixteenth century saw also the emergence of numerous emirates, sultanates, and Muslim principalities along the coast. Harar was one among them and it acquired a certain power because of its prosperous agriculture and trade. It had become a small trading state and influential centre for the instruction of Islam and succeeded in freeing itself from the Sultanate with the advent of the Ali Ibn Daud Dynasty (1647). During almost three centuries, it was an independent city which minted coinage, was surrounded by walls and governed by its own emir.

But it was also a period of withdrawal during which the city saw its population fall from 40/50000 to 12/14000 inhabitants. Politically isolated and militarily weak, the city was able to subsist only due to its trade, the essential basis of its economy. Harari caravans reached the rich provinces of southern Ethiopia, of Shoa and Ogaden, as well as the ports on the Red Sea, Zayla, and Berbera. Nevertheless, Harar upheld its fundamental role as a well-established bastion of Islam—a centre of learning—while at the same time an active trading city.

Most important for the diffusion of Islam was undoubtedly the Islamization of a considerable part of the Oromo population by the merchants coming from the East—principally from Harar, but also from Yemen. As for the South Oromo tribes (Arusi, Borana, Lega), of which many were nomads or semi-nomadic, they also fell under the influence of the Muslim city from the nineteenth century. Islam and trade became one. In the Oromo language, "Muslim" becomes *naggâdi*, an Ethiopian word meaning "merchant."

At the end of the eighteenth century, the Oromo and Somali tribes were still expanding in the Harar region and invaded some new areas adjacent to the city. But conversions to Islam continued and numerous tribes became sedentary. The majority of them recognized the authority of the Emir to whom they paid tribute and offered gifts in exchange for his protection. In order to pacify their relations with the Oromo, the Harar emirs, moreover, carried out a policy of matrimonial alliances. At the same time, Harari merchants and Oromo and Somali peasants compromised in order to allow for the development of commercial trade between city and country. Some small Oromo and Somali trade caravans were daily authorized to enter the city, on condition they left their arms at the gate, and the number of foreigners in the city was constantly controlled.

Up until the end of the nineteenth century the city, thus, drew its richness as a result of its privileged position on one of the two principal trade routes connecting the south and the north of Ethiopia. At the end of the nineteenth century, contemporaries report testimonies of a very lively city where products of cultivation are exchanged—and the region is fertile—such as coffee, sorghum, bananas, *khat*, but also skins and leathers in great quantities, salt, gold, and incense.

The Emirs of Harar were the greatest tradesmen of the city before the arrival of the Egyptians. Free from harbour taxes, they exported coffee and ivory from Zayla, the large port on the Red Sea. The Emir sold ivory (a royal monopoly) in Berbera via the intermediary of a *wakil* or agent. The other tradesmen sold their slaves, ivory, and rubber from Harar in Aden, where they bought bottles of glass, clothing, etc. Then they went to Tadjurah and Ifat where they exchanged their goods for slaves, mules, and cotton.

The Egyptian Conquest

The Egyptian Rauf Pasha, who had already taken Zayla and Berbera in 1870 after having conquered the Sudan, occupied Harar from 1874 to 1884. Between 1883 and 1890, Menelik, King of Shoa from 1864, then Emperor of Ethiopia in 1889, conquered in his turn the province of Harar and annexed the city in 1887 to the Kingdom. He named his cousin Makonnen Governor of Harar. The most striking symbol of the defeat of Harar was the destruction of the Great Mosque that was situated on Faras Magala, the central square, and its replacement with an octagonal Orthodox church designed by an Italian engineer.

Harar, a city of the Ethiopian Empire

Educated by French priests in Harar, Ras Makonnen was preoccupied with establishing contact with Western civilization. In this perspective he travelled the East and Europe as emissary of the Empire. When he died in 1906, his son Tafari, born in Harar in 1892, succeeded him as governor of the Province of Harar. His home, the Ras Tafari House, still dominates the city. He became Emperor Haile Selassie in November 1930. It was during his reign that the road network between the capital city and the various provinces was developed and that the railroad linking Djibouti to Dire Dawa and Addis Ababa was created. Yet the commercial activity of Harar started its slow but inexorable retreat. This can be explained by internal political factors such as the loss of its independence on one part, and, thus, of its freedom of action, and on another part, the disappearance of the emirs who were the greatest tradesmen of the city. Moreover, the political disturbances continued to affect the safety of the roads and disorganize its trade.

The rise to power of new commercial centres also disturbs its activity. The installation of the railroad, for example, proves to be one of the key factors of its decline: not being able to pass by Harar which is in a mountainous zone, the line connecting Djibouti to Addis Ababa passes by Dire Dawa, in the plain. Thus, contrary to the predictions of Makonnen, it is not Harar, of which he is the governor, which develops but rather Dire Dawa, to the detriment of its historical neighbour.

The Italian Occupation

The city was taken by the Italians in 1936 and liberated in 1942. The Italians carried out major urban development throughout the city. Outside the ramparts, in the western part beyond the city walls, they built the embryo of a new city including the Governor's Palace and other administrative buildings. They, furthermore, built a new straight thoroughfare which links Harar Bari, the western gate, to the central square, Faras Magala, to allow for the passage of automobiles. Inside *Jugal* (the historical city), they also built a permanent market, accommodating arcades indoors, and thus enabling businesses to set up real shops. The Italians who counted on the Muslims to fight against Amhara resistance conferred many advantages to them. They built mosques everywhere, named *qadi*s in the centres, and encouraged the teaching of Arabic, which was declared the official language in Harar. This policy favoured the Ethiopian Muslim community, which was not, as in the past, kept at the periphery of political life.

The structure of the city

The historical city is surrounded by a continuous wall interrupted by six gates, one of which—the Harar Gate, is recent. Obviously, the gates are located according to the main roads connecting the city to its surrounding regions. The *Choa gate* allowed the entrance of the city from the west into what was the main east-west street before its enlargement by the Italian administration after 1936. The *Fallana Gate* is related to the north, the *Herer Gate* to the east, the *Sanga Gate* to southeast, the *Buda Gate* to the south. All these gates were opened to streets that led to the central area of the city. That one was occupied until 1887 by the central mosque and market. All the public buildings, including some modern facilities (like the hospital), are located in a central public area limited by:—the municipal hall on the western part of *Faras Magala*, facing the *Medhanealem* Church,—the main Mosque (Mosque Jamia) and the nearby hospital connected to the Catholic Church and school on the eastern part—and the *Gidir Megala* (central market) located on the southern part.

This central area is connected to the western gate by the "straight street," a modern thoroughfare bordered by contemporary dress-shops,

Andinnya Manget. This urban segment manifests a long sequence of modern commercial activities, where one finds all building material supplies, car parts, paper stores, photographic laboratories, as well as modern tailors, jewellery stores, etc.

The street of the Emir

A second sequence corresponds to the former principal street, the street of the Emir, which leads into Harar by the *Shoa* entry. The commercial urban fabric there is preserved; it is always dense and increases in density as one approaches the city gate. It is made up of shops constructed in hard materials for various activities (butchers, grocers, shoes, etc.) and of stalls on the edges of the street (vegetables, gasoline toward the top of the street, etc.). The street is highly frequented by pedestrians (because it is not accessible to cars). The inhabitants of the old city use it to go to the market through the *Shoa* entry, located just outside the wall, and benefit from this commercial path to do their shopping in the street of the Emir.

Faras Magala

The central place *Faras Magala*, located at the end of the principal straight street, presents the same typology as the latter, with high density due to the centrality of the place, which includes the cinema and outdoor cafes. In addition, the principal market of *khat* of Harar is located here. *Khat* is produced in the countryside, a specific cultivation of the Harar area, and consumed and exported in very great quantity. It is of a considerable commercial value for the peasants who live off the revenue from its cultivation. Collected every morning in the fields close to Harar, the *khat* is then sold in the city by the *Oromo* women.

Makina Girgir

The *Makina Girgir* street descends from *Faras Magala* towards the central market (*Gidir Magala*). This street is a very particular commercial sequence because of its specialization (craft industry at the top of the street, sales of textile and traditional tailors in the second lower half). There is no mix of the activities in this section, and the customers are very targeted. The street regroups the greatest part of artisan activities of the city and, in addition to the tailors, one finds mainly basket making. The baskets are manufactured generally at home by the Harari women. The women of the surrounding countryside villages also manufacture baskets that they bring to sell in Harar. These baskets form part of the decoration and the traditional furniture of the Harari house, even if the women today tend to replace them by enamelled iron basins imported from China and sold at a lower price.

Gidir Magala

At the bottom of *Makina Girgir* street, one arrives at the central market built under the Italian occupation, the only one to have a structure constructed in masonry. It is located in the middle of a large place, the previous open market, occupied by a great number of covered stalls, aligned in front of and along the arcades of the market. Inside the market are butchers; they sell halal meat for the Moslems. In the centre of the market, in the space located between the two U-shaped forms, are Oromo women who come from the countryside to sell faggots of wood. Outside the building, there are stalls for clothing, spices, fruits, and vegetables. Within the market, one can also find travelling sales-women of coffee (they move with a tray bearing cups and thermoses of hot coffee) and milk. These latter transport milk in containers which they carry on their back and sell it by pouring it into plastic bags.

The Mosques

Harar, which is known as being the fourth Holy city of Islam contained 99 mosques, from which only 82 remain, as well as 103 shrines dedicated to Muslim saints, scattered within the urban fabric. The two major mosques were located on the higher point of the city (the central one has been demolished and replaced by the church), very close to the centre, not far from the tomb of Emir Nur, the builder of the city walls. On the contrary, the tomb of Sheikh Abadir, the famous founder of the Holy city, is located on the southeast periphery of the city, nearby the city wall, in the middle of a large plot under the shadow of two large sycamores.

The traditional Harari mosque is a building with simple forms and is evolutionary in nature. The prayer room is rectangular in shape with a surface which varies from 24m² to 35m². The flat ceiling is supported by two pillars that divide the room into six spaces. The walls are covered with whitewash, *nora*, and have, besides the traditional *mihrab*, recesses which were traditionally used for keeping books, candles, and shoes. In the majority of the mosques we also find the *zawiya*, a covered room whose surface varies according to the places of worship. It can be situated within the perimeter of the mosque or outside. Inside, a masonry bench, or *nadaba*, and four recesses recall fulfil the functions of welcoming strangers and of teaching the Koran.

Whether it be a pool or installations with seats, taps, and a system of evacuation, a place for ablutions is to be found in almost all the courtyards. A few mosques have minarets the form of which varies with the date of construction. Always small in size, except for the great mosque, they are signs of the mosque in the urban landscape.

Some mosques house one or several tombs of imams, muezzins, and their families in the courtyard or the garden. When these graves belong to men who are considered to be holy men, or *awlia'*, ceremonies take place in the courtyard of the mosque every year.

The Tombs

In Harar, the Muslim tombs are called *awach* by the inhabitants and can be found in various forms: natural elements, constructed forms, and unmarked sites. These can be found just as easily inside as outside the limits of the historic city, although they are most numerous in *Jugal*.

The most important natural elements are trees and rocks. They were venerated in the Cushitic religion and there were cults practised around these sites with pre-Islamic origins. Upon the arrival of Islam, a synthesis between existing practices and new ones was established. In the case of the tree, it can be found alone or accompanied by a constructed form, which might be a buried grave. Ten lone trees can be found in *Jugal*.

The constructed tombs are called *qabri* in Harari, a word that signifies both the cemetery and the tomb. Some of them are accompanied by a tree, either *wanza* (sycamore) or *klinto*. When they are located in a mosque, the tombs are systematically of the rectangular form known as *mazar*, situated on the level of the ground with a stela of at least 50 cm. height and facing west.

The dome is a built element with a circular base, measuring 3 to 6 metres in height, called *qubbi*. The interior is entered through a narrow and low door. The smallness of these doors relates to those of the mosques and symbolizes the humility and modesty that one should assume through bowing when entering the tomb. Inside, one finds a tomb oriented towards the east, or sometimes west, above which there is a wooden catafalque covered with standards and green embroidered fabrics. The *qubbi* is painted either green or white. Sometimes the outer dome is dressed with stones which allow access to the upper part for the annual whitewashing.

The Mausoleums

The mausoleums of Abadir, located in the south of *Jugal*, and that of Abdulqadir al-Jilani, 15 kilometres further south from the town, are the two most important. These two complexes have the particularity of being organised around the tomb. They are made up of two distinct parts, each one surrounded by an enclosing wall and separated by a common passageway.

The tomb of Abadir is the most venerated and visited of the ones belonging to saints, as he is considered to be the "father" of the town and was said to have had a great role in its foundation during the thirteenth century. The ensemble is composed of two parts. The first is a cemetery, accessible by a prayer-room in which is found the tomb of the saint himself as well as the tombs of other saints, in the shadow of two superb sycamores. The second part, on the other side of an alley that separates the complex in two, includes a mosque and a group of mixed housing (traditional house on the ground floor, and Indian style above).

As for the tomb of Abdulqadir al-Jilani, it is built in the same manner as the former with its cemetery and three sycamores on the one hand, and on the other, a group of houses, a mosque, a *galma*, and Qur'anic schools, all assembled around a central plaza.

The unmarked sites are spaces where once existed the tomb of a saint, or a tree which was destroyed during the construction of streets or houses. Nonetheless, they can be considered as immaterial heritage for the inhabitants based on the fact that rites are still practiced on these sites. They are always designated by the name of the saint that they represent. Religious ceremonies continue to be practiced here, but with less frequency than in the case of constructed tombs or natural elements.

One can find close to some tombs a *galma*. The term is of oromifa origin: it refers to a prayer room used to celebrate a saint. The *galma* existed before the arrival of Islam and was transformed after into a place of Muslim worship. The forms are varied: there can be an open space simply covered with sheet metal, a rectangular covered room with some *nadaba*, or even (in two cases, one inside the city, the other outside) circular spaces with roofs made of branches. They are used during religious ceremonies or on an everyday basis by the *murid* (the person responsible for the tomb) when he receives visitors. The most frequently visited sanctuaries are those that possess a *galma*. Some are visited daily, such as those of Abadir and Ay Abida. Such a visit to the tomb by the faithful is known as *ziyara* and is an integral part of the social and religious practices of the Harari. This activity implies bringing offerings, namely *khat* and incense, sometimes sugar. These gifts are given to the *murid* who welcomes the visitors in the *galma* with a prayer and a blessing.

The feast days of the Muslim calendar are celebrated in the tombs rather than in the mosques. In the more important tombs, such as those of Abadir and Abdulqadir al-Jilani, the ceremonies are more frequent and can occur as many as twenty-four times per year. During these occasions, the holidays are celebrated by readings from the Koran and the practice of *zikr*, songs destined to the saints and prophets in the languages of Harari, Oromifa, Arabic, and Amharic. During the feast of Ashura, in the night of the ninth to the tenth day of the month of Moharram, there is a ceremony in the tombs outside of Jugal in which a meal is prepared for the hyenas. Myths tell how one day these animals attacked humans during a great famine. Since then a pact was concluded: each year a meal prepared with butter and cereals is prepared for them so that they do not attack. If this meal is not consumed, it is a bad sign. It means that there will be no marriages during the month and that it will be a bad year. The link between hyenas and tombs is systematic in the ceremonies because the beasts represent the savage dangerous aspect of night and the invisible world. This is also why, whenever an animal is sacrificed in a tomb, its stomach is offered to the hyenas.

The Ge Abad

The Harari traditional buildings are of the same architectural type. The house, *ge abad*, groups together several housing units, either separate units or, for a certain number of them, units juxtaposed one next to another. Traditionally and before the government (DERG period) expropriated the houses, these residences grouped together members of the same family. Today, families coming from various social groups and from different origins share the house.

The *ge abad* is made up of a principal rectangular unit, *ge gar*, comprising three rooms on the ground floor, the *gidir gar*, the *kirtat*, and the *dera*, as well as a room called *qutti qala* upstairs. The service areas, the W.C. and the kitchen, are always situated in the courtyard and are not directly adjoined to the main unit but are generally located alongside the house.

The main exterior place of the house is the courtyard. It is separate and isolated from the street by a wall. It is a shared space that accommodates various activities such as culinary preparations, basket weaving, washing, etc. It is regimented by the succession of two thresholds. The first, the door to the house, often closed, if not fully open, marks the separation between public space and the courtyard. The second, the door to the main unit, enables access to the main room, *ge gar*, often defined on the ground by a group of plants or a step.

The ge gar (*or* gidir gar)

The *gidir gar* (literally "large house") is the main reception room of the house. Entry is through a door of high and wide dimensions which reflects the social standing of the inhabitant and his family. Old doors were composed of double door leafs made of wooden boards from a single slab. The more recent (made from the end of the nineteenth century) are carved and sculpted with floral motifs, according to a generalized tradition known on the Swahili coast, in Iran and India, classified as "Indo-Iranian" and imported by Indian traders from the end of the nineteenth century. The room is lighted by this door and does not have any other opening, with the exception of a small window that lights the room upstairs.

The room is composed of different spaces arranged in a T shape. In the central part, facing the door, one finds a large niche, open to the entranceway. His ground is built with raised masonry platforms outfitted as seating and called *nadaba*. The niche and its *nabada* is called *ge gar*. Numbering five, the *nabada* constitute the hierarchical raised seats, as much for visitors as for members of the family. Each one of them carries a name. The platforms, just as the floor of the room, are painted a red colour that recalls, in a symbolical way, the memory of the many *ge usu* killed in the Battle of Chalenko (that allowed Menelik II to take over the city). This type of coating is called *qeh afar*, which means literally "red earth."

The Nadabas

They are built on several levels of 5 different heights. They are covered with matting, carpets, and bordered by cushions. The carpets are a part of the bride's trousseau. Each *nadaba* carries a name that designates him who occupies it (*amir nadaba*), the inviting agreeable aspect surrounding it (*soutri nadaba*), its size (*gedir nadaba, tait nadaba*), and its position in the room (*gebti her nadaba*, literally "next to the door."

Amir nadaba: In general this is the highest. A strategic place in the case of an attack upon the house or the city, it is traditionally reserved for the head of the household. Today, it is used by all members of the household and very few families still own or display the spears of yesteryear.

Soutri nadaba: A seat defined as intimate (*soutri*) placed in the innermost recess, on the right side of the niche. When there are cultural ceremonies, it is reserved for guests of honour or the elders, a place where they are seen neither by visitors, nor by the women. It is a nighttime space for elderly people and widows and is used by day as a rest or meditation space.

Gedir nadaba: This is the largest of the five *nadabas* that is placed opposite the door. It affords visual access to the room in general, and especially upon the wooden rods that still today hold the rolled carpets against the wall of the façade on the courtyard side, carpets given as dowry to the young girl to be married. This position enables one to know, without having to ask, if a girl of the household is marriageable. It is said that the number of carpets indicates to visitors the number of marriageable young girls. When there are ceremonies, it is reserved for educated men, that is to say, those who read the Quran and Arabic. It is on this *nadaba* that men and women pray. It is also a nighttime space for men and young boys. Place of rest, relaxation, or activity during the day: *chichi* (water pipe), coffee-ceremony, *khat*, reading, etc.

Tit nadaba: Located beneath the *"gedir nadaba,"* this is the lowest of all and allows one access to the *gedir* and *soutri nadabas*. During holidays or feast days it is traditionally reserved for adolescents who have the responsibility of serving the men who are on the higher seats. It is used by anyone at any time of the day for various activities.

Gebti her nadaba: This *nadaba* is exclusively reserved for women at the time of holidays. Located on the side of the entrance space, it is sheltered from view. It is here that meals are taken most often.

The walls of the *gidir gar* are hollowed out with niches, in general eleven in number. Five overhang the *gidir nadaba*, and are hollowed out of the wall opposite the entranceway. Two rectangular niches, the *eqed taqet* (from *eqed* "opposite"), are reserved for the Quran and some pious images. The more recent ones are sometimes carved with floral decorations. Three other niches, called *tele taqet*, (from *tele* which means "eagle" because of their high position towards the sky), are located above the first two. Of a form that is not rectangular but curved, they are used as receptacles for precious objects, lamps, or porcelain vessels. Traditionally, instruments for calligraphy were kept there.

Above the other *nadaba* can also be found two or three niches, carrying the names of the seats they overhang, such as the *gebtihair nadaba taqet* and the *amir nadaba taqet*. These niches are used today to exhibit fine dishes or personal belongings of members of the household (schoolbooks, cassette-radios, etc.).

On one side of the main alcove, above the *gebtihair nadaba*, is located a shelf called *marabaraba*, forming a niche and made up of little beams on which used to be stored musical instruments. Today dishes and other objects are placed there. On the opposite side a cupboard inserted in the wall closed by two carved wooden doors—the *nadaba dera*—in which clothes and fabric are kept. The *hamil*, a beam made of sycamore (*ouenza*) parallel to the front facade, separates the seating area from the entranceway. It is often covered with a wooden casing carved with floral motifs, similar to those of the front door. A number of wooden stakes with oblong heads, called *wontafinchi*, are implanted in a row over the front door. They are used to support the carpets woven by the lady of the house. The ceiling of the *gidir gar* is made of joined beams whose number allows one to measure the surface area of the room. They are whitewashed and remain exposed in most of the homes. However, in some houses today, they are hidden by wooden casing. In times past an ostrich egg was hung there to protect the house from lightening.

The walls are covered with a great number of decorative elements, such as woven baskets, *darat*, (shown in pairs), wooden dishes coated with black oil paint, *gabata*, and metal bowls with highly coloured floral motifs imported from China. Traditionally, only the wall opposite the entranceway was covered. Today, all the walls of the room are covered with these elements of decoration in a perfectly symmetrical way and arranged around the wall niches.

Today, a number of enamelled metal dishes are imported from China or Japan and contribute to the decorative whole. They are placed with the same precision and replace the former baskets that have been sold. That does not prevent the tradition of basketry to continue, preserved by the savoir-faire of Harari women of whom some opened a tourist market. Several workshops of associations and businesses specialized in the sale of these objects have cropped up in the city during the last few years, enabling young women from various social groups to practice a craft.

On the ground floor, two other rooms adjoin the prestigious *gidir gar*: the *kirtat* and the *dera*. The *kirtat* is in fact sort of an alcove partially open onto the main room, which is used for storage. The wall separating it from the *gidir gar* sometimes has a window closed by a screen made of crossed slats of wood that allow for ventilation. This is also the room that accommodates those of the household who might be sick. It includes a masonry platform.

The *dera* is a room closed by a door that faces the *kirtat*. As in the previous case, its ceiling is half the height of that of the *gidir gar* since it is beneath the room upstairs. It is used to store everyday objects, especially women's affairs. It is also used as a nuptial chamber for the young married couple until the conception or birth of the first child. A niche of rectangular form, carved out of the wall of the room that separates it from the *kirtat*, houses four pieces of black earthenware pottery called *aflala*, covered with "pointed hats" in wicker called *aflala uffa*. Each contains things precious for the house. They "read" right to left: the first contains seed, the second jewellery, the third dried medicinal plants, and the last silver. Today metal recipients or pots often replace the traditional black pottery.

Upstairs, above the *kirtat* and the *dera*, is a large room called *qutti qala*. Traditionally, this room was used for storing products from the fields (coffee, mangoes, etc.). Access is via a stairway located to the side of the front door. From the mid-nineteenth century, the wall separating this room from the *gidir gar* was replaced by a screen of carved wood (*moucharabieh* type), the *mandera*, and a wooden railing was added to the stairway. The upstairs room, thus, changed status and became a living space.

These rooms are today all used differently and fulfil various functions, that of a separate bedroom for the parents, distinct from that of the children, or storage space. Another room is often built onto one side of the *ge gar*, this is the *tit gar*, the "small house." For the use of the women, or for one of the children of the family, the room has only one *nadaba*, raised about 30 cm. from the floor and might accommodate a tenant, a student, or a guest. It is accessible either from indoors, or from outside or, when adjoining the main unit, from the courtyard.

The Indian House

The second housing type one can find in Harar is the Indian house built by the Indian merchants when they came after the conquest of Harar in 1887. Most of these houses have been built on the ridge, the highest point of the city. They are simple rectangular two stories buildings whose main characteristic is their first floor wooden veranda of the main facade overlooking the street or the courtyard. They are covered with a roof and are higher than the average Harari houses. They dominate the city landscape. The most beautiful, and the most famous, is the RIMBAUD house built in the beginning of the twentieth century. Restored recently by local authorities with the help of the French cultural services, the house functions now as cultural centre and a library. It is the best known building in Harar. There are about a dozen of this kind of houses located in the higher part of Jugol. Ras Tafari, inhabited by the future Haile Selassie when he was living in Harar, belongs to this type of house.

The mixed house

The third housing type is the mixed type made up from the traditional Harari nucleus with more recent "Indian" extensions on the first or second floor. When the new rooms have been added above the traditional type they are accessible by a wooden gallery open onto the courtyard. This type is relatively common and many traditional Harari houses, *Ge Gar*, have been enlarged and extended without being transformed.

Therefore, the original house is kept, whereas the new parts are inspired by the Indian model. It seems that the traditional house is not modified in the enlargement process since the solution is to build a new house, or new rooms, without touching the existing one. Then the house becomes a "double house" in which one can find the Harari traditional type associated with the new Indian building.

The new parts have a simple rectangular form and do not have the architectural complexity of the Harari type. On the first floor the new rooms have windows and are added to one another to form a linear set of rooms built along one side of the courtyard. On the second floor the same pattern of rooms is distributed by an outdoor wooden gallery accessible through an exterior staircase. In most of the rooms one finds one masonry bench which occupies a large part of the room area.

The Villa

In today's times, a number of Harar inhabitants have new houses built outside the ramparts. These houses are of a "villa" type and include two housing units on a single plot: the first, in a modern style, and the second, of typical traditional Harari type.

The new house, "modern," is a house on one level, rectangular, most often covered by a double-pitched roof and is open to the street through a veranda. It groups living rooms (on the street side) and bedrooms and service rooms (kitchen and bathroom) along a central distribution corridor. Traditional construction material is replaced by armed concrete for the weight-bearing walls and by cement blocks for the walls and partitions. It's in this house that the family lives everyday.

The second house, "traditional," actually is to be found at the back of the lot, beyond the "villa" house, which always takes the front position with the façade towards the street. One finds therein the traditional volumetric configuration of the typical Harari block-unit as well as the system of *nadaba* and niches. The most notable transformations to be found are in regard to the materials themselves, those same ones that are used for the modern house. Nevertheless, the very existence of this house shows how the Harari block-unit is perpetuated and continues to accommodate the former utilization since the new *gidir gar* keeps its role as reception room. It is in this house that festive occasions and religious ceremonies are held, as well as the everyday *khat* sessions, wedding ceremonies, funerals, etc.

Most of the houses had neither a well nor a cistern to collect water. Then the Harari women were obliged to bring water from two rivers which run outside the city walls. Today, the rivers are completely polluted and are used as garbage disposals. Recently, the houses have been connected with a municipal water network which, unfortunately, provides only undrinkable water. Until now, most of the dirty water is ejected from the houses into the streets, then towards an open-air sewer outside the city walls. The main streets have been recently paved with stone, but the lack of a sewage network does not allow the majority of the streets to be clean.

Nevertheless, the existing state of the urban and architectural fabric in Harar is pretty good, especially if we compare it to the Arab cities in the Islamic world. A large majority of the traditional houses are still well kept (between 80 and 85%), including their inner ornament and decoration. Few contemporary transformations are visible along the existing streets of the walled city and their present aspect is very traditional. Originally, the walls were made up of brown stones assembled with earth and gave a dark colour to the streets. Recently, many walls have been covered by limestone mortar and whitewashed for a better protection of the masonry, changing the dark coloured aspect of the streets. Nevertheless, the city of Harar whose inhabitants, very proud of their "Harari culture," were able to keep their architectural and urban heritage until today, is certainly one of the best preserved Islamic cities in the world.

Nota Bene: The present paper has been written using the documentation and surveys collected by the "Harar Workshops" which were held in 2000, 2001, and 2003 in the city with the financial help of the French Government. The workshops were managed by Philippe Revault and Serge Santelli, architects and professors in the postgraduate program "Cities, Architecture and Heritage. Maghreb and Near East." The social and architectural surveys concerning the religious and domestic buildings have been implemented by Nadia Ammi, Emma Greiner, and Nadège Chelhi.

RABAT – SALÉ.
HOLY CITIES OF THE TWO BANKS

Saïd Mouline

1. *Introduction*

At the heart of the capital of the Moroccan Kingdom, the Bou Regreg, a river rich in history, divides the agglomeration of Rabat and Salé, winding through the expanse of a magnificent valley of close to four thousand hectares. On both sides, endless landscapes extend as far as the eye can see, over a width of some fifteen kilometres. In this place, the water, the sky, the earth, the plants are animated in a magical orchestration, a source of fascination and emotion.

Human settlements at the mouth of the Bou Regreg—probably since the Phoenicians and the Carthaginians, and certainly since the Roman settlement at Sala Colonia—seem to have faced not the Atlantic Ocean but rather the banks of the river. Some hundred kilometres long, the river reaches the ocean through a substantial bar situated around seven hundred metres from the entrance channel, which runs almost parallel to the coast over a fairly long distance. Because the bar is so shallow, the draught of ships was long limited, up indeed to the beginning of the twentieth century.

Hence, along the length of the Bou Regreg, the medinas of Salé and Rabat have, since the construction of their initial urban nuclei, turned their backs to the sea. Fairly much equal in area, these medinas have, as their respective nuclei, the Banu ʿAshara quarter, built in the eleventh century on the right bank, and the Ribat of ʿAbd al-Muʾmin, built in 1150 on the left bank. Their presence on the two banks of the river is not limited to the elegant urban skylines they offered in the past. *Borj*s, belvederes, *sqala*s, semaphores, crenellated walls, decorated urban gates, frame the river and embellish it on both of its sides. Further back, the ochre minarets of the Jamaʿ al-ʿAtiq, of the Jamaʿ al-Aʿdam and Hasssan, built of the same ochre stone, and the curves of the whitened cupolas of the numerous *zawiya*s, accentuate the horizontal contrasts of the buildings, in the past very low, that embrace the smooth foundations of the medinas seen from the riverside.

Thanks to this river, and the respective fluvial ports of these medinas, a maritime destiny was assured, a destiny that made them famous at the time they were created, then, principally, in the fourteenth and seventeenth centuries. We often forget that these fluvial ports, established long ago on the Bou Regreg estuary, were the only ones on the Moroccan Atlantic coast never to be subjugated or subject to foreign domination, up to the French Protectorate in 1912. This fluvial port tradition now remains only in the toponymy, with Bab al-Bhar (Sea Gate) on the left bank and Bab Mrisa (Gate of the Small Port) on the right bank. It seems, today, to have been completely erased from the history of the two cities; and this has erased, too, just how much the two cities owe to the river that links them—and, consequently, the river itself, the vector of their history and their historical patrimony.

It is the river that marks the history of a number of highly important monuments in the Bou Regreg valley. Such is the case with Sala Colonia—which later contained the Marinid necropolis of Chellah—with the Qasba of the Oudaya, overhanging the mouth whose entrance it commands, with the Hassan minaret and the Almohad mosque. And it is likewise the case with Bab al-Bhar which led to the Street of Consuls in Rabat, and Bab Mrisa; and with the channel that linked the river to the dockyard within the walls, in the medina of Salé, and so on. More important and meaningful was the imprint of the sacred that these twin cities sealed, through and by virtue of the river.

In the sections that follow, we shall try to sketch this history from a fresh viewpoint: that of a river and of the holy cities on the two banks, devoted to the expansion of Islam, to the glorification of faith, and maritime *jihad*. We shall naturally give particular attention, over the period in question, to monuments, remains, and to the material traces of this sacred imprint, to be seen in the architectural and urban characteristics of the agglomerations at the mouth of the Bou Regreg. In this regard, we must pay homage to those who, like 'Abd al-Mu'min, Ya'qub al-Mansur, Sidi al-Yaburi, Sidi ben Asher, al-Ayyashi, and many others, have contributed to sanctifying the urban entities on the two banks, and to developing faith and piety in this estuary that devoted itself, very early on, to holy war in the furthest Muslim West. We shall also give attention to the relations developed, by the two banks, with al-Andalus: multiple relations whose effects showed through in many fields, and especially in that of the closed universes of dwellings in Rabat and Salé, in their design and their furnishing.

2. *Initial urban nuclei*

2.1   *The left bank: The Qasba of the Oudaya*

From the tenth century on, the site of Rabat was marked by its sacred character, reflected in a *ribat*, then in an Almoravid fortress on the edge of the cliff on the left bank of the Bou Regreg. In this natural defensive position, dominating the estuary from some thirty metres, ʿAbd al-Muʾmin, the first sovereign of the Almohad dynasty, built, in 1150, a fortress bringing together fighters for the faith, a staging point in the Almohad epic for the expansion of Islam and the conquest of Andalusia. The fortress contained a caliphal residence, a mosque, and reservoirs fed by aqueducts that took in their water from Ain Ghebula. Ramparts of dressed stone, with jutting elements, embraced the irregularities of the cliff, giving it further height and making it still more inaccessible. This construction, which largely corresponds to the present Qasba of the Oudaya, was called Mahdiya, in memory of Mahdi Ibn Tumart, creator of the unitary Almohad doctrine.

A small town of ten hectares or so, a city in miniature, this Almohad fortress, essentially designed to accommodate, around its walls, the assembly of fighters for the faith who were to go and wage a holy war in Spain, was to become the first nucleus of the city of Rabat. It is in the Qasba that is to be found the oldest mosque in Rabat, al-Jamaʿ al-ʿAtiq (the old mosque), which rises at the highest point of the Qasba and is one of the first Almohad sanctuaries.[1]

ʿAbd al-Muʾmin frequently stayed in this princely residence, where he died in 1163. Between Marrakesh, capital of the Almohad Empire, and the Straits of Gibraltar, the Ribat was essentially a place designed to accommodate, around its walls, the assembly of fighters for the faith who were to go and wage war against the Christians of Spain; a point in the road of *jihad*, which passed by al-Ksar al-Kebir and al-Ksar al-Sghir. It was not until the reign of Yaʿqub al-Mansur (1184–1199) that this sacred territory, easily accessible from the south and the north of

---

[1] Through the centuries, this agglomeration received further, successive designations: the Rabat Fortress, the Salé Citadel, the Qasba, the Palace, the Andalusian Qasba, etc. Its present appellation goes back to 1833, when the sultan Moulay ʿAbd al-Rahman expelled the Oudaya tribe from Fez; what remained of this tribe settled in the Qasba, which was then almost uninhabited and has since borne the name of its new inhabitants.

Morocco, at once distinct from and neighbour to the city of Salé on
the other bank of the Bou Regreg, would become a grandiose city,
starting from the Ribat.

2.2 *The right bank: the Banu ʿAshara quarter*

Seated on a slight eminence of some twenty metres at the mouth of
the Bou Regreg, on the right bank and facing its twin city of Rabat,
Salé is situated by the side of the sea, turning its back to the Atlantic
Ocean; this ocean which rocks it constantly with the murmuring and
sounds of its swell, has a mainly decorative value. A maritime city in
appearance, sometimes intensely so, Salé has remained land-based and
secret, and it has always had a reputation for piety.

This reputation was forged in the eleventh century and truly confirmed from the twelfth, when the whole Bou Regreg estuary region
made up a sacred territory dedicated to holy war, a rallying point for
volunteers of the faith for *jihad* in Andalusia and a port in constant
relation with Seville. The first urban nucleus was formed by Andalusi
families—notably that of the Banu ʿAshara, princes of Umayyad origin come from al-Andalus—which settled in Salé during the eleventh
century. Major patrons, the Banu ʿAshara proved to be especially
generous to the intellectuals, poets and musicians of al-Andalus.[2] In
1121, Ibn Tumart, who later founded the Almohad movement, was
accommodated in their palace, of which, however, no trace has been
found. From the twelfth century, Salé was to witness a noteworthy urban
development, and the first nucleus was to constitute, in the twelfth
century, the city's religious pole under the Almohad dynasty: one that
would be confirmed, enlarged and embellished under the Marinids in
the fourteenth century.

3. *The Almohad epic*

3.1 *The left bank: Ribat al-Fath*

Starting from the Ribat of ʿAbd al-Muʾmin on the left bank of the Bou
Regreg, his grandson Yaʿqub al-Mansur, heir to an empire stretching

---

[2] Prominent among them were the celebrated secretary Ibn Khazan, the great
philosopher and musician Ibn Bajja (Avempace) and his disciple Ibn al-Himara.

from Castille to Tripoli, was to plan a grandiose city, surrounded by imposing walls set with monumental gates and endowed with a gigantic mosque, Hassan, in which a whole army would be able to pray.

At the end of the twelfth century, a substantial surrounding wall was built to protect the south and west faces of the city. It was formed of two long rectilinear walls, intersecting at an acute angle; the total length was more than 5 kilometres, the thickness more than 2 metres, the average height around 8 metres. Thus, an area of about 420 hectares, comprising the high plateau that dominates the Chellah today, was enclosed to assure the security of the lower parts of the city in case of attack.[3]

At the highest point of this wall, Bab al-Ruah, a monumental artistic masterpiece, exhibited, like the gate of the Qasba, a design of intertwined elements around the opening, in the form of a Moorish arch set in a rectangular frame. As with Bab Agnaou in Marrakesh, large arches take up and enlarge the movement of the arch of the gate, encircling it with an aureole of winding acute points, topped with a large frieze of Kufic inscriptions.[4]

Within this surrounding wall, in the northeast part of the city above the river and facing the sea, at a height almost equal to that of the Qasba, Ya'qub al-Mansur ordered the building of a huge mosque that was never in fact to be completed; it would have been one of the greatest sanctuaries of the Muslim world.[5]

Extending over an area of some two-and-a-half hectares, the edifice was laid out in rigorously symmetrical fashion, by reference to a great central axis leading to the *mihrab*. At the other end of this axis, the minaret was inserted in the north façade, jutting on to the interior and exterior of the great courtyard. This was the only minaret in the whole of the Muslim West to occupy such a position. A minaret

---

[3] Like most of the walls erected by the Almohads, this surrounding structure, built in a very solid concrete rich in lime, has shown admirable resistance. Flanked by regular square towers, its curtain was crowned by a rampart walkway, bordered on the outside by a parapet whose tips were covered with small pyramids. The west rampart was set with four gates, at fairly regular intervals: Bab al-Alou, Bab al-Had, Bab al-Ruah, and the fourth being actually part of the Royal Palace. The south rampart had only one gate, Bab Zaer.

[4] "These Moroccan gates are indisputably among the most beautiful in the world." Henri Terrasse, in *L'art hispano-mauresque des origines au XIIIème siècle*, Publications de l'Institut des Hautes Etudes Marocaines (Paris: Éditions G. Van Oest, 1932).

[5] "In the rest of the Muslim world, only the Samarra Mosque in Iraq displayed a more extensive area." (Lévi-Provençal)

of exceptional amplitude,[6] today called the Hassan Tower, it spreads towards the sky a sumptuous decoration, distributed over four faces with distinct compositions.[7]

In 1199, the death of Ya'qub al-Mansur interrupted the works, and his great foundation, Ribat al-Fath—i.e., Victory Camp, in testimony to the success achieved in the holy war against the Christians in Spain—never received the population its walls could have sheltered. The mosque remained unfinished, and its famous minaret, though bereft of its upper part, remains the living symbol of the Almohad's greatest urban project, alongside the works they undertook in the two metropolises of Marrakesh and Seville. The three towers, the Koutoubia, the Giralda, and Hassan light up the Almohad path like beacons, testifying to the same artistic breath that animated the two shores of the Straits of Gibraltar.

3.2   The right bank: an oriented bi-polar city

Under the Almohads, Salé was given new ramparts on the north and southeast sides. The façades on the riverside and facing the sea remained open. In 1196, Ya'qub al-Mansur had built a new, quite vast mosque in place of the original one whose roof had collapsed. The Great Mosque is still today called al-Jama' al-A'dam, or Masjid al-Tal'a. This mosque still occupies the same site, but owes its present appearance to the restorations of the eighteenth century. It has a majestic minaret, in sculpted stone, that dominates the skyline of the whole city, and a monumental gate.

Thus, the urban fabric became organized between this religious pole in the northwest, centred around the mosque, and an economic pole in the southeast, centred around the suq and the Qissaria. It is to be noted that the whole urban layout would progressively take its form from the Tal'a quarter, being clearly oriented by reference to the Almohad mosque. In fact, the division into quarters, and, in particular, the layout of the main arteries, is either from east to west, parallel to the *qibla* wall of the Great Mosque (Bab al-Jdid to Bab Sibta, Bab bou Haja to Bab Ferth), or else from north to south (from Sidi ben Achir

---

[6] With a height of 44 metres and a square section of a little over 16 metres.

[7] It is in fact the most important of the three great Almohad minarets: its dimensions exceed (or at least would have exceeded) those of the two other minarets of Almohad mosques, the Koutoubiya in Marrakesh, and the Giralda in Seville.

to Bab Mrisa, from the north cemetery near Bab Chaf ʿa to Bab Fès), perpendicular to it. This shows the extent to which the *qibla* wall of the Jamaʿ al-Aʿdam regulates the urban layout of the town.

In contributing considerably to the urbanization of the mouth of the Bou Regreg, Yaʿqub al-Mansur also, for the first time in their history, linked the cities of the two banks, through a removable bridge: a remarkable feat of technology that won him the admiration of his contemporaries.

4. *Marinid rule*

4.1 *The left bank*

From the end of Almohad rule around the mid-thirteenth century up to the beginning of the seventeenth century, the importance of Rabat diminished considerably; only the monuments raised by the Marinids in the fourteenth century bear witness to this period. A case in point is the Jamaʿ al-Kbir, the "Great Mosque," which is today the largest sanctuary in the medina. Near this mosque there remain the traces of a beautiful fountain. A little apart, near Sidi Fatah street, the Hammam al-Jdid, built by the sultan Abu ʿInan, goes back to the same period.[8]

However, the most important monument of this period is the funerary mausoleum of the Marinid dynasty, or Chellah necropolis. On the site of Rabat, dominating the left bank of the Bou Regreg, Chellah displays the majestic remains of the Marinid royal necropolis, enclosing, within its walls, the ruins of Sala Antica. The latter, together with Volubilis, marked the furthest extent of the Roman province of Mauretania Tingitana. Sala is mentioned by ancient authors only from the first century on (Pomponius Mela and Pliny the Elder), but it seems to have been a staging post for the Phoenicians from the seventh century B.C.[9] It is not till the end of the thirteenth century that Sala re-appears (Chellah, in Arabic texts). The Marinid sultan Abu Yusuf Yaʿqub

---

[8] As with the Arab baths in Andalusia, in Murcia, Xerés, Granada, etc., it comprised, in alignment, the main rooms of Roman baths: rest room, cold room, warm room, and hot room.

[9] In the Mauretanian era (second to first centuries B.C.), the city developed around one of the region's most abundant springs. Reorganized in the Roman era, it was encircled by a wall in 144 A.D. In the fifth century it was abandoned, probably following the Vandal invasion of 429.

(d. 1286) chose this site for the royal necropolis of his dynasty. He built there a mosque and its dependencies, together with mausoleums for his remains and those of his family. In the mid-fourteenth century, his descendant Abu 'l-Hasan enlarged this latter nucleus, encircled it with a wall set with three gates, and built a madrasa with a minaret and a bath. Chellah was accessed through a main gate, facing Bab Zaer in the Rabat wall. It was a beautiful gate made of sandstone, richly decorated, having two towers with cut-off corners, broadened at their top. Inside, a path was laid out, dividing the two hills that formed the site. On the lower side, to the right, were the ancient ruins,[10] and facing them was the Marinid necropolis.

4.2 *The right bank*

Salé, the Castillians' first Moroccan target, was sacked in 1260. The Marinid Ya'qub re-conquered it, then plugged its breaches by reinforcing the ocean side and raising the great gate called Bab al-Mrisa (Gate of the Small Port). During the Marinid period, the defence system was supplemented and consolidated generally, and the city was endowed with numerous monuments. A beautiful wall in stone was raised on the riverside and a maritime dockyard was built, linked to the fluvial port by two channels within the city. Two monumental gates, one of them Bab al-Mrisa to the south, allowed the passage of boats.

Among the most important elements of this period, we should particularly mention the reinforcing of the religious pole of the city: in 1342, the magnificent Abu 'l-Hasan madrasa, regarded as one of the wonders of Marinid art, was completed near the Great Mosque. Although one of the smallest madrasas of the Marinid period, it is worthy of interest from various viewpoints. Adjacent to the Jama' al-A'dam, it has the feature, notable for this type of institution, of revealing

---

[10] The excavated part of old Salé is organized around the main roadway, the Decumanus Maximus. Here are to be found the main uncovered monuments: shops to the right of the roadway; the main temple of the Roman city and the capitol on the upper terrace; and, at the heart, the forum, laid out in the courtyard of a pre-Roman temple, where was discovered the statue of the last Mauretanian king, Ptolemy, a descendant of Cleopatra, tragically assassinated by Caligula. To the left of the Decumanus Maximus are the public baths, municipal storehouses, the curia, and a nymphaeum fronted by fountains; in the middle of the roadway are the remains of a triumphal arch. The principal roadway of Sala has been followed by means of sample digs carried out in the direction of the ancient port on the Bou Regreg, now silted up. Thus, the Roman city went beyond the Marinid wall, in the direction of the river.

a whole façade, testifying to a judicious architectural composition and urban integration. The monument's graduated portal, next to which a beautiful fountain was built, is assuredly one of the loveliest of its type. It combines, with a rare happiness, a tympanum of stone and a canopy of wood, both sculpted with refinement. The building is centred on an inner courtyard whose small dimensions[11] are forgotten in the exactness of the proportions, the richness and harmony of the decoration and the strength of the thrust towards the sky.

Moreover, a *maristan* (hospital for mental sickness),[12] an aqueduct whose starting point was the springs of Ain Baraka, the building of Zawiyat al-Nussak, a place for receiving learned men, ascetics, the pious, and so on—all these achievements reflect the interest the Marinids took, for close to a century, in Salé and, more generally, in the mouth of the Bou Regreg, where they built the funerary necropolis of their dynasty.

Between the eleventh and the fourteenth centuries, Salé knew real agricultural and commercial prosperity: it imported oil from Seville and exported grain, beeswax, skins, wool, and indigo. According to al-Idrisi, "ships from Seville and all the maritime cities of Andalusia anchored there... [they] took supplies towards the whole of maritime Andalusia."

During this era, illustrious men, theologians, men of learning, scholars, were active, notably Sidi Ahmad ben 'Asher, an interpreter of Shadhili thought and an important Moroccan mystical figure in a fourteenth century already blessed with ample enlightenment. He was one of the venerated saints of the city of Salé and became its patron. His mausoleum is a dominant feature of the splendid marine cemetery which bears his name,[13] and which, at once, extends the religious pole of Salé and divides it from the Atlantic Ocean.

5. *The Bou Regreg Republic*

At the beginning of the seventeenth century, the King of Spain, Philip III, issued a series of edicts[14] expelling Muslims from his kingdom; these

---

[11] Around 32 square metres.
[12] The present-day Funduq Askour.
[13] Of an initial area of some 20 hectares.
[14] Those of 4 August 1609, 3 December 1609, etc.

were known as Andalusians in Morocco and Moriscos in Spain. Among them were the inhabitants of the city of Hornachos, the Hornacheros,[15] who settled at the mouth of the Bou Regreg. They were subsequently joined by other Andalusian refugees, and so it was that, from 1610, the mouth area took in a large population of Muslim refugees driven out from Andalusia and settling and organizing themselves in the cities of the two banks.

In 1627, after numerous ups and downs,[16] the Republic of the Two Banks was proclaimed; and this united New Salé (Rabat) and Old Salé (Salé) for a few decades in a common destiny. "Thanks to the initiative of its inhabitants, and its position allowing it to command the entrance to the river and the port, the Qasba immediately became the capital of the new state."[17] The Bou Regreg estuary then, with the maritime *jihad*, entered the most tumultuous period of its history, became famous for the exploits of its Corsairs, who, as a vanguard of maritime Islam, scoured the Atlantic, showed their colours in British waters, at the mouth of the Thames, in Iceland, proving their prowess in distant and dangerous expeditions, as far as Acadia and Newfoundland.

In the seventeenth, then in the eighteenth centuries, those who came to be known as the "Salé Corsairs" privateered on board light boats of the Mediterranean or Lusitanian type (tartans, brigantines, xebecs, pinques, polacks, caravels, etc.). The most intense period of this activity corresponds to the duration of the Bou Regreg Republic (1627–1666), during which ships' manpower was around forty units. Privateering did in fact exist before Salé, but, according to Jacques Caillé and Roger Coindreau,[18] "it was neither well developed nor truly dangerous." It was not until the first half of the seventeenth century that it became "the veritable 'industry' of the inhabitants of the Bou Regreg Republic."[19]

In contrast to Algiers, Tunis, or Tripoli, which privateered at this time in the Mediterranean, the "Salé Corsairs," in the vanguard of maritime

---

[15] A city located in Estramadura, in the province of Badajoz, to the east of Mérida.

[16] Ups and downs resulting from the difficult relations both among the new arrivals themselves, according to their cities of origin, and between them and the inhabitants of Rabat and Salé. See Jacques Caillé, vol. 4, *La République du Bou Regreg*, 205–81.

[17] See Caillé, *La République*, 215.

[18] Roger Coindreau, *Les Corsaires de Salé*, Publications de l'Institut des Hautes Etudes Marocaines, vol. 47 (Paris, 1948).

[19] See Caillé, *La République*, 223–25. "From 1618 to 1626, just 6,000 Christians were captured, and the prize money amounted to more than fifteen million pounds. In ten years, from 1629 to 1639, customs, Moriscos customs, registered the figure of twenty-five or twenty-six million ducats."

Islam, essentially operated in the Atlantic. It was indeed on the vast, perilous ocean that they accomplished their most remarkable exploits. They launched highly dangerous expeditions, reaching Newfoundland, some two thousand miles from their base, and acquired a fearsome reputation, making the Bou Regreg estuary the cradle of holy war.

This period was naturally marked by numerous works and modifications to the urban entities on both banks of the Bou Regreg. The Qasba, mainly occupied by the Hornacheros, saw its surrounding defence set in order, its wall repaired; embrasures were pierced for cannon, houses and baths were built within the walls, along with numerous underground passages for which plans have been successfully established by Jacques Caillé.[20] Wishing to augment their strength and have people they could rely on, the Hornacheros brought further Andalusian refugees into Morocco, settling near the Qasba and in the already inhabited quarter close to the river. Thus, as the ribat of 'Abd al-Mu'min had been at the origin of Ribat al-Fath, so the Hornacheros' Qasba was to give birth to the Andalusian city of Rabat.

"The history of Morocco has preserved the memory of the 'Salé Corsairs.' However, this term may be confusing, leading us to believe the pirates lived in the present city of Salé. It is explained by the fact that, in the 17th century, the name Rabat was not known, only that of Salé: New Salé and Old Salé. In reality, the inhabitants of Old Salé remained strangers to piracy, whose instigators were the Moriscos who were settled on the left bank of the Bou Regreg...and who regarded this activity as one of the forms of holy war."[21] History, likewise, preserves the memory of a tumultuous port that bears, more than others, the marks of European civilization.

6. *Urban identities and specificities*

6.1　*The left bank: from Andalusian city to imperial residence*

In Rabat, the Andalusian city was to occupy a part of the interior within the Almohad surrounding wall: an urban area of some hundred hectares, including the Marinid elements and delimited to the southeast by the construction of a new wall. Beginning close to Bab al-Had, this

---

[20] See Caillé, *La République*, 214.
[21] See Caillé, *La République*, 224–226.

Andalusian wall links the twelfth-century curtain to the cliff dominating
the Bou Regreg, where Borj Sidi Makhlouf is located.[22] Thus the broad
lines of the city on the left bank or the medina of Rabat, sketched
in the twelfth, then in the fourteenth century, truly took shape in the
seventeenth century. During this period its opening to the maritime part
of the river became confirmed, and this orientation remains evident in
its urban framework defined by two main perpendicular arteries: the
Street of Consuls running alongside the river, which constituted the
city's economic pole, and Souiqa Street, a main axis running alongside
the Great Mosque in the fourteenth century and linking Bab al-Had
to the Street of Consuls, then to Bab al-Bhar, or the Sea Gate, which
opens on to the fluvial port.

The Street of Consuls, in view of its location between the Qasba
and the fluvial port, is certainly one of the oldest arteries of the city
and would play an important role in the seventeenth and eighteenth
centuries. The progressive opening up to Europe was demonstrated in
this street's cosmopolitan ambiance, vibrant as it was with the rhythm
of the fluvial port's activities. The agents in question, while concerned
to protect the interests of their nationals, also played a political role:
their governments charged them with negotiating and paying ransoms
for the liberation of captives. The Street of Consuls would progressively
become inhabited by the representatives of many foreign nations. First
the legations of Sweden, Denmark, Holland, and France; then would
come the representatives of England, Spain and Portugal, then those
of Italy, Austria-Hungary, Germany, the United States, etc.

Between the taking of the estuary in 1666 by Moulay al-Rashid,
founding father of the Alawi dynasty, and the beginning of the twentieth century, Rabat witnessed substantial changes. While these did not
affect the urban framework of the medina, the extensions and new
monuments set in place in the eighteenth and nineteenth centuries
progressively gave it another major character, that of imperial residence.
Initially, under the first Alawi sovereigns up to Moulay Sliman at the
beginning of the nineteenth century, the city remained dedicated to
its privateering activities. This explains the interest taken in the Qasba
which had become a *makhzan* fortress, and the numerous constructions

---

[22] Rectilinear and flanked by towers, the Andalusian wall, which extended for more
than 1,400 metres, had an average height of 5 metres and a width of more than a
metre and a half. It was set with three gates: Bab al-Tben, Bab al-Bououiba, and Bab
Chellah.

and modifications set in place there, and the work of maritime defence undertaken throughout this period. On the other hand, the construction by Sidi Muhammad ben 'Abd Allah, around the end of the eighteenth century, of a palace and a great mosque in the southwest part of the Almohad enclosure underlined the importance attributed to it by sovereigns.

During the reign of Moulay Sliman, this new character of the city was still further confirmed. Indeed, this sovereign had a palace built by the side of the sea, called Dar al-Bahr,[23] and a number of sanctuaries, including the mosque sited at the corner of Bouiba and Souiqa streets, which bears his name. He restored Bab al-Had and Bab Chellah, and ordered the construction of a *millah* (Jewish quarter) at the eastern end of the medina, on land occupied up till then by the last great orchards within the walls of the Andalusian city. In addition, at the beginning of the nineteenth century probably, an external rampart of a total length of 4,300 metres was built. It extended the Almohad enclosure to the south and doubled it in the west as far as the Atlantic, so enclosing an area of more than 840 hectares. Then, in the second half of the nineteenth century, Sidi Muhammad ben 'Abd al-Rahman completed the construction of a new palace in the southwest part of the Almohad enclosure and consequently revived the small imperial town previously created in the same place.

At the beginning of the twentieth century, Rabat took on a new face, forming just a single agglomeration. Even though the population was still concentrated in the medina, within the Andalusian wall, the monuments built in the space delimited by the Almohad wall marked the imperial residential character acquired by the city from that moment on.

6.2   The right bank

Up to the beginning of the twentieth century, Salé continued strongly to bear the imprint of a pious city: in the layout of the city, as seen above, but likewise in the number, nature and specific features of building or social tradition that had been preserved. The city has in fact sixty mosques, near which were *msid*s, or Quranic schools.[24] It has some forty saints, whose *zawiya*s were sited within or without the walls, and

---

[23] Now disappeared.

[24] Among the main ones, and in addition to those mentioned, there is the Mosque of Sidi Ahmad Hajj, the Shahba Mosque, the Zarqa Mosque, that of Sidi al-Hajj 'Abd Allah, those of the Hajjamin, Semmarin, Guezzarin, etc.

twenty-four public fountains, more than half of which still constantly
provided water.

In 1918, the city, which covered almost half of the area enclosed by
the walls,[25] was divided into a dozen quarters.[26] It contained a population of around 17,000 people, around ten per cent of them Jewish. The
substantial extent of this Jewish population goes back to the exodus
provoked by the Inquisition in Spain. The Jewish population of Salé
had settled near Bab Hsaien, in the Millah al-Qdim quarter. At the
beginning of the nineteenth century, the sultan Moulay Sliman had a
millah built to the southwest of the city; it was a new quarter, marked
out from others by the regular way it was laid out. The Jewish cemetery
was outside the city, and, in 1918, the Jewish population of Salé was
headed by the rabbi Raphael Angora, one of the best known authorities of the Jewish community in Morocco.[27]

Salé remained one of the main intellectual centres in Morocco. The
intellectual movement which had reached its peak during the Marinid[28]
period was prolonged, notably through the magisterial work of a high-
ranking Salé functionary from the Makhzan named Ahmed ben Khalid
al-Naciri, an important witness to nineteenth-century Morocco and
author of *Al-Istiqsa*, the last major compilation of the Muslim history
of Morocco. Finally, Salé is the only city in the whole of Morocco to
have kept alive the "procession of candles," celebrated there annually in
commemoration of the Prophet's birth.[29] On the eve of the Mouloud,
a procession is formed near Dar Chakroun, where, each year, imposing
candelabras are restored, whose sides are finely hung with thousands of
tiny wax motifs in the most various colours. Dressed in their glittering
outfits, the Salé boatmen bear the seven decorated candles that are
the chief ornaments of the procession. The procession is accompanied
by music, along a route that passes, notably, by the Sidi Ahmad Hajj

---

[25] As can be seen from the aerial views of the time. Between this urbanized zone
and the wall, there were mainly *sania*s, orchards, and agricultural land.

[26] Among the main ones we may mention La Tal'a, Ras al-Shajra, Blida, al-Guezzarin,
al-Millah al-Qdim, al-Soff, al-Souiqa, etc.

[27] The same decision had been taken in Rabat, where the new *millah* had been built
on the southeast edge of the medina.

[28] It was the period when illustrious men, such as Lisan al-Din ibn al-Khatib, came
to make a stay in Salé and sought an audience with Sidi ben Acher.

[29] This very popular and attractive custom had been introduced to Morocco at the
end of the sixteenth century on the initiative of the Sa'di sultan Ahmad al-Mansur
al-Dahbi, who had links with the Sublime Porte. At that time, it was celebrated in the
capital, Marrakesh, and in numerous towns in Morocco.

mausoleum, the Great Suq and the Great Mosque, before reaching the
sanctuary of Sidi ʿAbd Allah ben Hassun, where the most beautiful
candle is placed at the centre of the cupola dominating the catafalque.
Still today, this urban procession, experienced as the central moment
of a great religious feast, marks, throughout its route, the principal
moments and monuments attesting to the faith and piety that have
characterized the history of the Salé medina.

7. Spatial configuration and social organization

Analysis of the plan of Rabat's medina leads to a distinction between
a central zone on the one hand, and, on the other, peripheral quarters located to the west, north, and east sides of the medina. In the
central zone, access ways (streets, alleys, derbs) exhibit an irregular
layout, while the residential zones, in enclosed wholes, are made up
of urban blocks grouped around major residences. In the peripheral
quarters, al-Gza, Sidi Fateh, al-Alou and above all the Millah, land
division takes the form of a regular layout made up of a central axis
from whose two sides perpendicular and parallel streets service blocks
of a width of two parcels. The religious monuments erected in Rabat
under the Alawi dynasty, from the seventeenth to the beginning of the
twentieth century, constitute, by virtue of their number, an imposing
architectural array.[30]

In the Salé medina, whose main orientations have been noted above,
the religious pole is framed by major residences, some with riads, by
numerous dependencies and even by private cemeteries. The residential
quarters surrounding the economic pole are of a smaller size and are
often more modest. Aerial views from the beginning of the century
show how, between the central urbanized zone and the walls, there
were mainly sanias, orchards, and agricultural land. Among the main
residential quarters were La Talʿa, Ras al-Shajra, Blida, al-Guezzarin,
al-Millah al-Qdim, al-Soff, al-Souiqa, etc.

In both cities, the residential zones and quarters, of variable size,
comprise neighbouring units within the urban whole. Each quarter has

---

[30] In 1906, there were, in Rabat, 6 cathedral mosques, 33 secondary mosques, and
13 zawiyas, most of them built during the time of the Alawi sovereigns. See Caillé,
La République, 457.

collective services for the provision of residents' daily needs: bread oven, Quranic school, fountain, and small trades, plus, in a wider ring, concentric or not, a district mosque, a *zawiya*, a *hammam*, etc. In the medinas of Rabat and Salé, the quarter may not always have been distinct as a single physical entity, but it formed a social unity, or *huma*, essentially brought about by a community of interest between inhabitants. Each *huma* had a certain number of *derb*s, which constituted the fundamental social spaces of the medina. The *derb* was structured from the residence sited at the end of a cul-de-sac linked to a family of notables from which it often took its name. From the heart of the *derb* to its end, the two sides were lined with a certain number of houses reflecting kinship relations or client relations with the families owning them.

The difference in scale, atmosphere, and function to be observed between residential quarters and the great commercial arteries stems from a fundamental difference in architectural layout. The road networks crossing the suqs were delimited by organic structures built in linear series and opening on to the public space. The alleys and cul-de-sacs of the residential quarters were determined by the blind perimeters of organic structures built with a central courtyard. In this type of organization, the *derb* thus constituted a first degree of spacing, part of a larger mechanism whereby residential units were isolated vis-à-vis the exterior. This is a mode of grouping to be observed fairly generally in the urban fabrics of Arab-Muslim cities.

8. *The universe of houses in Rabat and Salé*

On the architectural level, each unit of residence was organized around a central courtyard; this was the focal space, the true nucleus from which and around which all the houses' constituent elements combined to form a spatial unit. The most prosperous residences were developed around a courtyard of large dimensions; they might indeed have two or more courtyards, including private gardens, a *hammam*, a stable, plus lodging for guests, servants, etc. We may likewise note, in Rabat and Salé, a large number of *menzeh*s on the terraces. Largely open on one or more sides, and providing a panoramic urban view (without, though, allowing any glimpse at neighbouring courtyards), the *menzeh* was a leisure space where the master of the house could receive at the end of the afternoon. Often adorned by a central basin or mural fountain, the courtyard was generally bordered by a gallery which could be partially or totally doubled on the first floor.

The construction systems and the materials used, similar in Rabat and Salé,[31] played their part in giving houses analogous volumetric compositions. This was the case, too, with the dimensions of the inner courtyards, the habitation rooms surrounding them, the types of galleries, and the lambrequin or festoon arches that bordered the galleries or accentuated the entrances to the main rooms. The use of stone[32] made it possible, in both cities, to build on fairly thin walls, to achieve light and elegant porticos and to use slender stone columns. This gave slim, light and even audacious proportions to porticos: in contrast, for instance, to the residences of Fez or Marrakesh, where pillars of a height of two metres often had diameters of 50 or 60 centimetres, while in Rabat or Salé it was common to see columns of 25 or 30 centimetres in diameter rise to a height of 3 or 4 metres. The stone adorning the galleries and entrances to rooms was entirely sculpted before being laid, even if designed for a complicated arcade. In Rabat and Salé, the mason was also a stone-cutter and a sculptor. He prepared his work on the ground, stone by stone, by composing it horizontally, before it was constituted on an improvised arch on the work site. Moreover, in Rabat and Salé, as in other coastal cities, the doors giving on to the streets were often adorned with frames in stone, made up of two pilasters topped by an archivolt, a design which was probably alien to Muslim art. We may also note the phalloid form of knockers in wrought iron or copper.[33]

The Moorish elements marking out residences in Rabat and Salé are especially to be found in the nature and division of decoration. This influence appears in the entrance doors adorned by designs borrowed from Spain, and also in the *setwan*s, long arched vestibules leading to the inner courtyard. In the latter, the overall decoration—marble-squared floors, chiselled plaster, carved wooden ceiling—supplies a perspective ending on a central panel of *zellij*, the *shuwwaf*, notably displayed on the corner of the hallway, which runs throughout its length between two rows of benches interspersed with columns topped by lambrequin arches.

---

[31] See the chapter, "Particularités des maisons de Rabat," in Jean Gallotti, *Le Jardin et la maison arabes au Maroc* (Paris: Editions Albert Levy, 1926), vol. 2.

[32] There are numerous quarries in the plateau where the Bou Regreg has hollowed out its broad estuary: quarries of a smooth ochred limestone, easy to cut and to bake.

[33] See P. Ricard and A. Delpy, "Note au sujet de vieilles portes marocaines," *Hespéris* 15, 2nd trimester (1932), fasc. 1.

This influence also appears in the layout and design of the inner courtyard, whose symmetrical composition makes openings harmonious and gives rise to a succession of stone-cut arches along the gallery: large median lambrequin arches between two smaller festoon arches. The inversion of these forms in the gallery on the first floor makes its contribution to an overall elegance, balance and harmony. Marble, cut stone, sculpted plaster, wrought iron, painted carved wood, *zellij*, are deployed on the courtyard's ground and façades; and these, by the richness and refinement of their execution, give the house its true status.[34]

Furniture is essentially made up of thick and comfortable couches, topped by cushions and encircling each room. The Moorish influence is also very evident in the sumptuous silk embroideries specific to Rabat and Salé. Original in their designs and their colours, they give the cushions, drapes and curtains the happy harmony possessed by the interiors of traditional residences in the two cities. It is quite clear that the Andalusians who settled the Qasba, in Rabat or Salé, preserved their art and their skill in the new forms of urbanism to which arranged spaces lent themselves. It was thus possible for certain of their practices to endure and develop, such as gardening, irrigation by waterwheels (*arsat* and *jnanat*), the growing of new varieties of fruits,[35] artistic shoemaking, tapestry, the art of binding, furniture of the Spanish Renaissance and baroque styles, with their succession of canopied beds and small cabled columns, together with the Andalusian music known as Gharnati (i.e., from Granada); even family names still reflect this Spanish origin.[36]

---

[34] See Saïd Mouline, "Trois demeures de Rabat: Dâr Caïd Souissi, dâr Reghaye et dâr Hassani," in *L'habitat traditionnel dans les pays musulmans autour de la Méditerranée*, vol. 1, *L'héritage architectural: formes et fonctions*, Groupe de Recherches et d'Etudes sur le Proche-Orient (Cairo: Publications de l'Institut Français d'Archéologie Orientale, 1988), 243–63.

[35] Among them the famous grapes of Rabat-Salé. "The inhabitants [of the two cities]...are especially gifted in the culture of vines and produce every variety of table grape. They are so passionate about them, and such connoisseurs, that they produce them in their homes. In fact, the majority of houses have climbing vines...The grapes are very light and sweet especially the varieties called 'silky' (*hariri*). Their juice is highly refined and was, in the past, exported to Andalusia. Even the Muscat variety is a specialty of the cities of the two banks..." M. Ben Ali Doukkali, trans. Halima Ferhat, quoted by Hamid Triki in *Itinéraire Culturel des Almoravides et des Almohades. Maghreb et Péninsule Ibérique*, published by the foundation *El legato andalus* (March 1999), 137.

[36] Such as, for instance, the families Pirou, Tredano, Bargach, Balafrej, Mouline, etc., in Rabat, and the families Zniber, Fennich, Brital, Al-Krombi, A'mar, etc., in Salé.

9. *Conclusion*

The urban and architectural patrimony stems from the work of builders, from the distinctive local art, and from social, cultural, historical, ecological, and other relations, multiple and differentiated; but this comes not from a single source, rather from a number of sources and a multitude of exchanges. Hence, in the long run, the patrimony is the result of multiple determining factors, the fruit of a cultural crossbreeding, or rather—to avoid any pejorative connotations that might be attached to this last term—the outcome of "cross-fertilization."

In his remarkable work devoted to the Mediterranean, Fernand Braudel writes that "civilizations are firmly attached to a geographical space and find, in their confrontation, their raison-d'être." It is this viewpoint of confrontation as a motor of evolution in civilizations that interests us here, with specific reference to the historical evolution of the holy cities on the two banks of the Bou Regreg. It is of interest to us since the urban and architectural patrimony, at once a product and a factor of civilization, bears witness to exchanges, ruptures, changes that are displayed, placed, and archived within time. We might almost say they form strata and sediments within time, and so forge unique sites and urban landscapes.

It is this unique character, resulting from a particular ambiance and atmosphere, that is remarkably reflected in the 1918 description of the estuary and the cities of the two banks by Jérome and Jean Tharaud, who had been invited by Hubert Lyautey, Resident-General of the French Protectorate in the Sharifi Kingdom since 1912: "At the mouth of a slow African river, where the sea enters broadly in long billows fringed with foam, two prodigious white cities, two cities from the *Thousand and One Nights*, Rabat al-Fath, the Camp of Victory, and Barbary Salé, send back, from one bank to the other, like two stanzas from the same poem, their whiteness and their terraces, their minarets and their gardens, their walls, their towers, their great cemeteries like Breton lands, like huge carpets of grey stone spread out by the side of the sea. Further on, further up the river, in the midst of red lands and itself red, rises the high square tower of a vanished mosque. Still further on, a further city, or rather the ramparts of a ruined fortress, which is now a mere dream, a memory of stone in a grove of orange trees. And from Rabat the white to white Salé, over the river's broad estuary, from the solitary tower of Hassan in Chellah the mysterious, there is, from dawn to dusk, a slow coming and going of storks, which, through the course of their flight, link with an invisible thread these three cities of Islam gathered in a narrow space, this whiteness, this greenness, these waters."

> Is it my imagination or is it my eyes that see in this place one of the loveliest spots in the world? As with the great birds, my gaze falls on all of these dispersed beauties, one by one, without ever growing weary.[37]

---

[37] Jérome and Jean Tharaud, *Rabat ou les heures marocaines* (Paris: Emile-Paul Frères, 1928), 4, 5.

THE SUB-SAHARAN CITY:
RULES AND BUILT FORM

Besim Hakim and Zubair Ahmed

This case study from sub-Sahara Africa will examine the rules that were followed by all parties concerned with decisions affecting the built environment, particularly at the neighbourhood level. The material presented is derived from manuscripts written during the Sokoto Caliphate in the nineteenth century. The built form example is from the traditional historic area of Zaria city in Northern Nigeria. By understanding the rules and the issues they addressed, it will be possible to appreciate how they affected the outcome of the built form, as shown by the selected example from Zaria of numerous compounds forming a neighbourhood cluster.

It is generally recognized that the Sokoto Caliphate commenced in 1808 A.D. with the successes of the Jihad of Uthman dan Fodio until its demise at the hands of the British colonists in 1903. We studied the underlying rules that were followed in the processes of decision-making that affected the layout of towns, their sectors comprising groups of neighbourhoods and the typical neighbourhood cluster. To discover those rules with accuracy, we have studied the relevant manuscripts written at the outset of this period by the Fodiawa trio—Shehu Uthman, his brother Abdallah (known in the region as Abdullahi), and son Muhammad Bello—and, subsequently, by other scholars.[1]

It soon became clear that the writings of the Fodiawa trio are rooted in the works of earlier Muslim scholars from North Africa and the Middle East. Our consultation of those works clarified the intentions of the trio, namely, to revive Islamic law and to establish a society that would be governed according to the Shariʿa. They did what others before them had done: re-establish the links to earlier sources and scholarship in Islamic culture.

---

[1] For an explanation of the term "Fodiawa" see John O. Hunwick, *Arabic Literature of Africa*, vol. 2, *The Writings of Central Sudanic Africa* (Leiden, 1995), 53–55. *Trio* refers to Shehu Uthman, his brother Abdallah, and his son Muhammad Bello. For their biographies see this reference by Hunwick.

Uthman's teachers, his family, and others who followed him were members of the Maliki *madhhab* (school of law). They affirmed their respect for the *Qur'an* and Sunnah of the Prophet (i.e. the Prophet's sayings and deeds), and for the opinions and scholarship of the four Imams and the precedents set by the four righteous caliphs.[2] Whenever appropriate and necessary, they consulted the opinions of scholars from other schools of law to clarify aspects of certain rulings.

In addition to the treatises of the *Fodiawa*, we have also consulted the work of other scholars from the Sokoto Caliphate whose identity and work will be mentioned.

Rules for decision-making

After analyzing the treatises written in nineteenth-century northern Nigeria and the characteristics of the morphology of cities in that region, we determined that the rules developed for managing the processes of growth and change in the built environment fit under one or more of the issues in the following framework:

1. *Harim*: zone surrounding a city, town, property or structure that is necessary for its viability and function.
2. *Ihya al-Mawat*: revivification of dead land, i.e. land not owned or utilized.
3. *Haqq al-Irtifaq*: rights of abutting adjacent properties, and rights related to access and servitude.
4. *al-Turuq al-Amma wa Haqquha*: rights of public streets.
5. *al-Marafiq wa Man' al-Darar*: preventing damages to adjacent structures and facilities.
6. *al-Daman wa al-Mas'uliyya 'Inda Ihdath al-Darar*: liability and responsibility for creating damage(s).

---

[2] The four Caliphs are known to Sunni Muslims as al-Rashidun (The Rightly Guided). They are Abu Bakr (reigned 10–13/632–634), Umar b. al-Khattab (r. 13–23/634–644), Uthman b. Affan (r. 23–36/644–656), and Ali b. Abi Talib (r. 36–41/656–661). The four Sunni Imams are Abu Hanifa (80–150/699–767), Malik (96–179/715–795), al-Shafi'i (150–205/767–820), and Ibn Hanbal (163–241/780–855).

The following are the rules for each of the above six categories:

1. Rules for the *Harim*. Abdallah Fodio, in his treatise *Ta'lim al-Radi*, explains how the *Harim* for different entities is established and recognized:[3]

- Village: the area surrounding it that is usually used for gathering firewood and for grazing. The distance is based on walking back and forth in one day, which is about 10 kilometres each way for a total of 20 km. Sometimes the area for collecting firewood is beyond the grazing area or within it. In that situation the *Harim* includes the further of the two.
- River: 1000 cubits or about 500 metres, and an area adequate for those who come to benefit from it.
- Abundant spring: 500 cubits or about 250 metres.
- Well used for livestock: the area of land that does not inconvenience anyone who brings his flock to drink at the well.
- Well used for agricultural purposes: space needed to protect it from damage and to allow its users to benefit from it.
- Well used for agriculture, a house, or small tributary or a river in land not owned by anybody: 20 cubits or about 10 metres.
- House surrounded by dead land: Its *Harim* is the areas needed for access and egress, its built-in benches, space for accumulating soil for construction and maintenance purposes, space for discharge of rainwater and wastewater.
- House surrounded by other houses or owned properties: No single owner is allowed to occupy an area as *Harim* for his sole purpose, but rather each owner can benefit from the *Harim* abutting his property without harming or inconveniencing his neighbour(s).
- Palm orchard and other trees: The *Harim* is the area on the edges of the orchard and areas allowing entrances and egresses.
- Streets: Seven cubits or about 3.5 metres. It is not allowed to sit and occupy space within the minimum width of the street, unless more space is available. If a structure is built in the street's right-of-way, it

---

[3] Abdallah Fodio's treatise, *Ta'lim al-radi fi asbab al-ikhtisas bi-mawat al-aradi* [On teaching about the revivification of dead land]. The author did not indicate the date when he completed writing this treatise.

must be demolished, even if it does not create harm. It is also not allowed to take space from the street's right-of-way and incorporate it within one's boundaries. Other stipulations are mentioned regarding streets.

2. *Ihya al-Mawat*: Abdallah Fodio, in his treatise *Ta'lim al-Radi*, stipulates the following rules for revivification of dead land:

If land is within the *Harim* of a built up area, it can be revived with the permission of the Imam, ruler or his representative. If it is outside of the *Harim* of a built up area, there is no need for permission. Those who revive dead land acquire ownership rights to it. However, there are various rules and conditions regarding the loss of ownership of a revived land, and how ownership may be claimed by another reviver of the same land when the first reviver allows the land in question to revert to its previous condition. Its location and distance from the built up area is a factor that affects ownership rights when it is allowed to revert to its original condition by its initial reviver. *Ihya* is deemed legitimate when any one or more of these conditions occurs: (i) finding water within the land by digging a well or opening up a spring so that it is possible to cultivate the land; (ii) removing water from a flooded land; (iii) building a permanent structure on the land; (iv) substantial planting on the land; (v) cultivation by ploughing and breaking up the soil. It is to be noted that cultivation without prior ploughing does not constitute revivification; (vi) removing trees from the land by cutting or burning; and (vii) breaking up stones on the land and levelling its steep slopes.

Tahjir signifies the boundary delimitation of a land selected for *Ihya* by using stone markers. Some scholars, such as Ibn al-Qasim, do not recognize this act as *Ihya*, others, like Ashhab, accept *Tahjir* as an indicator of intention to revive the chosen land within a short period of time. Grazing and digging a well for watering flocks is not recognized as an act of *Ihya*.

3. *Haqq al-Irtifaq*: The right to abut a neighbour, and the right of servitude, i.e. a right that grants access through another's property. One of the earlier references to this right is found in Khalil bin Ishaq's *Mukhtasar*, where he indicates that the owner of a structure should allow his neighbour to use the structure for inserting beams in his wall, and give him other rights, such as access through his property or the

sharing of a water source.[4] Ibn Salmun al-Kinani (d. 741/1340), who lived in Granada one generation before Khalil, also explains the right of *Irtifaq*.[5] He explains that such a right may be given in perpetuity or for a limited period of time. In either case a contract or agreement should be written. Ibn Asim (d. 829/1426) of Granada also discusses the right of *Irtifaq*.[6]

Abd al-Qadir b. al-Mustafa from the Sokoto Caliphate who was married to Muhammad Bello's daughter, Khadija, quoted his father-in-law on the issue of houses abutting a public right-of-way. Bello's view, as quoted by Abd al-Qadir, was that such streets cannot be infringed upon by the owners of abutting houses and must always be kept clean and accessible for the public. Bello uses the term *Irtifaq*, i.e. the public has the right of servitude or access to these public streets.[7]

4. *al-Turuq al-Amma wa Haqquha*: Generally the public has the right of unimpeded access to public streets.[8] Khalil b. Ishaq stipulates the following rights regarding public streets: (i) it is not permissible to build within the public-right-of-way, whether or not such construction creates impediments and damage to passers-by. Any infringement of this type must be demolished; (ii) Vendors who use the sides of streets to display their goods are allowed to do so, if usage of such spaces is temporary and does not impinge upon the traffic of passers-by. The use of a particular space on the side of a public street is determined by who occupies that space first, by analogy to a person who occupies a space within the confines of a mosque for the purposes of study or teaching; (iii) On a public street, one neighbour cannot open a shop or a stable opposite the front door of another, as this would create a nuisance and the potential for invading the privacy of the neighbour on

---

[4] Khalil b. Ishaq al-Maliki (d. 776/1374), *Mukhtasar al-allama Khalil fi fiqh al-imam Malik* (Beirut, 1995), 218, section *al-Shirka* (Partnership and its rules).

[5] Ibn Salmun al-Kinani (d. 741/1340), *Kitab al-ʿqd al-Munazzam lil-Hukkam*, published on the margins of *Tabsirat al-Hukkam* by Ibn Farhun (Cairo, 1301/1884; reprinted Beirut, n.d.), 2:129–130.

[6] Ibn Asim (d. 829/1426), *Tuhfat al-Hukkam fi nakt al-uqud wa al-ahkam*. His treatise was commented on by a number of scholars, including al-Tusuli from Fez (d. 1258/1842), *al-Bahja fi Sharh al-Tuhfa*.

[7] Abd al-Qadir b. al-Mustafa, *Nubdhat Ibn Mustafa min Kutub al-Aʾimma*. He was born 1219/1804 and died in 1281/1864. See his biography and writings in Hunwick, *Arabic Literature of Africa* (full citation in note 1 above).

[8] Ibid.

the other side of the street; (iv) It is permissible to build a projection or a *Sabat* (room bridging a street) as long as it does not create harm to the passer-by. A person who owns two buildings opposite each other across the street may build a *Sabat* between them.[9] Stipulations (i) and (iii) are also mentioned by Idris b. Khalid b. Muhammad, Qadi of Gwandu, in his *Kitab Jami Ahammu Masa'il al-Ahkam fi Qat'i al-Khisam*, completed on August 20, 1836. (The author refers primarily to the works of the Fodiawa Trio: Uthman, Abdallah, and Muhammad Bello.) In his *Diya al-Hukkam*, written in 1221/1806 while he was visiting Kano, Abdallah Fodio clarifies a number of issues that might cause problems in public streets, e.g. digging a well in a public street is not allowed, whereas directing rain gutters onto a public street is. Khalil's stipulation (iii), above, is also affirmed by Abdallah Fodio. Other stipulations related directly or indirectly to public streets are also documented.[10]

5. *al-Marafiq wa Man' al-Darar*: preventing damage to adjacent structures and facilities. Ibn Salmun of Granada (d. 741/1340) and two generations later, Ibn Farhun of Medina (d. 799/1397) both discussed the numerous conditions and situations that may arise between adjacent and opposite (across the street) facilities, i.e. damages of one to the other and how those potential and actualized damages may be prevented or eliminated.[11]

Abdallah Fodio devotes the thirteenth section of Part five (*al-Siyasat al-Shari'ya*) of his *Diya al-Hukkam* to the topic of *Nafi al-darar an al-jiran wa ghayrihum* (prevention of damages to neighbours and others). Idris b. Khalid b. Muhammad's book, *Jami ahammu...* completed in 1836, also includes a section on *al-Marafiq wa Man' al-Darar* (preventing damages to adjacent facilities). This is followed by a shorter section on *Man ahdathah dararan umira bi-qat'ihi* (he who causes damage(s) is ordered to eliminate it).[12]

---

[9] al-Kharashi's analysis and explanation of *Mukhtasar Khalil*. First published in 5 volumes, Cairo 1317/1900, 275–278. Muhammad b. Abdallah al-Kharashi al-Maliki lived and died in Cairo 1101/1690. This book was available in manuscript form to the Fodiawa Trio and other scholars of the Sokoto Caliphate.

[10] The full title of the treatise is: *Diya al-hukkam fi-ma lahum wa-alayhim min al-ahkam*. It was completed in 1806 while its author, Abdallah Fodio, was visiting Kano. He wrote it in response to repeated requests from friends and associates in Kano.

[11] Ibn Salmun, *Kitab al-'qd al-Munazzam lil-Hukkam*, and Ibn Farhun, *Tabsirat al-Hukkam*. The latter was very popular among the Fodiawa Trio and subsequent scholars in the Sokoto Caliphate.

[12] Idris b. Khalid b. Muhammad, *Jami ahammu masa'il al-ahkam fi qat'i al-khisam mimma ishtaddat ilayhi hajat al-hukkam*. Active in 1246/1830 as *Qadi* of Gwandu during the reign

The following are some of the issues applicable to the morphology of compounds as the nucleus of urban formation in cities of the Sokoto Caliphate. The primary justification for rules in this area, invoked by various scholars, including those from the Sokoto Caliphate, is the hadith "La Darar wa-la Dirar" which is a leading *Qa'ida* (principle) of *Qawa'id Fiqhiya*.[13] Abdallah Fodio's interpretation of this hadith follows that of al-Matiti (d. 570/1174): *Darar* is when one neighbour harms another, and *Dirar* is when both neighbours harm each other.[14]

In *Diya al-Hukkam* Abdallah Fodio provides the following list of phenomena that may create harm:

- Smoke from baths and bakeries.
- Dust from threshing wheat (*Ghubar al-Anadir*).
- Foul smell from a tanner's workshop (*Natn al-Dabbaghin*).
- Building a stable near a neighbour.
- Building a place for a grinding device, or a blacksmith workshop near a neighbour.
- An act considered to be damaging is usually viewed as being *hadith* (recent), unless it is proven to be *qadim* (old).
- Opening a window that overlooks a neighbour's private domain.
- Building a gargoyle that releases water onto a neighbour's property is not allowed even if it causes no harm, unless the neighbour grants permission.
- A door constructed in a house or structure on a public street must not face another door across the street, but must be set back from it to prevent a direct visual corridor. In a cul-de-sac owned by the people who have access from it, one is not allowed to build a projection or open a new door without the consensus of all the owners.

---

of Ibrahim Khalil b. Abdullah Fodio who died in 1276/1860. Date of the treatise's completion is August 20, 1836. The author's objective in writing it was to create a reference work for himself and also for other Qadis. His primary sources were the works of the Fodiawa Trio, Uthman, Abdallah, and Muhammad Bello. He also refers to well-known sources such as the *Mukhtasar* of Khalil b. Ishaq, the *Risala* by Ibn Abi Zayd al-Qayrawani, *Qawanin al-Ahkam* by Ibn Juzayy, *Kitab al-Nawazil* by Muhammad b. Salim, *al-Mi'yar* by al-Wansharisi, and others.

[13] For a brief discussion of *Qawa'id Fiqhiya* (Fiqh principles) and their impact on the formulation and nature of rules affecting the built environment, see the contribution in this book on "Law and the City" by Besim S. Hakim.

[14] al-Matiti (d. 570/1174) is a Maliki scholar from Fez whose book, *al-Nihaya wa al-Tamam fi Ma'rifat al-Watha'iq wa al-Ahkam*, known as *al-Matitiya*, influenced many later scholars.

- It is not permissible to plaster a wall, which belongs to an adjacent abutting neighbour, from the side of the other neighbour's property.
- Maintenance of a sewer/wastewater channel is based on the principle that each user is responsible for the portion that he uses, assisted by the neighbour(s) upstream using the channel, e.g. if the channel serves four houses, then the owner of the first house cleans his portion of the channel and helps the next neighbour clean, then both help the third neighbour, and so on.
- Owning trees on someone else's land: access must always be allowed, and the owner of the land can demand that access be the shortest and most direct route to the location of the trees.
- Location of a path used by the public but which passes through private property and has been there since the owner of the land purchased or inherited it. The owner cannot change the location of the path, even if it creates an inconvenience for him, because the path is used by the community. The owner may seek to obtain the permission of the Imam who, after examining the location, can determine if re-aligning the path is possible and beneficial to its owner and the public who use it. If the owner re-aligns it without the Imam's permission, the Imam, after examining the change, may allow it or may order that it be restored to its original alignment. However, if the path is used by only a specific number of individuals, then those individuals may grant permission to the property owner to re-align it.[15]

Idris b. Khalid b. Muhammad, who was active in the 1830s in Gwandu, mentioned other issues relating to the prevention of damages:

---

[15] Abdallah Fodio relied on some of the following sources in compiling the rules: Ashhab al-Qaysi (d. 204/819 in Egypt), a friend of Imam Malik (d. 179/795) from Medina; Ibn al-Majishun (d. 212/827) originally from Isfahan, lived and worked in Medina, and died in Baghdad; Asbagh b. al-Faraj b. Nafi' (d. 225/840) from Egypt; Ibn Habib (d. 238/853) from Cordoba, author of al-Wadiha; Sahnun (d. 240/854) originally Syrian, born and died in Qairouan, author of al-Mudawwana al-Kubra; Yahya b. Umar (d. 289/901) from Qairouan. Studied under Ibn Habib (d. 238/853) and Sahnun (d. 240/854). His book Ikhtisar al-Mustakhrajah is known as al-Muntakhabah; Ibn Abi Zayd al-Qairouani (d. 386/996), one of Qairouan's great scholars, author of al-Risala and the multi-volume work al-Nawadir wa al-Ziyadat; Ibn 'Attab (d. 462/1069) from Cordoba, a scholar in the science of al-Watha'iq; Al-Lakhmi (d. 478/1085) originally from Qairouan, resided in Sfax where he died, author of al-Tabsira; al-Matiti (d. 570/1174) from Fez, author of al-Nihaya wa al-Tamam fi Marifat al-Watha'iq wa al-Ahkam known as al-Matitiya; Ibn Juzayy al-Kalbi (d. 741/1340) from Granada, author of al-Qawanin al-Fiqhiya; Ibn Sahnun, Abu Muhammad (d. 741/1340) from Granada, author of al-Iqd al-Munazzam lil-Hukkam; Ibn Farhun (d. 799/1397) born, raised and died in Medina, author of Tabsirat al-Hukkam.

- How to determine ownership and usage rights regarding a wall
  between adjacent neighbours, e.g. what happens if a wall surrounding a jointly owned orchard falls into ruin and one of the partners
  wants to rebuild it, but the other refuses?
- If a jointly owned *Rahi* (mill) falls into ruin, and one of the partners
  rebuilds it, after the other refused, how should the revenue of the
  mill be shared?
- Who is responsible for a ceiling and its maintenance in a two- or
  three-storey structure if each level is owned by a different party? (This
  condition rarely applied in towns of the Sokoto Caliphate, due to
  the nature of the predominant architectural typology.)

Otherwise Idris repeats what Abdallah Fodio included in his treatise.
At the outset of his book Idris lists his sources, citing the Fodiawa Trio,
Uthman, Abdallah, and Muhammad Bello. He also cites other scholars
and their specific works which he consulted.[16]

Later scholars from the Sokoto Caliphate mention cases relating to
the management of the built environment, mostly repetitions of issues
listed above. They include: Abd al-Qadir b. al-Mustafa (d. 1280/1864),
the son-in-law of Muhammad Bello. His treatise is *Nubdha min kutub
al-a'imma*; Uthman b. Ishaq b. Umar (d. after 1303/1885), his treatise
Ajwiba li-Askia fi ma ashkala min al-tullab (completed in 1285/1868); Qadi
Abdullah b. al-Imam (d. 1321/1903), two short letters, one to Isma'il
b. Muhammad al-Bukhahri, Amir of Kebbi, the other to Banagha,
Chief of Maru.

6. *al-Daman wa al-Mas'uliyya inda ihdath al-darar*: The question of how
to determine and allocate responsibility for an act creating harm and
damages was addressed by scholars in the Sokoto Caliphate. In his
Kitab Tanbih al-Hukkam, Uthman Fodio discusses the conditions under
which responsibility for creating damage is determined. Part five (*Fi al-
Siyasat al-Shar'iya*) of Abdallah Fodio's treatise, *Diya al-Hukkam*, includes
numerous references to the context in which responsibility is assigned
for an act that has created harm. Section twelve of Part five, entitled

---

[16] *Al-Risala* by Ibn Abi Zayd al-Qairouani (d. 386/996) from Qairouan; *al-Qawanin
al-Fiqhiya* by Ibn Juzayy al-Kalbi (d. 741/1340) from Granada; *Mukhtasar Khalil* by
Khalil bin Ishaq (d. 776/1374) from Cairo; *Tuhfat al-Hukkam* by Ibn Asim (d. 829/1426)
from Granada; *Lamia fi al-Ahkam* known as *Lamiyat al-Zaq'qaq* by Ali bin al-Qasim al-
Zaqqaq (d. 912/1506) from Fez; *al-Miyar al-Mu'rib* by Ahmad b. Yahya al-Wansharisi
(d. 914/1508) from Fez.

Fi Tadmin al-Sunna' wa Ghayrihum (responsibility of workers and others), discusses various trades and the circumstances in which certain actions by a worker are determined to be an act of negligence for which the worker is responsible. In his book *Jami' Ahammu Masa'il al-Ahkam*, Idris b. Khalid, Qadi of Gwandu, refers to responsibility for various deeds and under what conditions the perpetrator has to assume responsibility. He repeats some of the material in Uthman and Abdallah Fodio's works.

In a recent study, Sharara discusses the theoretical and legal premises for actions that create damage and how the allocation of responsibility is determined.[17] He quotes al-Qarafi, a Maliki scholar, who indicates three reasons for allocating responsibility: (i) *al-'udwan*, or aggression, such as burning or demolishing; (ii) the result or consequence of an act, such as digging a well in a public street, and (iii) the hand of the offender, or the untrustworthy hand, such as usurping someone's rights or property. Also included in this third category is the illegal abrogation of a contract, such as a renter refusing to pay the rental fee.[18]

The essential criterion for allocating responsibility is to determine if damage or harm occurred. The elimination of damage or harm becomes the responsibility of the party, whose action created the damage in the first place, e.g. removing any damage that occurs in the public right-of-way of streets and paths. In a recent study, Abd al-Mejid al-Hakim observes that aggression on people's rights takes the form of aggression on a person or on assets and is the underlying basis for the principle, *Inna kulla fi'lin dar yuwajjib al-daman* (a person is liable for his/her act which is damaging to others). He bases this legal stipulation on the Prophet's saying, "La Darar wa-la Dirar," as interpreted by the *Fuqaha*.[19]

Example from Zaria

The old walled town of Zaria was the capital of the traditional Zaria emirate.[20] Formerly Zazzau or Zegzeg, the historic kingdom is said to

---

[17] Abd al-Jabbar Ahmad Sharara, *Nazariat Nefi al-Darar fi al-Fiqh al-Islami al-Muqaran* [Theory of preventing damage in comparative Islamic Fiqh] (Tehran, 1997), part 2, chap. 4, 278.

[18] Ibid., 262.

[19] Abd al Mejid al-Hakim, *al-Mujaz fi Sharh al-Qanun al-Madani* (Baghdad, n.d.). As quoted by Sharara on page 268.

[20] Zaria's geographic coordinates are latitude 11 degrees 3 minutes north, longitude 7 degrees 42 minutes east, at an elevation of 670 metres above sea level. The direction

date from the eleventh century C.E., when King Gunguma founded it as one of the original Hausa Bakwai (seven true Hausa states). Camel caravans from the northern Sahara came here to trade. Islam was introduced in about 1456, and there were Muslim Hausa rulers from the early sixteenth century C.E. Muhammad I Askia, a well known leader of the Songhai Empire, conquered Zazzau in 1512. Later in the century, Zazzau's ruler, Queen Amina, enlarged her domain by making numerous conquests. Zaria was probably founded in 1536, and later in the century became the capital of the Hausa state of Zazzau. Both the town and state were named after Queen Zaria (late sixteenth century C.E.), the younger sister and successor of Queen Amina.

In 1219/1804 the Muslim Hausa ruler of Zaria pledged allegiance to Uthman dan Fodio, which resulted in a Fulani becoming ruler of Zaria in 1223/1808. The emirate of Zaria was created in 1251/1835, retaining control of Keffi, Nasarawa, Jema'a, and Lapai to the south. It was governed by a representative of the Sultan at Sokoto as well as the local emir.[21]

The location of Zaria relative to the frontier of the Sokoto Caliphate in the nineteenth century, and the frontier of the modern state of Nigeria, is shown in figure 1. The town map of old Zaria (figure 2), circa 1970, shows primary streets, the built up area within the walls, and the gates of the city. It also shows the location of the major market, the palace complex, and the study area. Figure 3 is an air photo of a typical cluster of compounds located east of Zaria's major market.

The study area is a cluster of twenty-six compounds, which may be considered as a neighbourhood with its common spaces and local facilities. It is located northeast of the market and south of the Emir's palace. The compounds comprising the cluster are grouped around the oldest compound in the cluster belonging to the Chief Imam, and, together with the small mosque and square, form the focal point of the cluster. The inhabitants of the compounds that make up this cluster were originally the Chief Imam's sons, relatives, and relatives through marriage.[22]

All compounds in Hausa walled cities are surrounded by high walls. Their only entrance is a *Zaure*, an entrance hut that leads into the *Kofar*

---

to the *qibla* in Mecca is 67 degrees 16 minutes northeast.

[21] *Encyclopaedia Britannica*, CD-ROM, 1998 Standard edition, s.v. "Zaria."

[22] Barbara A. Urbanowicz, "Selected Aspects of House Form in Zaria Urban Area with Special Reference to Traditional Forms in Zaria Walled City" (Ph.D. thesis, Ahmadu Bello University, Zaria, 1979), 74.

Gida (forecourt). To reach the central and private part of the compound (*Cikin Gida*), one has to pass through a *Shigifa* or second entrance hut. Normally, the *Shigifa* acts as the transition space between the male and female zones (figure 4). Thus the area of the *Zaure*, *Kofar Gida*, and adjacent rooms or facilities is the men's and boys zone, and the rest of the compound beyond the *Shigifa* is the zone for the family, women and service areas. Compounds, on a citywide basis, average 500–600 square metres in area.[23]

A detailed account by Taylor and Webb of the construction process of a compound in Zaria during the early decades of the twentieth century is available in English and Hausa.[24] The account clearly demonstrates the involvement of the owner and builder and their mutual cooperation in decision-making relating to the planning and layout of the compound. The magnitude of the enterprise depends on the financial resources of the owner. The account provides valuable insight into the building materials used during the stages of the construction process and the approximate number of days that it took for a variety of construction activities. Schwerdtfeger describes the responsibilities of the compound head and the allocation of labour between members of the compound in maintaining walls, common rooms, and the construction of a new hut for a newly-wed couple. The compound is named after the compound head, who, as the primary decision-maker can take independent action. Dependent or semi-dependent household heads within the compound must acquire approval of the compound head for changes in the compound.[25]

Taylor and Webb also provide an account on farming. They observe, "If a man wants to make a farm, he chooses a place where there is good soil,…" This confirms the practice of *Ihya*, i.e. a person chooses a suitable plot to farm and by doing so he practices *Ihya al-Mawat*. The account continues: "…he thoroughly clears the weeds and cuts down the bushes;…"[26]

---

[23] Friedrich W. Schwerdtfeger, "Urban settlement patterns in northern Nigeria (Hausaland)," in *Man, Settlement and Urbanism*, ed. P. J. Ucko, R. Tringham, and G. W. Dimbleby (London: Duckworth, 1972), 547–556.

[24] F. W. Taylor and A. G. G. Webb, *Labarum Al'Adun Hausawa da Zantatukansu—* Accounts and conversations describing certain Customs of the Hausas (London: Oxford University Press, 1932), 169–191.

[25] Friedrich W. Schwerdtfeger, *Traditional Housing in African Cities* (New York: John Wiley and Sons, 1982), 35.

[26] Taylor and Webb, *Labarum Al'Adun*, 163–169.